Blackstone's

Police Ope

Blackstone's

Police Operational Handbook 2019

Police National Legal Database

Editor: Mark Hartley

Consultant Editor: Paul Connor

OXFORD
UNIVERSITY PRESS

OXFORD
UNIVERSITY PRESS

Great Clarendon Street, Oxford, OX2 6DP,
United Kingdom

Oxford University Press is a department of the University of Oxford.
It furthers the University's objective of excellence in research, scholarship,
and education by publishing worldwide. Oxford is a registered trade mark of
Oxford University Press in the UK and in certain other countries

First Edition published in 2006
Thirteenth Edition published in 2018

Impression: 1

Published in the United States of America by Oxford University Press
198 Madison Avenue, New York, NY 10016, United States of America

British Library Cataloguing in Publication Data
Data available

Library of Congress Cataloging in Publication Data
Data available

ISBN 978–0–19–883166–2

Printed in Great Britain by
Ashford Colour Press Ltd, Gosport, Hampshire

Preface

This is the thirteenth edition of the *Blackstone's Police Operational Handbook*, which has been specifically designed to meet the needs of the operational police officer, police community support officer, special constable, or other practitioner who has to interpret and apply the criminal law within our community.

Due to the success of previous editions and the positive comments that we have received it is apparent that the format and contents of the handbook are meeting the needs of our readers and proving to be an invaluable 'tool kit' for police officers, and where relevant, for community support officers and community support volunteers.

Formulated and written by qualified staff from the Police National Legal Database (PNLD) <http://www.pnld.co.uk>, the book covers a wide range of offences, and clearly explains and interprets the relevant legislation. It follows the style of the PNLD database by providing the wording of the offences, points to prove, meanings, explanatory notes, relevant cases, and practical considerations. To assist further, the law/guidance notes are all presented in a 'bullet point', easy-to-understand format; thus, at a glance, a quick and informed decision can be made in a host of everyday policing situations.

Although every effort has been made to include as many 'commonly dealt with offences' as possible, the size of the handbook dictates how many offences can be included. However, the number and variety of offences given within the areas of crime and road traffic, including a sample of PACE powers and procedures, together with the guidance chapters and useful appendices, provides sufficient information for most eventualities.

The handbook is fully up to date as of 1 June 2018.

Over the last year, additional sections of The Policing and Crime Act 2017 have come into force and relevant changes in this handbook include those made to s 38 of the Police Reform Act 2002 and the powers relating to civilians including Community Support Officers (formally PCSOs) and Community Support Volunteers. In addition, new powers have been revised relating to s 136 of the Mental Health Act 1983 and places of safety and powers to remove and to search and detain, with specific restrictions preventing detention of a child (under 18 years of age) at a police station. Additional inclusions relate to the Proceeds of Crime Act 2002 and unexplained wealth, the Criminal Finances Act 2017, Pyrotechnic Articles (Safety) Regulations 2015, a new offence under s 15A Sexual Offences Act for communication with a child, updates to s 14 Modern Slavery Act 2015, s 2 Homicide Act 1957, s 88A Environment Protection Act 1990 for littering from vehicles, s 4 Animal Welfare Act 2006, and s 28A Firearms Act 1968. There are also updates

Preface

to PACE Code C that defines a 'juvenile' for the purpose of detention and the meaning of an appropriate adult, Code D for identification procedures, and Code E for exemption to audio record interviews undertaken elsewhere than at a police station for certain offences. Finally there are changes to s 17 PACE, s 30(A) 'street bail', s 63B testing for class 'A' drugs, Sch 6A to the Anti-social Behaviour, Crime and Policing Act 2014, ss 4 and 4A Prevention from Harassment Act 1997, and s 51 Sexual Offences Act 2003.

Officers are required to know what offences are indictable or either way for their search or arrest powers—the mode of trial icons (within each offence) provided in the book give this important information.

Whilst every care has been taken to ensure that the contents of this handbook are accurate, neither the publisher nor the authors can accept any responsibility for any action taken, or not taken, based on the information contained within this handbook.

Please email <police.uk@oup.com> with any comments or queries.

Mark Hartley

Editor

June 2018

Acknowledgements

The Police National Legal Database (PNLD) (<http://www.pnld.co.uk>) is well known by all police forces in England and Wales, the Crown Prosecution Service, and other recognised organisations from within the criminal justice system.

Special thanks are extended to all the PNLD legal advisers and other staff who, over the years, have contributed to the production of the *Blackstone's Police Operational Handbook*.

Contents

Contents

Contents

Contents

Contents

Contents

Contents

Table of Cases

Table of Cases

Table of Cases

Table of Cases

Table of Cases

International

European Court of Human Rights

Table of Legislation

Table of Legislation

Table of Legislation

Table of Legislation

Table of Legislation

Table of Legislation

Table of Legislation

Table of Legislation

Table of Legislation

Table of Legislation

Codes of Practice

MOJ Circulars

EU Directives

Table of Conventions

List of Abbreviations

A-G	Attorney-General
ACPO	Association of Chief Police Officers (see NPCC)
ANPR	Automatic Number Plate Recognition (system/camera)
AOABH	assault occasioning actual bodily harm
ASBO	Anti-Social Behaviour Order
BB gun	ball bearing gun
BS	British Standard
BTP	British Transport Police
CBO	criminal behaviour order
CC	Chief Constable or County Court
CCTV	closed-circuit television
CED	conducted energy device
CEO	Chief Executive Officer
CEOP	Child Exploitation and On-line Protection Centre
CIE	Continuous Insurance Enforcement
CJ	criminal justice
CJA	Criminal Justice Act
COP	Code of Practice
CPC	Certificate of Professional Competence
CPN	community protection notice
CPR	cardiopulmonary resuscitation
CPS	Crown Prosecution Service
CRB	Criminal Records Bureau
CSE	child sexual exploitation
CS spray	named after the initials of the inventors—Corson and Staughton
CSO	Community support officer
CSV	Community support volunteer
DBO	Drink Banning Order
DBS	Disclosure and Barring Service (formerly ISA)
DC	Divisional Court
DEFRA	Department for Environment, Food, and Rural Affairs
DNA	deoxyribonucleic acid
DPP	Director of Public Prosecutions
DSA	Driving Standards Agency (now DVSA)
DVLA	Driver and Vehicle Licensing Agency

List of Abbreviations

DVPN	Domestic Violence Protection Notice
DVPO	Domestic Violence Protection Order
DVSA	Driver and Vehicle Standards Agency
ECHR	European Convention on Human Rights
ECtHR	European Court of Human Rights
EEA	European Economic Area
EPO	Emergency Protection Order
EU	European Union
FA	Football Association
FGM	female genital mutilation
FMU	Forced Marriage Unit at the Foreign and Commonwealth Office
FPN	fixed penalty notice
GB	Great Britain
GBH	grievous bodily harm
GHB	gamma-hydroxybutrate
GV	goods vehicle
HGV	heavy goods vehicle
HIV	human immunodeficiency virus
HL	House of Lords
HMCTS	Her Majesty's Courts and Tribunal Service
HMRC	Her Majesty's Revenue & Customs
HOC	Home Office Circular
HSE	Health and Safety Executive
ICO	Information Commissioner's Office
IOPC	Independent Office for Police Conduct
ISA	Independent Safeguarding Authority (now DBS—above)
LA	local authority
MAPPA	Multi-Agency Public Protection Agreements
MASH	Multi-Agency Safeguarding Hubs
MC	Magistrates' Court
MCA	Magistrates' Courts Act 1980
MIB	Motor Insurers' Bureau
MOD	Ministry of Defence
MOJ	Ministry of Justice
NCA	National Crime Agency

NHS	National Health Service
NIP	notice of intended prosecution
NPCC	National Police Chiefs' Council (formerly ACPO)
NPT	Neighbourhood Policing Team
NRM	National Referral Mechanism (modern slavery and human trafficking)
OAPA	Offences Against the Person Act 1861
OFCOM	Office of Communications
OPL	over the prescribed limit
PACE	Police and Criminal Evidence Act 1984
PCSO	Police Community Support Officer
PCV	passenger-carrying vehicle
PNC	Police National Computer
PND	Penalty Notice for Disorder/Police National Database
PND-E	Penalty Notice for Disorder—Education option
PNLD	Police National Legal Database
POA	Public Order Act 1986
POCA	Proceeds of Crime Act 2002
PolSA	Police Search Adviser
PSPO	public spaces protection order
PSV	public service vehicle
QBD	Queen's Bench Division
RTC	road traffic collision
SC	Supreme Court
SCGC	self-contained gas cartridge system
SI	Statutory Instrument
SIO	Senior Investigating Officer
SORN	Statutory Off-Road Notification
STPO	Slavery and Trafficking Prevention Order
STRO	Slavery and Trafficking Risk Order
TDA	taking and driving away
TFPN	traffic fixed penalty notice
TWOC	taking a conveyance without owner's consent
UK	United Kingdom
UKBA	UK Border Agency
UKMPB	UK Missing Persons Bureau
UKSC	United Kingdom Supreme Court
UTMV	unlawful taking of a motor vehicle

List of Abbreviations

VDRS	Vehicle Defect Rectification Scheme
VED	Vehicle Excise Duty
VEL	Vehicle Excise Licence
VOSA	Vehicle and Operator Services Agency (now DVSA)
VPS	victim personal statement
YOI	young offenders' institution
YOT	youth offending team

Icons List

SSS   **Stop, search, and seize powers** under the Police and Criminal Evidence Act 1984, s 1 or stop, search, and seize powers under a statutory authority given within that Act.

E&S   **Entry and search powers** under the Police and Criminal Evidence Act 1984, ss 17, 18, and 32.

PND   **Penalty Notices for Disorder offences** under the Criminal Justice and Police Act 2001, s 1.

TFPN   **Traffic Fixed Penalty Notices** under the Road Traffic Offenders Act 1988.

RRA   **Racially or religiously aggravated offences** under the Crime and Disorder Act 1998, ss 28–32.

CHAR   **Offences where evidence of bad character can be introduced** under the Criminal Justice Act 2003, s 103.

TRIG   **Trigger offences**—when police can test (request to take samples) for presence of Class A drugs, under the Criminal Justice and Court Services Act 2000, Sch 6.

Mode of trial
Indictable, either way, or summary.

Prosecution time limit.
The time limit allowed for submission of the file (laying of the information).

Penalty
Maximum sentence allowed by law.

NIP   **Notice of Intended Prosecution** to be issued under s 1 of the Road Traffic Offenders Act 1988.

Chapter 1

Introduction

1.1 **Human Rights**

The Human Rights Act 1998 affects operational policing, legislation, court decisions, and encompasses the fundamental rights and freedoms contained in the ECHR; this is illustrated in the following summarised sections relating to the police and criminal justice system:

Section 2

Requires a court to take account of the opinions/decisions of the ECtHR, the Commission, or Committee of Ministers when determining a question relating to a **Convention right**.

Section 3

Demands that all UK legislation must be construed and given effect in such a way as to be compatible with Convention rights.

Section 4

Permits the Supreme Court, High Court, or Court of Appeal to make a declaration on any question of UK law.

Section 6

Makes it unlawful for a **public authority** to act in a way incompatible with a Convention right. This includes a failure to act.

Section 7

Provides for an aggrieved party to take proceedings where a public authority has breached (or proposes to breach) s 6, but only if that person is (or would be) a victim of the unlawful act.

Section 8

Empowers a court to grant such remedy or **relief** within its powers as it considers just and appropriate.

Section 11

Preserves any other right or freedom enjoyed under UK law.

Meanings

Convention right

Means the following rights and freedoms given in **Schedule 1**:
• Articles 2 to 12 and 14 of the Convention;
• Articles 1 to 3 of the First Protocol;
• Article 1 of the Thirteenth Protocol.

Public authority

This includes:
• a court or tribunal;
• any person (eg a police officer) whose functions are of a public nature.

Relief

Includes an award of damages or payment of compensation given through the civil courts, such as the county court or the High Court.

Convention

Means the Convention for the Protection of Human Rights and Fundamental Freedoms, agreed by the Council of Europe at Rome on 4 November 1950 as it has effect for the time being in relation to the UK.

Protocol

Means a protocol to the Convention which the UK has ratified or has signed with a view to ratification.

Schedule 1—Articles/Protocols

Article 2—Right to life

This right shall be protected by law. No one shall be deprived of life intentionally. Deprivation of life shall not be regarded as being in contravention of this Article if force is used, being no more than absolutely necessary, in order to:
• defend from unlawful violence;
• effect a lawful arrest;
• prevent the escape of a person lawfully detained;
• perform a lawful action to quell a riot or insurrection.

Article 3—Prohibition of torture

No one shall be subjected to torture or to inhuman or degrading treatment or punishment.

Article 4—Prohibition of slavery and forced labour

No one shall be held in slavery or servitude or be required to perform forced or compulsory labour.

Article 5—Right to liberty and security

No one shall be deprived of these rights save in the following cases and in accordance with a procedure prescribed by law:
• lawful detention (after conviction) by a competent court;

- lawful arrest or detention for failing to comply with the lawful order of a court or in order to secure the fulfilment of any obligation prescribed by law;
- lawful arrest or detention for the purpose of bringing the person before the competent legal authority on reasonable suspicion of having committed an offence or when it is reasonably considered necessary to prevent committing an offence or fleeing after having done so;
- detention of a minor by lawful order for the purpose of educational supervision or lawful detention for the purpose of bringing before the competent legal authority;
- lawful detention for the prevention of the spreading of infectious diseases, of persons of unsound mind, alcoholics or drug addicts, or vagrants;
- lawful arrest or detention to prevent unauthorised entry into the country or with a view to deportation or extradition.

Article 5 also deals with:
- promptly being informed as to the reason for arrest/charge;
- entitlement to trial within a reasonable time or release pending trial;
- entitlement to take proceedings for unlawful detention and the right to compensation in these instances.

Article 6—Right to a fair trial

Everyone is entitled to a fair and public hearing within a reasonable time by an independent and impartial tribunal established by law. Protection shall be given against publicity (for all or part of the trial) in the interests of: morals, public order, national security, juveniles, the private lives of the parties, or if it would prejudice the interests of justice.

Furthermore, everyone charged with a criminal offence shall:
- be presumed innocent until proved guilty according to law;
- be informed promptly, in a language which they understand, of the detail, nature, and cause of the accusation against them;
- have adequate time and facilities for the preparation of their defence;
- be allowed to defend themselves in person or through legal assistance of their choosing or be provided with free legal assistance (if insufficient funds) when the interests of justice so require;
- be allowed to produce/examine witnesses for/against them;
- have the free assistance of an interpreter if they cannot understand or speak the language used in court.

Article 7—No punishment without law

No one shall be found guilty of a criminal offence arising out of actions which at the time were not criminal; neither shall a heavier penalty be imposed.

Article 8—Right to respect private/family life

Everyone has the right to respect for their private and family life, home, and correspondence, except where a public authority acts in accordance with the law and it is necessary in a democratic society in the interests of national security, public safety, or the economic well-being of the country, for the prevention of disorder or crime, for the protection of health or morals, or for the protection of the rights and freedoms of others.

Article 9—Freedom of thought, conscience, and religion

Everyone has this right, including the freedom to change their religion or belief. These rights can be limited in certain circumstances.

Article 10—Freedom of expression

Everyone has the right to hold opinions and express their views either on their own or in a group without interference by a public authority. These rights can only be restricted in specified circumstances.

Article 11—Freedom of assembly and association

Everyone has the right to assemble with other people in a peaceful way and to associate with other people, including the right to form and join trade unions for the protection of their interests. These rights may be restricted, but only in specified circumstances.

Article 12—Right to marry

Men and women of marriageable age have the right to marry and to found a family, according to the national laws governing the exercise of this right.

Article 14—Prohibition of discrimination

The enjoyment of the rights and freedoms set forth in this Convention shall be secured without discrimination on any ground such as sex, race, colour, language, religion, political or other opinion, national or social origin, association with a national minority, property, birth, or other status.

1st Protocol—Article 1 Protection of property, entitled to peaceful enjoyment of possessions

1st Protocol—Article 2 Right to education

1st Protocol—Article 3 Right to free elections

13th Protocol—Article 1 Abolition of the death penalty

Explanatory notes

- All action taken against an individual by the police must have a legal basis and the action should not unnecessarily interfere with the individual's human rights and freedoms. An officer must carefully consider the rights of the individual and the interests/rights of the community at large. Any action should be proportionate, in the interests of justice, accounted for and necessary.
- Public authorities include: central and local government; the police, including police and crime commissioners; UK Border Agency; prisons; courts; tribunals; and the core public activities of private utilities companies that were once publicly owned.
- Section 7(8) stipulates that nothing in the 1998 Act creates a criminal offence.
- A criminal trial judge does not have the power to award damages for an alleged breach of a Convention right. This will be a separate civil action.

- Infringement of an individual's human rights will be open to examination in every criminal trial, civil or care proceedings, and tribunals.

Related cases

Metropolitan Police Commissioner v DSD and another; Koraou v Chief Constable of Greater Manchester Police [2015] EWCA Civ 646 In this case, it was held that the duty to conduct an official investigation into alleged ill-treatment (including a person becoming a victim of crime) by private individuals to identify those responsible was inherent in Art 3. The courts will look at several key elements in assessing the liability of a police force including what information and resources were available to it at relevant times.

Austin v UK [2012] Crim LR 544, ECtHR In this case it was held that detaining people during a demonstration was not necessarily a breach of Art 5 (see **2.6.1** for details).

R (on the application of Saunders) v IPCC [2008] EWHC 2372 (Admin), QBD An investigation took place into a fatal shooting by the police and no steps were taken to prevent officers conferring prior to giving their first accounts. It was held that collaboration during the production of witness statements did not breach the Art 2 duty. However, this practice was criticised, particularly since the defence provided by s 3 Criminal Law Act 1967 (see **1.2**) is personal to the individual officer as to what they honestly believed at the time.

R (on the application of Bennett) v HM Coroner for Inner South London [2006] EWHC 196 (Admin), QBD If a police officer reasonably decides to use lethal force within the law of self-defence or s 3 (see **1.2**), then the reasonableness must be decided on the facts which the user of the force honestly believed to exist and an objective test as to whether they had reasonable grounds for that belief.

Osman v UK [1998] 29 EHRR 245, ECtHR This case involved a real and immediate risk to life and, amongst other matters, considered the responsibility of the police to warn the person in danger. If there is police intelligence that a person is in considerable danger of being killed or seriously wounded, they must inform that person and try to offer a solution. If the individual refuses police assistance and/or protection, the liability of the police/state is reduced. However, it was held that the protection given to the police against civil law proceedings (for negligence in most cases) being brought against them was designed to protect them from liability in policy or operation matters but the court should still have regard to the competing public interest and should not adopt an absolute rule to disbar such claims and grant immunity.

Practical considerations

- Section 6 makes it unlawful for police officers to act in a way which is incompatible with a Convention right. To ensure compliance with this requirement, officers should make themselves familiar with these 'rights' which have been incorporated into this legislation.

- The proportionality and necessity test asks, 'were the measures taken **necessary** in a democratic society and in **proportion** to the ultimate objective?' This test should always be borne in mind by a police officer when dealing with an incident, members of the public, or an individual (eg is the force being used proportionate and necessary to prevent disorder, protect life/property, or deal with offenders).

- This test is reflected in the statutory power of arrest (see **1.4**)—unless an officer can show that arrest was **necessary** (eg there was no alternative) then the arrest power cannot be used.

- Before using their powers, a police officer should consider this test in their decision-making process and ask themselves:
  a) What is the objective to be achieved?
  b) Is it urgent or (if desirable) could it be delayed?
  c) If action is needed now what are the alternative means of dealing with this incident/individual?
  d) Is the proposed action proportionate to the intended aim and the means to be used?
  e) Can the least intrusive means be deployed?
  f) If not, does a lawful power exist?

- The use of force must always be justified and reasonable otherwise an assault will be committed, and any action taken could be rendered unlawful (see **1.2**).

- Where excessive force is used, there is the possibility of a breach of Art 3 (inhuman or degrading treatment).

- If force is used disproportionately, this may amount to a breach of Art 8, as this Article guarantees not just the right to privacy, but also the right to physical integrity—the right not to be hurt in an arbitrary or unjustifiable way.

- There must be some objective justification for the decision or action taken.

- An important point, often overlooked, is the need to strike a proper balance between the interests and rights of the community at large as well as considering the rights of the individual.

- Lawful interference with an individual's human rights, especially depriving them of these rights, must be necessary and proportionate to the aim required to be achieved (eg lawful arrest/detention of a suspect meets the legitimate aim for the prevention and detection of crime).

- Always consider whether the aim can be met with minimal impact on the rights of the suspect and any other person likely to be affected.

- Article 15 allows governments to 'derogate' from the Convention in time of war or other public emergency threatening the life of the nation.

Links to alternative subjects and offences

1.2 **Lawful Authorities—Use of Force**

If a police officer uses force, this must be justified and reasonable and based on a lawful authority—otherwise it will be an assault and would, therefore, become an unlawful act. Statute, common law, and human rights set out the circumstances in which the use of force will be lawful, but each case will be decided upon its own peculiar facts.

Statute

Criminal Law Act 1967

(1) A person may use such force as is reasonable in the circumstances in the prevention of crime, or in effecting or assisting in the lawful arrest of offenders or suspected offenders or of persons unlawfully at large.

(2) Subsection (1) above shall replace the rules of the common law on the question when force used for a purpose mentioned in the subsection is justified by that purpose.

Criminal Law Act 1967, s 3

Police and Criminal Evidence Act 1984

Where any provision of this Act—

(a) confers a power on a constable; and

(b) does not provide that the power may only be exercised with the consent of some person, other than a police officer,

the officer may use reasonable force, if necessary, in the exercise of the power.

Police and Criminal Evidence Act 1984, s 117

Criminal Justice and Immigration Act 2008

(1) This section applies where in proceedings for an offence—

    (a) an issue arises as to whether a person charged with the offence ('D') is entitled to rely on a defence within subsection (2), and

    (b) the question arises whether the degree of force used by D against a person ('V') was reasonable in the circumstances.

(2) The defences are—

    (a) the common law defence of self-defence;

    (aa) the common law defence of defence of property; and

    (b) the defences provided by section 3(1) of the Criminal Law Act 1967 (use of force in prevention of crime or making arrest).

(3) The question whether the degree of force used by D was reasonable in the circumstances is to be decided by reference to the circumstances as D believed them to be, and subsections (4) to (8) also apply in connection with deciding that question.

(4) If D claims to have held a particular belief as regards the existence of any circumstances—

    (a) the reasonableness or otherwise of that belief is relevant to the question whether D genuinely held it; but

    (b) if it is determined that D did genuinely hold it, D is entitled to rely on it for the purposes of subsection (3), whether or not—

        (i) it was mistaken, or

        (ii) (if it was mistaken) the mistake was a reasonable one to have made.

(5) But subsection (4)(b) does not enable D to rely on any mistaken belief attributable to intoxication that was voluntarily induced.

(5A) In a householder case, the degree of force used by D is not to be regarded as having been reasonable in the circumstances as D believed them to be if it was grossly disproportionate in those circumstances.

(6) In a case other than a householder case, the degree of force used by D is not to be regarded as having been reasonable in the circumstances as D believed them to be if it was disproportionate in those circumstances.

(6A) In deciding the question mentioned in subsection (3), a possibility that D could have retreated is to be considered (so far as relevant) as a factor to be taken into account, rather than as giving rise to a duty to retreat.

(7) In deciding the question mentioned in subsection (3) the following considerations are to be taken into account (so far as relevant in the circumstances of the case)—

    (a) that a person acting for a legitimate purpose may not be able to weigh to a nicety the exact measure of any necessary action; and

    (b) that evidence of a person's having only done what the person honestly and instinctively thought was necessary for a legitimate purpose constitutes strong evidence that only reasonable action was taken by that person for that purpose.

(8) Subsections (6A) and (7) are not to be read as preventing other matters from being taken into account where they are relevant to deciding the question mentioned in subsection (3).

(8A) For the purposes of this section a householder case is a case where—

    (a) the defence concerned is the common law defence of self-defence;

    (b) the force concerned is force used by D while in or partly in a building, or part of a building, that is a dwelling or is forces accommodation (or is both);

    (c) D is not a trespasser at the time the force is used; and

(d) at that time D believed V to be in, or entering, the building or part as a trespasser.

(8B) Where—

(a) a part of a building is a dwelling where D dwells;

(b) another part of the building is a place of work for D or another person who dwells in the first part; and

(c) that other part is internally accessible from the first part,

that other part, and any internal means of access between the two parts, are each treated for the purposes of subsection (8A) as a part of a building that is a dwelling.

(8C) [*Relates to 'forces accommodation' under Armed Forces Act 2006, s 96.*]

(8D) Subsections (4) and (5) apply for the purposes of subsection (8A)(d) as they apply for the purposes of subsection (3).

(8E) The fact that a person derives title from a trespasser, or has the permission of a trespasser, does not prevent the person from being a trespasser for the purposes of subsection (8A).

(8F) In subsections (8A) to (8C) building includes a vehicle or vessel.

(9) This section, except so far as making different provision for householder cases, is intended to clarify the operation of the existing defences mentioned in subsection (2).

(10) In this section—

(a) 'legitimate purpose' means—

(i) the purpose of self-defence under the common law,

(ia) the purpose of defence of property under the common law, or

(ii) the prevention of crime or effecting or assisting in the lawful arrest of persons mentioned in the provisions referred to in subsection (2)(b);

(b) references to self-defence include acting in defence of another person; and

(c) references to the degree of force used are to the type and amount of force used.

Criminal Justice and Immigration Act 2008, s 76

Explanatory notes

- Section 76 provides a gloss on the common law of self-defence and the defences provided by section 3(1) of the Criminal Law Act 1967. It is intended to improve understanding of the practical application of these areas of the law. It uses elements of case law to illustrate how the defence operates. It does not change the current test that allows the use of reasonable force.

- In line with the case law, the defence will be available to a person if he honestly believed it was necessary to use force and if the degree of force used was not disproportionate in the circumstances as he viewed them (with the exception of householder cases). This reaffirms that a person who uses force is to be judged on the basis of the circumstances as he perceived them, that in the heat of the moment he will not be expected to have judged exactly what action was called for, and that a degree of latitude may be given to a person who only did what he honestly and instinctively thought was necessary. A defendant is entitled to have his actions judged on the basis of his view of the facts as he honestly believed them to be, even if that belief was mistaken.

- The Criminal Law Act 1967, s 3 allows the use of reasonable force in the prevention of crime or making a lawful arrest and applies to any person. '**Crime**' does not cover crimes recognised as against international law; it only refers to crimes committed against domestic law either by statute or judicial decision (*R v Jones and others; Ayliffe and others v DPP, Swain v DPP* [2006] UKHL 16) (see **4.4**).
- Section 117 of PACE relates to the use of **reasonable force** by a police officer whilst exercising their (PACE) powers (see **Chapter 12**).
- The Criminal Justice and Immigration Act 2008, s 76 provides a statutory test as to using reasonable force for self-defence and defence of property at common law, preventing crime, or making an arrest. This does not alter common law and is not a complete statement of the law, but it does set out the basic principles (*see R v Keane and McGrath* [2010] EWCA Crim 2514, CA).
- In a householder case, disproportionate force can be regarded as reasonable in the circumstances as the accused believed them to be when householders are acting to protect themselves or others from trespassers in their homes. The use of grossly disproportionate force is not permitted. The householder provisions extend to people who live and work in the same premises and armed forces personnel who may live and work in buildings such as barracks for periods of time. These provisions do not cover other scenarios where the use of force might be required, such as when people are defending themselves from attacks on the street, preventing crime or protecting property, but the law on use of reasonable force applies to these situations. For further advice see MOJ Circular 2/2013 and ACPO guidance in the same year titled 'Use of force in self-defence at a place of residence'.

Related cases

R v Ray [2017] EWCA Crim 1391 It was held in this case that the jury must first determine the circumstances as the defendant believed them to be and then whether, in those circumstances, the amount of force used was reasonable. In determining the reasonableness of the degree of force, the jury must decide whether it was grossly disproportionate or not.

R v Day [2015] EWCA Crim 1646 D, a student, stayed overnight at her friend's accommodation. She was partially dressed and preparing to go to bed when C, who was drunk, came into the room where she was staying. There followed an altercation during which D asked C to leave. She warned him that if he did not leave, she would shut the door on him. He did not leave, so she pushed him out of the door whereupon he fell and injured his head. D was charged with common assault and convicted. However, on appeal, it was held that as D was not a trespasser at the time she was in the accommodation and she believed C to be trespassing in that part of the building that she was in; the householder defence was available to her. Therefore, the defence of self-defence was available not just to the owner of a property, but to a person in lawful occupation of that property.

McDonnell v Commissioner of Police of the Metropolis and another (2015) CA An officer tackled M and brought him to the ground during his arrest resulting in the suspect breaking his shoulder. It was held not to be unreasonable or excessive use of force in accordance with s 117 of the Police and Criminal Evidence Act 1984 and s 3 of the Criminal Law Act 1967. The injury had resulted from the tackle, but it was accidental and had not been deliberately inflicted. If the tackle had been less vigorous, M might not have struck the wall and broken his shoulder, but that did not make the use of force unreasonable or excessive.

R v Hichens [2011] EWCA Crim 1626 It was held in this case that self-defence and the defence of using reasonable force in the prevention of crime under the Criminal Law Act 1967 s 3 was capable of extending to the use of force against an innocent third party to prevent a crime being committed by someone else.

Common law

- Whether force used is reasonable or excessive in the defence of self or property, the prevention of crime, or in making an arrest, will be determined by the court considering all the circumstances. The seminal words of Lord Morris in *Palmer v R* [1971] AC 814, HL emphasise the difficulties faced by a person confronted by an intruder or in taking any defensive action against attack.

If there has been an attack so that defence is reasonably necessary, it will be recognised that a person defending himself cannot weigh to a nicety the exact measure of his defensive action. If the jury thought that in a moment of unexpected anguish a person attacked had only done what he honestly and instinctively thought necessary, that would be the most potent evidence that only reasonable defensive action had been taken.

- Although this area of law is addressed by statute, the wider issues of self-defence under common law may still be relevant (see **2.1.2**).

Human rights

- In addition, under the provisions of the ECHR (see **1.1**), a further dimension in respect of the necessity and proportionality must be considered alongside the common law or statutory powers.
- Apart from using no more force than is necessary, considering proportionality will bring other factors into the equation, such as whether the force used is:
  - g) proportionate to the wrong that it seeks to avoid or the harm it seeks to prevent;
  - h) the least intrusive or damaging option available at the time.

- Striking a fair balance between the rights of the individual and the interests/rights of the community at large must be carefully considered.
- Any limited breaching of an individual's human rights must be both necessary and proportionate to the legitimate aim to be pursued (eg the lawful arrest or detention of that person is to pursue the legitimate aim of the prevention and detection of crime). Note, however, that certain Articles such as Art 3 cannot be lawfully breached.
- Therefore, any use of powers to cause inhuman or degrading treatment may amount to a breach—words alone may contribute to the demeaning treatment (eg of prisoners), and under extreme circumstances the use of words alone may suffice.
- If force is not used proportionately, then this may amount to a breach of various Articles of the ECHR (see **1.1** for details):
  - i) Article 2: Use of lethal force, unless the level of force used was strictly proportionate to the lawful aim pursued;
  - j) Article 3: If excessive force is used—inhuman or degrading treatment;
  - k) Article 8: Guarantees not only the right to privacy/family life, but also the right not to be hurt in an arbitrary or unjustifiable way.

Practical considerations

- Force used by an officer at an incident must be justified. When preparing evidence, state what the situation was like upon your arrival, the attitude of the individual(s) or group when they were approached, and what means were used (or attempted) to control the situation.
- Consider the NPCC 2010 Manual of Guidance on Keeping the Peace, which provides updated guidance on public order policing, planning and deployment, structure of command, communication, and tactical options.

Links to alternative subjects and offences

Powers and Procedures

1.3.1 **Stop and search powers**

The Police and Criminal Evidence Act 1984 (PACE) creates the generic stop and search powers for a constable in places to which the public has access.

1.3.2 **Search and detain**

Section 1 of PACE creates the power for a constable to stop and search people and vehicles for stolen property, offensive weapons, bladed/pointed articles, or prohibited fireworks.

> **Power—search and detain**
>
> (1) A constable may exercise any power conferred by this section—
>
>   (a) in any place to which at the time when he proposes to exercise the power the public or any section of the public has access, on payment or otherwise, as of right or by virtue of express or implied permission; or
>
>   (b) in any other place to which people have ready access at the time when he proposes to exercise the power, but which is not a dwelling.
>
> (2) Subject to subsection **(3)** to **(5)** below, a constable—
>
>   (a) may search—
>
>   (i) any person or vehicle;
>
>   (ii) anything which is in or on a vehicle;
>
>   for stolen or prohibited articles, any article to which subsection **(8A)** below applies or any firework to which subsection **(8B)** below applies; and
>
>   (b) may detain a person or vehicle for the purpose of such a search.
>
> Police and Criminal Evidence Act 1984, s 1

Meanings

Vehicle

This is not defined. In the *Oxford English Dictionary*, it means 'a conveyance, usually with wheels, for transporting people, animals, goods or other objects and includes (amongst others) a car, cart, truck, bus, train carriage or sledge'. However, this power also applies to vessels including any ship, boat, raft, or other apparatus constructed or adapted for floating on water (under s 118 of the Act), and aircraft, and hovercraft (under s 2(10) of the Act).

Stolen article (see 3.1)

Prohibited articles

Prohibited articles given under s 1(7) and (8) means:
- an offensive weapon (see **8.9.1**);
- an article made or adapted for use in the course of or in connection with the following offences **or** intended by the person having it with them for such use by them or by some other person:
  - ✦ burglary (see **3.3.1**);
  - ✦ theft (see **3.1**);
  - ✦ taking a conveyance without consent (see **4.3**);
  - ✦ fraud (see **3.8**);
  - ✦ criminal damage (see **4.5**).

Article to which s 1(8A) applies

Any pointed or bladed article, with which a person has committed, is committing, or is going to commit an offence under s 139 (see **8.10.1**) or s 139AA (see **8.10.3**) of the Criminal Justice Act 1988 (offences of having such articles in public place/on school premises).

Firework to which s 1(8B) applies

Any firework possessed in breach of prohibition imposed by fireworks regulations (see **8.8**).

Reasonable grounds for suspicion (subsection (3))

This section **does not** give a constable power to search a person or vehicle or anything in or on a vehicle **unless** (s)he has **reasonable grounds** for suspecting that (s)he will find stolen or prohibited articles, any article to which subsection (8A) applies or any firework to which subsection (8B) applies.

Meaning of 'reasonable grounds'

PACE Code A (updated March 2015) governs the exercise by police officers of statutory powers of stop and search. Paragraphs 2.2–2.11 provide an explanation of what are considered to be reasonable grounds for suspicion when conducting a search.

PACE Code of Practice A

Reasonable grounds for suspicion depend on the circumstances in each case:
- Officers must have formed a genuine suspicion in their own mind that they will find the object for which the search power being exercised allows them to search. This must be a reasonable suspicion, which means there must be an objective basis for that suspicion based on facts, information, and/or intelligence that are relevant to the likelihood of finding the object.
- Stop and search powers depend on the likelihood that the person searched is in possession of an item for which they may be searched; it does not depend on them being suspected of committing an offence.

- It can never be supported on the basis of personal factors alone without reliable supporting intelligence or information, or specific behaviour by the person concerned. For example, unless a suspect description is available, a person's physical appearance (including any of the 'protected characteristics' (see **13.6**) set out in the Equality Act 2010), or the fact that they have a previous conviction, cannot be used alone or in combination with each other as the reason for stopping and searching that person.
- It cannot be based on generalisations or stereotyping certain groups or categories of people as more likely to be involved in criminal activity.

Further points contained within this code are:
- Reasonable suspicion can be on the basis of behaviour of a person (eg an officer encountering someone on the street at night who is obviously trying to hide something). A hunch or an instinct which cannot be explained or justified to an objective observer can never amount to reasonable grounds.
- On reliable information or intelligence that members of a group or gang habitually carry knives unlawfully, or weapons, or controlled drugs, and they wear a distinctive item of clothing or denote their membership by other means, if that distinctive means of identification is displayed, that may provide the reasonable grounds to stop and search a person. A similar approach could be applied to organised protest groups.
- An officer who has reasonable grounds for suspicion may detain that person in order to carry out a search.
- Before carrying out a search, the officer may ask questions relating to the circumstances giving rise to the suspicion; as a result, the grounds for suspicion may be confirmed or, because of a satisfactory explanation, be eliminated.
- Reasonable grounds for suspicion cannot be provided retrospectively by such questioning during a person's detention or by refusal to answer any questions put.
- Once reasonable grounds to suspect that an article is being carried cease to exist, no search may take place. In the absence of any other lawful power to detain, the person is free to leave and must be so informed.
- There is no power to stop or detain a person in order to find grounds for a search.
- If a person is lawfully detained for the purpose of a search, but no search takes place, the detention will not subsequently be rendered unlawful.

Restrictions in a garden/yard (subsections (4) and (5))

If a person or vehicle is in a garden or yard occupied with and used for the purposes of a dwelling or on other land so occupied and used, a constable may not search that person or vehicle, in exercising the power

under s 1, unless the constable has reasonable grounds for believing that the suspect (or the person in charge of the vehicle):
- does not reside in the dwelling; **and**
- the vehicle is not in the place in question with the express or implied permission of a person who resides in the dwelling.

Power to seize

If in the course of such a search a constable discovers an article which he has reasonable grounds for suspecting to be a stolen or prohibited article, an article to which subsection (**8A**) applies or a firework to which subsection (**8B**) applies, he may seize it.

Police and Criminal Evidence Act 1984, s 1(6)

1.3.3 **Conduct of a search**

Section 2 of PACE provides safeguards for when a constable detains a person or vehicle under s 1 or in the exercise of any search powers prior to arrest. They are:
- a search can be abandoned if it is no longer required or it is impracticable to conduct one;
- the time for which a person or vehicle may be detained for a search is as reasonably required to permit the search to be carried out, either at the place detained or nearby;
- a search and detain power does not authorise a constable to:
  + require a person to remove any of his clothing in public other than an outer coat, jacket, or gloves; or
  + stop a vehicle, if not in uniform;
- before commencing a search (excepting an unattended vehicle), a constable shall take reasonable steps to bring to the attention of the detainee or person in charge of the vehicle the following matters and provide the following details:
  + name of constable and police station (where based), plus identification if the constable is not in uniform;
  + object of the proposed search;
  + grounds for proposing the search;
  + entitlement to a copy of the written stop and search record, unless it appears to the constable that it will not be practicable to make/ provide the record at the time of the search (see **1.3.4**);
- where an unattended vehicle is searched, a constable shall leave a notice inside the vehicle (unless it would damage the vehicle) stating that they have searched it; name of police station where based; that an application for compensation for any damage caused by the search may be made to that police station; the procedure as to the entitlement of a copy of the written stop and search record (see **1.3.4**).

1.3.3 Conduct of a search

Meaning of vehicle (see 1.3.2)

Terrorism stop and search powers

- A police officer may stop and search a person under s 43 of the Terrorism Act 2000, if they reasonably suspect that person to be a terrorist, to discover whether that person has in their possession anything which may constitute evidence that they are a terrorist. In exercising this power, if a constable stops a vehicle, they may search the vehicle and anything in or on it to discover evidence that the person is a terrorist and may seize and retain any such evidence found.
- Section 43A of the Terrorism Act 2000 provides that a constable on reasonable suspicion that a vehicle is being used for the purposes of terrorism may stop and search the vehicle and driver, passenger, or anything in or on the vehicle or carried by the driver or a passenger to discover evidence that the vehicle is being used for the purposes of terrorism. A constable may seize and retain anything discovered in the course of such a search and reasonably suspects may be evidence that vehicle is being used for the purposes of terrorism.
- Ensure compliance with the Code of Practice relating to the above stop and search powers under s 43, s 43A.
- Paragraph 4.13 of this Code deals with photography/film matters, as concerns had been raised among photographers and journalists about the use of stop and search powers in relation to photography. It is important to note that members of the public and media do not generally need any form of permit or express authority to take photographs nor is it an offence to take photographs/film in a public place or of a public building (unless there are any specific, advertised restrictions such as those applying to various Ministry of Defence buildings). Similarly, the police do not have any general power to stop people taking photographs.
- Digital images can be viewed as part of a search under ss 43, 43A, or 47 to discover whether the person has in their possession anything which may constitute evidence that they are a terrorist, or to determine whether the images are of a kind which could be used in connection with terrorism.
- Film and memory cards may be seized as part of such a search if the police officer reasonably suspects they are evidence that the person is a terrorist, or a vehicle is being used for the purposes of terrorism, but officers do not have a power to delete images, destroy film, or to require the person to do so.
- For further information and guidance on Terrorism Act powers, please see the *PNLD Counter-Terrorism Handbook* for further details.

1.3.4 Written records of stop and search

Section 3 of PACE details the following procedures to be adhered to when making written records of stop searches carried out by a constable, while exercising **any of their stop and search powers**, relating to a person or **vehicle**:

- If an arrest has been made as a result of a 'stop and search', a written record of the search must be included as part of the custody record. In any other case, if it is not practicable to make a record 'on the spot' then it shall be made as soon as practicable after the completion of the search.
- A record of the search of a person or vehicle shall include:
  - ✦ object of the search;
  - ✦ grounds for making it;
  - ✦ date and time made;
  - ✦ place where it was made;
  - ✦ except in the search of an unattended vehicle, the ethnic origins of the person searched or the person in charge of the vehicle searched (*ethnic origin is as described by that person, and if different as perceived by the constable*); and
  - ✦ shall identify the constable who carried out the search.
- Apart from the above mandatory fields, some forces continue to record all fields including name, outcome, and damage/injury caused.
- A person searched, or the owner/person in charge of a searched vehicle, is entitled to a copy of the record. This can be requested up to three months from the date when the search was made.

Meaning of vehicle (see **1.3.2**)

Explanatory notes

- Fireworks possessed in breach of prohibitions imposed by the Fireworks Regulations 2004 would give grounds for invoking the 'stop and search' powers (see **8.8** for details).
- Articles that are made, adapted, or intended for use for one of the listed offences could include:
  - ✦ crowbar/screwdriver (burglary);
  - ✦ car keys (for taking a vehicle without owner's consent);
  - ✦ stolen credit card (fraud); or
  - ✦ spray paint can/pens intending to cause graffiti (damage).
- This section does not give a constable power to search a person or vehicle, or anything in or on a vehicle unless they have reasonable grounds for suspecting that they will find stolen property, prohibited articles including fireworks.

Related cases (see also 5.4.1 cases)

Howarth v Commissioner of the Metropolitan Police [2011] EWHC 2818, QBD A police officer searched a protestor travelling to a demonstration for prohibited items. This action was justified by intelligence that the protestors were carrying items which had been used to cause criminal damage at previous demonstrations. It was held that it was well recognised that the threshold for the existence of reasonable grounds for suspicion was low. It was accepted that it was not necessarily essential in all cases for the searching officer reasonably to suspect every individual member of a suspected group to be carrying the offending items before the search of members of the group was lawful.

B v DPP [2008] EWHC 1655 (Admin), QBD Failure by a constable in plain clothes to produce their warrant card was a breach of s 2(2) of PACE and para 3.8 of Code A and consequently, the drugs search was deemed unlawful.

R v Bristol [2007] EWCA Crim 3214, CA If a person is searched for drugs under s 23 of the Misuse of Drugs Act 1971 (see **5.4**) then s 2 of PACE applies. As the officer had failed to state his name and police station, then s 2 was breached, the search was unlawful, and the conviction was set aside (following *Osman v DPP* (1999) 163 JP 725, QBD).

O'Hara v CC of the RUC [1997] 1 All ER 129, HL Reasonable grounds for suspicion can arise from information/intelligence passed to an officer by a colleague, an informant, or anonymously. But the mere fact that an officer had been instructed is not sufficient; it is necessary that the arresting officer had in his own mind the relevant suspicion.

R v Fennelley [1989] Crim LR 142, CC In this case, the defendant had not been properly informed of the reasons for a street search. It was held that the evidence obtained as an outcome of the search was unfair and was consequently excluded.

Practical considerations

- Paragraph 4.12 of Code A states that there is no longer a national requirement for an officer to make any record of a 'stop and account' incident or to give the person a receipt although, after consulting with local communities, forces can continue to record self-defined ethnicity if it is considered necessary to monitor any local 'disproportionality'.
- All COPs are legally binding; failure to comply with them could result in the CPS declining to institute or continue proceedings. A court case may be lost through evidence being disallowed and the police officer could be subject to severe penalties.
- Code A provides assistance and guidance to police officers in the exercise of their powers to stop and search people and vehicles.
- Searches based on up-to-date and accurate intelligence are likely to be effective and lawful, thus securing public confidence. Ensure that all stop and search powers are used objectively, fairly, and without any bias against ethnic or other groups within the community.
- Officers must be fully aware and ready to take account of the special needs of juveniles and other vulnerable groups.

Links to alternative subjects and offences

1.4 Powers of Arrest

Sections 24, 24A, and 28–31 of PACE deal with arrests made by a constable or other people and other related matters.

1.4.1 Arrest without warrant: constables

Arrest without warrant

Section 24 of PACE provides the power of arrest for a constable without a warrant and the conditions that must apply before the arrest power can be used.

Powers of arrest

Arrest

(1) A constable may arrest without a warrant—
   (a) anyone who is about to commit an offence;
   (b) anyone who is in the act of committing an offence;
   (c) anyone whom he has reasonable grounds for suspecting to be about to commit an offence;
   (d) anyone whom he has reasonable grounds for suspecting to be committing an offence.

(2) If a constable has reasonable grounds for suspecting that an offence has been committed, he may arrest without a warrant anyone whom he has reasonable grounds to suspect of being guilty of it.

(3) If an offence has been committed, a constable may arrest without a warrant—
   (a) anyone who is guilty of the offence;
   (b) anyone whom he has reasonable grounds for suspecting to be guilty of it.

Necessity criteria

(4) But the power of summary arrest conferred by subsection (1), (2), or (3) is exercisable only if the constable has reasonable grounds for believing that for any of the reasons mentioned in subsection (5) it is necessary to arrest the person in question.

Reasons

(5) The reasons are—
   (a) to enable the name of the person in question to be ascertained (in the case where the constable does not know, and cannot readily ascertain, the person's name, or has reasonable grounds for doubting whether a name given by the person as his name is his real name);
   (b) correspondingly as regards the person's address;

(c) to prevent the person in question—
  (i) causing physical injury to himself or any other person;
  (ii) suffering physical injury;
  (iii) causing loss of or damage to property;
  (iv) committing an offence against public decency (subject to subsection (6)); or
  (v) causing an unlawful obstruction of the highway;
(d) to protect a child or other vulnerable person from the person in question;
(e) to allow the prompt and effective investigation of the offence or of the conduct of the person in question;
(f) to prevent any prosecution for the offence from being hindered by the disappearance of the person in question.
(6) Subsection (5)(c)(iv) applies only where members of the public going about their normal business cannot reasonably be expected to avoid the person in question.

Police and Criminal Evidence Act 1984, s 24

Explanatory notes

- The use of this arrest power is governed by PACE Code G.
- If a person is arrested on suspicion of being a terrorist, then Code H would apply in connection with the detention, treatment, and questioning for persons arrested under s 41 of, and Sch 8 of the Terrorism Act 2000.
- If a person is arrested on suspicion of having committed a terrorist offence, but is arrested under s 24 of PACE, then PACE and Codes G and C will apply.
- The Director General of NCA may confer some or all of the s 24 powers on NCA staff and nominate them as 'designated persons' (with powers of constable).
- The s 24 power means that a constable/designated person may only arrest persons without a warrant under this general power where:
  + they are about to commit/in the act of committing an offence;
  + there are reasonable grounds to suspect they are about to commit/ to be committing an offence;
  + there are reasonable grounds to suspect that an offence has been committed;
  + has reasonable grounds to suspect they are guilty of it;
  + an offence has been committed: they are guilty of the offence; reasonable grounds to suspect they are guilty of it;

and the constable has reasonable grounds to believe (more than 'suspect') that it is **necessary** to arrest that person for any of the reasons listed.
- A lawful arrest requires both elements of:
  + a person's involvement or suspected involvement, or attempted involvement in the commission of a criminal offence; **and**
  + reasonable grounds to believe that the arrest is necessary.

1.4.1 **Arrest without warrant: constables**

- The requirement for reasonable grounds makes this an **objective test**—that is, it requires some verifiable material fact other than the belief of the arresting officer.
- The exercise of these arrest powers will be subject to a test of necessity, based on the nature and circumstances of the offence, and the interests of the criminal justice system.
- An arrest will only be justified if the constable believes it is necessary for any of the reasons set out, **and** they had reasonable grounds on which that belief was based.
- Criteria for what may constitute necessity remain an operational decision at the discretion of the arresting officer.
- Paragraph 4 of Code G deals with 'Records of Arrest' in that:
  + the arresting officer is required to record in his pocketbook or other methods used for recording information:
    - the nature and circumstances of the offence leading to arrest;
    - the reason or reasons why arrest was necessary;
    - the giving of the caution;
    - anything said by the person at the time of arrest;
  + such record should be made at the time of arrest unless impracticable to do so, in which case to be completed as soon as possible thereafter.
- Some of the reasons to consider under s 24(5)(e), as to a prompt and effective investigation, are given in para 2.9 of Code G; these may be where there are reasonable grounds to believe that the person:
  + has made false statements;
  + has made statements which cannot be readily verified;
  + has presented false evidence;
  + may steal or destroy evidence;
  + may make contact with co-suspects or conspirators;
  + may intimidate or threaten, or make contact with witnesses; or
  + where it is necessary to obtain evidence by questioning:
    - it is thought unlikely that the person would attend the police station voluntarily to be interviewed;
    - arrest would enable 'special warnings' to be given per Code C paras 10.10 and 10.11.
- If an arrest is for an indictable offence, there could be other reasons under s 24(5)(e) to consider such as a need to:
  + enter and search any premises occupied or controlled by a person;
  + search the person (in respect of **any** offence, not just indictable);
  + prevent contact with others.
- If arrest is for a recordable offence and it is necessary to secure and preserve evidence of that offence:
- take fingerprints, footwear impressions, samples, or photographs; or
  + ensure compliance with statutory drug testing requirements.
- Apart from arrest, other options such as:
  + report for summons;
  + grant street bail;
  + issue a fixed penalty notice, PND; or
  + other methods of disposal;

will have to be considered and excluded before arrest is decided upon.
* Some preserved powers of arrest under Sch 2 have been retained.
* Arrest (without warrant) by other people is subject to s 24A of PACE (see **1.4.4**).
* Use of reasonable force—see '**Use of force resolution**' at **1.2**.

Related cases

Sneyd v DPP [2006] EWHC 560 (Admin), QBD Once a positive breath test had been provided under s 6(1) of the Road Traffic Act 1988, the officer had grounds to suspect that an offence had been committed and was only then required to caution S.

1.4.2 Information to be given on arrest

Cautions

Code of Practice C deals with when a caution must be given.

PACE Code of Practice C

Police officers and other persons subject to observing PACE should be aware of the following paragraphs in this code of practice:
* A person whom there are grounds to suspect of an offence must be cautioned before any questions about an offence or further questions, if the answers provide the grounds for suspicion are put to them, if either the suspect's answers or silence (ie failure or refusal to answer or answer satisfactorily) may be given in evidence to a court in a prosecution.

A person need not be cautioned if questioned in order to:
  + solely establish identity or ownership of vehicle;
  + obtain information to comply with a statutory requirement;
  + in furtherance of the proper and effective conduct of a search, (eg to determine the need to search in the exercise of powers of stop and search or to seek co-operation while carrying out a search); or
  + seek clarification for a written record (para 10.1).
* A person who is arrested or further arrested, must also be cautioned unless:
  + it is impracticable to do so by reason of their condition or behaviour at the time;
  + they have already been cautioned immediately prior to arrest (para 10.4).

The **caution** that must be given on arrest; before a person is charged or informed they may be prosecuted; and **should** (unless the restriction on drawing adverse inferences from silence applies) **be in the following terms**:

'You do not have to say anything. But it may harm your defence if you do not mention when questioned something which you later rely

on in Court. Anything you do say may be given in evidence.' (Code C
para 10.5; for terrorism Code H para 10.4.)

- Anyone who appears to be **under 18** shall, in the absence of clear
  evidence that they are older, be treated as a juvenile and where a
  caution is given, it must be done in the presence of an appropriate
  adult (see below).

Meaning

Appropriate adult

PACE Code C (para 1.7) In the case of a juvenile (under 18):

(a) the parent, guardian or, if the juvenile is in the care of a local
authority or voluntary organisation, a person representing that
authority or organisation; or

(b) a social worker of a local authority; or

(c) failing these, some other responsible adult aged 18 or over
who is not
   + a police officer,
   + employed by the police,
   + under the direction or control of the chief officer of a police
     force; or a person who provides services under contractual
     arrangements (but without being employed by the chief officer
     of a police force), to assist that force in relation to the discharge
     of its chief officer's functions,

whether or not they are on duty at the time.

Note that a solicitor or independent custody visitor who is present at
the police station and acting in that capacity, may not be the appropriate adult (Note 1F).

Explanatory notes

- Whenever a person **not under arrest** is initially cautioned, or
  reminded that they are under caution, that person must at the same
  time be told they are not under arrest and must be informed that
  they need to agree to be interviewed, how they may obtain legal
  advice according to whether they are at a police station or elsewhere
  and the other rights and entitlements that apply to a voluntary
  interview (Code C para 3.21 and 10.2).
- Minor deviations from the words of any caution given in accordance
  with Code C do not constitute a breach of this code, provided the
  sense of the relevant caution is preserved (Code C, para 10.7).
- After any break in questioning under caution the person being
  questioned must be made aware that they remain under caution. If
  there is any doubt, the relevant caution shall be given again in full
  when the interview resumes (Code C, para 10.8).
- Failure to comply with cautioning procedures will allow the accused
  to claim a breach of this code at any subsequent court proceedings.
  By virtue of s 76 or s 78 of PACE, the court may then exclude the
  evidence of confession so obtained.

Statutory requirements

Section 28 of PACE determines the information that must be given to a person when arrested.

Information to be given on arrest

(1) Subject to subsection (5) below, where a person is arrested, otherwise than by being informed that he is under arrest, the arrest is not lawful unless the person arrested is informed that he is under arrest as soon as is practicable after his arrest.

(2) Where a person is arrested by a constable, subsection (1) above applies regardless of whether the fact of the arrest is obvious.

(3) Subject to subsection (5) below, no arrest is lawful unless the person arrested is informed of the ground for the arrest at the time of, or as soon as practicable after, the arrest.

(4) Where a person is arrested by a constable, subsection (3) above applies regardless of whether the ground for the arrest is obvious.

(5) Nothing in this section is to be taken to require a person to be informed—
    (a) that he is under arrest; or
    (b) of the ground for the arrest,

if it was not reasonably practicable for him to be so informed by reason of his having escaped from arrest before the information could be given.

Police and Criminal Evidence Act 1984, s 28

Explanatory notes

- A person who is arrested, or further arrested, must be informed at the time, or as soon as practicable thereafter, in a language they understand (see COP and ECHR), that they are under arrest and the grounds for their arrest.
- When arresting using the power under s 24, the officer must tell the person not only the offence/suspected offence involved but also the reason why the officer believes that arrest is necessary. The necessity criteria (see **1.4.1**) must also be recorded by the officer.
- If it becomes apparent that a more serious offence may have been committed the suspect must be made aware of these facts immediately (eg originally arrested and interviewed for sexual assault, which now transpires is rape).
- It would be manifestly unfair if the defendant did not know the true extent of the situation they were in and any interviews could be excluded at trial.

Related cases

Hayes v CC of Merseyside Police [2011] EWCA Civ 911, CA The arresting officer must believe that the arrest is necessary under s 24(4) for a s 24(5) reason and this belief must be objectively reasonable.

Dhesi v CC of West Midlands Police, The Times 9 May [2000] All ER (D) 1172 The officer informing the offender that they were under arrest and giving the grounds does not have to be the same officer as the one who is physically detaining that person.

1.4.3 **Arrest procedures**

Arrest at police station—voluntary attendance

Where for the purpose of assisting with an investigation a person attends voluntarily at a police station or at any other place where a constable is present, or accompanies a constable to a police station or any such other place without having been arrested:

(a) he shall be entitled to leave at will unless he is placed under arrest;
(b) he shall be informed at once that he is under arrest if a decision is taken by a constable to prevent him from leaving at will.

Police and Criminal Evidence Act, s 29

Explanatory notes

- Confusion sometimes arises about the status of a suspect who has attended at a police station voluntarily. If the investigating officer concludes that the suspect should not be allowed to leave, and an arrest is **necessary**, then the officer should caution the suspect (unless recently cautioned) and inform the suspect that they are under arrest and take them before the custody officer.
- Ensure that the **necessity test** is satisfied (see **1.4.1**). Simply giving the grounds for the arrest as 'for the prompt and effective investigation' is not a good enough reason, without further explanation.
- Under s 29 a person is free to leave the station interview at any time. If they do, then it may be lawful to arrest, and the necessity criteria may be met. This is because, under para 2.9(e)(i) of Code G (see **1.4.1**), it may be 'necessary to obtain evidence by questioning', and here the person has refused or failed to comply with arrangements for voluntary attendance/interview.
- There is no provision to bail voluntary attenders at a police station, PACE only contains provisions for bail after arrest (including 'street bail') (see below). If you need to speak to the voluntary attender again and do not want to arrest them then you can request that they re-attend at a set time and date but there is no power to enforce this.
- When a person who attends a police station as a volunteer and is not charged with an offence, there is no power to obtain biometric data, however, the taking of fingerprints etc may be done with a person's consent and an appropriate consent form should be provided and signed by the person.
- Where a person attends at a police station or elsewhere voluntarily the suspect has a right to legal advice and all other rights and entitlements that apply to all voluntary interviews in accordance with Code C, irrespective of where the interview takes place.
- For further guidance see Code C, 3.21.

Arrest—not at a police station

Section 30 of PACE provides the procedure to be applied when a constable either makes an arrest or takes a person into custody after arrest by a person other than a constable (at any place other than a police station). The relevant points are:
- the arrested person must be taken to a police station as soon as practicable after arrest;
- this must be a police station designated for dealing with 'PACE' prisoners, unless:
  + it is anticipated that the arrested person will be dealt with in less than six hours at any police station;
  + the arrest/taken into custody is without the assistance of any other constable(s) and none were available to assist;
  + it is considered that the arrested person cannot be conveyed to a designated police station without the arrested person injuring himself, the constable, or some other person;
- if the first police station to which an arrested person is taken after their arrest is not a designated police station, they shall be taken to a designated police station not more than six hours after their arrival at the first police station unless they are released previously;
- prior to arrival at the police station, the arrested person must be released without bail if the constable is satisfied that there are no longer grounds for keeping them under arrest or releasing them on bail; if this occurs the constable shall record the fact that they have done so and shall make the record as soon as practicable after release. This requirement should be read in conjunction with the necessity criteria as, once the relevant criterion making the arrest necessary has ceased, arguably the person should be released;
- a constable can delay taking a person to a police station or releasing them on bail, if the presence of the arrested person at a place (other than a police station) is necessary in order to carry out such investigations as it is reasonable to carry out immediately; if such delay occurs the reason(s) for the delay must be recorded when the person first arrives at a police station or (as the case may be) is released on bail.

Explanatory notes
- There is no requirement that a person must be taken to the nearest police station: s 30(1A) states 'the person must be taken by a constable to a police station as soon as practicable after the arrest'—there is no mention of the word 'nearest'.
- The type of record that has to be made, if the arrested person is 'de-arrested' prior to arrival at the police station, is not specified but could for example include completing a formal custody record: this depends on individual **force policies**.

Power to release a person prior to arrival at a police station

Section 30A provides that a constable has power to release a person at any time prior to arrival at a police station without bail or on bail, and if on bail, with or without conditions.

Power

A constable may release a person who is arrested or taken into custody in the circumstances mentioned in section 30(1)—

a) without bail unless subsection (1A) applies, or
b) on bail if subsection (1A) applies.

(1A) This subsection applies if—

a) the constable is satisfied that releasing the person on bail is necessary and proportionate in all the circumstances (having regard, in particular, to any conditions of bail which would be imposed), and
b) a police officer of the rank of inspector or above authorises the release on bail (having considered any representations made by the person).

Police and Criminal Evidence Act 1984 s 30A(1) and (1A)

Practical considerations

- A person may be released at any time before he arrives at a police station.
- If released on bail, the person must be required to attend at a police station.
- Under this section, bail cannot be granted with conditions, such as, securities, sureties, conditions of residence in a bail hostel as per s 30A(3A).
- **However, under s 30A(3B)** where a constable releases a person on bail under subsection (1) the constable may impose, as conditions of the bail, such requirements as appear to the constable to be necessary—
  a) to secure that the person surrenders to custody,
  b) to secure that the person does not commit an offence while on bail,
  c) to secure that the person does not interfere with witnesses or otherwise obstruct the course of justice, whether in relation to himself or any other person, or
  d) for the person's own protection or, if the person is under the age of 18 for the person's own welfare or in the person's own interests.

Explanatory notes

- This power includes the power to grant so-called 'street bail' and can only be used in the circumstances mentioned in s 30(1) ("only where a person is at any place other than a police station"); that means, only prior to a person's arrival at the police station. Once a person has arrived at a police station, for example after an arrest or when answering bail, s 30A powers cannot be used and the requirement to attend a police station and any conditions would be invalid. The person could therefore not be arrested if in breach of bail.

- There is a presumption that, where a police officer decides that it is appropriate to release an arrested person rather than take them to a police station, that release will be without bail, unless the requirements in s 30A(1A) are met.

- Officers can grant 'street bail' and consider attaching conditions relevant and proportionate to the suspect and the offence. The conditions that can be imposed must be necessary to secure that the person surrenders to custody, that the person does not commit an offence while on bail, or that the person does not interfere with witnesses or otherwise obstruct the course of justice. Where the person is under the age of 18 conditions may also be applied for their welfare, or in their own interest. No recognizance, security, or surety may be taken and no requirement to reside in a bail hostel may be imposed.

- Where a person has been bailed subject to conditions, they will have the right to apply for variation of conditions to a custody officer and to a magistrates' court. A record must be made of the exercise of the power and a copy provided to the person explaining their rights.

- The measures reflect bail provisions already available in relation to people at the charging stage of the process.

- Prior to release under s 30A a constable must give a notice in writing, setting out the offence for which he was arrested and the ground on which the arrest was made (see s 30B).

- Note that under s 30D(1) where a person fails to surrender to bail granted under s 30A, either to attend at the police station or to attend at the specified time, a constable may arrest without warrant and the person must then be taken to a police station as soon as practicable after the arrest. A power of entry under s 17 PACE may be used to effect the arrest (see **1.5.2**).

Arrest—for further offences

Where—

(a) a person—
   (i) has been arrested for an offence; and
   (ii) is at a police station in consequence of that arrest; and

(b) it appears to a constable that, if he were released from that arrest, he would be liable to arrest for some other offence,

he shall be arrested for that other offence.

Police and Criminal Evidence Act 1984, s 31

Explanatory notes

- Consider the necessity test under s 24(5) (see **1.4.1**).

1.4.4 **Arrest without warrant: other persons**

Section 24A of PACE provides a power of arrest without warrant to persons other than police officers.

Arrest power (other persons)

(1) A person other than a constable may arrest without a warrant—
  (a) anyone who is in the act of committing an indictable offence;
  (b) anyone whom he has reasonable grounds for suspecting to be committing an indictable offence.
(2) Where an indictable offence has been committed, a person other than a constable may arrest without a warrant—
  (a) anyone who is guilty of the offence;
  (b) anyone whom he has reasonable grounds for suspecting to be guilty of it.
(3) But the power of summary arrest conferred by subsection (1) or (2) is exercisable only if—
  (a) the person making the arrest has reasonable grounds for believing that for any of the reasons mentioned in subsection (4) it is necessary to arrest the person in question; and
  (b) it appears to the person making the arrest that it is not reasonably practicable for a constable to make it instead.
(4) The reasons are to prevent the person in question—
  (a) causing physical injury to himself or any other person;
  (b) suffering physical injury;
  (c) causing loss of or damage to property; or
  (d) making off before a constable can assume responsibility for him.
(5) This section does not apply in relation to an offence under Part 3 or 3A of the Public Order Act 1986.

Police and Criminal Evidence Act 1984, s 24A

Meaning of indictable offence

- An indictable offence includes triable 'either way offences'.
- The Anti-social Behaviour, Crime and Policing Act 2014, s 176(6) states:
  + any reference in PACE 1984 to an **indictable offence** has effect as if it included a reference to **low-value shoplifting**.
- The Magistrates' Courts Act 1980, s 22A states:
  + low-value shoplifting is triable only summarily—unless a person aged 18 or over elects trial at Crown Court before the summary trial begins;
  + **low-value shoplifting** means an offence under s 1 Theft Act 1968 where:
    ▪ the value of the stolen goods does not exceed £ 200;

- the goods were being offered for sale in a shop or any other premises, stall, vehicle, or place from which there is carried on a trade or business; and
- at the time of the offence, the person accused was, or was purporting to be, a customer or potential customer of the person offering the goods for sale.

Explanatory notes

- This power of arrest does not apply to offences under ss 17–29N of the Public Order Act 1986 (offences of racial/religious hatred, sexual orientation) (see **7.9**).

Practical considerations

- Consideration should be given to lawful authorities for using reasonable force and use of force resolution (see **1.2**).
- Arrest powers under ss 24 and 24A of PACE have effect in relation to any offence/indictable offence whenever committed.

Links to alternative subjects and offences

1.5 Entry, Search, and Seizure Powers

Sections 32 and 17–22 of PACE deal with matters relating to searching people/premises, seizure and retention of property, plus entry and access for copying of seized items. These powers, without warrant, apply either upon or after arrest.

1.5.1 Search upon arrest

Section 32 of PACE creates powers of search relating to arrested persons before they are conveyed to a police station. The relevant points are:

Person

A constable may search any person arrested at a place other than at a police station on reasonable grounds to believe that:
- the person may present a danger to themselves or others;
- concealed on the arrested person is anything which might be:
  + used to assist escape from lawful custody;
  + evidence relating to an offence.

Premises

- If a person is arrested for an **indictable offence**, at a place other than at a police station, a constable can enter and search any **premises** in which that person was:
  + when arrested;
  + immediately before they were arrested;

for evidence relating to the indictable offence for which arrested, providing reasonable grounds exist to believe that the evidence is on the premises.
- If the premises consist of two or more separate dwellings, the power to search is limited to:
  + any dwelling in which the arrest took place or in which the person arrested was immediately before their arrest; **and**
  + any parts of the premises which the occupier of any such dwelling uses in common with the occupiers of any other dwellings comprised in the premises.

Seizure from person

A constable searching a person in the exercise of this power may seize and retain anything found on that person on reasonable grounds to believe that:
- the person might use it to cause physical injury to that person or to any other person;

- the person might use it to assist him/her to escape from lawful custody;
- it is evidence of an offence or has been obtained in consequence of the commission of an offence (other than an item subject to **legal privilege**).

Meanings

Indictable offence (see **1.4.4**)

Premises

Premises includes any place, and in particular, includes:
- any vehicle, vessel, aircraft, or hovercraft;
- any offshore installation;
- any renewable energy installation; and
- a tent or movable structure.

Legal privilege

- Items subject to legal privilege relate to communications between:
  - ◆ the client and a professional legal adviser;
  - ◆ clients and any person representing them;
  - ◆ between such adviser/representative and any other person.
- This communication was made in connection with the:
  - ◆ giving of legal advice; or
  - ◆ contemplation of legal proceedings and for such purposes.
- It also includes items enclosed with or referred to in such communications, when they are in the possession of a person who is entitled to them.
- Items held with the intention of furthering a criminal purpose are not items subject to legal privilege (s 10 of PACE).

Explanatory notes

- This power to search a person does not authorise a constable to require a person to remove any items of clothing in public other than an outer coat, jacket, or gloves.
- It does authorise a search of a person's mouth.
- The power to search premises is only to the extent that is reasonably required for the purpose of discovering any thing or any such evidence as mentioned in section 32(2).
- Any search of premises must comply with Code B.
- This power does not apply to an arrest which takes place at a police station.
- Items held subject to legal privilege cannot be seized when discovered during a premises search or executing a search warrant for an indictable offence.
- Legal privilege does not extend to a conveyancing document, solicitor's time sheets, fee records, appointment books, and other similar documents.

- Generally, an expert working for the defence is covered by the same legal privilege as the rest of a defence team.
- If it is suspected that the person is a terrorist then stop and search powers given under the Terrorism Act 2000, s 43 will apply.

1.5.2 **Power of entry to arrest, save life, or prevent damage**

Section 17 of PACE creates a power to enter and search premises to effect an arrest or to save life/prevent damage.

Power to enter premises

(1) Subject to the following provisions of this section, and without prejudice to any other enactment, a constable may enter and search any premises for the purpose—

    (a) of executing—

        (i) a warrant of arrest issued in connection with or arising out of criminal proceedings; or

        (ii) a warrant of commitment issued under s 76 of the Magistrates' Courts Act 1980;

    (a) of arresting a person for an indictable offence;

    (b) of arresting a person for an offence under—

        (i) s 1 (prohibition of uniforms in connection with political objects) of the Public Order Act 1936;

        (ii) any enactment contained in ss 6, 7, 8, or 10 of the Criminal Law Act 1977 (offences relating to entering and remaining on property);

        (iii) section 4 of the Public Order Act 1986 (fear or provocation of violence);

        (iiia) s 4 (driving etc when under influence of drink or drugs) or s 163 (failure to stop when required to do so by constable in uniform) of the Road Traffic Act 1988;

        (iiib) s 27 of the Transport and Works Act 1992 (which relates to offences involving drink or drugs);

        (iv) s 76 of the Criminal Justice and Public Order Act 1994 (failure to comply with interim possession order);

        (v) any of ss 4, 5, 6(1) and (2), 7, and 8(1) and (2) of the Animal Welfare Act 2006 (offences relating to the prevention of harm to animals);

        (vi) section 144 of the Legal Aid, Sentencing and Punishment of Offenders Act 2012 (squatting in a residential building);

    (ca) of arresting, in pursuance of s 32(1A) of the Children and Young Persons Act 1969, any child or young person who has been remanded to local authority or youth detention accommodation under s 91 of the Legal Aid, Sentencing and Punishment of Offenders Act 2012;

(caa) of arresting a person for an offence to which s 61 of the Animal Health Act 1981 applies;

(cab) of arresting a person under any of the following provisions—

    (i) s 30D(1) or (2A);

    (ii) s 46A(1) or (1A);

    (iii) s 5B(7) of the Bail Act 1976 (arrest where a person fails to surrender to custody in accordance with a court order);

    (iv) s 7(3) of the Bail Act 1976 (arrest where a person is not likely to surrender to custody etc);

    (v) s 97(1) of the Legal Aid, Sentencing and Punishment of Offenders Act 2012 (arrest where a child is suspected of breaking conditions of remand);

(cb) of recapturing any person who is, or is deemed for any purpose to be, unlawfully at large while liable to be detained—

    (i) in a prison, young offender institution, secure training centre or secure college, or

    (ii) in pursuance of s 92 of the Powers of Criminal Courts (Sentencing) Act 2000 (dealing with children and young persons guilty of grave crimes), in any other place;

(d) of recapturing any person whatever who is unlawfully at large and whom he is pursuing; or

(e) of saving life or limb or preventing serious damage to property (see 'Explanatory notes' below).

(2) Except for the purpose specified in paragraph (e) of subsection (1) above, the powers of entry and search conferred by this section—

  (a) are only exercisable if the constable has reasonable grounds for believing that the person whom he is seeking is on the premises; and

  (b) are limited, in relation to premises consisting of two or more separate dwellings, to powers to enter and search—

    (i) any parts of the premises which the occupiers of any dwelling comprised in the premises use in common with the occupiers of any other such dwelling; and

    (ii) any such dwelling in which the constable has reasonable grounds for believing that the person whom he is seeking may be.

(3) The powers of entry and search conferred by this section are only exercisable for the purposes specified in subsection (1)(c)(ii), (iv), or (vi) above by a constable in uniform.

(4) The power of search conferred by this section is only a power to search to the extent that is reasonably required for the purpose for which the power of entry is exercised.

(5) Subject to subsection (6) below, all the rules of common law under which a constable has power to enter premises without a warrant are hereby abolished.

(6) Nothing in subsection (5) above affects any power of entry to deal with or prevent a breach of the peace.

Police and Criminal Evidence Act 1984, s 17

1.5.2 Power of entry to arrest, save life, or prevent damage

Conditions

- A concern for welfare may be too low a threshold for entry under s 17(1)(e) (see the *Syed* case, below), as this power is for saving life or limb or preventing serious damage to property.
- Apart from entry under s 17(1)(e), to save life or limb or prevent serious damage to property, the s 17(1) powers are only exercisable if the constable has reasonable grounds for believing that the person whom they are seeking is on the premises.
- In relation to premises consisting of two or more separate dwellings, these powers are limited to:
  - ✦ any parts of the premises which the occupiers of any dwelling comprised in the premises use in common with the occupiers of any other such dwelling; **and**
  - ✦ any such dwelling in which the constable has reasonable grounds for believing that the person whom they are seeking may be.
- The power to search is only given to the extent that is reasonably required for the purpose for which the power of entry is exercised.

Explanatory notes

- Code B must be complied with when this power is exercised.
- This section does not apply to s 4A of the Public Order Act 1986 (intentional harassment, alarm or distress) (see **7.7**).
- Section 17(1)(e) life and limb refers to humans only but animals can be property.
- A **warrant of commitment** is a commitment warrant to prison issued under the Magistrates' Courts Act 1980, s 76 for failing to pay fines. It does not include 'default warrants' where an offender has defaulted on their payment of a fine.
- An **indictable offence** includes triable 'either way offences' and low-value shoplifting (see **1.4.4**).
- A designated CSO or CSV has the same powers as a police constable to enter and search premises for the purpose of saving life or limb or preventing serious damage to property (see **11.1.2**).
- Nothing in this section affects any power of entry to deal with or prevent a breach of the peace at common law (see **7.3**).
- The powers of entry and search conferred by this section are only exercisable for the purposes of subsection (1)(c)(ii), (iv), or (vi) by a constable in uniform (s 17(3)).

Related cases

Syed v DPP [2010] EWHC 81 (Admin), QBD In this case, a neighbour reported screaming and shouting from S's house. On arrival, the police found no sign of a disturbance. S came to the door, stating that there had been an argument between two brothers, but evaded further questions. Officers said they had a power of entry as there were concerns for a person's welfare. S refused entry, spat in the face of one officer, and head-butted the other. It was held that the police were not acting in the execution of their duty; there were no signs of injury, damage, or disturbance and the occupants had no complaints. Concern for welfare was too low a threshold for entry under s 17(1)(e). The power is for saving life or limb or preventing serious damage to property.

Baker v CPS [2009] EWHC 299 (Admin), QBD on a report that B had 'gone berserk with a knife' inside her home, officers entered the property 'to save life or limb' under s 17(1)(e). The defendant was sitting on the floor rocking to and fro, with blood on her head, pyjama bottoms, and arm, and a rolling pin between her legs. On asking her to stand up during the search for the knife, she punched the officer in the stomach and was arrested for police assault. It was held that 'Saving life or limb' covered saving a person from causing serious harm to him/herself, or third parties. Police entry and search powers under s 17(1)(e) does not require consent of the occupier. Though it might be desirable to give reasons for search and entry, it may be impossible or impracticable to do so.

Blench v DPP [2004] EWHC 2717, QBD A call was received from a female that a drunken man was taking her baby; she then told the police not to attend. It was held that the police could enter the property as they had reason to believe that a child was at risk and there had been a breach of the peace and was likely to be another. Therefore, their presence was lawful, and they were not trespassers.

O'Loughlin v CC of Essex [1998] 1 WLR 374, CA When entry to premises is made to arrest a person for an offence, any occupier present should be informed of the reason for the entry, unless circumstances make it impossible, impracticable, or undesirable; otherwise the constable would be acting unlawfully.

D'Souza v DPP [1992] 4 All ER 545, HL Entry was forced to a dwelling by police officers to recapture a person unlawfully at large from a secure hospital (under the Mental Health Act). Section 17(1)(d) of PACE gives a power of entry when in pursuit of persons unlawfully at large. The court ruled that the pursuit had to be within a few seconds or minutes of the entry (now known as 'immediate pursuit'). Officers were not entitled to form an intention to arrest and then go to premises where the person might be found. Here, although the wife was unlawfully at large, there was no power of entry, therefore the officers had exceeded their authority. **Note:** This 'immediate pursuit' requirement does not apply to people unlawfully at large from prison/custody/remand/serving a sentence.

1.5.3 Searching of premises after arrest

Section 18 of PACE creates a power to enter and search premises after someone has been arrested for an indictable offence and provides a power to seize relevant items.

1.5.3 Searching of premises after arrest

Power to enter/search after arrest

(1) Subject to the following provisions of this section, a constable may enter and search any premises occupied or controlled by a person who is under arrest for an indictable offence, if he has reasonable grounds for suspecting that there is on the premises evidence other than items subject to legal privilege, that relates—
  (a) to that offence; or
  (b) to some other indictable offence which is connected with or similar to that offence.

(2) A constable may seize and retain anything for which he may search under subsection (1) above.

(3) The power to search conferred by subsection (1) above is only a power to search to the extent that is reasonably required for the purpose of discovering such evidence.

(4) Subject to subsection (5) below, the powers conferred by this section may not be exercised unless an officer of the rank of inspector or above has authorised them in writing.

(5) A constable may conduct a search under subsection (1)—
  (a) before the person is taken to police station or released under section 30A; and
  (b) without obtaining an authorisation under subsection (4),
  if the condition in subsection (5A) is satisfied.

(5A) The condition is that the presence of the person at a place (other than a police station) is necessary for the effective investigation of the offence.

(6) If a constable conducts a search by virtue of subsection (5) above, he shall inform an officer of the rank of inspector or above that he has made the search as soon as practicable after he has made it.

(7) An officer who—
  (a) authorises a search; or
  (b) is informed of a search under subsection (6) above, shall make a record in writing—
    (i) of the grounds for the search; and
    (ii) of the nature of the evidence that was sought.

(8) If the person who was in occupation or control of the premises at the time of the search is in police detention at the time the record is to be made, the officer shall make the record as part of his custody record.

Police and Criminal Evidence Act 1984, s 18

Meanings

Occupied

This refers to premises where the arrested person resides or works, and may include occupancy as an owner, tenant, or 'squatter'.

Controlled

This includes premises in which the arrested person holds some interest, such as owning, renting, leasing, or has use of the premises.

Indictable (see **1.4.4**)

Legal privilege (see **1.6.4**)

Explanatory notes

- A search should only be conducted if the officer has reasonable grounds for suspecting that evidence of that or another connected or similar indictable offence is on the premises.
- The search must be conducted in accordance with Code B.
- A person does not have to be in police detention before a s 18 authority can be issued, as s 18(1) just requires them to be arrested for an indictable offence.
- Another power to search premises immediately after arrest is created by s 32 (see **1.5**).

Related cases

Cowan v Commissioner of the Metropolitan Police [2000] 1 WLR 254, CA Where a constable may seize 'anything' which is on premises, there is no reason why 'anything' could not mean 'everything' that was movable, and it was practicable to remove. It does not matter that property itself could be considered to be premises, so the removal of a vehicle (being premises) is lawful and can be seized if necessary.

1.5.4 **Powers of seizure from premises**

Section 19 of PACE provides a constable who is lawfully on premises with a general power to seize property.

> **Power to seize**
>
> (1) The powers conferred by subsections (2), (3), and (4) below are exercisable by a constable who is lawfully on any premises.
> (2) The constable may seize anything which is on the premises if he has reasonable grounds for believing—
>   (a) that it has been obtained in consequence of the commission of an offence; and
>   (b) that it is necessary to seize it in order to prevent it being concealed, lost, damaged, altered or destroyed.
> (3) The constable may seize anything which is on the premises if he has reasonable grounds for believing—
>   (a) that it is evidence in relation to an offence which he is investigating or any other offence; and

(b) that it is necessary to seize it in order to prevent the evidence being concealed, lost, altered or destroyed.

(4) The constable may require any information which is stored in electronic form and is accessible from the premises to be produced in a form in which it can be taken away and in which it is visible and legible or from which it can readily be produced in a visible and legible form, if he has reasonable grounds for believing—

(a) that—

(i) it is evidence in relation to an offence which he is investigating or any other offence; or

(ii) it has been obtained in consequence of the commission of an offence; and

(b) that it is necessary to do so in order to prevent it being concealed, lost, tampered with or destroyed.

(5) The powers conferred by this section are in addition to any power otherwise conferred.

(6) No power of seizure conferred on a constable under any enactment (including an enactment contained in an Act passed after this Act) is to be taken to authorise the seizure of an item which the constable exercising the power has reasonable grounds for believing to be subject to legal privilege.

Police and Criminal Evidence Act 1984, s 19

Explanatory notes

- Officers using this power can (while they are on the **premises lawfully**) seize any evidence whether it is owned by the defendant or by someone else, provided the seizure of it is necessary for the purpose(s) described. However, this Act does not provide a specific power for seizure of an innocent person's property when it is in a public place.
- As vehicles are deemed to be '**premises**' for the purposes of this Act, they can be seized under the same power (*Cowan v MPC* [2000] 1 WLR 254, CA).
- Motor vehicles, if owned by an innocent party and in a public place, may also be searched under authority of a s 8 warrant (see **1.6.1**) to search premises for evidence.
- A designated civilian investigating officer has the same seizure powers as a police constable.

Seizure of computerised information

Section 20 of the Police and Criminal Evidence Act 1984 relates to the seizure of computerised information from premises.

(1) Every power of seizure which is conferred by an enactment to which this section applies on a constable who has entered premises in the exercise of a power conferred by an enactment shall be construed as including a power to require any information stored in any electronic form and accessible from the premises to be produced in a form in

which it can be taken away and in which it is visible and legible or from which it can readily be produced in a visible and legible form.

(2) This section applies—
   (a) to any enactment contained in an Act passed before this Act;
   (b) to sections 8 and 18 above;
   (c) to paragraph 13 of Schedule 1 to this Act; and
   (d) to any enactment contained in an Act passed after this Act.

Police and Criminal Evidence Act 1984, s 20

Seizure of bulk material

The Criminal Justice and Police Act 2001 allows seizure of bulk material in order to examine it elsewhere ('seize and sift').

Premises

Section 50 of the 2001 Act allows a person who is lawfully on premises to seize bulk material when using existing seizure powers, providing:

- there are reasonable grounds to believe that it is material which can be searched for and seized;
- in all the circumstances, it is not reasonably practicable for this to be ascertained whilst on the premises;
- it is necessary to remove it from the premises to enable this to be determined and the material to be separated;
- the existing seizure powers are listed in Pt 1 of Sch 1 to the Act.

Person

Section 51 of the 2001 Act gives the police additional powers of seizure of bulk material from the person, where there is an existing power to search as shown in Pt 2 of Sch 1 to the Act.

Explanatory notes

- Powers given under s 50 also include any other authorised people such as HMRC or designated policing support officer.
- What is reasonably practicable will differ in each case. Factors to consider include the time to examine and separate the material, and the type and number of people involved. In addition, the need to reduce the risk of accidentally altering or damaging any of the material may be relevant.
- Where legally privileged material forms part of the 'whole thing' then this can be seized in order to separate from the bulk of the material.
- Section 51 (seizure from person) could apply, for example, where the person has a hand-held computer or computer disk which holds relevant electronic data, or a briefcase containing bulk correspondence which could not be examined in the street.
- Section 52 requires the occupier and/or some other person or persons from whom material has been seized to be given a notice specifying what has been seized and why, and that they can apply to

1.5.4 Searching of premises after arrest

a judge for the return of the material or for access to and copying of the seized material.

- Section 21 of PACE provides a person, from whom material has been lawfully seized by the police, with certain rights to access to and/or copies of it.
- Section 22 of PACE provides powers to retain items that have been seized by the police.

Links to alternative offences or subjects

1.6 **Enter and Search Warrants**

Procedures for premises search warrants, the application and execution process for warrants, and applying for access to excluded or special procedure material are all controlled by PACE.

There are several warrants provided under other legislation such as s 23 of the Misuse of Drugs Act 1971 and s 46 of the Firearms Act 1968. When executed they should be conducted in accordance with PACE and the COP, although they do retain individual powers peculiar to themselves.

1.6.1 **Premises search warrant**

Section 8 of the Police and Criminal Evidence Act 1984 provides the grounds and procedure to be followed when applying for a search warrant relating to an indictable offence. It also provides a power to seize certain incriminating items.

> ### Search warrant—application and procedure
>
> (1) If on an application made by a constable a justice of the peace is satisfied that there are reasonable grounds for believing—
>   (a) that an indictable offence has been committed; and
>   (b) that there is material on premises mentioned in subsection (1A) below which is likely to be of substantial value (whether by itself or together with other material) to the investigation of the offence; and
>   (c) that the material is likely to be relevant evidence; and
>   (d) that it does not consist of or include items subject to legal privilege, excluded material or special procedure material; and
>   (e) that any of the following conditions specified in subsection (3) below applies in relation to each set of premises specified in the application,
>
> he may issue a warrant authorising a constable to enter and search the premises.
>
> (1A) The premises referred to in subsection (1)(b) above are—
>   (a) one or more sets of premises specified in the application (in which case the application is for a 'specific premises warrant'); or
>   (b) any premises occupied or controlled by a person specified in the application, including such sets of premises as are so specified (in which case the application is for an 'all premises warrant').
>
> (1B) If the application is for an all premises warrant, the justice of the peace must also be satisfied—
>   (a) that because of the particulars of the offence referred to in paragraph (a) of subsection (1) above, there are reasonable

grounds for believing that it is necessary to search premises occupied or controlled by the person in question which are not specified in the application in order to find the material referred to in paragraph (b) of that subsection; and

(b) that it is not reasonably practicable to specify in the application all the premises, which he occupies or controls and which might need to be searched.

(1C) The warrant may authorise entry to and search of premises on more than one occasion if, on the application, the justice of the peace is satisfied that it is necessary to authorise multiple entries in order to achieve the purpose for which he issues the warrant.

(1D) If it authorises multiple entries, the number of entries authorised may be unlimited, or limited to a maximum.

(2) A constable may seize and retain anything for which a search has been authorised under subsection (1) above.

(3) The conditions mentioned in subsection (1)(e) above are—

(a) that it is not practicable to communicate with any person entitled to grant entry to the premises;

(b) that it is practicable to communicate with a person entitled to grant entry to the premises, but it is not practicable to communicate with any person entitled to grant access to the evidence;

(c) that entry to the premises will not be granted unless a warrant is produced;

(d) that the purpose of a search may be frustrated or seriously prejudiced unless a constable arriving at the premises can secure immediate entry to them.

Police and Criminal Evidence Act 1984, s 8

Meanings

Indictable offence (see **1.4.4**)

Premises (see **1.5.1**)

Relevant evidence

In relation to an offence, means anything that would be admissible in evidence at a trial for the offence—s 8(4).

Legal privilege (see **1.6.4**)

Excluded material (see **1.6.4**)

Special procedure material (see **1.6.4**)

Specific premises warrant

This consists of one or more sets of premises named/specified in the application.

All premises warrant

Being all premises occupied or controlled by an individual.

Explanatory notes

- Section 8(5) state that the power to issue a warrant under this section is in addition to any other powers to issue warrants.
- Warrants under s 8 only apply to indictable offences, and can be for entry to:
  + named/specific premises—'**specific premises warrant**'; or
  + premises 'occupied or controlled by' an individual—'**all premises warrant**'.
- An all premises warrant will apply when it is necessary to search all premises occupied or controlled by an individual, but it is not reasonably practicable to specify all such premises at the time of application. The warrant will allow access to all premises occupied or controlled by that person, both those which are specified on the application and those which are not.
- Section 16(3) states that a warrant for entry and search must be executed within three months from the date of its issue.
- Where items falling outside those which may be seized under s 8(2) are found on the premises, consider the seizure provided by s 19 of PACE (see **1.5.4**).
- When applying for and executing warrants then s 15 (see **1.6.2**) and s 16 (see **1.6.3**) together with Code B must be complied with in relation to application, safeguards, and execution.
- In any application also consider the procedures for access to excluded material/special procedure material, if relevant, provided by s 9 of PACE (see **1.6.4**).
- Failure to comply with statutory requirements will make the entry and subsequent seizure of property unlawful (*R v CC of Lancashire, ex parte Parker* [1993] Crim LR 204, QBD).
- Officers should be aware of the extensive powers to search without a warrant on arrest under s 32 (see **1.5**) or after arrest under s 18 (see **1.5.3**).
- Warrants issued under the provision of s 8 only authorises searching of the premises not people who are in them.
- Such people may only be searched if arrested, but there can be a specific power to search people in warrants issued under s 23(2) of the Misuse of Drugs Act 1971 (see **5.5**) and s 46(2) of the Firearms Act 1968 (see **8.6.3**) (providing the application includes to search people in the premises).

When applying for search warrants, 'reasonable grounds to believe' under s 8 PACE imposes a higher threshold test than 'reasonable grounds to suspect' under s 46(1) of the Firearms Act 1968 (*R (on the application of Eastenders Cash and Carry plc) v South Western Magistrates' Court* [2011] 2 Cr App Rep 123).

- In relation to seizure and examination of bulk material (see **1.5.4**).

1.6.2 **Application procedures for a search warrant**

Section 15 of PACE sets out the procedure to be followed when applying for a search warrant. For quick reference s 15 is given in bulleted form as follows:

Application procedure

- This section (and s 16) relates to the issue of warrants (**under any enactment**) for constables to enter and search premises.
- Entering or searching of premises under a warrant is unlawful unless it complies with this section and s 16 (see **1.6.3**).
- Where a constable applies for such warrant the following details must be given:
  - ✦ grounds on which application made;
  - ✦ enactment under which the warrant would be issued;
  - ✦ identify (as far as practicable) the articles or persons sought.
- Furthermore, if the application is for:
  - ✦ a warrant authorising entry and search on more than one occasion
    - ■ ground on which application made;
    - ■ whether unlimited number of entries is sought;
    - ■ otherwise the maximum number of entries desired.
  - ✦ a 'specific premises warrant' (see **1.6.1**)
    - ✦ each set of premises to be entered and searched;
  - ✦ an 'all premises warrant' (see **1.6.1**)
    - ■ specify (as far as reasonably practicable) the sets of premises to be entered and searched;
    - ■ the person who is in occupation or control of those premises and any others which require entering and searching;
    - ■ why it is necessary to search more premises than those specified and why it is not reasonably practicable to specify all the premises to be entered and searched.
- Such a warrant shall specify:
  - ✦ the name of the person who applied for it;
  - ✦ the date on which it is issued;
  - ✦ the enactment under which it is issued;
  - ✦ the articles or persons to be sought (identified as far as is practicable);
  - ✦ each set of premises to be searched;
  - ✦ in the case of an 'all premises warrant':
    - ■ the person who is in occupation or control of premises to be searched, together with any premises under his occupation or control which can be specified and which are to be searched.
- The following points also have to be complied with:
  - ✦ applications shall be supported by an information in writing and made *ex parte* (subject does not have to be present);

✦ the constable shall answer on oath any question that the justice of the peace or judge hearing the application puts to them;

✦ a warrant shall authorise an entry on one occasion only—unless multiple entries are authorised, in which case it must specify whether the number of entries is unlimited, or limited to a specified maximum;

✦ two copies shall be made of a specific premises warrant that specifies only one set of premises and does not authorise multiple entries. Otherwise, as many copies as are reasonably required may be made of any other kind of warrant;

✦ copies shall be clearly certified as copies.

Explanatory notes

• Advice and guidance are given in Code B, under search warrants.

• Where premises are multiple occupancy (eg a single house converted into flats) the warrant must specify all the rooms required to be searched (including the common living areas), and not just give the main address.

• Section 15(1) states that entering or searching premises under authority of a warrant is unlawful, unless procedures given in ss 15 and 16 (see **1.6.2**) are complied with.

Related cases

R (on the application of Lees) v Solihull MC [2013] EWHC 3779 (Admin), QBD Search warrants granted under s 8 to HMRC did not specify what material was sought. As a result, the entry, search, and seizure were unlawful because the warrants breached s 15(6)(b) by failing to identify the articles or persons sought.

R (on the application of Bhatti) v Croydon MC [2010] EWHC 522 (Admin), QBD In an 'all premises warrant' issued under s 8, all premises that can be identified at the time of application must be so identified. Premises identified later must be added to the schedule attached to the warrant and signed by an inspector before attending the property. Failure to supply the occupier with a copy of the warrant/schedule at entry naming the premises or adding the address by hand as a warrant is executed breaches s 16(5), so entry, search, and seizure become unlawful under s 15(1).

1.6.3 **Execution of search warrants**

Section 16 of PACE sets out the procedure to be followed when executing a search warrant. For quick reference s 16 is given in bulleted form as follows:

Execution procedure

A warrant to enter and search premises:
• may be executed by any constable;

1.6.3 Execution of search warrants

- may authorise persons to accompany any constable who is executing it;
  - ✦ such a person has the same powers as the constable, but only whilst in the company and under the supervision of a constable;
  - ✦ such a person will then be able to execute the warrant, and seize anything to which the warrant relates;
- must be executed within three months from the date of its issue;
- must be executed at a reasonable hour unless it appears that the purpose of a search may be frustrated on an entry at a reasonable hour;
- will only authorise a search to the extent required for the purpose for which the warrant was issued.

Specifically, no premises may be entered or searched unless an inspector (or above) authorises, in writing, entry for:
- an 'all premises warrant':
  - ✦ premises which are not specified;
- a 'multiple entries warrant':
  - ✦ for the second or subsequent entry and search.

Notification requirements exist: when a constable is seeking to execute a warrant to enter and search premises, the constable shall:
- where the occupier is present:
  - ✦ identify themselves to the occupier. If not in uniform documentary evidence produced to show that they are a constable;
  - ✦ produce the warrant and supply a copy of the warrant/schedule to the occupier;
- if the occupier is not present, but some other person is present who appears to the constable to be in charge of the premises:
  - ✦ the constable shall deal with that person as if they were the occupier and comply with the above requirements;
- if there is no person present (occupier or in charge):
  - ✦ the constable shall leave a copy of the warrant in a prominent place on the premises.

Where a constable has executed a warrant, they shall:
- endorse the warrant stating whether:
  - ✦ the articles or persons sought were found;
  - ✦ any articles were seized, other than articles which were sought;
- unless the warrant is for one set of premises only:
  - ✦ separately endorse each set of premises entered and searched providing the above details.

A warrant shall be returned to the **appropriate person**:
- when it has been executed;
- in the case of:
  - ✦ a **'specific premises warrant'** (not been executed);
  - ✦ an 'all premises warrant';
  - ✦ any warrant authorising multiple entries;

upon the expiry of the three-month period or sooner.

Meanings

Premises (see **1.5.1**)

All premises warrant (see **1.6.3**)

Multiple entries warrant (see **1.6.3**)

Appropriate person

If the warrant was issued by:
- a justice of the peace, it will be the designated officer for the local justice area in which the justice was acting when the warrant was issued;
- a judge, it will be the appropriate officer of the court from which the judge issued it.

Specific premises warrant (see **1.6.1**)

Explanatory notes

- A warrant returned to the appropriate person shall be retained by that person for twelve months from its return.
- An occupier of premises to which the warrant relates can inspect the warrant (and should be allowed to do so) during the twelve-month retaining period.
- When executing a search warrant, advice and guidance should be obtained from Code B, under search warrants.
- A person authorised in the warrant to accompany the constable may be an expert in computing or financial matters. Such an expert will then be able to take a more active role in the search and in seizing material, rather than merely being present in an advisory or clerical capacity.
- In practical terms the supervising constable must identify any accompanying persons to the occupier of premises prior to the start of any search and explain that person's role in the process. The constable in charge will have overall supervisory responsibility and will be accountable for any action taken.

1.6.4 **Access to excluded and special procedure material**

Section 9 of PACE provides the procedures to be adopted in order to gain access to excluded material and special procedure material.

Access procedure

(1) A constable may obtain access to excluded material or special procedure material for the purposes of a criminal investigation by making an application under Schedule 1 and in accordance with that Schedule.

1.6.4 **Access to excluded and special procedure material**

(2) Any Act (including a local Act) passed before this Act under which a search of premises for the purposes of a criminal investigation could be authorised by the issue of a warrant to a constable shall cease to have effect so far as it relates to the authorisation of searches—

    (a) for items subject to legal privilege; or

    (b) for excluded material; or

    (c) for special procedure material consisting of documents or records other than documents.

Police and Criminal Evidence Act 1984, s 9

Meanings

Excluded material

Means:

- **personal records** acquired or created in the course of any trade, business, profession, or other occupation or for the purposes of any paid or unpaid office;
- human tissue or tissue fluid taken for the purposes of diagnosis or medical treatment held in confidence;
- both sets of material held in confidence subject to:
    - ✦ an express or implied undertaking to do so;
    - ✦ a disclosure restriction or an obligation of secrecy contained in any legislation;

or

- **journalistic material** which consists of documents or records other than documents, being held or continuously held in confidence (by one or more persons), subject to an undertaking, restriction, or obligation of confidence since it was first acquired or created for the purposes of journalism.

Personal records

Means documentary and other records concerning an individual (whether living or dead) who can be identified from them and relates to:

- their physical or mental health;
- spiritual counselling or assistance given/to be given to them; or
- counselling or assistance given/to be given for their personal welfare, by any voluntary organisation or individual who by reason of:
    - ✦ their office or occupation has responsibilities for this; or
    - ✦ an order by a court has responsibilities for their supervision.

Journalistic material

- Is material acquired or created for the purposes of journalism.
- Providing it is in the possession of a person who acquired or created it for this purpose.
- It will be acquired if a person receives the material from someone who intends that the recipient uses it for that purpose.

Special procedure material

- Includes journalistic material, other than excluded material.
- Includes material, other than items subject to legal privilege and excluded material, in the possession of a person who acquired or created it in the course of any trade, business, profession, or for the purpose of any paid or unpaid office; and holds it in confidence subject to:
  - ✦ an express or implied undertaking to do so;
  - ✦ a disclosure restriction or an obligation of secrecy contained in any legislation.
- Where material is acquired by:
  - ✦ an employee from their employer in their course of employment;
  - ✦ a company from an associated company;

it is only special procedure material if it was special procedure material immediately before the acquisition.

- Where material is created by:
  - ✦ an employee in the course of their employment;
  - ✦ a company on behalf of an associated company;

it is only special procedure material if it would have been special procedure material had the employer/associated company created it.

Schedule 1

This gives full details of the procedure to be followed when making an application to a judge in order to gain access to excluded material or special procedure material.

Premises (see **1.5.1**)

Legal privilege (see **1.6.4**)

Explanatory notes

- Code B provides guidance regarding the conduct of searches and advice on Sch 1 searches.
- The CPS makes Sch 1 applications and advice should be sought from them in any application.
- Case law has established that:
  - ✦ police cannot routinely examine hospital records;
  - ✦ search warrant not lawful without the proper paperwork;
  - ✦ a Sch 1 notice should specify the documents being sought.
- In relation to seizure and examination of bulk material (see **1.5.4**).
- Officers should be mindful of the powers to search (without a warrant) on arrest or after arrest (see **1.4**).
- Special procedure and excluded material can be searched for and seized under PACE, ss 18 and 32, provided:
  - ✦ lawful arrest is made, in good faith; **and**
  - ✦ the search is carried out strictly within the terms of those sections.

Related cases

R v Blackfriars CC and the Commissioner of Police of the Metropolis [2014] EWHC 1541 (Admin), QBD A warrant was the authority to go onto premises; if s 15(6)(b) was not complied with (eg by failing to specify in detail the article(s) sought), then the warrant—and therefore the entry—could be invalidated.

R (on application of Faisaltex Ltd) v Preston CC [2008] EWHC 2832 (Admin), QBD A computer and hard drive counted as a single item within 'material' under s 8(1) of PACE. This power was sufficient without using s 51 of the Criminal Justice and Police Act 2001 as well.

R v Bristol CC, ex parte Bristol Press and Picture Agency (1986) 85 Cr App R 190, QBD A 'Picture Agency' took photographs during two nights of rioting in Bristol. The police applied under s 9 and Sch 1 of PACE for an order allowing them access to the pictures, on the grounds that the photographs might help the police to identify offences and offenders. A High Court judge granted the order, but the agency appealed, saying that since individual photographs were not specified, and it was not known if they would be of any use, the access conditions under the Schedule were not satisfied. It was held that the judge was entitled to grant the order as there were sufficient grounds in this case to believe that the photographs might help, and it was in the public interest to grant the order.

Links to alternative subjects and offences

Chapter 2
Assaults and Violence

2.1 Assault (Common/Actual Bodily Harm)

A common assault under s 39 of the Criminal Justice Act 1988 is in fact two separate matters: an assault and/or a battery. This area of law is dealt with first, before covering the more serious assault occasioning actual bodily harm (AOABH) under the Offences Against the Person Act 1861. Defences which may be available to assaults are then discussed.

2.1.1 Common assault—battery

Offence

Common assault and battery shall be summary offences

Criminal Justice Act 1988, s 39

Points to prove

Assault
- ✓ unlawfully
- ✓ assaulted
- ✓ another person

Battery
- ✓ all points above
- ✓ application of unlawful force (eg by beating)

Meanings

Assault

Any act, which **intentionally** or **recklessly**, causes another person to apprehend immediate and **unlawful** personal violence (*Fagan v Metropolitan Police Commissioner* [1968] 3 All ER 442, QBD).

2.1.1 Common assault-battery

Battery

An act by which a person intentionally or recklessly applies force to the complainant.

Intent (see 4.1.2)

Reckless (see 2.3.1)

Unlawful (see 2.3.1)

Explanatory notes

- There are two offences covered by this legislation: 'assault' and 'assault by beating' (battery).
- There is also a civil wrong of assault/battery.
- An 'assault' does not have to involve an actual application of force: it may just be threatening words used, although if violence is threatened, there must be the ability to carry out the threat at the time. A mere omission to act cannot be an assault.
- In both offences, there must be either an intentional causing of apprehension of immediate unlawful violence or subjective recklessness as to that apprehension.

Defences (see 2.1.2)

Related cases

ZH v Metropolitan Police Commissioner [2012] EWHC 604 (Admin), QBD It was held in this case that a police officer's failure to consider disabilities appropriately can result in liability for assault, false imprisonment, disability discrimination, and breaches of human rights.

Wood v DPP [2008] EWHC 1056 (Admin), QBD A police officer, without any intention to arrest, grabbed a person's arm to stop them walking away to question them about an incident at a public house. It was held that this action amounted to an unlawful assault. Where a police officer restrains someone but does not at the time intend to arrest him/her that police officer risks committing an assault even if an arrest at a later time would have been justified.

Haystead v CC Derbyshire Police [2000] 3 All ER 890, QBD In this case, a mother was punched by her boyfriend and, as a result, dropped and injured the baby she was carrying. The defendant was convicted of assault by battery directly on the mother, and indirectly on the baby.

Mepstead v DPP [1996] Crim LR 111, QBD Police officers were issuing a fixed penalty notice to a car when the owner returned and became abusive to the officers. One officer took hold of his arm and told him to calm down. It was held that touching someone to draw his/her attention to what was being said was acceptable by the ordinary standards of everyday life.

Fagan v Metropolitan Police Commissioner [1968] 3 All ER 442, QBD It is irrelevant whether the battery is inflicted directly by the body of the offender, or with a weapon or instrument such as a car.

Practical considerations

- If racially or religiously aggravated, consider the more serious racially/religiously aggravated offence (see **7.10**).
- An individual should be charged with either 'assault' or 'battery'—the inclusion of both in the same charge is bad for duplicity and could result in the charge being dismissed (*DPP v Little* (1994) 95 Cr App R 28, CA).
- Ensure that visible injuries are photographed.
- Include in your CJA witness statement evidence as to intent or recklessness.
- Ascertain whether any of the defences could apply.

Assault

- Unless extenuating circumstances apply, the police/CPS will invariably invite the aggrieved party to take their own action either by criminal prosecution or by civil action.
- Where a court decides that the assault or battery has not been proved or that it was justified, or so trifling as not to merit any punishment, they must dismiss the complaint and forthwith make out a certificate of dismissal. This certificate releases the defendant from any further proceedings (civil or criminal) (Offences Against the Person Act 1861, s 44).
- If the conduct involves threatening acts, words, gestures, or a combination of these, then consider alternative offences under the Public Order Act 1986, breach of the peace or harassment (see **7.7**).

Battery

- Ascertain the degree/severity of injury before charging.
- CPS guidelines specify the following injuries should normally be charged as battery: grazes, scratches, abrasions, minor bruising, swellings, reddening of the skin, superficial cuts, and a 'black eye'.

Consider s 47, s 20, or s 18 of the Offences Against the Person Act 1861 for more serious injuries.

 Summary   6 months

6 months' imprisonment and/or a fine

2.1.2 **Assault occasioning actual bodily harm (AOABH)/Defences to assaults**

Offences

Whosoever shall be convicted upon an indictment of any assault occasioning actual bodily harm shall be guilty of an offence.

Offences Against the Person Act 1861, s 47

Points to prove

- ✓ unlawfully
- ✓ assaulted
- ✓ another person
- ✓ occasioning him/her
- ✓ actual bodily harm

Meaning of actual bodily harm

Actual bodily harm has been defined as 'any hurt which interferes with health or comfort but not to a considerable degree'.

Explanatory notes

- Bodily harm has its ordinary meaning and is that which is calculated to interfere with the health or comfort of the victim but must be more than transient or trifling.
- Examples of 'actual bodily harm' physical/mental injuries are given in **Practical considerations**.
- A conviction can be obtained if actual bodily harm is caused to the victim by some action which is the natural and reasonably foreseeable result of what the defendant said or did.

Defences to assault

Accident (as long as malice is not present)
Consent

- This can be expressly given to an application of force (such as tattooing or an operation), providing the activity is not illegal itself (injection of illegal drugs); or it can be implied (by getting into a crowded train where contact is unavoidable).
- An honestly held belief that consent had been given (or would have been given—emergency surgery to save life).
- Submitting to an assault is not consent. Similarly, consent is negated if given due to duress or fraud (a trick), but the burden of proof is on the prosecution to prove that this was how consent was obtained.
- Consent cannot be given by a child or young person if they fail to understand the true nature of the act (what is involved).

- A teacher at a school with children who had behavioural problems did not impliedly consent to being assaulted by the children (*H v CPS* [2010] EWHC 1374, QBD).
- Consent cannot be given to an assault that inflicts substantial bodily harm, such as in sadomasochism (*R v Brown and others* [1994] 1 AC 212, HL), although some body mutilation in limited and non-aggressive circumstances may be acceptable (*R v Wilson* [1996] 2 Cr App R 241, CA).

Lawful sport

- Properly conducted lawful sports are considered to be for the public good and injuries received during the course of an event kept within the rules are generally accepted.
- Players are taken to have consented to any injuries which they might reasonably expect to suffer during the course of the match or contest.
- Criminal charges and proceedings should only be instigated in situations where the player acted outside the rules of the sport and the conduct was sufficiently serious as to be properly regarded as criminal.

Lawful correction

The Children Act 2004, s 58 ensures that parents no longer have the right to use force in the course of reasonable chastisement of their child that would go beyond a s 39 'common assault'.

Section 58 states that in relation to the following offences under:
- s 18 or s 20 (wounding and causing grievous bodily harm);
- s 47 (assault occasioning actual bodily harm);
- s 1 of the Children and Young Persons Act 1933 (cruelty under 16); the battery of a child cannot be justified on the ground that it constituted reasonable punishment.

Self-defence (case law)

'A jury must decide whether a defendant honestly believed that the circumstances were such as required him to use force to defend himself from an attack or threatened attack; the jury has then to decide whether the force used was reasonable in the circumstances' (*R v Owino* [1996] 2 Cr App R 128, CA and *DPP v Armstrong-Braun* (1999) 163 JP 271, CA).

Self-defence (statutory test—reasonable force)

Criminal Justice and Immigration Act 2008, s 76 (see 1.2).

Statutory authorities—using reasonable force (see 1.2)

Related cases

R v Keane and McGrath [2010] EWCA Crim 2514, CA Self-defence could be available to an aggressor where the violence offered by the victim was so out of proportion that the roles were effectively reversed.

H v DPP [2007] EWHC 960, QBD It is not necessary to identify which injury had been caused by which defendant provided that some injury resulting in actual bodily harm had been caused by the defendant.

2.1.2 AOABH/Defences to assaults

DPP v Smith [2006] 1 WLR 1571, QBD Cutting hair, or applying some unpleasant substance that marked or damaged the hair, was capable of being AOABH. Harm is not limited to injury and includes hurt or damage.

R v Barnes [2004] EWCA Crim 3246, CA Provides guidance on consent in contact sports (see **'Defences to assaults—Lawful sports'**).

T v DPP [2003] EWHC 266 (Admin), QBD Actual bodily harm can include loss of consciousness (even if there is no other physical injury) as it involves an impairment of the victim's sensory functions.

R v Chan-Fook [1994] All ER 552, CA Actual bodily harm can include psychiatric injury, but does not include mere emotions such as fear, distress, or panic.

R v Brown and others [1994] 1 AC 212, HL Sadomasochists engaged in torture with each other cannot give consent, even though the 'victims' were all willing participants.

Practical considerations

- If racially or religiously aggravated, consider the more serious racially/religiously aggravated offence (see **7.10**).
- Ensure that visible injuries are photographed.
- Include in your CJA witness statement details of injuries, circumstances of the incident, and any evidence as to intent or recklessness.
- Obtain medical evidence (hospital or doctor).
- Could any of the defences apply or be used by the defendant?
- CPS guidance gives examples of injuries which could amount to 'actual bodily harm':
  - ✦ loss or breaking of a tooth or teeth;
  - ✦ temporary loss of sensory functions (includes loss of consciousness);
  - ✦ extensive or multiple bruising;
  - ✦ displaced broken nose;
  - ✦ minor fractures;
  - ✦ minor cuts (not superficial), may require stitches (medical treatment);
  - ✦ psychiatric injury (proved by appropriate expert evidence) which is more than fear, distress, or panic.
- Consider s 20 or s 18 of the Offences Against the Person Act 1861 for more serious injuries (see **2.3**).

 Either way   None

 Summary: 6 months' imprisonment and/or a fine

Indictment: 5 years' imprisonment

SSS Stop, search, and seize powers   **E&S** Entry and search powers   **RRA** Racially or religiously aggravated offences

Links to alternative subjects and offences

2.2 Assault/Resist/Impersonate and Obstruct—Police or Designated/Accredited Person or Emergency Workers

This area of law concerns offences involving assault with intent to resist or prevent arrest; assault, resist, or wilfully obstruct a police constable, designated or accredited person in the execution of their duty; and obstruct or hinder emergency workers.

2.2.1 Assault with intent to resist or prevent lawful arrest

Section 38 of the Offences Against the Person Act 1861 creates the offence of 'assault with intent to resist or prevent lawful arrest'.

> **Offences**
>
> Whosoever shall assault any person with intent to resist or prevent the lawful apprehension or detainer of himself or of any other person for any offence shall be guilty of an offence.
>
> Offences Against the Person Act 1861, s 38

Points to prove

✓ assaulted
✓ with intent to resist/prevent
✓ the lawful apprehension/detention of
✓ self/other person
✓ for the offence of (specify)

Meanings

Assault (see 2.1.1)

Intent (see 4.1.2)

Resist or prevent

The *Oxford English Dictionary* offers the following meanings:
- resist—'to strive against, oppose, try to impede or refuse to comply with';
- prevent—'stop from happening or doing something; hinder; make impossible'.

Explanatory notes

- The assault itself need not be any more serious than a common assault (which could be considered as an alternative charge).
- The intention to resist the lawful arrest (either of themselves or another person) must be proved.

Defences to assault (see 2.1.2)

Related cases

R v Lee (2000) 150 NLJ 1491, CA In this case, the defendant was driving a motor car when he was stopped by police for a routine check. His breath smelled of alcohol and he was breathalysed. The test was positive and he was arrested. A scuffle developed in which he punched the two officers. He argued that he had a defence to these assaults because he believed the arrest was unlawful. It was held that a genuine or honest mistake might offer a defence in relation to many criminal offences that required '*mens rea*' (intent). Such a mistake might provide a defence in relation to assault with intent to resist arrest or assaulting an officer in the execution of his duty if it related to the question of whether the person assaulted was a police officer. However, to allow such a defence, the mistake had to be one of fact and not a mistake of law as to the authority of the person acting as a police officer. The conviction was, therefore, upheld by the court.

Practical considerations

- It must be proved that:
  - ✦ the arrest/detention was lawful and
  - ✦ the person concerned knew that an arrest was being made on himself or another.
- Intention (at the time of commission of the offence) can be proved by:
  - ✦ interviewing defendant—admissions made and explanations as to their state of mind, actions, and intentions and/or
  - ✦ inferences drawn from the circumstances of the offence, evidence from witnesses, property found on defendant or in their control, and any other incriminating evidence.
- If this offence is committed by the person initially being arrested, the power of arrest comes from the original offence. Otherwise consider assaulting a police officer in the execution of their duty or breach of the peace.
- Could any of the general assault defences apply?
- Consider CPS guidelines and charging standards for assault with intent to resist arrest.

SSS   E&S   RRA

🕐 Either way   🕐 None

▦ **Summary:** 6 months' imprisonment and/or a fine

   Indictment: 2 years' imprisonment

2.2.2 Assault constable in execution of duty

The Police Act 1996, s 89(1) provides the offences of assaulting a constable or person assisting a constable acting in the execution of their duty.

> **Offences**
>
> Any person who assaults a constable in the execution of his duty, or a person assisting a constable in the execution of his duty, shall be guilty of an offence.
>
> **Police Act 1996, s 89(1)**

Points to prove

✓ assaulted a constable **or** person assisting a constable
✓ in execution of their duty

Meanings

Assault (see 2.1.1)

Execution of duty

The officer must be acting lawfully and in the execution of their duty (see **'Related cases'**).

Explanatory notes

- The duties of a constable have not been defined by any statute (see 'Related cases').
- This offence also applies to police officers from Scotland or Northern Ireland (while in England or Wales) who are acting within statutory powers or executing a warrant.
- Section 30 of the Police Act 1996 defines the jurisdiction of a constable as being throughout England and Wales and the adjacent

UK waters. Special constables have the same jurisdiction, powers, and privileges of a constable.

Defences to assault (see 2.1.2)

Related cases (see 2.1.1 and s 17 entry at 1.5.2 for more cases)

Oraki v CPS [2018] EWHC 115 (Admin) In this case the defendant intervened to pull a police officer away from his mother believing that the officer had assaulted her. He was charged and convicted of offences under s 89(1) and (2). On appeal the conviction was quashed. The Court held that *being mistaken* as to whether his mother was in fact being assaulted does not make the defence unavailable to a charge of obstruction.

Walker v Commissioner of Police of the Metropolis [2014] EWCA Civ 897, CA In this case, a police officer attended a domestic incident and restricted the suspect's movements in a doorway while appraising the situation. This action had not deprived the defendant of his liberty, albeit freedom of movement was restricted for a few seconds. The subsequent public order arrest had been lawful, but the common law power to detain, short of arrest, to prevent a breach of the peace (see 7.3) can only apply if the officer had this power in mind at the relevant time.

DPP v Hawkins [1988] 1 WLR 1166, QBD In this case it was held that an arrest was rendered unlawful by a failure to provide the reason for arrest as soon as practicable after arrest.

Collins v Wilcock [1984] 3 All ER 374, QBD In this case, a police officer was assaulted after holding the arm of the defendant in order to detain her to answer questions. It was held that this act went beyond acceptable lawful physical contact and so constituted a battery. Consequently, the officer had not been acting in the execution of his/her duty when assaulted by the defendant.

Robson v Hallett [1967] 2 All ER 407, QBD An officer may be a trespasser (and, therefore, not acting in the execution of their duty) if permission to enter or remain on property is withdrawn, but reasonable time must be given to leave property.

Practical considerations

- Officers should ensure they are acting within their powers and following relevant requirements or procedures (eg information to be given prior to search or at time of arrest under ss 2 and 28 PACE (see 1.4.2), otherwise they may no longer be acting within the execution of their duty (*Sobczak v DPP* [2012] EWHC 1319 (Admin)).
- The offence does not require proof that the defendant knew or ought to have known that the victim was a constable or that they were acting in the execution of their duty.

- A plain clothes officer should produce identification, as a failure to do so could mean that the officer was acting outside the execution of their duty.
- Section 68 of the Railways and Transport Safety Act 2003 and s 68 of the Energy Act 2004 stipulate that the s 89(1) and s 89(2) (see **2.2.3**) offences also apply to BTP and members of the Civil Nuclear Constabulary.
- Do any of the general assault defences apply?
- Consider CPS guidelines and 2012 revised charging standards for this offence relating to injuries received amounting to a battery (see **2.1.1**).
- If the injuries justify a s 47 charge (see **2.1.2**) for a member of the public, then this will also be the appropriate charge for a constable.

 Summary   6 months

 6 months' imprisonment and/or a fine

2.2.3 **Resist/obstruct constable in execution of duty**

Section 89(2) of the Police Act 1996 deals with the offences of resisting or wilfully obstructing a constable in the execution of their duty.

> ### Offences
>
> Any person who resists or wilfully obstructs a constable in the execution of his duty, or a person assisting a constable in the execution of his duty, shall be guilty of an offence.
>
> Police Act 1996, s 89(2)

Points to prove

✓ resisted/wilfully obstructed a constable or person assisting
✓ in the execution of constable's duty

Meanings

Resists (see 2.2.1)

Wilful obstruction

In this context, it must be a deliberate obstruction.

66   SSS Stop, search, and
seize powers   RRA Racially or religiously
aggravated offences

Execution of duty (see 2.2.2)

Explanatory notes

- Resists does not imply that any assault has taken place and where a person in the process of being lawfully arrested tears himself away from the constable or person assisting, this will constitute resistance.
- The obstruction must be some form of positive act which prevents or impedes the officer in carrying out their duty.
- For the constable's duty and jurisdiction, see **2.2.2**.
- It must be proved that the officer was acting in the execution of their duty.

Related cases

Aznanag v CPS (2015) Unreported QBD In this case, several police officers were attempting to arrest a person inside premises resulting in unrest from a crowd that had formed outside. The defendant tried to push past a police officer and enter the premises. The officer put her hand out to stop him and requested that he go no further. He ignored the request and grabbed the officer's wrist which caused her pain. It was held that the police were acting in the exercise of their duty in trying to prevent people from moving forward and the officer had been entitled to try to stop the defendant.

Marsden v CPS [2014] All ER (D) 199 (Oct), CA In this case, the police were invited into a house by H (partner of M) to deal with a domestic dispute but were unable to rouse M who was sleeping on the couch. After M had awoken, he shouted 'Fuck off' to the officer, and a violent struggle then ensued while the officer was trying to arrest him. It was held that consent given by H to enter the house was enduring. M's words ('fuck off') did not 'revoke' the licence (permission) for the officer to remain on the property.

Smith v DPP (2001) 165 JP 432, QBD Three police officers went to the house responding to a discontinued 999 call. The defendant, who lived at the premises, was banging on the door. An officer tried to move him away by taking his arm (knowing full well that he lived at that address). The defendant hit him and in the ensuing struggle assaulted all three officers. He was arrested and charged with three offences of assaulting a police constable in the execution of his duty. It was held that it was perfectly reasonable for the police officer to require the defendant to move away so that the others could investigate the call without interference.

Practical considerations (see **2.2.2**)

 Summary 6 months

 1 month imprisonment and/or a level 3 fine

2.2.4 **Impersonate constable or wear/ possess article of police uniform**

Section 90 of the Police Act 1996 deals with the offences of impersonating a member of a police force or special constable or unlawfully wearing/being in possession of any article of police uniform.

Offences

(1) Any person who with intent to deceive impersonates a member of a police force or special constable or makes any statement or does any act calculated falsely to suggest that he is such a member or constable, shall be guilty of an offence.

(2) Any person who, not being a constable, wears any article of police uniform in circumstances where it gives him an appearance so nearly resembling that of a member of a police force as to be calculated to deceive shall be guilty of an offence.

(3) Any person who, not being a member of a police force or special constable, has in his possession any article of police uniform shall, unless he proves that he obtained possession of that article lawfully and has possession of it for a lawful purpose, be guilty of an offence.

Police Act 1996, s 90

Points to prove

s 90(1) offence

- ✓ impersonated
- ✓ special constable/member of police force
- ✓ with intent to deceive

or

- ✓ with intent to deceive
- ✓ made a statement/did an act
- ✓ which calculated falsely to suggest
- ✓ that you were a special constable/member of a police force

s 90(2) offence

- ✓ not being a constable
- ✓ wore article(s) of police uniform
- ✓ in circumstances which made you appear to resemble
- ✓ being a member of police force
- ✓ so as to be calculated to deceive

s 90(3) offence

- ✓ not being a special constable/member of police force
- ✓ possessed article(s) of police uniform

Meanings

With intent (see **4.1.2**)

Deceive

Means to induce a person to believe a thing to be true which is in fact false: in this case that the person is a police officer.

Special constable

A special constable has the same jurisdiction, powers, and privileges as a constable.

Article of police uniform

Means any article of uniform or any distinctive badge, or mark, or document of identification usually issued to members of police forces or special constables, or anything having the appearance of such an article, badge, mark, or document.

Explanatory notes

- Section 68 of the Railways and Transport Safety Act 2003 states that s 90 (impersonation of constable) applies to a constable/special constable of the BTP.
- In s 90(2) 'calculated to deceive' has been held to mean 'likely to deceive' (*Turner v Shearer* [1973] 1 All ER 397), although this does not require the defendant to have a specific intent to deceive as with the more serious offence under s 90(1).

Defence—applicable to s 90(3) only

Proof that they obtained possession of the article of police uniform lawfully and possession of it was for a lawful purpose.

Related cases

Cooke v DPP [2015] EWHC 3312 (Admin) The defendant was the owner of a business dealing in old military and police uniforms. He was charged with an offence under s 90(3). If the possession of the articles of police uniform was for the purpose of supply, whether by sale or otherwise, to an end user who intended to use them for an unlawful purpose, for example, to impersonate a police officer with intent to deceive, then on the face of it, the possession by the seller would be for an unlawful purpose. However, the court held that where the possession was for a purpose of sale to a person who, unknown to the seller, had such an unlawful purpose, this would not be an offence under this section and the statutory defence would apply.

Practical considerations

- The burden of proof in relation to the defence of lawful possession under s 90(3) is on the defendant, to prove on the balance of probabilities.
- For the s 90(1) and s 90(2) offences it is not necessary to prove intent to deceive a specific individual, or to prove that the person obtained any form of benefit or advantage as a result of the deception.

 Summary   6 months

 s 90(1)—6 months' imprisonment and/or a fine

s 90(2)—Level 3 fine

s 90(3)—Level 1 fine

2.2.5 **Assault/resist/obstruct designated or accredited person in execution of duty**

Section 46 of the Police Reform Act 2002 refers to offences in respect of suitably designated and accredited people as follows:

Offences

(1) Any person who assaults—
   (a) a designated person in the execution of his duty,
   (b) an accredited person in the execution of his duty,
   (ba) an accredited inspector in the execution of his duty, or
   (c) a person assisting a designated or accredited person or an accredited inspector in the execution of his duty,
   is guilty of an offence.

(2) Any person who resists or wilfully obstructs—
   (a) a designated person in the execution of his duty,
   (b) an accredited person in the execution of his duty,
   (ba) an accredited inspector in the execution of his duty, or
   (c) a person assisting a designated or accredited person or an accredited inspector in the execution of his duty,
   is guilty of an offence.

Police Reform Act 2002, s 46

Points to prove

✓ assaulted or resisted/wilfully obstructed
✓ a designated/accredited person/accredited inspector or person assisting
✓ while in the execution of their duty

Meanings

Assaults (see 2.1.1)

Designated person

(a) Designated persons are to be within the meaning given by
    s 47(1), and
(b) a person in relation to whom a designation under s 38B is for the
    time being in force.

Accredited person

Means a person accredited under s 41.

Accredited inspector

Means a weights and measures inspector accredited under s 41A.

Resists or wilfully obstructs (see 2.2.3)

Explanatory notes

- Designated person under s 47(1) means person designated under s
  38 or 39, and includes community support officer, policing support
  officer, community support volunteers, policing support volunteers,
  and contracted-out staff (see 11.1).
- The term accredited person relates to community safety
  accreditation schemes set up by the chief officer under ss 40 and 41.
  The accredited person is given the powers defined in Schedule 5.
- References to the execution of their duties relate to exercising any
  power or performing any duty by virtue of their designation or
  accreditation.
- Under s 41A a chief officer of police may grant accreditation to a
  weights and measures inspector who is an inspector of weights and
  measures appointed under s 72(1) of the Weights and Measures
  Act 1985.

Defences to assault (see 2.1.2)

Related cases (see 2.2.2 and 2.2.3)

Practical considerations (see also 2.2.2 and 2.2.3)

- Given the extensive and detailed restrictions on the powers of these
  individuals, the precise activities that were involved at the time will
  be closely scrutinised by a court. It will be critical to establish that the
  person was acting within the lawful limits of their powers at the time.
- It is also an offence under s 46(3) for any person who, with intent to
  deceive, impersonates the above persons.
- It is a summary offence to intentionally obstruct a person acting
  lawfully as an enforcement agent (formerly certified bailiffs) under
  the Tribunals, Courts and Enforcement Act 2007, Sch 12, para 68(1).

Summary   🕐 6 months

🏛 ***Assaulted/assaulted a person assisting and impersonation:***
6 months' imprisonment and/or a fine

Resisted/wilfully obstructed or resisted/obstructed a person assisting: 1 month imprisonment and/or a level 3 fine

2.2.6 Obstruct/hinder emergency workers and persons assisting

The Emergency Workers (Obstruction) Act 2006 creates offences of obstructing/hindering certain emergency workers responding to an emergency, and obstructing/hindering persons assisting such emergency workers.

Offences against emergency workers

A person who without reasonable excuse obstructs or hinders another while that other person is, in a capacity mentioned in subsection (2) below, responding to emergency circumstances, commits an offence.

Emergency Workers (Obstruction) Act 2006, s 1(1)

Points to prove

✓ without reasonable excuse
✓ obstructed or hindered
✓ emergency worker as described in s 1(2) who is
✓ attending/dealing/preparing to deal
✓ with emergency circumstances as given in s 1(3) and s 1(4)

Meanings

Capacity (of emergency worker)

(2) The capacity referred to in subsection (1) above is—
   (a) that of a person employed by a fire and rescue authority in England and Wales;
   (b) in relation to England and Wales, that of a person (other than a person falling within paragraph (a)) whose duties as an employee or as a servant of the Crown involve—
     (i). extinguishing fires; or
     (ii). protecting life and property in the event of a fire;

    (c) that of a person employed by a **relevant NHS body** in the provision of ambulance services (including air ambulance services), or of a person providing such services pursuant to arrangements made by, or at the request of, a relevant NHS body;

    (d) that of a person providing services for the transport of organs, blood, equipment or personnel pursuant to arrangements made by, or at the request of, a relevant NHS body;

    (e) that of a member of Her Majesty's Coastguard;

    (f) that of a member of the crew of a vessel operated by—

        (i) the Royal National Lifeboat Institution, or

        (ii) any other person or organisation operating a vessel for the purpose of providing a rescue service,

    or a person who musters the crew of such a vessel or attends to its launch or recovery.

Responding to emergency circumstances

(3) For the purposes of this section and section 2 of this Act, a person is **responding** to emergency circumstances if the person—

    (a) is going anywhere for the purpose of dealing with emergency circumstances occurring there; or

    (b) is dealing with emergency circumstances or preparing to do so.

(4) For the purposes of this Act, circumstances are '**emergency circumstances**' if they are present or imminent and—

    (a) are causing or are likely to cause—

        (i) serious injury to or the serious illness (including mental illness) of a person;

        (ii) serious harm to the environment (including the life and health of plants and animals);

        (iii) serious harm to any building or other property; or

        (iv) a worsening of any such injury, illness or harm; or

    (b) are likely to cause the death of a person.

Emergency Workers (Obstruction) Act 2006; s 1

Offences against person assisting

(1) A person who without reasonable excuse obstructs or hinders another in the circumstances described in subsection (2) below commits an offence.

(2) Those circumstances are where the person being obstructed or hindered is assisting another while that other person is, in a capacity mentioned in section 1(2) of this Act, responding to emergency circumstances.

Emergency Workers (Obstruction) Act 2006, s 2

2.2.6 Obstruct/hinder emergency workers and persons assisting

Points to prove

✓ without reasonable excuse
✓ obstructed or hindered
✓ a person who was assisting
✓ an emergency worker as described in s 1(2) who was
✓ attending/dealing/preparing to deal
✓ with emergency circumstances as given in s 1(3) and s 1(4)

Explanatory notes

- In s 1(2) a **'relevant NHS body'** is an NHS foundation trust, NHS trust, Special Health Authority, a clinical commissioning group, or Local Health Board.
- A person may be convicted of the offence under s 1 or s 2 of this Act notwithstanding that it is affected by: means other than physical means; or action directed only at any vehicle, vessel, apparatus, equipment, or other thing, or any animal used, or to be used by a person referred to in that section.
- For the purposes of ss 1 and 2, circumstances to which a person is responding are to be taken to be emergency circumstances if the person believes and has reasonable grounds for believing they are or may be emergency circumstances.
- Further details on this 2006 Act are dealt with in HOC 3/2007.
- The 2006 Act does not include police or prison officers because obstruction of a police constable is an offence under the Police Act 1996 (see **2.2.3**). This 1996 Act also covers prison officers by virtue of s 8 of the Prison Act 1952 which stipulates that prison officers, whilst acting as such, shall have all the powers, authority, protection, and privileges of a constable.
- See **2.2.5** for assault or resist/wilfully obstruct a suitably designated or accredited person.

 Summary   6 months

 Fine

Links to alternative subjects and offences

2.3 Wounding/Grievous Bodily Harm

2.3.1 Wounding or inflicting grievous bodily harm

Section 20 of the Offences Against the Person Act 1861 provides the offence of 'wounding or inflicting grievous bodily harm'.

Offences

Whosoever shall unlawfully and maliciously wound or inflict any grievous bodily harm upon any other person, either with or without any weapon or instrument shall be guilty of an offence.

Offences Against the Person Act 1861, s 20

Points to prove
✓ unlawfully
✓ maliciously
✓ wounded **or** inflicted grievous bodily harm
✓ upon another person

Meanings

Unlawfully

Means without excuse or justification at law.

Maliciously

- Means malice (ill-will or an evil motive) must be present.
- 'Maliciously requires either an actual intention to do the particular kind of harm that was done or **recklessness** whether any such harm should occur or not; it is neither limited to, nor does it require, any ill-will towards the person injured' (*R v Cunningham* [1957] 2 All ER 412, CA).

Recklessness

Defendant being aware of the existence of the risk but nonetheless had gone on and taken it (*R v Cunningham* [1957] 2 All ER 412, CA).

Wound

Means any break in the continuity of the whole skin.

Inflict

- Inflict does not have as wide a meaning as 'cause'—grievous bodily harm can be inflicted without there being an assault.
- 'Grievous bodily harm may be inflicted either by: directly and violently assaulting the victim; or something intentionally done which although in itself is not a direct application of force to the body of the victim, does directly result in force being applied to the body of the victim so that he suffers grievous bodily harm' (*R v Wilson and Jenkins* [1983] 3 All ER 448, HL).

Grievous bodily harm

- Means 'serious or really serious harm' (*R v Saunders* [1985] Crim LR 230, CA).
- Bodily harm can include inflicting/causing a psychiatric harm/illness (silent/heavy breathing/menacing telephone calls—*R v Ireland* [1998] AC 147, HL) or include psychiatric injury, in serious cases, as well as physical injury (stalking victim—*R v Burstow* [1997] 4 All ER 225, HL).

Explanatory notes

- If it appears that the target of the attack was not the actual victim, then the 'doctrine of transferred malice' provides that if a person mistakenly causes injury to a person other than the person whom he intended to attack, they will commit the same offence as if they had injured the intended victim. The doctrine only applies if the crime remains the same and the harm done must be of the same kind as the harm intended (*R v Latimer* (1886) 17 QBD 359, QBD).
- As wounding and grievous bodily harm are both different, the distinction as to which offence is appropriate should be made.

Defences

May be available to a s 20 offence (see **2.1.2**).

Related cases

R v Golding [2014] EWCA Crim 889 In this case, the defendant had a sexual relationship with C and infected her with an incurable genital herpes virus. He was charged with inflicting grievous bodily harm contrary to s 20. At interview, he admitted that he had infected C and that he should have informed her of his condition. The case involved speculation as to whether herpes could be described as 'really serious bodily harm'. It was held that C's painful symptoms and their effect and indefinite recurrence without effective cure was sufficient for a jury to consider that it was really serious bodily harm. The serious harm did not have to be either permanent or dangerous.

2.3.1 Wounding or inflicting grievous bodily harm

R v Dica [2005] EWCA Crim 2304, CA Inflicting grievous bodily harm was held to include infecting the victim with HIV through unprotected consensual sexual intercourse.

R v Konzani [2005] EWCA Crim 706, CA In this case, it was held that for a valid defence, there must be a willing and informed consent by the other party to the specific risk of their contracting HIV—this cannot be inferred from consent to unprotected sexual intercourse alone.

R v Brown and others [1994] 1 AC 212, HL In this case it was held that consent cannot be given to an assault that inflicts bodily harm of a substantial nature such as in sadomasochism other than in very limited circumstances such as a regulated boxing match.

R v Savage [1992] 1 AC 699, HL and **DPP v Parmenter [1991] 3 WLR 914, HL** In s 20 wounding/GBH cases:
- s 47 assault (AOABH) can be an alternative verdict if it includes implications of assault occasioning actual bodily harm.
- 'Cunningham malice' will suffice. It is enough that the defendant should have foreseen that some physical harm might result—of whatever character.

R v Wilson and Jenkins [1983] 3 All ER 448, HL In this case, the victim, frightened by the defendant, jumps through a window and breaks a leg. It was held that grievous bodily harm has been 'inflicted' by the offender by inducing substantial fear, even though there is no direct application of force.

R v Cunningham [1957] 2 All ER 412, CA Meaning of 'maliciously' and recklessness test (above).

Practical considerations

- Consider the more serious racially/religiously aggravated offence (see **7.10**).
- In cases of 'transferred malice' the charge must specify at whom the intent was aimed (eg 'A wounded C with intent to cause GBH to B').
- The distinction between 'wound' and 'GBH' must be identified and considered, as they do not have the same meaning.
- Where both a wound and grievous bodily harm have been inflicted, choose which part of s 20 reflects the true nature of the offence (*R v McCready* [1978] 1 WLR 1376, CA).
- The s 18 offence requires intent while s 20 is 'unlawfully and maliciously'.
- Consider CPS advice and guidance for unlawful wounding or inflicting GBH:
  - ✦ The distinction between charges under s 18 and s 20 is one of **intent**. The gravity of the injury may provide some evidence of intent.
  - ✦ Wounding means the breaking of the continuity of the whole of the outer skin, or the inner skin within the cheek or lip. It does not include the rupturing of internal blood vessels.

+ Minor wounds, such as a small cut or laceration, should be charged under s 47. Section 20 should be reserved for those wounds considered to be serious (thus equating the offences with the infliction of grievous or serious bodily harm).
+ Grievous bodily harm means serious bodily harm, such as:
  - injury resulting in permanent disability or permanent loss of sensory function; injury which results in more than minor permanent, visible disfigurement;
  - broken or displaced limbs or bones, including fractured skull, compound fractures, broken cheekbone/jaw or ribs;
  - injuries which cause substantial loss of blood, usually necessitating a transfusion, or resulting in lengthy treatment or incapacity;
  - psychiatric injury (expert evidence is essential to prove the injury).
* Obtain medical evidence to prove extent of injury.
* Obtain photographs of victim's injuries.

 Either way   None

 Summary: 6 months' imprisonment and/or a fine

Indictment: 5 years' imprisonment

2.3.2 Wounding or grievous bodily harm—with intent

Section 18 of the Offences Against the Person Act 1861 creates the offences of 'wounding or causing grievous bodily harm with intent'.

Offences

Whosoever shall unlawfully and maliciously by any means whatsoever wound or cause any grievous bodily harm to any person with intent to do some grievous bodily harm to any person, or with intent to resist or prevent the lawful apprehension or detainer of any person, shall be guilty of felony.

Offences Against the Person Act 1861, s 18

Points to prove

✓ unlawfully and maliciously
✓ caused grievous bodily harm or wounded a person
✓ with intent to
✓ do grievous bodily harm or resist/prevent lawful apprehension/detention of self/another

2.3.2 Wounding or grievous bodily harm—with intent

Meanings

Unlawfully (see **2.3.1**)

Maliciously (see **2.3.1**)

Any means whatsoever

This is given its literal meaning. A connection between the means used and the harm caused must be proved.

Wound (see **2.3.1**)

Cause

Defined as 'anything that produces a result or effect'.

Grievous bodily harm (see **2.3.1**)

Intent (see **4.1.2**)

Resist or prevent (see **2.2.1**)

Explanatory notes

- Cause has a wider meaning than 'inflict'. All that needs to be proved is some connection between the action (the means used) and the injury (sometimes called the chain of causation). There does not need to be a direct application of force.
- The issue of causation is separate from the test for intent.
- If appropriate consider the 'causation test' (see *R v Roberts* (1972) 56 Cr App R 95, CA—see '**Related cases**').
- Intent must be proved either from verbal admissions on interview and/or other incriminating evidence (eg subsequent actions).
- The statutory test under s 8 of the Criminal Justice Act 1967 must be considered (see **4.1.2**).
- In relation to the offence of wounding or causing GBH with intent to resist or prevent lawful arrest/detention it must be proved:
  - ✦ arrest/detention was lawful;
  - ✦ defendant must have known that arrest was being made on them/ another person.

> **Defences** (see **2.1.2**)

Related cases

R v Roberts (1972) 56 Cr App R 95, CA In this case, a victim of an ongoing sexual assault jumped out of a car to escape and was seriously injured in doing so. The court considered the 'chain of causation' and applied the 'causation test':

- If the victim's actions are reasonable ones which could be foreseen and were acceptable under the circumstances, then the defendant will be liable for injuries resulting from them.

• If the harm/injury was caused by a voluntary act on the part of the victim, which could not reasonably be foreseen, then the chain of causation between the defendant's actions and the harm/injury received will be broken and the defendant will not be liable for them.

Practical considerations (see also 2.3.1)

• Section 18 does not come under racially or religiously aggravated assaults (see **7.10.2**), although this will be considered when determining sentence.
• Knowledge that GBH was a virtually certain consequence of their action will not amount to an intention, but it *will* be good evidence from which a court can infer such intention.
• Other factors which may indicate the specific intent include:
  ✦ a repeated or planned attack;
  ✦ deliberate selection of a weapon or adaptation of an article to cause injury, such as breaking a glass before an attack;
  ✦ making prior threats;
  ✦ using an offensive weapon against, or kicking, the victim's head.
• Proof is required that the wound/GBH was inflicted maliciously. This means that the defendant must have foreseen some harm—although not necessarily the specific type or gravity of injury suffered or inflicted.
• Generally, an assault under this section may be:
  ✦ wounding with intent to do GBH;
  ✦ causing GBH, with intent to do GBH;
  ✦ wounding with intent to resist or prevent the lawful arrest/detention of self/any person;
  ✦ maliciously causing GBH with intent to resist or prevent the lawful arrest of self/any person.
• Where evidence of intent is absent, but a wound or grievous bodily harm is still caused, then both s 18 and s 20 should be included on the indictment.
• Consider CPS advice and guidance for wounding/causing GBH with intent.
• In cases involving GBH, remember that s 20 requires the infliction of harm, whereas s 18 requires the causing of harm, although this distinction has been greatly reduced by the decisions in *R v Ireland* [1998] AC 147, HL and *R v Burstow* [1997] 4 All ER 225, HL (see **2.3.1**).
• Section 18 is of assistance in more serious assaults upon police officers, where the evidence of an intention to prevent arrest is clear, but the evidence of intent to cause GBH is in doubt.
• Section 6(3) of the Criminal Law Act 1967 permits a conviction for s 20 (inflicting GBH) in respect of a count for s 18 (causing GBH with intent), as 'cause' includes 'inflict' (*R v Wilson and Jenkins* [1983] 3 All ER 448, HL).

2.3.2 Wounding or grievous bodily harm—with intent

- Obtain medical evidence to prove extent of injury.
- Obtain photographs of victim's injuries.

 Indictable only

 None

Life imprisonment

Links to alternative subjects and offences

SSS Stop, search, and seize powers

RRA Racially or religiously aggravated offences

2.4 **Child Cruelty and Taking a Child into Police Protection**

2.4.1 **Child cruelty**

The Children and Young Persons Act 1933 was introduced to prevent children and young persons from being exposed to moral and physical danger. The Act addresses such problem areas as cruelty, neglect, safety, employment, and performing in entertainments. It also provides rules and guidance in relation to children and young persons who are involved in the criminal justice process.

Offences

If any person who has attained the age of 16 years and has responsibility for any child or young person under that age, wilfully assaults, ill-treats (whether physically or otherwise), neglects, abandons, or exposes him, or causes or procures him to be assaulted, ill-treated (whether physically or otherwise), neglected, abandoned, or exposed, in a manner likely to cause him unnecessary suffering or injury to health (whether the suffering or injury is of a physical or a psychological nature), that person shall be guilty of an offence.

Children and Young Persons Act 1933, s 1(1)

Points to prove

✓ being a person 16 years or over
✓ having responsibility
✓ for a child/young person (under 16 years)
✓ did wilfully or caused/procured the child/young person to be
✓ assaulted/ill-treated (whether physical or otherwise)/neglected/abandoned/exposed
✓ in manner likely to cause unnecessary suffering/injury (physical or psychological) to health

Meanings

Responsibility (s 17)

- The following shall be presumed to have responsibility for a child or young person:
  (a) any person who:
    (i) has **parental responsibility** for the child/young person; or
    (ii) is otherwise legally liable to maintain the child/young person; and
  (b) any person who has care of the child/young person.

2.4.1 Child cruelty

- A person who is presumed to be responsible for a child or young person by virtue of (a) shall not be taken to have ceased to be responsible by reason only that they do not have care of the child/young person.

Parental responsibility

Means all the rights, duties, powers, responsibilities, and authority which by law a parent of a child has in relation to that child and their property.

Child

Means a person under 14 years of age.

Young person

Person who has attained the age of 14 but is under the age of 18 years.

Neglect in a manner likely to cause injury to health

- A parent or other person legally liable to maintain a child or young person, or the **legal guardian** of such a person, is deemed to have neglected in a manner likely to cause injury (physical or psychological) to health if they have failed to provide adequate food, clothing, medical aid, or lodging, or if, having been unable to do so, they have failed to take steps to procure it to be provided under relevant enactments.
- A person may be convicted of this offence:
  - ✦ even though actual suffering or injury (physical or psychological) to health, or the likelihood of it, was prevented by the action of another person;
  - ✦ notwithstanding the death of the child or young person in question.

Legal guardian

Means a **guardian** of a child as defined in the Children Act 1989.

Guardian

Includes any person who, in the opinion of the court having cognisance of any case in relation to the child or young person or has for the time being the care of the child or young person.

Explanatory notes

- The Serious Crime Act 2015, s 66 added 'whether physically or otherwise' and 'psychological' to the physical suffering or injury. See HOC 8/2015 for further details.
- The term 'ill-treated' is not specifically defined, but will include bullying, frightening, or any conduct causing unnecessary suffering or injury to physical or mental health.

- Battery of a child cannot be justified on the grounds of reasonable punishment (see **2.1.2 'Defences to assault'**).

Practical considerations

- Section 548 of the Education Act 1996 prevents teachers in any school from giving corporal punishment.
- The prosecution must prove a deliberate or reckless act, or failure to act. The test is **subjective**, not based on the notion of a reasonable parent or person in charge.
- Consider taking the child/young person into police protection (see **2.4.2**).

 Either way   None

 Summary: 6 months' imprisonment and/or a fine

Indictment: 10 years' imprisonment and/or a fine

2.4.2 Taking a child at risk into police protection

The Children Act 1989, s 46 provides police powers to take children under 18 years old who are at risk of significant harm into police protection.

Powers

(1) Where a constable has reasonable cause to believe that a child would otherwise be likely to suffer significant harm, he may—
   (a) remove the child to suitable accommodation and keep him there; or
   (b) take such steps as are reasonable to ensure that the child's removal from any hospital, or other place, in which he is being accommodated is prevented.
(2) For the purposes of this Act, a child with respect to whom a constable has exercised his powers under this section is referred to as having been taken into police protection.
(3) As soon as is reasonably practicable after taking a child into police protection, the constable concerned shall—
   (a) inform the local authority within whose area the child was found of the steps that have been, and are proposed to be,

taken with respect to the child under this section and the
reasons for taking them;

(b) give details to the authority within whose area the child is
ordinarily resident ('the appropriate authority') of the place at
which the child is being accommodated;

(c) inform the child (if he appears capable of understanding)—
  (i) of the steps that have been taken with respect to him under
  this section and of the reasons for taking them; and
  (ii) of the further steps that may be taken with respect to him
  under this section;

(d) take such steps as are reasonably practicable to discover the
wishes and feelings of the child;

(e) secure that the case is inquired into by an officer designated
for the purposes of this section by the chief officer of the police
area concerned; and

(f) where the child was taken into police protection by being
removed to accommodation which is not provided—
  (i) by or on behalf of a local authority; or
  (ii) as a refuge, in compliance with the requirements of
  section 51,
secure that he is moved to accommodation which is so provided.

(4) As soon as is reasonably practicable after taking a child into police
protection the constable concerned shall take such steps as are
reasonably practicable to inform—

(a) the child's parents;

(b) every person who is not a parent of his but who has parental
responsibility for him; and

(c) any other person with whom the child was living immediately
before being taken into police protection,

of the steps that he has taken under this section with respect to the
child, the reasons for taking them and the further steps that may be
taken with respect to him under this section.

(5) On completing any inquiry under subsection (3)(e), the officer
conducting it shall release the child from police protection unless he
considers that there is still reasonable cause for believing that the
child would be likely to suffer significant harm if released.

(6) No child may be kept in police protection for more than 72 hours.

(7) While a child is being kept in police protection, the designated
officer may apply on behalf of the appropriate authority for an
emergency protection order to be made under s 44 with respect to
the child.

(8) An application may be made under subsection (7) whether or not
the authority knows of it or agree to its being made.

(9) While a child is being kept in police protection—

(a) neither the constable concerned, nor the designated officer
shall have parental responsibility for him; but

(b) the designated officer shall do what is reasonable in all the
circumstances of the case for the purpose of safeguarding or

> promoting the child's welfare (having regard in particular to the
> length of the period during which the child will be so protected).
> (10) Where a child has been taken into police protection, the designated
> officer shall allow—
> (a) the child's parents;
> (b) any person who is not a parent of the child but who has
> parental responsibility for him;
> (c) any person with whom the child was living immediately before
> he was taken into police protection;
> (d) any person named in a child arrangements order as a person
> with whom the child is to spend time or otherwise have
> contact;
> (e) any person who is allowed to have contact with the child by
> virtue of an order under s 34; and
> (f) any person acting on behalf of any of those persons,
> to have such contact (if any) with the child as, in the opinion of the
> designated officer, is both reasonable and in the child's interests.
>
> Children Act 1989, s 46

Meanings

Child

Means a person under the age of 18.

Hospital

Has the same meaning as in the Mental Health Act 1983, except
that it does not include a hospital at which high security psychiatric
services are provided. The 1983 Act states a hospital is 'any health
service hospital within the meaning of the National Health Service
Act 2006 ... and any accommodation provided by a local authority
and used as a hospital by or on behalf of the Secretary of State under
that Act'.

Explanatory notes

- The police have a duty to protect the child until more formal
  arrangements can be made. It is possible for a child to be in police
  protection without physically moving them. For example, if a child
  is in hospital having been battered, they may be taken into police
  protection while leaving the child in the hospital.
- This power is appropriate for detaining and returning children
  missing from home as long as they are at risk from significant harm.

Related cases

Langley and others v Liverpool City Council [2006] 1 WLR 375, CA
If practicable, removal of a child should be authorised by an emergency
protection court order under s 44 and carried out by the local authority.

2.4.2 Taking a child at risk into police protection

If such an order is in force the police should not exercise their s 46 powers, unless there are compelling reasons for doing so.

Practical considerations

- HOC 17/2008 provides guidance as follows:
  - ◆ The designated officer under s 46(3)(e) will usually be an officer of the rank of Inspector.
  - ◆ These powers should only be used when the child would be likely to suffer significant harm.
  - ◆ Except in exceptional circumstances (eg imminent threat to a child's welfare), no child is to be taken into police protection until the investigating officer has seen the child and assessed their circumstances.
  - ◆ Consider entry powers under s 17 PACE (see **1.5.2**) as no power of entry is provided under these police protection powers.
  - ◆ A police station is not suitable accommodation for these purposes but may be used as a temporary or emergency measure until suitable accommodation is identified.
- The Children Act 1989 includes other powers to protect children:
  - ◆ s 43—Child assessment orders;
  - ◆ s 44—Emergency protection orders;
  - ◆ s 47—Duty of local authority to investigate welfare;
  - ◆ s 48—Warrant/powers to ascertain if child requires protection;
  - ◆ s 50—Recovery of abducted children.
- A Local Safeguarding Children Board for each area should protect children from abuse and neglect. This involves a range of parties providing children's services and the police liaising with each other, including an information database whereby information can be shared between all partners.

Links to alternative subjects and offences

2.5 **Threats to Kill**

Section 16 of the Offences Against the Person Act 1861 provides the offence of threats to kill.

Offences

A person who, without lawful excuse makes to another a threat intending that the other would fear it would be carried out, to kill that other or a third person shall be guilty of an offence.

Offences Against the Person Act 1861, s 16

Points to prove

✓ without lawful excuse
✓ made threat to kill
✓ intending to cause fear threat would be carried out

Meaning of intending (see **4.1.2**)

Explanatory notes

- There is no need to show that the defendant intended to kill anyone. The relevant intent must be that the person receiving the threat would fear the threat (to kill them or a third person) would be carried out.

Defences

- Having a lawful excuse, such as the prevention of crime or self-defence.
- It must be reasonable in all the circumstances to make the threat.

Related cases

R v Tait [1990] 1 QB 290, CA An unborn child (foetus in utero) is not a third person distinct from its mother for the purposes of this section. Therefore, a threat to a pregnant woman to kill her unborn baby is not an offence under this section. However, it would appear that a threat to kill a child after its birth made at a time when it was still a foetus may come within the scope of this offence.

2.5 Threats to Kill

R v Williams (1987) 84 Cr App R 299, CA In this case it was held that evidence of a past assault committed against the victim was admissible to show that the defendant had intended the threats to be taken seriously.

Practical considerations

- The onus is on the prosecution to prove that there was no lawful excuse for making a threat and it is for the jury to decide what is reasonable and what amounts to a threat.
- Consider hearsay and bad character admissibility under the Criminal Justice Act 2003.
- Proof of the '*mens rea*' ('guilty mind'), as to the intention that the other person would fear the threat would be carried out to kill that person or a third person, is required.
- Evidence of previous history between the parties is admissible as tending to prove that the defendant intended his words to be taken seriously.
- Detail in your file and CJA witness statements the following points:
  - ✦ nature of the threats made—exact words used and in what context, include any previous threats made;
  - ✦ the fact that the threat was **understood** by the person to whom it was made, and that the person feared the threat would be carried out;
  - ✦ describe the full circumstances of the incident and antecedent history details of the relationship between the defendant and complainant.
- Communications that constitute threats to another person may also amount to other offences. Consider intimidation of witnesses and jurors under s 51 Criminal Justice and Public Order Act 1994 (see **4.8.1**); threats of violence under ss 4 and 4A Protection from Harassment Act 1997 (see **7.11.2**); s 1 malicious Communications Act 1988 and s 127 Communications Act 2003 (see **7.12.1**).

 Either way   🕐 None

Summary: 6 months' imprisonment and/or a fine

Indictment: 10 years' imprisonment

Links to alternative subjects and offences

2.6 **False Imprisonment, Kidnapping, and Child Abduction**

Contained within this topic area are the common law offences of kidnapping, false imprisonment, and child abduction under the Child Abduction Act 1984. Officers should be familiar with this area of law when dealing with any violent domestic incidents, sexual offences, or where people are taken against their will.

2.6.1 **False imprisonment**

False imprisonment is an offence at common law.

Offences

The unlawful and total restraint of the personal liberty of another, whether by constraining them or compelling them to go to a particular place or by confining them in a prison or police station or private place or by detaining them against their will in a public place.

Common law

Points to prove

✓ imprisoned, detained, or arrested
✓ another person
✓ against his/her will
✓ unlawfully

Explanatory notes

- The wrongful act ('actus reus') of false imprisonment is the act of placing an unlawful restriction on the victim's freedom in the absence of any legal right to do so.
- There must also have been an element of intent ('mens rea') to restrain, either deliberately or recklessly.
- There is no offence if the victim is not physically restrained, unless the offender detains/intends to detain them by use of fear/threats. Unlawfully locking someone in a vehicle may be sufficient for this offence.

Defences

That the taking or detaining was in the course of a lawful arrest or
detention under PACE (see **1.4**) or acting under another statutory or
common law power.

Related cases

Austin v UK [2012] Crim LR 544, ECtHR The police imposed a cordon
to isolate and contain a large crowd of protestors in volatile and dangerous conditions to prevent serious injury or damage. It was held that in
the circumstances, an absolute cordon had been the least intrusive and
most effective means to be applied. Those within the cordon had not
been deprived of their liberty in breach of Art 5 (see **1.1**). The police
were fulfilling their duty of maintaining order and protecting the public, as required under both national and Convention law.

**R (on the application of McClure and Moos) v Commissioner of
Police of the Metropolis [2012] EWCA Civ 12, CA** Two large demonstrations, each one having about 4,000 protestors, took place in London
to protest against the G20 Summit. The police contained the first disorderly demonstration to avoid the two camps joining forces, thus
preventing widespread violence occurring. It was held that the police
'kettling' tactics used were, on this occasion, a lawful means of preventing imminent and serious breach of the peace (see **7.3**).

Bird v Jones (1845) 7 QB 742, QBD Preventing a person from proceeding along a particular way is not false imprisonment.

Practical considerations

- A parent has no right to imprison their own child, although a parent
  is allowed to detain a child for purposes of reasonable parental
  discipline. Whether it is reasonable in all the circumstances is for a
  jury to decide.
- A victim could bring a civil action for damages (invariably after
  unlawful arrest by the police). Consider kidnapping (**2.6.2**) or child
  abduction (**2.6.3**) as alternatives.

 E&S

 Indictable   None

 Life imprisonment and/or a fine

2.6.2 **Kidnapping**

Kidnapping is another offence at common law.

Offences

The taking or carrying away of one person by another, by force or fraud, without the consent of the person so taken or carried away, and without lawful excuse.

Common law

Points to prove

- ✓ without lawful excuse
- ✓ by force/fraud
- ✓ took/carried away
- ✓ another person
- ✓ without their consent

Meaning of fraud

Means deceit, guile, or trick. It should not be confused with the narrower meaning given to it for the purposes of consent in sexual offences.

Explanatory notes

- The important points to prove are the deprivation of liberty and carrying away even where a short distance is involved—and the absence of consent.
- In the case of a child it is the child's consent that should be considered (rather than the parent/guardian) and in the case of a very young child, absence of consent may be inferred.

Defences

Consent or lawful excuse.

Related cases

R v Cort [2003] 3 WLR 1300, CA The defendant went to bus stops telling lone women that the bus they were waiting for had broken down and offering/providing lifts in his vehicle. It was held that the fact that the defendant had lied about the absence of the bus meant that, although they had got into the car voluntarily, the women had not given true consent to the journey and the offences of kidnap (and attempts) were complete.

Practical considerations

- A man or woman may be guilty of this offence in relation to their spouse or partner.
- Under s 5 of the Child Abduction Act 1984, consent of the DPP is required to prosecute for an offence of kidnapping if it was committed:
  - ◆ against a child under 16;
  - ◆ by a person connected with the child under s 1 (see **2.6.3**).
- In all other cases the consent of the DPP is not required.

 Indictable   None

 Life imprisonment and/or a fine

2.6.3 **Child abduction**

The Child Abduction Act 1984 provides two distinct child abduction offences: s 1—person connected to child (parent/guardian) and s 2—committed by other persons.

Person connected with child

> **Offences**
>
> Subject to subsections (5) and (8) below, a person connected with a child under the age of 16 commits an offence if he takes or sends the child out of the United Kingdom without the appropriate consent.
>
> Child Abduction Act 1984, s 1(1)

Points to prove

- ✓ being a parent/person connected with
- ✓ a child under 16 years of age
- ✓ took/sent that child
- ✓ out of the United Kingdom
- ✓ without the appropriate consent

Meanings

Person connected (s 1(2))

A **person connected** with a child for the purposes of this section is:
(a) a parent of the child; or

(b)   in the case of a child whose parents were not married to each other at the time of birth, there are reasonable grounds for believing that he is the father of the child; or

(c)   the guardian of the child; or

(ca) a special guardian of the child; or

(d)   a person named in a child arrangements order as a person with whom the child is to live; or

(e)   has custody of the child.

Takes

A person is regarded as **taking** a child if they cause or induce the child to accompany them, or any other person, or causes the child to be taken.

Sends

A person is regarded as **sending** a child if they cause the child to be sent.

Appropriate consent (s 1(3))

(a)   This means the consent of each of the following:
  (i)   the child's mother;
  (ii)   the child's father, if he has parental responsibility for him;
  (iii)   any guardian of the child;
  (iiia) any special guardian of the child;
  (iv)   any person named in a child arrangements order as a person with whom the child is to live;
  (v)   any person who has custody of the child; or

(b)   the leave of the court granted under or by virtue of any provision of Pt 2 of the Children Act 1989; or

(c)   if any person has custody of the child, the leave of the court which awarded custody to him.

Explanatory notes

- A court could deal with a parent who had abducted his/her child in three ways. First, for contempt of court (flouting a court order); secondly, prosecution for an offence under the 1984 Act; and thirdly, prosecution for kidnapping, either based on force, or fraud in achieving the removal of the child from the other parent (*R v Kayani; R v Sollim* [2011] EWCA Crim 2871, CA).

- This offence can also be committed (subject to the statutory defences given below) when a child is in the care of a local authority, or voluntary organisation, or place of safety whilst subject to adoption proceedings.

Defences

(4) A person does not commit an offence under this section by taking or sending a child out of the United Kingdom without obtaining the appropriate consent if—

   (a) he is a person named in a child arrangements order as a person with whom the child is to live, and he takes or sends the child out of the United Kingdom for a period of less than one month; or

   (b) he is a special guardian of the child and he takes or sends the child out of the United Kingdom for a period of less than three months.

(4A) Subsection (4) above does not apply if the person taking or sending the child out of the United Kingdom does so in breach of an order under Pt 2 of the Children Act 1989.

(5) A person does not commit an offence under this section by doing anything without the consent of another person whose consent is required under the forgoing provisions if—

   (a) he does it in the belief that the other person—

     i. has consented; or

     ii. would consent if he was aware of all the relevant circumstances; or

   (b) he has taken all reasonable steps to communicate with the other person but has been unable to communicate with him; or

   (c) the other person has unreasonably refused to consent.

(5A) Subsection (5)(c) above does not apply if—

   (a) the person who refused to consent is a person—

     (i) named in a child arrangements order as a person with whom the child is to live; or

     (ia) who is a special guardian of the child; or

     (iii) who has custody of the child; or

   (b) the person taking or sending the child out of the United Kingdom is, by so acting, in breach of an order made by a court in the United Kingdom.

Child Abduction Act 1984, s 1

Abduction of child by another person

This is an offence in relation to the taking or detaining of a child where the offender is not connected with that child.

Offences

Subject to subsection (3), a person other than one mentioned in subsection (2) below, commits an offence if, without lawful authority or reasonable excuse, he takes or detains a child under the age of 16—

(a) so as to remove him from the lawful control of any person having lawful control of the child; or

2.6.3 Child abduction

(b) so as to keep him out of the lawful control of any person entitled to lawful control of the child.

Child Abduction Act 1984, s 2(1)

Points to prove

✓ without lawful authority/reasonable excuse
✓ detained or took
✓ a child under 16 years of age
✓ so as to remove/keep him/her
✓ from/out of the lawful control
✓ of a person having/entitled to lawful control
✓ of that child

Meanings

Takes (see s 1(1))

Detains

A person is regarded as detaining a child if they cause the child to be detained or induces the child to remain with them or any other person.

Remove from lawful control

This can be satisfied if the child is induced to take some action that they would not normally have done.

Explanatory notes

- The offence is subject to a statutory defence of consent (s 2(3)—below).
- This offence does not apply to persons listed in s 2(2) namely:
  - ✦ the child's father and mother—being married to each other at the time of the birth;
  - ✦ the child's mother—where the father was not married to her at the time of the birth;
  - ✦ any other person mentioned in s 1(2)(c) to (e) above.

Defences

It shall be a defence for that person to prove—

(a) where the father and mother of the child in question were not married to each other at the time of his birth—
   (i) that he is the child's father
   (ii) that, at the time of the alleged offence, he believed, on reasonable grounds, that he was the child's father, or

(b) that, at the time of the alleged offence, he believed that the child had attained the age of 16 years.

Child Abduction Act 1984, s 2(3)

Related cases

R v Wakeman [2011] EWCA 1649, CA In this case, the defendant took the hands of two children and walked them 30 metres across a park to show them something interesting, without the consent of the nearby parents. It was held that the prosecution need only prove an intentional or reckless taking, or detention, the consequence of which was removing a child from the control of any person having lawful control of that child.

R v Mohammed [2006] EWCA Crim 1107, CA See **6.7.2 'Related cases'**.

Foster and another v DPP [2005] 1 WLR 1400, QBD Section 2 has two separate offences and alternative charges cannot be made. The '*mens rea*' of s 2 is an intentional or reckless taking or detention. It is immaterial that the child consents to removal from lawful control, but the s 2(3)(b) defence is available if it is believed that the child was 16 or over.

Practical considerations

- Child Abduction Warning Notices (formerly known as Harbourers Warning Notices) have provided useful evidence in many prosecutions, including large-scale 'grooming cases'. They have no statutory basis but, if properly used, can help to safeguard vulnerable youngsters and provide supportive evidence for criminal or other proceedings.
- Consider the more serious offence of kidnapping but be aware that consent from the DPP may be required under s 5 (see **2.6.2**).
- The s 1 offence (person connected with child) can only be committed by those people listed in s 1(2) **and** they must take or send that child out of the UK; the prosecution must rebut the defence of consent.
- Section 2 (other people not connected with the child) will cover the situation where an agent snatches a child for an estranged parent. The parent in such a case may commit the offence of aiding and abetting the principal offence.

 Either way   None

Summary: 6 months' imprisonment and/or a fine

Indictment: 7 years' imprisonment

Links to alternative subjects and offences

2.7 **Suspicious Deaths**

Police officers investigating sudden/suspicious deaths should have a basic knowledge of the relevant law and powers. Apart from informing supervision, following **force policies/procedures**, and requesting the assistance of scenes of crime officers, be mindful of scene preservation and the obtaining of forensic evidence (see **1.3**).

2.7.1 **Murder**

The offence of murder comes under the common law and is defined as:

> **Offence**
>
> Where a person of sound mind and discretion unlawfully kills any reasonable creature in being and under the Queen's peace, with intent to kill or cause grievous bodily harm.
>
> Common law

Points to prove

✓ unlawfully killed a human being
✓ with intent to kill or cause grievous bodily harm

Meanings

Sound mind and discretion

Every person of the age of discretion is presumed to be sane and accountable for his actions, unless the contrary is proved. This means anyone who is not insane or under 10 years old.

Unlawfully

Means without lawful authority, legal justification, or excuse.

Kills

This is 'the act' ('actus reus') which is the substantial cause of death (stabbed, shot, strangled, suffocated, poisoned, etc).

Reasonable creature in being

Any human being, including a baby born alive having an independent existence from its mother.

2.7.1 Murder

Under the Queen's peace

This is meant to exclude killing in the course of war. A British subject takes the Queen's peace with them everywhere in the world.

Intent

An intention to kill or to cause grievous bodily harm is the '*mens rea*' of murder (see **4.1.2**).

Cause/causation

If there is an 'intervening factor' between the defendant's actions and the death of the victim, the jury will consider whether the defendant's act contributed significantly to the death.

Grievous bodily harm (see **2.3**)

Explanatory notes

- It shall be conclusively presumed that no child under the age of 10 years can be guilty of any offence (Children and Young Persons Act 1933, s 50).
- If a defendant wishes to plead **insanity**, they will be judged on the M'Naghten Rules from *M'Naghten's Case* (1843) 10 Cl & F 200. This examines the extent to which, at the time of the commission of the offence, the person was 'labouring under such defect of reason from disease of the mind that either: (a) the defendant did not know what they were doing, **or** (b) they did know what they were doing but did not know it was wrong'.
- If a person intentionally causes GBH and the victim subsequently dies as a result, that person is guilty of murder.
- The jury will consider whether the defendant's act **contributed significantly** to the death by applying the 'substantial test' as set out in *R v Smith* [1959] 2 All ER 193, Court Martial CA.
- Whether the defendant intended or foresaw the results of their actions will be determined by several factors including the statutory test under the Criminal Justice Act 1967, s 8 (see **4.1.2**).

Defences to murder

Insanity

See the meaning of 'sound mind and discretion' and 'Explanatory notes' as to 'insanity'.

Lawful killing

Means with lawful authority; legal justification or excuse, including self-defence (see 1.2.1).

At war

This is self-explanatory, not being under the 'Queen's peace' (see 'Meanings').

Specific defences

Loss of control

Where a person ('D') kills or is a party to the killing of another ('V'), D is not to be convicted of murder if—

(a) D's acts and omissions in doing or being a party to the killing resulted from D's loss of self-control,

(b) the loss of self-control had a qualifying trigger, and

(c) a person of D's sex and age, with a normal degree of tolerance and self-restraint and in the circumstances of D, might have reacted in the same or in a similar way to D.

Coroners and Justice Act 2009, s 54(1)

Diminished responsibility

(1) A person ('D') who kills or is a party to the killing of another is not to be convicted of murder if D was suffering from an abnormality of mental functioning which—

(a) arose from a recognised medical condition,

(b) substantially impaired D's ability to do one or more of the things mentioned in subsection (1A), and

(c) provides an explanation for D's acts and omissions in doing or being a party to the killing.

(1A) Those things are—

(a) to understand the nature of D's conduct;

(b) to form a rational judgment;

(c) to exercise self-control.

Homicide Act 1957, s 2

Suicide pact

Means a common agreement between two or more persons having for its object the death of all of them, whether or not each is to take his own life, but nothing done by a person who enters into a suicide pact shall be treated as done by him in pursuance of the pact unless it is done while he has the settled intention of dying in pursuance of the pact.

Homicide Act 1957, s 4(3)

Related cases

R v Golds [2016] UKSC 61 The Supreme Court in this case clarified the meaning of 'substantially' in relation to a partial defence of diminished responsibility set out in s 2 of the Homicide Act 1957. Diminished responsibility involves an impairment of one or more of the abilities listed in the statute to an extent which **the jury** judges to be 'substantial' and which it is satisfied significantly contributed to the commission of the offence. Illustrative expressions, as an ordinary English word, of 'substantially' may be employed so the jury can clearly understand it, but the judge should not attempt to define the meaning.

R v Gnango [2011] UKSC 59, SC In this case, the defendants had a gun fight with each another in a public place; both had the intent to kill the other. During the shooting a shot from one killed a passerby. It was held that by virtue of transferred malice, both were guilty of the passerby's murder.

R v Hatton [2005] EWCA Crim 2951, CA Self-defence is not possible if mistake was induced by intoxication.

R v Malcherek and **R v Steel (1981) 73 Cr App R 173, CA** A defendant (who causes injury necessitating medical treatment) could not argue that the sole cause of death was the doctor's action in switching the life support system off.

Practical considerations

- The killing must be causally related to the acts of the defendant and not through an intervening factor which breaks the chain of causation.
- If there is doubt whether death was caused by some supervening event (such as medical negligence when treated), the prosecution does not have to prove that the supervening event was not a significant cause of death.
- Intention—'*mens rea*' ('guilty mind')—has to be proved (see **4.1.2**).
- Consent of the A-G is required where:
  - ✦ the injury was sustained more than three years before death; **or**
  - ✦ the accused has been previously convicted of the offence alleged to be connected with the death.
- If a person is suffering from a terminal disease and receives a wound that hastens their death, this killing would (with the required intent) be murder or manslaughter.
- A murder or manslaughter committed by a British citizen outside the UK may be tried in this country as if it had been committed here.
- Motivation will form a key part of any prosecution and the availability of any defences should be considered.
- The meaning of '**qualifying trigger**' for the partial defence to murder is where the defendant lost self-control because:
  - ✦ of fear of serious violence against defendant or another person; **or**
  - ✦ it was attributable to things done or said (or both) which constituted circumstances of an extremely grave character and caused the defendant to have a justifiable sense of being seriously wronged.
- Guidance and details regarding the partial defences to murder for loss of control, diminished responsibility, and infanticide, made by the Coroners and Justice Act 2009, is given in MOJ Circular 13/2010.
- Offences Against the Person Act 1861, s 4 is the offence of soliciting to murder: 'Whosoever shall solicit, encourage, persuade, or endeavour to persuade, or shall propose to any person, to murder any other person, shall be guilty of an offence and liable to imprisonment for life.'
- Section 2(1) of the Suicide Act 1961 deals with encouraging or assisting suicide, whereby a person commits an offence if they do an act capable of encouraging or assisting suicide or attempted suicide of another person, and the act was intended to encourage or assist suicide or an attempt at suicide.

- MOJ Circular 3/2010 explains the above encourage or assist suicide offence, as replaced by the Coroners and Justice Act 2009. Consider the CPS policy in respect of this offence, which requires DPP consent before prosecution.

 Indictable None

Life imprisonment

2.7.2 **Manslaughter**

Offence

Manslaughter is the unlawful killing of another human being which can either be a voluntary or involuntary manslaughter offence.

Common law

Points to prove

✓ unlawful act or gross negligence
✓ killed a human being

Meanings

Unlawful killing (see 2.7.1)

Voluntary manslaughter

When a murder charge is reduced to voluntary manslaughter by reason of one of the specific defences to murder (see **2.7.1**).

Involuntary manslaughter

An unlawful killing without an intention to kill or cause grievous bodily harm. Apart from the required intent, the elements of the offence are the same as for murder (see **2.7.1**).

Manslaughter can be caused by:

- **unlawful act** (not omission): the unlawful act must be unlawful in itself (eg another criminal offence such as an assault or a threat to kill) and must involve a risk that someone would be harmed by it;
- **gross negligence** (involving breach of duty): gross negligence manslaughter requires a breach of a duty of care owed by the defendant to the victim under circumstances where the defendant's conduct was serious enough to amount to a crime.

Related cases

R v Rose [2017] EWCA Crim 1168 This case followed the test in *R v Rudling* (see below) that for gross negligence manslaughter, there had to be a serious and obvious risk of death at the time of the statutory breach, not merely serious illness.

R v Rudling [2016] EWCA Crim 741 This case involved a charge of gross negligence manslaughter against a doctor. The offence requires a breach of an existing duty of care which is reasonably foreseeable as giving rise to the serious and obvious risk of death and the conduct of the defendant amounts to a criminal act or omission. It was held that in medical cases, that at the time of the breach of duty, a reasonably prudent person would conclude there was a risk of death and not merely serious illness.

R v Evans [2009] EWCA Crim 650, CA This case considered the duty required in gross negligence manslaughter. Where a person has contributed to a state of affairs which they knew or ought reasonably to have known had created a threat to life, a duty arose for them to act by taking all reasonable steps to save the life at risk.

R v Misra and Srivastava [2004] All ER (D) 150, CA Grossly negligent medical treatment, which exposes the patient to the risk of death and causes the death of the victim would be manslaughter.

Practical considerations (for further considerations see **2.7.1**)

- Consider corporate manslaughter (see **2.7.3**) in work-related deaths involving negligence by the company/organisation.
- Previous convictions or past behaviour of the defendant in homicide cases may well be relevant, both to the issue of '*mens rea*'/intent and to sentence.
- The burden of proof in relation to claiming diminished responsibility or acting in pursuance of a suicide pact lies with the defendant.
- Section 2(1) of the Suicide Act 1961 gives an **offence** of encouraging or assisting suicide of another (see **2.7.1**).

 Indictable None

 Life imprisonment

2.7.3 **Corporate manslaughter**

The Corporate Manslaughter and Corporate Homicide Act 2007 sets out the offence of corporate manslaughter for an organisation, where a gross failure in the way its activities were managed or organised resulted in a person's death.

Offences

(1) An organisation to which this section applies is guilty of an offence if the way in which its activities are managed or organised—
  (a) causes a person's death, and
  (b) amounts to a gross breach of a relevant duty of care owed by the organisation to the deceased.

Corporate Manslaughter and Corporate Homicide Act 2007, s 1

Points to prove

✓ being an organisation to which s 1 applies
✓ managed or organised its activities
✓ in a way that caused the death of a person
✓ by an act or omission
✓ which amounted to a gross breach of a relevant duty of care owed to that person

Meanings

Organisations to which s 1 applies

- **corporation**;
- department or other body listed in **Sch 1**;
- **police force**;
- partnership, or a trade union or employers' association, that is an employer.

Schedule 1

This Schedule lists over forty government departments and other similar bodies, such as: CPS; DEFRA; Department for Transport; Department of Health; Foreign and Commonwealth Office; HMRC; Home Office; Ministry of Defence; and the Serious Fraud Office.

Explanatory notes

- An organisation will commit this offence if the way in which its activities are managed or organised causes a death and amounts to a gross breach of a duty of care owed to the deceased.
- The conduct must fall far below what would reasonably have been expected for it to be a gross breach. Any breaches of health and safety legislation will have to be considered—and how serious and dangerous those failures were.
- A duty of care exists for example in respect of the systems of work and equipment used by employees, the condition of work sites or premises occupied by the organisation, or to products or services supplied to customers. This Act does not create new duties; they are

already owed in the civil law of negligence and the offence is based on these.

Practical considerations

- Officers dealing with fatal/potentially fatal work incidents that appear to involve negligence by the organisation should inform the HSE (see **Appendix 1**), as well as protecting the crime scene.
- Section 2 deals with the **'relevant duty of care'** owed by an organisation under the law of negligence to its employees or other persons working for them, as occupier of premises, or duty owed with the supply of goods or services, carrying out of any construction or maintenance operations or other commercial activity, or the use/keeping of any plant, vehicle, or other thing.
- This Act applies to a police force, so making them liable for the corporate manslaughter offence if a person dies whilst detained in police custody. MOJ Circular 7/2011 gives guidance in relation to deaths of persons in police custody under s 2(2) who are owed a duty of care under the Act.
- Section 2(1)(d) states that a duty owed to a person, being a person within s 2(2), is someone for whose safety the organisation is responsible.
- Directors, senior managers, or other individuals cannot be held liable for this offence. It will be the organisation that will be prosecuted. However, individuals can still be prosecuted for gross negligence manslaughter (*R v Winter* [2010] EWCA Crim 1474—see **2.7.2**) and for health and safety offences. Individuals will continue to be prosecuted where there is sufficient evidence and it is in the public interest to do so.
- Consent of the DPP is needed before a case of corporate manslaughter can be taken to court. Cases will be prosecuted by the CPS and Health and Safety charges will probably be dealt with at the same time.

 Indictable   None

 An unlimited fine

2.7.4 **Death or serious physical harm to a child/vulnerable adult**

Section 5 of the Domestic Violence, Crime and Victims Act 2004 creates the offences of causing or allowing the death of or serious physical harm to a child or a vulnerable adult by means of an unlawful act.

Offences

A person ('D') is guilty of an offence if—
(a) a child or vulnerable adult ('V') dies or suffers serious physical harm
    as a result of the unlawful act of a person who—
    (i) was a member of the same household as V, and
    (ii) had frequent contact with him,
(b) D was such a person at the time of that act,
(c) at that time there was a significant risk of serious physical harm
    being caused to V by the unlawful act of such a person, and
(d) either D was the person whose act caused the death or serious
    physical harm or—
    (i) D was, or ought to have been, aware of the risk mentioned in
        paragraph (c),
    (ii) D failed to take such steps as he could reasonably have been
        expected to take to protect V from the risk, and
    (iii) the act occurred in circumstances of the kind that D foresaw or
        ought to have foreseen.

Domestic Violence, Crime and Victims Act 2004, s 5(1)

Points to prove

✓ being a member of the same household and having had
  frequent contact with a person who was at that time a child/
  vulnerable adult
✓ caused that person's death or
✓ caused that person to suffer serious physical harm or
✓ was, or ought to have been, aware that there was a significant
  risk of serious physical harm being caused to that person
✓ by the unlawful act of a member of their household
✓ which occurred in circumstances of the kind that the defendant
  foresaw or ought to have foreseen and
✓ the defendant failed to take such steps as they could reasonably
  have been expected to take to protect them from that risk

Meanings

Child

Means a person under the age of 16 years.

Vulnerable adult

Means a person aged 16 or over whose ability to protect themselves
from violence, abuse, or neglect is significantly impaired through physical or mental disability or illness, through old age or otherwise. This
includes a temporary vulnerability as well as one which is permanent.

Unlawful act *(see 2.7.2)*

2.7.4 Death or serious physical harm to a child/vulnerable adult

Act

This includes a course of conduct and includes omission.

Member of the same household

This includes people who do not live in that household, providing they visit often and for such periods of time that they are regarded as a member of it.

Serious physical harm

Means grievous bodily harm for the purposes of the Offences Against the Person Act 1961 (see **2.3**).

Explanatory notes

- The meaning of a **vulnerable adult** also includes a temporary vulnerability as well as one which is permanent.
- If D was not the mother or father of V, D may not be charged with an offence under this section if he was under the age of 16 at the time of the act that caused the death or serious harm; and for the purposes of subsection (1)(d)(ii) (see above), D could not have been expected to take any such step as is referred to there before attaining that age.

Related cases

R v Uddin [2017] EWCA Crim 1072 The appeal in this case focused upon the interpretation of the phrase 'or otherwise' in the definition of 'vulnerable adult' in s 5 (see **meanings** above). The meaning of 'otherwise' could be an external cause, through which the victim's ability to protect him or herself from violence, abuse or neglect was significantly impaired. There are no limits to the facts or circumstances that might lead to the victim finding him or herself in a state of impaired ability to obtain protection and would include those who are not suffering from illness, disability or old age.

R v Khan and others [2009] EWCA Crim 2, CA There was a history of the defendant using violence against the victim and on this occasion the injuries he inflicted proved fatal. There was other medical evidence that suggested that she had sustained injuries from three previous attacks. It was held that this offence imposes a duty on members of the same household to protect children/vulnerable adults where their ability to protect themselves was impaired and vulnerability may be short- or long-term. Furthermore, the defendant was aware of the risk of serious harm and foresaw or ought reasonably to have foreseen that an unlawful act or course of conduct would result in death and failed to take reasonable steps to prevent the risk.

Practical considerations

- If D was not the mother or father of V then they may not be charged with this offence if they were under the age of 16 at the time of the act that caused the death or serious harm. Similarly, they could not have been expected to take any such preventative steps to protect the victim before attaining that age.

- If V dies, the death should still be thoroughly investigated to establish whether the person is responsible for murder or manslaughter. As the offence is limited to an unlawful act, it will not apply to accidental or cot deaths.
- Further details on allowing/causing the death are dealt with in HOC 9/2005, whereas MOJ Circular 3/2012 concerns the Domestic Violence, Crime and Victims (Amendment) Act 2012, which extended the original offence to now include serious physical harm.

 Indictable None

 Causing/allowing death: 14 years' imprisonment and/or a fine
Causing/allowing serious physical harm: 10 years' imprisonment and/or a fine

2.7.5 **Overlaying/suffocation of infant under 3**

The Children and Young Persons Act 1933 provides for circumstances where a child has been suffocated while lying next to an adult.

> ### Offences
>
> Where it is proved that the death of an infant under three years of age was caused by suffocation (not being suffocation caused by disease or the presence of any foreign body in the throat or air passages of the infant) while the infant was in bed with some other person who has attained the age of sixteen years, that other person shall, if he was, when he went to bed or at any later time before the suffocation, under the influence of drink or a prohibited drug, be deemed to have neglected the infant in a manner likely to cause injury to its health.
>
> Children and Young Persons Act 1933, s 1(2)(b)

Points to prove

✓ being a person 16 years or over
✓ caused the death of an infant under 3 years of age
✓ by suffocation
✓ while the infant was lying next to that person
✓ person under the influence of drink/prohibited drug
✓ when they went in to/on a bed/any furniture/surface for the purpose of sleeping

---

Meanings

In bed/went to bed

This includes a reference to the infant lying next to the adult in or on any kind of furniture or surface being used by the adult for the purpose of sleeping.

Prohibited drug

If possession of the drug immediately before taking it would be an offence under s 5(2) of the Misuse of Drugs Act 1971 (see **5.2.1**).

Explanatory notes

- The Serious Crime Act 2015, s 66 added a 'prohibited drug' to this offence and expanded on the infant being 'in bed' and when the adult 'went to bed'. HOC 8/2015 provides guidance on these changes.
- Consider a more serious charge, such as manslaughter (see **2.7.2**) or causing/allowing the death of a child (see **2.7.4**).
- Further details relating to s 1 are given at **2.4.1**.

 Either way   None

 Summary: 6 months' imprisonment and/or a fine

Indictment: 10 years' imprisonment and/or a fine

2.7.6 Infanticide/child destruction/ concealment of birth

This offence is committed by the mother of a child (under 12 months old), who by any wilful act or omission, causes the death of her child whilst mentally unbalanced (such as post-natal depression) due to childbirth or lactation.

Offences

Where a woman by any wilful act or omission causes the death of her child being a child under the age of twelve months, but at the time of the act or omission the balance of her mind was disturbed by reason of her not having fully recovered from the effect of giving birth to the child or by reason of the effect of lactation consequent upon the birth of the child, then, if the circumstances were such that but for this Act the offence would have amounted to murder or manslaughter, she shall be guilty of infanticide, and may for such offence be dealt with and punished as if she had been guilty of the offence of manslaughter of the child.

Infanticide Act 1938, s 1(1)

Points to prove

✓ a woman
✓ caused the death of her own child (being under 12 months of age)
✓ by wilful act/omission
✓ whilst balance of her mind disturbed

Practical considerations

- This offence reduces the act to manslaughter as the responsibility for her actions may have been reduced by the disturbance of her mind caused by childbirth.
- There is no reference to any intention to kill or cause serious bodily harm, only a wilful act or omission (*R v Gore* [2007] EWCA Crim 2789, HL).

Child destruction

- The Infant Life (Preservation) Act 1929, s 1(1) makes it an indictable offence for any person, by any wilful act, to intentionally destroy a child capable of being born alive, before it has an existence independent of its mother.
- Evidence that a woman had at any material time been pregnant for a period of twenty-eight weeks or more shall be *prima facie* proof that she was at that time pregnant with a child capable of being born alive.
- It has been held that a foetus of between eighteen and twenty-one weeks is not 'capable of being born alive' since it would be incapable of breathing even with the aid of a ventilator, and a termination of a pregnancy of that length is not an offence under this Act.
- No person shall be found guilty of this offence if it is proved that the act was done in good faith for saving the life of the mother.
- A registered medical practitioner does not commit this offence if the pregnancy is terminated in accordance with the provisions of the Abortion Act 1967, s 5(1).
- Section 58 of the Offences Against the Person Act 1861 relates to administering drugs or using instruments to procure a miscarriage (abortion) at any time between conception and the birth of the child alive; whereas the 1929 Act prohibits the killing of any child capable of being born alive.

Concealment of birth

- Under s 60 of the 1861 Act, if any woman delivers a child, every person who shall, by any *secret disposition* of the dead body of the said child, whether such child died before, at, or after its birth, endeavour to conceal the birth thereof, shall be guilty of an either way offence.

2.7.6 Infanticide/child destruction/concealment of birth

- This offence relates to secret disposal, hiding of the dead body of a baby, where the baby has died before, at, or shortly after birth.
- If the living body of a child is concealed, which then dies where it is concealed, clearly a more serious offence of homicide may be committed.
- The offence is specific in that it must be a **'secret disposition'** *after the child has died*, the test being whether there is likelihood that the body would be found.

Indictable None

Life imprisonment

Links to alternative subjects and offences

2.8 **Domestic Violence**

The Serious Crime Act 2015, s 76 creates an offence in relation to a person who repeatedly or continuously engages in behaviour towards another (this person being personally connected to them) that is controlling or coercive.

Offence

A person (A) commits an offence if—
(a) A repeatedly or continuously engages in behaviour towards another person (B) that is controlling or coercive,
(b) A and B are personally connected at the time of the behaviour,
(c) the behaviour has a serious effect on B, and
(d) A knows or ought to know that the behaviour will have a serious effect on B.

Serious Crime Act 2015, s 76(1)

Points to prove

- ✓ date and location
- ✓ repeatedly/continuously engaged in controlling/coercive behaviour
- ✓ towards person to whom they were personally connected
- ✓ the behaviour had a serious effect on victim
- ✓ knew/ought to know the behaviour would have a serious effect

---

Meanings

Domestic violence

In HOC 3/2013 Domestic violence is defined as: 'Any incident or pattern of incidents of controlling, coercive, threatening behaviour, violence or abuse between those aged 16 or over who are or have been intimate partners or family members regardless of gender or sexuality. The abuse can encompass, but is not limited to, psychological, physical, sexual, financial and/or emotional abuse.'

Controlling behaviour

A range of acts designed to make a person subordinate and/or dependent by isolating them from sources of support, exploiting their resources and capacities for personal gain, depriving them of the means needed for independence, resistance and escape, and regulating their everyday behaviour.

Coercive behaviour

An act or a pattern of acts of assault, threats, humiliation and intimidation, or other abuse that is used to harm, punish, or frighten their victim.

2.8 Domestic Violence

This definition includes violence that is sometimes described as 'honour'-based violence, female genital mutilation (FGM), and forced marriage (see **13.5**), and it is clear that victims are not confined to one gender or ethnic group.

Personally connected

A and B are 'personally connected' if:
(a) A is in an intimate personal relationship with B, or
(b) A and B live together and—

   (i) they are members of the same family, or
   (ii) they have previously been in an intimate personal relationship with each other.

Serious Crime Act 2015, s 76(2)

But A does not commit an offence under this section if at the time of the behaviour in question:
(a) A has responsibility for B, for the purposes of Part 1 of the Children and Young Persons Act 1933 (see s 17 of that Act), (see **2.4.1**) and
(b) B is under 16.

Serious effect

A's behaviour has a 'serious effect' on B if:
(a) it causes B to fear, on at least two occasions, that violence will be used against B, or
(b) it causes B serious alarm or distress which has a substantial adverse effect on B's usual day-to-day activities.

For the purposes of subsection (1)(d) A 'ought to know' that which a reasonable person in possession of the same information would know.

Members of the same family

For the purposes of subsection (2)(b)(i) A and B:
(a) are, or have been, married to each other;
(b) are, or have been, civil partners of each other;
(c) are relatives;
(d) have agreed to marry one another (whether or not the agreement has been terminated);
(e) have entered into a civil partnership agreement (whether or not the agreement has been terminated);
(f) are both parents of the same child;
(g) have, or have had, parental responsibility for the same child.

Civil partnership agreement

This has the meaning given by s 73 of the Civil Partnership Act 2004 (see **3.8.6**). It is a relationship between two people of the same sex (civil partners) registered as civil partners under the act and ends only on death, dissolution, or annulment.

Child

This means a person under the age of 18 years.

Parental responsibility

This has the same meaning as in the Children Act 1989 (see **2.4.1**).

Relative

This has the meaning given by s 63(1) of the Family Law Act 1996.

> ### Defence
>
> In proceedings for an offence under this section it is a defence for A to show that—
>
> (a) in engaging in the behaviour in question, A believed that he or she was acting in B's best interests, and
>
> (b) the behaviour was in all the circumstances reasonable.
>
> Serious Crime Act 2015, s 76(8)

Explanatory notes

- The defence in subsection (8) is not available to A in relation to behaviour that causes B to fear that violence will be used against B.
- See Home Office 'Controlling or Coercive Behaviour in an Intimate or Family Relationship' Statutory Guidance Framework relating to the investigation of offences under s 76.

Police powers of entry

- PACE, s 17(1)(b)—enter premises for the purpose of arresting a person for an indictable offence (see **1.5.2**).
- PACE, s 17(1)(e)—enter premises for the purpose of saving life or limb or preventing serious damage to property (see **1.5.2**).
- Breach of the peace—enter premises to prevent or deal with a breach of the peace (see **7.3**).

Restraining orders/injunctions

- Consider offences and powers available under the Protection from Harassment Act 1997 in relation to harassment or stalking (see **7.11**). This Act also deals with restraining orders (under s 5) and injunctions (under s 3).
- The victim should be made aware that they have certain rights enforceable in a civil court but should be advised that civil action can be costly and also the consequence of civil action instead of involving the police.
- Victims should be told that if a civil injunction is obtained under s 3 (see **7.11.6**) **with a power of arrest**, then details would be recorded on police computer systems.
- Sections 24–30 of the Crime and Security Act 2010 allow a Domestic Violence Protection Notice (DVPN) to be issued by a superintendent (or above) to an alleged domestic abuse perpetrator (P), if they have

reasonable grounds to believe the person has threatened or used violence against the victim. Under s 25(1)(b) a constable can arrest P for breach of the DVPN. Within forty-eight hours of the DVPN being served, the police must make an application for a Domestic Violence Protection Order (DVPO) to a magistrates' court for the area, at which point the court can remand P.

- A DVPN and DVPO could be issued where the victim did not consent and was not willing to attend court; all available material should be considered when making the decision (see *Kerr v Chief Constable of Surrey Police* [2017] EWHC 2936 (Admin)).

 Indictable   None

 Summary: 12 months' imprisonment and/or a fine

Indictment: 5 years' imprisonment and/or a fine

Links to alternative subjects and offences

Chapter 3

Crime: Dishonesty

3.1 Theft

The Theft Act 1968 provides for the offence of theft and other connected offences. Section 1 of the Act provides for the offence of theft, while s 11 covers the offence of removing articles from places open to the public and s 23 concerns advertising rewards for the return of stolen or lost goods.

3.1.1 Theft (general)/theft of scrap metal

Theft is defined by s 1 of the Act, while ss 2–6 explain the elements contained within that definition.

Offences

A person is guilty of theft if he dishonestly appropriates property belonging to another with the intention of permanently depriving the other of it; and 'thief' and 'steal' shall be construed accordingly.

Theft Act 1968, s 1(1)

Points to prove
- ✓ dishonestly
- ✓ appropriates
- ✓ property
- ✓ belonging to another
- ✓ intention to permanently deprive the other of it

Meanings

Dishonestly

Section 2 defines what will not be considered as 'dishonest'.

3.1.1 Theft (general)/theft of scrap metal

- It is not considered dishonest if a person takes possession of property belonging to another, whether for themselves or a third person, believing that they have a legal right to deprive the other of it.
- It is not considered dishonest to take property belonging to another believing that, if the other had known about it and the circumstances, they would have consented.
- It will not be dishonest if, not being a trustee or personal representative, a person takes possession of property believing that, by taking reasonable steps, the owner could not be discovered.
- Taking property belonging to another may be dishonest even if the perpetrator is willing to pay for it.

Appropriates

'Appropriates' is defined in s 3.
- If a person assumes the rights of an owner over property they are deemed to have appropriated it. This includes where they obtain the property without stealing and later assume such rights by keeping or dealing with it as the owner.
- Where property or a right or interest in property is or purports to be transferred for value to a person acting in good faith, no later assumption by him of rights which he believed himself to be acquiring shall, by reason of any defect in the transferor's title, amount to theft of the property.

Property

'Property' is defined by s 4.
- It includes money and all other property (real or personal) including 'things in action' and other intangible property. Unless expressly excluded by s 4, 'property' covers all property even if possession or control of it is prohibited or unlawful (eg drugs).
- Land, or things forming part of it, and taken from it by a person or on their instructions, can only be stolen if:
  + the person is a trustee or personal representative, or is authorised by power of attorney, as a company liquidator, or in some other way, to sell or dispose of land belonging to somebody else, and they appropriate it or anything forming part of it, by dealing with it in breach of the confidence entrusted in them; or
  + when the person is not in possession of the land, they appropriate anything forming part of it by severing it, causing it to be severed, or after it has been severed; or
  + when, being in possession of the land under a tenancy, they appropriate all or part of a fixture or structure let for use with that land.
- Mushrooms (and other fungi), flowers, plants (including shrubs and trees), and fruit or foliage from a plant are all capable of being 'property' for the purposes of theft. Picking mushrooms, flowers, fruit, or foliage **growing wild** on land is not theft unless it is done for reward, sale, or other commercial purpose.

- Wild creatures, tamed or untamed, are regarded as property. However, a wild creature which is not tamed or normally kept in captivity (or the carcass of such animal) cannot be stolen unless it has been taken into possession by or on behalf of another, and such possession has not been lost or given up, or it is in the process of being taken into possession.

Belonging to another

'Belonging to another' is defined by s 5.
- Property belongs to any person having possession or control of it or having a proprietary right or interest in it.
- Where property is subject to a trust, ownership includes the right to enforce that trust, and any intention to break it is regarded as intending to deprive a person having such right.
- Where a person receives property from or on account of another and is under an obligation to the other to retain and deal with that property or its proceeds in a particular way, the property or proceeds shall be regarded (as against them) as belonging to the other.
- When a person obtains property because of another's mistake, and they are obliged to repay all or part of it, its proceeds, or value then, to the extent of that obligation, the property or proceeds are regarded as belonging to the person entitled to restoration, and any intent not to repay it is an intention to deprive them of it.

Intention to permanently deprive

'Intention to permanently deprive' is defined by s 6.
- Appropriation of property belonging to another without meaning them permanently to lose it still has the intention of 'permanently depriving' them of it, if the appropriator intends to treat it as their own to dispose of regardless of the other's rights.
- Borrowing or lending the property may amount to treating it as their own if it is for a period and in circumstances equating to an outright taking or disposal.
- Where a person has possession or control of another's property, for their own purposes and, without the other's permission, loans it to a third person with unachievable conditions for its return, they treat it as their own to dispose of regardless of the other's rights (eg pawning property belonging to another when not able to redeem it).

Explanatory notes

- It is immaterial whether the appropriation is made with a view to gain or is made for the thief's own benefit.
- 'Things in action' include a cheque drawn to a payee, giving them an action (demand for payment) which they may enforce against the payer. It is, therefore, the property of the payee.
- 'Intangible property' includes patents, applications for patents, copyrights.
- 'Tenancy' means a tenancy for any period and includes a tenancy agreement, but a person who, when a tenancy ends, remains in

possession as statutory tenant or otherwise will be treated as having possession under the tenancy.

* Possession, in general terms, means having the right to use property as your own without having any legal title to it (eg hiring a car— you have possession while legal ownership remains with the hire company).
* Possession may be 'actual' (an item in your hand or pocket) or 'constructive' (an item at your home while you are elsewhere).
* Control means having the power to use or manage items without having legal title to them (eg a delivery service having control of letters and packages for delivery—it does not actually own any of them and may not even have 'possession' at all times).
* Proprietary right or interest means ownership or having legal title to property or similar rights.
* An obligation to make restoration of property belonging to another must be a legal obligation, not a moral or social one.
* Simple and genuine borrowing of property is insufficient to constitute theft because the necessary '*mens rea*' is missing, unless the person intends to return the property in such a state that it loses its value or goodness (eg exam papers borrowed for copying would not be 'stolen' as they had not lessened in their intrinsic value).
* The theft or attempted theft of mail bags or postal packages, or their contents, whilst in transit between British postal areas is, even if it happens outside England and Wales, triable in England and Wales.

Related cases

Ivey v Genting Casinos (UK) Ltd (trading as Crockfords) [2017] UKSC 67 Where dishonesty is in question but s 2 of the Theft Act is of no assistance (s 2 will not cater for every circumstance), the magistrates/jury will first have to ascertain that actual state of the individual's knowledge or belief as to the facts (this does not have to be a reasonable belief—the question is whether the belief is genuinely held). Once his/her actual state of mind as to knowledge or belief is established, the question of whether his/her conduct had been honest or dishonest was to be determined by the magistrates/jury by applying the (objective) standards of ordinary decent people. There is no requirement that the defendant had to appreciate that what he/she had done was, by those standards, dishonest. Taking this approach means that to prove dishonesty, a prosecutor need only place before a court, the facts of what the defendant did and thought and then invite the court to hold that he was dishonest according to the standards of ordinary decent people.

R v Hayes [2015] EWCA Crim 1944 the defendant was charged with conspiracy to defraud by manipulating financial trade markets but the defence was that he had not acted dishonestly in that what he had done was common practice and had been encouraged by his managers. His conviction was upheld, and the court reaffirmed that his conduct should be tested by the standards of the first **objective** limb of *R v Ghosh*

[1982] 2 All ER 689; by the ordinary standards of the honest and reasonable person and **not** by the standards of a particular market.

R v Smith and others [2011] EWCA Crim 66, CA In this case, S contacted V (a known drug dealer) and arranged a meeting to sell £50 worth of heroin. V handed the drugs over to avoid violence. It was held that unless expressly excluded by s 4, 'property' covers all property even if possession or control of it is prohibited or unlawful (eg drugs).

R (on the application of Ricketts) v Basildon MC [2010] EWHC 2358 (Admin), QBD It was held in this case that taking bags of donated items left outside a charity shop or from its waste bins was still theft.

R v Hinks [2000] 4 All ER 833, HL In this case, the defendant influenced, coerced, or encouraged the complainant who was naive, gullible, and of limited intelligence to hand over large sums of money. It was held that receiving a valid gift is appropriation. If the circumstances surrounding the acceptance of the property would be considered dishonest (by a reasonable person), then that conduct becomes theft.

R v Ngan [1998] 1 Cr App R 331, CA Appropriation must take place in England and Wales.

Practical considerations

- Consider stop, search, and seizure powers under s 1 of PACE (see **1.3.2**).
- All five of the elements contained within the theft definition must be proved to obtain a conviction.
- In the absence of a reliable admission of dishonesty, this evidence will have to be proved by other evidence such as: Where was the property found? Had it been hidden? What were the subsequent actions of the defendant?
- Other matters that should be addressed include:
  - ✦ Evidence of who owns the property and/or that the defendant does not.
  - ✦ Does the offender have any claim on the property?
  - ✦ Does the offender own any similar property/have the means to have paid for it?
  - ✦ Any attempts to alter the property or change its appearance.
  - ✦ Proof that only some of the property was stolen is sufficient for a conviction.
  - ✦ The current location of the property.
  - ✦ The value of the property stolen/recovered.
- The fact that a man and woman are married or are civil partners, does not preclude one from stealing property belonging to the other.
  - ✦ A person is not exempt from answering questions in recovery proceedings on the grounds that to do so would incriminate them or their spouse or civil partner.
  - ✦ However, a statement or confession made in recovery proceedings is not admissible in proceedings for an offence under this Act as evidence against them or their spouse or civil partner.

3.1.1 Theft (general)/theft of scrap metal

- PACE Code E para 3.1(a)(iii) provides exemption from the requirement to audio record interviews that are undertaken elsewhere than at a police station for certain indictable offences that includes where a person has been cautioned for retail theft (shoplifting) contrary to s 1. This exemption is subject to a number of conditions, but the suspect must be aged 18 years or over, and does not require an appropriate adult, the value of the property must not exceed £100 inclusive of VAT; the stolen property has been recovered and is fit for sale, and the suspect is not employed (whether paid or not) by the person, company, or organisation to which the property belongs. (See **Code E** for full details.)
- An interviewer who is not sure or has any doubt about the suitability of a place or location for carrying out an interview elsewhere than at a police station, should consult an officer of the rank of Sergeant or above for advice.
- The above exemption to audio record interviews applies to an attempt to commit the offence under s 1 Criminal Attempts Act 1981 (see **4.1.1**).
- Consider issuing a PND for retail/commercial thefts under £100 (see **7.1.1**).
- Consider additional evidence (eg security video, CCTV footage).
- Low-value shoplifting (value that does not exceed £200) may be triable only as a summary offence under the MCA 1980, s 22A; but it is still considered an 'indictable offence' for PACE purposes (see **1.4.4**).

Theft of scrap metal

- The Scrap Metal Dealers Act 2013 was passed in order to curb metal theft from a range of sectors—including the rail network, electric/telecommunication distribution, memorials, and street furniture.
- It is a summary offence under s 1 of the Act for a person to carry on business as a scrap metal dealer unless authorised by a licence under this Act.
- A person carries on business as a scrap metal dealer if the business:
  + consists wholly or partly in buying or selling scrap metal, whether or not the metal is sold in the form in which it was bought, or
  + carries on as a motor salvage operator.
- Scrap metal includes:
  + any old, waste, or discarded metal or metallic material, and
  + any product, article, or assembly which is made from or contains metal and is broken, worn out or regarded by its last holder as having reached the end of its useful life.
- But gold, silver, or alloy which contains by weight 2 per cent or more gold or silver, are not scrap metal.
- Section 12(1) of the Act stipulates that a scrap metal dealer must not pay for scrap metal except by 'non-transferable' cheques, or by an electronic transfer of funds (authorised by credit or debit card or otherwise). Payment cannot be made by cash or 'paying in kind' (with goods or services).

- Under s 12(4), if scrap metal is paid for in breach of s 12(1), the following commit a summary offence:
  - ✦ the scrap metal dealer;
  - ✦ the site manager (if payment on site);
  - ✦ any person who makes the payment acting for the dealer.
- It is a defence for the scrap metal dealer or site manager to prove that they:
  - ✦ made arrangements to ensure payment was not in breach of s 12(1), and
  - ✦ took all reasonable steps to ensure compliance with those arrangements.
- Section 15(6) makes it a summary offence if comprehensive records of receipt or disposal of scrap metal are not recorded as required by s 13 or s 14 or kept for three years from receipt or disposal. This ensures that the seller/purchaser of the scrap metal can be readily identified.
- Under s 16 of the Act a constable or local authority officer may:
  - ✦ enter and inspect a licensed site at any reasonable time on notice to the site manager, but are not entitled to use force to enter the site;
  - ✦ require production of and inspect any scrap metal kept on site or records kept under s 13 or s 14 for receipt/disposal of scrap metal; and
  - ✦ make copies/extracts from such records.
- A justice of the peace may issue a warrant authorising entry onto premises to ensure compliance with the Act.
- It is a summary offence (s 16(13)) if a person: obstructs a right of entry or inspection, or fails to produce a record when so required, under the s 16 powers.

 Either way   None

 Summary: 6 months' imprisonment and/or a fine
Indictment: 7 years' imprisonment and/or a fine

3.1.2 Removal of articles from places open to the public

Section 11 of the Theft Act 1968 covers the offence of removing articles from places open to the public.

Offences

Subject to subsections (2) and (3) below, where the public have access to a building in order to view the building or part of it, or a collection or part of a collection housed in it, any person who without lawful authority

---

3.1.2 Removal of articles from places open to the public

removes from the building or its grounds the whole or part of any article displayed or kept for display to the public in the building or that part of it or in its grounds shall be guilty of an offence.

Theft Act 1968, s 11(1)

Points to prove

✓ without lawful authority
✓ removed from building/grounds of building
✓ to which public have access
✓ to view building/collection/part thereof
✓ the whole/part of article displayed/kept for display to public

Meaning of collection

This includes a collection displayed to the public for a temporary purpose (*R v Durkin* [1973] 2 All ER 872, CA), but references in this section to a collection do not apply to a collection made or exhibited for the purpose of effecting sales or other commercial dealings.

Explanatory notes

- Access to grounds alone is insufficient. The public must have access to a building to view it, part of it or a collection or part of it housed therein.
- Payment for the privilege of viewing the collection is irrelevant, as is whether such payment merely covers expenses or makes a profit.
- Articles displayed are not confined to works of art, the test being that the article, which may be priceless or valueless, is displayed or kept for public display.
- Note that this offence does not require any intent to permanently deprive the owner of the article taken.

Defences

A person does not commit an offence under this section if he believes that he has lawful authority for the removal of the thing in question or that he would have it if the person entitled to give it knew of the removal and the circumstances of it.

Theft Act 1968, s 11(3)

Defence notes

The burden is on the prosecution to prove the absence of genuine belief on the part of the defendant.

Practical considerations

- Ascertain the dates on which the building/articles is/are on display.
- Public access to a building for other purposes (eg a shopping mall) when a collection is displayed as an incidental to the main purpose of access (shopping) is unlikely to fall into this section.
    - ✦ However, if the collection was displayed in a separate part of the building with access given purely to view it, it would fall into this section.
- Removal need not be during the times the public have access. It can occur even when the buildings/grounds are closed. However, per s 11(2), if the display is temporary, removal must take place on a day when the public have access to the buildings/grounds in order to view.
- Does the defendant have any claim on the property?
- Current location of the article(s).
- Value of property taken/recovered.
- Obtain CJA witness statements.
- Consider additional evidence (eg security video, CCTV footage).

 Either way None

 Summary: 6 months' imprisonment and/or a fine
Indictment: 5 years' imprisonment and/or a fine

Links to alternative subjects and offences

3.2 **Robbery**

The Theft Act 1968 provides for the offence of theft and other connected offences. Section 8 provides for the offences of robbery and assault with intent to rob, whilst s 21 concerns the offence of blackmail.

3.2.1 **Robbery**

Offences

A person is guilty of robbery if he steals, and immediately before or at the time of doing so, and in order to do so, he uses force on any person or puts or seeks to put any person in fear of being then and there subjected to force.

Theft Act 1968, s 8(1)

Points to prove
✓ stole property
✓ immediately before/at the time of doing so
✓ and in order to do so
✓ used force on a person or put/sought to put person in fear of immediate force

Meanings

Steals (see **3.1.1**)

Force

Means the ordinary meaning and whether force has been used is a matter for the court to decide.

Explanatory notes

- The offence of theft must be proved before robbery can be substantiated.
- Section 8(2) deems that a person guilty of robbery is guilty of an offence.
- Force or the threat of force must be used immediately before or at the time of the theft.
- A threat to use force must be made with the intention that something should happen immediately.

- The purpose of the use of force is to facilitate the theft; using force to escape is not robbery.
- If the offence is carried out by a number of assailants, but only one uses violence towards the victim, the others cannot be held responsible for the violence unless a prior agreement between them to use that degree of violence in order to achieve their objective is shown.
- In order to seek to put somebody in fear, the state of mind of the offender is what is important (rather than that of the victim).
- If a person, while stealing or attempting to steal mailbags or postal packages, or their contents, whilst in transit between British postal areas, commits robbery or attempted robbery, the offence is triable in England and Wales, even if it is committed outside England and Wales.

Defences

If an honest belief that a legal claim of right to the property exists (*R v Skivington* [1967] 1 All ER 483, CA).

Related cases

R v DPP [2012] EWHC 1657 (Admin), QBD Snatching a cigarette did not constitute 'force' required for an offence of robbery to be made out.

R v Clouden [1987] Crim LR 56, CA It was held in this case that very little force is required and a push or nudge to put the victim off balance to enable a theft to take place can be sufficient.

Corcoran v Anderton (1980) 71 Cr App R 104, CA Two defendants tried to steal a handbag carried by the complainant by tugging at it and hitting her on the back causing the bag to fall to the ground. Both defendants made off empty handed. It was held that while tugging at the handbag could be seen by some not to be an appropriation, sufficient assumption of the rights of an owner for an appropriation to have taken place had occurred when the handbag fell to the ground.

Practical considerations

- Ownership and value of any property stolen/recovered.
- The fear of being subjected to force must be genuine and can be proved in the victim's statement (although it is the defendant's intention to cause fear that is the key element).
- Specific words used by the defendant will be critical.
- It is not necessary to prove that somebody was put in fear, only that the accused sought to put somebody in fear of force.
- The force used must be to enable the theft to take place.
- The use of force after the theft is complete is not robbery.

- A threat of force can also be implied, if the victim believes that force will be used against them and therefore allows the theft to take place.
- An assault committed as an afterthought following a theft is not robbery, but it is assault and theft.
- Obtain CJA witness statements.
- Consider blackmail (see **3.2.3**) when the threats are for force to be used on a future occasion.
- Any additional evidence (eg security video, CCTV footage).

SSS	E&S	CHAR	TRIG

  ♿ Indictment   🕐 None

🏛 Life imprisonment

3.2.2 **Assault with intent to rob**

> **Offences**
>
> A person guilty of robbery, or of an assault with intent to rob, is guilty of an offence.
>
> Theft Act 1968, s 8(2)

Points to prove
- ✓ assault
- ✓ intended to rob

Meanings

Robbery (see **3.2.1**)

Intent (see **4.1.2**)

Explanatory notes

- This offence is committed if a victim is assaulted in order to rob them, but the robbery is not completed because of interference or resistance, or it could not be completed because the assailant demanded property which the victim did not have.
- If a person, whilst stealing or attempting to steal mailbags, or postal packages, or their contents, whilst in transit between British postal areas, commits assault with intent to rob, the offence is triable in England and Wales, even if it is committed outside England and Wales.

Defences (see **3.2.1**)

Practical considerations

- What was the purpose of the assault?
- Was there an unsuccessful attempt to steal property from the victim?
- There is no need for actual violence, as an assault does not require it. However, where no force is used immediately before or at the time of the unsuccessful attempt to rob, consider attempted robbery (see **4.1.1**).
- If the assault occurs when the assailant has a firearm in their possession, consider offences under the Firearms Act 1968 (see **8.3**).
- What was the degree of violence used towards the victim?
- Obtain CJA witness statements.
- Consider any additional evidence (eg security video, CCTV footage).
- If the defence to robbery is available, consider the assault in isolation.

 Indictment None

 Life imprisonment

3.2.3 **Blackmail**

Section 21 of the Theft Act 1968 deals with the offence of blackmail.

> ### Offences
>
> A person is guilty of blackmail if, with a view to gain for himself or another or with intent to cause loss to another, he makes any unwarranted demand with menaces; and for this purpose, a demand with menaces is unwarranted unless the person making it does so in the belief—
> (a) that he has reasonable grounds for making the demands; and
> (b) that the use of the menaces is a proper means of reinforcing the demands.
>
> Theft Act 1968, s 21(1)

Points to prove
✓ with view to gain for self/another or intent to cause loss to another
✓ made unwarranted demand with menaces

3.2.3 Blackmail

Meanings

Intent (see 4.1.2)

Menaces

The ordinary meaning of menaces applies (eg threats).

Explanatory notes

- The nature of the act or omission demanded is immaterial.
- It is also immaterial whether the menaces relate to action to be taken by the person making the demand or a third party.
- The words 'with a view to gain' and 'with intent to cause loss' are alternative, separate, and distinct phrases.
- The posting, making, or receipt of the threat must occur in this country.

Defences

In the belief that:
- they had reasonable grounds for making the demands; and
- the use of the menaces is a proper means of reinforcing the demands.

Defence notes

- Belief in both s 21(1)(a) and (b) must be present for this defence. If only one is present the offence of blackmail will still be made out.
- The onus is on the defendant to prove the belief, but the prosecution must cover this defence in interview or by other means to negate it.

Related cases

R v Lambert [2009] EWCA Crim 2860 The defendant was owed money by the grandson of the victim and he had tried to get his money from the victim instead of her grandson. He telephoned her, pretending to be her grandson, saying that he was being held by people who would harm him unless she gave them £5,000. The defendant was charged with blackmail contrary to s 21. It was held that it made no difference whether the defendant was pretending to be a victim or an aggressor, or whether he could cause harm to a fictional person. There had to be an unwarranted demand and it could be made in a way that was not aggressive or pressured. The more sophisticated and gentle the request, the more sinister it could be.

Practical considerations

- The menaces do not need to relate to action to be taken by the person making the demand.
- Cover the defence in interview or other means in order to negate it.
- Obtain CJA witness statement.

- If the evidence for 'gain' or 'loss' is vague, consider s 1 of the Malicious Communications Act 1988 (see **7.12**).
- Identify any evidence of contact/threats made to the complainant by the defendant (eg notes, letters, telephone, or social media).
- Consider confiscation of cash and property as this blackmail offence is listed as a 'criminal lifestyle' offence under Sch 2 of the Proceeds of Crime Act 2002 (see **5.5.** for details).

 Indictment None

14 years' imprisonment

Links to alternative subjects and offences

3.3 **Burglary/Aggravated Burglary**

The Theft Act 1968 provides for the offence of theft and other connected offences. Section 9 creates the offence of burglary and s 10 aggravated burglary.

3.3.1 **Burglary**

Offences

(1) A person is guilty of burglary if—
   (a). he enters any building or part of a building as a trespasser and with intent to commit any such offence as is mentioned in subsection (2) below; or
   (b). having entered any building or part of a building as a trespasser he steals or attempts to steal anything in the building or that part of it or inflicts or attempts to inflict on any person therein any grievous bodily harm.

(2) The offences referred to in subsection (1)(a) above are offences of stealing anything in the building or part of a building in question, of inflicting on any person therein any grievous bodily harm or of doing unlawful damage to the building or anything therein.

Theft Act 1968, s 9

Points to prove

✓ entered a building/part of a building
✓ as a trespasser
✓ with intent
✓ to steal property therein/inflict grievous bodily harm on person therein/do unlawful damage to the building or anything therein

or

✓ having entered a building/part of a building
✓ as a trespasser
✓ stole or attempted to steal anything therein/inflicted or attempted to inflict grievous bodily harm on any person therein

Meanings

Building

'Building' includes an outhouse, a shed, an inhabited vehicle, or a vessel irrespective of whether the resident is there or not.

Trespasser

Trespass means to pass over a limit or boundary or to unlawfully enter another's building or land. An offender must either know or be reckless as to whether they are a trespasser. Entry gained by fraud is still trespass.

Intent (see 4.1.2)

Steal (see 3.1)

Grievous bodily harm (see 2.3.1)

Unlawful damage (see 4.4)

Explanatory notes

- There does not have to be a forced entry into the building, merely proof that the person has entered as a trespasser.
- Entry into a building may be an actual physical entry, by use of an instrument (eg a hook on a stick through an open window), or by an innocent agent (eg a child under 10 years old).
- The offence does not differentiate between different types of building—but the punishment does (see below).
- A person who has entered one part of a building legally and then enters into another part of the same building as a trespasser falls within this section.
- In s 9(1)(a) the original intention need not be completed—it is sufficient that the intention existed at the time of entry.
- In s 9(1)(b) no specific intention is required at the time of entry as the intruder commits one of the acts having entered as a trespasser.

Related cases

Hudson v CPS [2017] EWHC 841 (Admin) The defendants were charged with burglary contrary to s 9 having entered a fully furnished rental property with utilities connected but at the time there were no tenants. The court held in this case that although vacated and not occupied, the property was still a dwelling ready for use as a home and the offence was complete. Deciding whether premises are a dwelling for the purpose of burglary is essentially a matter of fact and degree in each case.

R v Brown [1985] Crim LR 212, CA The least degree of entry is sufficient to constitute this element of the offence (eg putting a hand or instrument through an open window or letterbox).

R v Wilson and Jenkins [1983] 3 All ER 448, HL If force is applied either directly or indirectly then harm is inflicted (eg if a victim is so intimidated by an intruder that they jump from a window thereby causing injury then harm has been caused although no actual force is used).

R v Walkington [1979] 2 All ER 716, CA A person who enters a building as a trespasser with the intention of committing a relevant offence therein but gets caught before they manage to commit that offence, will still commit burglary.

Practical considerations

- Consider stop, search, and seizure powers under s 1 of PACE (see **1.3.2**).
- Ensure a degree of entry into the building can be proved; otherwise consider other offences relevant to the circumstances.
- If satisfied the offender entered the building gather evidence as to right to be there—CJA witness statements.
- A building may include structures made of wood, steel, or plastic, but it would not include a tent (inhabited or not), articulated trailer (on wheels), open-sided bus shelter, or carport.
- An inhabited caravan would be a building under this legislation.
- A static caravan permanently connected to mains water, sewers, and gas/electricity would probably be a building even when it was not occupied.
- A touring caravan parked in the driveway of a house is a vehicle. However, if it was no longer used for touring, and instead used for storage as a garden shed, it may well then be a building.
- A person who enters a shop legally and then goes into a store room may be a trespasser.
- A person who legally enters premises and later becomes a trespasser due to hostilities by them does not become a trespasser for burglary. They must have been a trespasser at the time of entry into that part of the building.
- A person acting as a lookout should be treated as a joint principal.
- Is there any other evidence available (eg security video, CCTV)?
- Is there any evidence of the intent for an offence under s 9(1)(a)? For theft this may be easy to prove (eg the possession of burgling tools), but it may be more difficult for GBH or damage.
- The type of building may affect the sentence.
- If any person in the dwelling was subjected to violence (or threat) then the case is triable on indictment only.
- If the defendant had a firearm/imitation firearm with them, then consider also s 17(2) of the Firearms Act 1968 (see **8.3.5**).

 Either way   None

 Summary: 6 months' imprisonment and/or a fine

Indictment: 10 years' imprisonment (dwelling—14 years' imprisonment)

3.3.2 **Aggravated burglary**

Section 10 of the Theft Act 1968 creates the offence of aggravated burglary, where the trespasser has with them, at the time of committing the burglary, one or more of the specified articles.

Offences

A person is guilty of aggravated burglary if he commits any burglary and at the time has with him any firearm or imitation firearm, any weapon of offence, or any explosive.

Theft Act 1968, s 10

Points to prove

✓ committed burglary
✓ had with them
✓ firearm/imitation firearm/weapon of offence/explosive

Meanings

Burglary (see **3.3.1**)

Has with him

This phrase has a narrower meaning than 'possession' (see **8.3.6**).

Firearm (see **8.1.1**)

Includes an airgun or air pistol (see **8.7.2**).

Imitation firearm

Anything which has the appearance of being a firearm, whether capable of being discharged or not.

Weapon of offence

Any article made or adapted for use for causing injury to or incapacitating a person or intended by the person having it with him for such use.

Explosive

Means any article manufactured for the purpose of producing a practical effect by explosion or intended by the person having it with him for that purpose.

Related cases

R v Daubney (2000) 164 JP 519, CA Defendant must know that they had the article with them.

R v Klass [1998] 1 Cr App R 453, CA Entry into a building with a weapon is an essential element of this offence. Therefore, if there is only one weapon and it is with an accomplice who remains outside the building, neither of the offenders would commit aggravated burglary.

R v Kelly (1993) 97 Cr App R 245, CA A burglar who used a screwdriver to break into premises then, when challenged by the occupants, used that same screwdriver to threaten them, was held to have a weapon of offence with him at the time.

3.3.2 Aggravated burglary

R v Stones [1989] 1 WLR 156, CA A burglar in possession of a knife for self-protection while carrying out a burglary may be tempted to use it if challenged and may therefore commit this offence.

Practical considerations

- Was the burglary committed under s 9(1)(a) or (b)? This affects the point in time at which the offence occurred.
- If there is more than one offender, is there evidence that somebody entered the building with the weapon? If not, charge with burglary or the relevant offence.
- What reason did the offender have for possessing the article?
- Where it is unclear whether the offender had the article with them at the relevant time, charge them with burglary and charge possession of the article separately.
- The offence may be committed where the offender takes possession of an article in one part of a building and then enters another part of the building with it.
- Obtain evidence of ownership and right of entry into building.
- Obtain CJA witness statements.
- Is there any other evidence (eg security video, CCTV footage)?

♿ Indictable	**🕐 None**	

🏛 Life imprisonment

Links to alternative subjects and offences

SSS Stop, search, and seize powers **E&S** Entry and search powers
CHAR Offences where evidence of bad character can be introduced **TRIG** Trigger offences

3.4 **Dishonestly—Abstract Electricity/Retain a Wrongful Credit**

Further offences provided for by the Theft Act 1968 are dishonestly abstracting electricity under s 13 and dishonestly retaining a wrongful credit under s 24A.

3.4.1 **Dishonestly abstracting electricity**

Offences

A person who dishonestly uses without due authority, or dishonestly causes to be wasted or diverted, any electricity commits an offence.

Theft Act 1968, s 13

Points to prove

✓ dishonestly
✓ used without due authority or caused to be wasted/diverted
✓ electricity

Meanings

Dishonestly

This means a state of mind as opposed to conduct.

Uses

Consumption of electricity that would not have occurred without an action by the accused.

Without due authority

Means without the proper authorisation.

Explanatory notes

- This section is made necessary by the fact that electricity does not fit into the definition of property under s 4 for theft (see **3.1.1**) and, therefore, it cannot be stolen. This also means that entering a building and abstracting electricity (or intending to) will not be burglary.

3.4.1 Dishonestly abstracting electricity

- A tramp who obtains warmth by an electric fire, which is already switched on, would not commit this offence, but if they switched the fire on they would commit this offence.
- Employees using their employer's electrically powered machinery for their own use would commit an offence under this section.
- It is not necessary for anybody to benefit from the wasted or diverted electricity. A person who, out of spite, switches on an electrical appliance before leaving a building would commit this offence.

Related cases

R v McCreadie and Tume [1992] Cr App Rep 143 In this case, squatters were charged with abstracting electricity, but they argued that they had not tampered with the meter. It was held that the suggestion that the meter had to be tampered with in some way to constitute the offence was quite wrong. It is sufficient for the prosecution to show that electricity was used without the authority of the electricity authority and that there was no intention to pay for it.

Practical considerations

- Obtain evidence of dishonest use, waste, or diversion of electricity (eg note the state of the meter, cash box missing).
- The person using the electricity does not have to be the person who reconnects the supply (eg a person using electricity with no intention to pay for it after a disconnected supply has been unlawfully reconnected by a third person would commit this offence).
- Check for sign of break-in to the premises, which may negate or support the story of the householder.
- Utilities bill may assist to prove diversion to bypass the meter.
- There is no requirement for the electricity to be supplied through the mains (eg it may be supplied from a car battery). Thus a person who takes a pedestrian-controlled electric vehicle which is not classed as a conveyance (see **4.3.1**) may commit this offence.
- Obtain CJA witness statement from electricity supplier.

 Either way   None

 Summary: 6 months' imprisonment and/or a fine

Indictment: 5 years' imprisonment

3.4.2 **Dishonestly retain a wrongful credit**

Offences

A person is guilty of an offence if—
(a) a wrongful credit has been made to an account kept by him or in respect of which he has any right or interest;
(b) he knows or believes that the credit is wrongful; and
(c) he dishonestly fails to take such steps as are reasonable in the circumstances to secure that the credit is cancelled.

Theft Act 1968, s 24A(1)

Points to prove

✓ knowing/believing
✓ wrongful credit made to account
✓ kept by them in which they had right or interest
✓ dishonestly
✓ failed to take reasonable steps to cancel the credit

Meanings

Wrongful credit

A **credit** to an account is wrongful to the extent that it derives from:
• theft (see **3.1.1**);
• blackmail (see **3.2.3**);
• fraud (see **3.8.1**); or
• stolen goods (see **3.5**).

Credit

Means a credit of an amount of money.

Explanatory notes

• In determining whether a credit to an account is wrongful, it is immaterial (in particular) whether the account is overdrawn before or after the credit is made.
• Any money dishonestly withdrawn from an account to which a wrongful credit has been made may be regarded as stolen goods.

Practical considerations

• Where did the credit originate?
• Obtain supplementary evidence (eg bank statements, cheque book).

3.4.2 Dishonestly retain a wrongful credit

- What steps could/have been taken to cancel the credit.
- Obtain CJA witness statement.

 Either way   None

 Summary: 6 months' imprisonment and/or a fine

Indictment: 10 years' imprisonment

Links to alternative subjects and offences

3.5 **Handling Stolen Goods**

Section 22 of the Theft Act 1968 creates various combinations of offences of handling stolen goods knowing or believing them to be stolen.

Offences

A person handles stolen goods if (otherwise than in the course of the stealing) knowing or believing them to be stolen goods he dishonestly receives the goods, or dishonestly undertakes or assists in their retention, removal, disposal or realisation by or for the benefit of another person, or he arranges to do so.

Theft Act 1968, s 22(1)

Points to prove

✓ otherwise than in the course of stealing
✓ knowing/believing goods to be stolen
✓ dishonestly received them or
✓ dishonestly undertook/assisted
✓ in the retention/removal/disposal/realisation of them
or
✓ arranged to do so
✓ by/for the benefit of another

Meanings

Stolen goods (s 24(2))

References to stolen goods shall include—**in addition** to the **goods** originally stolen and parts of them (whether in their original state or not)—**any other goods** which directly or indirectly represent or have at any time represented the stolen goods in the hands of the thief or handler of the goods (or any part of them) as being the proceeds of any disposal or realisation of the whole or part of the goods stolen or stolen goods handled by him of goods so representing the stolen goods.

Goods

Includes money and every other description of property except land, and includes things severed from the land by stealing (see **3.1.1**).

Knowing

Means actually having been told by somebody having first-hand knowledge (eg the thief or burglar) that the goods had been stolen (*R v Hall* (1985) 81 Cr App R 260, CA).

3.5 Handling Stolen Goods

Believing

Means the state of mind of a person who cannot be certain that goods are stolen, but where the circumstances indicate no other reasonable conclusion (*R v Elizabeth Forsyth* [1997] 2 Cr App R 299, CA).

Dishonestly (see **3.1.1**)

Receives

Means gaining **possession** or control of the goods.

Possession

Means either actual physical possession or constructive possession (storing the goods in premises belonging to them).

Undertakes

Includes where the person agrees to perform the act(s) that constitute the offence.

Retention

Means keeping possession of, not losing, continuing to have (*R v Pitchley* [1972] Crim LR 705, CA).

Realisation

Means the conversion of the goods, invariably into money (*R v Deakin* [1972] Crim LR 781, CA).

Arranges to do so

Means arranging to receive, retain, remove, dispose, or convert the stolen goods. This can be done without seeing or having had anything to do with the goods.

Explanatory notes

- Where a person is being proceeded against for handling stolen goods only, s 27(3)(a) provides for '**special evidence**' (eg their previous dealings with stolen goods within the twelve months prior to the current incident) to be introduced into the proceedings. No charge or conviction regarding the previous incident is necessary.
- Similarly, s 27(3)(b) allows the introduction of evidence of a previous conviction for theft or handling within five years of the present incident. In this case a notice must be served on the defence seven days prior to use of the evidence in court.
- Where the only evidence on a charge of handling stolen goods is circumstantial in that an accused person is in possession of property recently stolen (doctrine of recent possession), a court may infer guilty knowledge if: (a) the accused offers no explanation to account for their possession, or (b) the court is satisfied that the explanation they offer is untrue.

- Any benefit to the receiver is irrelevant.
- Someone who handles stolen goods, whilst having no knowledge or reason to believe them to be stolen, will not commit this offence.
- Actions taken for the benefit of another are only relevant in the offence of handling stolen goods—they have no significance in relation to the receiving of such goods.

Related cases

R v Bloxham (1982) 74 Cr App R 279, HL The defendant agreed to buy a car for £1,300. Unknown to him, the car had been stolen. The documents were never produced and some months later he suspected that the car had been stolen and subsequently he sold the car to an unidentified person. He was charged and convicted with handling stolen goods. On appeal his conviction was quashed. The court held that, on the true construction of s 22(1), a purchaser could not be 'another person' for whose benefit goods were realised or sold since it was the purchase, not the sale, which was for the purchaser's benefit. This means that a person who innocently buys goods for value and later discovers they were, in fact, stolen goods cannot commit the offence of assisting in their disposal by selling them as they benefited from their purchase not their sale.

R v Figures [1976] Crim LR 744, CC The defendant was found at Southampton to have in his possession goods that had been stolen in France. He admitted receiving them and paying for them in France knowing them to be stolen. He was charged with handling by assisting in their retention in England. The court dismissed the case and held that handling of goods stolen abroad is only an offence in England when the handling takes place in England. In this case, the offence was complete in France when the goods were received and paid for.

Practical considerations

- Under s 24(3), **goods** are **not regarded** as **still being stolen** goods after return to the person from whom stolen or to other lawful possession or custody, or after that person and any other person having a claim to them ceases, as regards those goods, to have any right to restitution regarding the theft.
- Ownership of the goods and evidence of theft must be established.
- Check for any evidence of previous dealings with stolen goods within the previous twelve months.
- Check previous convictions for theft or handling within the previous five years.
- Check for communications between the handler, the thief, or any potential buyers or distributors.
- Check for evidence of removal or alteration of identifying features.
- Obtain evidence of the true value of the goods.

3.5 Handling Stolen Goods

- If the facts fit both theft and handling stolen goods, use the relevant alternative charges and let the court decide which offence, if any, is committed.
- Several people may be charged on one indictment, concerning the same theft, with handling all or some of the goods at the same or various times, and all such persons may be tried together. This does not apply to a summary trial.

 Either way None

 Summary: 6 months' imprisonment and/or a fine
Indictment: 14 years' imprisonment

Links to alternative subjects and offences

SSS Stop, search, and seize powers   E&S Entry and search powers
CHAR Offences where evidence of bad character can be introduced   TRIG Trigger offences

3.6 **Going Equipped**

The Theft Act 1968 provides for several other key offences of which theft is a constituent part. Section 25 creates the offences of going equipped for any burglary or theft.

> ### Offences
>
> A person shall be guilty of an offence if, when not at his place of abode, he has with him any article for use in the course of or in connection with any burglary or theft.
>
> Theft Act 1968, s 25(1)

Points to prove
✓ not at place of abode
✓ had with them
✓ article(s) for use in course of/in connection with
✓ a burglary/theft

Meanings

Place of abode

This normally means the place or site where someone lives. Using its natural meaning it normally includes the garage and garden of a house, but it is ultimately a matter for the court or jury to decide.

Has with him

This phrase has a narrower meaning than 'possession' (see **8.3.6**).

Article

This has a wide meaning. It may include a whole range of items and substances, from treacle and paper to assist in breaking a window quietly, a car jack for spreading bars, or pieces of spark plug ceramic for breaking car windows.

Burglary (see 3.3.1)

Theft (see 3.1.1)
Includes taking a conveyance without owner's consent (see **4.3.1**).

Explanatory notes
- A direct connection between the article and a specific act of burglary or theft does not need to be proved.
- You do not need to prove that the person found with the article intended to use it themselves—intended use by another will suffice.

Related cases

R v Bundy [1977] 2 All ER 382, CA The defendant was living rough and sleeping in his car. He was stopped one day after a woman complained that he was following her. When his car was searched a pipe wrench, three pieces of stocking, a hammer, and some pipe were found. He was charged with 'going equipped' and convicted. He appealed on the grounds that his car was his 'place of abode'. His conviction was upheld, and the court stated that although the car was his abode, he did not intend to occupy it at the place where he was stopped by the police. He was at that time in transit from one place to another and was, therefore, in transit at the time of commission of this offence.

Practical considerations

- What articles were with or available to the defendant?
- Where were the articles?
- What were their possible/intended uses?
- Did the defendant have a lawful purpose for having the article(s) in their possession at that particular time/place?
- Has the defendant used such articles in committing the offence previously?
- Obtain CJA witness statements.
- This offence caters for some preparatory acts prior to the commission of one or more of the specified acts.
- This offence can only be committed before the intended burglary or theft, not afterwards.
- Possession of the article(s) after arrest is not sufficient for this offence.
- When two or more people are acting in concert the possession of housebreaking implements by one of them would be deemed to be possession by all of them.
- A person who has a relevant article with them but has not yet decided whether to use the article, does not have the necessary intent to commit the offence.
- Taking a conveyance without the owner's consent is, for the purposes of this section, to be treated as theft.
- Once it has been proved that the defendant had a relevant article with them, the defendant will need to prove possession for a purpose other than burglary or theft.

 Either way   None

 Summary: 6 months' imprisonment and/or a fine

Indictment: 3 years' imprisonment

Links to alternative subjects and offences

3.7 **Making off without Payment**

The Theft Act 1978 creates specific offences relating to fraudulent conduct. Section 3 creates the offence of making off without payment (also known as 'bilking') when on-the-spot payment is required or expected for goods or a service and the perpetrator intends to avoid payment.

Offences

Subject to subsection (3) below, a person who, knowing that payment on the spot for any goods supplied or service done is required or expected from him, dishonestly makes off without having paid as required or expected and with intent to avoid payment of the amount due shall be guilty of an offence.

Theft Act 1978, s 3(1)

Points to prove

✓ knowing immediate payment is required/expected
✓ for goods supplied/service done
✓ dishonestly
✓ made off
✓ without having paid as required/expected
✓ with intent to avoid payment of amount due

Meanings

Payment on the spot

This includes payment at the time of collecting goods on which work has been done or in respect of which service has been provided.

Goods (see 3.5)

Dishonestly (see 3.1.1)

Intent (see 4.1.2)

Explanatory notes

- The term **'goods supplied or service done'** will include making off without payment for fuel at a self-service petrol station, meals at restaurants, or hotel accommodation/services where the charge is levied after supplying the goods/service.
- If a motorist forgets to pay for petrol and drives off, but later remembers that they had not paid, and then returns to the filling

station to pay, they may not commit the offence due to lacking the necessary intent.

- Where there is an agreement to defer payment, any such agreement would normally eliminate the expectation of payment on the spot.

Defences

Subsection (1) above shall not apply where the supply of the goods or the doing of the service is contrary to law, or where the service done is such that payment is not legally enforceable.

Theft Act 1978, s 3(3)

Defence notes

A payment not being legally enforceable may be where the service provider breaks a contract (eg a taxi driver who fails to complete a journey) or where the contract cannot be enforced through the courts.

Related cases

R v Brooks and Brooks (1983) 76 Cr App R 66, CA This case involved the defendants leaving a restaurant without making payment. The point outlined by the court was that the defendant had left the premises with intent to avoid payment which he knew was expected. The words 'dishonestly makes off' were to be given their natural meaning (a departure from the spot where payment is required) and it was a matter of fact on which the jury could decide.

Practical considerations

- What goods or services have been provided?
- The goods or services provided must be specified in the charge.
- It is important to prove that the person knew that 'payment on the spot' was required.
- Did the accused have money or means with which to pay the bill?
- Is the payment legally enforceable?
- There must be an intention to avoid payment completely and not merely intent to defer or delay it.
- Obtain CJA witness statement.
- Is there any further evidence (eg CCTV footage)?

 Either way   None

 Summary: 6 months' imprisonment and/or a fine
Indictment: 2 years' imprisonment

Links to alternative subjects and offences

3.8 **Fraud Offences**

The Fraud Act 2006, ss 1–4 detail the three different ways of committing fraud, s 12 the liability of company officers, s 13 evidential matters relating to fraud, and ss 6 and 7 possess/make articles for use in fraud.

3.8.1 **Fraud offence**

Section 1 creates the general offence of fraud, and ss 2–4 detail three different ways of committing fraud by false representation, failing to disclose information, or by abuse of position.

Offences

(1) A person is guilty of fraud if he is in breach of any of the sections listed in subsection (2) (which provide for different ways of committing the offence).

(2) The sections are—
   (a) section 2 (fraud by false representation),
   (b) section 3 (fraud by failing to disclose information), and
   (c) section 4 (fraud by abuse of position).

Fraud Act 2006, s 1

Points to prove

False representation

✓ dishonestly made a false representation
✓ intending to make a gain for yourself/another or
✓ intending to cause loss to another/expose another to a risk of loss

Failing to disclose information

✓ dishonestly failed to disclose to another
✓ information which you were under a legal duty to disclose
✓ intending, by that failure
✓ to make a gain for yourself/another or
✓ to cause loss to another/expose another to a risk of loss

Fraud by abuse of position

✓ occupying a position in which you were expected
✓ to safeguard, or not to act against, the financial interests of another
✓ dishonestly abused that position
✓ intending to make a gain for yourself/another or
✓ intending to cause loss to another/expose another to a risk of loss

Meanings

Fraud by false representation (see **3.8.2**)

Fraud by failing to disclose information (see **3.8.3**)

Fraud by abuse of position (see **3.8.4**)

Gain and loss

(1) The references to gain and loss in sections 2 to 4 are to be read in accordance with this section.

(2) 'Gain' and 'loss'—
   (a) extend only to gain or loss in money or other property;
   (b) include any such gain or loss whether temporary or permanent; and 'property' means any property whether real or personal (including things in action and other intangible property).

(3) 'Gain' includes a gain by keeping what one has, as well as a gain by getting what one does not have.

(4) 'Loss' includes a loss by not getting what one might get, as well as a loss by parting with what one has.

Fraud Act 2006, s 5

Dishonestly (see **3.1.1**)

Intention (see **4.1.2**)

Explanatory notes

- Section 1 creates the general offence of fraud, and ss 2–4 detail three different ways of committing the fraud offence.
- All three fraud offences require an intention to make a gain for oneself or another or cause loss to another/expose another to a risk of loss.
- Similarly, intention must be proved (see **4.1.2**).
- Property covers all forms of property, including intellectual property, although in practice this is rarely 'gained' or 'lost'.
- If any offences are committed by a company, the company officers may also be liable under s 12 (see **3.8.5**).
- Section 13 deals with evidential matters under this Act, conspiracy to defraud or any other offences involving any form of fraudulent conduct or purpose (see **3.8.6**).

3.8.2 Meaning of fraud by false representation

Meanings

Fraud by false representation

(1) A person is in breach of this section if he—
   (a) dishonestly makes a false representation, and

(b) intends, by making the representation—
  (i) to make a **gain** for himself or another, or
  (ii) to cause **loss** to another or to expose another to a risk of loss.
(2) A representation is false if—
  (a) it is untrue or misleading, and
  (b) the person making it knows that it is, or might be, untrue or misleading.
(3) '**Representation**' means any representation as to fact or law, including a representation as to the state of mind of—
  (a) the person making the representation, or
  (b) any other person.
(4) A representation may be express or implied.
(5) For the purposes of this section a representation may be regarded as made if it (or anything implying it) is submitted in any form to any system or device designed to receive, convey or respond to communications (with or without human intervention).

Fraud Act 2006, s 2

Gain and loss (see **3.8.1**)

Dishonestly (see **3.1.1**)

Intention (see **4.1.2**)

Explanatory notes

- The offence of fraud by false representation comes under fraud s 1 (see **3.8.1**) and **not** s 2.
- The gain or loss does not actually have to take place.
- There is no restriction on the way in which the representation may be expressed. It can be spoken, written (hardcopy or electronically), or communicated by conduct.
- An example of a representation by conduct is where a person dishonestly uses a credit card to pay for goods. By tendering the card, they are falsely representing that they have the authority to use it for that transaction. It is immaterial whether the retailer accepting the card is deceived by this representation.
- The practice of 'phishing' (eg sending an email purporting to come from a legitimate financial institution in order to obtain credit card and bank account details, so that the 'phisher' can access and fraudulently use those accounts) is another example of false representation.
- Subsection (5) is given in broad terms because it may be difficult to distinguish situations involving modern technology and/or human involvement. It could well be that the only recipient of the false statement is a machine or a piece of software, where a false statement is submitted to a system for dealing with electronic communications and not to a human being (eg postal or messenger systems). Another example of fraud by electronic means can be entering a number into a 'chip and pin' machine.

3.8.3 **Meaning of fraud by failing to disclose information**

Meanings

Fraud by failing to disclose information

A person is in breach of this section if he—
(a) **dishonestly** fails to disclose to another person information which he is under a **legal duty** to disclose, and
(b) **intends**, by failing to disclose the information—
    (i) to make a **gain** for himself or another, or
    (ii) to cause **loss** to another or to expose another to a risk of loss.

Fraud Act 2006, s 3

Gain and loss (see **3.8.1**)

Dishonestly (see **3.1.1**)

Intention (see **4.1.2**)

Explanatory notes

- The offence of fraud by failing to disclose information comes under fraud s 1 (see **3.8.1**) and **not** s 3.
- A legal duty to disclose information may include duties under both oral and/or written contracts.
- The concept of **'legal duty'** may derive from statute; a transaction that requires good faith (eg contract of insurance); express, or implied terms of a contract; custom of a particular trade/market; or a fiduciary relationship between the parties (eg between agent and principal).
- This legal duty to disclose information may be where the defendant's failure to disclose gives the victim a cause of action for damages, or the law gives the victim a right to set aside any change in their legal position to which they may consent as a result of the non-disclosure. An example of an offence under this section could be where a person intentionally failed to disclose information relating to their physical condition when making an application for life insurance.

3.8.4 **Meaning of fraud by abuse of position**

Meanings

Fraud by abuse of position

(1) A person is in breach of this section if he—
    (a) occupies a **position** in which he is expected to safeguard, or not to act against, the financial interests of another person,

(b) **dishonestly** abuses that position, and

(c) **intends**, by means of the abuse of that position—

    (i) to make a **gain** for himself or another, or

    (ii) to cause **loss** to another or to expose another to a risk of loss.

(2) A person may be regarded as having **abused** his position even though his conduct consisted of an omission rather than an act.

Fraud Act 2006, s 4

Gain and loss (see **3.8.1**)

Dishonestly (see **3.1.1**)

Intention (see **4.1.2**)

Explanatory notes

- The offence of fraud by abuse of position comes under fraud s 1 (see **3.8.1**) and **not** s 4.
- The offence of committing fraud by dishonestly abusing their **position** applies in situations where they are in a privileged position, and by virtue of this position are expected to safeguard another's financial interests or not act against those interests.
- The necessary relationship could be between trustee and beneficiary, director and company, professional person and client, agent and principal, employee and employer, or even between partners. Generally, this relationship will be recognised by the civil law as importing fiduciary duties. This relationship and existence of their duty can be ruled upon by the judge or be subject of directions to the jury.
- The term '**abuse**' is not defined because it is intended to cover a wide range of conduct. Furthermore, the offence can be committed by omission as well as by positive action.
- Examples of offences under this section are:
  - ✦ purposely failing to take up the chance of a crucial contract in order that an associate or rival company can take it up instead to the loss of their employer;
  - ✦ a software company employee uses their position to clone software products with the intention of selling the products to others;
  - ✦ where a carer for an elderly or disabled person has access to that person's bank account and abuses their position by transferring funds for their own gain.

3.8.5 Liability of company officers for offence by company

Liability

(1) Subsection (2) applies if an offence under this Act is committed by a body corporate.

(2) If the offence is proved to have been committed with the consent
or connivance of—
   (a) a director, manager, secretary or other similar officer of the
   body corporate, or
   (b) a person who was purporting to act in any such capacity,
   he (as well as the body corporate) is guilty of the offence and
   liable to be proceeded against and punished accordingly.

(3) If the affairs of a body corporate are managed by its members,
subsection (2) applies in relation to the acts and defaults of a
member in connection with his functions of management as if he
were a director of the body corporate.

Fraud Act 2006, s 12

Explanatory notes

- This section provides that if people who have a specified corporate
role are party to the commission of an offence under the Act by their
body corporate, they will be liable to be charged for the offence as
well as the corporation.
- Liability for this offence applies to directors, managers, company
secretaries, and other similar officers of companies and other bodies
corporate.
- Furthermore, if the body corporate is charged with an offence and
the company is managed by its members, the members involved in
management can be prosecuted too.

3.8.6 **Admissible evidence**

Evidence

(1) A person is not to be excused from—
   (a) answering any question put to him in proceedings relating to
   property, or
   (b) complying with any order made in proceedings relating to
   property, on the ground that doing so may incriminate him
   or his spouse or civil partner of an offence under this Act or a
   related offence.

(2) But, in proceedings for an offence under this Act or a related
offence, a statement or admission made by the person in—
   (a) answering such a question, or
   (b) complying with such an order, is not admissible in evidence against
   him or (unless they married or became civil partners after the
   making of the statement or admission) his spouse or civil partner.

(3) 'Proceedings relating to property' means any proceedings for—
   (a) the recovery or administration of any property,
   (b) the execution of a trust, or
   (c) an account of any property or dealings with property,
   and 'property' means money or other property whether real

or personal (including things in action and other intangible property).

(4) 'Related offence' means—
   (a) conspiracy to defraud;
   (b) any other offence involving any form of fraudulent conduct or purpose.

Fraud Act 2006, s 13

Explanatory notes

- This means that during any proceedings for:
   + the recovery or administration of any property;
   + the execution of a trust; or
   + an account of any property or dealings with property;
   a person cannot be excused from answering any question or refuse to comply with any order made in those proceedings on the grounds of incrimination under this Act, conspiracy to defraud, or an offence involving any form of fraudulent conduct or purpose.
- However, any statement or admission made in answering such a question, or complying with such an order, is not admissible in evidence against them or their spouse or civil partner (unless they married or became civil partners after the making of such a statement or admission).
- Although this section is similar to s 31(1) of the Theft Act 1968 where a person/spouse/civil partner is protected from incrimination, while nonetheless being obliged to cooperate with certain civil proceedings relating to property, it goes beyond that section by removing privilege in relation to this Act, conspiracy to defraud, and any other offence involving any form of fraudulent conduct or purpose.
- A civil partnership is a relationship between two people of the same sex ('civil partners') registered as civil partners under the Civil Partnerships Act 2004 and ends only on death, dissolution, or annulment.

Related cases

R v Minet [2009] All ER (D) 215, CA The defendant was in financial difficulties with his plumbing business and made fraudulent transactions using his customers' credit card details. It was held that this was a clear breach of trust. The defendant had been allowed into the victims' homes and been entrusted with their credit cards and details. He had been under an obligation to deal honestly with them.

Kensington International Ltd v Congo and others [2007] EWCA Civ 1128, CA This case provides guidance relating to disclosure, evidence, and other aspects of s 13.

Practical considerations

- Consider stop, search, and seizure powers under s 1 of PACE (see **1.3.2**).
- The words used may be spoken or written. Alternatively, there may be nothing done or said in circumstances where a reasonable and honest person would have expected something to be said/done (eg to correct a mistake).
- The fraud may be proved by admissions, the defendant's actions, or a combination of both.
- Acts may be dishonest even if the perpetrator genuinely believed them to be morally justified.
- If committed by a body corporate with the consent or connivance of one of its officers they, as well as the body corporate, are liable to be proceeded against (see **3.8.5**).

3.8.7 **Possess or control article for use in fraud**

Section 6 deals with the offence of having in their possession or under their control an article for use in fraud.

> ### Offences
>
> A person is guilty of an offence if he has in his possession or under his control any article for use in the course of or in connection with any fraud.
>
> Fraud Act 2006, s 6(1)

Points to prove

✓ had in your possession/under your control
✓ an article
✓ for use in the course of/in connection with a fraud

Meanings

Possession (see **8.1.1**)

Article

Means an article:

- made or adapted for use in the course of or in connection with an offence of fraud; or
- **intended** by the person having it with them for such use by them or by some other person.

It also includes any program or data held in electronic form.

Fraud (see **3.8.1**)

Intention (see **4.1.2**)

Explanatory notes

- Having the article after the commission of the fraud is not sufficient for this offence.
- The prosecution must prove that the defendant was in possession of the article and intended the article to be used in the course of or in connection with some future fraud. It is not necessary to prove that they intended it to be used in the course of or in connection with any specific fraud; it is enough to prove a general intention to use it for fraud.
- Similarly, it will be sufficient to prove that they had it with them with the intention that it should be used by someone else.
- Examples of electronic programs or data which could be used in fraud are: a computer program that can generate credit card numbers; computer templates that can be used for producing blank utility bills; computer files containing lists of other people's credit card details; or draft letters in connection with 'advance fee' frauds.

 Either way   None

 Summary: 12 months' imprisonment and/or a fine
Indictment: 5 years' imprisonment and/or a fine

3.8.8 Making or supplying article for use in fraud

Section 7 deals with the offences of making or supplying an article for use in fraud.

Offences

A person is guilty of an offence if he makes, adapts, supplies or offers to supply any article—

(a) knowing that it is designed or adapted for use in the course of or in connection with fraud, or

(b) intending it to be used to commit, or assist in the commission of, fraud.

Fraud Act 2006, s 7(1)

3.8.8 Making or supplying article for use in fraud

Points to prove

✓ made/adapted/supplied/offered to supply
✓ an article
✓ knowing that it was designed/adapted for use in the course of/in connection with fraud

or

✓ intending it to be used to commit/assist in the commission of fraud

Meanings

Article (see 3.8.7)

Fraud (see 3.8.1)

Intention (see 4.1.2)

Explanatory notes

- The offence is to make, adapt, supply, or offer to supply any article, knowing that it is designed or adapted for use in the course of or in connection with fraud, or intending it to be used to commit or facilitate fraud.
- Such an example would be where a person makes devices which, when attached to electricity meters cause the meter to malfunction. The actual amount of electricity used is concealed from the provider, who thus suffers a loss.

Practical considerations

- A general intention to commit fraud will suffice rather than a specific offence in specific circumstances (eg credit card skimming equipment may provide evidence of such an intention).
- Proof is required that the defendant had the article for the purpose of or with the intention that it be used in the course of or in connection with fraud, and a general intention to commit fraud will suffice.
- Consider s 12 (see **3.8.5**) as to liability of company officers for offences under this Act if they are committed by a body corporate. Similarly, s 13 deals with evidential matters for offences under this Act.

 SSS E&S TRIG

 Either way None

 Summary: 12 months' imprisonment and/or a fine

Indictment: 10 years' imprisonment and/or a fine

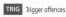

Links to alternative subjects and offences

3.9 **Obtaining Services Dishonestly**

The Fraud Act 2006 provides for the offence of fraud and other fraudulent offences of which dishonesty is a constituent part. Section 11 makes it an offence for any person, by any dishonest act, to obtain services for which payment is required, with intent to avoid payment.

Offences

(1) A person is guilty of an offence under this section if he obtains services for himself or another—
  (a) by a dishonest act, and
  (b) in breach of subsection (2).
(2) A person obtains services in breach of this subsection if—
  (a) they are made available on the basis that payment has been, is being or will be made for or in respect of them,
  (b) he obtains them without any payment having been made for or in respect of them or without payment having been made in full, and
  (c) when he obtains them, he knows—
    (i) that they are being made available on the basis described in paragraph (a), or
    (ii) that they might be, but intends that payment will not be made, or will not be made in full.

Fraud Act 2006, s 11

Points to prove

✓ obtained services for yourself/another by a dishonest act
✓ services were available on the basis that payment made for/in respect of them
✓ you obtained them without any payment/in full
✓ when you obtained them, you knew that they were being/might be made available on the basis described above
✓ but you intended that payment would not be made/made in full

---

Meanings

Dishonest act (see **3.1.1**)

Intention (see **4.1.2**)

Explanatory notes

- This section makes it an offence for any person, by any dishonest act, to obtain services for which payment is required, with intent to avoid payment.
- This offence replaced the offence of obtaining services by deception in s 1 of the Theft Act 1978, although this offence contains no deception element.
- It is not possible to commit the offence by omission alone and it can be committed only where the dishonest act was done with the intent not to pay for the services as expected.

Practical considerations

- The person must know that the services are made available on the basis that they are chargeable, or that they might be.
- There is nothing to suggest that the services obtained need to be lawful for this offence to be committed (eg services of a prostitute).
- There must be some action or communication by the defendant rather than an error wholly initiated by the supplier of the service which is unaffected by behaviour on the part of the defendant.
- The offence is not inchoate. It requires the actual obtaining of the service, for example data or software that is only available on the internet once you have paid for access rights to that service.
- Examples of this offence would be where a person:
  ✦ dishonestly uses false credit card details or other false personal information to obtain the service;
  ✦ climbs over a wall and watches a sports event without paying the entrance fee—such a person is not deceiving the provider of the service directly, but is obtaining a service which is provided on the basis that people will pay for it;
  ✦ attaches a decoder to a television set in order to view/have access to cable/satellite channels for which they have no intention of paying.
- Consider s 12 (see **3.8.5**) as to liability of company officers for offences under this Act if they are committed by a body corporate.

 Either way   None

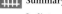 **Summary:** 12 months' imprisonment and/or a fine

Indictment: 5 years' imprisonment and/or a fine

Links to alternative subjects and offences

Chapter 4

Crime: General

4.1 Criminal Attempts/Meaning of Intent/Meaning of Aid, Abet, Counsel, and Procure/ Encourage or Assist Crime

4.1.1 Criminal attempts

The Criminal Attempts Act 1981 creates an offence of 'attempting' to commit certain crimes. It is imperative to prove intent (*mens rea*) for attempt offences, as well as other offences requiring intent. Intent is therefore discussed in detail.

Offence

(1) If, with intent to commit an offence to which this section applies, a person does an act which is more than merely preparatory to the commission of the offence, he is guilty of attempting to commit the offence.

(2) A person may be guilty of attempting to commit an offence to which this section applies even though the facts are such that the commission of the offence is impossible.

(3) In any case where—

    (a) apart from this subsection a person's intention would not be regarded as having amounted to an intent to commit an offence; but

    (b) if the facts of the case had been as he believed them to be, his intention would be so regarded

then, for the purposes of subsection (1) above, he shall be regarded as having had an intent to commit that offence.

Criminal Attempts Act 1981, s 1

4.1.1 Criminal attempts

Points to prove
- ✓ with intent
- ✓ attempted
- ✓ (wording of the offence attempted)

Meanings

Intent (see **4.1.2**)

Offence to which this section applies

- This section applies to any offence which if it were completed, would be triable as an indictable or an either way offence, **other than**:
  - ◆ conspiracy (at common law or under s 1 of the Criminal Law Act 1977 or any other enactment);
  - ◆ aiding, abetting, counselling, procuring, or suborning the commission of an offence (see **4.1.3**);
  - ◆ an offence under s 2(1) of the Suicide Act 1961 (encouraging or assisting suicide) (see **2.7.1**);
  - ◆ offences under s 4(1) (assisting offenders) or s 5(1) (accepting or agreeing to accept consideration for not disclosing information about a relevant offence) of the Criminal Law Act 1967.
- This section also applies to low-value shoplifting as defined by the Magistrates' Courts Act 1980, s 22A (see **1.4.4**).

More than merely preparatory (see 'Explanatory notes' below)

Explanatory notes

- Therefore, a person may attempt an offence that is either indictable or triable either way. However, offences that are 'summary only' cannot be attempted.
- Whether an act is more than merely preparatory to the commission of an offence is ultimately for the jury/court to decide. However, two tests have been set out over the years and have been accepted by the higher courts. These are:
  - ◆ the decision in *Davey v Lee* (1967) 51 Cr App R 303: the offence of attempt is complete if the defendant does an act which is a step towards the commission of the specific crime, which is immediately (and not just remotely) connected with the commission of it, the doing of which cannot reasonably be regarded as having any other purpose than the commission of the specific crime.
- Remember—a criminal **attempt** is not the same as having the **intent** to commit the offence. If an act is only preparatory (eg obtaining an insurance claim form to make a false claim), then it is not an attempt. There would have to be some other act such as actually filling the form out and posting it. Mere intent is not enough.

Related cases

R v Tosti and White [1997] EWCA Crim 222 The defendants were trying to break into premises and it was held that the first action to that end was the examination of the padlock. This amounted to an act that was more than merely preparatory to the commission of the substantive offence (burglary).

R v Shivpuri [1986] UKHL 2, HL The defendant was arrested by customs officers in possession of a suitcase in which he believed he had hidden heroin. The 'drugs' turned out to be harmless powder, but by receiving and hiding the powder in the suitcase, he had completed an act that was more than merely preparatory to the commission of the offence. The court held that the defendant was guilty of attempting to import heroin—even by attempting what was impossible—under s 1(2).

Practical considerations

- Criminal attempt offences can only occur where the principal offence is either an indictable offence or one that is triable either way.
- Even though damage under £5,000 can be dealt with at magistrates' court, a suspect can still be charged with attempting to damage property under £5,000, because the attempted damage offence is still an 'either way' offence. It is not a purely summary offence in the normal sense (*R v Bristol Justices, ex parte Edgar* [1998] 3 All ER 798).
- Where a person commits the full offence of aid, abet, counsel, or procure, the offender should be charged as principal to the main offence where the offence is indictable or either way (Accessories and Abettors Act 1861, s 8).
- When investigating attempted murder consideration must be given to the CPS advice offered in the assault charging standards (see **'Assault' 2.1** and **'Murder' 2.7.1**).
- Powers of arrest, search, mode of trial, penalty, and time limits are the same as those relating to the principal offence.
- Consider confiscation of cash and property for an offence of attempting, conspiring, or inciting, the commission of a 'criminal lifestyle' offence under Sch 2 to the Proceeds of Crime Act 2002 (see **5.5.** for details).

E&S

CHAR Where substantive theft/sexual offences apply

TRIG Only in relation to attempt of the following offences—
- **Theft**—s 1 (see **3.1**)
- **Robbery**—s 8 (see **3.2**)
- **Burglary**—s 9 (see **3.3.1**)
- **Handling stolen goods**—s 22 (see **3.5**)
- **Fraud**—s 1 (see **3.8.1**)

 As principal offence   As principal offence

 As principal offence

4.1.2 **Meaning of intent**

The *mens rea*, which is Latin for 'guilty mind', must be proved—more so in 'attempts' than in any other offence.

Intent

This can be proved by drawing on various sources of information:

- admissions made by the defendant in interview which reveal their state of mind at the time of commission of the offence;
- answers given by the defendant to questions regarding their actions and intentions at the time of the offence;
- by inference from the circumstances of the offence;
- evidence from witnesses;
- actions of the defendant before, during, and after the event, and property found on them or in their control (such as a vehicle for transporting property).

To prove intent, you need to take all the above into account. However, the important thing is that you must **prove** the defendant's **state of mind** at the time. A jury/magistrates' court must consider the circumstances and decide whether the defendant would have intended or foreseen the results which occurred by way of a subjective test.

> **Statutory test**
>
> A court or jury in determining whether a person has committed an offence—
> (a) shall not be bound by law to infer that he intended or foresaw a result of his actions by reason only of its being a natural and probable consequence of those actions; but
> (b) shall decide whether he did intend or foresee that result by reference to all the evidence, drawing such inferences from the evidence as appear proper in the circumstances.
>
> Criminal Justice Act 1967, s 8

Subjective/objective tests

The difference between 'objective' and 'subjective' tests are important here. *Black's Law Dictionary* defines the terms as:

- *Objective*: 'of, relating to, or based on externally verifiable phenomena, as opposed to an individual's perceptions, feelings, or intentions'. This is sometimes used in the context of the 'reasonable person' test—what would a reasonable man or woman perceive to be the rights or wrongs of the matter in question or the likely outcome?
- *Subjective*: 'based on an individual's perceptions, feelings, or intentions, as opposed to externally verifiable phenomena'. In a legal context, this is the opposite of objective. Instead of the hypothetical reasonable person, subjectivity requires a court to establish whether the offender was in fact conscious of a risk or other factor.

Strict liability

For some rare criminal offences, 'strict liability' will be enough to secure a conviction. The liability for committing this type of offence does not depend on an intention (such as causing harm) or state of mind (eg recklessness), but is based on the breach of a duty. Beyond road traffic offences, the occasions where strict liability offences will be encountered by police officers are few.

4.1.3 **Meaning of aid, abet, counsel, and procure**

To be convicted as an 'aider or abettor' a person must have knowledge of all the circumstances that constitute the offence. Whether the 'aider' realises that the circumstances constitute an offence is immaterial.

> **Offences**
>
> Whosoever shall aid, abet, counsel or procure the commission of any indictable offence whether the same be an offence at common law or by virtue of any Act passed or to be passed, shall be liable to be tried, indicted and punished as a principal offender.
>
> Accessories and Abettors Act 1861, s 8

Aid

This means to provide help or assistance to a principal offender, whether before or at the time of committing the offence.

Abet

This is somewhat difficult to describe, but abetting could include where an individual incites, instigates, or encourages the principal to commit the offence.

Counsel

This means to advise or solicit the commission of an offence.

Procure

Lord Widgery described this as 'to produce by endeavour'. It has also been defined as 'obtaining by care and effort'. A course of action is procured by setting out to see that it happens and taking the appropriate steps to produce that happening. A causal link must be established between what the procurer did and what the principal did.

Explanatory notes

- Section 44 of the Magistrates' Courts Act 1980 provides that it is an offence to aid, abet, counsel, or procure any offence that is triable summarily, including either way offences (unless specifically excluded by statute).

- Section 4 of the Criminal Law Act 1967 creates an offence of assisting a person who has committed a 'relevant' offence (see **4.1.1**) i.e. one to which s 1 of the Criminal Attempts Act 1981 applies.

4.1.4 **Encourage, assist, or accessory to commit crime**

Part 2 (ss 44–67) of the Serious Crime Act 2007 abolishes the common law offence of incitement and creates three encouraging or assisting crime offences. This area of law is far too wordy and involved to give full details here, but the relevant law is discussed to develop an understanding of the key issues as to what is involved.

Offences

A person commits an offence if—

(a) he does an act capable of encouraging or assisting the commission of an offence; and

(b) he intends to encourage or assist its commission.

Serious Crime Act 2007, s 44(1)

Points to prove

✓ did an act which was capable of encouraging or assisting

✓ in the commission of an offence namely (*detail offence*)

✓ intending to

✓ encourage or assist in its commission

Meanings

Does an act

This includes a reference to a course of conduct.

Capable of encouraging or assisting

(1) A reference in this Part to a person's doing an act that is capable of encouraging the commission of an offence includes a reference to his doing so by threatening another person or otherwise putting pressure on another person to commit the offence.

(2) A reference in this Part to a person's doing an act that is capable of encouraging or assisting the commission of an offence includes a reference to his doing so by—

(a) taking steps to reduce the possibility of criminal proceedings being brought in respect of that offence;

(b) failing to take reasonable steps to discharge a duty.

(3) But a person is not to be regarded as doing an act that is capable of encouraging or assisting the commission of an offence merely because he fails to respond to a constable's request for assistance in preventing a breach of the peace.

Serious Crime Act 2007, s 65

Encouraging or assisting commission of an offence

Reference in Pt 2 to encouraging or assisting the commission of an offence is to be read in accordance with s 47.

Intends (see **4.1.2**)

Explanatory notes

- A person is not taken to have intended to encourage or assist the commission of an offence merely because such encouragement or assistance was a foreseeable consequence of that person's act.
- If a person (D1) arranges for a person (D2) to do an act that is capable of encouraging or assisting the commission of an offence, and D2 does the act, D1 is also to be treated for the purposes of this Part as having done it.
- **Section 47** provides further meanings, assumptions, and sets out what is required to prove intent or belief and whether an act would amount to the commission of an offence.

Accessory to an offence

Being an accessory to an offence can occur in three ways:

1. An accessory **before the fact** (a person who counsels or procures the commission of a crime) (see **4.1.3**). Also, the offences of encouraging and assisting an offender (ss 44–49 of the Serious Crime Act 2007) and the offence of conspiracy under s 1 of the Criminal Law Act 1977.

2. Someone involved with the principal in a **joint enterprise**. Though not committing the crime itself, the person is involved with the principal offender to a greater or lesser degree at the time of the crime. If involved in that way, he is said to have secondary liability.

3. An accessory **after the fact** (now replaced by the offence of 'assisting an offender' under s 4 of the Criminal Law Act 1967), which states that where a person has committed a relevant offence, any other person who knowing or believing him to be guilty of the offence or some other relevant offence, does without lawful authority or reasonable excuse, any act, with intent to impede his apprehension or prosecution shall be guilty of an offence. (For more information, see www.pnld.co.uk, document reference D5930.)

For an accessory involved at the time of the offence as a **joint enterprise** (known as the doctrine of 'parasitic accessory liability') the Supreme Court in the case of *R v Jogee; R v Ruddock* in 2016 is the leading precedent on this subject (see related cases below).

Defences of acting reasonably

(1) A person is not guilty of an offence under this Part if he proves—
   (a) that he knew certain circumstances existed; and
   (b) that it was reasonable for him to act as he did in those circumstances.

(2) A person is not guilty of an offence under this Part if he proves—
   (a) that he believed certain circumstances to exist;
   (b) that his belief was reasonable; and
   (c) that it was reasonable for him to act as he did in the circumstances as he believed them to be.

(3) Factors to be considered in determining whether it was reasonable for a person to act as he did include—
   (a) the seriousness of the anticipated offence (or, in the case of an offence under section 46, the offences specified in the indictment);
   (b) any purpose for which he claims to have been acting;
   (c) any authority by which he claims to have been acting.

Serious Crime Act 2007, s 50

Related cases

R v Jogee; R v Ruddock [2016] UKSC 8 The Supreme Court was asked to review the doctrine of parasitic accessory liability where defendants had acted in a joint enterprise. The case came as the result of two appeals against convictions for murder. The doctrine had previously been laid down by the Privy Council in 1985 in the case of *Chan Wing Siu v R*. In that case it was held that if two people set out to commit an offence and in the course of that joint enterprise the first person committed another offence, the second person would be guilty as an accessory to the other offence if he had *foreseen the possibility* that the first person might act as he did. It was held by the Supreme Court that the principle in Chan Wing Siu could not be supported and that the mental threshold to establish guilt was too low. It must be proved that the defendant *intended* that the offence should be committed and that mere foresight of what another might do was not enough.

Practical considerations

- Other sections worthy of note in Pt 2 of the Act are as follows:
  - ✦ s 45—Encouraging or assisting an offence believing it will be committed;
  - ✦ s 46—Encouraging or assisting offences believing one or more will be committed;
  - ✦ s 47—Proving an offence under Pt 2;
  - ✦ s 48—Further provision as to proving a s 46 offence;
  - ✦ s 49—Supplemental provisions;
  - ✦ s 51—Protective offences: victims not liable;
  - ✦ s 56—Persons who may be perpetrators or encouragers.

- A person may commit an offence under Pt 2 whether or not any offence capable of being encouraged or assisted by his act is committed. MOJ Circular 4/2008 provides further details and guidance on Pt 2 of the Act.
- Consider confiscation of cash and property for an offence under s 44, which is listed as a 'criminal lifestyle' offence under Sch 2 to the Proceeds of Crime Act 2002 (see **5.5** for details). Similarly aiding, abetting, counselling, or procuring the commission of the s 46 offence is also listed under Sch 2.
- For a s 46 offence, a defendant might believe that his conduct would assist in the commission of one or more different offences by another individual without necessarily knowing, or being able to identify, the precise offence or offences which the person to whom he offered encouragement or assistance intended to commit or would commit (*R v Sadique* [2013] EWCA Crim 1150, CA).

 s 46—Indictment   None

 s 44 or s 45—Per anticipated offence   Variable as to trial venue

 ss 44–6—Penalty per anticipated offence, subject to s 58

Links to alternative subjects and offences

4.2 Vehicle Interference and Tampering with a Motor Vehicle

The Criminal Attempts Act 1981 and the Road Traffic Act 1988 creates offences which protect motor vehicles such as vehicle interference and tampering with motor vehicles. Although a defendant may be trying to take a vehicle without the owner's consent, the 1981 Act does not allow 'criminal attempts' for purely summary offences.

4.2.1 Vehicle interference

Offences

(1) A person is guilty of the offence of vehicle interference if he interferes with a motor vehicle or trailer or with anything carried in or on a motor vehicle or trailer with the intention that an offence specified in subsection (2) below shall be committed by himself or some other person.

(2) The offences mentioned in subsection (1) above are—
  (a) theft of the motor vehicle or part of it;
  (b) theft of anything carried in or on the motor vehicle or trailer; and
  (c) an offence under section 12(1) of the Theft Act 1968 (taking a conveyance)

and if it is shown that a person accused of an offence under this section intended that one of those offences should be committed, it is immaterial that it cannot be shown which it was.

Criminal Attempts Act 1981, s 9

Points to prove

✓ interfere with a
✓ motor vehicle/trailer/part of/anything carried in/on it
✓ with intent that an offence of
✓ theft/taking and drive away without consent
✓ should be committed

Meanings

Interferes (see 'Related cases' below)

Motor vehicle

Means a mechanically propelled vehicle intended or adapted for use on a road (see **10.1.3**).

Trailer

Means a vehicle drawn by a motor vehicle (see **10.1.3**).

Intention (see **4.1.2**)

Explanatory notes

This offence 'fits' between the offence of going equipped (an offence which may be committed prior to any contact with a 'conveyance') and the offence of taking a conveyance without the owner's consent or theft (which is dependent on whether an intention to permanently deprive can be established).

Related cases

Reynolds and Warren v Metropolitan Police [1982] Crim LR 831, CC In this case the suspects were seen to look into four vehicles. In each case one of them touched one door handle (not always the driver's door). It was held that there was no case to answer on charges of interfering with vehicles contrary to s 9 of the 1981 Act and that more than looking into vehicles and touching them was necessary.

Practical considerations

- Has the suspect possession of any implements for use in the offence that would not necessarily complete the offence of going equipped?
- Is there any CCTV evidence available?
- Check on the availability of witness evidence for CJA statements.

 Summary   6 months

 3 months' imprisonment and/or a level 4 fine

4.2.2 **Tampering with motor vehicles**

Offences

If while a motor vehicle is on a road or on a parking place provided by a local authority, a person—
(a) gets on to the vehicle, or
(b) tampers with the brake or other part of its mechanism without lawful authority or reasonable cause he is guilty of an offence.

Road Traffic Act 1988, s 25(1)

4.2.2 Tampering with motor vehicles

Points to prove
✓ without lawful authority or reasonable cause
✓ got on to/tampered with
✓ the brakes/other mechanism of a motor vehicle
✓ on a road/parking place provided by local authority

Meanings

Motor vehicle/vehicle (see **10.1.3**)

Road (see **10.1.1**)

Tampers

Means improperly interfering with something.

Other part of its mechanism

Means any mechanical part and not just those of a similar type to the brake.

Explanatory notes
- The motor vehicle must be on a road (see **10.1.1**) and/or on a parking place provided by the local authority.
- It is for the prosecution to prove the above and that the accused got onto or tampered with the motor vehicle without lawful authority or reasonable cause.

Defences
People with lawful authority and reasonable cause will have a defence. Lawful authority might take the form of a police officer or fire-fighter releasing the brake of a vehicle to move it in an emergency.

Practical considerations
- Has the suspect possession of any implements for use in the offence that would not necessarily complete the offence of going equipped?
- Is there any CCTV evidence available?
- Check on the availability of witness evidence for CJA statements.

 Summary   6 months

 Level 3 fine

Links to alternative subjects and offences

4.3 **Taking a Conveyance without Owner's Consent**

The following topic covers three aspects: taking a conveyance without the owner's consent (TWOC), aggravated vehicle-taking, and the taking of pedal cycles. TWOC can also be known as unlawful taking of a motor vehicle (UTMV) or taking and driving away (TDA).

4.3.1 **Taking a conveyance without owner's consent**

Offences

subject to subsections (5) and (6) below, a person shall be guilty of an offence if, without having the consent of the owner or other lawful authority, he takes any conveyance for his own or another's use or, knowing that any conveyance has been taken without such authority, drives it or allows himself to be carried in or on it.

Theft Act 1968, s 12(1)

Points to prove

There are several sets of circumstances depending on the role taken in the offence. Following relates to initial taker only:
- ✓ without the consent
- ✓ of the owner/other lawful authority
- ✓ took a conveyance
- ✓ for own/another's use

Meanings

Owner

If the conveyance is subject to a hiring or hire purchase agreement, this means the person in possession of the conveyance under that agreement.

Takes

Some movement of the conveyance is essential (*R v Bogacki* [1973] 2 All ER 864).

Conveyance

Means any conveyance constructed or adapted for the carriage of a person or persons whether by land, water, or air, **except** that it **does not include** a conveyance constructed or adapted for use only under the control of a person not carried in or on it.

Explanatory notes

- An important point is that the conveyance must be capable of carrying a person. A machine such as a small domestic lawnmower is not a conveyance, but one upon which the operator sits would be.
- A horse is an animal and therefore not 'constructed or adapted', so it is not a 'conveyance'.
- Pedal cycles are catered for in s 12(5) (see **4.3.3**).
- You must prove the use or intended use as a means of transport. If the conveyance is not used in this way (eg pushing a car away from a drive entrance to remove an obstruction), then there is no 'taking'.
- If it is used to ride on while being pushed, then there may be a taking (*R v Bow* [1977] Crim LR 176).
- A dinghy on a trailer that is to be used as a dinghy at some future time is still 'taken' for the taker's/another's own use. Use has been held to mean 'use as a conveyance' and future intended use is sufficient (*R v Marchant and McAllister* (1985) 80 Cr App R 361).
- The term **'carried in or on'** requires some movement of the conveyance. In *R v Miller* [1976] Crim LR 147, a man found sitting in a boat that had been moored was found not guilty of the offence. The normal movement of the waves was deemed insufficient for the ingredients of the offence. However, the vertical movement of a hovercraft would be sufficient, because that is not a 'natural' movement taking place independently of the use of the conveyance.
- The term **'consent of the owner'** does not arise simply on occasions where specific permission has been given. Problems tend to arise where the owner has given some form of conditional consent; case law suggests that if the borrower of a car, for instance, makes a reasonable detour to their journey, then that detour will still be made 'with the consent of the owner'. However, using the conveyance for a wholly or substantially different purpose may well be an offence. This element is also relevant to one of the statutory defences.
- To prove the term **'allows himself'**, it is necessary to show that the defendant knew that the conveyance had been taken without the consent of the owner or other lawful authority. The person may not know that when they get into the conveyance, but if they find out subsequently, they are expected to make some attempt to leave.
- The essential difference between this offence and the offence of theft is that in this offence there is an absence of any intention to permanently deprive the owner of their property.

Defences

A person does not commit an offence under this section by anything done in the belief that he has lawful authority to do it or that he would have the owner's consent if the owner knew of his doing it and the circumstances of it.

Theft Act 1968, s 12(6)

Defence notes

- The prosecution must prove that the defendant did not believe that they had lawful authority (such as a police or local authority power of removal, or repossession by a finance company).
- Apart from the belief that the owner would have consented if they had known of the using of the conveyance, it must also be shown that they believed that the owner would have consented had they known of the circumstances of the taking and the using of it.

Related cases

R v Vaid [2015] EWCA Crim 298 In this case it was held that DNA evidence taken from an airbag after a vehicle had been involved in a collision to establish who had been driving at the time was admitted in offences of TWOC and dangerous driving.

R v Marchant and McAllister (1985) 80 Cr App R 361, CA The defendants were seen by police officers to push a car a few feet from where its owner had parked it. They were arrested and charged with taking the vehicle without the owner's consent. The owner did not realise it had been moved until told by police. It was held that even though the car had not been used, it had been taken and it had been intended for 'his own or another's use'.

Whittaker v Campbell [1983] 3 All ER 582, QBD In this case, the suspect did not have a driving licence. He found one belonging to someone else and then used it as false evidence of identity to hire a vehicle in the name shown on the licence. He was stopped by the police and charged and first convicted with taking a conveyance. On appeal, his conviction was quashed. It was held that, on the true construction of s 12(1), the consent of the owner of a motor vehicle to its use by another was not vitiated where that consent was obtained fraudulently.

McKnight v Davies [1974] Crim LR 62, CA The defendant was employed as a delivery driver. He damaged the lorry after completing deliveries. He then drove to a pub, took three friends home on the lorry, drove to another pub, then parked near his home. The next morning, he took the lorry back to the yard. It was held that his use of the vehicle exceeded the terms of consent to its use given to him by his employer and as such, committed the offence under s 12. He had 'taken' the vehicle when he left the first pub, as he had then assumed possession in a legal sense.

Practical considerations

- Note that, each deviation from the authorised route should not be regarded as 'taking' for s 12. So long as the driver is still performing the duties s/he is employed to perform, even if in an unauthorised manner, s/he is acting in the character of an employee. When the purpose of the journey is something other than the employer's business, as in this case, then s/he has 'taken' the vehicle.
- Consider stop, search, and seizure powers under s 1 of PACE (see **1.3.2**).
- If on the trial of an indictment for theft of a conveyance, the jury are not satisfied that the accused committed theft, they may find the accused guilty of the s 12(1) offence.
- As the offence is only summary, there is no such thing as an 'attempted taking of a conveyance' (see **4.1.1**).
- Consider the more serious offence of aggravated vehicle-taking (see **4.3.2**).
- In the interview, the situation where the person becomes aware that the conveyance has been taken after they had entered it should be covered along with any subsequent efforts to leave the conveyance.
- The Act allows for the extension of **prosecution time limits**, where proceedings shall not be commenced after the end of the period of three years beginning with the day on which the offence was committed. Subject to the three-year maximum period, proceedings may be commenced at any time within the period of six months beginning with the **relevant day**.
- The '**relevant day**' means the day on which sufficient evidence is available to justify proceedings.

 Summary

 Complex—see '**Prosecution time limits**' in '**Practical considerations**' above

 6 months' imprisonment and/or a fine. Discretionary disqualification.

4.3.2 **Aggravated vehicle-taking**

Section 12A of the Theft Act 1968 creates the various offences of 'aggravated vehicle-taking'.

Offences

(1) Subject to subsection (3) *[defence]* a person is guilty of aggravated taking of a vehicle if—
    (a) he commits an offence under section 12(1) (taking a conveyance without consent) (in this section referred to as the 'basic offence') in relation to a mechanically propelled vehicle, and
    (b) it is proved that, at any time after the vehicle was unlawfully taken (whether by him or another) and before it was recovered, the vehicle was driven, or injury or damage was caused, in one or more of the circumstances set out in paragraphs (a) to (d) of subsection (2).

(2) The circumstances referred to in subsection (1)(b) are—
    (a) that the vehicle was driven dangerously on a road or other public place;
    (b) that, owing to the driving of the vehicle, an accident occurred by which injury was caused to any person;
    (c) that, owing to the driving of the vehicle, an accident occurred by which damage was caused to any property, other than the vehicle;
    (d) that damage was caused to the vehicle.

Theft Act 1968, s 12A

Points to prove

✓ without the consent
✓ of the owner/other lawful authority
✓ took (being the initial taker)
✓ a mechanically propelled vehicle for
✓ own/another's use
✓ (The 'basic offence')

And after it was taken and before it was recovered—

✓ the vehicle was driven dangerously on a road/public place **or**
✓ accident which caused injury to person(s), damage to any property or the vehicle

Meanings

Dangerously (see **10.7.1**)

A vehicle is driven dangerously if:
• it is driven in a way which falls far below what would be expected of a competent and careful driver; **and**

- it would be obvious to a competent and careful driver that driving the vehicle in that way would be dangerous.

Accident

Means 'any unintended occurrence which has an adverse physical result' and the legislation does not specify that it must occur on a road or even in a public place.

Damage

Means any damage not just criminal damage.

Explanatory notes

- 'Owner' has the same meaning as s 12(1) (see **4.3.1**).
- Consider the offence of dangerous driving (see **10.7.1**).
- A vehicle is recovered when it is restored to its owner or to other lawful possession or custody.
- A vehicle has been recovered once the police, owner, or some other person with the authority of the owner, takes responsibility for the vehicle. However, if the police have been informed of the location of a taken vehicle, it has yet to be decided whether 'recovered' is from the time of the call or the time the police arrive at the scene and take physical control.
- This offence only applies to mechanically propelled vehicles and not to all conveyances.
- Passengers in a vehicle involved in such an offence can also be liable to prosecution. Their culpability would be increased depending upon the extent or degree of encouragement they may have given to the driver.

Defences

A person is not guilty of an offence under this section if he proves that, as regards any such proven driving, injury or damage as is referred to in subsection (1)(b) (aggravating factors) above, either—

(a) the driving, accident or damage referred to above occurred before he committed the basic offence; or

(b) he was neither in, nor on, nor in the immediate vicinity of, the vehicle when that driving, accident or damage occurred.

Theft Act 1968, s 12A(3)

Related cases

R v Taylor [2016] UKSC 5 In this case it was held that for an offence under s 12A and the circumstances listed in subsections (2)(b) and (c), there must be at least some act or omission in the control of the car which involves some element of fault in the driving that is more than minimal to contribute to the accident. The driving alone could not be said to be the cause of the accident if it merely explains how the vehicle came to be in the place where the accident occurred.

4.3.3 Take pedal cycle without owner's consent

R v Wheatley and another [2007] EWCA Crim 835, CA In this case it was held that passengers can also be criminally liable, and the degree of their culpability will depend upon the amount of encouragement they give the actual driver of the vehicle.

Dawes v DPP [1995] 1 Cr App R 65, QBD The defendant was arrested after unlawfully taking a vehicle that had been set up by the police with a device which automatically secured the car preventing his escape. During the short time before being arrested the defendant damaged the car trying to get out. It was held that the subsequent damage caused was sufficient to create an offence under s 12A.

Practical considerations

- The fact that the person who originally took the vehicle is not the person who caused the accident resulting in personal injury is irrelevant—the initial taker can still be prosecuted for the aggravated offence. Nor is there any requirement that the driver of the 'taken vehicle' must be at fault when a personal injury accident occurs (*R v Marsh* [1996] 8 CL 54).
- Always bear in mind the above defences when interviewing.
- The aggravated offence never becomes statute-barred as it is an either way offence. Even if the damage caused is under £5,000 and the offence is triable only summarily, it is still an either way offence.
- By virtue of s 12A(5), a person who is found not guilty of this offence can still be found guilty of taking a vehicle without consent as an alternative.

 Either way   None

 Summary: 6 months' imprisonment and/or a fine

Indictment: 2 years' imprisonment, **but** where a person dies as a result of an accident involving the offence, 14 years' imprisonment
Obligatory disqualification—licence endorsed 3 to 11 penalty points

4.3.3 Take pedal cycle without owner's consent

Taking or riding a pedal cycle without the consent of the owner or other lawful authority is an offence.

Offences

Taking a conveyance shall not apply in relation to pedal cycles; but, subject to subsection (6) below *[defences]*, a person who, without having the consent of the owner or other lawful authority takes a pedal cycle for his own or another's use, or rides a pedal cycle knowing it to have been taken without such authority, shall be guilty of an offence.

Theft Act 1968, s 12(5)

Points to prove

- ✓ without consent of the owner/lawful authority
- ✓ takes/rides
- ✓ pedal cycle
- ✓ for own or other's use

Explanatory notes

- A pedal cycle is neither propelled by mechanical power nor is it electrically assisted.
- There are many types of 'hybrid' vehicles, such as motorised scooters, that may qualify as mechanically propelled vehicles or conveyances. Ultimately this is a question of fact for the court to decide.

Defences (see **4.3.1**)

Practical considerations

- The prosecution must prove that the accused did not have lawful authority, such as a police or local authority power of removal, or repossession by a finance company.
- As this is a summary offence, there is no offence of 'attempting to take a pedal cycle' (see **4.1.1**).

 Summary   6 months

 Level 3 fine

Links to alternative subjects and offences

4.4 **Criminal Damage**

The offence of criminal damage is designed to protect people's property from the unlawful actions of others. Section 1 of the Criminal Damage Act 1971 creates the offence of simple 'criminal damage'.

Offences

A person who without lawful excuse destroys or damages any property belonging to another intending to destroy or damage any such property or being reckless as to whether any such property would be destroyed or damaged shall be guilty of an offence.

Criminal Damage Act 1971, s 1(1)

Points to prove

- ✓ without lawful excuse
- ✓ destroyed/damaged
- ✓ property to value of
- ✓ intending to
- ✓ destroy/damage such property or
- ✓ being reckless whether it was destroyed/damaged

Meanings

Destroyed

Means property which is incapable of being repaired and can only be replaced.

Damaged

Means property that has suffered some physical harm, impairment, or deterioration.

Property (s 10(1))

Means property of a tangible nature, whether real or personal, including money and:

(a) wild creatures which have been tamed or are ordinarily kept in captivity, and any other wild creatures or their carcasses if, but only if, they have been reduced into possession which has not been lost or abandoned or are in the course of being reduced into possession; but

(b) not including mushrooms growing wild on any land or flowers, fruit, or foliage of a plant growing wild on any land.

4.4 Criminal Damage

Belonging to another

This is property that belongs to another person who has custody or control of it, or who has a right or an interest in it or has a charge over it.

Intending (see **4.1.2**)

Reckless

The test set out in *R v G and R* [2003] UKHL 50 applies, which states that a person acts 'recklessly' for the purposes of s 1 with respect to:

- circumstances where that person is aware of a risk that exists or will exist;
- a result when they are aware of a risk that it will occur;
  and it is, in the circumstances known to them, unreasonable to take the risk.

The **first part** provides for those existing or future circumstances known to the defendant which, in the circumstances as known to them, made it unreasonable to take the risk they took. An example would be a tramp taking shelter in a barn full of dry hay: aware of the risk they light a fire to boil water for a cup of tea and set the barn alight.

The **second part** of the test applies if the person is aware that the result of their actions is a risk and, in the circumstances as known to them, it would be unreasonable to take that risk. An example would be an adult who lets off a large rocket and ignores instructions which state that the firework should be launched from a tube embedded in the ground and instead launches it from a bottle standing upright on the pavement. As a result, the rocket goes through the window of a house opposite and causes a fire.

The case of *G and R* involved two children aged 11 and 12 who set fire to a shop when lighting newspapers in a yard at the back. It was argued in their defence that, although the act might have been an obvious risk to the average person, it might not be obvious to such young children. The House of Lords agreed and overturned the previous '**objective**' test in the case of *R v Caldwell* [1981] 1 All ER 961.

Explanatory notes

The important thing to prove or disprove (in addition to the damage itself) is the state of mind (intent) or that they were reckless in their actions, in destroying/damaging the property.

Defences

Lawful excuse

(1) This section applies to any offence under section 1(1) and any offence under section 2 or 3 other than one involving a threat by the person charged to destroy or damage property in a way which he knows is likely to endanger the life of another or involving an intent by the person charged to use or cause or permit the use

of something in his custody or under his control so to destroy or damage property.

(2) A person charged with an offence to which this section applies shall, whether or not he would be treated for the purposes of this Act as having a lawful excuse apart from this subsection, be treated for those purposes as having a lawful excuse—

   (a) if at the time of the act or acts alleged to constitute the offence he believed that the person or persons whom he believed to be entitled to consent to the destruction of or damage to the property in question had so consented, or would have so consented to it if he or they had known of the destruction or damage and its circumstances; or

   (b) if he destroyed or damaged or threatened to destroy or damage the property in question or, in the case of a charge of an offence under section 3, intended to use or cause or permit the use of something to destroy or damage it, in order to protect property belonging to himself or another or a right or interest in property which was or which he believed to be vested in himself or another, and at the time of the act or acts alleged to constitute the offence he believed—

      (i) that the property, right or interest was in immediate need of protection; and

      (ii) that the means of protection adopted or proposed to be adopted were or would be reasonable having regard to all the circumstances.

(3) For the purposes of this section it is immaterial whether a belief is justified or not if it is honestly held.

Protect life or property

(4) For the purposes of subsection (2) above a right or interest in property includes any right or privilege in or over land, whether created by grant, licence or otherwise.

(5) This section shall not be construed as casting doubt on any defence recognised by law as a defence to criminal charges.

Criminal Damage Act 1971, s 5

Defence notes

Damage caused to protect life, prevent injury, or stop unlawful imprisonment of a person is also a valid defence (*R v Baker and Wilkins* [1997] Crim LR 497, CA).

Related cases

R v Jones and others; Ayliffe and others v DPP; Swain v DPP [2006] UKHL 16, HL The defendants took part in protests at military bases against the war in Iraq and damaged the perimeter fence and vehicles. It was claimed that the damage done was to prevent the international crime of aggression and so was a 'lawful excuse' under s 5. It was held that the right of citizens to use force or cause damage on their own initiative is limited when not defending their own person or property and furthermore it does not cover customary international law.

Chamberlain v Lindon [1998] 2 All ER 538, QBD The requirement of immediacy (under s 5(2)(b)(i) above) will still be satisfied if the threat to property (or rights in property) is already taking place. In this case, the defendant was charged with criminal damage after destroying a wall erected by his neighbour which obstructed a right of access to his property. It was held that the defendant had a lawful excuse for his action because the obstruction to his rights had already happened and he believed rights would be further prejudiced if the wall remained in place.

Johnson v DPP [1994] Crim LR 673, QBD The defendant was a squatter and damaged a door in a house which he was occupying by chiselling off the locks and replacing them with his own. He was charged with criminal damage but his defence was that he had lawful excuse under s 5(2)(b). The appeal against conviction was rejected. It was held that when lawful excuse is the defence, two questions need to be asked. The first is an objective question (eg whether the act of damage was done to protect property); *and* second, a subjective question (whether the defendant believed that the property was in immediate need of protection and the means of protection used were reasonable).

Practical considerations

- Consider stop, search, and seizure powers under s 1 of PACE (see **1.3.2**).
- If property has been destroyed, the value specified in the charge should reflect the full replacement cost.
- Charging that property was both 'destroyed' and 'damaged' is an unnecessary duplication, so wherever possible a choice should be made.
- Consider applying for a warrant (under s 6) to search for and seize anything in custody or control of suspect on their premises.
- If the destruction or damage has been caused by fire, an offence of arson under s 1(3) should be charged (see **4.5.2**).
- Consider the more serious offence of racially or religiously aggravated criminal damage (see **7.10**).
- PACE Code E para 3.1(a)(iii) provides exemption from the requirement to audio record interviews that are undertaken elsewhere than at a police station for certain indictable offences that includes where a person has been cautioned for criminal damage to property contrary to s 1(1). This exemption is subject to a number of conditions, but the suspect must be aged 18 years or over and does not require an appropriate adult, the value of the damage must not exceed £300, and the suspect is not employed (whether paid or not) by the person, company, or organisation to which the property belongs. (See **Code E** for full details.)
- The above exemption to audio record interviews applies to an attempt to commit the offence under s 1 Criminal Attempts Act 1981 (see **4.1.1**).

- Consider issuing a PND if damage value is below £300 (see **7.1.1**).
- If the full offence is not committed, consider attempt at criminal damage (see **4.1**).
- The same incident may involve separate activities, some causing ordinary damage and some damage by fire (eg protestors break into a laboratory building, smash laboratory equipment, and set fire to some files). In such circumstances, they are separate offences and best charged as such.
- There is a special offence of criminal damage to an ancient monument under the Ancient Monuments and Archaeological Areas Act 1979, s 28. The advantage of using this offence is that the owner can also be liable for damaging the protected monument which they own.
- Consider the offences of having an article with intent to commit damage (see **4.7**) or making threats to cause damage (see **4.6**).

 Either way None

 Summary: *Value below* £5,000—3 months' imprisonment and/or a level 4 fine. *Value* £5,000 *or above*—6 months' imprisonment and/or a fine

Indictment: 10 years' imprisonment

Links to alternative subjects and offences

4.5 Damage with Intent to Endanger Life and Arson

Damage with intent to endanger life is also known as aggravated damage. This and arson are serious offences because of their potential to have disastrous effects on other people's lives and the wider community.

This section is presented in two parts: damage with intent to endanger life and then arson.

4.5.1 Damage with intent to endanger life

Section 1(2) of the Criminal Damage Act 1971 creates the serious offence of destroying or damaging property intending that or being reckless as to whether life would be endangered.

Offences

A person who without lawful excuse, destroys or damages any property, whether belonging to himself or another—

(a) intending to destroy or damage any property or being reckless as to whether any property would be destroyed or damaged; and

(b) intending by the destruction or damage to endanger the life of another or being reckless as to whether the life of another would be thereby endangered;

shall be guilty of an offence.

Criminal Damage Act 1971, s 1(2)

Points to prove

✓ without lawful excuse
✓ destroy/damage
✓ property
✓ whether belonging to self or another
✓ with intent destroy/damage or reckless destroy/damage and
✓ intending by destruction/damage to endanger life of another or
✓ being reckless as to whether such life would thereby be endangered

Meanings

Lawful excuse (see 'Defences' below)

Intent (see 4.1.2)

Destroy (see **4.4**)

Damage (see **4.4**)

Property (see **4.4**)

Belonging to another (see **4.4**)

Endanger life

Does not require an attempt to kill or injury to occur. It is sufficient that life was endangered.

Reckless (see **4.4**)

Explanatory notes

- Consider attempted murder or manslaughter (see **4.1**. and **2.7**).
- No actual injury need occur; all that is required is evidence that life was endangered. For example, if a jealous person cuts the brake pipe of his rival's car, no harm may come to the intended victim, but the potential for harm exists. Either intention to endanger the life of another or recklessness in that regard must be proved and the potential for harm to someone other than the defendant must be proved.
- The actual damage caused must also be the cause of the danger. For example, shooting at a person in a room (through a window) both endangers life and damages the window, but it is not the damage that endangers the life.

Defences

- Lawful excuse could be attempting to effect, a rescue to save life, but in doing so it could endanger life.
- Statutory lawful excuse defence for damage given in s 5 (see **4.4**) specifically precludes damage with intent to endanger life and arson.

Related cases

R v Wenton [2010] EWCA Crim 2361, CA The defendant smashed a dwelling house window, after which an open can of petrol was thrown through the window along with a piece of paper that had been set alight. The petrol spilled, but did not ignite, so there was no fire. The house had a family with children living in it at the time of the attack. The defendant was charged and convicted of the s 1(2) offence. However, on appeal, it was held that any endangerment to life must directly arise from the act of damage/destruction. The damage to the window was unrelated to the incident which gave rise to the risk of danger to life and consequently the appeal was allowed and the conviction quashed.

R v Webster and others [1995] 2 All ER 168, CA In this case, a coping stone was pushed from a bridge onto a moving train. It landed on top of a carriage, piercing through the outer skin, showering the passengers with debris. However, no one was injured. The defendants were charged and convicted of 'damage with intent to endanger life'. It was held that where the intention was for the stone to injure the passengers the damage caused was not relevant and that the correct offence was 'recklessness causing damage which could endanger life'.

Practical considerations

- The same incident may involve separate activities, some causing ordinary damage and some damage by fire (eg protestors break into a laboratory building, smash laboratory equipment, and set fire to files). In such circumstances, they are separate offences and should be charged as such.
- Damage by fire is arson (see **4.5.2**).

 Indictable None

Life imprisonment

4.5.2 **Arson**

Section 1(3) of the Criminal Damage Act 1971 creates the offence of 'arson'.

> ### Offences
>
> An offence committed under this section by destroying or damaging property by fire shall be charged as arson.
>
> Criminal Damage Act 1971, s 1(3)

> ### Points to prove
>
> #### Arson
>
> ✓ without lawful excuse
> ✓ destroy/damage
> ✓ by fire
> ✓ property with intent to destroy/damage it or
> ✓ being reckless whether such property was destroyed/damaged
>
> #### Arson—endanger life
>
> ✓ all points to prove for arson (above) and
> ✓ intending by destruction/damage to endanger life of another or
> ✓ being reckless as to whether such life would be endangered

---

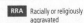

Meanings

Destroy (see 4.4)

Damage (see 4.4)

Property (see 4.4)

Explanatory notes

For the offence to be complete, some of the damage must be by fire; this does not include smoke damage. It is enough, however, that wood is charred (*R v Parker* [1839] 173 ER 733).

Defences

There is no specific defence for arson.

Related cases

R v Drayton [2005] EWCA Crim 2013, CA A charge of causing criminal damage by fire under s 1(3) still constitutes a charge of arson even if 'arson' is not specifically stated in the charge.

Practical considerations

- Intention or recklessness must be proved. A burglar who accidentally dropped a lighted match used for illumination could be reckless.
- The same incident may involve separate activities, some causing ordinary damage and some damage by fire. These are separate offences and should be so charged.
- Most arsons involve the use of **'accelerants'** such as petrol or lighter fuel to start the fire. If it is suspected that accelerants might have been used, special procedures need to be implemented to obtain forensic samples.
- An accelerant is used to increase the speed of a chemical reaction. For police purposes, this usually means something to speed up the spread of a fire during an arson attack. Accelerants (such as petrol) are volatile and will evaporate if left in the open air. Do not confuse accelerants with oils and greases, which demand different treatment.
- Procedures for the careful preservation and packaging which must be carried out to enable the detection of accelerants can be divided into three basic areas:
  - ✦ clothing;
  - ✦ at the scene;
  - ✦ fragile items.
- Submit the control sample of the suspected accelerant in a clean metal container with a well-fitting cap, sealed inside a **nylon bag**. If no metal can is available, use a clean glass container but protect any rubber insert in the cap with a nylon film. For this purpose, cut up part of one of the nylon bags, and use the rest as a control—see below. Isolate from all other samples.

4.5.2 **Arson**

- Control sample of nylon bag used to seal any sample: in a case where a nylon bag has been employed to seal a sample, a control nylon bag from the same batch as the one used to contain the samples should be submitted. This should be sealed but should only contain air.
- Important—never dry out items suspected of containing fire accelerants before packaging. Never store or transport items for examination for the presence of fire accelerant materials near a control sample of fire accelerant or anything taken from the defendant. Even a suspicion of contamination will destroy the evidential value of the samples.

 Either way   None

 Summary: 6 months' imprisonment and/or a fine

Indictment: Life imprisonment

Links to alternative subjects and offences

4.6 **Threats to Destroy or Damage Property**

Section 2 of the Criminal Damage Act 1971 creates specific offences relating to threats to destroy or damage property.

Offences

A person who without lawful excuse makes to another a threat, intending that the other would fear it would be carried out—
(a) to destroy or damage any property belonging to that other or a third person; or
(b) to destroy or damage his own property in a way which he knows is likely to endanger the life of that other or a third person

shall be guilty of an offence.

Criminal Damage Act 1971, s 2

Points to prove

✓ without lawful excuse
✓ threatened to destroy/damage property of a person
✓ intending
✓ a person would fear that the threat would be carried out

Threaten damage to own property to endanger life

✓ without lawful excuse
✓ threatened to destroy/damage
✓ own property
✓ in a way knew
✓ was likely to endanger life of another
✓ intending a person would fear threat would be carried out

Meanings

Lawful excuse (see 'Defences' **4.4**)

Intending (see **4.1.2**)

Destroy (see **4.4**)

Damage (see **4.4**)

Property (see **4.4**)

Endanger life (see **4.5.1**)

Explanatory notes

- It is not necessary to show the other person is in fear that the threat will be carried out; what must be proved is that the defendant intended the other to fear it will be carried out.
- It does not matter that the defendant may not actually intend to carry out the threats and/or the victim may not even believe them. The offender's **intention** to create such a fear is sufficient—and necessary—to complete the offence.
- The test for whether the action amounts to a threat, is objective (ie 'would the reasonable person conclude that a threat had been made?') (*R v Cakmak and others* [2002] EWCA Crim 500). Only intention will do; unlike s 1, there is no mention of 'reckless' in this section.
- The threat must be to another person and can relate to a third party—such as 'I will smash up your son's car if you don't do what I say'—the threat is to one person about their or a third person's property.
- In s 2(b) above, the offender can threaten to damage their own property in a way that is likely to endanger the life of another, such as a landlord threatening to burn down a house he owns if a tenant will not leave.
- In relation to the meaning of 'threats in criminal damage', two points must be considered:
  - ✦ the type of conduct threatened; and
  - ✦ the threat itself.
- There is no specific requirement for the threatened act to be immediate and a threat to do damage to a property at some time in the future may well suffice; each case will depend on the circumstances surrounding it.

Defence

Having a lawful excuse will be a defence under s 5 (see **4.4**).

Related cases

R v Ankerson [2015] EWCA Crim 432, CA The defendant made threats to burn down his estranged wife's house regardless of whether their children were inside or not, and then to burn himself in the town centre. It was held that the intention of the defendant must have been to create a genuine fear that the threat might be carried out, even where the listener was not certain that the threat would be carried out. The critical word was 'fear'. It was enough if the intention was to create in the mind of an objective listener the genuine fear that the threat might be carried out. The listener could have that fear, even where he/she was not certain that the threat would be carried out.

 Either way None

 Summary: 6 months' imprisonment and/or a fine

Indictment: 10 years' imprisonment

Links to alternative subjects and offences

4.7 **Custody/Control of Articles with Intent to Damage and Sale of Paint Aerosols to Persons under 16**

Even when criminal damage has not been committed or threatened, there may be an offence of possessing articles with an intention to cause damage. An offence of selling paint aerosols to children is designed to curb criminal damage to property by way of graffiti.

4.7.1 **Custody/control of articles with intent to damage**

Section 3 of the Criminal Damage Act 1971 creates the offence of 'going equipped' intending to destroy or damage property.

> **Offences**
>
> A person who has anything in his custody or under his control intending without lawful excuse to use it or cause or permit another to use it—
> (a) to destroy or damage any property belonging to some other person or
> (b) to destroy or damage his own or the user's property in a way which he knows is likely to endanger the life of some other person;
> shall be guilty of an offence.
>
> Criminal Damage Act 1971, s 3

Points to prove

- ✓ had in custody/control
- ✓ an article/object/substance/anything at all
- ✓ intending
- ✓ without lawful excuse
- ✓ to destroy/damage or to cause/permit another to use the article, etc
- ✓ property belonging to another/own or user's property knowing life of another is likely to be endangered

Meanings

Anything

Has its natural/everyday meaning and can range from explosives to a box of matches or a hammer.

Custody or control

It must be proved that the defendant had custody or control of the article in question. This is a wider term than possession and could cover occasions where the defendant does not have the article with them.

Intent (see 4.1.2)

Lawful excuse (see 4.4)

Cause

Means some degree of dominance or control, or some express or positive authorisation, from the person who 'causes'.

Permit

Requires general or particular permission, as distinguished from authorisation, and the permission may be express (eg verbal/written) or implied (eg the person's actions). A person cannot permit unless they are in a position to forbid and no one can permit what they cannot control.

Destroy (see 4.4)

Damage (see 4.4)

Property (see 4.4)

Belonging to another (see 4.4)

Endanger life (see 4.5.1)

Explanatory notes

- The offence is split into two parts, but certain elements are common to both. Intent to use/cause/permit must be proved in all cases, as must the element of having anything in the defendant's custody/control and the absence of lawful excuse.
- The act intended does not have to be immediate; it can be at some time in the future (eg someone storing bomb-making materials for future use).
- The only difference between s 3(a) and s 3(b) offences is that in (b) there is an element of knowledge of the likelihood of endangering the life of someone else and the offender's own property can be the object of the intended damage (eg a person carrying a can of petrol to set fire to their own house with their partner inside).

Defence

Having a lawful excuse (see **4.4**).

Related cases

R v Fancy [1980] Crim LR 171, CC The defendant was seen carrying a bucket of white paint and a roller in a crowd of some 25 people. When questioned, he stated that he had been 'white washing' National Front slogans from walls. He admitted that he had no authority or permission to do this and was charged with an offence of having articles to cause damage contrary to s 3. The case was dismissed, and it was held that the prosecution must show that the defendant intended to damage property with the paint and roller. In this case, there might be an element of recklessness involved, but s 3 does not include the concept of recklessness. On these facts, there was no evidence to say that a wall would be damaged.

 Either way   None

Summary: 6 months' imprisonment and/or a fine

Indictment: 10 years' imprisonment

4.7.2 Sale of aerosol paints to children

Section 54 of the Anti-social Behaviour Act 2003 makes it an offence to sell aerosol spray paints to persons under 16, to reduce the incidence of graffiti criminal damage caused by young persons.

Offence

A person commits an offence if he sells an aerosol paint container to a person under the age of sixteen.

Anti-social Behaviour Act 2003, s 54(1)

Points to prove

✓ sale
✓ an aerosol paint container
✓ to a person under the age of 16

Meaning of aerosol paint container

Means a device which contains paint stored under pressure and is designed to permit the release of the paint as a spray.

Defences

(4) It is a defence for a person charged with an offence under this section in respect of a sale to prove that—
   (a) he took all reasonable steps to determine the purchaser's age, and
   (b) he reasonably believed that the purchaser was not under the age of sixteen.
(5) It is a defence for a person charged with an offence under this section in respect of a sale effected by another person to prove that he (the defendant) took all reasonable steps to avoid the commission of an offence under this section.

Anti-social Behaviour Act 2003, s 54

Practical considerations

- You will need to show that the sale was concluded, rather than simply the advertising or negotiating.
- There is no need to prove any intention by the purchaser or any specific knowledge/suspicion of intended knowledge on the part of the seller.
- Age to be proved by birth certificate or valid ID card.

 Summary   6 months

 Level 4 fine

Links to alternative subjects and offences

4.8 Intimidation of a Witness/ Juror and Perverting the Course of Justice

Witnesses and/or jurors involved in the investigation or trial of criminal offences are protected from intimidation and/or threat by s 51 of the Criminal Justice and Public Order Act 1994. This area of law is presented in two parts: intimidation of a witness/juror, and perverting the course of justice.

4.8.1 Intimidation of a witness/juror

Offences

Intimidation

(1) A person commits an offence if—
   (a) he does an act which intimidates, and is intended to intimidate, another person ('the victim'),
   (b) he does the act knowing or believing that the victim is assisting in the investigation of an offence or is a witness or potential witness or a juror or potential juror in proceedings for an offence; and
   (c) he does it intending thereby to cause the investigation or the course of justice to be obstructed, perverted or interfered with.

Threats

(2) A person commits an offence if—
   (a) he does an act which harms, and is intended to harm, another person or, intending to cause another person to fear harm, he threatens to do an act which would harm that other person,
   (b) he does or threatens to do the act knowing or believing that the person harmed or threatened to be harmed ('the victim'), or some other person, has assisted in an investigation into an offence or has given evidence or particular evidence in proceedings for an offence, or has acted as a juror or concurred in a particular verdict in proceedings for an offence; and
   (c) he does or threatens to do it because of that knowledge or belief.

Criminal Justice and Public Order Act 1994, s 51

Points to prove

Intimidate a witness/juror

✓ knew/believed person was
✓ assisting investigation of offence or a witness/potential witness or juror/potential juror
✓ in proceedings for offence
✓ did an act which
✓ intimidated that person and was intended to do so
✓ intending to cause investigation/course of justice to be obstructed or perverted or interfered with

Harm/threaten a witness/juror

✓ knew/believed person or another had assisted in investigation/ given evidence inproceedings/acted as juror/concurred in particular verdict
✓ because of that knowledge/belief
✓ threatened/did an act which
✓ harmed/was intended to harm/would have harmed person

Meanings

Investigation into an offence

Means such an investigation by the police or other person charged with the duty of investigating offences or charging offenders.

Offence

Includes an alleged or suspected offence.

Potential juror

Means a person who has been summonsed for jury service at the court at which proceedings for the offence are pending.

Act intending to intimidate

If, in proceedings against a person for an **offence under subsection (1)**, it is proved that he did an act falling within paragraph (a) with the knowledge or belief required by paragraph (b), he shall be presumed, unless the contrary is proved, to have done the act with the intention required by paragraph (c) of that subsection.

Criminal Justice and Public Order Act 1994, s 51(7)

Intended (see 4.1.2)

Act intending to threaten/harm

In proceedings against a person for an offence under subsection (2) (**threats**) if it can be proved by the prosecution that within the **relevant period** he did or threatened to do an act described by (a) above with the knowledge or belief of (b) above, then he shall be presumed,

---

unless the contrary is proved, to have done the act (or threatened to do the act) with the motive required by (c) above.

Criminal Justice and Public Order Act 1994, s 51(8)

The relevant period

In this section 'the relevant period'—

(a) in relation to a witness or juror in any proceedings for an offence, means the period beginning with the **institution of the proceedings** and ending with the first anniversary of the conclusion of the trial or, if there is an appeal or a reference under s 9 or s 11 of the Criminal Appeal Act 1995, of the conclusion of the appeal;

(b) in relation to a person who has, or is believed by the accused to have, assisted in an investigation into an offence, but was not also a witness in proceedings for an offence, means the period of one year beginning with any act of his, or any act believed by the accused to be an act of his, assisting in the investigation; and

(c) in relation to a person who both has, or is believed by the accused to have, assisted in the investigation into an offence and was a witness in proceedings for the offence, means the period beginning with any act of his, or any act believed by the accused to be an act of his, assisting in the investigation and ending with the anniversary mentioned in paragraph (a) above.

Criminal Justice and Public Order Act 1994, s 51(9)

Institution of proceedings

For the purposes of the definition of the relevant period in subsection (9) above—

(a) proceedings for an offence are instituted at the earliest of the following times:
   (i) when a justice of the peace issues a summons, or warrant under s 1 of the Magistrates' Courts Act 1980 in respect of the offence;
   (ii) when a person is charged with the offence after being taken into custody without a warrant;
   (iii) when a bill of indictment is preferred by virtue of s 2(2)(b) of the Administration of Justice (Miscellaneous Provisions) Act 1933;

(b) proceedings at a trial of an offence are concluded with the occurrence of any of the following, the discontinuance of the prosecution, the discharge of the jury without a finding, the acquittal of the accused or the sentencing of or other dealing with the accused for the offence of which he was convicted; and

(c) proceedings on an appeal are concluded on the determination or abandonment of the appeal.

Criminal Justice and Public Order Act 1994, s 51(10)

Explanatory notes

- For equivalent offences in some civil proceedings see ss 39 and 40 of the Criminal Justice and Police Act 2001.
- In respect of the relevant period, this subsection means that the statutory presumption can only be used during the relevant period. It is still possible to bring a prosecution for this offence many years after that period, but the prosecution will not have the advantage of being able to use this presumption.
- In relation to both offences, it will be immaterial whether the act is (or would be) done, or that the threat is made:
  + otherwise than in the presence of the victim or
  + to a person other than the victim.
- Two cases regarding the above provision have determined the following:
  + Relating to both offences, the person making the threats still commits an offence if they use a third party to convey them to the witness/juror. The 'messenger' could be an innocent agent (eg a victim's relative), who simply passes on a message without understanding its meaning or effect (*A-G's Reference (No 1 of 1999)* [2000] QB 365).
  + The threats can be made by telephone, letter, or by other means. It is not necessary for the offender and victim to be in the same place at the same time (*DPP v Mills* [1996] 3 WLR 1093).
- The harm done or threatened may be financial as well as physical (whether to the person or a person's property) and the same applies regarding any intimidatory act that consists of threats.
- This offence is in addition to, and does not necessarily replace, any offence which currently exists at common law (eg perversion of the course of justice, which is usually charged as an attempt, conspiracy, or incitement).
- Communications that constitute threats to another person may also amount to other offences. Consider threats to kill under s 16 Offences Against the Person Act 1861 (see **2.5**); threats of violence under ss 4 and 4A Protection from Harassment Act 1997 (see **7.11.2**); s 1 malicious Communications Act 1988; and s 127 Communications Act 2003 (see **7.12.1**).

Related cases

R v ZN [2013] EWCA Crim 989, CA It was held in this case that for witness intimidation, the victim must be 'intimidated'. If the victim was not intimidated, then consider an offence of attempting witness intimidation (see **4.8.1**).

Van Colle and another v CC of Hertfordshire [2008] UKHL 50, HL In the absence of special circumstances, the police owed no common law duty of care to protect a witness from harm, unless a threat assessment found the need to warrant further action (*Osman v UK* (1998) 29 EHRR 245, for test in relation to Art 2 claim—see **1.1**).

4.8.2 Perverting the course of justice

R v Singh (B), Singh (C) and Singh (J) [2000] Cr App R 31, CA The defendants visited the victim and threatened him. The men were prosecuted for witness intimidation contrary to s 51(1) (b). It was held that to prove the case, there must be evidence that the investigation had started. This is required as an objective fact under s 51(1)(c). It is not sufficient for the defendant to believe there is an investigation underway.

Practical considerations

* *R v Davis* [2008] UKHL 26 concerned the use of anonymous witness evidence at trial. The House of Lords judgment placed a restriction on the court's ability to allow evidence to be given anonymously during criminal trials; as a result, protection is now provided through s 89 of the Coroners and Justice Act 2009.
* Sections 74–85 of the Coroners and Justice Act 2009 deal with anonymity in criminal investigations for murder/manslaughter where a firearm or knife was used, and the issue of investigation anonymity orders to prohibit disclosure of information to prevent identification of potential witnesses. MOJ Circular 6/2010 provides guidance on these orders.
* Sections 86–97 of the Coroners and Justice Act 2009 concern the anonymity of witnesses, and the issue, discharge, or variation of witness anonymity orders to protect a witness or prevent the identity of a witness in criminal proceedings being disclosed. MOJ Circular 8/2009 provides guidance on these witness anonymity provisions.

E&S

 Either way   None

 Summary: 6 months' imprisonment and/or a fine

Indictment: 5 years' imprisonment and/or a fine

4.8.2 **Perverting the course of justice**

Offences

Committed where a person or persons—
* acts or embarks upon a course of conduct
* which has a tendency to, and
* is intended to pervert,
* the course of public justice.

Common law

Points to prove

✓ with intent to pervert
✓ the course of public justice
✓ do an act/series of acts
✓ tending to pervert course of public justice

Explanatory notes

- Examples where conduct is capable of amounting to this offence are:
  - ◆ making false allegations;
  - ◆ perjury;
  - ◆ concealing offences;
  - ◆ obstructing the police;
  - ◆ assisting others to evade arrest;
  - ◆ failing to prosecute;
  - ◆ procuring and indemnifying sureties;
  - ◆ interference with witnesses, evidence, and jurors;
  - ◆ publication of matters calculated to prejudice a fair trial.
- A positive act is required (eg failing to respond to a summons was insufficient to warrant a charge of perverting the course of justice).
- Any act or course of conduct that tends or is intended to interfere with the course of public justice can amount to an offence. To get a conviction, it is not sufficient to prove that the conduct did, or tended to, pervert the course of justice. The evidence must prove that the offender intended that it would do so.
- It is not necessary for the offender's motives to be the procurement of a false verdict or the defeat of the ends of justice. Trying to introduce genuine evidence by unlawful means is perverting the course of justice (eg a witness takes incriminating photos but refuses to give evidence). Steps are then taken by the investigator to get another witness to introduce them as evidence (*A-G's Reference (No 1 of 2002)* [2002] EWCA Crim 2392).

Related cases

R v T [2011] EWCA Crim 729, CA The defendant deleted child pornography files from a memory stick, intending to prevent a criminal investigation against her husband. It was held that an act which might mislead the police or make their investigation more difficult could pervert the course of justice.

R v Headley (1996) 160 JP 25, CA The defendant was the brother of a man who was stopped by police and asked to produce his driving documents. The brother gave the defendant's details and did not subsequently produce any documents. A summons was issued with the defendant's details on it and he was subsequently convicted and fined in his absence after failing to attend Court. It was held that the defendant had not done any act or embarked on any course of action which could amount to a deliberate attempt to pervert justice. Passive inaction is not sufficient for this offence.

Practical considerations

- Putting the term 'attempting to pervert the course of justice' in a common law indictment was misleading because it is a substantive rather than an inchoate (incomplete) offence. It should be charged as 'doing acts tending and intended to pervert the course of justice' (*R v Williams* (1991) 92 Cr App R 158).
- Perverting the course of justice is usually charged as an attempt, conspiracy, or incitement.
- There has been comment by the courts where this offence has been used for relatively minor attempts to pervert the course of justice and it is charged alongside an offence that is serious enough to permit the offender's conduct to be considered when sentencing for the main offence. In *R v Sookoo* [2002] EWCA Crim 800, a shoplifter had attempted to hide his identity and inevitably failed, the prosecutors should not include a specific count of perverting the course of justice. Such conduct may serve to aggravate the original offence and the judge may increase the sentence as a result. However, in *R v Pendlebury* [2003] EWCA Crim 3426, P gave a positive breath test but a false name to police and had four previous convictions for doing the same thing. He argued that he should not be charged with perverting the course of justice, but it should simply be an aggravating factor. Held that P's conduct was not too trifling to amount to the offence because it was the third occasion on which he had given false particulars against a background of persistent and serious offending.
- A more appropriate use for this offence will be where a great deal of police time and resources are involved in putting the matter right, or there may be cases where innocent members of the public have their names given and they have been the subject of questioning and even detention.

 Indictment   None

 Life imprisonment

Links to alternative subjects and offences

4.9 Slavery and Human Trafficking

Article 4 of the Council of Europe Convention on Action against Trafficking in Human Beings defines **human trafficking** as:

- recruiting, transporting, harbouring or receiving of people;
- by threatening or using:
  - ✦ force or other forms of coercion
  - ✦ abduction
  - ✦ fraud
  - ✦ deception
  - ✦ the abuse of power or a position of vulnerability, or
  - ✦ the giving or receiving of payments or benefits;
- to achieve the consent of a person having control over another person;
- for the purpose of exploitation.

Exploitation shall include, at a minimum, the exploitation of the prostitution of others or other forms of sexual exploitation, forced labour or services, slavery or practices similar to slavery, servitude, or the removal of organs.

Article 10 of the Convention requires the UK to adopt legislative or other measures to identify, support, and protect victims of trafficking.

Article 26 of the Convention requires that the UK allows for the possibility of not imposing penalties on human trafficking victims, if they have been compelled to break the law.

4.9.1 The Modern Slavery Act 2015

The Modern Slavery Act ensures that the National Crime Agency, the police, and other law enforcement agencies have the powers they need to pursue, disrupt, and bring to justice those engaged in human trafficking and slavery, servitude, and forced or compulsory labour. The 2015 Act also introduces measures to enhance the protection of victims of slavery and trafficking.

Sections 1–6 consolidate and simplify existing slavery and trafficking offences into one Act. This aims to provide clarity and focus when investigating and prosecuting those involved in modern slavery offences. It also clarifies important aspects of the existing offences, for example to make it clearer that the offences can be used effectively where the victim is vulnerable, such as a child.

The Act includes two main modern slavery offences and creates a defence for victims.

4.9.2 **Slavery, servitude, and forced or compulsory labour**

Section 1(1) provides an offence of slavery, servitude, and forced or compulsory labour.

Offences

A person commits an offence if—

(a) the person holds another person in slavery or servitude and the circumstances are such that the person knows or ought to know that the other person is held in slavery or servitude, or

(b) the person requires another person to perform forced or compulsory labour and the circumstances are such that the person knows or ought to know that the other person is being required to perform forced or compulsory labour.

Modern Slavery Act 2015 s 1(1)

Points to prove

For s 1(1)(a)

✓ date and location
✓ held person in slavery or servitude
✓ knew or ought to have known that the person was in slavery or solitude

For s 1(1)(b)

✓ date and location
✓ required person to perform forced/compulsory labour
✓ knew or ought to have known that he/she was being required to perform forced/compulsory labour

Explanatory notes

- The s 1 offence is committed where a person holds another person in slavery or servitude or requires another person to perform forced or compulsory labour, and the first person knows or ought to know that the second person is being held in slavery or servitude or is being required to perform forced or compulsory labour. The offence should be interpreted in accordance with Art 4 of the European Convention on Human Rights, which proscribes slavery, servitude, and forced or compulsory labour.

- The personal circumstances of the victim, including any that make the individual more vulnerable, can be considered when assessing whether the offence has taken place.

- An individual's consent to the conduct alleged to amount to slavery, servitude, or forced or compulsory labour does not prevent the offence being committed. This provision could be particularly relevant in cases where the victim is vulnerable to abuse, for example a child.

- In relation to the forced or compulsory labour offence, the court can consider any work or services provided by the person including any work or services provided in circumstances that amount to exploitation under s 3(3)–(6). This makes it clear that the forced and compulsory labour offence can cover a broad range of types of work and services, such as begging or picking pockets, that could amount to exploitation under s 3(5) or s 3(6).
- See HO Circular 024/2015.

4.9.3 **Human trafficking**

Section 2(1) of the Modern Slavery Act 2015 provides for a single offence of human trafficking covering sexual and non-sexual exploitation.

Offence

A person commits an offence if the person arranges or facilitates the travel of another person ('V') with a view to V being exploited.

Modern Slavery Act 2015, s 2(1)

Points to prove

✓ date and location
✓ being a UK national (see '**Explanatory notes**' below regarding non-UK nationals)
✓ **arranged or facilitated** the **travel** of another person with a view to
✓ him or her being **exploited**

Meanings

Travel

This means:
- arriving in, or entering, any country;
- departing from any country;
- travelling within any country.

Arrange or facilitate

Section 2 clarifies that it is irrelevant whether or not V consents to the travel and that, in particular, a person may arrange or facilitate V's travel by recruiting V, transporting or transferring V, harbouring or receiving V, or transferring or exchanging control over V.

Exploit

For the offences in s 2, s 3 defines 'exploit' as including slavery, servitude, and forced or compulsory labour; sexual exploitation; removal of organs; securing services, etc by force, threats, or deception; and securing services, etc from children and vulnerable persons.

Explanatory notes

- Section 2(6) provides that a UK national commits an offence regardless of: where in the world the arranging or facilitating takes place; or the countries of arrival, entry, travel, or departure. For example, a UK national who traffics a person from Spain to France could be prosecuted in England and Wales for this offence.
- Under s 4, committing one offence with a view to going on to commit a trafficking offence under s 2 is a separate offence. Thus, preparatory criminal conduct that constitutes a lesser offence can attract higher penalties. For example, if someone supplies false documents intending them to be used to facilitate human trafficking, or steals a vehicle intending to use it to traffic individuals, that person can be tried *both* for the lesser offence (supplying false documents; vehicle theft) *and* for an offence preparatory to human trafficking.
- A person who is not a UK national commits an offence under this section if:
  (a) any part of the arranging or facilitating takes place in the United Kingdom, or
  (b) the travel consists of arrival in or entry into, departure from, or travel within, the United Kingdom.
- See HO Circular 024/2015.

Related cases

R v Ali and another [2015] EWCA Crim 1279 This case considered (among other issues) the meaning of 'trafficking', in which the defendants were convicted of various sexual offences arising out of the grooming of young girls for sexual purposes. It was held that the key factor was travel and that a journey was contemplated. The fact that the journey might be short did not affect whether the offence had been committed. The legislation does not specify a minimum distance or duration and, therefore, victims could be 'trafficked' within or across a small geographical area.

R (on the application of SF) v Secretary of State for the Home Department [2015] EWHC 2705 (Admin) In determining whether a 17-year-old girl (SF) had been trafficked, it was held that the competent authority had wrongly attached significant weight to a police inspector's conclusion that there was insufficient evidence of trafficking. The decision that SF had not been trafficked had to be quashed, as the CA had failed to take into account the evidence of the experts, fortified by the guidance, relating to the reasons why an honest person who had been trafficked might give inconsistent or late evidence.

Practical considerations

What to look for: indications that a person might be a victim of trafficking

Trafficking victims are often arrested on the following charges:

- cannabis cultivation
- drug importation
- immigration offences
- document offences
- prostitution
- dishonesty offences, including theft, picking pockets, and begging.

The following is a non-exhaustive list of common factors that may also help identify possible victims:

- from a place known to be a source of human trafficking
- possession of false identity or travel documents
- showing signs of fear or anxiety
- exhibiting distrust of the authorities
- evidence of violence or threats of violence
- fear of revealing immigration status
- lack of knowledge of home or work address
- signs that the individual's movements are being controlled or that they are taking instructions from a third party
- inconsistent about name and age.
- Section 7 amends Sch 2 to the Proceeds of Crime Act 2002 (POCA) to make both the s 1 offence (slavery, servitude, and forced or compulsory labour) and the s 2 offence (human trafficking) 'criminal lifestyle' offences (see **5.5**).
- Sections 1 and 2 of the Modern Slavery Act 2015 are being added to the list of either way offences, so a simple caution can only be used in exceptional circumstances and with the agreement of an **Inspector**, in accordance with s 17(3) of the Criminal Justice and Courts Act 2015.
- In relation to the s 2 offence and child sexual exploitation, also consider the Serious Crime Act 2015 s 69(8) (possession of paedophile manual) (see **6.5.1**).
- Sections 11 and 12 of the Modern Slavery Act 2015 allow a senior immigration officer or **constable** to detain a **land vehicle, ship, or aircraft** where a person has been arrested for a s 2 offence (human trafficking) and there are reasonable grounds to believe that a forfeiture order could be made if that person was convicted.

Either way

 None

 For both s 1 and s 2 offences:

> **Summary:** 12 months' imprisonment and/or a fine
> **Indictment:** Life imprisonment

4.9.4 Slavery and trafficking prevention orders on sentencing

Section 14 of the Modern Slavery Act 2015 provides for slavery and trafficking prevention orders ('STPO') on conviction

> A court may make a slavery and trafficking prevention order against a person ("the defendant") where it deals with the defendant in respect of—
>
> (a) a conviction for a slavery or human trafficking offence,
> (b) a finding that the defendant is not guilty of a slavery or human trafficking offence by reason of insanity, or
> (c) a finding that the defendant is under a disability and has done the act charged against the defendant in respect of a slavery or human trafficking offence.
>
> Modern Slavery Act 2015, s 14(1)

Explanatory notes

- The prohibitions that may be included in the order are those which the court is satisfied are necessary for the purpose of protecting persons generally, or particular persons, from the physical or psychological harm which would be likely to occur if the defendant committed a slavery or human trafficking offence.
- Section 14(2) provides that the court may make the order only if it is satisfied that—
  - (a) there is a risk that the defendant may commit a slavery or human trafficking offence, and
  - (b) it is necessary to make the order for the purpose of protecting persons generally, or particular persons, from the physical or psychological harm which would be likely to occur if the defendant committed such an offence.
- A slavery or human trafficking offence means an offence listed in Sch 1 of the Act.
- Section 17 of the Act provides that the STPO may prohibit the defendant from doing things in any part of the United Kingdom, and anywhere outside the United Kingdom and will have effect for

a fixed period of at least five years (save for restrictions on foreign travel) or until a further order is made.

- The STPO is intended to restrict the activity of individuals who have been convicted of a slavery or human trafficking offence, including an equivalent offence in a country outside the UK.
- A court may make an STPO against an individual when sentencing that person for a slavery or human trafficking offence. Alternatively, a **chief officer of police**, an immigration officer, or the Director General of the National Crime Agency can apply to a magistrates' court for an STPO.
- An STPO can be used for individuals under 18. In these cases, the application will be dealt with by a youth court.
- Under s 23 a slavery and trafficking risk order (STRO) can be made by a magistrates' court. The court may make the order only if it is satisfied that the defendant has acted in a way which means that—
  (a) there is a risk that the defendant will commit a slavery or human trafficking offence, and
  (b) it is necessary to make the order for the purpose of protecting persons generally, or particular persons, from the physical or psychological harm which would be likely to occur if the defendant committed such an offence.
- Section 24 gives the effect to an STRO to prohibit the defendant from doing anything described in the order for a fixed period of at least two years, or until a further order is made.

4.9.5 **Defence for victims of slavery or trafficking**

Section 45 of the 2015 Act provides a defence for victims of slavery or trafficking who have committed a criminal offence. The defence is intended to provide further encouragement to victims to come forward and give evidence without fear of being prosecuted and convicted for offences connected to their slave or trafficked status.

The statutory defence set out in s 45 applies a different test in the defence for people aged 18 or over and those under the age of 18. This emphasises that children can be influenced into committing crimes without compulsion being used and reflects DPP guidance.

> **Defence**
>
> For a person under the age of 18 when an act that constitutes an offence is committed, s 45 defence applies where:
> - the child commits the offence as a direct consequence of their being a victim of slavery or relevant exploitation; and

- a reasonable person in the same situation and having the child's relevant characteristics (including their age) would have committed the offence.

Where a person is aged 18 or over when an act that constitutes an offence is committed, s 45 defence applies where that person:
- commits the offence because they were compelled to do so;
- was compelled as a result of slavery or relevant exploitation (compulsion is further defined at s 45(3)); and
- a reasonable person in the same situation and having the relevant characteristics would have committed the offence.

Defence note

See 'Criminal prosecutions of victims of trafficking', Law Society Practice Notes, 29 October 2015.

4.9.6 **Duty to notify the Home Office of suspected victims of modern slavery**

Section 52 introduced a duty to notify the Home Office about suspected victims of slavery or human trafficking. Potential victims should be referred to the National Referral Mechanism (NRM). The duty is placed on specified public authorities to which the section applies and is triggered where that authority has reasonable grounds to believe that a person may be a victim of slavery or human trafficking.

Explanatory notes

- The public authorities to which the duty applies currently include a chief officer of police for a police area, the Chief Constable of the British Transport Police, the National Crime Agency, and council authorities.
- The NRM team has a target date of five working days from receipt of referral in which to decide whether there are reasonable grounds to believe the individual is a potential victim of human trafficking. This may involve seeking additional information from the first responder or from specialist non-governmental organisations, social services, or the individual's legal representative.
- See HO Circular 025/2015.

4.9.6 Duty to notify the Home Office

Links to alternative subjects and offences

4.10 Ill-treatment or Neglect by a Care Worker

It is an offence for an individual who has the care of another individual by virtue of being a care worker to ill-treat or wilfully to neglect that individual.

Criminal Justice and Courts Act 2015, s 20(1) and (2)

Points to prove

✓ date and location
✓ has the care of another
✓ by virtue of being a care worker
✓ ill-treated/wilfully neglected that individual

Meanings

Care worker

An individual who, as **paid work**, provides:

(a) **health care** for an **adult** or **child**, other than excluded health care, or
(b) **social care** for an adult,

including an individual who, as paid work, supervises or manages individuals providing such care or is a director or similar officer of an organisation that provides such care.

Paid work

An individual does something as paid work if they receive or are entitled to payment for doing it other than:

(a) payment of reasonable expenses;
(b) payment to which the individual is entitled as a foster parent;
(c) a social security benefit; or
(d) a payment made under s 2 of the Employment and Training Act 1973 (arrangements to assist people to select, train for, obtain, and retain employment).

Health care

This includes:

(a) all forms of care provided for individuals relating to physical or mental health, and care provided for or in connection with the protection or improvement of public health; and

(b) procedures similar to forms of medical or surgical care that are not provided in connection with a medical condition, and 'excluded health care' is defined in Sch 4.

Social care

This includes all forms of personal care and other practical assistance provided for individuals who need such care or assistance by reason of age, illness, disability, pregnancy, childbirth, dependence on alcohol or drugs, or any similar circumstances.

Adult

This means an individual aged 18 or over.

Child

This means an individual aged under 18.

Explanatory notes

- Section 20 makes it an offence for an individual who has the care of another individual by virtue of being a care worker to ill-treat or wilfully neglect that individual. The offence applies in England and Wales.
- A person providing health care or social care that is merely incidental to the person's other activities is not included. So, for example, a prison officer who assisted a prisoner in adjusting a hearing aid, could be perceived as providing practical assistance within the definition of 'social care'; but in this example, the prison officer would have provided the assistance incidentally to their custodial duties, not by virtue of being a care worker. The same principles would apply, for example, to police officers and office workers in similar circumstances.
- The *care provider* may also commit an offence under s 21 of the Act (subject to s 22).
- The definition of 'care worker' is intended to ensure that the individual offence can apply to any individual perpetrator, not just those on the 'front line' of care provision. However, it will only apply where the individual supervisor, director, etc has themselves directly committed ill-treatment or wilful neglect. They will not commit the individual offence by virtue of the acts or omissions of others they supervise or manage.
- The offence is limited to those performing 'paid work', as defined, to ensure that informal carers, such as unpaid family and friends, are not captured by the offence. The intention is also to exclude from the definition situations where an individual works as an unpaid volunteer but, for example, travel costs to and from the place where they volunteer are reimbursed. Similarly, this exclusion would also cover a family carer who occasionally receives a contribution towards the personal costs they incur in providing that care from the person for whom they care. Such reimbursement is not to be treated

as amounting to paid work. The intention is also to exclude any social security benefit where, for example, claimants are required to undertake unpaid work as a condition of receiving that benefit. So, for example, an individual working in an adult care home as part of the Department for Work and Pensions' 'Work Programme' will not be treated as being in paid work.

- 'Health care' includes services provided as part of the protection or improvement of public health, for example smoking cessation support, and is also intended to capture services, such as cosmetic surgery, that are not necessarily directly related to a medical condition.
- For more information, see MOJ Circular 2015/01.

 Either way   None

 Penalty

> **Summary:** 12 months' imprisonment and/or a fine
> **Indictment:** 5 years' imprisonment and/or a fine

Links to alternative subjects and offences

4.11 **Forced Marriages**

The Anti-social Behaviour, Crime and Policing Act 2014 deals with the criminal offence of forced marriage. In addition, the Family Law Act 1996 provides civil remedies regarding forced marriage and the offence of breaching a forced marriage protection order.

4.11.1 **Forced marriage offences**

Section 121 of the Anti-social Behaviour, Crime and Policing Act 2014 gives various offences relating to forced marriage.

> **Offences**
> (1) A person commits an offence under the law of England and Wales if he or she—
>   (a) uses violence, threats or any other form of coercion for the purpose of causing another person to enter into a marriage, and
>   (b) believes, or ought reasonably to believe, that the conduct may cause the other person to enter into the marriage without free and full consent.
> (2) A person commits an offence under the law of England and Wales if he or she—
>   (a) practises any form of deception with the intention of causing another person to leave the United Kingdom, and
>   (b) intends the other person to be subjected to conduct outside the United Kingdom that is an offence under subsection (1) or would be an offence under that subsection if the victim were in England or Wales.
>
> Anti-social Behaviour, Crime and Policing Act 2014, s 121

Points to prove

s 121(1) offence

✓ used violence/threats/other form of coercion
✓ in order to cause a person to enter into marriage
✓ believed/ought reasonably to have believed
✓ this conduct may cause that person
✓ to marry without free and full consent

s 121(3) offence

✓ practised any form of deception
✓ with intent to cause a person to leave UK
✓ intending that person to be subject of s 121(1) offence outside UK or
✓ would be subject to s 121(1) offence if victim were in England and Wales

Meaning of marriage

This means any religious or civil ceremony of marriage (whether or not legally binding).

Explanatory notes

- If the intended victim lacks capacity (under the Mental Capacity Act 2005) to consent to marriage, the offence under s 121(1) is capable of being committed by any conduct carried out for the purpose of causing the victim to enter into a marriage (whether or not the conduct amounts to violence, threats, or any other form of coercion).
- It is irrelevant whether the conduct mentioned in s 121(1)(a) is directed at the victim or another person.

Practical considerations

- A person commits an offence under s 121(1) or (3) only if, at the time of the conduct or deception:
  ✦ the person or the victim or both of them are in England or Wales;
  ✦ neither the person nor the victim is in England or Wales but at least one of them is habitually resident in England and Wales; or
  ✦ neither the person nor the victim is in the United Kingdom but at least one of them is a **UK national**.
- The term **UK national** means an individual who is:
  ✦ a British citizen, a British Overseas Territories citizen, a British National (Overseas), or a British Overseas citizen;
  ✦ a person who under the British Nationality Act 1981 is a British subject; or
  ✦ a British protected person within the meaning of that Act.
- HOC 10/2014 provides guidance, further information for these offences.
- If a forced marriage protection order is breached, then this is an offence under s 63CA of the Family Law Act 1996 (see **13.5.2**).
- Obtain a certified copy of the religious or civil marriage certificate whether or not it is a legally binding marriage.
- Schedule 6A (para 1) to the Anti-social Behaviour, Crime and Policing Act 2014 provides for the anonymity of victims of forced marriage in England and Wales. It creates a prohibition (summary offence) on the identification of victims in publications; penalties where the prohibition is breached; but also a defence to a defendant who can prove that at the time of the alleged offence, he or she was not aware, and did not suspect or have reason to suspect, that the publication included the matter in question, or that the allegation in question had been made.

Either way   None

🏛 **Summary:** 12 months' imprisonment and/or a fine

Indictment: 7 years' imprisonment

4.11.2 **Forced marriage: protection orders/guidance**

Section 120 of the Anti-social Behaviour, Crime and Policing Act 2014 inserted the offence of breaching a forced marriage protection order under s 63CA of the Family Law Act 1996 (see below).

It is important that the difference between an arranged marriage and a forced marriage is recognised and understood.

An **arranged** marriage is an **agreement** between both parties (usually prompted by the parents) entered into freely and is a practice that has worked successfully in several cultures for many centuries.

A **forced** marriage is where one or both parties have **not agreed** to marry and have been forced to do so **against their own free will**. Although it is mostly women who are affected by this, there are cases of men who are also forced to marry, and they should be treated in the same way as a woman making the report.

Sections 63A–63S of the Family Law Act 1996 make provision for protecting individuals against being forced into marriage without their free and full consent. The Act provides powers for the courts to issue protection orders, and deal with other associated matters, together with the offence of breaching a marriage protection order, as follows:
- s 63A—Forced marriage protection orders;
- s 63B—Contents of forced marriage protection orders;
- s 63C—Applications and other occasions for making orders;
- s 63CA—Offence of breaching order:
  - ✦ s 63CA(1): A person who without reasonable excuse does anything that the person is prohibited from doing by a forced marriage protection order is guilty of an offence;
  - ✦ s 63CA(2): Where an order is made under s 63D(1) a person is liable for the s 63CA offence only if that person was aware of the existence of the order;
  - ✦ s 63CA(3): If a person is convicted of the s 63CA offence, that conduct is not punishable as a contempt of court;
  - ✦ s 63CA(4): If any conduct has been punished as a contempt of court, a person cannot be convicted of the s 63CA offence;
  - ✦ s 63CA(5): This is an 'Either way' offence and is the defendant is liable to:

Summary: 6 months' imprisonment and/or a fine;

Indictment: 5 years' imprisonment and/or a fine.
- s 63D—*Ex parte* orders;
- s 63E—Undertakings instead of orders;
- s 63F—Duration of orders;
- s 63G—Variation of orders and their discharge;
- s 63J—Arrest under warrant;
- s 63K—Remand: General;
- s 63L—Remand: medical examination and report;
- s 63M—Jurisdiction of courts;
- s 63O—Contempt proceedings;
- s 63P—Appeals;
- s 63Q—Guidance;
- s 63R—Other protection or assistance against forced marriage;
- s 63S—Interpretation of sections 63A to 63R.

Apart from the above powers, there are criminal offences that can be committed by the family and (potential) husband/wife of the person when forcing someone into marriage such as forced marriage (see **4.11.1**), assaults (see **2.1**), false imprisonment or kidnapping (see **2.6**), and sexual offences (see **Chapter 6**).

Information contained in this section is based on official guidelines. However, any force policy must be adhered to and the information below is intended as a guide to be read in conjunction with any such policy.

Section 173 of The Policing and Crime Act 2017 has improved the protection to victims of forced marriages by providing them with lifelong anonymity by amending s 122 of the Anti-social Behaviour, Crime and Policing Act 2014.

The initial report

The most important factors when dealing with cases of forced marriage are the safety of the person, assurance, and confidentiality.
- Reassure the victim about the confidentiality of police involvement.
- It is important to establish a safe and discreet means of contact with the victim in the future.
- Treat the victim in a respectful and sensitive manner and consider their feelings and concerns.
- Ask the victim if they would prefer an officer of a certain gender, race, nationality, or religion to deal with the report.
- Obtain full details of the victim, including National Insurance number, and a copy of their passport.
- Make a record of any birthmarks, distinguishing features.
- Obtain a recent photograph or take a photograph of the victim (with the victim's consent).
- Create a restricted entry on the local intelligence system.
- Perform a risk assessment in every case.
- Consider the forced marriage offence (see **4.11.1**), identify any other criminal offences, and if appropriate, submit a crime report.

- Secure any evidence in case of any future prosecutions.
- Keep a full record of all decisions made and the explanations for those decisions (including decisions not to act).
- With the victim's consent refer them to local and national support groups (eg Honour Network—see **Appendix 1**).
- Tell them of their right to seek legal advice and representation.

Apart from taking the above actions, **do not**:
- send them back to the family home against their wishes;
- approach the family without express consent of the victim;
- inform anyone of the situation without express consent of the individual;
- attempt to mediate and reconcile the family.

There are different types of situations where the issue of forced marriage can arise:
- fear of being forced to marry in the UK or abroad;
- already in a forced marriage;
- a third-party report;
- a spouse brought from abroad.

It is likely that the nominated officer will take over enquiries; however, it is advisable to be aware of the action to be taken in these situations.

Fear of being forced to marry in the UK or abroad

Additional steps to be taken as well as those listed above are:
- obtain as much detail as possible about the victim's family both here and abroad including the intended spouse's details;
- consider the offence of forced marriage (see **13.4.1**);
- discuss with the person if there is any way of avoiding going abroad and if they did not go what difficulties that could cause;
- obtain exact details of where the victim would be staying abroad;
- ascertain if there is a family history of forced marriage;
- report details of the case to the Forced Marriage Unit (FMU) at the Foreign and Commonwealth Office and pass on contact details (see **Appendix 1**) to the victim. The FMU provides advice and assistance to potential and actual victims of forced marriage. It works with partnership agencies both in the UK and abroad to assist those affected by forced marriage.

If the victim does travel abroad ensure the following:
- that they have details of their passport in a safe place;
- that they can learn at least one telephone number and email address of a trusted person;
- ensure that they contact you on their return **without fail** and ask for an approximate return date;
- decide on a code word so that, if contact is made, verification of identity can be made;
- advise they take emergency cash and details of a trusted person in that country;

- ask the victim for details of a trusted person in the UK with whom they will be keeping in touch and whom you can contact in case of problems (eg if they do not return on specified date). Contact that person prior to the departure of the victim and pass on your or the nominated officer's contact details;
- ensure they have the details of the nearest Embassy/British High Commission in the country they are visiting.

Already in a forced marriage

The offence of forced marriage (see **13.4.1**) came into force on 16 June 2014. Additional steps to be taken as well as those listed above are:
- obtain details of the marriage, where, when, who, etc;
- ascertain if any other family members are at risk;
- take a statement about adverse behaviour towards the victim, such as threats and harassment (if appropriate);
- refer the victim with their consent to local and national support groups;
- establish a safe way to contact the victim and maintain contact with them;
- refer the matter to the FMU (see **Appendix 1** for contact details) who not only provide advice and assistance to victims of forced marriage, but also assist with concerns about visa issues for parties who are overseas;
- make a referral to social services and Child Protection Department if the victim is, or has children, under 18.

A third-party report

Additional steps to be taken as well as those listed above are:
- obtain contact details of the informant and stay in contact with them and advise them against making their own enquiries as this may jeopardise the official investigation;
- ascertain the relationship between the informant and the potential victim;
- find out as many details as possible such as where the victim is being held and in what circumstances, and if there is any evidence available to corroborate the story;
- check missing persons reports to see if the victim is reported missing;
- obtain as much information as possible about the victim's family and the intended spouse's family, and extended family in the UK and overseas;
- obtain a recent photograph of the victim;
- obtain some details (about the victim) that only the victim would know (an aid for verification of identity);
- prior to contacting the police overseas, it is essential to establish if any reliable links exist within that police force (this can be done through other police forces, Interpol, and the Foreign and

4.11.2 Forced marriage: protection orders/guidance

Commonwealth Office). **Do not** contact the force directly without making these enquiries.

A spouse brought from abroad

Additional steps to be taken as well as those listed above are:
- ensure that an independent authorised interpreter is available if required;
- ensure the victim is put at ease as they may be very frightened, vulnerable, and isolated;
- refer the victim with their consent to the relevant agencies and support groups, such as solicitors, immigration, and counselling;
- notify domestic violence vulnerable witness coordinator if applicable;
- refer to social services and Child Protection Department if the victim is, or has children under, 18.

Support and assistance

A national charity called Karma Nirvana has launched a confidential helpline called the 'Honour Network' which provides support to victims of 'honour'-based violence and forced marriages. (see **Appendix 1** for contact details).

Links to alternative subjects and offences

Chapter 5

Drugs

5.1 Produce/Supply a Controlled Drug and Supply of Articles

The Misuse of Drugs Act 1971 regulates certain drugs and designates which drugs are controlled by assigning them to certain categories (A, B, or C). If the drug is a controlled drug it will be unlawful, with exceptions, to import, export, produce, supply, or possess that drug. Section 4 deals with producing or supplying a controlled drug and s 9A supplying or offering articles for the purpose of administering or preparing controlled drugs.

5.1.1 Produce/supply a controlled drug

Section 4 of the Misuse of Drugs Act 1971 provides a prohibition on the production, supply, and offering to supply of controlled drugs, with offences for contravening such prohibitions.

Offences

(1) Subject to any regulations under section 7 of this Act, or any provision made in a temporary class drug order by virtue of section 7A for the time being in force, it shall not be lawful for a person—
  (a) to produce a controlled drug; or
  (b) to supply or offer to supply a controlled drug to another.
(2) Subject to section 28 of this Act, it is an offence for a person—
  (a) to produce a controlled drug in contravention of subsection (1) above; or
  (b) to be concerned in the production of such a drug in contravention of that subsection by another.
(3) Subject to section 28 of this Act, it is an offence for a person—
  (a) to supply or offer to supply a controlled drug to another in contravention of subsection (1) above; or

(b) to be concerned in the supplying of such a drug to another in contravention of that subsection; or

(c) to be concerned in the making to another in contravention of that subsection of an offer to supply such a drug.

Misuse of Drugs Act 1971, s 4

Points to prove

s 4(2)(a) offence

✓ produced
✓ controlled drug of Class A/B/C

s 4(2)(b) offence

✓ concerned in the production
✓ by another of
✓ controlled drug of Class A/B/C

s 4(3)(a) offence

✓ supply or offered to supply (type of drug)
✓ a controlled drug of Class A/B/C

s 4(3)(b) offence

✓ was concerned in
✓ supplying (type of drug)
✓ a controlled drug of Class A/B/C

s 4(3)(c) offence

✓ was concerned in making an offer
✓ to supply (type of drug)
✓ a controlled drug of Class A/B/C

Meanings

Regulations under section 7

Currently the Misuse of Drugs Regulations 2001—see '**Defences**' below.

Temporary class drug order

This is an order under s 2A that temporarily makes a substance or product a Class A, B, or C controlled drug until it can be formally classified and added to Sch 2 to the Act.

Provision made by virtue of s 7A

Section 7A provides the secretary of state with the power to make further provision in relation to a drug subject to temporary control.

Produce

Means producing by manufacture, cultivation, or any other method, and 'production' has a corresponding meaning. Stripping a cannabis plant of its leaves comes within the term 'any other method' for the purposes of production (*R v Harris and Cox* [1996] Crim LR 36).

Defendants who supply hydroponic equipment have been convicted of conspiracy to be concerned in the production of cannabis by another (*R v Dang and others* [2014] EWCA Crim 348).

Controlled drug

Means (per s 2) a substance or product that is classified under Class A, B, or C in Sch 2 to the Act; or a drug subject to a temporary class drug order.

Supply

Furnishing or providing a person with something that person wants or requires for their purpose. Including where an offender is looking after drugs whether voluntarily or involuntarily if they intend returning them to the person for whom they were being 'minded' or even anyone else (*R v Maginnis* [1987] 1 All ER 907 (voluntary minding) and *R v Panton* [2001] EWCA Crim 611 (involuntary minding, eg after threats have been made against them)).

Subject to section 28 (see 'Defences' below)

Explanatory notes

- The offence of offering to supply a controlled drug is complete when the offer is made. It does not matter whether the defendant intended ever to follow the offer through (see *R v Goddard* [1992] Crim LR 588).
- Section 37 (interpretation) states that supplying includes distributing.
- Undercover or 'test purchase' officers are trained to a National Standard and comply with NPCC guidelines. Where appropriate, authority is obtained under Pt 2 of the Regulation of Investigatory Powers Act 2000, before surveillance takes place.

Defences

Section 28 of the Misuse of Drugs Act 1971

This applies to offences under s 4(2) and (3), s 5(2) and (3), s 6(2), and s 9 of this Act and provides that it shall be a defence if the defendant proves that they:

- neither believed nor suspected nor had reason to suspect that the substance or product in question was a controlled drug; or
- believed the substance or product in question to be a controlled drug or a controlled drug of a description such that, if it had been that controlled drug or a controlled drug of that description, they would not at the material time have been committing any offence to which this section applies.

Regulation 5—Licences to produce, supply, possess

Where any person is authorised by a licence of the Secretary of State issued under this regulation and for the time being in force to produce, supply, offer to supply or have in his possession any controlled drug, it shall not by virtue of section 4(1) or 5(1) of the Act be unlawful for that person to produce, supply, offer to supply or have in his possession that drug in accordance with the terms of the licence and in compliance with any conditions attached to the licence.

Misuse of Drugs Regulations 2001, reg 5

Regulation 6—General authority to supply and possess

(1) Notwithstanding the provisions of section 4(1)(b) of the Act, any person who is lawfully in possession of a controlled drug may supply that drug to the person from whom he obtained it.

(2) Notwithstanding the provisions of section 4(1)(b) of the Act, any person who has in his possession a drug specified in Schedule 2, 3, 4 or 5 which has been supplied by or on the prescription of a practitioner, an extended formulary nurse prescriber, a registered nurse, a pharmacist independent prescriber, a supplementary prescriber or a person specified in Schedule 8 acting in accordance with a patient group direction for the treatment of that person, or of a person whom he represents, may supply that drug to any doctor, dentist or pharmacist for the purpose of destruction.

(3) Notwithstanding the provisions of section 4(1)(b) of the Act, any person who is lawfully in possession of a drug specified in Schedule 2, 3, 4 or 5 which has been supplied by or on the prescription of a veterinary practitioner or veterinary surgeon for the treatment of animals may supply that drug to any veterinary practitioner, veterinary surgeon or pharmacist for the purpose of destruction.

(4) It shall not by virtue of section 4(1)(b) or 5(1) of the Act be unlawful for any person in respect of whom a licence has been granted and is in force under section 16(1) of the Wildlife and Countryside Act 1981 to supply, offer to supply or have in his possession any drug specified in Schedule 2 or 3 for the purposes for which that licence was granted.

(5) Notwithstanding the provisions of section 4(1)(b) of the Act, any of the persons specified in paragraph (7) may supply any controlled drug to any person who may lawfully have that drug in his possession.

(6) Notwithstanding the provisions of section 5(1) of the Act, any of the persons so specified may have any controlled drug in his possession.

(7) The persons referred to in paragraphs (5) and (6) are—
   (a) a constable when acting in the course of his duty as such;
   (b) a person engaged in the business of a carrier when acting in the course of that business;
   (c) a person engaged in the business of a postal operator (within the meaning of the Postal Services Act 2000) when acting in the course of that business;
   (d) an officer of customs and excise when acting in the course of his duty as such;
   (e) a person engaged in the work of any laboratory to which the drug has been sent for forensic examination when acting in the course of his duty as a person so engaged;

> (f) a person engaged in conveying the drug to a person who may
> lawfully have that drug in his possession.
>
> Misuse of Drugs Regulations 2001, reg 6

Related cases

R v Abi-Khalil, R v Porja [2017] EWCA Crim 17, CA Two defendants
cannot be concerned in the supply of drugs to another, where the supply is to one of the defendants themselves, unless the facts suggest an
onward supply of the drugs.

R v Marron [2011] EWCA Crim 792, CA At the airport M's luggage
was found to contain 44kg of a fine white powder. M was convicted
of conspiracy to supply cocaine, by importing a non-controlled drug
(Phenacetin) that is used as a 'cutting agent' for cocaine.

R v Hodgson [2001] EWCA Crim 2697, CA The number of visitors, for
short periods, to a property may be evidence from which drug dealing
may be inferred.

R v Leeson [2000] 1 Cr App R 233, CA It does not matter whether a
person thinks they are dealing in a specific type of controlled drug if
they are in fact dealing in another.

R v Gill (Simon Imran) (1993) 97 Cr App R 215, CA An 'offer to supply' fake drugs is an offence.

R v Russell [1992] Crim LR 362, CA Making crack from cocaine is
'producing'.

R v Shivpuri [1986] 2 All ER 334, HL Attempting to supply something that
in fact was not a controlled drug can nevertheless be a criminal attempt.

R v Hunt [1987] 1 All ER 1, HL In this case, it was made clear that
the onus is on the prosecution to prove all elements, including the fact
that the drug could not be lawfully possessed by the defendant in the
circumstances.

R v Maginnis [1987] 1 All ER 907, HL This case involved possession of
a packet of cannabis that was being kept for a friend (a drug trafficker).
The return of the drugs to the trafficker was deemed to be supply.

Practical considerations

- Consider offences under s 23 or s 24 of the Offences Against the
  Person Act 1861 relating to unlawfully administering poison or
  noxious things, etc to another.
- Section 4A of the Misuse of Drugs Act 1971 aggravates the offence
  of supplying a controlled drug where the offender (drug dealer)
  commits the offence in the vicinity of school premises (including
  school land) or uses a courier under the age of 18.
- HOC 82/1980 recommends that cultivation of cannabis (see **5.3.1**) be
  charged under s 4 instead of s 6 of the Misuse of Drugs Act 1971 in
  view of s 37(1) of this Act which provides a definition of 'produce'.

5.1.2 Supply articles to administer or prepare drugs etc.

- The specific power to search, detain a person or vehicle/vessel, and seize any drugs is given in s 23(2) (see **5.4.1**). Ensure that s 2 of PACE (see **1.3.3**) is complied with.
- Fungus (of any kind) that contains psilocin or an ester of psilocin, commonly known as 'magic mushrooms', is a Class A drug under the Misuse of Drugs Act 1971.
- Consider confiscation of cash and property for the s 4(2) and (3) offences of unlawful production/supply of controlled drugs; these are listed as 'criminal lifestyle' offences under Sch 2 to the Proceeds of Crime Act 2002 (see **5.5** for details).

E&S   TRIG

 Either way   None

 Class A drug

    Summary: 6 months' imprisonment and/or a fine
    Indictment: Life imprisonment and/or a fine

    Class B drug
    Summary: 6 months' imprisonment and/or a fine
    Indictment: 14 years' imprisonment and/or a fine

    Class C drug
    Summary: 3 months' imprisonment and/or a fine
    Indictment: 14 years' imprisonment and/or a fine

5.1.2 Supply articles to administer or prepare drugs/drug-cutting agents

Section 9A of the Misuse of Drugs Act 1971 creates a prohibition on the supply or offering to supply articles for administering or preparing a controlled drug.

Offences

(1) A person who supplies or offers to supply any article which may be used or adapted to be used (whether by itself or in combination with another article or other articles) in the administration by any person of a controlled drug to himself or another, believing that the article (or the article as adapted) is to be so used in circumstances where the administration is unlawful, is guilty of an offence.

(3) A person who supplies or offers to supply any article which may be used to prepare a controlled drug for administration by any person to himself or another believing that the article is to be used in circumstances where the administration is unlawful is guilty of an offence.

                           Misuse of Drugs Act 1971, s 9A

Points to prove

✓ supplied/offered to supply article(s)
✓ which might be used/adapted
✓ for administration of a controlled drug
✓ to self/another
✓ believing article(s)
✓ was/were to be used
✓ in circumstances where administration unlawful

Meanings

Supplies (see **5.1.1**)

Offers (see '**Related cases**' **5.1.1**)

Controlled drug (see **5.1.1**)

Administration

Includes administering it with the assistance of another.

Defences

...
(2) It is not an offence under subsection (1) above to supply or offer to supply a hypodermic syringe, or any part of one.
(3) For the purposes of this section, any administration of a controlled drug is unlawful except—
  (a) the administration by any person of a controlled drug to another in circumstances where the administration of the drug is not unlawful under section 4(1) of this Act,
  (b) the administration by any person of a controlled drug, other than a temporary class drug, to himself in circumstances where having the controlled drug in his possession is not unlawful under section 5(1),
  (c) the administration by any person of a temporary class drug to himself in circumstances where having the drug in his possession is to be treated as excepted possession for the purposes of this Act (see section 7A(2)(c)).

Misuse of Drugs Act 1971, s 9A

Practical considerations

• The scope of the 'article(s)' is wide and includes, for example, plastic bottles which are intended to be used or adapted for smoking controlled drugs.
• Specified health care professionals are exempted from s 9A regarding certain articles per reg 6A of the Misuse of Drugs Regulations 2001; this includes their supplying aluminium foil as part of a drug treatment plan; see HOC 14/2014 for further details.

- Section 9 of the Misuse of Drugs Act 1971 provides for offences related to opium.

Drug-cutting agents

- Drug-cutting agents are substances added to drugs by dealers in order to increase the volume of a drug to maximise their profits. For example, benzocaine, lidocaine, and phenacetin are commonly added to cocaine without the user noticing.
- These substances are often not in themselves illegal, for example benzocaine and lidocaine are used in health and veterinary care but using legal substances for illegal purposes to substantially increase criminal profits has become a serious problem.
- Part 4 of the Serious Crime Act 2015 (ss 52–65) confers new powers on a constable, officer of the NCA, or HMRC customs officer to seize, retain, and destroy substances intended to be used as cutting agents for controlled drugs (in Sch 2 or subject to a temporary class drug order) under the Misuse of Drugs Act 1971 (see **5.1.1**).
- A drug-cutting agent is defined as a substance which is added to a controlled drug in connection with the unlawful supply or exportation of the drug. Therefore, it can be any substance intended for use in this way.
- The powers in Pt 4 of the Act enable a police or customs officer to enter and search premises for suspected drug-cutting agents, pursuant to a search and seizure warrant under s 52, and to seize and retain these substances. The process for application and execution of the warrant mirrors that given in the 1971 Act. When lawfully on premises (eg at a port) police and customs officers can seize substances under s 56, on reasonable grounds to suspect they are intended for use as drug-cutting agents.
- Section 54(4) makes it a summary offence for a person, without reasonable excuse, to obstruct a police or customs officer executing or seeking to execute a search and seizure warrant.
- Consider the offence of conspiracy to supply Class A drugs (*R v Marron* [2011] EWCA Crim 792, CA—see **5.1.1**) or assisting in the commission of an offence under the Serious Crime Act 2007 (see **4.1.3**).
- Further details and guidance are provided in 'Guidance on Part 4 of the Serious Crime Act 2015: The seizure and forfeiture of drug-cutting agents' (Home Office—April 2015), and HOC 8/2015.

 Summary   6 months

 6 months' imprisonment and/or a fine

Links to alternative subjects and offences

5.2 **Possession of/with Intent to Supply a Controlled Drug**

The Misuse of Drugs Act 1971 makes a distinction between people who are lawfully allowed to possess controlled drugs and people who are unlawfully in possession of such drugs. Possession (unless exempt) of a controlled drug is unlawful, as is possession of controlled drugs with intent to supply.

5.2.1 **Possessing a controlled drug**

Offences

(1) Subject to any regulations under section 7 of this Act for the time being in force, it shall not be lawful for a person to have a controlled drug in his possession.

(2) Subject to section 28 of this Act and to subsection (4) below, it is an offence for a person to have a controlled drug in his possession in contravention of subsection (1) above.

(2A) Subsections (1) and (2) do not apply in relation to a temporary class drug.

Misuse of Drugs Act 1971, s 5

Points to prove

✓ possess [name of drug]
✓ a controlled drug of Class A/B/C

Meanings

Regulations under section 7 (see **5.1.1**)

Controlled drug (see **5.1.1**)

Possession

Proof of unlawful possession requires the following three elements:
- the drug must be in the custody or control (actual or **constructive**) of the defendant;
- the defendant must know or suspect the existence of the drug in question;
- the drug must be a controlled drug within the meaning of the Act.

Temporary class drug (see 5.1.1)

Constructive control/possession

The defendant does not have immediate physical possession of the drugs but has almost as much control over them (see '**Explanatory notes**').

Explanatory notes

- Simple possession of a temporary class drug will not be an offence. However, all other offences will apply to temporary class drugs; see HOC 12/2011 for further details.
- An example of 'constructive possession' is where a person leaves drugs in a 'left luggage' locker and retains the keys. Although they no longer have 'actual' custody of the drugs, they have a high degree of control over them which amounts to possession. If the defendant handed the keys to an innocent agent who holds them as a favour, the defendant still has constructive possession. Similarly, if that other person knows that drugs are in the locker then, by keeping the keys, they are also in constructive possession of the drugs.

Defences

Section 28 and Regulations under s 7 (see 'Defences' 5.1.1)
Section 5(4)

In any proceedings for an offence under subsection (2) above in which it is proved that the accused had a controlled drug in his possession, it shall be a defence for him to prove—

(a) that, knowing or suspecting it to be a controlled drug, he took possession of it for the purpose of preventing another from committing or continuing to commit an offence in connection with that drug and that as soon as possible after taking possession of it he took all such steps as were reasonably open to him to destroy the drug or to deliver it into the custody of a person lawfully entitled to take custody of it; or

(b) that, knowing or suspecting it to be a controlled drug, he took possession of it for the purpose of delivering it into the custody of a person lawfully entitled to take custody of it and that as soon as possible after taking possession of it he took all such steps as were reasonably open to him to deliver it into the custody of such a person.

Misuse of Drugs Act 1971, s 5(4)

Defence notes

The defence under s 5(4) is to cater for situations such as:
- a parent discovers his or her child has a controlled drug, takes possession of it, and flushes it down the lavatory;

5.2.1 Possessing a controlled drug

- a passerby discovers heroin lying on the pavement, takes possession of it, and then gives it to the police.

Related cases

R v Altham [2006] EWCA Crim 7, CA Using cannabis to alleviate chronic pain was still unlawful possession.

Adams v DPP [2002] All ER (D) 125 (Mar) The defendants' flat was searched on a drug warrant while she was present with some visitors. Heroin was found on the sofa between two guests, and she said it was hers. She withdrew the admission when she was interviewed. It was held that 'possession' means (in brief): actual or potential physical control; and an intention to possess. The defendant's knowledge that one of the visitors to her home had brought heroin, and that one had intended to take the heroin, was insufficient to conclude that she had control over the drugs to establish the offence under s 5.

Practical considerations

- For produce/supply a controlled drug (see **5.1.1**).
- The Misuse of Drugs Regulations 2001 allows a person to possess some drugs for certain legitimate reasons (eg medicinal, research) (see **5.1.1**). Regulation 4(2) deals with drugs in Pt 2 of Sch 4 (anabolic steroids and human growth hormones) and states that the importation or exportation of these drugs is to be carried out in person and only for that person's use. This prevents access to these drugs through postal, freight, or courier services. HOC 9/2012 provides further details.
- HOC 15/2012 states that substances suspected to be controlled drugs must be sent to a forensic science laboratory for analysis unless they are seizures of:
  - ✦ cannabis, including cannabis resin but excluding cannabis (hash) oil; or
  - ✦ a small quantity (for personal use only) of certain controlled drugs, which gave a positive result when tested with a Home Office-approved kit (see below).

This is providing the case is dealt with at magistrates' court (some cases Crown Court), a trained law enforcement member confirms that it is that drug, and the identification of the drug is not in dispute.

- Section 63B of the Police and Criminal Evidence Act 1984 provides for the testing of adult persons for specified Class A drugs. The test can be carried out when a person has been arrested for or charged with either a 'trigger' offence or any offence when authorised by a police officer of inspector rank or above who has reasonable grounds to suspect that misuse of a specified Class A drug caused or contributed to the offence.
- Home Office-approved kits (operated by trained officers) (HOC 13/2014) can be used to identify the following drugs for evidential purposes: heroin; morphine; amphetamine; cocaine; MDMA (ecstasy); ketamine (now a Class B drug—see HOC 8/2014 for details); and methylmethcathinone (including mephedrone).

- The specific power to search, detain a person or vehicle/vessel, and seize any drugs is given in s 23(2) (see **5.4.1**). Ensure that s 2 of PACE (see **1.3.3**) is complied with.
- Cannabis and its derivatives are a Class B controlled drug. HOC 1/2009 provides guidance on cannabis offences.
- PACE Code E para 3.1(a)(iii) provides exemption from the requirement to audio record interviews that are undertaken elsewhere than at a police station for certain indictable offences that includes where a person has been cautioned for possession of a controlled drug under s 5(2) if the drug is cannabis or khat (but not cannabis oil), and possession is for personal use. This exemption is subject to a number of conditions, but the suspect must be aged 18 years or over and does not require an appropriate adult (see Code E for full details).
- The above exemption to audio record interviews applies to an attempt to commit the offence under s 1 Criminal Attempts Act 1981 (see **4.1.1**).
- Possession of cannabis under s 5(2) can be dealt with by PND for offenders 18 and over. ACPO guidance gives a three-stage escalation procedure (see **7.1.2**).

 (Cannabis)

 Either way None

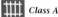 *Class A*

    Summary: 6 months' imprisonment and/or a fine
    Indictment: 7 years' imprisonment and/or a fine

    Class B
    Summary: 3 months' imprisonment and/or a level 4 fine
    Indictment: 5 years' imprisonment and/or a fine

    Class C
    Summary: 3 months' imprisonment and/or a level 3 fine
    Indictment: 2 years' imprisonment and/or a fine

5.2.2 **Possession with intent to supply**

The Misuse of Drugs Act 1971 creates a specific offence of possessing a controlled drug with intent to supply it.

Offences

Subject to section 28 of this Act, it is an offence for a person to have a controlled drug in his possession, whether lawfully or not, with intent to supply it to another in contravention of section 4(1) of this Act.

Misuse of Drugs Act 1971, s 5(3)

PND Penalty notice for disorder offences   **SSS** Stop, search, and seize powers   **E&S** Entry and search powers   **245**

TRIG Trigger offences

5.2.2 Possession with intent to supply

Points to prove
- ✓ possesses
- ✓ [name of drug]/an unspecified controlled drug of class A/B/C
- ✓ with intent to supply

Meanings

Controlled drug (see 5.1.1)

Possession (see 5.2.1)

Intent (see 4.1.2)

Supply (see 5.1.1)

Section 4 (see 5.1.1)

Explanatory notes (see 5.1.1 and 5.2.1)

Defences

Section 28 (lack of knowledge defence) (see 5.1.1)

Related cases (see also 5.1.1 and 5.2.1 cases)

R v Lambert [2001] UKHL 37, HL A judge must treat the s 28 defence as an evidential burden on the defendant rather than a legal requirement to be proved on the balance of probabilities.

R v Griffiths [1998] Crim LR 567 CA Evidence of large sums of cash in the defendant's house along with the drugs may be used as part of the prosecution case to show that the defendant was in possession of those drugs with intent to supply.

R v Scott [1996] Crim LR 652, CA Lifestyle may prove possession, but not intent to supply.

Practical considerations (see also 5.1.1 and 5.2.1)

- Lifestyle/paraphernalia can sometimes be used to help prove the 'possession' element but not 'intent to supply' where dealers are being prosecuted (*R v Edwards* [1998] Crim LR 207, CA).
- Provided a controlled drug is involved, it does not matter that a dealer thought they were supplying another controlled drug.
- The specific power to search, detain a person or vehicle/vessel, and seize any drugs is given in s 23(2) (see **5.4.1**). Ensure that s 2 of PACE (see **1.3.3**) is complied with.
- Consider confiscation of cash and property for the s 5(3) offence of possession of controlled drug with intent to supply; this is listed as a 'criminal lifestyle' offence under Sch 2 to the Proceeds of Crime Act 2002 (see **5.5** for details).

Either way None

 Class A

Summary: 6 months' imprisonment and/or a fine
Indictment: Life imprisonment and/or a fine

Class B
Summary: 6 months' imprisonment and/or a fine
Indictment: 14 years' imprisonment and/or a fine

Class C
Summary: 3 months' imprisonment and/or a level 4 fine
Indictment: 14 years' imprisonment and/or a fine

Links to alternative subjects and offences

5.3 Cultivate Cannabis, Possess Khat, and Psychoactive Substances

This chapter deals with the offences of cultivating cannabis, possessing khat, and possessing or dealing in psychoactive substances.

5.3.1 Cultivate cannabis/possess khat

Section 6 of the Misuse of Drugs Act 1971 makes it an offence to cultivate cannabis plants.

Offences

(1) Subject to any regulations under section 7 of this Act for the time being in force, it shall not be lawful for a person to cultivate any plant of the genus cannabis.

(2) Subject to section 28 of this Act, it is an offence to cultivate any such plant in contravention of subsection (1) above.

Misuse of Drugs Act 1971, s 6

Points to prove

✓ cultivation of cannabis plant(s) being a Class B drug

Meanings

Regulations under section 7

Allow cultivation of the cannabis plant under licence (see 'Defences' below).

Cannabis

This includes the whole plant.

Section 28 (see 'Defences' below)

Explanatory notes

- The mere growing of the cannabis plant is regarded as an act of 'production'.
- It is necessary to prove that the defendant gave some attention to the plant in order to show 'cultivation'—watering, heating, and lighting would be common examples.

Defences

Section 28 (lack of knowledge) (see 5.1.1)
Regulations under section 7

Where any person is authorised by a licence of the Secretary of State issued under this regulation and for the time being in force to cultivate plants of the genus Cannabis, it shall not by virtue of section 6 of the Act be unlawful for that person to cultivate any such plant in accordance with the terms of the licence and in compliance with any conditions attached to the licence.

Misuse of Drugs Regulations 2001, reg 12

Defence notes

- Acting without a valid licence or failing to comply with the conditions of the licence is an offence under s 18 of the Misuse of Drugs Act 1971 (although other more serious offences may also have been committed).
- Certain people can lawfully possess/supply a controlled drug and/or can be licensed to do so (see **5.1.1**).
- There is no general defence of medical necessity to the offence of production/possession/supply of cannabis (*A-G's Reference (No 2 of 2004)* [2005] EWCA Crim 1415, CA).

Practical considerations

- HOC 82/1980 recommends that the cultivation of cannabis be charged under s 4(2) 'producing cannabis' or being 'concerned in the production of cannabis' (see **5.1.1**). This is because under s 37(1) the definition of 'produce' has a much wider meaning than just chemically making a drug, and means by manufacture, cultivation, or any other method. Stripping a cannabis plant of its leaves comes within the term 'any other method' for the purposes of production (*R v Harris and Cox* [1996] Crim LR 36).
- Any equipment used at 'cannabis farms', which usually consists of hydroponic equipment to provide the lighting and heating, electrical fans, air ventilation systems, transformers. and other equipment, can be seized under s 19 of PACE (see **1.5.4**).
- Instead of storing this bulky equipment, which has been seized as evidence, consider s 22 of PACE which states that photographs of the equipment will be sufficient evidence.
- Supplying hydroponic equipment could be an offence of conspiring to be concerned in the production of cannabis by another (*R v Dang and others* [2014] EWCA Crim 348, CA—see **5.1.1** for details).
- In order to ascertain whether a building is being used as a 'cannabis farm' consider the use of a thermal camera or heat-seeking equipment to detect high infrared values; for example, in the roof area. This is due to the intensive use of heating and lighting equipment in the growing environment.

5.3.2 **Psychoactive substances**

- Cannabis and its derivatives are classified as a Class B controlled drug. As regards possession under s 5(2) (see **5.2.1**), ACPO guidance gives a three-stage escalation procedure which involves issuing a PND for offenders 18 and over (see **7.1.2**).

Possess khat

- Khat is a herbal product from the leaves and shoots of the shrub Catha edulis, and is used socially in homes, parties, and khat cafes. When chewed for several hours it gives a mild stimulant effect, so providing an increase in energy levels, alertness, and self-esteem. Due to the risks and potential harm associated with khat it has been classified as a Class C controlled drug.
- PACE Code E para 3.1(a)(iii) provides exemption from the requirement to audio record interviews undertaken elsewhere than at a police station for certain indictable offences that includes where a person has been cautioned for possession of khat (see **5.2.1**).
- The above exemption to audio record interviews applies to an attempt to commit the offence under s 1 Criminal Attempts Act 1981 (see **4.1.1**).
- Possession of khat is an offence under s 5(2) of the 1971 Act (see **5.2.1**) and can be dealt with by a (lower tier) PND (see **7.1.1**), although with the bulky nature of khat and its reliance on international freight, law enforcement will also focus on UK borders.
- HOC 11/2014 provides further details and gives a three-stage escalation procedure for dealing with possession for personal use only—not for possession with intent to supply or other offences. This is similar to that used for possession of cannabis (see **7.1.2**): with a 'khat warning' for a first offence, PND for a second offence, and prosecution for a third offence.
- Annex B of HOC 11/2014 provides guidelines for identifying khat, being visual for khat warnings and PND issue, but in other cases done forensically.

 Either way   None

 Summary: 6 months' imprisonment and/or a fine

Indictment: 14 years' imprisonment and/or a fine

5.3.2 **Psychoactive substances**

The Psychoactive Substances Act 2016 introduces several new offences (subject to statutory exemptions) that include the production, supply or offer to supply any psychoactive substance, and possession of a substance with intent to supply, if the substance is likely to be used for its psychoactive effects, regardless of its potential for harm. Note that there is no offence of possession of a psychoactive substance for personal use in the same way that there is for controlled drugs, except for possession while in a custodial institution, where separate provisions are made.

5.3.3 **Producing a psychoactive substance**

Section 4 of the Psychoactive Substances Act 2016 provides for an offence of producing a psychoactive substance.

Offences

(1) A person commits an offence if—
  (a) the person intentionally produces a psychoactive substance,
  (b) the person knows or suspects that the substance is a psychoactive substance, and
  (c) the person—
    (i) intends to consume the psychoactive substance for its psychoactive effects, or
    (ii) knows, or is reckless as to whether, the psychoactive substance is likely to be consumed by some other person for its psychoactive effects.

Psychoactive Substances Act 2016, s 4

Points to prove

✓ date and location
✓ intentionally produce psychoactive substance
✓ knows/suspects it is a psychoactive substance
✓ intends to consume it for psychoactive effects

OR

✓ knows/is reckless as to whether
✓ it is likely to be consumed by other person for psychoactive effects

Meanings

Psychoactive substance

Means any substance that:
(a) is capable of producing a psychoactive effect in a person who consumes it, and
(b) is not an **exempted substance** (see 'Other useful information' below).

Psychoactive effect

A substance produces a psychoactive effect in a person if, by stimulating or depressing the person's central nervous system, it affects the person's mental functioning or emotional state; and references to a substance's psychoactive effects are to be read accordingly.

5.3.4 Supply of a psychoactive substance

Consumes

A person consumes a substance if (s)he causes or allows the substance, or fumes given off by the substance, to enter his/her body in any way. For example, this includes injecting, eating or drinking, snorting, inhaling, and smoking.

Exempted substance

Means a substance listed in Sch 1 to the Psychoactive Substances Act 2016. Exempted substances are included in Sch 1 either because they are already controlled through existing legislation (alcohol, tobacco, medicines, and controlled drugs) or because their psychoactive effect is negligible (caffeine and foodstuffs such as nutmeg and chocolate).

Explanatory notes

- Section 2(2) provides that a substance produces a psychoactive effect in a person if, by stimulating or depressing the person's central nervous system, it affects that person's mental functioning or emotional state. The main effect of psychoactive substances is on a person's brain, the major part of the central nervous system. By speeding up or slowing down activity in the central nervous system, psychoactive substances cause an alteration in the individual's state of consciousness by producing a range of effects including, but not limited to, hallucinations; changes in alertness, perception of time and space, mood or empathy with others; and drowsiness.

 Either way   None

 Summary: maximum 12 months' imprisonment and/or a fine

Indictment: maximum 7 years' imprisonment and/or a fine
Region: United Kingdom

5.3.4 Supply of a psychoactive substance and offering to supply a psychoactive substance

Section 5 of the Psychoactive Substances Act 2016 provides for two separate offences, namely supply of a psychoactive substance and offering to supply a psychoactive substance.

Offences

(1) A person commits an offence if—
   (a) the person intentionally supplies a substance to another person,
   (b) the substance is a psychoactive substance,

(c) the person knows or suspects, or ought to know or suspect, that the substance is a psychoactive substance, and

(d) the person knows, or is reckless as to whether, the psychoactive substance is likely to be consumed by the person to whom it is supplied, or by some other person, for its psychoactive effects.

(2) A person ('P') commits an offence if—

(a) P offers to supply a psychoactive substance to another person ('R'), and

(b) P knows or is reckless as to whether R, or some other person, would, if P supplied a substance to R in accordance with the offer, be likely to consume the substance for its psychoactive effects.

Psychoactive Substances Act 2016, s 5

Points to prove

s 5(1) offence

✓ date and location
✓ offer to supply psychoactive substance
✓ to another
✓ knowing/being reckless as to whether that/another person would
✓ if supplied in accordance with offer
✓ be likely to consume it for psychoactive effects

s 5(2) offence

✓ date and location
✓ intentionally supply a substance to another
✓ the substance was psychoactive substance
✓ knows/suspects/ought to know/suspect the substance was psychoactive substance
✓ knows/was reckless as to whether substance likely to be consumed for psychoactive effects

---

Meanings

Psychoactive substance (see 5.3.3)

Psychoactive effect (see 5.3.3)

Consumes (see 5.3.3)

Explanatory notes

• For the purposes of s 5(2)(b), the reference to a substance's psychoactive effects includes a reference to the psychoactive effects that the substance would have if it were the substance that P had offered to supply to R.

5.3.5 Intent to supply psychoactive substances

- Section 6 provides for a statutory aggravating factor when sentencing an offender for an offence under s 5, where the supply, or offer to supply, took place at or in the vicinity of a school, involved the use of a courier under the age of 18, or took place in a custodial institution.
- For custodial institutions, the same offence of possession with intent to supply exists, which is aggravated if the supply occurs on the premises of the institution. There is an additional offence for a detained person to possess a psychoactive substance in a custodial institution under s 9 of the Act.
- Section 79 Serious Crime Act 2015 provides an offence to throw or project any article or substance into a prison and this will include drugs, mobile phones, and psychoactive substances.

 Either way   None

 Summary: maximum 12 months' imprisonment and/or a fine

Indictment: maximum 7 years' imprisonment and/or a fine
Region: United Kingdom

5.3.5 Possession with intent to supply psychoactive substances

Section 7 of the Psychoactive Substances Act 2016 provides for an offence of possession with intent to supply psychoactive substances.

Offences

A person commits an offence if—
(a) the person is in possession of a psychoactive substance,
(b) the person knows or suspects that the substance is a psychoactive substance, and
(c) the person intends to supply the psychoactive substance to another person for its consumption, whether by any person to whom it is supplied or by some other person, for its psychoactive effects.

Psychoactive Substances Act 2016, s 7

Points to prove

✓ date and location
✓ possession of psychoactive substance
✓ knows/suspects it is a psychoactive substance
✓ intends to supply substance to another
✓ for its consumption
✓ for psychoactive effects

Meanings

Psychoactive substance (see **5.3.3**)

Psychoactive effect (see **5.3.3**)

Consumes (see **5.3.3**)

Explanatory notes

- Section 7 is a possession offence but is aimed at those in the supply chain. Simple possession of a psychoactive substance for personal use would not be caught by this offence and is only criminalised by the Act when it occurs in a custodial institution. The offence in this section would, however, cover social supply—that is, circumstances where a person acquires a psychoactive substance on behalf of a group of friends and then supplies the substance to those friends.

Other useful information

- Offences under ss 4, 5, 7, and 8 are lifestyle offences for the purposes of confiscation proceedings (see **5.5**).
- Section 11 provides the exceptions to offences under the Act: including the offences under ss 4, 5, and 7: it is not an offence for a person to carry on any activity listed in s 11(3) if, in the circumstances in which it is carried on by that person, the activity is an exempted activity. In this section 'exempted activity' means an activity listed in Sch 2.
- Other exemptions include controlled drugs (see Misuse of Drugs Act 1971) (see **5.2**), medicinal products, alcohol, nicotine, tobacco, caffeine, and foods.
- Sections 36–39 inclusive provide powers to stop and search persons, vehicles, vessels, aircraft, and premises where an officer has reasonable grounds to suspect that a person has committed, or is likely to commit, an offence under any of the ss 4–9.
- CSOs and CSVs may seize and retain a psychoactive substance where he or she finds a psychoactive substance in a person's possession (whether or not the CSO or CSV finds it in the course of searching the person in the exercise of a power or duty conferred or imposed by his or her designation (see **11.1.6**)).
- There is no power to stop and search where an officer suspects that a person has in his or her possession a psychoactive substance intended for personal use; the officer will need to have reasonable grounds to suspect that the person has committed or is likely to commit an offence under the Act: for example, the person is likely to commit the offence of possession with intent to supply a psychoactive substance.
- Section 43 provides a power to seize and retain anything found during the course of a search which the officer believes is a psychoactive substance.

5.3.5 Intent to supply psychoactive substances

- Retention and disposal of psychoactive substances are covered by ss 49 to 51 and 53 but should also be undertaken in accordance with force policy.
- There are no Home Office kits to identify psychoactive substances, with forensic testing being the only option. In terms of other offences consider selling/supplying controlled drugs (see **5.1.1**), drugs articles (see **5.1.2**), or breaching consumer protection legislation.
- Test purchases could establish if an item sold as a psychoactive substance contains controlled drugs (including temporary controlled drugs) by forensic testing, in which case a s 23(3) drugs warrant (see **5.4.1**) can be applied for.
- Consider approaching the local authority for them to issue a PSPO (see **7.15.2**), which could ban people using psychoactive substances in a public place, with a power to seize such substances and if appropriate to issue a fixed penalty notice.

Related cases

R v Chapman [2017] EWCA Crim 1743 In this case the defendant was convicted of possessing a psychoactive substance with intent to supply, namely nitrous oxide. He was stopped when driving his car and 408 canisters were found in the vehicle. A self-storage unit owned by the defendant was also searched and 13,800 canisters of nitrous oxide were seized. The defendant's case was that the canisters, save for a small number for personal use, were for use in his small catering business, in particular for whipping cream, which is what they were designed for. It was not disputed that nitrous oxide was a psychoactive substance capable of producing a psychoactive effect of the sort described in s 2. The question to be considered was whether it was an exempted substance under Sch 1 to the Act, in particular a medicinal product, the defence arguing that nitrous oxide may bring benefits to human health, however, the prosecution submitted that as it was produced for catering purposes as a recreational drug it fell outside the concept of a medicinal product and the Court of Appeal agreed: the convictions were upheld.

 Either way   None

 Summary: maximum 12 months' imprisonment and/or a fine

Indictment: maximum 7 years' imprisonment and/or a fine
Region: United Kingdom

Links to alternative subjects and offences

5.4 **Drug Search Powers/Permit Drug Use on Premises**

5.4.1 **Power to search, detain, and seize drugs**

Search powers under s 23 or s 23A of the Misuse of Drugs Act 1971 confer powers on a constable to stop, detain, and search a person, vehicle, or vessel for controlled drugs and an obstruction offence for failing to comply.

Power to search, detain, and seize drugs

If a constable has reasonable grounds to suspect that any person is in possession of a controlled drug in contravention of this Act or of any regulations or orders made thereunder, the constable may—
(a) search that person, and detain him for the purpose of searching him;
(b) search any vehicle or vessel in which the constable suspects that the drug may be found, and for that purpose require the person in control of the vehicle or vessel to stop it;
(c) seize and detain, for the purposes of proceedings under this Act, anything found in the course of the search, which appears to the constable to be evidence of an offence under this Act.

Misuse of Drugs Act 1971, s 23(2)

Offences

A person commits an offence if he—
(a) intentionally obstructs a person in the exercise of his powers under this section.

Misuse of Drugs Act 1971, s 23(4)

Points to prove
✓ intentionally obstructed
✓ constable/authorised person in exercise of s 23 powers

Meanings

Reasonable grounds (see 1.3.2)

Controlled drug (see 5.1.1)

Vehicle (see 10.1.3)

Vessel

Includes a hovercraft within the meaning of the Hovercraft Act 1968.

Intentionally obstructs

Where a person deliberately does an act which, though not necessarily aimed at or hostile to the police, makes it more difficult for the police to carry out their duty and they intentionally do the act knowing that their conduct will have an obstructive effect (*Lewis v Cox* [1984] Crim LR 756, QBD).

Explanatory notes

- Section 23(1) gives a constable/authorised person power to enter premises relating to producing or supplying (eg chemists) any controlled drugs, to inspect the drug stocks or demand production and inspection of books or documents regarding dealings in such drugs.
- Where a person is acting under s 23(1), it is an offence (s 23(4) (b)–(c)) to conceal books, documents, stocks, or drugs; or when demanded, to fail (without reasonable excuse) to produce the books or documents.
- Section 23A provides further powers to search and detain for the purpose of searching, a person (or vehicle or vessel) where a constable has reasonable grounds to suspect that the person is in possession of a temporary class drug (see **5.1.1**). Also, to seize, detain, and dispose of such a drug. It is an offence under s 23A(6) to intentionally obstruct a constable exercising this power; guidance is provided in HOC 12/2011 regarding temporary class drug offences and powers.
- These powers are exercisable *anywhere* and must be conducted in accordance with the related COP and PACE (see **1.3**).
- Paragraph 5 of Sch 3C Police Reform Act 2002 confers powers for Community Support Officers (CSOs) and Community Support Volunteers (CSVs) to seize and detain controlled drugs found in the possession of a person (see **11.1.5**).

Related cases

Browne v Commissioner of Police for the Metropolis [2014] EWHC 3999, QBD Failure by the officer to comply with s 2 PACE (see **1.3.3**) and use of excessive force, rendered a search unlawful and led to damages being awarded for assault.

R v Bristol [2007] EWCA Crim 3214, CA The officer failed to give his name and police station prior to a s 23 drug search, in breach of s 2 PACE (see **1.3.3**), making the search unlawful. As a result, the officer was not acting in the execution of his duty and the s 23(4) offence was not committed.

5.4.1 Power to search, detain, and seize drugs

Practical considerations

Personal safety

- Contact with the blood or saliva of drug abusers (particularly those users who inject) carries a risk of infection with serious diseases such as AIDS, HIV, and hepatitis.
- Every effort should be made to avoid such fluids entering your own body through cuts, eyes, or the mouth. Should such contact occur, the possibility of infection is minimised by the contact area being thoroughly washed immediately and medical advice sought as soon as practicable.

Searching of suspects

- Care should always be taken to avoid unguarded needles piercing the skin; if such an event does occur seek medical advice as soon as practicable.
- When conducting a search initially request the suspect/prisoner to turn out their own pockets, before patting the outside of pockets to detect the presence of a syringe.
- Drug abusers will go to extreme lengths to conceal drugs on or in their bodies. Drugs are commonly found in body orifices (s 55 of PACE 1984 provides the circumstances in which intimate searches can be carried out).
- Search a person minutely: small amounts of drugs can be concealed, for example, in the lining of clothing, under plasters supposedly covering an abrasion, or stuck to the skull under the hairline.
- Searching inside a person's mouth does not constitute an intimate search.

Handling of drugs

- Certain drugs may be absorbed through the skin; it is therefore always advisable to wear gloves when handling drugs.
- Never under any circumstances taste the drugs.
- There will be occasions when the name of the drug seized is unknown and there is doubt as to whether it is controlled. Always seek advice and assistance from a supervisory officer or the drug squad.

Drug abusers' equipment

- Abusers use a wide range of paraphernalia to prepare and administer their drugs. The following list (which is not exhaustive) may provide evidence of that activity where premises are searched:
    - ✦ syringes and needles; scorched tinfoil and spoons; small mirrors, razors, and straws; tubes of tinfoil; ligatures; lemon juice or citric acid; cigarette papers and home-made cigarettes; bloodstained swabs; square folds of paper which may contain powder; cling film; small self-sealing bags; weighing scales; hookah pipes.

General

- Section 23(3) of the Misuse of Drugs Act 1971 allows a warrant to be issued for any constable to enter (if need be by force) premises named in the warrant and to search the premises and any persons found therein for evidence of offences relating to controlled drugs (see **1.5** for application procedures).
- Ensure all s 23(3) search powers are in the warrant; a warrant authorising premises search only does not give grounds to search people found therein (*CC of Thames Valley v Hepburn* [2002] EWCA Civ 1841). If the warrant authorises the search of premises and people, it is reasonable to restrict their movement to conduct a proper search (*DPP v Meadon* [2003] EWHC 3005 (Admin)).
- Comply with PACE and the COP for the grounds for searching people, conduct of the search, and completion of a search record (see **1.3**); using reasonable force to detain and carry out the search (see **1.3.2**).
- When using s 23 search powers, ensure that the s 2 PACE requirements are met (see **1.4.2**) (eg police officer fails to state name and police station), otherwise the search will be deemed unlawful and may affect the admissibility of any evidence obtained.
- Although s 23(2) authorises detention of a suspect for the purpose of searching, it does not give the officer a general right to question the suspect. However, they may ask questions incidental to exercising that power.
- Section 23(2)(b) does not give an officer the right to stop a vehicle or to search it simply because they suspect the vehicle (not the occupants) has been used in connection with a drug offence on a previous occasion (*R v Littleford* [1978] CLR 48).
- Nothing in s 23(2) prejudices any other powers available to a constable to search or seize/detain property.
- Consider road traffic law to stop the vehicle (see **10.2**).

 Either way   None

 Summary: 6 months' imprisonment and/or a fine

Indictment: 2 years' imprisonment and/or a fine

5.4.2 **Occupier/manager permits drug use on premises**

Section 8 of the Misuse of Drugs Act 1971 makes it an offence for occupiers and managers of premises to permit certain activities relating to drugs to take place on those premises.

5.4.2 Occupier/manager permits drug use on premises

Offences

A person commits an offence if, being the occupier or concerned in the management of any premises, he knowingly permits or suffers any of the following activities to take place on those premises, that is to say—

(a) producing or attempting to produce a controlled drug in contravention of section 4(1) of this Act;

(b) supplying or attempting to supply a controlled drug to another in contravention of section 4(1) of this Act, or offering to supply a controlled drug to another in contravention of section 4(1);

(c) preparing opium for smoking;

(d) smoking cannabis, cannabis resin or prepared opium.

Misuse of Drugs Act 1971, s 8

Points to prove

✓ being the occupier/concerned in managing of premises
✓ knowingly
✓ permitted/suffered to take place
✓ on premises
✓ the production/attempted production or
✓ supplying/attempted to supply/offering to supply to another
✓ Class A/B/C drug namely [if known] or
✓ preparing of opium for smoking or
✓ smoking of cannabis, cannabis resin, or prepared opium

Meanings

Occupier

Whether a person is in lawful occupation of premises has created some difficulty. In *R v Tao* [1976] 3 All ER 65, a college student who paid rent for a room on the campus was deemed to be the occupier of that room; Lord Justice Roskill commented that it would be 'somewhat astonishing' if a squatter could not be an 'occupier' under the Act. Similarly, there may be different occupiers at different times or an occupier who only had that status for certain periods. The question was always one of fact (*R v Coid* [1998] Crim LR 199, CA).

Management

Implies a degree of control over the running of the affairs of the venture or business. If a person controls premises by running, planning, or organising them they will be managing. Sharing or assisting in the running of premises is sufficient for the purposes of 'being concerned in the management'.

Knowingly (see 9.1.3)

Permits (see 10.14.1)

Suffers

Means an unwillingness or failure to prevent.

Producing (see **5.1.1**)

Controlled drug (see **5.1.1**)

Section 4(1) (see **5.1.1**)

Supplying (see **5.1.1**)

Explanatory notes

- If the defendant is aware that the premises are being used to supply controlled drugs, it does not matter, for the purposes of establishing guilt, which type of drug is involved (*R v Bett* [1999] 1 All ER 600). However, there is a difference so far as the penalty is concerned as to which class of drugs were used.
- This offence is limited to the activities specified at (a)–(d). It is not committed, for example, by a landlord who knows that one of their tenants is in their room injecting themselves with amphetamines. They may commit the offence if, for example:
  - ✦ a drug is being supplied to others on the premises;
  - ✦ a controlled drug is being produced on the premises;
  - ✦ the occupants are smoking cannabis.
- The Misuse of Drugs Regulations 2001 allows a person to possess some drugs for certain legitimate reasons (eg medicinal, research) (see '**Defences**' **5.1.1**).

Related cases

R v McGee [2012] EWCA Crim 613, CA Where a person permits the supply of Class A drugs to take place on their premises, the prosecution must prove that the supply took place 'on the premises' rather than 'from the premises'.

R v Lunn [2008] EWCA Crim 2082, CA It is more serious where the manager of a public house allows premises to be used for drugs compared to the owner of a private house. This is because it is drug taking in public, thus making it appear to be an acceptable activity, and may encourage others to partake.

R v Auguste [2003] EWCA Crim 3929, CA In this case, during a police raid, a block of cannabis resin and two reefers were found. Although several men were in the house, there was no smell of cannabis having been smoked. It was held that activity of actually smoking cannabis must be carried out before this offence is committed.

R v Brock and Wyner (2001) 2 Cr App R 3, CA The offence under s 8(b) has two elements: (i) knowingly permits—knowledge of the dealing, which could be actual knowledge or the defendant closing their eyes to the obvious; or (ii) suffers—unwillingness to prevent the dealing, which could be inferred from the failure to take reasonable steps

5.4.2 Occupier/manager permits drug use on premises

to prevent it. A belief that they had taken reasonable steps does not provide them with a defence.

Practical considerations

* Whenever the decision to search premises can be planned in advance, a warrant should be obtained under the Misuse of Drugs Act 1971, s 23(3) (see **5.4.1** and **1.6**).
* The police have a power to close premises associated with nuisance or disorder by issuing a closure notice under the Anti-social Behaviour, Crime and Policing Act 2014, s 76 (see **7.13.5**).
* Consider confiscation of cash and property for premises relating to controlled drugs under s 8, as this is listed as a 'criminal lifestyle' offence under Sch 2 to the Proceeds of Crime Act 2002 (see **5.5** for details).

 Either way None

 Class A/B
Summary: 6 months' imprisonment and/or a fine
Indictment: 14 years' imprisonment and/or a fine

Class C
Summary: 3 months' imprisonment and/or a fine
Indictment: 14 years' imprisonment and/or a fine

Links to alternative subjects and offences

5.5 **Proceeds of Crime**

The Proceeds of Crime Act 2002, s 75 sets out the criminal lifestyle criteria which could be subject to a confiscation order; this is to be read in conjunction with Sch 2 (lifestyle offences) and s 6 (confiscation order procedure).

Criminal lifestyle criteria

(1) A defendant has a criminal lifestyle if (and only if) the following condition is satisfied.

(2) The condition is that the offence (or any of the offences) concerned satisfies any of these tests—
   (a) it is specified in Schedule 2;
   (b) it constitutes conduct forming part of a course of criminal activity;
   (c) it is an offence committed over a period of at least six months and the defendant has benefited from the conduct which constitutes the offence.

(3) Conduct forms part of a course of criminal activity if the defendant has benefited from the conduct and—
   (a) in the proceedings in which he was convicted he was convicted of three or more other offences, each of three or more of them constituting conduct from which he has benefited, or
   (b) in the period of six years ending with the day when those proceedings were started (or, if there is more than one such day, the earliest day) he was convicted on at least two separate occasions of an offence constituting conduct from which he has benefited.

(4) But an offence does not satisfy the test in subsection (2)(b) or
   (c) unless the defendant obtains relevant benefit of not less than £5,000.

(5) Relevant benefit for the purposes of subsection (2)(b) is—
   (a) benefit from conduct which constitutes the offence;
   (b) benefit from any other conduct which forms part of the course of criminal activity and which constitutes an offence of which the defendant has been convicted;
   (c) benefit from conduct which constitutes an offence which has been or will be taken into consideration by the court in sentencing the defendant for an offence mentioned in paragraph (a) or (b).

(6) Relevant benefit for the purposes of subsection (2)(c) is—
   (a) benefit from conduct which constitutes the offence;
   (b) benefit from conduct which constitutes an offence which has been or will be taken into consideration by the court in sentencing the defendant for the offence mentioned in paragraph (a).

Proceeds of Crime Act 2002, s 75

Criminal lifestyle offences

Schedule 2 lists the criminal lifestyle offences:

Drug trafficking

Misuse of Drugs Act 1971

- s 4(2) or (3) (unlawful production/supply of controlled drugs) (see **5.1.1**);
- s 5(3) (possession of controlled drug with intent to supply) (see **5.2.2**);
- s 8 (premises relating to controlled drugs) (see **5.4.2**);
- s 20 (assisting/inducing offence outside UK).

Psychoactive Substances Act 2016

- s 4 (producing a psychoactive substance);
- s 5 (supplying, or offering to supply, a psychoactive substance);
- s 7 (possession of psychoactive substance with intent to supply);
- s 8 (importing or exporting a psychoactive substance).

Customs and Excise Management Act 1979

Committed in breach of import or export drug restriction:
- s 50(2) or (3) (improper importation of goods);
- s 68(2) (exportation of prohibited or restricted goods);
- s 170 (fraudulent duty evasion).

Criminal Justice (International Co-operation) Act 1990

- s 12 (manufacture/supply substance used for drugs);
- s 19 (using a ship for illicit traffic in controlled drugs).

Money laundering

- s 327 (concealing, etc criminal property);
- s 328 (assisting another to retain criminal property).

Slavery etc

- Modern Slavery Act 2015, s 1 (slavery, servitude and forced or compulsory labour).

Directing terrorism

- Terrorism Act 2000, s 56 (directing the activities of a terrorist organisation).

People trafficking

- offence under ss 25, 25A, or 25B of the Immigration Act 1971 (assisting unlawful immigration, etc) (see **11.3**);
- offences of slavery, servitude, and forced or compulsory labour (s 1), and human trafficking offence (s 2), under the Modern Slavery Act 2015 (see **4.9**).

Arms trafficking

Customs and Excise Management Act 1979

In connection with a firearm or ammunition:
- s 68(2) (exportation of prohibited goods);
- s 170 (fraudulent duty evasion).

Firearms Act 1968, s 3(1)

- dealing in firearms or ammunition by way of trade or business (see **8.1.2**).

Counterfeiting

Forgery and Counterfeiting Act 1981

- s 14 (making counterfeit notes or coins);
- s 15 (passing, etc counterfeit notes or coins);
- s 16 (having counterfeit notes or coins);
- s 17 (make/possess materials or equipment for counterfeiting).

Intellectual property

Copyright, Designs and Patents Act 1988

- s 107(1) (make/deal in article which infringes copyright);
- s 107(2) (make/possess article designed or adapted to make copy of a copyright work);
- s 198(1) (making or dealing in an illicit recording);
- s 297A (making or dealing in unauthorised decoders).

Trade Marks Act 1994, s 92(1), (2), or (3)

- unauthorised trade mark use.

Prostitution and child sex

Sexual Offences Act 1956, ss 33 or 34

Keeping or letting premises for use as a brothel.

Sexual Offences Act 2003

- s 14 (arranging or facilitating commission of a child sex offence) (see **6.5.3**);
- s 48 (causing or inciting sexual exploitation of a child);
- s 49 (controlling a child in relation to sexual exploitation);
- s 50 (arranging or facilitating sexual exploitation of a child);
- s 52 (causing or inciting prostitution for gain);
- s 53 (controlling prostitution for gain) (see **6.11.3**).

Blackmail

Theft Act 1968, s 21

Blackmail (see **3.2.3**).

Gangmasters (Licensing) Act 2004, s 12(1) or (2)

Acting as a gangmaster without a licence, possession of false documents.

Inchoate offences

- offence of attempting, conspiring, or inciting the commission of an offence specified in this Schedule (see **4.1.1**);
- offence under s 44 of the Serious Crime Act 2007 of doing an act capable of encouraging or assisting the commission of an offence specified in this Schedule (see **4.1.3**);
- offence of aiding, abetting, counselling, or procuring the commission of such an offence.

Explanatory notes

- The criminal lifestyle tests are designed to identify individuals who may be living off crime and make them account for their assets, which are liable to be confiscated if the person is unable to account for their lawful origin.
- The first test is that s/he is convicted of an offence specified in Sch 2.
- The second test is that the defendant is convicted of an offence of any description, provided it was committed over a period of at least six months, and obtained not less than £5,000 from that offence and/or any others taken into consideration by the court on the same occasion.
- The third test is that the defendant is convicted of a combination of offences amounting to 'a course of criminal activity'.
- This third test is more complicated than the other two. The defendant satisfies it if s/he has been convicted in the current proceedings:
  - ◆ of four or more offences of any description from which s/he has benefited; or
  - ◆ of any one such offence and has other convictions for any such offences on at least two separate occasions in the last six years. In addition, the total benefit from the offence(s) and/or any others taken into consideration by the court must be not less than £5,000.
- The purpose of confiscation proceedings under s 6 is to recover the financial benefit that the offender has obtained from his criminal conduct. Proceedings are conducted according to the civil standard of proof, being on the balance of probabilities.
- In certain circumstances the court is empowered to assume that the defendant's assets, and their income and expenditure during the period of six years before proceedings were brought, have been derived from criminal conduct and to calculate the confiscation order accordingly.
- Confiscation orders may be made in the Crown Court following conviction. Where the conviction takes place in the magistrates' court, a confiscation order can only be made if the defendant is committed to the Crown Court either for sentence or for sentence and confiscation under s 70.

- The Policing and Crime Act 2017 introduced new provisions relating to '**unexplained wealth**'. Under s 362A(2) and s 362B Proceeds of Crime Act 2002, the High Court may make an order that requires the respondent to provide a statement setting out the nature and extent of his or her interest in the property in respect of which an order is made to explain how the property was obtained, etc. To make the order, the court must be satisfied that the respondent holds the property which must have a value greater than £50,000.
- The Criminal Finances Act 2017 makes the legislative changes necessary to give law enforcement agencies and partners new capabilities and powers to recover the proceeds of crime, and to tackle money laundering, corruption, and terrorist financing.

Links to alternative subjects and offences

Chapter 6

Sexual Offences and Assaults

6.1 **Rape**

Rape and other sexual offences were consolidated by the Sexual Offences Act 2003.

6.1.1 **Rape**

The offence of rape is covered by ss 1 (rape) and 5 (rape of a child under 13) of the Sexual Offences Act 2003.

> **Offences**
>
> A person (A) commits an offence if—
> (a) he intentionally penetrates the vagina, anus or mouth of another person (B) with his penis,
> (b) B does not consent to penetration, and
> (c) A does not reasonably believe that B consents.
>
> Sexual Offences Act 2003, s 1(1)

Points to prove
- ✓ intentionally
- ✓ without consent
- ✓ penetrated anus/vagina/mouth
- ✓ of another person
- ✓ with the defendant's penis
- ✓ not reasonably believing that s/he had consented

Meanings

Intentionally (see also **4.1.2**)

This is the defendant's aim or purpose in pursuing a particular course of action. If the defendant intended to penetrate but was physically unable to do so or he admitted that it was his intent, then the law states that he still had the necessary intent.

Penetration

Means a continuing act from entry to withdrawal.

Vagina

Includes vulva.

Consent

Both s 75 (evidential presumptions about consent) and s 76 (conclusive presumptions about consent) apply to this offence (see **'Defences'** below).

Reasonable belief

Whether a belief is reasonable is to be determined having regard to all the circumstances, including any steps A has taken to ascertain whether B consents.

Explanatory notes

- As the definition of vagina includes vulva, then full penetration is not essential to commit rape.
- The offence of rape includes penile penetration not only of the vagina and anus but also of the mouth as this act could be just as traumatising and damaging for the victim.
- As penetration can be proved by reference to scientific evidence (sperm, semen, bruising, etc), consent often becomes the major, if not only, issue.
- The offence of rape is gender specific in that only a male (over the age of 10) can commit the offence; the gender of the complainant is irrelevant. This section and s 5 (see **6.1.2**) are the only offences throughout the whole Act that are gender specific because they refer to penile penetration.

Defences

A critical issue in rape cases is consent and ss 74–76 deal specifically with these issues.

Consent

A person consents if he agrees by choice and has the freedom and capacity to make that choice.

Sexual Offences Act 2003, s 74

Evidential presumptions about consent

(1) If in proceedings for an offence to which this section applies it is proved—
    (a) that the defendant did the relevant act,

(b) that any of the circumstances specified in subsection (2) existed, and

(c) that the defendant knew that those circumstances existed, the complainant is to be taken not to have consented to the relevant act unless sufficient evidence is adduced to raise an issue as to whether he consented, and the defendant is to be taken not to have reasonably believed that the complainant consented unless sufficient evidence is adduced to raise an issue as to whether he reasonably believed it.

(2) The circumstances are that—

(a) any person was, at the time of the relevant act or immediately before it began, using violence against the complainant or causing the complainant to fear that immediate violence would be used against him;

(b) any person was, at the time of the relevant act or immediately before it began, causing the complainant to fear that violence was being used, or that immediate violence would be used, against another person;

(c) the complainant was, and the defendant was not, unlawfully detained at the time of the relevant act;

(d) the complainant was asleep or otherwise unconscious at the time of the relevant act;

(e) because of the complainant's physical disability, the complainant would not have been able at the time of the relevant act to communicate to the defendant whether the complainant consented;

(f) any person had administered to or caused to be taken by the complainant, without the complainant's consent, a substance which, having regard to when it was administered or taken, was capable of causing or enabling the complainant to be stupefied or overpowered at the time of the relevant act.

(3) In subsection (2)(a) and (b), the reference to the time immediately before the relevant act began is, in the case of an act that is one of a continuous series of sexual activities, a reference to the time immediately before the first sexual activity began.

Sexual Offences Act 2003, s 75

Conclusive presumptions about consent

(1) If in proceedings for an offence to which this section applies it is proved that the defendant did the relevant act and that any of the circumstances specified in subsection (2) existed, it is to be conclusively presumed—

(a) that the complainant did not consent to the relevant act, and

(b) that the defendant did not believe that the complainant consented to the relevant act.

(2) The circumstances are that—

(a) the defendant intentionally deceived the complainant as to the nature or purpose of the relevant act;

> (b) the defendant intentionally induced the complainant to consent
> to the relevant act by impersonating a person known personally
> to the complainant.
>
> Sexual Offences Act 2003, s 76

Defence notes

Meaning of 'relevant act' (s 77)

References to the term 'relevant act' in ss 75 and 76 vary according to
the offence committed and are where the defendant intentionally:
- penetrates, with his penis, the vagina, anus or mouth of another
  person [*Rape (s 1)*];
- penetrates, with a part of his body or anything else, the vagina or
  anus of another person, where the penetration is sexual [*Assault by
  penetration (s 2)*];
- touches another person, where the touching is sexual [*Sexual assault
  (s 3)*];
- causes another person to engage in a sexual activity [*Causing a person
  to engage in sexual activity without consent (s 4)*].

Consent (s 74)

The **freedom** to **agree** is intended to stress that a lack of protest, injury,
or consent by the victim does not necessarily signify consent.
- Freedom is not defined in the Act so it must be a matter of fact as to
  whether the victim was free to agree or whether pressure or threats
  ruled out that agreement.
- A person might not have sufficient **capacity** if they suffer from a
  mental disorder, was incapacitated due to drink/drugs, or their age
  prevents them from being able to do so.
- Capacity is not defined so it will be for the court to decide from all
  the available evidence.

Evidential presumptions about consent (s 75)

- The term '**substance**' in s 75(2)(f) is not defined, so anything capable
  of stupefying or overpowering would be covered; this would include
  substances such as alcohol, GHB, or Rohypnol.
- Section 75(3) covers the situation where there have been a number
  of sexual acts, of which penetration is the culmination, and the
  defendant is being prosecuted for them and the threats occurred
  immediately before the first sexual act. In that case the presumption
  still applies.
- Where the prosecution proves that the defendant did a **relevant
  act** (in this case rape), and the situations described in s 75(2)
  existed and the defendant knew they existed, then the complainant
  will be presumed not to have consented and the defendant will
  be presumed not to have reasonably believed the complainant
  consented.

Conclusive presumptions about consent (s 76)

- Where the prosecution prove that the defendant did a **relevant act** and any of the circumstances described above existed then it is conclusively presumed that the complainant did not consent, and the defendant did not believe that the complainant consented to the relevant act. Therefore, evidence as to the existence of the intentional deception will be critical.
- Deceiving the complainant as to the nature or purpose of the act could be where the complainant is told that digital penetration of her vagina is necessary for medical reasons when in fact it is only for sexual gratification of the defendant.
- Impersonation would cover circumstances where the defendant deceives the complainant into believing that he is her partner causing the complainant to consent to the sexual act.

General

- If none of the situations described in ss 75 and 76 apply, then the prosecution must show that the circumstances of the offence were such that the defendant could not reasonably believe that the complainant consented.
- If the defendant states that he did reasonably believe that the complainant consented, then it would be a matter for the jury to decide as to whether a reasonable person would come to the same belief having regard to all the circumstances. In interview he should be asked what assured him that the victim consented or that it was consensual.
- The circumstances will include the personal characteristics of the defendant. The defendant's age; general sexual experience; sexual experience with this complainant; learning disability; and any other factors that could have affected his ability to understand the nature and consequences of his actions which may be relevant depending on the circumstances of the case.
- The Act makes it clear there is an onus on parties involved in a relevant sexual activity to ensure that they have the true consent of the other person(s) and that they took reasonable steps to make sure true consent has been freely given prior to any sexual act taking place.

Related cases

R v Bree [2007] EWCA Crim 804, CA This case considered the issue of consent where the complainant had consumed a considerable amount of alcohol. Consent is defined in s 74 of the Sexual Offences Act 2003 and it was held that if, as a result of consuming alcohol or for any other reason, capacity to choose whether to have sexual intercourse was temporarily lost, then no consent was present and dependent upon enquiries into the state of mind of the victim, if intercourse takes place, then it would be rape.

Practical considerations

- Ejaculation does not have to occur for the rape to be committed.
- All reports of rape must be treated as genuine and the victims treated with sensitivity. Only a suitably trained or qualified person should be used to take a statement or obtain evidence from the victim.
- The crime scene should be identified and preserved, ensuring that cross-contamination does not occur (see **1.3**).
- Evidence of the offence should be seized, including clothing and any articles used, such as condoms.
- Consider medical and forensic examination of the victim and offender.
- Consider DPP Guidance on consent in rape cases regarding capacity, steps taken to obtain consent, and reasonable belief in the consent. In January 2015, CPS published a joint protocol setting out how the police and CPS will deal with all rape cases from the initial complaint through to end of trial.
- HOC 1/2015 gives guidance on the 'date rape' drug GHB, now under Sch 2 to the Misuse of Drugs Regulations 2001, so ensuring stricter control to reduce the risks of diversion and misuse.
- Obtain evidence of first complaint if appropriate and available.
- Advise the victim not to shower, bathe, drink, or smoke, and to retain the clothing they were wearing at the time of the attack.
- Consider CCTV and other potential evidence from independent witnesses.

 Indictable   None

 Life imprisonment

6.1.2 **Rape of a child under 13**

This is covered by s 5 of the Sexual Offences Act 2003.

> **Offences**
>
> A person commits an offence if—
> (a) he intentionally penetrates the vagina, anus or mouth of another person with his penis, and
> (b) the other person is under 13.
>
> Sexual Offences Act 2003, s 5(1)

6.1.2 Rape of a child under 13

> **Points to prove**
> ✓ intentionally
> ✓ penetrated the anus/vagina/mouth
> ✓ of a person under 13
> ✓ with the defendant's penis

Meanings

Intentionally (see **6.1.1**)

Penetrates (see **6.1.1**)

Vagina (see **6.1.1**)

Explanatory notes

- There is no issue of consent under this section. Whether the child consented or not is irrelevant, making this almost an offence of 'strict liability'.
- This section also includes not only penetration of the vagina and anus but also penile penetration of the mouth as in s 1.
- This section replaces the offence of unlawful sexual intercourse with a girl under 13 in the Sexual Offences Act 1956, s 5.

Related cases

R v G [2008] UKHL 37, HL The defendant, a boy aged 15, had intercourse with a girl of 12 years old in his room with her consent. At the time he believed her to be aged 15 years of age. It was held that reasonable belief as to consent or age was irrelevant as the offence was absolute and imposed strict liability.

Practical considerations

- Full penetration does not have to occur, and it is not necessary to prove any additional consequences (eg that the hymen was broken).
- Once it can be proved that penetration occurred, it will be very hard to show that this was anything other than intentional, but it is still a necessary ingredient of the offence.
- Prove age of child. Only a suitably trained or qualified person should be used to take a statement or obtain evidence from the child/victim.
- Specific provisions for the police and other agencies to protect the welfare and safety of children are given in the Children Act 2004 (see **2.4.2**).
- Whilst offences between adults and children will always be viewed as serious, account should be taken of Art 8 ECHR (respect for private life) in relation to the criminalisation of consenting children.

- Consider CPS charging principles based on the Code for Crown Prosecutors.
- Consider all the evidential responsibilities highlighted as with the s 1 offence of rape.

 Indictable   None

 Life imprisonment

Links to alternative subjects and offences

6.2 **Sexual Assault by Penetration**

These offences are covered by ss 2 and 6 (child under 13) of the Sexual Offences Act 2003.

6.2.1 **Assault by penetration of a person aged 13 or over**

Offences

A person (A) commits an offence if—
(a) he intentionally penetrates the vagina or anus of another person (B) with a part of his body or anything else,
(b) the penetration is sexual,
(c) B does not consent to the penetration, and
(d) A does not reasonably believe that B consents.

Sexual Offences Act 2003, s 2(1)

Points to prove

✓ intentionally
✓ sexually penetrated
✓ the anus/vagina of another person aged 13 or over
✓ with a part of the body and/or a thing
✓ without consent
✓ not reasonably believing that s/he had consented

Meanings

Intentionally (see **6.1.1**)

Penetration (see **6.1.1**)

Vagina (see **6.1.1**)

Part of his body (see s 79(3))

References to a part of the body include references to a part surgically constructed (in particular, through gender reassignment surgery).

Anything else

This term has not been defined but it is an extremely wide category and will cover anything that can be used to penetrate the body of another.

Sexual

For the purposes of this Part (except section 71), penetration, touching or any other activity is sexual if a reasonable person would consider that—

(a) whatever its circumstances or any person's purpose in relation to it, it is because of its nature sexual, or

(b) because of its nature it may be sexual and because of its circumstances or the purpose of any person in relation to it (or both) it is sexual.

Sexual Offences Act 2003, s 78

Consent (see 6.1.1)

Reasonable belief (see 6.1.1.)

Explanatory notes

- Section 79(3) takes into account surgically reconstructed genitalia. Medical examination could reveal that a person has undergone reconstructive surgery. A person can have their birth certificate changed to reflect their new gender under the Gender Recognition Act 2004.
- Once penetration has been proved, it will be difficult for the defendant to show that it was not their intention to do this. However, as partial penetration will suffice, there may be occasions (such as during sporting or gymnastic contact) where the defendant claims partial penetration by, say, a finger was inadvertent. It would then be for the prosecution to prove otherwise.
- If the defendant states that they reasonably believed that the complainant consented, then it will be a matter for the jury to decide as to whether a reasonable person would come to the same belief having regard to all the circumstances.
- The circumstances include the personal characteristics of the defendant; the defendant's age; general sexual experience; sexual experience with this complainant; learning disability; and any other factor that could have affected their ability to understand the nature and consequences of their actions may be relevant depending on the circumstances of the case.
- The reasonableness test does not oblige the defendant to have taken any specific steps to ascertain consent, but any taken will be highly pertinent to the case.
- Parties to relevant sexual activity must ensure that they have the true consent of the other person(s) and that they took reasonable steps to make sure true consent had been freely given prior to any sexual act taking place.
- This offence was created to reflect the seriousness of assault by penetration, previously being indecent assault, which was perceived not to carry the appropriate penalties for such a serious offence. It carries the same penalty as rape (life imprisonment), thus reflecting its gravity.

- **Section 78 which defines 'sexual'** is a mixed test consisting of an objective test based on what a reasonable person would consider to be sexual and the purpose of the person involved:
  - ✦ subsection (a) where there is no doubt that the activity is sexual, such as oral sex or penetration by vibrator; and
  - ✦ subsection (b) where the activity could also have some purpose apart from a sexual one, and where the defendant's act was not sexually motivated. This would cover situations where the defendant penetrates his victim with an object with the sole intent of committing a violent act not a sexual one (eg penetration with the handle part of a knife to humiliate and assert their power over the victim).
- The defendant may not have intended the act to be sexual but, from a reasonable person's point of view and because of its nature, a reasonable person would consider that it might be sexual.
- Medical examinations or intimate searches by the relevant authorities (such as police and customs), or such other treatment where penetration is involved but is not sexual (eg in colonic irrigation), will not normally be deemed sexual.
- Unlike rape, this offence can be committed by digital penetration and penetration by any other part of the body, such as a fist, tongue, and toes.
- Full penetration is not essential to commit the offence.
- Items included in the term 'anything else' can be such objects as bottles, vibrators, and other similar objects and substances.

Defences

Sections 75 and 76 apply to this offence; see **6.1.1 'Defences'** for further details.

Practical considerations

- Any reports of serious sexual assault must be treated as genuine and the victims with sensitivity.
- Evidence of the offence should be seized and includes clothing, condoms, and articles used.
- Ensure cross-contamination does not occur.
- Obtain evidence of first complaint if appropriate and available.
- Advise the victim not to shower, bathe, drink, or smoke and to retain the clothing they were wearing at the time of the attack.
- Consider CCTV and other evidence from potential witnesses.

Indictable None

Life imprisonment

6.2.2 **Assault by penetration of a child under 13**

This offence is the same as s 2 above, except that the complainant is under 13 and there is no issue of consent.

Offences

A person commits an offence if—
(a) he intentionally penetrates the vagina or anus of another person with a part of his body or anything else,
(b) the penetration is sexual, and
(c) the other person is under 13.

Sexual Offences Act 2003, s 6

Points to prove

✓ intentionally
✓ sexually penetrated
✓ anus/vagina of a girl aged under 13
✓ anus of a boy aged under 13
✓ with a part of the body and/or a thing

Meanings

Intentionally (see **6.1.1**)

Penetrates (see **6.1.1**)

Vagina (see **6.1.1**)

Part of his body (see **6.2.1**)

Anything else (see **6.2.1**)

Sexual (see **6.2.1**)

Explanatory notes (see **6.2.1** notes)

Practical considerations (also see 6.2.1 considerations)

• This is an offence of strict liability (see **6.1.2**).

6.2.2 Assault by penetration of a child under 13

- It is not necessary for the victim to know or explain what they were penetrated with.
- The offence can be used in cases where the child does not possess the knowledge to identify the nature of what they had been penetrated with.
- Prove age of child. Only a suitably trained or qualified person should be used to take a statement or obtain evidence from the victim.
- The Children Act 2004 (see **2.4.2**) makes specific provision for the police and other agencies to protect the welfare and safety of children.

 Indictable None

 Life imprisonment

Links to alternative subjects and offences

6.3 Sexual Assault by Touching

6.3.1 Sexual assault by touching a person aged 13 or over

This offence is covered by s 3 of the Sexual Offences Act 2003.

Offences

A person (A) commits an offence if—
(a) he intentionally touches another person (B),
(b) the touching is sexual,
(c) B does not consent to the touching, and
(d) A does not reasonably believe that B consents.

Sexual Offences Act 2003, s 3

Points to prove

✓ intentionally touched
✓ another person aged 13 or over
✓ by touching her/his body
✓ that touching was sexual
✓ not reasonably believing that s/he was consenting

Meanings

Intentionally (see 6.1.1)

Touches

This includes touching:
• with any part of the body;
• with anything else;
• through anything;

and in particular includes touching amounting to penetration.

Sexual (see 6.2.1)

Consent (see 6.1.1)

Reasonable belief (see 6.1.1)

Explanatory notes

• This section covers non-penetration sexual assaults on another person aged 13 or over. It will cover a wide spectrum of behaviour that would include the defendant rubbing up against the complainant's private parts through the person's clothes for their sexual gratification.

- Touching includes touching through clothes, touching with anything, and touching that amounts to penetration. It does not have to involve using the hands and can involve any part of the body being used or touched or even an object such as a sex toy.
- The offence does not require that the defendant intended that the touching be sexual, only that the touching itself was intentional. The sexual aspect of the touching is a separate element.
- Whilst there could not be many examples of 'accidental' or inadvertent penetration, accidental touching occurs all the time. Jostling in a crowded street, travelling on a busy train or bus, and attending sports events can all lead to some form of contact with others.
- It will normally be apparent that the defendant intentionally touched the victim (because of the part of the body touched or used, or because of accompanying circumstances) but there will still be far more room for a defence of lack of intent than in penetration offences.
- In most cases of sexual assault, the sexual element will be non-contentious. For example, where a man gropes a female's genitals, it would be hard to imagine a set of circumstances where this would not be sexual and in those cases s 78(a) (see **6.2.1**) will be relied on.
- If with regard to all the circumstances, the purpose and nature of the touching, a reasonable person would consider it sexual then it will be covered by s 78(b). However, it is not certain if the more obscure sexual fantasies would be covered at all by s 78. Would a reasonable person consider the removal of a shoe as sexual, looking at the purpose and nature of it? If not, then this would not constitute 'sexual' touching even if the offender received sexual gratification from doing it. This reflects the former common law position with regard to such offences (see **'Explanatory notes'** under **6.2.1** for further details on 'sexual' and s 78).

Defences

Sections 75 and 76 apply—see **6.1.1 'Defences'** for further details.

Related cases

R v Ciccarelli [2011] EWCA Crim 2665, CA The defendant claimed that, at a party, the complainant had touched him between the legs and tried to kiss him. Later, while the complainant was asleep, he went to her bedroom and climbed into bed, and touched her with his erect penis from behind, tried to pull her knickers down and climbed on top of her. She woke up and made him leave the room. The defendant was convicted of sexual assault but appealed on a question of consent. Because the defendant made no attempt to awaken the complainant prior to his sexual advances, it was held that there was insufficient evidence for him to raise the issue of reasonable belief under s 75.

R v Heard [2007] EWCA Crim 125, CA In this case, police officers took the defendant, who was drunk, emotional, and injured, to hospital. He was abusive, singing noisily, and danced suggestively towards one of the police officers. He then punched the officer in the stomach and took out his penis, rubbing it up and down the officers' thigh. He was convicted of sexual assault with intent but argued that because of his voluntary intoxication he could not form sufficient intent. It was held that, in this instance, the touching was plainly intentional despite the intoxication. His drunkenness may have made him lose inhibitions or behave out of character but did not detract from the fact that his intent to touch the officer with his penis was deliberate.

Practical considerations

- Reports of serious sexual assault must be treated as genuine and the victims treated with sensitivity.
- As with all serious sexual offences, identify any scene, preserve it, and seize any articles or associated items relevant to the offence for which the offender has been arrested.
- Prevent any potential for cross-contamination.
- Keep the offender and victim separate.
- Consider medical and forensic examination for victim and offender.

 Either way   None

Summary: 6 months' imprisonment and/or a fine

Indictment: 10 years' imprisonment

6.3.2 **Sexual assault by touching a child under 13**

This offence is covered by s 7 of the Sexual Offences Act 2003 and is the same as s 3 but there is no need to prove lack of consent by the child; any such consent is irrelevant.

> ### Offences
>
> A person commits an offence if—
> (a) he intentionally touches another person,
> (b) the touching is sexual, and
> (c) the other person is under 13.
>
> Sexual Offences Act 2003, s 7

6.3.2 Sexual assault by touching a child under 13

Points to prove
- ✓ intentionally touched
- ✓ a girl/boy aged under 13
- ✓ and the touching was sexual

Meanings

Intentionally (see **6.1.1**)

Touches (see **6.3.1**)

Sexual (see **6.2.1**)

Explanatory notes

- Consent is not an issue as this is an offence of strict liability (see **6.1.2**).
- Points raised in **6.3.1** relating to the touching and its sexual nature are still relevant to this offence.

Related cases

R v Weir [2005] EWCA Crim 2866, CA The defendant was on trial for sexual assault by touching a 10-year-old girl. Despite not being the same offence category, a previous caution for taking an indecent photograph of a child was disclosed at court under s 103(2)(b) of CJA 2003. This was allowed as it showed a propensity to commit the s 7 offence.

Practical considerations

- Prove age of child. Only a suitably trained or qualified person should be used to take a statement or obtain evidence from the victim.
- The Children Act 2004 (see **2.4.2**) makes specific provision for the police and other agencies to protect the welfare and safety of children.
- If possible, identify and preserve a scene and seize any articles suspected of being used in the offence. Always consider the potential for cross-contamination (see **1.3**).

 Either way   None

 Summary: 6 months' imprisonment and/or a fine

Indictment: 14 years' imprisonment

Links to alternative subjects and offences

6.4 **Sexual Activity with a Child**

This offence is covered by s 9 of the Sexual Offences Act 2003.

Offences

(1) A person aged 18 or over (A) commits an offence if—
   (a) he intentionally touches another person (B),
   (b) the touching is sexual, and
   (c) either—
      (i) B is under 16 and A does not reasonably believe that B is 16 or over, or
      (ii) B is under 13.
(2) A person is guilty of an offence under this section, if the touching involved—
   (a) penetration of B's anus or vagina with a part of A's body or anything else,
   (b) penetration of B's mouth with A's penis,
   (c) penetration of A's anus or vagina with a part of B's body, or
   (d) penetration of A's mouth with B's penis.

Sexual Offences Act 2003, s 9

Points to prove

Non-penetrative, under 13

✓ defendant aged 18 or over
✓ intentionally touched
✓ a girl/boy under 13
✓ the touching was sexual

Penetrative, under 13

✓ defendant aged 18 or over
✓ intentionally touched complainant sexually
✓ sexual touching involved penetration of:
   ✦ complainant's anus/vagina with part of D's body or thing or
   ✦ complainant's mouth with D's penis or
   ✦ D's anus/vagina with part of complainant's body or
   ✦ D's mouth with complainant's penis
✓ complainant being under 13

Penetrative, between 13 and 15

✓ per points to prove of 'Penetrative under 13' except
✓ complainant is aged 13/14/15
✓ not reasonably believing complainant was 16 or over

Non-penetrative, aged between 13 and 15

✓ defendant aged 18 or over
✓ intentionally touched a girl/boy aged 13/14/15
✓ not reasonably believing s/he was 16 or over
✓ the touching was sexual

Meanings

Intentionally (see **6.1.1**)

Touching (see **6.3.1**)

Sexual (see **6.2.1**)

Reasonable belief (see 'Defence' below)

Explanatory notes

This offence is very similar to ss 3 and 7 (see **6.3**), but the defendant is aged 18 or over and touching involved in s 9(2) is specified in terms of what was used on/in what part of the body. Consent is not mentioned in s 9, but—per s 7—if the complainant is under 13 then consent is irrelevant.

Defences

Proving a reasonable belief that the child was 16 or over at the time. This only applies if the victim is aged between 13 and 15. If under 13 the offence is one of strict liability.

Defence notes

- If the victim is aged between 13 and 15 the prosecution must provide evidence that the defendant's belief was not reasonable. For example, that the defendant knew that a girl attended school and had not yet taken her GCSE examinations.
- However, if the defendant and the complainant met for the first time over the internet, the complainant provided photographs of herself in which she looked much older than she in fact was, and if she told the defendant that she was 18 and looked 18, then the belief might be reasonable.
- If the prosecution can provide such evidence it is open to the defendant to rebut it, if he can show on the balance of probabilities that his belief was reasonably held.

Practical considerations

- This offence is gender neutral.
- Consent is not an issue, but if complainant is under 13, consent is irrelevant as the offence will be one of strict liability.

6.4 Sexual Activity with a Child

- Identify and preserve any scene. Prevent cross-contamination.
- Seize any articles/clothing or associated equipment which is relevant.
- Consider charging principles in the Code for Crown Prosecutors.
- Consider factors which include the age and emotional maturity of the arties, whether they entered into the sexual relationship willingly, any coercion or corruption by a person, relationship between the parties, and whether there was any existence of a duty of care or breach of trust.
- The discretion of the CPS not to charge where it is not in the public interest would be partially relevant where the two parties were close in age, for instance an 18-year-old and a 15-year-old and had engaged in mutually agreed sexual activity.

s 9(1) offence

 Either way

 None

 Summary: 6 months' imprisonment and/or a fine

Indictment: 14 years' imprisonment

s 9(2) offence

 Indictment

 None

 14 years' imprisonment

Links to alternative subjects and offences

6.5 Child Sexual Exploitation Offences

6.5.1 Cause/incite child under 16 to engage in sexual activity

The offence of causing/inciting a child under 16 to engage in sexual activity, where the offender is aged 18 or over, is under the Sexual Offences Act 2003, s 10.

Offences

(1) A person aged 18 or over (A) commits an offence if—
  (a) he intentionally causes or incites another person (B) to engage in an activity,
  (b) the activity is sexual, and
  (c) either—
    (i) B is under 16 and A does not reasonably believe that B is 16 or over, or
    (ii) B is under 13.
(2) A person is guilty of an offence under this section, if the activity caused or incited involved—
  (a) penetration of B's anus or vagina,
  (b) penetration of B's mouth with a person's penis,
  (c) penetration of a person's anus or vagina with a part of B's body or by B with anything else, or
  (d) penetration of a person's mouth with B's penis.

Sexual Offences Act 2003, s 10

Points to prove

Non-penetration

✓ offender aged 18 or over
✓ intentionally
✓ caused/incited
✓ a girl or boy 13/14/15, not reasonably believing s/he was 16 or over or
✓ under 13
✓ to engage in sexual activity
✓ of a non-penetrative nature

Penetration

✓ per first six points of '**Non-penetration**'
✓ involving the penetration of
✓ girl/boy's anus/vagina **or**

6.5.1 Cause/incite child under 16 to engage in sexual activity

> ✓ girl/boy's mouth with another person's penis **or**
> ✓ a person's anus/vagina with part of girl/boy's body or by girl/boy with anything else **or**
> ✓ a person's mouth with the boy's penis

Meanings

Intentionally (see **6.1.1**)

The defendant's aim or purpose in pursuing a particular course of action.

Causes

Defined by the *Concise Oxford Dictionary* as 'be the cause of, make happen'. This implies that the defendant must take some positive action rather than omit acting. Examples could be the use of force, threats, deception, or intimidation.

Incites

Defined by the *Concise Oxford Dictionary* as 'encourage, stir up, urge or persuade'. Examples could be bribery, threats, or pressure.

Sexual (see 6.2.1)

Reasonably believe (see 6.4)

Explanatory notes

- The sexual activity that is caused or incited involves the victim being engaged in that sexual activity. This can be, for example, where the defendant causes or incites the child to sexually touch themselves or the child to masturbate or strip for the defendant's sexual gratification.
- It may be with a third person (eg where the defendant causes or incites the child to have oral sex with the penis of another person).
- The incitement itself is an offence so the sexual activity does not have to take place for the offence to be committed.
- Section 10(2) replicates some of the other offences covered in the Act, such as rape, assault by penetration. This duplication is intended to cover every possible scenario that could be envisaged, ensuring that offenders do not escape prosecution because of a loophole in the law.
- Examples of an adult causing or inciting a child to engage in sexual activity could be promising a reward, persuading the child that it is perfectly acceptable behaviour that other children engage in all the time and they would be abnormal not to agree, or saying that the activity was necessary to check the child's body for bruises, lice, etc, or to try on clothes.
- Where the child is under 13, the offender should be charged with the s 8 offence (see **6.5.2**), especially if it involves penetration, as it then carries life imprisonment. However, s 10 might be used where the offender is under 18 or the child is under 13 and it only became known during trial that the child was under 13. The extension of s 10

to under-13s now means that the trial could continue with the original charge where necessary, thus closing a potential loophole in the law.

Practical considerations

- Prove age of child. Only a suitably trained or qualified person should be used to take a statement or obtain evidence from the victim.
- Section 10 is not intended to cover health professionals, nor anyone providing sex education, advice, or contraception to children.
- This offence could be considered where the offender and victim are very close in age (eg an offender of 18 and a victim of 15), and are in a relationship, and both have entered into a sexual relationship willingly.
- Where the child is aged 13 or over, but under 16, the prosecution must prove that the defendant did not reasonably believe that s/he was 16 or over. If the child is under 13 the offence is one of strict liability.
- If possible identify and preserve crime scene and seize any articles and evidence relevant to the offence.

Child sexual exploitation (CSE) offences

- It is an offence under the Sexual Offences Act 2003, s 47 to intentionally obtain for oneself the sexual services of a child aged under 18, where those services have been paid for or where payment has been promised.
- HOC 8/2015 provides guidance on CSE offences under s 47 (above) and ss 48–50 of the 2003 Act:
  - ✦ s 48—Causing or inciting sexual exploitation of a child;
  - ✦ s 49—Controlling a child in relation to sexual exploitation;
  - ✦ s 50—Arranging or facilitating sexual exploitation of a child.
- Under s 51(2) for the purposes of ss 48–50, a person (B) is sexually exploited if:
  - (a) on at least one occasion and whether or not compelled to do so, B offers or provides sexual services to another person in return for payment or a promise of payment to B or a third person, or
  - (b) an indecent image of B is recorded, or streamed, or otherwise transmitted and 'sexual exploitation' to be interpreted accordingly.
- In s 51(2)(a) *'Payment'* means any financial advantage, including the discharge of an obligation to pay or the provision of goods or services (including sexual services) gratuitously or at a discount.
- Section 51 ensures that the definition of sexual exploitation also covers situations where indecent images of children are not only recorded, but also streamed, eg via the internet, or transmitted by some other technological means, such as CCTV.
- The Serious Crime Act 2015, s 69 makes it an either way offence to be in possession of a paedophile manual, being an item (which includes anything in which information of any description is recorded) that contains advice or guidance about abusing children sexually. This covers offences under Pt 1 (ss 1–79) of the 2003 Act or the Protection of Children Act 1978, s 1 (see **6.6.1**).
- Section 116 of the Anti-social Behaviour, Crime and Policing Act 2014 provides that a police officer (inspector or above) may issue a

notice to the owner, operator, or manager of a hotel, on reasonable belief that the hotel has been or will be used for the purposes of CSE or conduct preparatory to or connected with CSE.

- A constable may require a person issued with such a notice to provide the police with name and address details of guests staying at the hotel. It is a summary offence under s 118(1) if a person fails without reasonable excuse to comply with this requirement.

s 10(1) offence

Either way   None

Summary: 6 months' imprisonment and/or a fine

Indictment: 14 years' imprisonment

s 10(2) offence

Indictment   None

14 years' imprisonment

6.5.2 Cause/incite child under 13 to engage in sexual activity

The offence of causing/inciting a child under 13 to engage in sexual activity is covered by s 8 of the Sexual Offences Act 2003.

Offences

(1) A person commits an offence if—
   (a) he intentionally causes or incites another person (B) to engage in an activity,
   (b) the activity is sexual, and
   (c) B is under 13.

(2) A person is guilty of an offence under this section, if the activity caused or incited involved—
   (a) penetration of B's anus or vagina,
   (b) penetration of B's mouth with a person's penis,
   (c) penetration of a person's anus or vagina with a part of B's body or by B with anything else, or
   (d) penetration of a person's mouth with B's penis.

Sexual Offences Act 2003, s 8

Points to prove

Non-penetration

- ✓ intentionally caused/incited
- ✓ a boy/girl under 13
- ✓ to engage in sexual activity
- ✓ of a non-penetrative nature

Penetration

- ✓ the first three points of '**Non-penetration**'
- ✓ involving the penetration of
- ✓ boy/girl's anus/vagina or
- ✓ boy/girl's mouth with another person's penis or
- ✓ a person's anus/vagina with a part of boy/girl's body or by boy/girl with anything else or
- ✓ a person's mouth with the boy's penis

Meanings

Intentionally (see 6.1.1)

Cause (see 6.5.1)

Incite (see 6.5.1)

Sexual (see 6.2.1)

Explanatory notes

- This offence is the same as the s 10 offence save that the defendant can be of any age and that the victim is under 13.
- In relation to sexual activity caused or incited, the offence covers the same situations as does the offence under s 4 except that, for this offence, consent is irrelevant.

Practical considerations

- Section 8 consists of four separate offences: causing or inciting penetrative or non-penetrative sexual activity; you must specify which offence it is. The sexual activity must be of the child (*R v Grout* [2011] EWCA Crim 299, CA).
- If possible, identify and preserve crime scene, and seize any articles and documentation relevant to the offence.
- Prove age of child. Only a suitably trained or qualified person should be used to take a statement or obtain evidence from the victim.

s 8(1) offence

 Either way

 None

Summary: 6 months' imprisonment and/or a fine

Indictment: 14 years' imprisonment

s 8(2) offence

Indictment　　　　　　　　None

Life imprisonment

6.5.3 **Arrange/facilitate commission of a child sex offence**

This offence is covered by s 14 of the Sexual Offences Act 2003.

Offences

A person commits an offence if—
(a) he intentionally arranges or facilitates something that he intends to do, intends another person to do, or believes that another person will do, in any part of the world, and
(b) doing it will involve the commission of an offence under any of sections 9 to 13.

Sexual Offences Act 2003, s 14(1)

Points to prove

✓ intentionally
✓ arranged/facilitated
✓ an act which the defendant
✓ intended to do or
✓ intended/believed another person would do
✓ in any part of the world
✓ and doing it will involve the commission of an offence under any of ss 9–13

Meanings

Intentionally (see **6.1.1**)

Arranges

Organise, plan, or reach agreement about an action or event in advance.

Facilitates

Make it happen, make it easier to achieve or promote.

Explanatory notes

- The defendant does not have to be the one who will commit the sexual offence; it will be enough if they intended/believed that they or another person would commit the relevant offence in any part of the world.
- The offence covers a situation where the defendant takes a person to a place where there is a child in the belief that the person is likely to engage in sexual activity with that child.
- It also caters for situations where the defendants arrange for themselves or another the procurement of a child with whom they propose to engage in sexual activity. For example, the defendant is going on holiday and plans to engage in sexual activity with children whilst there and so arranges through an agency to meet children.
- The sexual activity does not have to occur for the offence to be committed.
- The relevant offences are—
  - ✦ s 9—Sexual activity with a child;
  - ✦ s 10—Causing or inciting a child to engage in sexual activity;
  - ✦ s 11—Engaging in sexual activity in the presence of a child;
  - ✦ s 12—Causing a child to watch a sexual act;
  - ✦ s 13—Child sex offences committed by children or young persons.

Defences

(2) A person does not commit an offence under this section if—
  (a) he arranges or facilitates something that he believes another person will do, but that he does not intend to do or intend another person to do, and
  (b) any offence within subsection (1)(b) would be an offence against a child for whose protection he acts.

(3) For the purposes of subsection (2), a person acts for the protection of a child if he acts for the purposes of—
  (a) protecting the child from sexually transmitted infection,
  (b) protecting the physical safety of the child,
  (c) preventing the child from becoming pregnant, or
  (d) promoting the child's emotional well-being by the giving of advice,
  and not for the purpose of obtaining sexual gratification or for the purpose of causing or encouraging the activity constituting the offence within subsection (1)(b) or the child's participation in it.

Sexual Offences Act 2003, s 14

Defence notes

This is intended to protect those people such as health care workers who are aware that a person is having sex with a child under 16 and give them condoms as they believe that if they do not the child will have unprotected sex. It appears that the health care worker must warn the person that what they are doing is illegal but can give the condoms without committing an offence under this section.

Practical considerations

- The specified offence (under ss 9–13) does not have to take place. If it does occur or would have occurred if it were not for there being facts which made the commission of the offence impossible, then it might be easier to prove the above offence.
- Obtain any evidence which proves the links (eg advertisement, emails, and bookings for hotels).
- Seize mobile phone, computer hard drive, and any other physical evidence relevant to the offence.
- This offence is listed as a 'criminal lifestyle' offence under Sch 2 to the Proceeds of Crime Act 2002 (see **5.5** for details).
- The Child Sex Offender disclosure scheme is operated by CEOP (see **Appendix 1**). For further guidance and details about this matter see HOC 7/2010.

 Either way None

 Summary: 6 months' imprisonment and/or a fine

Indictment: 14 years' imprisonment

6.5.4 **Meeting a child following sexual grooming**

This offence is covered by s 15 of the Sexual Offences Act 2003.

> ### Offences
>
> A person aged 18 or over (A) commits an offence if—
> (a) A has met or communicated with another person (B) on one or more occasions and subsequently—
>   (i) A intentionally meets B,
>   (ii) A travels with the intention of meeting B in any part of the world or arranges to meet B in any part of the world, or
>   (iii) B travels with the intention of meeting A in any part of the world,

(b) A intends to do anything to or in respect of B, during or after the
      meeting mentioned in paragraph (a)(i) to (iii) and in any part of the world,
      which if done will involve the commission by A of a relevant offence,
(c) B is under 16, and
(d) A does not reasonably believe that B is 16 or over.

Sexual Offences Act 2003, s 15(1)

Points to prove

✓ being a person 18 or over, (A)
✓ has on one or more occasions met/communicated
✓ with a person under 16
✓ not reasonably believing that person to be 16 or over
✓ intentionally met or travelled intending to meet, or arranged
   to meet, that person or that person has travelled with the
   intention of meeting (A)
✓ in any part of the world
✓ intending to do anything to/in respect of that person
✓ during/after the meeting and in any part of the world
✓ which if done would involve commission by (A)
✓ of a relevant offence

Meanings

Has met or communicated

The reference to A having met or communicated with B is a reference to
A having met B in any part of the world or having communicated with
B by any means from, to, or in any part of the world.

Intentionally (see **6.1.1**)

Relevant offence

Means an offence under Pt 1 (ss 1–79 inclusive) and anything done outside England and Wales being an offence within Pt 1.

Reasonably believe (see 'Defences' below)

Explanatory notes

• A defendant must have communicated on one or more occasions
  or had one prior meeting with the person. The communication
  could be by telephone, texting, or email. These communications
  do not have to contain sexually explicit language or pornography
  but could, for example, be something as seemingly innocuous as
  the offender giving the victim swimming lessons or meeting them
  incidentally through a friend.
• Where person A has met, or communicated with, person B only
  once before the event mentioned in s 15(1)(a)(i)–(iii), an offence
  under s 15 is committed only if these events took place on or after

6.5.4 Meeting a child following sexual grooming

13 April 2015, when s 15 was amended by the Criminal Justice and Courts Act 2015, s 36. Prior to that date it would have to be 'on at least two occasions'. MOJ Circular 1/2015 provides further details.

- They must intentionally meet or travel with the intention of meeting or arrange to meet each other. This meeting can take place anywhere in the world as long as some part of the journey took place in England, Wales, or Northern Ireland.
- The meeting itself does not have to take place, arranging will suffice, although the intent to commit the relevant offence (in any part of the world) will have to be proved.
- This offence is intended to deal with predators who groom young children by gaining their trust, lying about their age, then arranging to meet them to sexually abuse them. This offence is preventative, in that the relevant sexual offence does not have to occur for the offence to be committed.

Defences

Reasonable belief that the victim is 16 or over (see **6.4** 'Defence notes').

Related cases

R v H [2010] EWCA Crim 1693, CA The defendant communicated with the victim and arranged to meet her at her school. It was held that there is no requirement that communication is sexual in nature, but a sexual intent must exist at the time of arranging the meeting. The statutory offence does not require the meeting to take place; it is sufficient if, with the intention of meeting, A travels to B or B travels to A. In each case, however, A must intend to commit a relevant (sexual) offence. A's sexual intention must be proved to have been formed either when A travels to B, waits for B to arrive or at the moment of meeting. It is not enough that, during the course of a meeting, started without any such intention, A then decides to take advantage of the situation and commit an offence: the crime then will be the commission of or the attempt to commit that offence. The offence contained within s 15 is not engaged.

R v Mohammed [2006] EWCA Crim 1107, CA The defendant sent intimate text messages to a vulnerable 13-year-old girl with severe learning difficulties and behavioural problems. Both were found together 8 miles from her foster home. He confirmed the complainant had visited his home; the abduction was short-lived, with the girl being willing and initiating contact, but no sexual act taking place. It was held that the defendant's motivation was sexual, and he had blatantly taken her from the control of carers and he was convicted.

Practical considerations

- Prove that the victim is under 16. Only a suitably trained or qualified person should be used to take a statement or obtain evidence from the victim.

- Any articles in the defendant's possession such as condoms, pornography, rope, and lubricant could help to prove intent.
- The Children Act 2004 (see **2.4.2**) makes specific provision for the police and other agencies to protect the welfare and safety of children.
- Offence applies to all offences in Pt 1 of the Act (ss 1–79).
- All evidence in relation to the grooming should be seized (eg any communications, bookings, or other documents which link the defendant and victim).
- Consider CCTV evidence.
- Seize any computer and mobile phone that could have been used.
- Section 72 allows sexual offences committed outside the UK to be dealt with in England and Wales, as if the person had committed the act in the UK, provided certain conditions are met. The conditions are that the defendant is a UK national or resident who commits an act in a country outside the UK, and the act, if committed in England and Wales, would constitute a sexual offence given in Sch 2.

 Either way   None

 Summary: 6 months' imprisonment and/or a fine

     Indictment: 10 years' imprisonment

6.5.5 **Sexual communication with a child**

This offence of sexual communication with a child helps ensure that young people are fully protected by the law and allow the authorities to intervene earlier to prevent more serious offending against children.

> **Offence**
>
> A person aged 18 or over (A) commits an offence if—
> (a) for the purpose of obtaining sexual gratification, A intentionally communicates with another person (B),
> (b) the communication is sexual or is intended to encourage B to make (whether to A or to another) a communication that is sexual, and
> (c) B is under 16 and A does not reasonably believe that B is 16 or over.
>
> *Sexual Offences Act 2003 s 15A(1)*

6.5.5 Sexual communication with a child

Meanings

Sexual activity

An activity that a reasonable person would, in all the circumstances but regardless of any person's purpose, consider to be sexual.

Practical considerations

- Subsection (2) provides that for the purposes of this section, a communication is sexual if—
    (a) any part of it relates to sexual activity, or
    (b) a reasonable person would, in all the circumstances but regardless of any person's purpose, consider any part of the communication to be sexual.
- This offence criminalises conduct where an adult intentionally communicates (eg, by email, text message, written note or orally) with a child under 16 (whom the adult does not reasonably believe to be aged 16 or over) for the purpose of obtaining sexual gratification if the communication is sexual or intended to encourage the child to make a communication that is sexual (s 15A(1) and (2)) often referred to as 'sexualised chat'.
- This offence means that action can be taken at a much earlier stage in the grooming process and/or in cases where the suspect does not intend or go on to arrange to meet a child.
- There are existing offences under ss 8 and 10 of the Sexual Offences Act 2003 (see **6.5.2**) that make it an offence to cause or incite a child under 13 or 16 respectively to engage in sexual activity. However, these offences are unlikely to apply if a communication (for example, in the form of an email or a text message) sent to a child contains sexual content but does not in any way ask the child to engage in sexual activity but the offence in section 15A covers such scenarios.
- Scenarios likely to be covered by the offence include talking sexually to a child via a chatroom or sending sexually explicit text messages to a child as well as inviting a child to communicate sexually (irrespective of whether the invitation is itself sexual).
- This offence is designed to ensure that it does not criminalise, for example, ordinary social or educational interactions between children and adults or communications between young people themselves.
- The term 'sexual gratification' has been described in case law as having a wide meaning and may take any of the myriad forms which sexual pleasure or indulgence may take.
- Section 127 of the Communications Act 2003 (see **7.12.2**) makes it an offence to send a message by means of a public electronic communications network (including the internet) if its content is grossly offensive, indecent, obscene, or menacing. Depending on the content of the message, this offence could apply where sexual messages are sent to a child by some form of electronic communication, such as text, email, or phone (although it would

not cover non-electronic written messages or verbal communication, or electronic messages sent by a private network such as a school intranet). However, this offence is not a sexual offence and does not attract sex offender registration. It would not be appropriate to change that position as the offence criminalises behaviour that may not be sexual in any way.

 Either way

 None

 Summary: 12 months' imprisonment and/or a fine

Indictment: 2 years' imprisonment

Links to alternative subjects and offences

6.6 Indecent Photographs/ Images: Persons under 18/ Disclose with Intent to Cause Distress

6.6.1 Take, make, distribute, publish indecent photographs of person under 18

This offence is covered by s 1 of the Protection of Children Act 1978.

Offences

Subject to sections 1A and 1B [defences], it is an offence for a person—
(a) to take, or permit to be taken, or to make, any indecent photograph or pseudo-photograph of a child; or
(b) to distribute or show such indecent photographs or pseudo-photographs; or
(c) to have in his possession such indecent photographs or pseudo-photographs, with a view to their being distributed or shown by himself or others; or
(d) to publish or cause to be published any advertisement likely to be understood as conveying that the advertiser distributes or shows such indecent photographs or pseudo-photographs or intends to do so.

Protection of Children Act 1978, s 1(1)

Points to prove

s 1(1)(a), (b)

✓ made/permitted to be taken/took/showed/distributed
✓ indecent photograph(s)/pseudo-photograph(s)
✓ of a child/children

s 1(1)(c)

✓ possessed
✓ indecent photograph(s)/pseudo-photograph(s)
✓ of child/children
✓ with a view to it (them) being distributed/shown to another

s 1(1)(d)

✓ published/caused to be published
✓ an advertisement which is likely to convey or be understood
✓ that the advertiser
✓ distributes/shows or intends to distribute/show

> ✓ indecent photograph(s)/pseudo-photograph(s)
> ✓ of child/children

Meanings

Make

Includes downloading images from the internet and storing or printing them (*R v Bowden* [2000] 1 WLR 1427).

Indecent photographs

- Includes indecent **film**, a copy of an indecent photograph or film, and an indecent photograph comprised in a film.
- Photographs (including those comprised in a film) shall, if they show children and are indecent, be treated for all purposes of this Act as indecent photographs of children and so as respects pseudo-photographs.

Photograph

References to a photograph include:
- the negative as well as the positive version; and
- data stored on a computer disc or by other electronic means which is capable of conversion into a photograph;
- a tracing or other image, whether made by electronic or other means (of whatever nature):
  + which is not itself a photograph or pseudo-photograph; but
  + which is derived from the whole or part of a photograph or pseudo-photograph (or a combination of either or both); **and** data stored on a computer disc or by other electronic means which is capable of conversion into the above tracing or image.

Notes: If the impression conveyed by a pseudo-photograph is that of a child, the pseudo-photograph shall be treated as showing a child and so shall a pseudo-photograph where the predominant impression conveyed is that the person shown is a child notwithstanding that some of the physical characteristics shown are those of an adult.

Film

This includes any form of video recording.

Pseudo-photograph

Means an image, whether made by computer graphics or otherwise howsoever, which appears to be a photograph.

Indecent pseudo-photograph

This includes a copy of an indecent pseudo-photograph, and data stored on a computer disc or by other electronic means which is capable of conversion into an indecent pseudo-photograph.

6.6.1 Take, make, distribute, publish indecent photographs

Child

A person under the age of 18.

Distribute

Means to part with possession to another person or exposes or offers for acquisition by another person.

Shown by himself

Means shown by the defendant to other people.

Explanatory notes

- The image does not have to be stored in a way that allows it to be retrieved. However, the image must be made deliberately. Innocently opening a file from the internet may not be an offence: see s 1(4)(b) in '**Defences**' below.
- The attendant circumstances of the way in which the images have been downloaded, stored, labelled, and filed will be important in demonstrating the extent to which the defendant was or should have been aware of their indecent nature. Other correspondence (by email or otherwise) with the defendant will also be useful here, as will any evidence of a general interest in paedophilia (*R v Mould* [2001] 2 Crim App R (S) 8).

Defences

1(4) Where a person is charged with an offence under subsection 1(b) or (c), it shall be a defence for him to prove—

    (a) that he had a legitimate reason for distributing or showing the photographs or pseudo-photographs or (as the case may be) having them in his possession; or

    (b) that he had not himself seen the photographs or pseudo-photographs and did not know, nor had any cause to suspect, them to be indecent.

Marriage and partnership

1A(1) This section applies where, in proceedings for an offence under s 1(1)(a) of taking or making an indecent photograph or pseudo-photograph of a child, or for an offence under s 1(1)(b) or (c) relating to an indecent photograph or pseudo-photograph of a child, the defendant proves that the photograph or pseudo-photograph was of the child aged 16 or over, and that at the time of the offence charged the child and he—

    (a) were married or civil partners of each other, or

    (b) lived together as partners in an enduring family relationship.

1A(2) Subsections (5) and (6) also apply where, in proceedings for an offence under s 1(1)(b) or (c) relating to an indecent photograph or pseudo-photograph of a child, the defendant proves that the photograph or pseudo-photograph was of the child aged 16 or over, and that at the time when he obtained it the child and he—

    (a) were married or civil partners of each other, or

    (b) lived together as partners in an enduring family relationship.

1 A(3) This section applies whether the photograph or pseudo-photograph showed the child alone or with the defendant, but not if it showed any other person.

1 A(4) In the case of an offence under s 1(1)(a), if sufficient evidence is adduced to raise an issue as to whether the child consented to the photograph or pseudo-photograph being taken or made, or as to whether the defendant reasonably believed that the child so consented, the defendant is not guilty of the offence unless it is proved that the child did not so consent and that the defendant did not reasonably believe that the child so consented.

1A(5) In the case of an offence under s 1(1)(b), the defendant is not guilty of the offence unless it is proved that the showing or distributing was to a person other than the child.

1A(6) In the case of an offence under s 1(1)(c), if sufficient evidence is adduced to raise an issue both—

    (a) as to whether the child consented to the photograph or pseudo-photograph being in the defendant's possession, or as to whether the defendant reasonably believed that the child so consented, and

    (b) as to whether the defendant had the photograph or pseudo-photograph in his possession with a view to its being distributed or shown to anyone other than the child,

the defendant is not guilty of the offence unless it is proved either that the child did not so consent, and that the defendant did not reasonably believe that the child so consented, or that the defendant had the photograph or pseudo-photograph in his possession with a view to its being distributed or shown to a person other than the child.

Instances when defendant is not guilty of the offence

1B(1) In proceedings for an offence under s 1(1)(a) of making an indecent photograph or pseudo-photograph of a child, the defendant is not guilty of the offence if he proves that—

    (a) it was necessary for him to make the photograph or pseudo-photograph for the purposes of the prevention, detection or investigation of crime, or for the purposes of criminal proceedings, in any part of the world,

    (b) at the time of the offence charged he was a member of the Security Service or the Secret Intelligence Service, and it was necessary for him to make the photograph or pseudo-photograph for the exercise of any of the functions of that Service, or

    (c) at the time of the offence charged he was a member of GCHQ, and it was necessary for him to make the photograph or pseudo-photograph for the exercise of any of the functions of GCHQ.

6.6.1 Take, make, distribute, publish indecent photographs

> 1B(2) In this section 'GCHQ' has the same meaning as in the Intelligence Services Act 1994.
>
> Protection of Children Act 1978, ss 1(4), 1A, and 1B

Defence notes

- The defence given in s 1(4)(b) as to 'not seeing and did not know, nor had any cause to suspect, them to be indecent' would cover situations where an email attachment was opened innocently and not subsequently deleted owing to a genuine lack of IT skills (eg may still be in a 'deleted' directory, 'recycle bin', or other 'temporary' directory), or innocently downloading an image from the web, then immediately deleting the image without realising that it was also stored as a back-up copy in a temporary internet directory.
- In a Crown Court case the 'Trojan Horse' virus defence was successful. In short, expert evidence confirmed the likelihood of this virus being responsible for fourteen depraved images saved on the defendant's personal computer. It was accepted that these could have been saved remotely, without the defendant's knowledge. Although this case is not binding on other courts, and each case will be determined according to its own particular facts, officers should be aware of the possibility of this defence being raised.

Related cases

R v Porter [2006] EWCA Crim 560, CA In this case it was held that if a person cannot gain access to retrieve deleted images on a computer then he was no longer in custody or control of those images.

R v Dooley [2005] EWCA Crim 3093, CA If downloaded material was accessible to all club members, then it is downloaded with a view to its distribution or showing to others.

R v Smith and Jayson [2002] 1 Cr App R 13, CA Deliberately opening an indecent computer email attachment or downloading an indecent image from the internet, so it can be viewed on a screen, is 'making' a photograph.

R v Fellows [1996] 10 CL 42 it was held that a digital image held on computer for display over the 'internet' was a photograph for the purposes of this legislation.

Practical considerations

- Problems arise when young people take and share indecent photos of themselves, invariably on mobile phones (known as 'sexting'), and if prosecuted for the s 1 offence means that the young person would be placed on the sex offenders register.
- NPCC and CEOP consider that a safeguarding approach should apply to children and young people involved in 'sexting'. The Children Act 1989, s 1(1) states that with statutory intervention the welfare of the child is paramount; this is reinforced by the Children

Act 2004, s 11, which places a duty on key persons and bodies to safeguard and promote the welfare of children.

- It is not an offence under this Act to possess photographs to show to yourself although this is an offence under s 160 of the Criminal Justice Act 1988 (see **6.6.2**).
- MOJ Circular 6/2010 provides guidelines about extending the 'marriage/other relationships' provisions to offences relating to indecent pseudo-photographs of persons under 18.
- Proceedings for this offence require the consent of the DPP.
- Ascertain how the photographs or pseudo-photographs were made, discovered, and whether stored.
- Seize all computer equipment as evidence under s 20 of PACE (see **1.5.4**).
- The 1978 Act schedule permits forfeiture of indecent images of children and the devices that hold them without the involvement of a court, unless the owner or other person with an interest in the material gives notice of a legitimate claim to the property.
- There are some authoritative factors in deciding whether or not a defence may apply, depending on whether the person(s):
  ✦ acted reasonably in all the circumstances;
  ✦ reported the photographs or pseudo-photographs as soon as was practicable and to the appropriate authority;
  ✦ stored the photographs or pseudo-photographs in a secure and safe manner;
  ✦ copied or distributed the photographs or pseudo-photographs unnecessarily.

E&S **CHAR**

 Either way   None

 Summary: 6 months' imprisonment and/or a fine

Indictment: 10 years' imprisonment

6.6.2 Possession of indecent photograph(s) of person under 18

Section 160 of the Criminal Justice Act 1988 concerns the offence of simple possession of indecent photographs or pseudo-photographs of a person under 18.

Offences

Subject to section 160A it is an offence for a person to have any indecent photograph or pseudo-photograph of a child in his possession.

Criminal Justice Act 1988, s 160(1)

6.6.2 Possession of indecent photograph(s)

Points to prove

✓ possessed
✓ indecent photograph(s)/pseudo-photograph(s)
✓ of a child/children

Meanings

Section 160A (see 'Defences' below).

Photograph (see **6.6.1**)

Indecent photograph (see **6.6.1**)

Pseudo-photograph (see **6.6.1**)

Child (see **6.6.1**)

Explanatory notes

Where there is evidence of intent to distribute or show then the offence under s 1 of the Protection of Children Act 1978 (see **6.6.1**) should be used.

Defences

160(2) Where a person is charged with an offence under subsection
(1) above it shall be a defence for him to prove—
(a) that he had a legitimate reason for having the photograph or pseudo-photograph in his possession; or
(b) that he had not himself seen the photograph or pseudo-photograph and did not know, nor had any cause to suspect, it to be indecent; or
(c) that the photograph or pseudo-photograph was sent to him without any prior request made by him or on his behalf and that he did not keep it for an unreasonable time.

160A(1) This section applies where, in proceedings for an offence under section 160 relating to an indecent photograph or pseudo-photograph of a child, the defendant proves that the photograph or pseudo-photograph was of the child aged 16 or over, and that at the time of the offence charged the child and he—
(a) were married or civil partners of each other, or
(b) lived together as partners in an enduring family relationship.

160A(2) This section also applies where, in proceedings for an offence under section 160 relating to an indecent photograph or pseudo-photograph of a child, the defendant proves that the photograph or pseudo-photograph was of the child aged 16 or over, and that at the time when he obtained it the child and he—
(a) were married or civil partners of each other, or
(b) lived together as partners in an enduring family relationship.

160A(3) This section applies whether the photograph or pseudo-
photograph showed the child alone or with the defendant, but
not if it showed any other person.

160A(4) If sufficient evidence is adduced to raise an issue as to whether
the child consented to the photograph or pseudo-photograph
being in the defendant's possession, or as to whether the
defendant reasonably believed that the child so consented, the
defendant is not guilty of the offence unless it is proved that
the child did not so consent and that the defendant did not
reasonably believe that the child so consented.

Criminal Justice Act 1988, ss 160 and 160A

Defence notes

The conditions for the defence are listed under s 160A(1)–(4). If any of
these conditions are not satisfied, the prosecution need only prove the
offence as set out in s 160. But if the three conditions are satisfied, the
defendant is not guilty of the offence unless the prosecution proves that
the child did not consent, and that the defendant did not reasonably
believe that the child consented.

Related cases

R v Miller [2010] EWCA Crim 2883, CA A conviction for possession of
indecent computer images of children was safe despite the fact that the
images had been deleted from the active part of the hard drive before
the computer's seizure.

R v Porter [2006] EWCA Crim 560, CA (see **6.6.1**).

Atkins v DPP and **Goodland v DPP [2000] 2 All ER 425, QBD** Images
stored in a temporary directory unbeknown to the defendant did not
amount to possession; knowledge was required.

Practical considerations

- Ensure that the photographs or pseudo-photographs are seized.
- It is for a jury to decide the age of an unknown child seen in a
  photograph.
- Seize the computer or storage mechanism as evidence under s 20 of
  PACE (see **1.5.4**).
- The schedule in the Protection of Children Act 1978 permits
  forfeiture of indecent images of children and the devices that hold
  them without the involvement of a court, unless the owner or
  some other person with an interest in the material gives notice of a
  legitimate claim to the property.
- Check on the audit chain for the photograph and documents
  relating to them to ensure possession is the only suitable charge.
- Consent of the DPP is required.

6.6.3 Disclose indecent photographs/films

- MOJ Circular 6/2010 provides guidelines about extending the 'marriage/other relationships' provisions to offences relating to indecent pseudo-photographs of persons under 18.
- Section 62 of the Coroners and Justice Act 2009 gives the offence of possession of a prohibited **image** of a person under 18, being a non-photographic image, which is pornographic and is grossly offensive, disgusting, or otherwise of an obscene character. MOJ Circular 6/2010 provides guidance on this matter. Any such image found in possession of a school pupil by a member of staff at the school can be given to a police constable (see **8.10.5**).
- Section 63 of the Criminal Justice and Immigration Act 2008 deals with the offence of possession of **extreme pornographic images**, **being** an image that portrays, in an explicit and realistic way, any act which involves:
  + threatening a person's life;
  + serious injury to a person's anus, breasts, or genitals;
  + sexual interference with a human corpse;
  + a person performing intercourse or oral sex with an animal (whether dead or alive);
  + rape of a person's vagina, anus, or mouth by another with the other person's penis; or
  + rape of a person's vagina or anus by another with a part of the other person's body or anything else,

and a reasonable person looking at the image would think that any such person or animal was real. Any such images found in possession of a school pupil by a member of staff at the school can be given to a police constable (see **8.10.5**).

E&S **CHAR**

 Either way   None

 Summary: 6 months' imprisonment and/or a fine

Indictment: 5 years' imprisonment and/or a fine

6.6.3 Disclose indecent photographs/ films with intent to cause distress

This offence is dealt with by s 33 of the Criminal Justice and Courts Act 2015.

> **Offences**
>
> (1) It is an offence for a person to disclose a private sexual photograph or film if the disclosure is made—
>   (a) without the consent of an individual who appears in the photograph or film, and
>   (b) with the intention of causing that individual distress.

(2) But it is not an offence under this section for the purpose to disclose the photograph or film to the individual mentioned in subsection (1)(a)or (b).

Criminal Justice and Courts Act 2015, s 33

Points to prove

✓ disclose
✓ private sexual photograph(s)/film(s)
✓ without consent of person who appears in photograph(s)/film(s)
✓ intending to cause that person distress

Meanings

Disclose

By any means, s/he **gives** or **shows** it to a person or **makes it available** to a person.

Gives/shows/makes available

Something that is given, shown or made available to a person is disclosed whether or not:

- it is given, shown, or made available for reward; and
- it has previously been given, shown, or made available to the person.

Private

If it shows something that is not of a kind ordinarily seen in public.

Sexual

A photograph or film is sexual if:

- it shows all or part of an individual's exposed genitals or pubic area;
- it shows something that a reasonable person would consider to be sexual because of its nature; or
- its content, taken as a whole, is such that a reasonable person would consider it to be sexual.

Photograph or film

Means a still or moving image in any form that:

- appears to consist of or include one or more **photographed or filmed images**; and
- in fact consists of or includes one or more **photographed or filmed images** (including images that have been altered in any way).

Photographed or filmed image

Means a still or moving image that was, or is part of, an image originally captured by photography or **filming**.

6.6.3 Disclose indecent photographs/films

Filming

Means making a recording, on any medium, from which a moving image may be produced by any means.

Consent

Consent to a disclosure includes general consent covering the disclosure, as well as consent to the particular disclosure.

Intention (see **4.1.2**)

Explanatory notes

- This offence, otherwise known as 'revenge porn', will generally apply to a finished relationship where a partner publishes a photograph or film of a sexual nature to get back at their ex-partner.
- A person charged with this offence is not to be taken to have disclosed a photograph or film with the intention of causing distress merely because that was a natural and probable consequence of the disclosure.
- Further to the meaning above, a 'photograph or film' includes a negative version of an image, and data stored by any means which is capable of conversion into an image so described.

Defences

(3) It is a defence for a person charged with an offence under this section to prove that he or she reasonably believed that the disclosure was necessary for the purposes of preventing, detecting or investigating crime.

(4) It is a defence for a person charged with an offence under this section to show that—
   (a) the disclosure was made in the course of, or with a view to, the publication of journalistic material, and
   (b) he or she reasonably believed that, in the particular circumstances, the publication of the journalistic material was, or would be, in the public interest.

(5) It is a defence for a person charged with an offence under this section to show that—
   (a) he or she reasonably believed that the photograph or film had previously been disclosed for reward, whether by the individual mentioned in subsection (1)(a) and (b) or another person, and
   (b) he or she had no reason to believe that the previous disclosure for reward was made without the consent of the individual mentioned in subsection (1)(a) and (b).

Criminal Justice and Courts Act 2015, s 33

Defence notes

- A person is taken to have shown the matters mentioned in subsection (4) or (5) if:
  - ✦ sufficient evidence of the matters is adduced to raise an issue with respect to it; and
  - ✦ the contrary is not proved beyond reasonable doubt.
- For the purposes of subsections (1)–(5):
  - ✦ consent to a disclosure includes general consent covering the disclosure, as well as consent to the particular disclosure; and
  - ✦ publication of journalistic material means disclosure to the public at large or to a section of the public.

Practical considerations

- This offence involves the sharing of private, sexual materials (either as photographs or film images) without the victim's consent and with the purpose/intention of causing them embarrassment or distress.
- The sexual material is not restricted to the genital/pubic area, but anything a reasonable person would consider to be sexual; for example, someone who is engaged in sexual behaviour or posing in a sexually provocative way.
- It concerns images shared electronically or in hard copy, including uploading of images onto the internet, sharing by text/email, or showing someone a physical or electronic image.
- This offence could apply to an image which appears to be originated from a film or photograph, even if the original has been altered in some way or where two or more images are combined.
- Photograph or film images that are completely computer-generated but made to look like an original photograph/film image, would not come under this offence because they are not a record of a real private event.
- Annex C in MOJ Circular 1/2015 provides further details and guidelines regarding this offence.

 Either way None

 Summary: 6 months' imprisonment and/or a fine

Indictment: 2 years' imprisonment and/or a fine

Links to alternative subjects and offences

6.7 Indecent Exposure and Outraging Public Decency

6.7.1 Indecent exposure

This offence is covered by s 66 of the Sexual Offences Act 2003.

Offences

A person commits an offence if—
(a) he intentionally exposes his genitals, and
(b) he intends that someone will see them and be caused alarm or distress.

Sexual Offences Act 2003, s 66(1)

Points to prove

✓ intentionally
✓ exposed genitals
✓ intending
✓ someone would see them
✓ and be caused alarm/distress

Meanings

Intentionally (see 6.1.1)

Genitals

Means male or female sexual organs.

Explanatory notes

- Offence would generally exclude naturists and streakers whose intention is not to cause alarm or distress.
- Exposure of the genitals must be intentional and not accidental.
- The offence applies to either sex. However, genitals do not include a female's breasts or the buttocks of either sex, so a female flashing her breasts or someone mooning (exposing their buttocks) will not be caught within this offence.
- Offence can be committed anywhere and is not restricted to public places.

Practical considerations

- CPS guidance in relation to naturists/nudity states that where there is no intention to cause alarm or distress and there is no sexual context then it would be appropriate to take no action. However, if people were caused harassment, alarm, and distress then consider the s 5 public order offence (see **7.8**), as 'disorderly' describes this behaviour since it does not conform to the normal standards of society which require people to be clothed in public.

- Proof of the relevant intent (both as to the genitals being seen and alarm or distress being caused thereby) will be critical to a successful prosecution.
- The precise location and the time of day could be important in showing a likely intention by the defendant.
- The accompanying words/conduct of the defendant will be relevant here, along with any preparatory or subsequent actions.
- Is this offence isolated or one of a series?

 Either way None

▥ **Summary:** 6 months' imprisonment and/or a fine

Indictment: 2 years' imprisonment

6.7.2 **Outraging public decency**

This is an offence at common law.

> ### Offences
>
> It is an offence to commit an act of a lewd, obscene, and disgusting nature, which is capable of outraging public decency, in a public place where at least two members of the public who were actually present at the time could have witnessed it.
>
> Common law

Points to prove
- ✓ in a public place
- ✓ committed an act capable of being seen by two or more persons present
- ✓ of a lewd/obscene/disgusting nature thereby outraging public decency
- ✓ by behaving in indecent manner

Meanings

Lewd

Means lustful or indecent.

Obscene

Means morally repugnant or depraved.

Disgusting

Means repugnant or loathsome.

Public place

Means a place to which the public have access or a place which is visible to the public.

Explanatory notes

- Consider if statutory offences would be more suitable, such as the Sexual Offences Act 2003, or the Public Order Act 1986.
- Such conduct can also be an offence of public nuisance at common law (see **7.13.4**).

Related cases

R v F [2010] EWCA Crim 2243, CA It was held in this case that the two-person rule applicable to outraging public decency had not been satisfied where, on the agreed evidence, the defendant had stopped the act of masturbating in his car whenever other people came into the area but continued once they had gone.

R v Hamilton [2007] EWCA Crim 2062, CA The defendant admitted positioning a camera to film up the skirts of women in a supermarket, but it was argued that since no one had seen him filming there had been no outrage of public decency and, therefore, no offence committed. It was held that a jury was capable of judging his conduct as lewd, obscene, or disgusting and were justified in reaching that conclusion despite no one actually seeing the filming. The act must also be done in a place that the public had access to or where the act was a capable of being viewed by at least two members of the public who were actually present. Filming in the supermarket satisfied that requirement.

R v Walker [1996] 1 Cr App R 111, CA The defendant exposed himself and masturbated in front of two young girls in his living room. It was held that as the public could not see into his living room then it was not a public place for this offence.

R v Gibson [1990] 2 QB 619 The 'act' does not have to be a 'live' activity, nor does it have to be of a sexual nature. It may be the act of putting a disgusting object on public display, such as displaying a sculpted head with a real human foetus dangling from it in a public art gallery.

Practical considerations

- More than one person must be able to witness the lewd act.
- Conduct must grossly cross the boundaries of decency and be likely to seriously offend the reasonable person (rather than simply upsetting or even shocking).

6.7.2 Outraging public decency

- In sexual offences, this offence is reserved for offences where masturbation or sexual intercourse occurs (as with the current fad of 'dogging'). There is no requirement to prove that those persons who witnessed the act were actually disgusted or outraged by it. The test is an objective one based on whether a reasonable person would be disgusted.
- Where the circumstances are appropriate, positive evidence of disgust can be given by a police officer.

 Either way   None

 Summary: 6 months' imprisonment and/or a fine

Indictment: Imprisonment and/or a fine

Links to alternative subjects and offences

E&S Entry and search powers   **CHAR** Offences where evidence of bad character can be introduced

6.8 **Voyeurism**

This offence is created by s 67 of the Sexual Offences Act 2003.

Offences

(1) A person commits an offence if—
   (a) for the purpose of obtaining sexual gratification, he observes another person doing a private act, and
   (b) he knows that the other person does not consent to being observed for his sexual gratification.

(2) A person commits an offence if—
   (a) he operates equipment with the intention of enabling another person to observe, for the purpose of obtaining sexual gratification, a third person (B) doing a private act, and
   (b) he knows that B does not consent to his operating equipment with that intention.

(3) A person commits an offence if—
   (a) he records another person (B) doing a private act,
   (b) he does so with the intention that he or a third person will, for the purpose of obtaining sexual gratification, look at an image of B doing the act, and
   (c) he knows that B does not consent to his recording the act with that intention.

(4) A person commits an offence if he installs equipment or constructs or adapts a structure or part of a structure, with the intention of enabling himself or another person to commit an offence under subsection (1).

Sexual Offences Act 2003, s 67

Points to prove

Observing (s 67(1))

✓ for purpose of obtaining sexual gratification
✓ observed another person
✓ doing a private act
✓ knowing that the person
✓ does not consent to being observed
✓ for defendant's sexual gratification

Operating equipment to observe (s 67(2))

✓ operated equipment
✓ with the intention of enabling another person
✓ for the purpose of obtaining sexual gratification
✓ to observe a third person doing a private act
✓ knowing that person does not consent
✓ to defendant operating equipment with that intention

> ### Recording a private act (s 67(3))
>
> ✓ recorded another person doing a private act
> ✓ with intention that
> ✓ defendant or a third person
> ✓ would for the purpose of obtaining sexual gratification
> ✓ look at an image of that other person doing the act
> ✓ knowing that the other person does not consent
> ✓ to defendant recording the act with that intention
>
> ### Install equipment/construct/adapt a structure (s 67(4))
>
> ✓ installed equipment **or**
> ✓ constructed/adapted a structure/part of a structure
> ✓ with intent
> ✓ to enable defendant or third person
> ✓ to commit an offence under s 67(1)

Meanings

Private act

A person is doing a private act if they are in a place where they could reasonably expect privacy and their genitals, breasts, or buttocks are exposed or covered only by underwear, they are using the toilet, or doing a sexual act that is not normally done in public.

Consent

Defendant must **know** that the person does not consent to being observed for **sexual gratification**. They may have consented to being observed for some other reason.

Sexual gratification

In s 67(1) the sexual gratification must be for the defendant; in the other subsections it could be for a third party's sexual gratification.

Structure

Includes a tent, vehicle, or vessel, or other temporary or movable structure.

Explanatory notes

- For s 67(2)–(4), it is irrelevant whether or not any third parties knew that the person did not consent.
- Section 67(2) is aimed at those who install webcams or other recording equipment for their own gratification or for that of others. An image is defined as 'a moving or still image and includes an image produced by any means and, where the context permits, a three-dimensional image'.

- Section 67(4) would cover a person who installed a two-way mirror or a spy-hole in a hotel room. The offender would commit the offence even if the peephole or mirror was discovered before it was ever used.

Related cases

R v Burke [2012] EWCA Crim 770, CA In relation to voyeurism, the jury had to be satisfied not only that the observation was deliberate, but also that it was for the purpose of sexual gratification.

R v Bassett [2008] EWCA Crim 1174, CA It was held in this case that whether a person had a reasonable expectation of privacy would depend on the facts and would be closely related to the nature of the observation taking place. The parts of the body that fall within the scope of the 2003 Act are those parts for which people conventionally expect privacy. 'Breasts' were to mean female breasts as opposed to the bare male chest.

Practical considerations

- Any equipment used requires seizing.
- CCTV footage may be of use.
- Search for films made and evidence of equipment hire.
- Medium/equipment used for recording/storing image can be seized for examination and evidence.

 Either way None

 Summary: 6 months' imprisonment and/or a fine

Indictment: 2 years' imprisonment

Links to alternative subjects and offences

E&S Entry and search powers   **CHAR** Offences where evidence of bad character can be introduced

6.9 **Sexual Activity in a Public Lavatory**

This offence is covered by s 71 of the Sexual Offences Act 2003.

Offences

A person commits an offence if—
(a) he is in a lavatory to which the public or a section of the public has or is permitted to have access, whether on payment or otherwise,
(b) he intentionally engages in an activity, and,
(c) the activity is sexual.

Sexual Offences Act 2003, s 71(1)

Points to prove

✓ being in a lavatory
✓ to which the public/a section of the public
✓ have/are permitted to have access
✓ whether on payment/otherwise
✓ intentionally
✓ engaged in a sexual activity

Meanings

Intentionally (see 6.1.1)

Sexual activity

An activity is sexual if a reasonable person would, in all the circumstances but regardless of any person's purpose, consider it to be sexual.

Explanatory notes

- Offence covers lavatories to which the public, or a section of the public, have access, whether or not payment is involved. This would include staff toilets in large/small premises where the public could have access.
- The sexual activity does not have to be specified; it would be enough to record details of what was seen or heard.
- There is no requirement to prove that anyone was alarmed or distressed by the activity.
- This offence replaced the former offence known as 'cottaging'.

Practical considerations

- 'Sexual' in s 71 is different than where used elsewhere throughout the Act, in that it is what a reasonable person would consider sexual, regardless of the person's purpose.
- The offence is gender neutral, so the sexual activity could be committed by a male or female against a male or female.
- If possible obtain independent evidence.

 Summary   6 months

 6 months' imprisonment and/or a fine

Links to alternative subjects and offences

6.10 Administer Substance Intending to Commit a Sexual Offence

This offence is covered by s 61 of the Sexual Offences Act 2003.

Offences

A person commits an offence if he intentionally administers a substance to, or causes a substance to be taken by, another person (B)—
(a) knowing that B does not consent, and
(b) with the intention of stupefying or overpowering B, so as to enable any person to engage in a sexual activity that involves B.

Sexual Offences Act 2003, s 61(1)

Points to prove

✓ intentionally
✓ administered a substance to or
✓ caused a substance to be taken by
✓ another person
✓ knowing that s/he did not consent
✓ with intention of stupefying/overpowering
✓ so as to enable any person
✓ to engage in a sexual activity involving victim

Meanings

Intentionally (see 6.1.1)

Administer

In *R v Gillard* (1988) 87 Cr App Rep 189 'administer' was held to include conduct that brings a substance into contact with the victim's body, directly or indirectly, for example by injection or by holding a cloth soaked in the substance to the victim's face.

Causes to be taken

This would cover such conduct as slipping a date rape drug directly into a drink or deceiving the victim as to the nature of the substance (eg telling the victim it is a painkiller when in fact it is a sedative).

Sexual (see 6.2.1)

Explanatory notes

- This offence is intended to cover situations where so-called 'date rape' drugs (such as Rohypnol or GHB (gamma-hydroxybutrate)—see **6.1.1**) are given to a person to allow the defendant or someone else to engage in sexual activity with them. It also covers the spiking of a person's drink with alcohol when they believed they were drinking a soft drink.
- It does not matter how the substance is administered (eg by drink, injection). The offence has a very wide ambit in that it allows for one person to administer the substance or cause the substance to be taken and another to engage in the sexual activity (although no sexual activity need take place).
- The required consent refers to the taking/administering of the substance as opposed to the intended sexual activity. In s 76(2)(f) there is an evidential presumption that the victim does not consent to the sexual activity under s 1 (see **6.1.1**) where a substance which would stupefy or overpower has been administered.

Practical considerations

- The offence is committed whether or not there is any sexual activity as long as the substance was administered and there was the relevant intention.
- If there was no sexual activity, it may be hard to prove this offence. However, consider offences under s 23 or s 24 of the Offences Against the Person Act 1861 as to administering a poison or other noxious thing (see **5.1.1**).
- Also consider offences under s 61 Sexual Offences Act 2003 for trespass with intent to commit a sexual offence and s 62 of the same Act to commit an offence with intent to commit a sexual offence.
- If there was sexual activity then consider other offences, not just this one.
- Consider taking samples and medical examinations where appropriate.
- Gather evidence by seizing any appropriate documentation.
- Seize mobile phones where there is evidence of a link between defendants and victims at the relevant time.
- Consider CCTV footage.

 Either way   None

 Summary: 6 months' imprisonment and/or a fine

    Indictment: 10 years' imprisonment

Links to alternative subjects and offences

6.11 Prostitution: Soliciting and Paying for Services of Prostitute (Subject Exploitation)

6.11.1 Persistently loitering/soliciting in street/public place for prostitution

This offence is contrary to s 1 of the Street Offences Act 1959.

> **Offences**
>
> It shall be an offence for a person aged 18 or over (whether male or female) persistently to loiter or solicit in a street or public place for the purpose of prostitution.
>
> Street Offences Act 1959, s 1(1)

> **Points to prove**
>
> ✓ person aged 18 or over
> ✓ persistently
> ✓ loitered or solicited
> ✓ in street/public place
> ✓ for purpose of prostitution

Meanings

Persistently

Conduct is persistent if it takes place on two or more occasions in any period of three months.

Prostitute

Means any person who offers sexual services for reward and includes a person acting as a 'clipper' (a person who offers a sexual service but does not provide it themselves).

Loiter

Means to dawdle or linger idly about a place, proceeding with frequent pauses (see '**Related cases**' below).

6.11.1 Persistently loitering etc.

Solicit

Means to accost and offer oneself.

Street

Includes any bridge, road, lane, footway, subway, square, court, alley, or passage, whether a thoroughfare or not, which is for the time being open to the public; and the doorways and entrances of premises abutting on a street, and any ground adjoining and open to a street.

Public place

Any highway and any place to which at the material time the public has access, on payment or otherwise, as of right or by virtue of express or implied permission.

Explanatory notes

- Section 68(7) of the Serious Crime Act 2015 amended this offence to apply only to persons aged 18 and over, thus recognising that a person under 18 is a victim (child sexual exploitation). It is an offence to pay for the sexual services of a child under the Sexual Offences Act 2003, s 47 (see **6.5.1**). HOC 8/2015 provides guidance on this matter.
- Any reference to a person loitering or soliciting for the purposes of prostitution is a reference to a person loitering or soliciting for the purposes of offering services as a prostitute.
- Men or women aged 18 or over can be prostitutes.

Practical considerations

- A court can make an order requiring a person convicted of this offence to attend three meetings with a named supervisor or with such other person as the supervisor may direct. If such order is made, the court may not impose any other penalty for the offence.
- The purpose of this order is to assist the offender by addressing the cause and finding ways to cease engaging in such conduct in the future.
- HOC 6/2010 provides guidance on the amendments to loitering for the purposes of prostitution.
- Official guidelines for dealing with prostitution ensure that all the relevant agencies work in partnership to ensure that individuals do not become involved in prostitution in the first place or to create opportunities to leave prostitution.
- **Prostitution adverts**: s 46 of the Criminal Justice and Police Act 2001 makes it an offence to place on, or in the immediate vicinity of, a public telephone an advertisement relating to prostitution

services, with the intention that the advertisement should come to the attention of any prospective customers.
• Consider seizing CCTV for evidential purposes.

  Summary   6 months

Level 2 fine (after a previous conviction: level 3)

6.11.2 **Soliciting to obtain services of a prostitute**

This offence is covered by s 51A of the Sexual Offences Act 2003.

Offences

It is an offence for a person in a street or public place to solicit another (B) for the purpose of obtaining B's sexual services as a prostitute.

Sexual Offences Act 2003, s 51A

Points to prove

✓ solicited
✓ another person (B)
✓ for purpose of obtaining
✓ B's sexual services as a prostitute

Meanings

Solicit (see **6.11.1**)

Prostitute

Means a person (A) who, on at least one occasion and whether or not compelled to do so, offers or provides sexual services to another person in return for payment or a promise of **payment** to A or a third person; and 'prostitution' is to be interpreted accordingly.

Payment

Means any financial advantage, including the discharge of an obligation to pay or the provision of goods or services (including sexual services) gratuitously or at a discount.

Street (see **6.11.1**)

Public place (see **6.11.1**)

6.11.3 Paying for sexual services

Explanatory notes

The reference to a person in a street or public place includes a person in a vehicle in a street or public place.

Practical considerations

HOC 6/2010 provides guidance on this s 51A soliciting offence.

 Summary   6 months

 Level 3 fine

6.11.3 **Paying for sexual services of a prostitute subject to exploitation**

Section 53A of the Sexual Offences Act 2003 makes it an offence for a person to pay or promise payment for sexual services of a prostitute who has been subject to exploitative conduct.

Offences

A person (A) commits an offence if—
(a) A makes or promises payment for the sexual services of a prostitute (B),
(b) a third person (C) has engaged in exploitative conduct of a kind likely to induce or encourage B to provide the sexual services for which A has made or promised payment, and
(c) C engaged in that conduct for or in the expectation of gain for C or another person (apart from A or B).

Sexual Offences Act 2003, s 53A(1)

Points to prove

✓ (A) made or promised payment
✓ for sexual services of a prostitute (B)
✓ B subject to exploitative conduct of a kind likely to induce/ encourage B to provide the sexual services
✓ third person (C) engaged in exploitative conduct
✓ for/expectation of gain for C or another person (apart from A or B)

Meanings

Payment (see **6.11.2**)

Prostitute (see **6.11.2**)

Exploitative conduct

Conduct which involves the use of: force; threats (whether or not relating to violence); any other form of coercion; or any form of deception.

Gain

Means any financial advantage, including the discharge of an obligation to pay or the provision of goods or services (including sexual services) gratuitously or at a discount; or the goodwill of any person which is or appears likely, in time, to bring financial advantage.

Explanatory notes

- It is irrelevant where in the world the sexual services are to be provided and whether those services are provided, and/or whether A is, or ought to be, aware that C has engaged in exploitative conduct.
- This is a strict liability offence which is committed if someone pays or promises payment for sexual services of a prostitute who has been subject to exploitative conduct.
- The person responsible for the exploitative conduct must have been acting for or in the expectation of gain for him/herself or another person, other than the payer or the prostitute.
- The use of threats is not restricted to threats of physical violence: it could be 'psychological' threats, such as threatening to inform immigration/police, to withdraw accommodation or financial support, or to stop supplying drugs.

Practical considerations

- This offence is aimed at protecting vulnerable/exploited females by trying to reduce the demand for prostitution by placing the emphasis of the law on the user, rather than the prostitute.
- HOC 6/2010 provides guidance on the Policing and Crime Act 2009 provisions relating to prostitution: paying for sexual services of a prostitute subject to exploitation; loitering for purposes of prostitution; soliciting; and closure notices/orders.
- Section 53 of the Sexual Offences Act 2003 makes it an offence for a person to intentionally control another person's activities relating to prostitution, in any part of the world, where the defendant does so for, or in the expectation of, gain for him/herself or a third party.
- Part 2A (ss 136A–136R) of the Sexual Offences Act 2003 deals with court orders and closure notices (issued by superintendent or above) for premises used for specified prostitution or pornography offences under s 136B or specified child sex offences under s 136BA.

 Summary   6 months

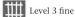 Level 3 fine

Links to alternative subjects and offences

Chapter 7

Public Disorder/Nuisance

7.1 **Penalty Notices for Disorder**

Penalty Notices for Disorder (PNDs) were established by s 2 of the Criminal Justice and Police Act 2001.

7.1.1 **Penalty notices for disorder offences**

A PND can no longer be issued to a person under 18. Offences for which a PND can be issued are as follows:

Upper tier

Penalty—£90 (18 and over)

Throwing fireworks in a thoroughfare
Explosives Act 1875, s 80 (see **8.8.6**).

Wasting police time or giving false report
Criminal Law Act 1967, s 5(2) (see **11.4.1**).

Disorderly behaviour while drunk in a public place
Criminal Justice Act 1967, s 91 (see **7.2.1**).

Theft (under £100 retail/commercial only) (see 7.1.2 'Shoplifting and criminal damage' for guidance)
Theft Act 1968, ss 1–7 (see **3.1.1**).

Destroying or damaging property (under £300) (see 7.1.2 'Shoplifting and criminal damage' for guidance)
Criminal Damage Act 1971, s 1(1) (see **4.4**).

Possess cannabis and its derivatives, being a Class B controlled drug (see 7.1.2 'Cannabis possession' for guidance)
Misuse of Drugs Act 1971, s 5(2) (see **5.2.1** and **5.3.1**).

7.1.1 Penalty notices for disorder offences

Behaviour likely to cause harassment, alarm, or distress

Public Order Act 1986, s 5 (see **7.7**).

Send offensive/false messages on public communications network

Communications Act 2003, s 127(2) (see **7.12.2**).

Breach Fireworks Regulations 2004 prohibitions: curfew/possess Category 4

Fireworks Act 2003, s 11 (see **8.8**).

Sale of alcohol anywhere to a person under 18

Licensing Act 2003, s 146(1) (see **9.1.2**).

Supply of alcohol by or on behalf of a club to a person aged under 18

Licensing Act 2003, s 146(3) (see **9.1.2**).

Buy or attempt to buy alcohol on behalf of a person under 18

Licensing Act 2003, s 149(3)(a) (see **9.1.4**).

Buy/attempt to buy alcohol for consumption by under 18 on relevant premises

Licensing Act 2003, s 149(4) (see **9.1.4**).

Sell or attempt to sell alcohol to a person who is drunk

Licensing Act 2003, s 141 (see **9.2.1**).

Deliver/allow delivery of alcohol to person under 18

Licensing Act 2003, s 151 (see **9.1.6**).

Knowingly give a false alarm of fire

Fire and Rescue Services Act 2004, s 49 (see **7.12.3**).

Lower tier

Penalty—£60 (18 and over)

Being drunk in a highway, public place, or licensed premises

Licensing Act 1872, s 12 (see **7.2.2**).

Trespassing on a railway

British Transport Commission Act 1949, s 55.

Throw stone, matter, or thing at a train/apparatus on railway

British Transport Commission Act 1949, s 56.

Possess khat or preparation/product containing khat, being a
Class C controlled drug (see **7.1.2** '**Khat possession**' for guidance)

Misuse of Drugs Act 1971, s 5(2) (see **5.3.1**).

Leave/deposit litter

Environmental Protection Act 1990, s 87(1) (see **7.16.2**)—issuing restrictions apply (see **7.16** and **11.1.4**).

Allow person under 18 to consume alcohol on relevant
licensed premises

Licensing Act 2003, s 150(2) (see **9.1.5**).

7.1.2 **Police operational guidance for issuing PNDs**

Police operational guidance on PNDs was updated by the MOJ on 24 June 2014.

PND scheme

- The main aim of the PND scheme is to provide a quick and effective alternative disposal option for dealing with low-level, anti-social, and nuisance offending. The PND is a type of fixed penalty notice for specified offences (see **7.1.1**). It does not prevent other means of disposal, and arrest should be considered where appropriate.
- A person has twenty-one days from being issued with the PND to either pay the penalty or request a court hearing or (in some cases— see '**Educational course schemes**' below) attend an educational course. Failure to do this within that period will mean a fine of one and a half times the penalty being registered at court for fine enforcement.
- Payment of the penalty or completing the course is not an admission of guilt and will discharge any liability to be convicted of the offence. A PND is not a criminal conviction, but for recordable offences a PNC entry may be made which may be disclosed under an enhanced DBS check.
- PNDs can be issued by constables (including special constables), CSOs, CSVs (see **11.1.2**), trading standards officers, or accredited persons for certain offences. No one can demand a PND; similarly, no one should be forced to accept a PND. Where a person is uncooperative consider an alternative disposal.
- PNDs are only available to a person aged 18 or over, providing they are suitable (see '**Persons**' below), and the evidential test in the Code for Crown Prosecutors is satisfied. The PND may be given either on the spot, at a police station or any other place later.

Preconditions for issuing a PND

A PND may **only** be issued where:
- they have reason to believe a person has committed a PND offence and they have sufficient evidence to support a successful prosecution (interviews and questioning must be consistent with the practice and procedures established by PACE 1984, Code C). Also note the provisions of PACE Code E para 3.1(a)(iii) relating to the power to issue a PND for retail theft (shoplifting) offences under s 1 Theft Act 1968;
- the offence is not too serious and is suitable for being dealt with by PND;
- the suspect is suitable, compliant, and able to understand what is going on;
- a second or subsequent offence, which is known, does not overlap with the PND offence (see **'Offences'** below);
- the offence(s) involve(s) no one below the age of 18;
- sufficient evidence as to the suspect's age, identity, and place of residence exists.

Offences

A PND will not be appropriate where:
- there has been any injury (or any realistic threat or risk of injury) to any person;
- there has been a substantial financial/material loss to the private property of an individual;
- a penalty offence is committed in association with another offence, including a penalty offence;
- the provisions of the Protection from Harassment Act 1997 might apply;
- the behaviour constitutes part of a pattern of intimidation;
- the offence involves domestic violence;
- it is a football-related offence;
- an offence has been committed jointly with a person under 18;
- any designated premises supervisor has committed an offence (but may be appropriate for bar staff when taking action against premises found or known to be serving alcohol to underage drinkers).

Shoplifting and criminal damage

- PND disposal for 'shoplifting' will only be appropriate where the value of goods does not exceed £100. The property must be recovered and remains fit for sale unless the items stolen comprised drink or food and have been consumed, and that the person suspected of stealing the property is not employed (whether paid or not) by the person, company, or organisation to which the property belongs.
- Label swapping can be dealt with by PND if they opt to deal with the offence as theft. A PND cannot be issued for the offence of making off without payment (see **3.7**).

- PND disposal may only be used for criminal damage up to a value of £300 so long as the suspect is not employed (as above).
- PND disposal for shop theft/criminal damage will not be appropriate for substance misusers. The reason is that they may be better dealt with by court or conditional caution which can direct them to treatment.

Throwing fireworks

A PND may be appropriate where fireworks are thrown to cause annoyance and nuisance, but this will not be the case if it is part of a pattern of intimidation or there was intention to cause harm.

False reports

- When dealing with offences under the Communications Act 2003, s 127(2), Criminal Law Act 1967, s 5(2), and the Fire and Rescue Service Act 2004, s 49, a PND may be appropriate if the 999 service is misused or the person has made nuisance calls, but this will not be the case for serious misuse such as making a hoax bomb threat.
- A PND may be issued without DPP consent for wasting police time. Where the offender requests a hearing, a summons will be raised in the normal way and the CPS will give delegated DPP consent.

Possession of cannabis or khat

- A PND may be issued for possession of cannabis (which is not cannabis oil), or khat and any preparation or other product containing khat for personal use. A PND cannot be given for other drug offences or possession with intent to supply.
- ACPO guidance on cannabis possession and the national framework guidance on khat possession for personal use provides a three-stage escalation procedure where an offender will receive a cannabis or khat warning for a first offence, a PND for a second offence, and prosecution for a third or subsequent offence.

Associated with other offences

- If a PND offence is clearly associated with another offence, including a penalty offence, a PND should not be issued and the offences should be charged together (eg drunk and disorderly and damage, due to being drunk).
- A PND may be issued if a penalty offence does not 'overlap with' or is 'associated with' another offence—for example, a PND s 5 public order offence then found in possession of stolen credit cards—for which a charge is deemed appropriate.
- A PND may be issued in addition to dealing with a second or subsequent offence in another way, although ensure that a PND is not issued in addition to dealing with a very serious offence.
- Where a PND is issued for a penalty offence and it subsequently comes to light after the incident that a more serious or non-penalty

offence was committed on the same occasion, officers may bring a charge for the subsequent offence. Payment of a penalty does not discharge liability to conviction for a more serious offence (*R v Gore* [2009] EWCA Crim 1424, CA). Ultimately, it will be for the CPS to determine, based on the facts of the case, whether a prosecution may be brought in respect of a subsequent or more serious offence.

Persons

A PND will not be appropriate where the suspect is:
- below the age of 18;
- unable to provide a satisfactory address for enforcement purposes;
- unable to understand the language, PND procedure, or what is being given to them;
- under the influence of drugs or alcohol, in which case consider arrest or issuing the PND at another time;
- a known Class A drug or substance misuser, then it would be better dealt with by court or a conditional caution which can direct a person to suitable substance treatment;
- uncooperative, non-compliant, or presents a considerable risk of not paying the penalty or completing the educational course;
- subject to: a custodial sentence, including home detention curfew, or a suspended sentence order; or a community penalty other than a fine, including an ASBO (under which the conduct may constitute a breach);
- known to have previous convictions for disorder offences, recently issued with a PND, or given a simple or conditional caution for such offences—but consideration could be given to issuing a PND, depending on the circumstances.

Jointly committed offences

Where a person under 18 and a person aged 18 or over jointly commit a penalty offence, then a PND will not be appropriate for the person aged 18 or over. In such cases, other forms of disposal should be considered.

Identification

- Age, identity, and address checks must be rigorous. The PNC and PentiP (the national system for recording the issuing and collection of penalty notices and the collection of related penalties) must be thoroughly checked, including the disposals page. If doubt as to identity exists consider exercising s 24 PACE arrest powers.
- Fingerprints may be taken with consent under s 61 PACE and Part 4 of Code D; this will support identification for any PND issued for a penalty offence.

Victims

- Consider the seriousness of the offence and its effect on the victim. Consult with the victim about the potential issue of a PND and take their views into account before reaching a decision.

- Be mindful that PND disposal removes the possibility of a compensation order, although the victim can still seek redress through civil litigation. The victim should be made aware of this.

Educational course schemes

- The Criminal Justice and Police Act 2001 permits a chief officer of police to establish a PND educational course scheme in relation to one or more penalty offences, but this is not mandatory. It means a constable can give a person a PND with an education option (**PND-E**) where appropriate.
- A PND-E gives a person the opportunity to discharge their liability to be convicted of the penalty offence by paying for and completing an educational course that relates to the penalty offence (although a record of the PND-E will remain on PentiP and the PNC (if given for a recordable offence) as with a 'standard' PND). Alternatively, a person can opt to pay the penalty in full or request to be tried (as with a PND).

Links to alternative subjects and offences

7.2 Drunkenness in Public Places

Section 91 of the Criminal Justice Act 1967 and s 12 of the Licensing Act 1872 deal with offences relating to drunkenness in public places, namely those of being drunk and disorderly and of being drunk in a highway.

7.2.1 Drunk and disorderly

Offences

Any person who in any public place is guilty, while drunk, of disorderly behaviour shall be liable to a summary conviction.

Criminal Justice Act 1967, s 91(1)

Points to prove
- ✓ while in a public place
- ✓ whilst drunk
- ✓ guilty of disorderly behavior

Meanings

Disorderly behaviour

Is defined by the *Oxford English Dictionary* as 'unruly or offensive behaviour'.

Public place

Includes any highway and other premises or place to which at the material time the public have or are permitted to have access, whether on payment or otherwise.

Drunk

Drunk is defined by the *Collins* and *Oxford English Dictionaries* as 'intoxicated with alcohol to the extent of losing control over normal physical and mental functions' and 'having drunk intoxicating liquor to an extent which affects steady self-control' (*R v Tagg* [2001] EWCA Crim 1230, CA).

Explanatory notes

- It does not apply to a person who is disorderly because of **sniffing glue** or **using drugs**. The common meaning of 'drunk' does not cater for such conduct, as confirmed by *Neale v RMJE (a minor)* (1985) 80 Cr App R 20.

- If the offender has taken liquor and drugs, the court must be satisfied that the loss of self-control was due to the liquor and not the drugs.
- Whether or not someone is in a state of drunkenness is a matter of fact for the court/jury to decide.
- A landing in a block of flats, to which access was gained by way of key, security code, tenant's intercom, or caretaker, has been held **not** to be a public place because only those admitted by or with the implied consent of the occupiers had access.

Related cases

H v DPP [2005] EWHC 2459 (Admin), QBD It was held in this case that conduct must be disorderly while the defendant is drunk to satisfy the offence. The offence is not committed if the defendant only becomes disorderly after the arrest.

Williams v DPP [1993] 3 All ER 365, QBD In this case the defendant was arrested and convicted of the s 91 offence which took place on the landing of the tenth floor of a block of flats. His conviction was quashed, and the court held that for the purposes of this offence, public place included premises to which, at the material time, the public had or were permitted to have access whether on payment or otherwise. The landing was not a public place because only people with implied consent, or those who had been given admission by one of the occupiers (such as building maintenance), could have access.

Practical considerations

- This offence can be dealt with by PND (see **7.1.1**).
- Home Office guidance relates to issuing a PND for this offence (see **7.1.2**).
- Comply with CPS public order charging standards and guidance for drunk and disorderly.
- Consider applying for a criminal behaviour order (see **7.13.2**).

 PND

 Summary   6 months

 Level 3 fine

7.2.2 Drunk on a highway

Section 12 of the Licensing Act 1872 creates the offence of being 'drunk and incapable' in a highway, public place, or licensed premises, whilst in possession of a loaded firearm or being in charge of various conveyances or animals.

7.2.2 Drunk on a highway

Offences

Every person found drunk in any highway or other public place, whether a building or not, or on any licensed premises, shall be liable to a penalty.

Every person who is drunk while in charge on any highway or other public place of any carriage, horse, cattle, or steam engine, or who is drunk when in possession of any loaded firearms, shall be liable to a penalty.

Licensing Act 1872, s 12

Points to prove

Drunk and incapable
- ✓ drunk and incapable
- ✓ highway/public place/licensed premises

Other drunk offences
- ✓ drunk
- ✓ whilst in charge of
- ✓ pedal cycle/carriage/horse/cattle/steam engine **or** when in possession of a loaded firearm
- ✓ on/in a highway/public place

Meanings

Drunk (see 7.2.1)

Highway/public place (see 7.2.1)

Incapable

Means 'incapable of looking after oneself and getting home safely'.

Carriage

Includes vehicles such as trailers and bicycles (whether being ridden or pushed).

Cattle

Includes sheep and pigs.

Firearm (see **8.1.1**)

Explanatory notes

- A motor vehicle is a 'carriage'. However, it may be more appropriate to consider the offence of driving or being in charge while over the prescribed limit under s 4 of the Road Traffic Act 1988 (see **10.10**).
- Case law suggests that residents in licensed premises cannot be convicted of this offence outside the permitted hours when the premises are closed to the public. However, the duty of the licensee to prevent drunkenness on the premises is unaffected.

- See also the related offences of drunk and disorderly in a public place (see **7.2.1**).
- Section 2 of the Licensing Act 1902 makes it an offence to be drunk in charge of a child who appears to be under the age of 7 years.

Practical considerations

- This offence can be dealt with by means of a PND (see **7.1.1**).
- If this offence involves a firearm, consider s 19 of the Firearms Act 1968 (carrying a firearm in a public place) which has a far greater penalty (see **8.5**).
- Officers should frequently assess the condition of drunks which can sometimes be life threatening (eg inhalation of vomit).
- Be aware that other medical conditions could give the impression that somebody is drunk (eg diabetic coma). It is best to convey the person to hospital if there are any doubts.
- Section 34 of the Criminal Justice Act 1972 provides a police constable with a power to take a drunken offender to a 'detoxification' or alcohol treatment centre. While a person is being so taken they shall be deemed to be in lawful custody.

PND

 Summary   6 months

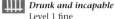 *Drunk and incapable*
Level 1 fine

Drunk in charge of firearm/carriage/horse/steam engine
1 month imprisonment or a level 1 fine

Links to alternative subjects and offences

7.3 **Breach of the Peace**

'Breach of the peace' is a common law concept which involves various powers in order to prevent a breach of the peace in both public and private places: these are arrest, intervene, or detain by force.

It is not a criminal offence, but a 'complaint', laid before the court with an application made for a person to be bound over to keep the peace.

Complaint

Breach of the peace

The power of a magistrates' court on the complaint of any person to adjudge any other person to enter into a recognizance, with or without sureties, to keep the peace or to be of good behaviour towards the complainant shall be exercised by order on complaint.

Magistrates' Courts Act 1980, s 115(1)

Points to prove

✓ behave in a manner
✓ whereby breach of the peace
✓ was occasioned/likely to be occasioned

Meaning of breach of the peace

A breach of the peace may occur where harm is done or is likely to be done to a person, or to their property in their presence, or they are in fear of being harmed through assault, affray, riot, or other disturbance (*R v Howell* [1982] QB 416, QBD).

Court powers

- Section 115 of the Magistrates' Courts Act 1980 provides magistrates' courts with the power to order a person to be 'bound over' to keep the peace and/or be of good behaviour towards a particular person.
- The power of a magistrates' court on the complaint of any person to adjudge any other person to enter into a recognizance, with or without sureties, to keep the peace or to be of good behaviour towards the complainant shall be exercised by order on complaint.
- If any person fails to comply with the order, the court may commit that person to custody for a period not exceeding six months or until they comply with the order.

Explanatory notes

- Notwithstanding that for some purposes proceedings under s 115 are treated as criminal proceedings, since the procedure is by way of complaint it is primarily a civil process. The jurisdiction of the justices does not depend on a summons being issued, nor does the absence of a complaint in the form prescribed invalidate the procedure.

Related cases

R (on the application of Laporte) v CC of Gloucestershire [2006] UKHL 55, HL In this case, three coaches were stopped by police and searched under a s 60 authority (see **8.11.3**) on intelligence that occupants would cause disorder at an RAF base in Gloucestershire. They were turned back and escorted back to London. Although the police actions were based on a reasonable and honestly held belief in preventing an apprehended breach of the peace, they had acted unlawfully and disproportionately because a breach of the peace was not 'imminent' at the time the coaches were stopped; thus, interfering with the protesters' rights under Arts 10 and 11 (see **1.1**).

McGrogan v CC of Cleveland Police [2002] EWCA Civ 86, CA It was held in this case that if a person is detained for an actual or threatened breach of the peace, then continued detention is limited to circumstances where there is a real, rather than a fanciful, fear, based on all the circumstances, that if released the detained person would commit/renew a breach of the peace within a relatively short time. It cannot be justified solely on the ground that sooner or later the prisoner, if released, is likely to breach the peace. The officer must have an honest belief, based on objectively reasonable grounds, that further detention was necessary to prevent such a breach of the peace.

Practical considerations

- A breach of the peace is not an offence, so bail cannot be given.
- Breach of the peace can occur on private premises. If the police have genuine grounds to apprehend such a breach, they have a power of entry to deal with or prevent a breach of the peace (see s 17(6) of PACE, **1.5.2**). This right of entry is not absolute but must be weighed against the degree of disturbance that is threatened.
- A police officer must not remain on private premises once a breach has finished (assuming it is not likely to **reoccur**), but as long as the officer is lawfully on the premises in the first instance, they are entitled to be given the opportunity to withdraw.
- Officers attending private premises with officials such as bailiffs may have to enter them to prevent a breach of the peace while a Court Order is being enforced.
- An individual arrested to prevent a breach of the peace does not have to be taken before a court. There is no power to continue the person's detention beyond the time where a recurrence or renewal of the breach of the peace is likely. If there is such danger they should be detained for court (see *McGrogan v CC of Cleveland Police* [2002] EWCA Civ 86, CA above).

- There is a continuing role for the common law power to detain short of arrest in order to prevent a breach of the peace, although in order for it to apply an officer would need to have it in mind at the relevant time (*Walker v Commissioner of Police of the Metropolis* [2014] EWCA Crim 897, CA—see **2.2.2**).
- Release may occur at any stage: at the scene, after they have been taken from the scene, or at the police station.

 Summary   6 months

 Breach of the order may result in up to 6 months' imprisonment

Links to alternative subjects and offences

7.4 **Riot and Violent Disorder**

The Public Order Act 1986 provides the statutory offences of riot and violent disorder.

7.4.1 **Riot**

Offences

Where twelve or more persons who are present together use or threaten unlawful violence for a common purpose and the conduct of them (taken together) is such as would cause a person of reasonable firmness present at the scene to fear for his personal safety, each of the persons using unlawful violence for the common purpose is guilty of riot.

Public Order Act 1986, s 1(1)

Points to prove

✓ 12 or more persons present together used/threatened unlawful violence for common purpose
✓ and conduct would cause fear for personal safety
✓ to a person of reasonable firmness

Meanings

Present together

Means that all the people concerned were actually present at the scene of the incident, aiming for a common purpose.

Common purpose (s 1(3))

The common purpose may be inferred from conduct.

Violence

Includes violent conduct towards property as well as violent conduct towards persons. It is not restricted to conduct causing, or intended to cause, injury or damage, but includes any other violent conduct (eg throwing at or towards a person a missile of a kind capable of causing injury, which does not hit or falls short).

Person of reasonable firmness

This test is an objective one by which the court can judge the seriousness of the disturbance using a fixed standard—namely whether or not a person of reasonable firmness would be put in fear by the conduct.

7.4.1 Riot

Explanatory notes

- It is immaterial whether or not the 12 or more use or threaten unlawful violence simultaneously.
- No **person of reasonable firmness** need actually be, or be likely to be, present at the scene.
- A court will not consider this hypothetical person (of reasonable firmness) to be someone who is the target for the people who are involved in the disturbance, but someone who is a bystander to the incident (*R v Sanchez* [1996] Crim LR 572, CA).
- Riot may be committed in private as well as in public places.
- The common purpose can be either lawful or unlawful, and must be proved either by admission or as above by inference from conduct.

Defences

Intention

(1) A person is guilty of riot only if he intends to use violence or is aware that his conduct may be violent.

(2) A person is guilty of violent disorder or affray only if he intends to use or threaten violence or is aware that his conduct may be violent or threaten violence.

(3) (7) Subsections (1) and (2) do not affect the determination for the purposes of riot or violent disorder of the number of persons who use or threaten violence.

Effect of intoxication

(4) For the purposes of this section a person whose awareness is impaired by intoxication shall be taken to be aware of that of which he would be aware if not intoxicated, unless he shows either that his intoxication was not self-induced or that it was caused solely by the taking or administration of a substance in the course of medical treatment.

(5) In subsection (5) 'intoxication' means any intoxication, whether caused by drink, drugs or other means, or by a combination of means.

Public Order Act 1986, s 6

Defence notes

- Intent or awareness must be proved. Even if intent can only be proved against two people but they were part of a group of, say, 13 who can be shown to have used unlawful violence, the two can still be convicted of riot.
- The intoxication defence applies to the following offences:
  + s 1—Riot—unlawful violence;
  + s 2—Violent disorder—unlawful violence;
  + s 3—Affray—unlawful violence;
  + s 4—Threatening words or behaviour; and
  + s 5—Harassment, alarm, or distress.

Practical considerations

- Refer to **8.11** for details of powers to stop and search when it is anticipated that serious violence may take place, and to remove masks.
- Consent of the DPP is required.
- Consider the CPS public order charging standards.
- A person who was feeling threatened does not actually have to be a 'person of reasonable firmness', but their evidence may support other evidence that will satisfy the court that such a person would have been in fear of their personal safety had they been present.

This evidence could be provided by:
   ✦ witnesses including police officers and bystanders (who may or may not be of reasonable firmness);
   ✦ the types of injuries sustained;
   ✦ damage to property;
   ✦ security cameras;
   ✦ news photographs or film footage.

 Indictable only   None

 10 years' imprisonment

7.4.2 **Violent disorder**

Offences

Where three or more persons who are present together use or threaten unlawful violence and the conduct of them (taken together) is such as would cause a person of reasonable firmness present at the scene to fear for his personal safety, each of the persons using or threatening unlawful violence is guilty of violent disorder.

Public Order Act 1986, s 2(1)

Points to prove

✓ used/threatened unlawful violence
✓ three persons present together
✓ use/threaten unlawful violence and their conduct (taken together)
✓ would cause a person of reasonable firmness present at the scene
✓ to fear for their personal safety

7.4.2 Violent disorder

Meanings

Present together

Means no more than being in the same place at the same time.

Person of reasonable firmness (see 7.4.1)

Violence (see 7.4.1)

Explanatory notes

- It is immaterial whether or not the three or more use or threaten unlawful violence simultaneously.
- No **person of reasonable firmness** need actually be, or likely to be, present at the scene.
- Violent disorder may be committed in private as well as in public places.
- If three or more people had been present together and using violence, even if intent can only be proved against one person, then that person can be convicted—it is not necessary that 'three or more persons' be charged with the offence. Following *R v Mahroof* [1988] Crim LR 72, CA (see below) it is good practice to specify 'others' in the charge, even if their identity is not known and they were not arrested.

Defences

Intention (see **s 6(2)** and **s 6(7), 7.4.1**)
Effect of intoxication (see **7.4.1**)

Defence notes

Intent

To use or threaten violence must, therefore, be proved for each individual. This means that even if only one person has the intent they can still be charged if it can be proved that at least two others were using, or threatening violence and they were present together. Words alone may suffice for the threats.

Related cases

R v NW [2010] EWCA Crim 404, CA It was held in this case that the term 'present together' in s 2, is intended to mean no more than being in the same place at the same time. There is no requirement in that there be a common purpose among those using or threatening the use of violence. Therefore, the offence which it created was not confined to situations in which the individual members of the crowd were acting together to achieve a common aim or even with a common motive. The phrase did not require any degree of cooperation between those using or threatening violence.

Practical considerations

- Refer to **8.11** for details of powers to stop and search when it is anticipated that serious violence may take place, and powers to remove masks.
- Consider CPS public order charging standards for violent disorder.
- Sections 34–49 of the Policing and Crime Act 2009 deal with injunctions to prevent gang-related violence. The Serious Crime Act 2015 substituted s 34 so it now includes drug-dealing activity as well. HOC 8/2015 provides guidance on this matter.

 Either way None

 Summary: 6 months' imprisonment and/or a fine

Indictment: 5 years' imprisonment and/or a fine

Links to alternative subjects and offences

7.5 **Affray**

The purpose of the offence of affray is to prevent incidents of public disorder and the fear of it. For the offence of affray to be committed, the threat of violence needs to be capable of affecting others.

Offences

A person is guilty of affray if he uses or threatens unlawful violence towards another and his conduct is such as would cause a person of reasonable firmness present at the scene to fear for his personal safety.

Public Order Act 1986, s 3(1)

Points to prove

✓ used/threatened unlawful violence
✓ towards another
✓ and conduct was such as would cause
✓ a person of reasonable firmness to fear for personal safety

Meanings

Threatens

A threat cannot be made by the use of words alone.

Violence

See **7.4**, except affray **does not include** violent conduct towards property.

Conduct

Where two or more persons use or threaten the unlawful violence, it is the conduct of them taken together that must be considered for the purpose of the offence.

Person of reasonable firmness

No person of reasonable firmness need actually be, or be likely to be, present at the scene. The concept meets the same criteria as riot (see **7.4.1**).

Explanatory notes

- Affray may be committed in private as well as in public places.
- Notionally there are at least three parties involved in an affray:
  + the individual making threats;
  + the person subject of the threats;

✦ the bystander of reasonable firmness who does not need to be physically present as long as evidence is available to prove that such a person would be affected.

Defences

Intent (see s 6(2) **7.4.1**)

Effects of intoxication (see 'Defences' **7.4.1**)

Defence notes (see 'Defence notes' **7.4.2**)

Related cases

R v Plavecz [2002] Crim LR 837, CA In this case, a doorman pushed a customer out of a nightclub doorway who then fell over. The defendant was charged with assault and affray. However, the court stated that where the incident was basically a 'one-on-one', it was inappropriate to use the public order offence of affray.

I v DPP; M v DPP; H v DPP [2001] UKHL 10, HL In this case, about 40 young people were 'hanging around' with some carrying petrol bombs. None of them lit or waved a petrol bomb about in a threatening way and there was no actual disturbance. On arrival of the police, the gang scattered, and the three defendants threw away their petrol bombs as they ran off. It was held that the mere possession of a weapon, without the threatening situation, would not be enough to constitute a threat of unlawful violence. Affray requires that the offender must be 'using/threatening unlawful violence towards another'. What amounted to such a threat was a question of fact in each case, but in this instance, there were no threats made and no violence was used.

Practical considerations

- Unlike riot and violent disorder, affray can be committed by one person acting alone. However, where two or more people are involved in the violence or threatened violence, it is the conduct of them taken together that will determine whether the offence is made out.
- Refer to **8.11.3** for details of powers to stop and search when it is anticipated that serious violence may take place and to remove masks.
- Consider CPS public order charging standards for affray.
- for powers to stop and search for knives and offensive weapons (see **1.3.1**).
- The person feeling threatened does not have to be a 'person of reasonable firmness', but evidence may support other evidence that will satisfy the court that a 'person of reasonable firmness' would have been in fear of their personal safety (see **7.4.1** for 'other evidence' examples).

7.5 **Affray**

 Either way None

Summary: 6 months' imprisonment and/or a fine
Indictment: 3 years' imprisonment

Links to alternative subjects and offences

7.6 **Fear or Provocation of Violence**

The Public Order Act 1986 deals with offences and powers relating to public order. Section 4 creates the offence of causing fear or provocation of violence, often known as 'threatening behaviour'.

Offences

A person is guilty of an offence if he—
- uses towards another person threatening, abusive or insulting words or behaviour, or
- distributes or displays to another person any writing, sign or other visible representation which is threatening, abusive or insulting,

with intent to cause that person to believe that immediate unlawful violence will be used against him or another by any person, or to provoke the immediate use of unlawful violence by that person or another, or whereby that person is likely to believe that such violence will be used or it is likely that such violence will be provoked.

Public Order Act 1986, s 4(1)

Points to prove

s 4(1)(a) offence

✓ use towards another person
✓ threatening/abusive/insulting words or behaviour
✓ with intent to **either**
✓ cause that person to believe
✓ that immediate unlawful violence
✓ would be used against them or another
✓ by any person **or**
✓ provoke the immediate use of unlawful violence
✓ by that person/another **or**
✓ that person was likely to believe
✓ that such violence would be used **or**
✓ likely that such violence would be provoked

s 4(1)(b) offence

✓ distribute/display
✓ to another
✓ a writing/sign/visible representation
✓ which was threatening/abusive/insulting
✓ with intent to **either**
✓ *(continue from this point in above offence—to end)*

7.6 Fear or Provocation of Violence

Meanings

Threatening

Includes verbal and physical threats, and also violent conduct.

Abusive

Means using degrading or reviling language.

Insulting

Has been held to mean scorning, especially if insolent or contemptuous.

Intent (see 'Defences' and 'Intent' below)

Distribute

Means spread or disperse.

Display

Means a visual presentation.

Explanatory notes

- An offence under this section may be committed in a public or
  a private place, except that no offence is committed where the
  words or behaviour are used, or the writing, sign, or other visible
  representation is distributed or displayed, by a person inside
  a **dwelling** and the other person is also inside that or another
  dwelling (s 4(2)).
- **Dwelling**—means any **structure** or part of a structure occupied as
  a person's home or as other living accommodation (whether the
  occupation is separate or shared with others) but does not include
  any part not so occupied, and for this purpose 'structure' includes
  a tent, caravan, vehicle, vessel, or other temporary or movable
  structure.
- No offence will be committed if the display is inside a dwelling, if
  it is displayed only to people also inside, although if it is displayed
  from inside to people outside the dwelling, then an offence under s
  4 may be committed.
- Whether behaviour is insulting or not is a question of fact for the
  justices/court to decide (*Brutus v Cozens* [1972] 2 All ER 1297, HL).

Defences

Intent

A person is guilty of an offence under s 4 only if he intends [see **4.1.2**] his
words or behaviour, or the writing, sign or other visible representation,
to be threatening, abusive or insulting, or is aware that it may be
threatening, abusive or insulting.

Public Order Act 1986, s 6(3)

Intoxication (see **'Defences' 'Effect of intoxication' 7.4.1**)

Related cases

Hughes v DPP [2012] EWHC 606 (Admin), QBD A blow delivered in such a way as to avoid giving the victim any advanced warning or perception that immediate unlawful violence was going to be used against them, could not constitute an offence under s 4(1).

DPP v Ramos [2000] Crim LR 768, QBD If the victim believes that the threatened violence will occur at any moment, this will be sufficient for the 'immediacy' requirement.

Swanston v DPP (1996) 161 JP 203, QBD A witness, (such as a police officer) who was present when the offence took place can give evidence to prove the threatening behaviour and intent, even if the victim does not give evidence.

Atkin v DPP [1989] Crim LR 581, QBD It was held in this case that the person threatened should be present. The threatening words must be addressed directly to another person who is present and either within earshot or aimed at someone thought to be in earshot.

Practical considerations

- Section 17(1)(c)(iii) of PACE gives a constable a specific power to enter and search premises for the purpose of arresting a person for an offence under s 4 (see **1.5.2**).
- If this offence is **racially or religiously aggravated** the more serious offence under s 31(1)(a) of the Crime and Disorder Act 1998 should be considered (see **7.10.4**). It is not open to the court to convict on both the simple and aggravated offences if they arise out of the same facts (*R (on the application of Dyer) v Watford MC* [2013] All ER (D) 88 (Jan)).
- Consider religious or racial hatred offences (see **7.9**).
- It is not duplicitous if the three alternatives 'threatening, abusive or insulting', are charged, though all three need not be present.
- Consider CPS public order charging standards.

 Summary   6 months

 6 months' imprisonment and/or a fine

Links to alternative subjects and offences

RRA Racially or religiously aggravated offences   E&S Entry and search powers

7.6 Fear or Provocation of Violence

7.7 Intentional Harassment, Alarm, or Distress

Section 4A of the Public Order Act 1986 creates the offences of intentionally causing a person harassment, alarm, or distress by using threatening, abusive, insulting words or behaviour, or disorderly behaviour; or displaying any writing, sign, or other representation that is threatening, abusive, or insulting.

Offences

A person is guilty of an offence if, with intent to cause a person harassment, alarm or distress, he—

- uses threatening, abusive or insulting words or behaviour, or disorderly behaviour, or
- displays any writing, sign or other visible representation which is threatening, abusive or insulting,

thereby causing that or another person harassment, alarm or distress.

Public Order Act 1986, s 4A(1)

Points to prove

s 4A(1)(a) offence

✓ used threatening/abusive/insulting words/behaviour **or** used disorderly behaviour
✓ towards another person
✓ with intent to cause harassment/alarm/distress
✓ and caused that/another person
✓ harassment/alarm/distress

s 4A(1)(b) offence

✓ displayed threatening/abusive/insulting writing/sign/other visible representation
✓ with intent to cause a person harassment/alarm/distress
✓ and caused that/another person
✓ harassment/alarm/distress

Meanings

Harassment

Means to subject someone to constant and repeated physical and/or verbal persecution.

Alarm

Means a frightened anticipation of danger.

Distress

Means to cause trouble, pain, anguish, or hardship.

Intent (see 4.1.2)

Threatening (see 7.6)

Abusive (see 7.6)

Insulting (see 7.6)

Disorderly behaviour

The *Oxford English Dictionary* states 'unruly, unrestrained, turbulent or riotous behaviour'.

Explanatory notes

- This offence is similar to the s 5 offence (except 'insulting'—see **7.8**), but this offence requires proof of **intent** to cause alarm, harassment, or distress.
- An offence under this section may be committed in a public or private place, but no offence is committed if it takes place inside a dwelling and the affected person is also inside that or another dwelling.
- Although this offence can be committed on private premises there is no specific power of entry.

Defences

It is a defence for the accused to prove—

(a) that he was inside a dwelling and had no reason to believe that the words or behaviour used, or the writing, sign or other visible representation displayed, would be heard or seen by a person outside that or any other dwelling, or

(b) that his conduct was reasonable.

Public Order Act 1986, s 4A(3)

Related cases

S v CPS [2008] EWHC 438 (Admin), QBD When posting offensive material on the internet, the defendant had the required intent and had taken the risk that the intended harm would be caused to the complainant. The fact that the complainant had not seen the material until being shown it by the police later did not break the chain of causation for the purposes of this offence.

R (on the application of R) v DPP [2006] EWHC 1375 (Admin), QBD In this case, a 12-year-old boy gestured and shouted obscenities at the police and was arrested for a s 4A offence. Although maybe intending to insult and annoy there was no intention to cause the officer alarm or distress. It was held that for a police officer to be distressed evidence of real emotional disturbance or upset is required, showing more than is normally experienced during their course of duty.

Dehal v CPS [2005] EWHC 2154 (Admin), QBD In this case, the defendant placed a poster on a notice board in a Sikh Temple which contained what was alleged to be abusive and insulting comments regarding an incorrect translation of the Holy Book. A defence under s 4A(3)(b) was submitted that this amounted to 'reasonable conduct'. It was held that however insulting or unjustified the contents of the poster, a criminal prosecution was unlawful by virtue of s 3 of the Human Rights Act 1998 and Article 10 of the ECHR unless it can be shown that a prosecution was necessary in order to prevent public disorder and there was no such finding or justification given by the court in this case. It is imperative that there is no restriction placed on what amounts to no more than legitimate protest.

Practical considerations

- There must be evidence of intent to cause harassment, alarm, or distress and one of those forms of abuse must be caused to someone (not necessarily the person who was its original target).
- Consider s 5 (see **7.8**) where there is no evidence of intent.
- Where the extent of the behaviour results in the fear or realisation of violence consider s 4(1) (see **7.6**) or assault charges (see **2.1**, **2.2**, or **2.3**).
- If there is repeated harassment, consider s 1 of the Protection from Harassment Act 1997 (see **7.11.1**).
- If a power of entry is required, consider s 17 of PACE (see **1.5.2**). Note that there is no power of entry for s 4A but consider an ongoing breach of the peace (see **7.3**), or a power of entry related to s 4 Public Order Act 1986 (see **7.6** and **1.5.2**).
- Consider the behaviour in the context of the circumstances— behaviour that causes distress to an elderly woman may not be distressing to a young man.
- If other people, besides the police officer and the defendant, are present include that fact in your evidence.
- If this offence is racially and/or religiously aggravated, consider the more serious offence under s 31 of the Crime and Disorder Act 1998 (see **7.10.4**) or ss 17–23 of the Public Order Act 1986 which relate to racial hatred offences (see **7.9**).

 Summary   6 months

 6 months' imprisonment and/or a fine

Links to alternative subjects and offences

7.8 Threatening/Abusive Words/Behaviour

Section 5 of the Public Order Act 1986 creates an offence of being threatening or abusive in a way which is likely to cause harassment, alarm, or distress.

Offences

A person is guilty of an offence if he—
(a) uses threatening or abusive words or behaviour, or disorderly behaviour, or
(b) displays any writing sign or other visible representation which is threatening or abusive,

within the hearing or sight of a person likely to be caused harassment, alarm or distress thereby.

Public Order Act 1986, s 5(1)

Points to prove

✓ used threatening/abusive words/behaviour or disorderly behaviour **or**
✓ displayed writing/sign/visible representation being
✓ threatening/abusive
✓ within hearing/sight of a person likely to be caused
✓ harassment/alarm/distress
✓ with intention/awareness that conduct/actions
✓ would have that effect

Meanings

Threatening or abusive (see 7.6)

Harassment, alarm, and distress (see 7.7)

Disorderly behaviour (see 7.7)

Explanatory notes

- What may distress an old woman of 75 years might not distress a young man of 20 years. The conduct must be **likely to cause** distress. However, you can fear for the safety of someone else (particularly if you are a police officer), and it does not necessarily have to be for yourself.
- An offence under this section may be committed in a public or a private place except that no offence is committed when the

words or behaviour are used, or the writing, sign, or other visible representation is displayed, by a person inside a dwelling and the other person is also inside that or another dwelling. Subject to particular facts, a dwelling does not include a garden to the front or rear of a property (see *R v Distill* [2017] EWHC 2244).

Defences

Specific

5(3) It is a defence for the accused to prove—

(a) that he had no reason to believe that there was any person within hearing or sight who was likely to be caused harassment, alarm or distress; or

   a. that he was inside a dwelling and had no reason to believe that the words or behaviour used, or the writing, sign or other visible representation displayed, would be heard or seen by a person outside that or any other dwelling; or

(b) that his conduct was reasonable.

Intent

6(4) A person is guilty of an offence under section 5 only if he intends his words or behaviour, or the writing, sign, or other visible representation, to be threatening, or abusive, or is aware that it may be threatening, or abusive, or (as the case may be) he intends his behaviour to be or is aware that it may be disorderly.

Public Order Act 1986, ss 5(3) and 6(4)

Intoxication (see **'Defences' 'Effect of intoxication' 7.4.1**)

Defence notes

Article 6 (right to a fair trial—see **1.1**) does not prohibit rules which transfer the burden of proof to the accused, provided it is only an 'evidential burden' where the defendant only needs to give believable evidence which justifies the defence and does not need to reach any specific standard of proof. Proving the guilt of the defendant still remains with the prosecution (eg s 28 of the Misuse of Drugs Act 1971—see **5.1.1**).

Intoxication (see **'Defence notes' 7.4.1**)

Related cases

Harvey v DPP [2011] All ER (D) 143 (Admin), QBD Two police officers stopped a group of people in the public area of a block of flats. The defendant objected to a cannabis drug search and said, 'Fuck this man, I ain't been smoking nothing.' He was warned about swearing, but continued and was arrested for s 5. It was held that police officers regularly hear this language so are unlikely to be affected by it. The swearing had not caused the officers, young people in the group, or anyone in the area harassment, alarm, or distress.

Abdul and others v DPP [2011] EWHC 247 (Admin), QBD This case involved a group of five men who hurled abuse and waved placards with offensive slogans such as 'Butchers of Basra', 'British soldiers go to hell', 'terrorists', and 'cowards' at soldiers marching through a town on return from Afghanistan. Freedom of expression under Art 10 (see **1.1.**) was not an unqualified right. It was held that not all speech is protected by freedom of expression rights, and that not all protest is legitimate in the eyes of the state. The words in question went well beyond legitimate protest and there was a very clear threat to public order. Their words were 'potentially defamatory and undoubtedly inflammatory'.

Taylor v DPP [2006] EWHC 1202 (Admin), QBD The Court considered the wording 'within the sight or hearing of a person'. It was held that this requires evidence that there was someone able to hear or see the conduct, but the prosecution does not have to call evidence to prove that the words were heard or behaviour seen. It is not sufficient that a person may have happened upon the scene and observed what was occurring but where there are several people on the scene near enough to hear, this equates to being able to hear, and so falls within the requirement of 'within the hearing of'.

Norwood v DPP [2003] EWHC 1564 (Admin), QBD The defendant displayed a poster in his flat window, visible from the street, which said, 'Islam out of Britain' and 'Protect the British People'. It bore a reproduction of one of the 'twin towers' in flames along with a Crescent and Star surrounded by a prohibition sign. It was held that the poster was capable of causing harassment, alarm or distress. The defence of reasonable conduct and the rights of freedom of expression under Art 10 carry a duty to avoid unreasonable or disproportionate interference with the rights of others; if they do interfere disproportionately the state has a duty to intervene.

Practical considerations

- If an offence under this section is racially or religiously aggravated, consider the more serious version of this offence under s 31 of the Crime and Disorder Act 1998 (see **7.10**).
- Consider racial and religious hatred offences (see **7.9**).
- Ensure any possible defences raised are covered in interview or rebutted by other evidence.
- The s 5 offence should be distinguished from the similar s 4A offence, which requires specific intent (see **7.7**).
- Words or behaviour are alternatives and one or other should be specified in the charge and must be proved.
- Consider issuing a PND for this offence (see **7.1**).
- It is not duplicitous if both alternatives are charged, 'threatening or abusive', though both need not be used.
- When investigating this offence, consideration must be given to the CPS public order charging standards (available at www.cps.gov.uk).

7.8 Threatening/Abusive Words/Behaviour

 Summary

 6 months

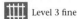 Level 3 fine

Links to alternative subjects and offences

7.9 **Racial, Religious, or Sexual Orientation Hatred Offences**

Sections 17–29 of the Public Order Act 1986 relate to racial hatred offences, whereas ss 29A–29N refer to religious or sexual orientation hatred offences.

7.9.1 **Use of words/behaviour or display of written material (racial)**

Section 18 creates the offence of using words or behaviour, or displaying written material, intending or likely to stir up racial hatred.

Offences

A person who uses threatening, abusive or insulting words or behaviour, or displays any written material which is threatening, abusive or insulting, is guilty of an offence if—
(a) he intends thereby to stir up racial hatred, or
(b) having regard to all the circumstances racial hatred is likely to be stirred up thereby.

Public Order Act 1986, s 18(1)

Points to prove

✓ used/displayed threatening/abusive/insulting
✓ words/behaviour/written material
✓ intended/likely to stir up racial hatred

Meanings

Threatening, abusive, and insulting (see 7.6)

Display (see 7.6)

Written material

Includes any sign or other visible representation.

Intention (see 4.1.2)

Racial hatred

Means hatred against a group of persons defined by reference to colour, race, nationality (including citizenship), or ethnic or national origins.

7.9.1 Use of words/behaviour or display of written material (racial)

Explanatory notes

- Racial hatred can be directed against a racial or religious group outside Great Britain.
- 'Insulting' does not mean behaviour which might give rise to irritation or resentment.
- Offence may be committed in a public or private place, but if committed inside a dwelling then the s 18(4) defence may apply—see below.
- An intention to stir up racial hatred must be proved, or if having regard to all the circumstances, racial hatred is likely to be stirred up.

Defences

(4) For the accused to prove that he was inside a dwelling and had no reason to believe that the words or behaviour used, or the written material displayed, would be heard or seen by a person outside that or another dwelling.

(5) A person who is not shown to have intended to stir up racial hatred is not guilty of an offence under this section if he did not intend his words or behaviour, or the written material, to be, and was not aware that it might be, threatening, abusive or insulting.

Public Order Act 1986, s 18

Defence notes

For meaning of 'Dwelling', see 7.6 'Explanatory notes'.

Practical considerations

- If the s 18, s 19, s 21, or s 23 offences relate to the display of written racial hatred material, the court may order forfeiture of the material.
- The following applies to all racially aggravated offences:
  + every section from s 18 to s 23 creates a separate offence (see 7.9.2 list) and one or more such offences may be charged together;
  + if the offence is committed by a body corporate, with the consent or connivance of a director, manager, company secretary, or other similar officer or person acting as such, then under s 28 they as well as the company are guilty of the offence;
  + consider the CPS public order charging standards for racial hatred offence;
  + consent of Attorney-General/Solicitor-General required.

 Either way   None

 Summary: 6 months' imprisonment and/or a fine

Indictment: 7 years' imprisonment and/or a fine

7.9.2 **Publishing/distributing written material (racial)**

Section 19 of the Public Order Act 1986 creates the offence of publishing or distributing written material intending or likely to stir up racial hatred.

Offences

A person who publishes or distributes written material which is threatening, abusive or insulting is guilty of an offence if—

(a) he intends thereby to stir up racial hatred, or

(b) having regard to all the circumstances racial hatred is likely to be stirred up thereby.

Public Order Act 1986, s 19(1)

Points to prove

✓ published/distributed
✓ threatening/abusive/insulting written material
✓ intended/likely to stir up racial hatred

Meanings

Publishes or distributes

Means its publication or distribution to the public or a section of the public.

Written material *(see 7.9.1)*

Threatening, abusive, or insulting *(see 7.6)*

Intends *(see 4.1.2)*

Racial hatred *(see 7.9.1)*

Defences

For accused who is not shown to have intended to stir up racial hatred to prove that he was not aware of the content of the material and did not suspect nor had reason to suspect, that it was threatening, abusive or insulting.

Public Order Act 1986, s 19(2)

Related cases

R v Sheppard [2010] EWCA Crim 65, CA In this case, the defendant created and uploaded onto the internet written material which cast doubt on the Holocaust and made disparaging racial remarks. Although taking place in the UK, the website was hosted by a server in California. The court had jurisdiction as a 'substantial measure' of these activities took place in the UK. It was held that written material includes articles in electronic form and it was also published/distributed over the internet for general access to the public.

Practical considerations (see 7.9.1)

- References to publication and distribution of written material are to its publication or distribution to the public or a section of the public.
- Other racial hatred offences under Pt 3A are:
  - ✦ public performance of play—s 20;
  - ✦ distributing, showing, or playing a recording—s 21;
  - ✦ broadcasting or including programme in programme service—s 22;
  - ✦ possession of racially inflammatory material—s 23.

 Either way None

 Summary: 6 months' imprisonment and/or a fine

Indictment: 7 years' imprisonment and/or a fine

7.9.3 Religious or sexual orientation hatred offences

Section 29B creates the offence of using words or behaviour, or displaying written material, intending or likely to stir up religious or sexual orientation hatred.

Offences

A person who uses threatening words or behaviour, or displays any written material which is threatening, is guilty of an offence if he intends thereby to stir up religious hatred or hatred on the grounds of sexual orientation.

Public Order Act 1986, s 29B(1)

Points to prove

✓ used threatening words or behaviour or displayed threatening written material
✓ intended to stir up religious or sexual orientation hatred

Meanings

Threatening (see **7.6**)

Displays (see **7.6**)

Written material (see **7.9.1**)

Intention (see **4.1.2**)

Religious hatred

Means hatred against a group of persons defined by reference to religious belief or lack of religious belief.

Hatred on the grounds of sexual orientation

Means hatred against a group of persons defined by reference to sexual orientation (whether towards persons of the same sex, the opposite sex, or both).

Explanatory notes

Racial or sexual orientation hatred may be committed in a public or a private place, but if committed inside a dwelling the s 29B(4) defence may apply.

> ### Defences
>
> For the accused to prove that he was inside a dwelling and had no reason to believe that the words or behaviour used, or the written material displayed, would be heard or seen by a person outside that or another dwelling.
>
> Public Order Act 1986, s 29B(4)

Defence notes (see **7.9.1**)

Practical considerations

- If the offence under s 29B relates to the display of written material, the court may, under s 29I, order forfeiture of the material. Forfeiture applies to publishing or distributing written material (s 29C), distributing/showing/playing a recording (s 29E), and possession of inflammatory material (s 29G).
- The following apply to religious or sexual orientation hatred offences:
  - ✦ every section from s 29B to s 29G creates a separate offence and one or more such offences may be charged together;
  - ✦ if the offence is committed by a body corporate with the consent or connivance of a director, manager, company secretary, or other similar officer or person acting as such, then under s 29M, they as well as the company are guilty of the offence;
  - ✦ consider CPS public order charging standards;
  - ✦ consent of the Attorney-General is required.

7.9.3 Religious or sexual orientation hatred offences

- HOC 29/2007 introduced Pt 3A on religious hatred, stating that for each offence the words, behaviour, written material, recordings, or programmes must be threatening and intended to stir up religious hatred. Part 3A was created with the offences of stirring up hatred against persons on religious grounds because Jews and Sikhs have been deemed by courts to be racial groups, but Muslims and Christians are religious rather than racial groups.
- MOJ Circular 5/2010 gives some explanatory guidance to the offences of intentionally stirring up hatred on the grounds of sexual orientation which have been added to the Pt 3A religious hatred offences.

Protection for freedom of expression

Religious hatred

Section 29J states that nothing in Pt 3A shall be read or given effect in a way which prohibits or restricts discussion, criticism, or expressions of antipathy, dislike, ridicule, insult, or abuse of particular religions, or the beliefs or practices of their adherents, or of any other belief system, or the beliefs or practices of its adherents, or proselytising, or urging adherents of a different religion or belief system to cease practising their religion or belief system.

Sexual orientation

Section 29JA states that in Pt 3A, for the avoidance of doubt, the discussion or criticism of sexual conduct or practices, or the urging of persons to refrain from or modify such conduct or practices, shall not be taken of itself to be threatening or intended to stir up hatred.

- Other religious or sexual orientation hatred offences under Pt 3A are:
  - ✦ publishing or distributing written material—s 29C;
  - ✦ public performance of play—s 29D;
  - ✦ distributing, showing, or playing a recording—s 29E;
  - ✦ broadcasting or including programme in programme service—s 29F; and
  - ✦ possession of inflammatory material—s 29G.

They are all either way offences and carry the same penalty as s 29B offence.

 Either way   None

 Summary: 6 months' imprisonment and/or a fine

    Indictment: 7 years' imprisonment and/or a fine

Links to alternative subjects and offences

7.10 Racially/Religiously Aggravated Offences

Sections 28–32 of the Crime and Disorder Act 1998 relate to racially or religiously aggravated offences.

7.10.1 Meaning of 'racially or religiously aggravated'

Section 28 states when a specific offence is deemed 'racially or religiously aggravated'.

Definition

An offence is racially or religiously aggravated for the purposes of ss 29 to 32 below if—

(a) at the time of committing the offence, or immediately before or after doing so, the offender demonstrates towards the victim of the offence hostility based on the victim's membership (or presumed membership) of a racial or religious group; or

(b) the offence is motivated (wholly or partly) by hostility towards members of a racial or religious group based on the membership of that group.

Crime and Disorder Act 1998, s 28(1)

Meanings

Membership

In relation to a racial or religious group, includes association with members of that group.

Presumed

Means presumed by the defendant (even if it is a mistaken presumption).

Racial group

Means a group of people defined by reference to race, colour, nationality (including citizenship), or ethnic or national origins.

Religious group

Means a group of people defined by religious belief or lack of religious belief.

Explanatory notes

It is immaterial whether or not the offender's hostility is also based, to any extent, on any other factor not mentioned in s 28(1).

Related cases

Jones v DPP [2011] 1 WLR 833, QBD The motive does not have to be proved for each limb of s 28(1). No subjective intent is required for s 28(1)(a) as the test is objective, with just the need to show racial hostility. However, under s 28(1)(b) the motivation behind the behaviour must be proved.

R v Rogers [2007] UKHL 8, HL In this case, the defendant called three Spanish women 'bloody foreigners' and told them to 'go back to their own country' before pursuing them in an aggressive manner. It was held that it is immaterial whether the hostility was based on factors other than simple racism or xenophobia. The denial of equal respect and dignity to people seen as different can be more deeply hurtful, damaging, and disrespectful than if it were based on a more specific racial characteristic.

Practical considerations

A police officer is just as entitled to protection under these provisions as anyone else (eg a person committing the offence of threatening behaviour by using racial taunts against the police could be prosecuted for the racially aggravated version of the offence).

7.10.2 **Racially or religiously aggravated assaults**

Section 29 relates to racially or religiously aggravated assault offences.

Offences

A person is guilty of an offence under this section if he commits—
(a) an offence under s 20 of the Offences Against the Person Act 1861 [see **2.3.1**]; or
(b) an offence under s 47 of that Act [see **2.1.2**]; or
(c) a common assault [see **2.1.1**],

which is racially or religiously aggravated for the purposes of this section.

Crime and Disorder Act 1998, s 29(1)

Points to prove

✓ committed offence under s 20 or s 47 of OAPA 1861; or s 39 of CJA 1988
✓ such offence was racially/religiously aggravated

7.10.3 Racially or religiously aggravated criminal damage

Meaning of racially or religiously aggravated (see 7.10.1)

Explanatory notes

- If, on the trial on indictment of a person charged with this offence, the jury find the defendant not guilty of the offence charged, they may find them guilty of the relevant 'basic' offence (eg s 20 or s 47 of the OAPA 1861; or s 39 of CJA 1988).
- There have now been a series of cases regarding the meaning of racial aggravation. Each is based on its own facts. It is important to prove racial hostility towards the victim or a racial motivation for the offence. In most cases the surrounding circumstances and actions should be sufficient, but there will be occasions when the hostility is not based on race (as below in *DPP v Pal*).

Related cases

DPP v Woods [2002] EWHC 85 (Admin), QBD A friend of the defendant was refused entry to licensed premises due to intoxication. The doorman was called a 'black bastard' and assaulted by the defendant. It was held that although the words were used out of frustration and the victim was unconcerned and did not consider the words racially offensive, the offence of racially aggravated common assault was still committed.

Practical considerations

Always charge the defendant with the relevant 'basic' offence, as there is no provision for an alternative verdict at a magistrates' court.

 Either way None

 Offence under s 29(1)(a) or (b)
   Summary: 6 months' imprisonment and/or a fine
   Indictment: 7 years' imprisonment and/or a fine

   Offence under s 29(1)(c)
   Summary: 6 months' imprisonment and/or a fine
   Indictment: 2 years' imprisonment and/or a fine

7.10.3 Racially or religiously aggravated criminal damage

Section 30 creates an offence of racially or religiously aggravated criminal damage.

Offences

A person is guilty of an offence under this section if he commits an offence under s 1(1) of the Criminal Damage Act 1971 (destroying or damaging property belonging to another) which is racially or religiously aggravated for the purposes of this section.

Crime and Disorder Act 1998, s 30(1)

Points to prove

✓ committed s 1(1) criminal damage offence (see **4.4**)
✓ offence was racially/religiously aggravated

Meaning of racially or religiously aggravated (see 7.10.1)

Explanatory notes

- For the purposes of this section, s 28(1)(a) (see **7.10.1**) has effect as if the person to whom the property belongs or is treated as belonging for the purposes of that Act was the victim of the offence.
- If, on the trial on indictment of a person charged with this offence, the jury find the defendant not guilty of the offence charged, they may find them guilty of the relevant 'basic' offence.

Practical considerations

- Where this offence is shown to be motivated by racial hostility under s 28(1)(b) (see **7.10.1**) there is no need to identify a specific victim (eg painting racist graffiti on a wall would be likely to constitute this offence).
- This offence is triable either way irrespective of the value of the damage caused (unlike the relevant 'basic' offence).

 Either way   None

 Summary: 6 months' imprisonment and/or a fine

Indictment: 14 years' imprisonment and/or a fine

7.10.4 Racially or religiously aggravated public order offences

Section 31 relates to racially or religiously aggravated public order offences.

Offences

A person is guilty of an offence under this section if he commits—

(a) an offence under s 4 of the Public Order Act 1986 (fear/provocation of violence) [see **7.6**]; or

(b) an offence under s 4A of that Act (intentional harassment, alarm, or distress) [see **7.7**]; or

(c) an offence under s 5 of that Act (harassment, alarm, distress) [see **7.8**],

which is racially or religiously aggravated for the purposes of this section.

Crime and Disorder Act 1998, s 31(1)

Points to prove

✓ committed an offence
✓ under s 4, s 4A, or s 5 of the Public Order Act 1986
✓ such offence was racially/religiously aggravated

Meaning of racially or religiously aggravated (see 7.10.1)

Explanatory notes

• If, on the trial on indictment of a person charged with an offence under s 31(1)(a) or (b), the jury find him not guilty of the offence charged, they may find him guilty of the 'basic' offence.

• For the purposes of s 31(1)(c), s 28(1)(a) (see **7.10.1**) shall have effect as if the person likely to be caused harassment, alarm, or distress were the victim of the offence.

Related cases

DPP v McFarlane [2002] EWHC 485, QBD During an argument over a disabled parking bay, the defendant (a white man) referred to the complainant (a black man) as a 'jungle bunny', a 'black bastard', and a 'wog' and was charged with racially aggravated threatening behaviour. It was held that the words used by the defendant had been racially inspired and anger about another's inconsiderate behaviour was not an excuse for racial comments.

DPP v Ramos [2000] Crim LR 768, QBD After a serious bomb attack, threatening letters were sent to an organisation offering help and advice to the Asian community making threats that a bombing hate campaign would be started, although no time frame was specified. Because there was no threat of immediate unlawful violence the defendant was acquitted. The appeal by the DPP was allowed and it was held that for the purposes of s 4(1), it was the state of mind of the victim which was central, rather than the statistical likelihood of violence taking place within a short space of time. Where the wording of a letter was very threatening and suggested that immediate violence may occur, it was open to the magistrate to decide whether or not the victim believed or was likely to believe that something could happen at any time.

Practical considerations

If the defendant is found not guilty of the offence charged under s 31(1)(a) or (b) at the magistrates' court there is no provision for an alternative verdict, therefore it is good practice to include the relevant 'basic' offence as an alternative charge.

Offence under s 31(1)(a) or (b)

 Either way   None

Summary: 6 months' imprisonment and/or a fine

Indictment: 2 years' imprisonment and/or a fine

Offence under s 31(1)(c)

 Summary   6 months

 Level 4 fine

7.10.5 Racially or religiously aggravated harassment/stalking

Section 32 concerns the offences of harassment/stalking or putting a person in fear of violence or stalking involving fear of violence or serious alarm or distress which is racially or religiously aggravated.

Offences

A person is guilty of an offence under this section if he commits—
(a) an offence under section 2 or 2A of the Protection from Harassment Act 1997 (offences of harassment and stalking); or
(b) an offence under section 4 or 4A of that Act (putting people in fear of violence and stalking involving fear of violence or serious alarm or distress),

which is racially or religiously aggravated for the purposes of this section.

Crime and Disorder Act 1998, s 32(1)

Points to prove

✓ committed an offence
✓ under s 2, s 2A, s 4, or s 4A of the Protection from Harassment Act 1997
✓ such offence was racially/religiously aggravated

7.10.5 Racially or religiously aggravated harassment/stalking

Meaning of racially or religiously aggravated (see 7.10.1)

Explanatory notes

- Offences relating to the Protection from Harassment Act 1997 (above) are harassment (s 2—see **7.11.1**), stalking (s 2A—see **7.11.3**), putting people in fear of violence (s 4—see **7.11.2**), and stalking involving fear of violence or serious alarm or distress (s 4A—see **7.11.4**).
- If, on the trial on indictment of a person charged with an offence under s 32(1)(a), the jury find them not guilty of the offence charged, they may find them guilty of the basic offence. Similarly, if found not guilty of an offence under s 32(1)(b), they may find them guilty of an offence under s 32(1)(a).
- If the matter is dealt with at the magistrates' court (summary) for an offence under s 32(1)(a) and found not guilty, there is no provision for an alternative verdict, so it is good practice to include the relevant basic offence as an alternative. Similarly, for a s 32(1)(b) offence, include the s 32(1)(a) offence as an alternative.

Practical considerations

Section 5 of the Protection from Harassment Act 1997 provides a court with the power to make a restraining order (see **7.11.5**).

 Either way None

Offence under s 32(1)(a)
Summary: 6 months' imprisonment and/or a fine
Indictment: 2 years' imprisonment and/or a fine

Offence under s 32(1)(b)
Summary: 6 months' imprisonment and/or a fine
Indictment: 14 years' imprisonment and/or a fine

Links to alternative subjects and offences

7.11 **Harassment/Stalking**

The Protection from Harassment Act 1997 provides criminal and civil remedies to restrain conduct amounting to harassment or stalking. Sections 42 and 42A of the Criminal Justice and Police Act 2001 concern prevention of harassment of a person in their own home.

7.11.1 **Harassment—no violence**

Section 1 prohibits harassment, while s 2 creates the offence of harassment.

Offences

1(1)   A person must not pursue a course of conduct—
  (a) which amounts to harassment of another, and
  (b) which he knows or ought to know amounts to harassment of the other.
1(1A) A person must not pursue a course of conduct—
  (a) which involves harassment of two or more persons, and
  (b) which he knows or ought to know amounts to harassment of those persons, and
  (c) by which he intends to persuade any person (whether or not one of those mentioned above)—
    (i)   not to do something that he is entitled or required to do, or
    (ii) to do something that he is not under any obligation to do.
2(1)   A person who pursues a course of conduct in breach of section 1(1) or (1A) is guilty of an offence.

Protection from Harassment Act 1997, ss 1(1), 1(1A), and 2(1)

Points to prove

✓ pursued a course of conduct
✓ on at least two occasions
✓ amounting to harassment
✓ which knew/ought to have known amounted to harassment

Meanings

Course of conduct

- Must involve to a single person under s 1(1), conduct on at least two occasions in relation to that person, **or** to two or more persons under s 1(1A), conduct on at least one occasion in relation to each of those persons.
- Conduct includes speech.

Harassment

Includes causing the person(s) alarm or distress.

Explanatory notes

- If a reasonable person in possession of the same information as the defendant would think the course of conduct amounted to harassment, then the offender should have realised this as well (*Kellett v DPP* [2001] EWHC 107 (Admin)).
- A person may be subjected to harassment by writing (eg emails or letters), orally (eg in person or by telephone), or by conduct.
- An offender does not have to act in a malicious, threatening, abusive, or insulting way. It could be that they may be infatuated with the victim and intend them no harm.
- The court can issue a 'restraining order' against the defendant. If required ask the CPS to apply for one (see **7.11.5**).

Defences

Section 1(1) or (1A) does not apply to a course of conduct if the person who pursued it shows—

(a) that it was pursued for the prevention or detection of crime,

(b) that it was pursued under any enactment or rule of law or to comply with any condition or requirement imposed by any person under any enactment, or

(c) that in the particular circumstances the pursuit of the course of conduct was reasonable.

Protection from Harassment Act 1997, s 1(3)

Defence notes

- These defences would apply to the police, customs, security services, including the private sector (eg private detective or store detective).
- A suspect suffering from some form of obsessive behaviour or schizophrenia cannot use their mental illness as a defence because of the 'reasonable person' test.

Related cases

Plavelil v DPP [2014] EWHC 736 (Admin), QBD The facts of this case involved numerous allegations being made against the complainant that were unproven and a complaint of harassment was made against the defendant. The argument that repeated untrue, malicious allegations could not be oppressive because they could so easily be rebutted was not be accepted and the conviction was upheld.

Kosar v Bank of Scotland [2011] EWHC 1050 (Admin), QBD It was held in this case that a company was not precluded from being able to commit a criminal offence of harassment contrary to s 2(1) of the 1997 Act.

7.11.2 Harassment (fear of violence)

DPP v Baker [2004] EWHC 2782 (Admin), QBD Harassment may occur either continuously or intermittently over a period of time. Providing at least one of the incidents relied on by the prosecution occurred within the six-month limitation period.

Practical considerations

- Evidence of previous complaints of harassment to prove continuance of the harassment on at least two separate occasions.
- Two isolated incidents do not constitute a course of conduct.
- Consider serving a harassment warning notice on the suspect. Have any previous warning notices been served on the suspect?
- A campaign of collective harassment applies equally to two or more people as it does to one. Namely, conduct by one person shall also be taken, at the time it occurs, to be conduct by another if it is aided, abetted, counselled, or procured by that other person.
- Consider the intentional harassment, alarm, or distress offence under s 4A of the Public Order Act 1986 (see **7.7**).
- If it is racially or religiously aggravated harassment see **7.10.5**.
- Obtain CJA witness statements.
- Obtain all available evidence (eg other witnesses, CCTV camera footage, detailed telephone bills, entries in domestic violence registers, harassment notice).
- The Court can also impose a Restraining Order on anyone convicted of this offence. A breach of such order is in itself an offence under s 5 (see **7.11.5**).
- Consider the offence of stalking under s 2A (see **7.11.3**).

RRA

 Summary   6 months

 6 months' imprisonment and/or a fine

7.11.2 **Harassment (fear of violence)**

Section 4 relates to a course of conduct, which, on at least two occasions, causes another to fear that violence will be used against them.

> ### Offences
>
> A person whose course of conduct causes another to fear, on at least two occasions, that violence will be used against him is guilty of an offence if he knows or ought to know that his course of conduct will cause the other so to fear on each of those occasions.
>
> Protection from Harassment Act 1997, s 4(1)

Points to prove

✓ caused fear of violence
✓ by a course of conduct on at least two occasions
✓ which you knew/ought to have known
✓ would cause fear of violence on each occasion

Meaning of course of conduct (see **7.11.1**)

Explanatory notes

- The person whose course of conduct is in question ought to know that it will cause another to fear that violence will be used against him on any occasion if a reasonable person with the same information would think it would cause the other so to fear on that occasion.
- A defendant found not guilty of this offence (at trial on indictment) may be convicted of s 2 harassment (see **7.11.1**) or s 2A stalking (see **7.11.3**).
- The court can issue a 'restraining order' against the defendant (see **7.11.5**).
- Communications that constitute threats to another person may also amount to other offences. Consider threats to kill under s 16 Offences Against the Person Act 1861 (see **2.5**); Intimidation of witnesses and jurors under s 51 Criminal Justice and Public Order Act 1994 (see **4.8.1**); and s 127 Communications Act 2003 (see **7.12.1**).

Defences

It is a defence for a person charged with an offence under this section to show that—

(a) his course of conduct was pursued for the purpose of preventing or detecting crime,

(b) his course of conduct was pursued under any enactment or rule of law or to comply with any condition or requirement imposed by any person under any enactment, or

(c) the pursuit of his course of conduct was reasonable for the protection of himself or another or for the protection of his or another's property.

Protection from Harassment Act 1997, s 4(3)

Defence notes (see 7.11.1)

Related cases

R v Widdows [2011] EWCA Crim 1500, CA A charge of harassment is not normally appropriate for use as a means of criminalising conduct during incidents in a long and predominantly affectionate relationship in which both parties persisted and wanted to continue.

7.11.3 **Stalking**

R v Curtis [2010] EWCA Crim 123, CA It was held in this case that the prosecution must establish that a course of conduct amounts to harassment. The conduct must be an oppressive, unreasonable, and unacceptable campaign, to a degree that would be a criminal matter.

Howard v DPP [2001] EWHC 17 (Admin), QBD In this case, a family suffered continual abuse from their neighbours. One of the many threats made by the defendant was to kill their dog. It was held that this was sufficient grounds for the family to fear violence being used against them.

Practical considerations (see also 7.11.1)

- Offence could cover long-standing disputes where fear of violence is a possibility against one of the parties.
- Consider stalking involving fear of violence or serious alarm or distress (see **7.11.4**) or intentional harassment, alarm, or distress offence under s 4A of the Public Order Act 1986 (see **7.7**).

 Either way   None

Summary: 6 months' imprisonment and/or a fine

    Indictment: 10 years' imprisonment and/or a fine

7.11.3 **Stalking**

Section 2A creates the offence of stalking.

Offences

(1) A person is guilty of an offence if—
  (a) the person pursues a course of conduct in breach of section 1(1), and
  (b) the course of conduct amounts to stalking.
(2) For the purposes of subsection (1)(b) (and section 4A(1)(a)) a person's course of conduct amounts to stalking of another person if—
  (a) it amounts to harassment of that person,
  (b) the acts or omissions involved are ones associated with stalking, and
  (c) the person whose course of conduct it is knows or ought to know that the course of conduct amounts to harassment of the other person.

Protection from Harassment Act 1997, s 2A

Points to prove

✓ pursued a course of conduct in breach of s 1(1)
✓ that conduct amounted to stalking
✓ which you knew/ought to have known
✓ amounted to harassment

Meanings

Breach of section 1(1) (see **7.11.1**)

Harassment (see **7.11.1**)

Includes causing the person(s) alarm or distress.

Acts or omissions (s 2A(3))

The following are examples which, in particular circumstances, are associated with stalking:

- following a person;
- contacting, or attempting to contact, a person by any means;
- publishing any statement or other material—relating or purporting to relate to a person, or purporting to originate from a person;
- monitoring the use by a person of the internet, email, or any other form of electronic communication;
- loitering in any place (whether public or private);
- interfering with any property in the possession of a person;
- watching or spying on a person.

Explanatory notes

- Stalking is most often found where a person is fixated and/or obsessed with another. This can manifest itself in a pattern of persistent and repeated contact, or attempts to contact, the victim. Examples of behaviours associated with stalking are given in s 2A(3) (above).
- An offender does not have to act in a malicious, threatening, abusive, or insulting way. It could be that they may be infatuated with the victim and intend them no harm.
- The court can issue a 'restraining order' against the defendant (see **7.11.5**).

Practical considerations

- Refer the victim to relevant support agencies: National Stalking Helpline or Paladin, including victim support (see **Appendix 1**) and local domestic violence support groups. Ensure compliance with the Victim Code and that a VPS is taken (see **13.4**).
- Section 2B allows a justice of the peace to issue a warrant, which authorises a constable to enter and search premises on reasonable grounds for believing that:
    - ✦ a stalking offence under s 2A has been, or is being, committed; and
    - ✦ there is material on the premises which is likely to be of substantial value (whether by itself or together with other material) to the investigation of the offence.

- Section 4A concerns the offence of stalking involving fear of violence or serious alarm or distress (see **7.11.4**).
- HOC 18/2012 provides further details concerning the s 2A and s 4A stalking offences and power of entry under s 2B.
- If it is racially or religiously aggravated stalking (see **7.10.5**).
- Consider the offence of intentional harassment, alarm, or distress under s 4A of the Public Order Act 1986 (see **7.7**).

 Summary   6 months

 6 months' imprisonment and/or a fine

7.11.4 **Stalking (fear of violence/serious alarm or distress)**

Section 4A is a more serious stalking offence of causing another to fear, on at least two occasions, that violence will be used against them or causes them serious alarm or distress which has a substantial adverse effect on their usual day-to-day activities.

Offences

A person (A) whose course of conduct—
(a) amounts to stalking, and
(b) either—
   (i) causes another (B) to fear, on at least two occasions, that violence will be used against B, or
   (ii) causes B serious alarm or distress which has a substantial adverse effect on B's usual day-to-day activities,

is guilty of an offence if A knows or ought to know that A's course of conduct will cause B so to fear on each of those occasions or (as the case may be) will cause such alarm or distress.

Protection from Harassment Act 1997, s 4A(1)

Points to prove

✓ course of conduct that amounted to stalking
✓ caused another to fear on at least two occasions that violence would be used or
✓ caused serious alarm/distress which had a substantial adverse effect on B's usual day-to-day activities
✓ which knew/ought to have known
✓ would cause either fear of violence on each occasion or serious alarm/distress

---

Meaning of stalking (see **7.11.3**)

Explanatory notes

- The phrase '**substantial adverse effect** on the usual day-to-day activities' is not defined in s 4A. HOC 18/2012 states that evidence of a substantial adverse effect may include the victim:
  - ✦ changing their routes to work, work patterns, or employment;
  - ✦ arranging for friends or family to pick up children from school;
  - ✦ installing additional security in/around their home;
  - ✦ suffering from physical or mental ill-health;
  - ✦ suffering from stress due to deterioration in performance at work;
  - ✦ moving home; or
  - ✦ stopping/changing the way they socialise.
- If the victim continues with their existing routines in defiance of a stalker, they may still be able to evidence the substantial impact on their usual day-to-day activities.
- The person whose course of conduct is in question ought to know that it will cause another to fear that violence will be used against them on any occasion if a reasonable person in possession of the same information would think the course of conduct would cause the other to fear on that occasion.
- For the purposes of this section the person whose course of conduct is in question ought to know that their course of conduct will cause the victim serious alarm or distress which has a substantial adverse effect on the victim's usual day-to-day activities if a reasonable person in possession of the same information would think the course of conduct would cause the victim such alarm or distress.
- Other offences that may be considered in appropriate circumstances include threats to kill under s 16 Offences Against the Person Act 1861 (see **2.5**); Intimidation of witnesses and jurors under s 51 Criminal Justice and Public Order Act 1994 (see **4.8.1**); s 1 malicious Communications Act 1988 (see **7.12.1**); and s 127 Communications Act 2003 (see **7.12.2**).

Defences

It is a defence for A to show that—

(a) A's course of conduct was pursued for the purpose of preventing or detecting crime,

(b) A's course of conduct was pursued under any enactment or rule of law or to comply with any condition or requirement imposed by any person under any enactment, or

(c) the pursuit of A's course of conduct was reasonable for the protection of A or another or for the protection of A's or another's property.

Protection from Harassment Act 1997, s 4A(4)

Defence notes (see **7.11.1**)

Related cases

R v Qosja [2016] EWCA Crim 1543 In this case it was held that the offence was wide enough to cover a person who is caused to fear on a particular occasion that violence will be used on an uncertain future date. This does not need to be a specific threat of violence, but the requirement is that they fear that violence will (rather than may be) used.

Practical considerations (see also **7.11.3**)

- If on the trial on indictment of a person charged with a s 4A offence, the jury find that person not guilty, they may find the person guilty of an offence under s 2 (see **7.11.1**) or s 2A (see **7.11.3**).
- The court can issue a 'restraining order' against the defendant (see **7.11.5**).
- If it is racially or religiously aggravated stalking (see **7.10.5**).
- Consider intentional harassment, alarm, or distress offence under s 4A of the Public Order Act 1986 (see **7.7**).

E&S

 Either way   None

 Summary: 12 months' imprisonment and/or a fine

Indictment: 10 years' imprisonment and/or a fine

7.11.5 **Restraining orders**

Restraining orders can be made against a person convicted of any offence under s 5 or acquitted of an offence under s 5A.

> **Offences**
>
> If without reasonable excuse the defendant does anything which he is prohibited from doing by an order under this section, he is guilty of an offence.
>
> Protection from Harassment Act 1997, s 5(5)

> **Points to prove**
> - ✓ without reasonable excuse
> - ✓ did something prohibited by a restraining order

Explanatory notes

- A court sentencing or otherwise dealing with a defendant convicted of **any offence** may, as well as sentencing or dealing with the defendant in any other way, make a restraining order under s 5 or s 5A. HOC 17/2009 provides guidelines on restraining orders to protect a person from harassment or violence.
- Under s 5A a court can make a restraining order on a person acquitted of an offence, if the court believes a restraining order is necessary to protect a person from harassment or stalking. It is also an offence to breach a s 5A restraining order, as s 5A(2) states that s 5(3)–(7) applies to an order under s 5A as they apply to an order under s 5.
- The order may prohibit the defendant from doing anything described in the order, for the purpose of protecting the victim(s), or any other person mentioned in the order, from further conduct which amounts to harassment, stalking or will cause fear of violence or serious alarm or distress.
- The order may last for a specified period or until a further order is made.
- The prosecutor, defendant, or any person named therein may apply for it to be varied or discharged by a further order.

Related cases

R v Buxton [2011] EWCA Crim 2923, CA A restraining order can be made to protect a company.

R v Major [2010] EWHC 3016, QBD If a court issues a restraining order on acquittal there must be clear evidence that the victim needs protection from harassment from the defendant.

Practical considerations

- Unlike the previous sections of this Act, one incident is sufficient to breach an order.
- These are criminal matters and should not be confused with civil injunctions.
- When an order is made it must identify the protected parties, so ensure the details are available.
- Include a copy of the original order in the file for CPS attention.
- If you require a further order you must request CPS apply for one.

 E&S

 Either way   None

Summary: 6 months' imprisonment and/or a fine

Indictment: 5 years' imprisonment and/or a fine

7.11.6 **Civil remedies**

Section 3 provides a civil remedy for harassment, allowing the victim to obtain damages and/or an injunction. Section 3A provides for injunctions to protect persons from harassment within s 1(1A).

Offences

Where—
(a) the High Court or a county court grants an injunction for the purpose mentioned in subsection (3)(a), and
(b) without reasonable excuse the defendant does anything which he is prohibited from doing by the injunction,

he is guilty of an offence.

Protection from Harassment Act 1997, s 3(6)

Points to prove

✓ without reasonable excuse
✓ pursued course of conduct prohibited by injunction
✓ granted by High Court/county court

Meanings

Injunction

An order or decree issued by a court for a person to do or not do that which is specified for a specified amount of time.

Subsection (3)(a)

In such proceedings, the High Court or a county court grants an injunction for the purpose of restraining the defendant from pursuing any conduct which amounts to harassment.

Reasonable excuse (see '**Defence**' below)

Explanatory notes

- An actual or perceived breach of s 1 may result in a claim in civil proceedings by the victim of the course of conduct in question.
- On such a claim, damages may be awarded for, among other things, any anxiety caused by, and financial loss resulting from, the harassment.
- Where, in such proceedings, the court grants an injunction restraining the defendant from pursuing any conduct amounting to harassment, and the plaintiff considers that the defendant has done anything prohibited by the injunction, they may apply to have a warrant issued for the arrest of the defendant.
- The warrant application must be made to the court that issued the injunction.

- Section 3A stipulates that where there is an actual or apprehended breach of s 1(1A) (see **7.11.1**) by the relevant person, then any person who is or may be:
  + a victim of the course of conduct in question; or
  + a person falling within s 1(1A)(c) may apply to the High Court or a county court for an injunction restraining the relevant person from pursuing any conduct which amounts to harassment in relation to any person or persons mentioned or described in the injunction.

Defences
The defence of reasonable excuse was meant for a life-saving situation such as a rescue from a burning house or something similar (*Huntingdon Life Sciences v Curtin* [1997] EWCA Civ 2486).

Related cases
Thomas v News Group Newspapers Ltd [2001] EWCA Civ 1233 In this case, a national newspaper and journalists were sued for harassment under s 3 after publishing an article about police discipline which gave the complainant's name, place of work, and described them as 'a black clerk'. It was held that it was not the conduct of the offender that created the offence or civil wrong of harassment, but the effect of that conduct. There was a sound argument that the reference by the newspaper to the complainant's skin colour was not reasonable. Furthermore, it could be argued that the newspaper could have foreseen that some of its readers would send hate mail after the articles.

Practical considerations
If a person is convicted of a breach of an injunction under this section, their conduct is not punishable as a contempt of court, or vice versa.

 Either way   None

 Summary: 6 months' imprisonment and/or a fine

Indictment: 5 years' imprisonment and/or a fine

7.11.7 **Harassment of person in their home**

Sections 42 and 42A of the Criminal Justice and Police Act 2001 give the police power to direct a person to leave a dwelling to prevent harassment and an offence of harassing a person in their home.

7.11.7 Harassment of person in their home

Offences

42(7) Any person who knowingly fails to comply with a requirement in a direction given to him under this section (other than a requirement under subsection (4)(b)) shall be guilty of an offence.

42(7A) Any person to whom a constable has given a direction including a requirement under subsection (4)(b) commits an offence if he—

(a) returns to the vicinity of the premises in question within the period specified in the direction beginning with the date on which the direction is given; and

(b) does so for the purpose described in subsection (1)(b).

42A(1) A person commits an offence if—

(a) that person is present outside or in the vicinity of any premises that are used by any individual ('the resident') as his dwelling;

(b) that person is present there for the purpose (by his presence or otherwise) of representing to the resident or another individual (whether or not one who uses the premises as his dwelling), or of persuading the resident or such another individual—

(i) that he should not do something that he is entitled or required to do; or

(ii) that he should do something that he is not under any obligation to do;

(c) that person—

(i) intends his presence to amount to the harassment of, or to cause alarm or distress to, the resident, or

(ii) knows or ought to know that his presence is likely to result in the harassment of, or to cause alarm or distress to, the resident; and

(d) the presence of that person—

(i) amounts to the harassment of, or causes alarm or distress to, any person falling within subsection (2); or

(ii) is likely to result in the harassment of, or to cause alarm or distress to, any such person.

Criminal Justice and Police Act 2001, ss 42, 42A

Points to prove

s 42(7) offence

✓ outside/in vicinity of premises
✓ knowingly
✓ contravened the direction of a constable

s 42(7A) offence

✓ having been given a direction by a constable
✓ to leave the vicinity of premises
✓ not to return within a specified period
✓ returned there within that period
✓ to persuade the resident/another individual

✓ not to do something they are entitled to do/do something not
  obliged to do

s 42A(1) offence

✓ present outside/in vicinity of a dwelling
✓ to persuade resident/other individual
✓ not to do something entitled/required to do/to do something
  not obliged to do
✓ intended to harass/cause alarm/distress to the resident
✓ knew/ought to have known such presence was likely to do so
✓ and their presence amounted to harassment/caused alarm/
  distress/likely to do so

Meanings

Directions

(1) Subject to the following provisions of this section, a constable
    who is at the scene may give a **direction** under this section to any
    person if—
    (a) that person is present outside or in the vicinity of any
        premises that are used by any individual ('the resident') as his
        dwelling;
    (b) that constable believes, on reasonable grounds, that that
        person is present there for the purpose (by his presence
        or otherwise) of representing to the resident or another
        individual (whether or not one who uses the premises as
        his dwelling), or of persuading the resident or such another
        individual—
        (i) that he should not do something that he is entitled or
            required to do; or
        (ii) that he should do something that he is not under any
            obligation to do; and
    (c) that constable also believes, on reasonable grounds, that the
        presence of that person (either alone or together with that of
        any other persons who are also present)—
        (i) amounts to, or is likely to result in, the **harassment** of the
            resident; or
        (ii) is likely to cause alarm or distress to the resident.
(2) A direction under this section is a direction requiring the person
    to whom it is given to do all such things as the constable giving it
    may specify as the things he considers necessary to prevent one or
    both of the following—
    (a) the harassment of the resident; or
    (b) the causing of any alarm or distress to the resident.
(3) A direction under this section may be given orally; and where a
    constable is entitled to give a direction under this section to each
    of several persons outside, or in the vicinity of, any premises, he
    may give that direction to those persons by notifying them of his
    requirements either individually or all together.

(4) The requirements that may be imposed by a direction under this section include—

   (a) a requirement to leave the vicinity of the premises in question, and

   (b) a requirement to leave that vicinity and not to return to it within such period as the constable may specify, not being longer than 3 months;

   and (in either case) the requirement to leave the vicinity may be to do so immediately or after a specified period of time.

(5) A direction under this section may make exceptions to any requirement imposed by the direction, and may make any such exception subject to such conditions as the constable giving the direction thinks fit; and those conditions may include—

   (a) conditions as to the distance from the premises in question at which, or otherwise as to the location where, persons who do not leave their vicinity must remain; and

   (b) conditions as to the number or identity of the persons who are authorised by the exception to remain in the vicinity of those premises.

(6) The power of a constable to give a direction under this section shall not include—

   (a) any power to give a direction at any time when there is a more **senior ranking** police officer at the scene; or

   (b) any power to direct a person to refrain from conduct that is lawful under section 220 of the Trade Union and Labour Relations (Consolidation) Act 1992 (right peacefully to picket a work place);

but it shall include power to vary or withdraw a direction previously given under this section.

Criminal Justice and Police Act 2001, s 42

Dwelling

Means any structure or part of a structure occupied as a person's home or as other living accommodation (whether the occupation is separate or shared with others) but does not include any part not so occupied, and for this purpose 'structure' includes a tent, caravan, vehicle, vessel, or other temporary or movable structure.

Harassment (see **7.11.1**)

Explanatory notes

- A requirement in a direction under s 42(4)(b) means to leave that vicinity immediately or after a specified period of time and not to return within a specified period (no more than three months).
- Under the s 42A(1)(d)(i) offence a person falls within s 42A(2) if he is the resident, a person in the resident's dwelling, or a person in another dwelling in the vicinity of the resident's dwelling.
- Under s 42 a constable in attendance may give a direction to any person if that person is outside or in the vicinity of premises used

by a resident as their dwelling, having reasonable grounds to believe that the person's presence amounts to harassment of the resident or is likely to cause them alarm or distress.
- Such a direction requires the person to whom it is given to do everything specified by the constable as necessary to prevent the harassment of and/or the causing of alarm or distress to, the resident.
- A direction under s 42 may include a requirement to leave:
  + the vicinity of the premises in question; and
  + not return to it within such period as the constable may specify, not being longer than three months.
- The references in s 42A(1)(c) and (d) to a person's presence refer to their presence either alone or together with any other person(s) also present.
- For the s 42A offence a person ought to know that their presence is likely to result in the harassment of, or cause alarm or distress to, a resident if a reasonable person possessing the same information would think that their presence would likely have that effect.

Practical considerations
- Directions given under this section may be given orally, but it is important that the direction must be both heard and understood by the person concerned.
- If a direction is given to more than one person, the constable may give it to them either individually or all together.
- The power of a constable to give a direction under s 42 does not include where there is a more **senior-ranking** officer present. If the senior officers are of the same rank, then the greater length of service in that rank determines who should give the direction.
- Similarly, a constable cannot give a direction if the person(s) are exercising their right to peacefully picket a workplace.
- A constable may vary or withdraw any direction previously given.

 Either way   None

 Offence under s 42(7)
3 months' imprisonment and/or a level 4 fine

Offence under s 42(7A) or s 42A
51 weeks imprisonment and/or a level 4 fine

Links to alternative subjects and offences

7.11.7 Harassment of person in their home

7.12 **Offensive/False Messages**

The Malicious Communications Act 1988 concerns the sending and delivery of letters or other articles to cause distress or anxiety; the Communications Act 2003 regulates all types of media, including the sending of grossly offensive material via the public electronic communications network; whilst the offence of giving or causing to be given a false alarm of fire is dealt with by the Fire and Rescue Services Act 2004.

7.12.1 **Send letters, etc intending to cause distress/anxiety**

Section 1 of the Malicious Communications Act 1988 creates offences relating to the sending of indecent, offensive, or threatening letters, electronic communications, or articles with intent to cause distress or anxiety to the recipient.

Offences

Any person who sends to another person—
(a) a letter, electronic communication or article of any description which conveys—
    (i)   a message which is indecent or grossly offensive;
    (ii) a threat; or
    (iii) information which is false and known or believed to be false by the sender; or
(b) any article or electronic communication which is, in whole or part, of an indecent or grossly offensive nature,

is guilty of an offence if his purpose, or one of his purposes, in sending it is that it should, so far as falling within paragraph (a) or (b) above, cause distress or anxiety to the recipient or to any other person to whom he intends that it or its contents or nature should be communicated.

Malicious Communications Act 1988, s 1(1)

Points to prove

s 1(1)(a) offence

✓ sent a letter/an electronic communication/an article
✓ which conveys an indecent/grossly offensive message/threat/ false information which knew/believed to be false
✓ for the purpose of causing distress/anxiety ✓ to the recipient/ any other person
✓ to whom its contents/nature were intended to be communicated

---

s 1(1)(b) offence

✓ sent to another person
✓ an article/an electronic communication
✓ wholly/partly of an indecent/grossly offensive nature
✓ for the purpose of causing distress/anxiety
✓ to the recipient/any other person
✓ to whom its contents/nature were intended to be
   communicated

Meanings

Electronic communication

Includes any:
- oral or other communication by means of an **electronic communications network**; and
- communication (however sent) that is in electronic form.

Electronic communications network

Means:
- a transmission system for the conveyance, by the use of electrical, magnetic, or electro-magnetic energy, of signals of any description; and
- such of the following as are used, by the person providing the system and in association with it, for the conveyance of the signals:
  + apparatus comprised in the system;
  + apparatus used for the switching or routing of the signals; and
  + software and stored data.

Grossly offensive

This has to be judged by the standards of an open and just multiracial society. Whether a message falls into this category depends not only on its content but on the circumstances in which the message has been sent (*DPP v Collins* [2005] EWHC 1308, HL).

Explanatory notes

- Sending includes delivering or transmitting and causing to be sent, delivered, or transmitted; 'sender' will be construed accordingly.
- Offence only requires that the communication be sent—not that the intended victim actually received it.

Defences

A person is not guilty of an offence by virtue of subsection (1)(a)(ii) above [threat] if he shows—
(a) that the threat was used to reinforce a demand made by him on reasonable grounds; and

---

> (b) that he believed, and had reasonable grounds for believing, that the
> use of the threat was a proper means of reinforcing the demand.
>
> Malicious Communications Act 1988, s 1(2)

Related cases

Connolly v DPP [2007] EWHC 237, QBD In this case the defendant
telephoned chemist shops to ascertain whether they stocked the
morning-after pill, sending pictures of aborted foetuses to those that
did. These pictures were indecent and grossly offensive with the purpose
of causing distress or anxiety. It was held that rights of expression under
Art 9 or Art 10 (see **1.1**) did not excuse the distress and anxiety caused,
and conviction was necessary in a democratic society. The words 'indecent' and 'grossly offensive' have their ordinary meaning.

Practical considerations

- As well as letters and telephone systems this offence would include
  emails, fax, text messages, Facebook, Twitter, or other social media.
- What was the intended purpose of the defendant in sending the
  communication?
- If the intent is to cause the victim annoyance, inconvenience,
  or needless anxiety, then consider the offence under s 127 of the
  Communications Act 2003 (see **7.12.2**).
- If there has been more than one incident an offence under s 2 or s
  2A of the Protection from Harassment Act 1997 may be appropriate
  (see **7.11.1** or **7.11.3**).
- If any threat used includes an unwarranted demand, consider the
  more serious offence of blackmail (see **3.2.3**).
- Preserve the means or item that was used to deliver the message to
  the victim.
- The original message can be retrieved from phones or computers; the
  original letter or envelope can be fingerprinted or examined for DNA.

E&S

 Either way   None

 Summary: 12 months' imprisonment and/or a fine

Indictment: 2 years' imprisonment and/or a fine

7.12.2 **Improper use of electronic public communications network**

Section 127 of the Communications Act 2003 creates offences regarding
improper use of a public electronic communications network.

Offences

(1) A person is guilty of an offence if he—
   (a) sends by means of a public electronic communications network a message or other matter that is grossly offensive or of an indecent, obscene or menacing character; or
   (b) causes any such message or matter to be so sent.

(2) A person is guilty of an offence if, for the purpose of causing annoyance, inconvenience or needless anxiety to another, he—
   (a) sends by means of a public electronic communications network, a message that he knows to be false,
   (b) causes such a message to be sent, or
   (c) persistently makes use of a public electronic communications network.

Communications Act 2003, s 127

Points to prove

s 127(1) offence

✓ sent
✓ by means of a public electronic communications network
✓ a message/other matter
✓ being grossly offensive/indecent/obscene/menacing character

or

✓ caused such a message/matter to be so sent

s 127(2) offence

✓ to cause annoyance/inconvenience/needless anxiety to another
✓ sent by means of a public electronic communications network
✓ a message known to be false

or

✓ caused such a message to be sent

or

✓ persistently made use
✓ of a public electronic communications network

Meanings

Public electronic communications network

Means an **electronic communications network** provided wholly or mainly for the purpose of making electronic communications services available for use by members of the public.

Electronic communications network (see 7.12.1)

Grossly offensive (see 7.12.1)

Menacing

Means a message which conveys a threat; which seeks to create a fear in or through the recipient that something unpleasant is going to happen. Here the intended or likely effect on the recipient must ordinarily be a central factor (*DPP v Collins* [2005] EWHC 1308, HL).

Persistently

Includes any case in which the misuse is repeated on a sufficient number of occasions for it to be clear that the misuse represents a pattern of behaviour, or practice, or recklessness as to whether people suffer annoyance, inconvenience, or anxiety.

Explanatory notes

- 'Electronic communications network' covers current and future developments in communication technologies (eg telephone, computers (internet), satellites, mobile terrestrial networks, emails, text messages, fax, radio, and television broadcasting including cable TV networks).
- These offences do not apply to anything done in the course of providing a broadcasting service, such as a television programme; public teletext; digital television; radio programme; or sound provided by the BBC.
- Sections 128–130 empower OFCOM (Office of Communications) to enforce this Act to stop a person persistently misusing a public electronic communications network or services.

Related cases

DPP v Smith (Kingsley Anthony) [2017] EWHC 359 (Admin) It was held in this case that for s 127(1)(a) when deciding whether a particular message is *grossly offensive*, a court needs to be careful not to criminalise speech that, however contemptable, is no more than offensive. It has to be asked whether taking account of the context and all relevant circumstances by applying the standards of a reasonable person in a multi-racial and multi-faith society, that a message was grossly offensive to those whom it related and whether it would have created a sense of apprehension or fear in a person of reasonable fortitude who received or read it.

R v Johnson [1996] 2 Cr App R 434, CA Making numerous obscene/offensive telephone calls can amount to a public nuisance (see **7.13.4**).

R v Ireland [1998] AC 147, HL and R v Burstow [1997] 4 All ER 225, HL It was held in this case that silent telephone calls which caused psychiatric injury to a victim were capable of being an AOABH (see **2.1**) or grievous bodily harm (see **2.3**) if they caused the victim to fear imminent violence on themselves. Expert evidence confirmed that the victims had suffered palpitations, breathing difficulties, cold sweats, anxiety, sleeplessness, dizziness, and stress.

Practical considerations

- These offences do not apply to a private/internal network. In these instances, consider s 1 of the Malicious Communications Act 1988 (see **7.12.1**).
- Under subsection (1) there is no requirement to show any specific purpose or intent by the defendant.
- Consider s 1 of the Malicious Communications Act 1988 (see **7.12.1**) if the offence involves intent to cause the victim distress or anxiety.
- Also consider an offence under the Protection from Harassment Act 1997 (see **7.11**).
- If threats or information relate to bombs, noxious substances, or the placing of dangerous articles, consider offences under the Anti-terrorism, Crime and Security Act 2001 and the Criminal Law Act 1977 (see **11.4.2**).
- Section 125 creates the offence of dishonestly obtaining an electronic communications service with intent to avoid the applicable payment.
- Possession or control of apparatus which may be used dishonestly to obtain an electronic communications service, or in connection with obtaining such a service is also an offence under s 126.
- If communication is with a child for the purposes of sexual gratification, consider the offence under s 15A Sexual Offences Act 2003 (see **6.5.5**).
- Communications that constitute threats to another person may also amount to other more serious offences. Consider threats to kill under s 16 Offences Against the Person Act 1861 (see **2.5**); Intimidation of witnesses and jurors under s 51 Criminal Justice and Public Order Act 1994 (see **4.8.1**); threats of violence under ss 4 and 4A Protection from Harassment Act 1997 (see **7.11.2**).
- A PND may be issued by a police officer, CSO, or other accredited person for an offence under s 127(2) (see **7.1.1**).
- Prosecutions, if in the public interest, should only proceed with cases under s 1 Malicious Communications Act 1988 (see **7.11.1**), or under this section where there is sufficient evidence that the communication is more than offensive, shocking, disturbing, or satirical, iconoclastic, or rude. Or the expression of unpopular or unfashionable opinion about serious or trivial matters, or banter or humour (see also *Smith v ADVFN* [2008] 1797 QBD).

PND

 Summary

 Normally 6 months but no more than 3 years after the offence

6 months' imprisonment and/or a fine

7.12.3 **Giving/cause to be given false alarm of fire**

Section 49 of the Fire and Rescue Services Act 2004 creates an offence of giving or causing to be given a false alarm of fire.

Offences

A person commits an offence if he knowingly gives or causes to be given a false alarm of fire to a person acting on behalf of a fire and rescue authority.

Fire and Rescue Services Act 2004, s 49(1)

Points to prove

✓ knowingly
✓ gave/caused to be given
✓ a false alarm of fire
✓ to a person acting on behalf of a fire and rescue authority

---

Meanings

Knowingly (see 9.1.3)

Fire and rescue authority

A fire and rescue authority for the county/county borough/area or the London Fire and Emergency Planning Authority.

Practical considerations

- The prosecutor may apply to the court for an **injunction** (see **7.13.1**) or a **criminal behaviour order** (see **7.13.2**).
- PND can be issued by a police officer/CSO (see **7.1.1**).

 Summary   6 months

 51 weeks imprisonment and / or a fine not exceeding level four on the standard scale.

Links to alternative subjects and offences

7.12.3 Giving/cause to be given false alarm of fire

7.13 Anti-Social Behaviour

Anti-social behaviour is dealt with in this chapter under the Anti-social Behaviour, Crime and Policing Act 2014, the Criminal Justice and Immigration Act 2008, and the Police Reform Act 2002.

7.13.1 Injunctions—application/breach

Section 1 of the Anti-social Behaviour, Crime and Policing Act 2014 allows a court to grant an injunction against a person involved in anti-social behaviour for the purpose of preventing further behaviour, and if there is a risk of violence, s 4 allows a court to attach a power of arrest to the injunction.

Power to grant injunctions

(1) A court may grant an injunction under this section against a person aged 10 or over ('the respondent') if two conditions are met.

(2) The first condition is that the court is satisfied, on the balance of probabilities, that the respondent has engaged or threatens to engage in antis-social behaviour.

(3) The second condition is that the court considers it just and convenient to grant the injunction for the purpose of preventing the respondent from engaging in anti-social behaviour.

(4) An injunction under this section may for the purpose of preventing the respondent from engaging in anti-social behaviour—
   (a) prohibit the respondent from doing anything described in the injunction;
   (b) require the respondent to do anything described in the injunction.

Anti-social Behaviour, Crime and Policing Act 2014, s 1

Meanings

Anti-social behaviour

Means conduct:
- that has caused, or is likely to cause, harassment, alarm, or distress to any person;
- capable of causing nuisance or annoyance to a person in relation to that person's occupation of residential premises; or
- capable of causing **housing-related** nuisance or annoyance to any person.

Housing-related

Means directly or indirectly relating to the housing management functions of a housing provider or a local authority.

Explanatory notes

- This civil injunction could be used to deal with anti-social nuisance or annoyance across a wide range of behaviours. This can include vandalism, public drunkenness, drug issues, aggressive begging, irresponsible dog owners, noisy or abusive behaviour, or bullying against neighbours or others.
- If the county court, High Court (youth court if under 18) issues an injunction, this will prohibit the person from doing and require them to do what is described in the injunction, with the intention of addressing their anti-social behaviour.
- The injunction can provide protection for victims and communities and set a clear standard of behaviour in order to prevent escalation.
- If an injunction includes a requirement, it must specify the person responsible for ensuring compliance with the requirement. The person may be an individual or an organisation.
- Before including a requirement, the court must receive evidence about its suitability and enforceability. If two or more requirements are included, the court must consider their compatibility with each other.
- A respondent subject to a requirement must keep in touch with the person responsible for ensuring compliance, regarding any instructions given by that person, and notify that person of any change of address. These obligations are requirements of the injunction.
- These are civil proceedings, but the standard of proof is to the criminal standard.
- An injunction may be granted only on the application of: a local authority; a housing provider; the chief officer of police for a police area; the chief constable of the BT police; Transport for London; the Environment Agency; the Natural Resources Body for Wales; the Secretary of State; a Special Health Authority; or the Welsh Ministers.
- The court may vary or discharge an injunction under the application of the person who applied for the injunction, or the respondent.
- Under s 4 a court granting an injunction may attach a power of arrest to a prohibition or **requirement** of the injunction if the court thinks that:
  - ✦ the respondent has engaged or threatened to engage in violence against other persons, or
  - ✦ there is a significant risk of **harm** to other persons from the respondent.
- **Requirement** does not include the respondent participating in activities. **Harm** includes serious ill-treatment or abuse, whether physical or not.

Arrest without warrant—breach of injunction

Where a power of arrest is attached to a provision of an injunction under section 1, a constable may arrest the respondent without warrant if he or she has reasonable cause to suspect that the respondent is in breach of the provision.

Anti-social Behaviour, Crime and Policing Act 2014, s 9(1)

Practical considerations

- A person arrested under s 9(1) must, within twenty-four hours from the time of the arrest, be brought before the appropriate judge of the High Court or county court. Christmas Day, Good Friday, and any Sunday are to be disregarded when calculating the twenty-four hours.
- Examples of injunction requirements could be attending dog training or alcohol awareness classes, or mediation sessions with neighbours or victims.
- Prohibitions or requirements in the injunction can be for a fixed or indefinite period, but must have a specified time limit to a maximum of twelve months if the respondent is under 18.
- Although breach of an injunction is not a criminal offence, the breach procedure is to the criminal standard of proof. Breach is treated as contempt of court, and sanctions could be up to two years' imprisonment and/or unlimited fine or, if under 18, supervision, detention, curfew, or activity requirement.
- An injunction may have the effect of excluding the respondent from the place where they normally live ('the premises') only if:
  - ✦ the respondent is aged 18 or over;
  - ✦ the injunction is granted on the application of a local authority, the chief officer of police for the area where the premises are located, or if the premises are owned or managed by a housing provider, that housing provider; and
  - ✦ the court thinks that the respondent has used or threatened to use violence against other persons, or there is a significant risk of harm to other persons from the respondent.
- An ASBO under s 1 or s1B of the Crime and Disorder Act 1998 and a DBO under s 3 or s 4 of the Violent Crime Reduction Act 2006 continue to be effective for as long as the order is in force.

7.13.2 Criminal behaviour orders— application/breach

Section 22 of the Anti-social Behaviour, Crime and Policing Act 2014 empowers any criminal court to make a criminal behaviour order (CBO) against a person convicted of a criminal offence, whose behaviour has caused or was likely to cause harassment, alarm, or distress. It is a criminal offence under s 30 to breach such an order.

Offences

A person who without reasonable excuse—

(a) does anything he or she is prohibited from doing by a criminal behaviour order, or

(b) fails to do anything he or she is required to do by a criminal behaviour order, commits an offence.

Anti-social Behaviour, Crime and Policing Act 2014, s 30(1)

Points to prove

✓ without reasonable excuse
✓ did anything prohibited from doing **or**
✓ failed to do anything required to do
✓ by criminal behaviour order

Meanings

Criminal behaviour order

(1) This section applies where a person ('the offender') is convicted of an offence.

(2) The court may make a criminal behaviour order against the offender if two conditions are met.

(3) The first condition is that the court is satisfied, beyond reasonable doubt, that the offender has engaged in behaviour that caused or was likely to cause harassment, alarm, or distress to any person.

(4) The second condition is that the court considers that making the order will help in preventing the offender from engaging in such behaviour.

(5) A **criminal behaviour order** is an order which, for the purpose of preventing the offender from engaging in such behaviour—

(a) prohibits the offender from doing anything described in the order;

(b) requires the offender to do anything described in the order.

Anti-social Behaviour, Crime and Policing Act 2014, s 22

Explanatory notes

- The CBO can deal with a wide range of anti-social behaviours following conviction for a criminal offence; for example, threatening violence against others, being aggressive due to alcohol or drugs in public or causing or threatening criminal damage.

- The court may make a CBO only if it is in addition to a sentence imposed in respect of the offence or if the offender has been conditionally discharged, and on application by the prosecution (CPS or local authority).

- The CBO will include prohibitions to stop the behaviour, but can include requirements to get the offender to address the underlying cause of their behaviour.
- If the offender is under the age of 18 the prosecution must find out the views of the local youth offending team (YOT) before applying for a CBO.
- A CBO that includes a requirement must specify the person responsible for ensuring compliance with the requirement. The person may be an individual or an organisation.
- Before including a requirement, the court must receive evidence about its suitability and enforceability. If two or more requirements are included, the court must consider their compatibility with each other.
- A respondent subject to a requirement must keep in touch with the person responsible for ensuring compliance, regarding any instructions given by that person, and notify that person of any change of address. These obligations are requirements of the order.
- It is the duty of the responsible person to promote compliance, and if the offender has complied with all or failed to comply with any relevant requirement to inform the police and prosecution.
- The court may vary or discharge a CBO on the application of the offender or the prosecution.

Practical considerations

- Requirements of the CBO should aim to tackle the underlying cause of the behaviour and be made to suit the needs of each offender. They could include:
  + attendance at an anger management course;
  + youth mentoring;
  + substance misuse awareness sessions; and
  + a job readiness course to help an offender get employment.
- The duration of a CBO is a minimum of two years up to an indefinite period, but must be between one and three years if the offender is under 18.
- Consider making the public aware of the offender and the terms of the CBO. Each case should be decided carefully, whether it is necessary and proportionate, being balanced to reassure the victim and inform the community so they can report any breaches.
- An ASBO under the Crime and Disorder Act 1998, s 1 will still be in force for as long as the order remains in force.

E&S

Either way   None

Summary: 6 months' imprisonment and/or a fine

Indictment: 5 years' imprisonment and/or a fine

7.13.3 **Act in anti-social manner—fail to give name/address**

Section 50 of the Police Reform Act 2002 empowers a police officer to request the name and address of a person behaving in an anti-social manner and creates an offence of failing to comply with that request.

Offences

Any person who—
(a) fails to give his name and address when required to do so under subsection (1), or
(b) gives a false or inaccurate name or address in response to a requirement under that subsection,
is guilty of an offence.

Police Reform Act 2002, s 50(2)

Points to prove

✓ being a person whom a constable had reason to believe
✓ had been/was acting in anti-social manner
✓ failed or gave false/inaccurate details
✓ when required by the constable to provide their name and address

Meanings

Required under subsection (1)

If a constable in uniform has reason to believe that a person has been acting, or is acting, in an **anti-social manner**, he may require that person to give his name and address to the constable.

Anti-social manner (behaviour) (see **7.13.1**)

Explanatory notes

• A person who fails to give their name and address **or** provides a false or inaccurate name or address will commit an offence.

Practical considerations

A constable must be in uniform to make the request.

 Summary　　　　 6 months

 Level 3 fine

7.13.4 **Public nuisance**

Types of behaviour which used to be prosecuted as a 'public nuisance' are now covered by statute (eg food, noise, waste disposal, highways, animals, agriculture, medicines). However, 'public nuisance' is still an offence at common law.

Offences

A person is guilty of this offence if he—
(a)   does an act not warranted by law, or
(b)   omits to discharge a legal duty,

and the effect of the act or omission is to endanger the life, health, property, morals or comfort of the public, or to obstruct the public in the exercise or enjoyment of rights common to everyone.

Common law

Points to prove

✓ by doing an act not warranted by law or omitting to discharge a legal duty
✓ caused
✓ a public nuisance

Meanings

Act not warranted by law

Means illegal conduct but does not have to be a specific offence covered by legislation.

Legal duty

Means a duty under any enactment, instrument, or rule of law.

Explanatory notes

- This offence is described as 'a nuisance that is so widespread in its range or so indiscriminate in its effect that it would not be reasonable to expect any one person to take proceedings on their own responsibility to put a stop to it, but that it should be taken on the responsibility of the community at large'.
- The purpose that the defendant has in mind when they commit the act is immaterial if the probable result is to affect the public as described in the offence.
- Where some work is done by an employee in a manner that causes a nuisance it is no defence for the employer to claim that they did not personally supervise the work and had instructed that it be carried out in a different way.

Related cases

R v Johnson [1996] 2 Cr App R 434, CA Over several years, the defendant used the public telephone system to cause nuisance, annoyance, harassment, alarm, and distress to many women by making hundreds of obscene calls. It was held that the cumulative effect of all the calls was a public nuisance, as the number of individuals affected was sufficient for his actions to be public.

R v Shorrock [1993] 3 All ER 917, CA The defendant leased a field at his farm for a weekend which was used for an acid house party/rave while he was away and denied any knowledge that a public nuisance would be committed on the land. Upholding the conviction, it was held that, it was not necessary to prove that the defendant had actual knowledge of the nuisance, but merely that he was responsible for a nuisance which he knew or ought to have known (in the sense that the knowledge was available to him) would be the consequences of activities on his land.

Practical considerations

- This common law offence is still important because of its flexibility in adapting to those areas not covered by specific legislation.
- For extreme acts of unpleasantness or lewdness consider offences under the Sexual Offences Act 2003 (see **Chapter 6**) or the common law offence of outraging public decency (see **6.7.2**).
- Conspiracy to commit this offence is contrary to s 1(1) of the Criminal Law Act 1977.

 Either way   None

 Summary: 6 months' imprisonment and/or a fine

Indictment: Imprisonment and/or a fine

7.13.5 **Closure of premises (nuisance/disorder)**

Section 76 of the Anti-social Behaviour, Crime and Policing Act 2014 gives police powers to close premises by issuing a closure notice if satisfied that the use of the premises has resulted or is likely to result in nuisance to members of the public or disorder near those premises, and the notice will prevent the nuisance or disorder from continuing, recurring, or occurring. Section 86 deals with offences regarding a closure notice/order.

Offences

(1) A person who without reasonable excuse remains on or enters premises in contravention of a closure notice (including a notice continued in force under section 81) commits an offence.

(2) A person who without reasonable excuse remains on or enters premises in contravention of a closure order commits an offence.

(3) A person who without reasonable excuse obstructs a person acting under section 79 or 85(1) commits an offence.

Anti-social Behaviour, Crime and Policing Act 2014, s 86

Points to prove

Closure notice s 86(1)

✓ without reasonable excuse
✓ remained on/entered premises
✓ in contravention of a closure notice or s 81 continue notice

Closure order s 86(2)

✓ without reasonable excuse
✓ remained on/entered premises
✓ in contravention of a closure order

Obstruction s 86(3)

✓ without reasonable excuse
✓ obstructed person
✓ acting under
✓ s 79 (service notice)/s 85(1) (order enforcement)

Meanings

Premises

Includes any:
• land or other place (whether closed or not);
• outbuildings that are, or are used as, part of premises.

Closure notice (power to issue)

(1) A police officer of at least the rank of inspector, or the **local authority**, may issue a closure notice if satisfied on reasonable grounds—

(a) that the use of particular premises has resulted, or (if the notice is not issued) is likely soon to result, in nuisance to members of the public, or

(b) that there has been, or (if the notice is not issued) is likely soon to be, disorder near those premises associated with the use of those premises,

and that the notice is necessary to prevent the nuisance or disorder from continuing, recurring or occurring.

7.13.5 Closure of premises (nuisance/disorder)

(2) A closure notice is a notice prohibiting access to the premises for a period specified in the notice.

For the **maximum period**, see section 77.

(3) A closure notice may prohibit access—
   (a) by all persons except those specified, or by all persons except those of a specified description;
   (b) at all times, or at all times except those specified;
   (c) in all circumstances, or in all circumstances except those specified.

(4) A closure notice may not prohibit access by—
   (a) people who habitually live on the premises, or
   (b) the owner of the premises,
   and accordingly, they must be specified under subsection (3)(a).

(5) A closure notice must—
   (a) identify the premises;
   (b) explain the effect of the notice;
   (c) state that failure to comply with the notice is an offence;
   (d) state that an application will be made under section 80 for a closure order;
   (e) specify when and where the application will be heard;
   (f) explain the effect of a closure order;
   (g) give information about the names of, and means of contacting, persons and organisations in the area that provide advice about housing and legal matters.

(6) A closure notice may be issued only if reasonable efforts have been made to inform—
   (a) people who live on the premises (whether habitually or not), and
   (b) any person who has control of or responsibility for the premises or who has an interest in them,
that the notice is going to be issued.

(7) Before issuing a closure notice the police officer or local authority must ensure that any body or individual the officer or authority thinks appropriate has been consulted.

Anti-social Behaviour, Crime and Policing Act 2014, s 76

Local authority

In England: district council, county council (for area with no district council), London borough council, Common Council of the City of London, or the Council of the Isles of Scilly.

In Wales: a county council or a county borough council.

Maximum period (s 77—Duration of closure notices)

• The maximum period that may be specified in a closure notice is twenty-four hours. An extension notice may extend this for up to a further twenty-four hours, by a superintendent (issued by police) or CEO of the authority (issued by local authority).

- The maximum period of a notice issued by a superintendent or CEO is forty-eight hours. In calculating when the period of forty-eight hours ends, Christmas Day is to be disregarded.

The local authority CEO means the head of the paid service of the authority designated under s 4 of the Local Government and Housing Act 1989.

Notice continued in force under s 81

Where application has been made to a magistrates' court under s 80 for a closure order, if the court does not make a closure order it may instead order that the closure notice shall continue for a specified further period (maximum forty-eight hours), if satisfied that conditions for making a s 76 notice are met, and that the continuation of the notice is necessary to prevent the nuisance or disorder from continuing, recurring or occurring.

Similarly, the court may adjourn the application hearing for up to fourteen days to enable the occupier of the premises, the person in control of or responsible for the premises, or any other person with an interest in the premises, to show why a closure order should not be made. If adjourned, the closure notice will continue in force until the end of the adjournment period.

Closure order (power of court to make order)

(1) Whenever a closure notice is issued an application must be made to a magistrates' court for a closure order (unless the notice has been cancelled under section 78).
(2) An application for a closure order must be made—
   (a) by a constable, if the closure notice was issued by a police officer;
   (b) by the authority that issued the closure notice, if the notice was issued by a local authority.
(3) The application must be heard by the magistrates' court not later than 48 hours after service of the closure notice.
(4) In calculating when the period of 48 hours ends, Christmas Day is to be disregarded.
(5) The court may make a closure order if it is satisfied—
   (a) that a person has engaged, or (if the order is not made) is likely to engage, in disorderly, offensive or criminal behaviour on the premises, or
   (b) that the use of the premises has resulted, or (if the order is not made) is likely to result, in serious nuisance to members of the public, or
   (c) that there has been, or (if the order is not made) is likely to be, disorder near those premises associated with the use of those premises,
and that the order is necessary to prevent the behaviour, nuisance, or disorder from continuing, recurring, or occurring.

7.13.5 Closure of premises (nuisance/disorder)

(6) A closure order is an order prohibiting access to the premises for a period specified in the order. The period may not exceed 3 months.

(7) A closure order may prohibit access—
   (a) by all persons, or by all persons except those specified, or by all persons except those of a specified description;
   (b) at all times, or at all times except those specified;
   (c) in all circumstances, or in all circumstances except those specified.

(8) A closure order—
   (a) may be made in respect of the whole or any part of the premises;
   (b) may include provision about access to a part of the building or structure of which the premises form part.

(9) The court must notify the relevant licensing authority if it makes a closure order in relation to premises in respect of which a **premises licence** is in force.

Anti-social Behaviour, Crime and Policing Act 2014, s 80

Premises licence

Means a licence granted under Part 3 of the Licensing Act 2003, in respect of any premises, which authorises the premises to be used for one or more licensable activities.

Person acting under s 79 (service of notice)

(1) A closure notice, an extension notice a cancellation notice, or a variation notice must be served by—
   (a) a constable, in the case of a notice issued by a police officer;
   (b) a representative of the authority that issued the notice, in the case of a notice issued by a local authority.

(2) The constable or local authority representative must if possible—
   (a) fix a copy of the notice to at least one prominent place on the premises,
   (b) fix a copy of the notice to each normal means of access to the premises,
   (c) fix a copy of the notice to any outbuildings that appear to the constable or representative to be used with or as part of the premises,
   (d) give a copy of the notice to at least one person who appears to the constable or representative to have control of or responsibility for the premises, and
   (e) give a copy of the notice to the people who live on the premises and to any person who does not live there but was informed (under section 76(6)) that the notice was going to be issued.

(3) If the constable or **local authority representative** reasonably believes, at the time of serving the notice, that there are persons occupying another part of the building or other structure in

which the premises are situated whose access to that part will be impeded if a closure order is made under section 80, the constable or representative must also if possible serve the notice on those persons.

(4) The constable or local authority representative may enter any premises, using reasonable force if necessary, for the purposes of complying with subsection (2)(a).

Anti-social Behaviour, Crime and Policing Act 2014, s 79

Local authority representative

Means an employee of the authority, or a person, or employee of a person, acting on behalf of the authority.

Person acting under s 85(1) (enforcement of closure orders)

An authorised person may—

(a) enter premises in respect of which a closure order is in force;
(b) do anything necessary to secure the premises against entry.

Anti-social Behaviour, Crime and Policing Act 2014, s 85(1)

Authorised person

In relation to a closure order made on the application of a constable or a local authority:

- a constable means a constable or a person authorised by the chief officer of police for the area in which the premises are situated;
- a local authority means a person authorised by that authority.

Explanatory notes

- The closure notice is a fast, flexible power that allows the police or council to protect victims and communities by quickly closing premises that are causing, or likely to cause nuisance or disorder.
- A closure notice is issued by the police/council in the first instance, then if required a closure order can be applied for through the courts.
- The closure notice can close premises for up to forty-eight hours, but cannot stop the owner or those who habitually live there accessing the premises. Whereas an order can close the premises for up to six months and can restrict all access.
- Both the notice and order can cover any land or any other place, whether enclosed or not including residential, business, nonbusiness, and licensed premises.
- Under s 78, where a closure notice is in force and the police/ authority decide to cancel the notice, they can issue a cancellation notice (all the premises) or variation notice (if part of the premises). The court should then be informed prior to the hearing for the closure order.

7.13.5 Closure of premises (nuisance/disorder)

Defences

Having a reasonable excuse for remaining on or entering premises in contravention of a closure notice/order or obstructing a person under s 79 or 85(1) (as the case may be).

Anti-social Behaviour, Crime and Policing Act 2014, s 86

Practical considerations

* Consultation is required as part of the closure notice process. This should include the victim, others that may be affected, community representatives, other organisations and bodies, the police or local council (if not the issuing body), or others using the premises. Consider those who use the premises to access other premises, not subject to the closure notice.
* The method of consultation will depend on the situation and urgency. A record must be kept of those consulted if the case is challenged in court.
* Include in the closure notice the following information:
  + identify the premises;
  + explain the effect of the notice;
  + state that failure to comply with the notice is an offence;
  + state that an application will be made for a closure order;
  + specify when and where the application will be heard;
  + explain the effect of the closure order; and
  + contact details of providers giving advice about housing and legal matters.
* A criminal offence is committed when a person, without reasonable excuse:
  + remains on or enters premises in contravention of a closure notice/order;
  + obstructs a police officer or local council employee who is: serving a closure notice, cancellation notice, or variation notice; entering the premises; or securing the premises.
* A closure notice cannot be appealed. A closure order can be appealed to the Crown Court within twenty-one days from the date of the decision to which the appeal relates.
* Notices under ss 1 and 11A of the Anti-social Behaviour Act 2003; orders under ss 2, 11B, and 40 of the 2003 Act; and orders under ss 161 and 165(2)(b), (c), or (d) of the Licensing Act 2003 will continue to be effective for as long as the notice or order is in force.

 Summary   6 months

 s 86(2) or (5)—51 weeks imprisonment and/or a fine
s 86(1), (3), or (4)—3 months' imprisonment and/or a fine

7.13.6 **Causing nuisance/disturbance on NHS premises**

Sections 119 and 120 of the Criminal Justice and Immigration Act 2008 create both the offence of causing a nuisance or disturbance to NHS staff on NHS premises, and the power to remove a person suspected of committing or having committed the offence.

Offences

(1) A person commits an offence if—

    (a) the person causes, without reasonable excuse and while on NHS premises, a nuisance or disturbance to an NHS staff member who is working there or is otherwise there in connection with work,

    (b) the person refuses, without reasonable excuse, to leave the NHS premises when asked to do so by a constable or an NHS staff member, and

    (c) the person is not on the NHS premises for the purpose of obtaining medical advice, treatment or care for himself or herself.

          Criminal Justice and Immigration Act 2008, s 119

Power to remove

(1) If a constable reasonably suspects that a person is committing or has committed an offence under section 119, the constable may remove the person from the NHS premises concerned.

(2) If an authorised officer reasonably suspects that a person is committing or has committed an offence under section 119, the authorised officer may—

    (a) remove the person from the NHS premises concerned, or

    (b) authorise an appropriate NHS staff member to do so.

(3) Any person removing another person from NHS premises under this section may use reasonable force (if necessary).

(4) An authorised officer cannot remove a person under this section or authorise another person to do so if the authorised officer has reason to believe that—

    (a) the person to be removed requires medical advice, treatment or care for himself or herself, or

    (b) the removal of the person would endanger the person's physical or mental health.

          Criminal Justice and Immigration Act 2008, s 120

Points to prove

✓ while on NHS premises
✓ other than for the purpose of obtaining medical advice or treatment/care for self

7.13.6 Causing nuisance/disturbance on NHS premises

> ✓ caused without reasonable excuse while on those premises
> ✓ a nuisance **or**
> ✓ a disturbance to an NHS staff member who is working there **or**
> ✓ was otherwise there in connection with work
> ✓ refused without reasonable excuse to leave the premises
> ✓ when asked to do so by a constable/NHS staff member

Meanings

NHS premises

Means:
- any hospital vested in, or managed by, a **relevant NHS body**;
- any building or other structure, or **vehicle**, associated with the hospital and situated on **hospital grounds** (whether or not vested in, or managed by, a relevant NHS body); and
- the hospital grounds.

Relevant NHS body

Means:
- a National Health Service trust (see National Health Service Act 2006), all or most of whose hospitals, establishments, and facilities are situated in England;
- an NHS foundation trust (England).

Vehicle

Includes an air ambulance.

Hospital grounds

Means land in the vicinity of a hospital and associated with it.

NHS staff member

Means a person employed by a relevant English body, or otherwise working for such a body (whether as or on behalf of a contractor, as a volunteer, or otherwise).

Authorised officer

Means any NHS staff member authorised by a relevant NHS body to exercise the powers which are conferred by this section on an authorised officer in respect of NHS premises.

Explanatory notes

- For the purposes of s 119, a person ceases to be on NHS premises for the purpose of obtaining medical advice, treatment, or care for him/herself, once the person has received the advice, treatment, or care, or if the person has been refused the advice, treatment, or care during the last eight hours.

- This offence addresses behaviour which disrupts NHS staff in the performance of their duties. There is no requirement that the delivery of health care is impeded.
- This offence is quite restricted, as it does not apply to a person who is on the premises for the purpose of obtaining medical advice, treatment, or care, patients, and those attending for consultations, to collect medication or test results, or convalescing after treatment.

Practical considerations

- Although the offence/power relates to England and Wales, it is currently (June 2018) only in force for England.
- A nuisance or disturbance can include any form of non-physical behaviour which breaches the peace, such as verbal aggression or intimidating gestures towards NHS staff.
- A person will not commit the offence if s/he has a reasonable excuse. Behaviour consequent to the receipt of upsetting news or bereavement may, for example, constitute a reasonable excuse.
- The nuisance or disturbance must be towards an NHS staff member, rather than any other person. The NHS staff member must either be working at the premises or be there for some other purpose relating to their work, such as walking between buildings or taking a break.
- Where NHS bodies wish to have the option to exercise the power of removal without recourse to police, they will need to authorise a member of staff (known as the '**authorised officer**') to exercise the powers of removal. Any person exercising the power of removal may use reasonable force if necessary.

 Summary   6 months

Level 3 fine

Links to alternative subjects and offences

7.13.6 Causing nuisance/disturbance on NHS premises

7.14 **Vehicles Causing Annoyance**

Section 59 of the Police Reform Act 2002 empowers police officers to seize motor vehicles used in a way as to cause alarm, distress, or annoyance to members of the public. The Police (Retention and Disposal of Motor Vehicles) Regulations 2002 govern how such seized vehicles should be retained and disposed of.

7.14.1 **Vehicles used in a manner causing alarm, distress, or annoyance**

Section 59 of the Police Reform Act 2002 concerns the use of vehicles in a manner that causes alarm, distress, or annoyance to members of the public.

Police powers

(1) Where a constable in uniform has reasonable grounds for believing that a motor vehicle is being used on any occasion in a manner which—
   (a) contravenes section 3 or 34 of the Road Traffic Act 1988 (careless and inconsiderate driving and prohibition of off-road driving), and
   (b) is causing, or is likely to cause, alarm, distress or annoyance to members of the public,
   he shall have the powers set out in subsection (3).
(2) A constable in uniform shall also have the powers set out in subsection (3) where he has reasonable grounds for believing that a motor vehicle has been used on any occasion in a manner falling within subsection (1).
(3) Those powers are—
   (a) power, if the motor vehicle is moving, to order the person driving it to stop the vehicle;
   (b) power to seize and remove the motor vehicle;
   (c) power, for the purposes of exercising a power falling within paragraph (a) or (b), to enter any premises on which he has reasonable grounds for believing the motor vehicle to be;
   (d) power to use reasonable force, if necessary, in the exercise of any power conferred by any of paragraphs (a) to (c).
(4) A constable shall not seize a motor vehicle in the exercise of the powers conferred on him by this section unless—

    (a) he has warned the person appearing to him to be the person whose use falls within subsection (1) that he will seize it, if that use continues or is repeated; and

    (b) it appears to him that the use has continued or been repeated after the warning.

(5) Subsection (4) does not require a warning to be given by a constable on any occasion on which he would otherwise have the power to seize a motor vehicle under this section if—

    (a) the circumstances make it impracticable for him to give the warning;

    (b) the constable has already on that occasion given a warning under that subsection in respect of any use of that motor vehicle or of another motor vehicle by that person or any other person;

    (c) the constable has reasonable grounds for believing that such a warning has been given on that occasion otherwise than by him; or

    (d) the constable has reasonable grounds for believing that the person whose use of that motor vehicle on that occasion would justify the seizure is a person to whom a warning under that subsection has been given (whether or not by that constable or in respect of the same vehicle or the same or a similar use) on a previous occasion in the previous twelve months.

(6) Subsection (3)(c) does not authorise entry into a private dwelling house.

Police Reform Act 2002, s 59

Offence

A person who fails to comply with an order under subsection (3)(a) is guilty of an offence.

Police Reform Act 2002, s 59(6)

Points to prove

- ✓ failed to stop
- ✓ a moving vehicle
- ✓ on the order of a police constable in uniform
- ✓ having reasonable grounds for believing
- ✓ that the vehicle was being used in a manner given in s 59(1)

Meanings

Motor vehicle

Any mechanically propelled vehicle, whether or not it is intended or adapted for use on roads (see **10.1.3**).

Driving (see 10.1.4)

Private dwelling house

Does not include any garage or other structure occupied with the dwelling house, or any land appurtenant to the dwelling house.

Explanatory notes

- An offence is committed if the driver of the moving motor vehicle fails to stop the vehicle when ordered to do so by a constable in uniform.
- A constable in uniform has the power to seize the vehicle but only after warning the person. If, after the warning has been given, the driving continues or is repeated then the vehicle can be seized.
- The requirement to give the warning does not apply where it is impracticable to do so or where it has been given on a previous occasion in the previous twelve months.
- The powers under this section cannot be exercised unless the driver is **both** using the vehicle anti-socially **and** is driving contrary to s 3 (careless and inconsiderate driving, see **10.6.1**) or s 34 (prohibition of off-road driving, see **10.23**) of the Road Traffic Act 1988.

Practical considerations

- The warning under s 59(4) **must** be given and ignored before the vehicle can be seized (see **7.14.2**). Therefore it is important that the warning is both heard and understood.
- A warning given within the last twelve months does not have to have been given in respect of the same vehicle.
- Where a motor vehicle is seized a seizure notice must be given to the person who appears to be the owner of the vehicle.
- A previous warning given on the same occasion need not have been given by the same constable nor does it have to have been given to the same person **or** in respect of the same vehicle. It could have been given to the same person using another vehicle or to a different person using the same vehicle. This covers situations where people use their vehicles anti-socially and swap them around.
- Consider the dispersal powers or powers under a PSPO (see **7.15**) or the public nuisance offence (see **7.13.4**).

 Summary   6 months

 Level 3 fine

7.14.2 **Retention/disposal of seized motor vehicle**

The Police (Retention and Disposal of Motor Vehicles) Regulations 2002 relate to vehicles seized under s 59 of the Police Reform Act 2002 (see **7.14.1**).

7.14.2 Retention/disposal of seized motor vehicle

Power

A relevant motor vehicle shall be passed into and remain in the custody of a constable or other person authorised under this regulation by the chief officer of the police force for the area in which the vehicle was seized ('the authority') until—

(a) the authority permits it to be removed from their custody by a person appearing to them to be the owner of the vehicle; or

(b) it has been disposed of under these Regulations.

Police (Retention and Disposal of Motor Vehicles) Regulations 2002, reg 3(1)

Meanings

Relevant motor vehicle

As seized and removed under s 59(3)(b) of the Police Reform Act 2002 (see **7.14.1**).

The authority

Means a constable or other person authorised by the chief officer.

Explanatory notes

- A relevant motor vehicle will pass into and remain in the custody of a constable or other person authorised under this regulation by the chief officer of police in the area in which it was seized, until the authority permits a person appearing to them to be the owner of it to remove it, or it has been disposed of under these regulations.
- While the vehicle is in the custody of the authority, they must take any necessary steps for its safe keeping.
- As soon as reasonably practicable after taking a vehicle into their custody the authority must take reasonable steps to serve a seizure notice on the person who is, or appears to be, the owner, except where the vehicle has been released from their custody.
- If a person satisfies the authority that they are the owner of the vehicle and pays the charges accrued concerning its removal and retention, the authority shall permit them to remove it from custody.
- A person otherwise liable to pay charges concerning the removal and retention of the vehicle will not be liable if they were not the user when it was seized under s 59 and they did not know of its use leading to the seizure, had not consented to such use, and could not, by reasonable steps, have prevented such use.
- Where it has not been possible to serve a seizure notice on the relevant person, or such a notice has been served and the vehicle has

not been released from their custody under these regulations, they may dispose of the vehicle in accordance with reg 7.

- The authority may not dispose of the vehicle under reg 7:
  (a) during the period of fourteen days, starting with the date of seizure;
  (b) if the fourteen-day period has expired, until after the deadline specified in the seizure notice;
  (c) if (a) or (b) does not apply, during the period of seven working days starting with the date on which the vehicle is claimed.
- Where the authority disposes of the vehicle by way of selling, it must pay the net proceeds of the sale to any person who, within a year of the sale, satisfies them that they were the vehicle owner at the time of the sale.

Practical considerations

- A seizure notice may be served by personal delivery to the person addressed in it, by leaving it at their usual or last known address or by registered delivery to their last known address.
- If the owner is a body corporate (eg a company) the notice must be served or sent to the company secretary or clerk at its registered office.
- The seizure notice must inform the owner that they have seven working days to collect the vehicle and that charges are payable from when the vehicle is claimed by the owner under reg 5.

Links to alternative subjects and offences

7.15 Dispersal Powers/Public Spaces Protection Orders

7.15.1 Dispersal powers

Sections 34 and 35 of the Anti-social Behaviour, Crime and Policing Act 2014 provide, if the proper authority is in place, police powers to direct a person in a public place, to leave the area for up to forty-eight hours, and return persons under the age of 16 to their place of residence or a place of safety. Failure to comply is an offence under s 39.

Authorisation

(1) A police officer of at least the rank of inspector may authorise the use in a specified locality, during a specified period of not more than 48 hours, of the powers given by section 35.

(2) An officer may give such an authorisation only if satisfied on reasonable grounds that the use of those powers in the locality during that period may be necessary for the purpose of removing or reducing the likelihood of—
   (a) members of the public in the locality being harassed, alarmed or distressed, or
   (b) the occurrence in the locality of crime or disorder.

(3) In deciding whether to give such an authorisation an officer must have particular regard to the rights of freedom of expression and freedom of assembly set out in articles 10 and 11 of the Convention.

(4) An authorisation under this section—
   (a) must be in writing,
   (b) must be signed by the officer giving it, and
   (c) must specify the grounds on which it is given.

Anti-social Behaviour, Crime and Policing Act 2014, s 34

Directions to exclude person

(1) If the conditions in subsections (2) and (3) are met and an authorisation is in force under section 34, a constable in uniform may direct a person who is in a public place in the locality specified in the authorisation—
   (a) to leave the locality (or part of the locality), and
   (b) not to return to the locality (or part of the locality) for the period specified in the direction ('the exclusion period').

(2) The first condition is that the constable has reasonable grounds to suspect that the behaviour of the person in the locality has contributed or is likely to contribute to—
   (a) members of the public in the locality being harassed, alarmed or distressed, or
   (b) the occurrence in the locality of crime or disorder.

(3) The second condition is that the constable considers that giving a direction to the person is necessary for the purpose of removing or reducing the likelihood of the events mentioned in subsection (2)(a) or (b).

(4) The exclusion period may not exceed 48 hours. The period may expire after (as long as it begins during) the period specified in the authorisation under section 34.

(5) A direction under this section—
  (a) must be given in writing, unless that is not reasonably practicable;
  (b) must specify the area to which it relates;
  (c) may impose requirements as to the time by which the person must leave the area and the manner in which the person must do so (including the route).

(6) The constable must (unless it is not reasonably practicable) tell the person to whom the direction is given that failing without reasonable excuse to comply with the direction is an offence.

(7) If the constable reasonably believes that the person to whom the direction is given is under the age of 16, the constable may remove the person to a place where the person lives or a place of safety.

(8) Any constable may withdraw or vary a direction under this section; but a variation must not extend the duration of a direction beyond 48 hours from when it was first given.

(9) Notice of a withdrawal or variation of a direction—
  (a) must be given to the person to whom the direction was given, unless that is not reasonably practicable, and
  (b) if given, must be given in writing unless that is not reasonably practicable.

Anti-social Behaviour, Crime and Policing Act 2014, s 35

Directions to surrender property

(1) A constable who gives a person a direction under section 35 may also direct the person to surrender to the constable any item in the person's possession or control that the constable reasonably believes has been used or is likely to be used in behaviour that harasses, alarms or distresses members of the public.

(2) A direction under this section must be given in writing, unless that is not reasonably practicable.

(3) A constable who gives a person a direction under this section must (unless it is not reasonably practicable)—
  (a) tell the person that failing without reasonable excuse to comply with the direction is an offence, and
  (b) give the person information in writing about when and how the person may recover the surrendered item.

(4) The surrendered item must not be returned to the person before the end of the exclusion period.

(5) If after the end of that period the person asks for the item to be returned, it must be returned (unless there is power to retain it under another enactment).

(6) But if it appears to a constable that the person is under the age of 16 and is not accompanied by a parent or other responsible adult, the item may be retained until the person is so accompanied.

(7) If the person has not asked for the return of the item before the end of the period of 28 days beginning with the day on which the direction was given, the item may be destroyed or otherwise disposed of.

Anti-social Behaviour, Crime and Policing Act 2014, s 37

Offences

(1) A person given a direction under section 35 who fails without reasonable excuse to comply with it commits an offence.

(3) A person given a direction under section 37 who fails without reasonable excuse to comply with it commits an offence.

Anti-social Behaviour, Crime and Policing Act 2014, s 39

Points to prove

✓ failed
✓ without reasonable excuse
✓ to comply with a direction given under s 35 or s 37

Meanings

Specified

Means specified in the authorisation.

Convention (see 1.1)

Public place

Means a place to which at the material time the public or a section of the public has access, on payment or otherwise, as of right or by virtue of express or implied permission.

Exclusion period (see s 35(1)(b) 'Directions to exclude person' above)

Explanatory notes

- If there is likely to be anti-social behaviour, crime, or disorder in an area and it may be necessary to use the dispersal power, an inspector can authorise officers to use the power for a period of up to forty-eight hours.
- If a person's behaviour is causing or likely to cause harassment, alarm, or distress, or crime or disorder in the public place specified in the authorisation, then under s 35 a police officer can issue a direction for that person to leave the area.

- A CSO or CSV has a power to require the names and addresses of persons believed to have committed the s 39 offence. Failing to provide name and address is an offence and the CSO or CSV can detain a person for 30 minutes pending the arrival of a constable (see **11.1.3** and **11.1.7**).
- A direction can be issued to anyone over the age of 10, and if they are under 16 they can be taken home or to a place of safety.
- The direction must be given in writing, unless impracticable to do so. A written notice must specify the relevant area, when they must leave the area, and the route they must take. Any item possessed/ under control of that person can be confiscated under s 37. The person must also be told that failure to comply with the direction (excluded from area and/or surrender of such item), without reasonable excuse, is an offence.
- The information provided in the direction should be as clear as possible, ensuring that the person has understood it. If the direction is given verbally a written record of it must be kept in order to enforce it in the event that it is breached, and to be able to monitor use of the power. The written notice can be admitted in evidence in breach proceedings.

Defences

Having a reasonable excuse for failing to comply with a direction given under s 35 (exclude from area) or s 37 (surrender property).

Anti-social Behaviour, Crime and Policing Act 2014, s 39

Practical considerations

- When authorising the dispersal power, the inspector (or above) must have regard to Arts 10 and 11 of the ECHR, which provide for the rights to freedom of expression and freedom of assembly. Ensure that this power is used proportionately and reasonably so it is compatible with the Human Rights Act 1998 (see **1.1**).
- When pre-authorising or authorising an area, the locality should be clearly defined as a specific geographic location, for example by listing the streets to which it applies or the streets which form the boundary of the area. The authorisation should not cover an area larger than necessary.
- This power can only be used in the specific location authorised, so if the behaviour occurs outside the authorised area, the inspector (or above) will have to increase the area or the officer cannot issue the dispersal.
- The exclusion period may not exceed forty-eight hours, and it may be that this period expires after (as long as it begins during) the period specified in the authorisation under s 34.
- The police officer can require the person given the direction to hand over items causing or likely to cause anti-social behaviour under s 37. These items could be alcohol, fireworks, offensive material, noisy equipment, eggs, or spray paint, for example.

7.15.1 **Dispersal powers**

- An officer can confiscate an item handed over to them, but there is no power to seize the item, although they will commit an offence under s 39 if they do not hand over the item when directed to do so.
- Surrendered items can be collected at the expiry of the direction period, but if the item is not collected within twenty-eight days it can be destroyed or disposed of. A person under the age of 16 can be required to be accompanied by a parent/responsible adult to collect the item, thus ensuring that the adult is made aware of the incident to encourage parental responsibility.
- Section 36 places restrictions, so that a direction cannot be given to someone engaged in lawful conduct: peaceful picketing (Trade Union and Labour Relations (Consolidation) Act 1992, s 220) or taking part in a public procession (Public Order Act 1986, s 11). In addition, the direction cannot restrict access to where they live or work or prevent them from attending court/tribunal or education/training, or from receiving medical treatment during the direction time period.
- A person who is given a direction and feels they have been incorrectly dealt with should speak to the duty inspector at the local police station. Details should be given to the person on the written notice.
- This dispersal power is a more flexible tool for officers to deal with anti-social behaviour, crime, and disorder. This is not only when they have occurred or are occurring, but also when they are likely to occur and, in any locality, thus extending the capability of the police to prevent incidents before they happen.
- Dispersal powers under s 27 of the Violent Crime Reduction Act 2006 and s 30 of the Anti-social Behaviour Act 2003 will continue to have effect for as long as they are in force.
- Helpful features of this power under the 2014 Act are that:
    + there is no requirement to pre-designate a 'dispersal zone'—it can now be used in any locality forthwith;
    + publicity is no longer required to highlight an authorisation;
    + an individual can be dispersed rather than requiring two or more people to be engaged in the offending behaviour;
    + the power can be used across a broader spectrum of anti-social behaviour, crime, and disorder;
    + there is an additional power to confiscate items associated with the behaviour;
    + the exclusion period has been extended to a maximum of forty-eight hours;
    + there is no need to establish the person's age as the power applies to a person who appears to be aged 10 or over;
    + the requirement to keep a written record of when the power is used enables effective enforcement of any breach and will be evidentially important for prosecution of breaches.

 Summary   6 months

 s 39(1) and (2)—3 months' imprisonment or a level 4 fine
s 39(3) and (4)—Level 2 fine

7.15.2 **Public spaces protection orders (PSPOs)**

Section 59 of the Anti-social Behaviour, Crime and Policing Act 2014 provides the local authority (LA) with power to make a public spaces protection order (PSPO) with regard to activities in a public place that have a detrimental effect on the quality of life of those in the locality. It is an offence to fail to comply with a PSPO; breach can also be dealt with by a fixed penalty notice (FPN) under s 68.

Power to make orders

(1) A local authority may make a public spaces protection order if satisfied on reasonable grounds that two conditions are met.

(2) The first condition is that—
   (a) activities carried on in a public place within the authority's area have had a detrimental effect on the quality of life of those in the locality, or
   (b) it is likely that activities will be carried on in a public place within that area and that they will have such an effect.

(3) The second condition is that the effect, or likely effect, of the activities—
   (a) is, or is likely to be, of a persistent or continuing nature,
   (b) is, or is likely to be, such as to make the activities unreasonable, and
   (c) justifies the restrictions imposed by the notice.

(4) A public spaces protection order is an order that identifies the public place referred to in subsection (2) ('the restricted area') and—
   (a) prohibits specified things being done in the restricted area,
   (b) requires specified things to be done by persons carrying on specified activities in that area, or
   (c) does both of those things.

(5) The only prohibitions or requirements that may be imposed are ones that are reasonable to impose in order—
   (a) to prevent the detrimental effect referred to in subsection (2) from continuing, occurring or recurring, or
   (b) to reduce that detrimental effect or to reduce the risk of its continuance, occurrence or recurrence.

(6) A prohibition or requirement may be framed—
   (a) so as to apply to all persons, or only to persons in specified categories, or to all persons except those in specified categories;
   (b) so as to apply at all times, or only at specified times, or at all times except those specified;
   (c) so as to apply in all circumstances, or only in specified circumstances, or in all circumstances except those specified.

(7) A public spaces protection order must—
   (a) identify the activities referred to in subsection (2);

(b) explain the effect of section 63 (where it applies) and section 67;

(c) specify the period for which the order has effect.

(8) A public spaces protection order must be published in accordance with regulations made by the Secretary of State.

Anti-social Behaviour, Crime and Policing Act 2014, s 59

Offences

(1) It is an offence for a person without reasonable excuse—

(a) to do anything that the person is prohibited from doing by a public spaces protection order, or

(b) to fail to comply with a requirement to which the person is subject under a public spaces protection order.

Anti-social Behaviour, Crime and Policing Act 2014, s 67

Points to prove

✓ in a public place subject to a PSPO

✓ without reasonable excuse

✓ did anything prohibited from doing by

or

✓ failed to comply with a requirement to which subject under

✓ a public spaces protection order (PSPO)

Meanings

Local authority (LA) (see 7.13.4)

Public place (see 7.15.1)

Public spaces protection order (PSPO) (see s 59(4) above)

Section 63 (see 9.4)

Section 67 (see '*mens rea*' above)

Explanatory notes

- A PSPO can deal with a nuisance/problem in a public area being detrimental to the local community and quality of life, by imposing conditions on using the specified area which apply to everyone, intending that the law-abiding majority can use and enjoy public spaces, safe from anti-social behaviour.

- LAs are responsible for making the PSPO, although enforcement of the order will be broader, involving LA officials, police officers, designated groups, and officers accredited under the community safety accreditation scheme.

- Before a PSPO can be made, the LA must be satisfied, on reasonable grounds, that activities in a public space have had or will be likely to have a detrimental effect on the quality of life of those in the locality; it is/likely to be, persistent or continuing in nature, so making the activities unreasonable; and the order justifies the restrictions imposed.

- The meaning of a public space is wide and includes any place to which the public or any section of the public has access, on payment or otherwise, as of right or by virtue of express or implied permission, for example a shopping centre.
- Prior to making a PSPO, the LA must consult with the police, the landowner or occupier, together with appropriate community representatives (eg residents association). It could include an individual or group of individuals, for instance regular users of a park, or specific activities such as busking or other types of street entertainment.

Defences

(1) Having a reasonable excuse for failing to comply with a public spaces protection order.

(3) A person does not commit an offence under this section by failing to comply with a prohibition or requirement that the local authority did not have power to include in the public spaces protection order.

Anti-social Behaviour, Crime and Policing Act 2014, s 67

Practical considerations

- The maximum duration of a PSPO is three years, but this can be for a shorter period if required. If considered necessary, the LA can extend a PSPO before its expiry by up to three years, and if appropriate further consultation should again take place.
- If required a PSPO can be varied, such as changing the size of the restricted area or the specific requirements or restrictions. For example, a PSPO deals with controlling dogs in a park, but a year later, groups now congregate in the park drinking alcohol, so the LA could vary the PSPO to deal with both issues. The LA can also discharge a PSPO at any time.
- Section 63 can restrict the consumption of alcohol in a public space subject to a PSPO, and s 62 provides details of premises and places where a PSPO cannot apply. For details of restrictions and enforcing the order see **9.4**.
- In relation to dogs and their owners, a PSPO could, for example, exclude dogs from designated areas (eg a children's play area in a park); require dog faeces to be picked up by owners; require dogs to be kept on leads; and restrict the number of dogs that can be walked by one person at any one time.
- A PSPO must be published in accordance with regulations (SI 2591/ 2014), identifying the activities subject to the order, sanctions for breach, and the duration of the PSPO. The LA should publish details of making, extending, varying, or discharging a PSPO on its website

7.15.2 Public spaces protection orders (PSPOs)

and display notices with details of the PSPO at the public place to which the order relates.

- The PSPO or variation can be challenged in the High Court by an interested person (person who lives or regularly works in or visits the area) within six weeks of it being made/varied. Grounds could be that the LA did not have power to make the order, or include certain prohibitions or requirements, or that proper consultation had not taken place. The High Court can uphold the PSPO, quash it, or vary it.
- A person who fails to comply with a PSPO, without reasonable excuse, will commit an offence; except breach of a PSPO by consuming alcohol which is an offence under s 63 (see **9.4**). Both the s 63 and s 67 offences can be dealt with by an FPN (up to £100) under s 68.
- Section 64A(1B)(ca) of PACE provides the power to photograph person(s) who are given a direction by a constable under s 35.
- Current designated public place orders, gating orders, and dog control orders could remain in force for three years from the commencement day of PSPOs (20 October 2014).
- A PSPO takes precedence over a by-law in the restricted area, if the by-law prohibits the same activity that is now covered by the PSPO.

 Summary   6 months

 Level 3 fine

Links to alternative subjects and offences

7.16 Community/Environmental Protection

The Anti-social Behaviour, Crime and Policing Act 2014 deals with issuing a community protection notice (CPN) for environmental nuisances; other matters such as litter, abandoned vehicles, and refuse are dealt with by the Environmental Protection Act 1990, the Litter Act 1983, and the Refuse Disposal (Amenity) Act 1978.

7.16.1 Community protection notices (CPN)

Section 43 of the Anti-social Behaviour, Crime and Policing Act 2014 gives an authorised person power to issue a CPN to a person or body if their conduct is unreasonable and it has a detrimental effect on the quality of life of those in the locality. Failure to comply with a CPN is an offence under s 48, and breach can be dealt with by a fixed penalty notice (FPN) under s 52.

Power to issue notices

(1) An authorised person may issue a community protection notice to an individual aged 16 or over, or a body, if satisfied on reasonable grounds that—
   (a) the conduct of the individual or body is having a detrimental effect, of a persistent or continuing nature, on the quality of life of those in the locality, and
   (b) the conduct is unreasonable.

(3) A community protection notice is a notice that imposes any of the following requirements on the individual or body issued with it—
   (a) a requirement to stop doing specified things;
   (b) a requirement to do specified things;
   (c) a requirement to take reasonable steps to achieve specified results.

(4) The only requirements that may be imposed are ones that are reasonable to impose in order—
   (a) to prevent the detrimental effect referred to in subsection (1) from continuing or recurring, or
   (b) to reduce that detrimental effect or to reduce the risk of its continuance or recurrence.

(5) A person (A) may issue a community protection notice to an individual or body (B) only if—
   (a) B has been given a written warning that the notice will be issued unless B's conduct ceases to have the detrimental effect referred to in subsection (1), and
   (b) A is satisfied that, despite B having had enough time to deal with the matter, B's conduct is still having that effect.

(6) A person issuing a community protection notice must before doing so inform any body or individual the person thinks appropriate.

(7) A community protection notice must—
   (a) identify the conduct referred to in subsection (1);
   (b) explain the effect of sections 46 to 51.

(8) A community protection notice may specify periods within which, or times by which, requirements within subsection (3)(b) or (c) are to be complied with.

Anti-social Behaviour, Crime and Policing Act 2014, s 43

Offences

A person issued with a community protection notice who fails to comply with it commits an offence.

Anti-social Behaviour, Crime and Policing Act 2014, s 48(1)

Points to prove
✓ being a person/body having been issued with a CPN
✓ failed to comply with a requirement in the CPN
✓ by doing or not stopping doing or achieving things/results as specified in the CPN

Meanings

Authorised person

Means a constable or person designated by the relevant local authority (eg housing providers).

Local authority (LA) (see 7.13.4)

Community Protection Notice (CPN) (see s 43(3) above)

Conduct

This includes a failure to act.

Sections 46–51

These sections relate to the following:
- s 46—Appeals against notices;
- s 47—Remedial action by local authority;
- s 48—Offence of failing to comply with notice;
- s 49—Remedial orders;
- s 50—Forfeiture of item used in offence; and
- s 51—Seizure of item used in offence.

Explanatory notes

- A CPN cannot be issued until a written warning has been given to the person/body; this must make it clear that if they do not stop the anti-social behaviour, a CPN could be issued. Identify in the written warning the behaviour that has to be changed and give a time period for it to be achieved, advising them of potential sanctions on breaching a CPN if a notice is then issued.

- When a written warning has been issued, enough time should be given to allow the person or body to deal with the matter, before issuing a CPN. This will be on a case-by-case basis; for example, where an area is to be cleared several days or weeks may be required, but in a case of playing loud music this could require the behaviour to stop immediately.
- A CPN can be issued by a LA enforcement officer, social landlord (designated by LA), constable against a person aged 16 or over, business, or organisation, if satisfied on reasonable grounds that their conduct: is having a detrimental effect on the quality of life of those in the locality; is persistent or continuing in nature; and is unreasonable.
- A CPN requirement should be appropriate to the situation; it could be to stop doing or to do specified things, or to take reasonable steps to achieve specified results. This means that not only can the officer stop someone being anti-social; they can also put steps in place to ensure the behaviour does not recur.
- If a body, the CPN should be given to the most appropriate person, such as the shop owner or a store manager. The issuing officer has to be satisfied that the person can be reasonably expected to control, affect, or deal with the behaviour. The notice can be given directly to the person in question, posted to them, or posted on the premises (if the owner or occupier is not known).

Defences

A person does not commit an offence under this section if—

(a) the person took all reasonable steps to comply with the notice, or

(b) there is some other reasonable excuse for the failure to comply with it.

Anti-social Behaviour, Crime and Policing Act 2014, s 48(3)

Practical considerations

- Consider if a requirement or timescale is reasonable and achievable before issuing the notice. Furthermore, a CPN is designed to deal with short or medium-term issues, and while restrictions and requirements may be similar to those in civil injunctions (see **7.13.1**), more serious conditions, such as attending a drug rehabilitation course, should be dealt with by a court order.
- Failing to comply with a CPN is an offence under s 48(1). If appropriate, a police officer or LA officer could issue an FPN (up to £100) under s 52(1) for failing to comply with a CPN. Other options to consider could be remedial action or a court remedial, forfeiture, or seizure order.

7.16.2 Leaving litter/removing or interfering with litter bins

- Remedial action could be the LA or their agent clearing a garden on the perpetrator's behalf, and when completed charging the perpetrator with the cost for the clearance, which could include officer time, equipment, labour, and administration costs. Work undertaken on land 'open to the air' can be done without the consent of the owner or occupier, but any indoor work will require the permission of the owner or occupier.
- Issuing a CPN does not discharge the LA from its duty to issue an Abatement Notice if it is a statutory nuisance as listed in s 79(1) of the Environmental Protection Act 1990.
- On conviction for failing to comply with a CPN, the prosecutor may ask the court to impose a remedial and/or a forfeiture order as:
  + it is a serious matter that requires a court order;
  + remedial work is in an area that requires consent from the owner/ occupier and this is not forthcoming; or
  + forfeiture or seizure of items may be required as a result of the behaviour (eg sound-making equipment).
- The court can order the forfeiture of items used in committing the s 48 CPN offence; this might be spray paints, sound equipment, or dog (owner unable to control the dog). Forfeited items can be destroyed or disposed of appropriately (including rehoming a dog). A warrant issued under s 51 can authorise seizure of such items, and an officer may use reasonable force, if necessary, to do this.
- Failure to comply with any of the requirements in the court order constitutes contempt of court and could lead to a custodial sentence.
- Anyone issued with a CPN can appeal to a magistrates' court, but this must be within twenty-one days of issue of the notice. Appeal could be on the grounds that the behaviour: did not take place; was not persistent or continuing; was not unreasonable; or did not have a detrimental effect on the quality of life of those in the locality. Other grounds for appeal might be: unreasonable CPN requirements; was issued to the wrong person; or the individual cannot reasonably be expected to control or affect the behaviour.

 Summary   6 months

 Level 4 fine (person) or fine (body)

7.16.2 Leaving litter/removing or interfering with litter bins

Section 87 of the Environmental Protection Act 1990 creates an offence of defacing a place by the leaving of litter.

Offences

A person is guilty of an offence if he throws down, drops or otherwise deposits any litter in any place to which this section applies, and leaves it.

Environmental Protection Act 1990, s 87(1)

Points to prove

✓ threw down/dropped/deposited litter
✓ in a place to which this section applies
✓ and left it there

Meanings

Deposits

Means no more than places or puts (*Felix v DPP* [1998] Crim LR 657).

Litter

Includes the discarded ends of cigarettes, cigars, and like products, chewing gum, and the remains of other products designed for chewing.

Place

- Any place in the area of a **principal litter authority** that is open to the air. Land shall be treated as 'open to the air' notwithstanding that it is covered, providing it is open to the air on at least one side.
- This section does not apply to a place which is 'open to the air' if the public does not have access to it, with or without payment.

Principal litter authority

Means a county council; county borough council; district council; London borough council; Common Council of the City of London; and the Council of the Isles of Scilly.

Explanatory notes

- It is immaterial whether the litter is deposited on land or in water, so the offence extends to dropping or depositing litter in bodies of water such as rivers and lakes.
- Under s 88 an authorised officer of a litter authority or a suitably designated constable may, if they have reason to believe that a person has committed an offence under s 87, issue a fixed penalty notice to that person.

Defences

No offence is committed under subsection (1) above where the depositing of the litter is—
(a) authorised by law, or

(b) done with the consent of the owner, occupier or other person having control of the place where it is deposited.

Environmental Protection Act 1990, s 87(4A)

Defence notes

A person may only give consent under s 87(4A)(b) in relation to the depositing of litter in a lake, pond, or watercourse if they are the owner, occupier, or other person having control of all the land adjoining that lake, pond, or watercourse and all the land through or into which water in that lake, pond, or watercourse directly or indirectly discharges, otherwise than by means of a public sewer.

Practical considerations

- The area of a local authority which is on the coast extends down to the low-water mark (s 72 of the Local Government Act 1972). Therefore, it is an offence to deposit litter on the beach.
- Consider issuing a PND (see **7.1**) for this litter offence (applies to constable only).
- If a **fixed penalty notice** is issued under s 88, a copy of it must be sent to the relevant litter authority within twenty-four hours.
- **Littering from vehicles**—s 88A provides that the Secretary of State may make regulations under which a vehicle keeper may be required to pay a fixed penalty notice where a littering offence has been committed in respect of the vehicle. A littering offence is committed in respect of a vehicle if an offence under s 87(1) occurs as a result of litter being thrown, dropped or otherwise deposited from the vehicle (whether or not by the vehicle's keeper).

Meanings

Keeper

In relation to a vehicle, means the person by whom the vehicle is kept at the time when the littering offence in question occurs, which in the case of a registered vehicle is to be presumed, unless the contrary is proved, to be the registered keeper.

Removing or interfering with litter bins

It is a summary offence under s 5(9) of the Litter Act 1983 for any person to wilfully remove or otherwise interfere with any litter bin or notice board provided or erected under this section or s 185 of the Highways Act 1980.

 Summary   6 months

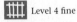 Level 4 fine

7.16.3 Unauthorised dumping/abandoned vehicles/fly tipping

Section 2 of the Refuse Disposal (Amenity) Act 1978 creates an offence of abandoning motor vehicles or any other thing on land in the open (fly tipping).

Offences

Any person who, without lawful authority—

(a) abandons on any land in the open air, or on any other land forming part of a highway, a motor vehicle or any thing which formed part of a motor vehicle and was removed from it in the course of dismantling the vehicle on the land; or

(b) abandons on any such land any thing other than a motor vehicle, being a thing which he has brought to the land for the purpose of abandoning it there,

shall be guilty of an offence.

Refuse Disposal (Amenity) Act 1978, s 2(1)

Points to prove

✓ without lawful authority
✓ abandoned on land
✓ in the open air/forming part of a highway
✓ a motor vehicle/part of a motor vehicle **or**
✓ an item brought to the land
✓ for the purpose of abandoning it there

Meanings

Motor vehicle

Means a mechanically propelled vehicle intended or adapted for use on roads, whether or not it is in a fit state for such use, and includes any trailer intended or adapted for use as an attachment to such a vehicle, any chassis or body, with or without wheels, appearing to have formed part of such a vehicle or trailer and anything attached to such a vehicle or trailer.

Abandoned

A person who leaves any thing on any land in such circumstances or for such a period that they may reasonably be assumed to have abandoned it or to have brought it to the land for the purpose of abandoning it there shall be deemed to have abandoned it there or, as the case may be, to have brought it to the land for that purpose unless the contrary is shown.

7.16.3 Unauthorised dumping/abandoned vehicles/fly tipping

Explanatory notes

In addition to any penalty, the court may order the defendant to pay any costs involved in the removal and disposal of the offending article.

Practical considerations

- Removal and disposal of items under this section is the responsibility of the local authority.
- Section 2A of the Refuse Disposal (Amenity) Act 1978 gives an authorised officer of a local authority the power to issue a fixed penalty in respect of the offence of abandoning a vehicle.
- Before contacting the local authority, consider checking the motor vehicle to ascertain whether it is stolen or used for involvement in crime.

 Summary   6 months

 3 months' imprisonment and/or a level 4 fine

Fixed penalty £200 or such amount as the appropriate person of a Local Authority may determine.

Links to alternative subjects and offences

7.17 **Trespassing on Premises/Land**

Section 144 of the Legal Aid, Sentencing and Punishment of Offenders Act 2012 relates to squatting in a residential building. Sections 61–62C of the Criminal Justice and Public Order Act 1994 deal with trespassers residing on land who fail to leave, whereas ss 6 and 7 of the Criminal Law Act 1977 concern the use or threat of violence to secure entry into premises and unauthorised entry or remaining on premises.

7.17.1 **Trespassers (squatting) in residential building/residing on land (failing to leave)**

Section 144 of the Legal Aid, Sentencing and Punishment of Offenders Act 2012 creates the offence of squatting in a residential building.

Offences

A person commits an offence if—

(a) the person is in a residential building as a trespasser having entered it as a trespasser,

(b) the person knows or ought to know that he or she is a trespasser, and

(c) the person is living in the building or intends to live there for any period.

Legal Aid, Sentencing and Punishment of Offenders Act 2012, s 144(1)

Points to prove

✓ being in a residential building
✓ having entered it as a trespasser
✓ lived/intended to live in the building

Meanings

Residential building

A building is residential if it is designed or adapted, before the time of entry, for use as a place to live.

Building

Includes any structure or part of a structure (including a temporary or moveable structure).

7.17.1 Trespassers (squatting) in residential building etc

Trespasser (see 7.17.2)

Explanatory notes

- The fact that a person derives title from a trespasser, or has permission from a trespasser, does not prevent the person from being a trespasser.
- For the purposes of s 144(1)(a) (above), it is irrelevant whether the person entered the building as a trespasser before or after this section came into force.

Defence

The offence is not committed by a person holding over after the end of a lease or licence (even if the person leaves and re-enters the building).

Legal Aid, Sentencing and Punishment of Offenders Act 2012, s 144(2)

Practical considerations

- MOJ Circular 4/2012 provides further details regarding this squatting offence, which requires that the trespasser 'is living' or 'intends to live' in the building for any period.
- Section 17(1)(c)(vi) of PACE provides a power of entry to arrest a person for the offence of squatting in a residential building (see 1.5.2).
- Section 6 of the Criminal Law Act 1977 provides the offence of using or threatening violence to secure entry to premises (see 7.17.2), but the police still have lawful authority to enter the property to arrest for the s 144 squatting offence.
- Section 7 of the 1977 Act concerns the offence of failing to leave residential premises once the lawful occupiers have gained legitimate entry (see 7.17.3).

Trespassers residing on land—failing to leave

- The Criminal Justice and Public Order Act 1994 gives the police powers for dealing with people, vehicles, and caravans trespassing on land.
- Section 61 gives the police power to direct two or more people trespassing on land, intending to reside there for a period of time, to leave that land and to remove any vehicles or other property they have with them on the land. This is providing that reasonable steps have been taken by or on behalf of the occupier to ask them to leave, and they have:
  - ✦ caused damage to the land or to property on the land; or
  - ✦ used threatening, abusive, or insulting words or behaviour towards the occupier or family member/employee/agent of the occupier; or
  - ✦ six or more vehicles on the land between them.

- It is a summary offence under s 61(4) if a person, knowing that a direction has been given which applies to them, either:
  - ◆ fails to leave the land as soon as is reasonably practicable, or
  - ◆ having left, again enters the land as a trespasser within the period of three months beginning with the day on which the direction was given.
- Section 62 provides that a constable may seize and remove a vehicle if a direction has been given under s 61 and they reasonably suspect that a person to whom it applies has, without reasonable excuse, failed to remove a vehicle which appears to belong to them, or to be in their possession or under their control; or they have entered the land as a trespasser with a vehicle within three months of the direction being given.
- Sections 62A–62C provide for the directing of trespassers to leave land and remove their vehicles/caravans, when there is a relevant caravan site in the local authority area, and it is managed by a relevant site manager.

 Summary

 6 months

 51 weeks imprisonment and/or a fine

7.17.2 **Violent entry to premises**

Section 6 creates the offences of using or threatening violence to secure entry to premises.

Offences

Subject to the following provisions of this section, any person who, without lawful authority, uses or threatens violence for the purpose of securing entry into any premises for himself or for any other person is guilty of an offence, provided that—

(a) there is someone present on those premises at the time who is opposed to the entry which the violence is intended to secure; and

(b) the person using or threatening the violence knows that that is the case.

Criminal Law Act 1977, s 6(1)

Points to prove

✓ without lawful authority
✓ used/threatened violence
✓ to secure entry to premises
✓ knowing someone present on the premises opposed entry

7.17.2 Violent entry to premises

Meanings

Premises

Any building, part of a building under separate occupation (eg flat), land ancillary to a building, and the site comprising any building(s) together with any land ancillary thereto.

Provisions of this section

Section 6(1) does not apply to a **displaced residential occupier** or a **protected intending occupier** of the relevant premises or a person acting on behalf of such an occupier. If the defendant produces sufficient evidence that they are, or were acting on behalf of, such an occupier they will be presumed to be so unless the prosecution proves the contrary.

Displaced residential occupier

Subject to the following **exception**, any person who was occupying any premises as a residence immediately before being excluded from occupation by anyone who entered those premises, or any **access** to those premises, as a **trespasser** is a displaced residential occupier of the premises so long as they continue to be excluded from occupation of the premises by the original trespasser or by any subsequent trespasser.

Exception

A person who was occupying the relevant premises as a trespasser immediately before being excluded from occupation shall not be a displaced residential occupier of the premises.

Access

Means, in relation to any premises, any part of any site or building within which those premises are situated that constitutes an ordinary means of access to those premises (whether or not that is its sole or primary use).

Trespasser

Someone who wrongfully enters onto someone else's premises.

Protected intending occupier

This is extensively defined in s 12A, but, in brief, means someone who has made a formal declaration to a commissioner of oaths that they were due to move into the affected premises.

Explanatory notes

- Anyone who enters, or is on or in occupation of, any premises under a title derived from a trespasser, or by a licence or consent given by a trespasser or by a person deriving title from a trespasser, will themselves be treated as a trespasser (whether or not they would be a trespasser apart from this provision).

- The fact that a person has an interest in, or right to possession or occupation of, the premises does not, for s 6(1), constitute lawful authority for the use or threat of violence by them or anyone else to secure entry into those premises.

Related cases

Wakolo v DPP [2012] EWHC 611 (Admin), QBD This case involved a married couple who had separated, and both were co-owners of the matrimonial home. The defendant, who had previously left the home, attempted to gain entry to the house but was refused admittance by his wife. Consequently, he used force to gain entry and he was convicted of s 6(1) and (5). He appealed and it was held that an individual who was the freeholder of a matrimonial property, from which he had not been formally excluded and which was occupied by his estranged wife, was not a protected intending occupier under the Criminal Law Act 1977, s 12A, could not avail himself of a defence under s 6 (1A), and could be convicted of the use of violence to gain entry to a property the front door of which he had damaged.

Practical considerations

- It is immaterial whether the violence is directed against a person or property and whether the violent entry is to acquire possession of the premises.
- A person who, by virtue of the definition of 'displaced residential occupier', is a displaced residential occupier of any premises is also deemed a displaced residential occupier of any access to those premises.
- A person on premises as a trespasser does not cease to be a trespasser under this legislation by being allowed time to leave there, nor does a person cease to be a displaced residential occupier of any premises because of any such allowance of time to a trespasser.
- Proceed with care where squatting appears to have lasted for a long time. It is possible for a squatter (someone who possesses premises without the lawful consent of the owner) to gain legal title if they have held the property for twelve years adversely but without disturbance or legal attempts to repossess it.

E&S

 Summary   None

6 months' imprisonment and/or fine

7.17.3 Adverse occupation of residential premises

Section 7 creates an offence of failing to leave residential premises once the lawful occupiers have gained legitimate entry.

Offences

Subject to the provisions of this section and s 12A(9), any person who is on any premises as a trespasser after having entered as such is guilty of an offence if he fails to leave those premises on being required to do so by or on behalf of—
(a) a displaced residential occupier of the premises; or
(b) an individual who is a protected intending occupier of the premises.

Criminal Law Act 1977, s 7(1)

Points to prove

✓ on premises
✓ as a trespasser
✓ having entered as such
✓ failed to leave when required
✓ by/on behalf of a displaced residential occupier/protected intending occupier

Meanings

Premises (see 7.17.2)

Trespasser (see 7.17.2)

Displaced residential occupier (see 7.17.2)

Protected intending occupier (see 7.17.2)

Explanatory notes

A reference to any premises includes a reference to any access to them, whether or not the access itself constitutes premises.

Defences

7(2) It is a defence for the accused to prove that he believed that the person requiring him to leave the premises was not a displaced residential occupier or protected intending occupier of the premises or a person acting on their behalf.

7(3) It is a defence for the accused to prove that—
  (a) the premises in question are, or form part of, premises used mainly for non-residential purposes; and
  (b) he was not on any part of the premises used wholly or mainly for residential purposes.

12A(9) Where the accused was requested to leave the premises by a person claiming to be or to act on behalf of a protected intending occupier of the premises—
  (a) it shall be a defence for the accused to prove that, although asked to do so by the accused at the time the accused was requested to leave, that person failed at that time to produce to the accused such a statement as is referred to in s 12A(2)(d) or s 12A(4)(d) or such a certificate as is referred to in s 12A(6)(d); and
  (b) any document purporting to be a document under 12A(6)(d) will be received in evidence and, unless the contrary is proved, will be determined to have been issued by or on behalf of the authority stated in the certificate.

Criminal Law Act 1977, ss 7 and 12A

Practical considerations

- Officers wishing to apply these provisions in an operational situation should make themselves conversant with the following terms: displaced residential occupier, squatters, and protected intending occupier (see **7.17.2**).
- A displaced residential occupier or a protected intending occupier (once they have completed the formalities) can use force (either personally or by others on their behalf) to break into the premises to regain possession. They can also demand that the premises be vacated and s 7 makes it an offence (subject to any defences) for the trespassers to remain.
- If the squatter is being evicted by a protected intending occupier (this does not apply to an eviction by a displaced residential occupier) then they are entitled to see a copy of the statement or certificate which must be held by the person making the eviction. They have a statutory defence if the certificate is not produced.

E&S

 Summary None

 6 months' imprisonment and/or fine

Links to alternative subjects and offences

7.18 Football/Sporting Event Offences/Banning Orders

At designated sporting events and grounds, the Sporting Events (Control of Alcohol) Act 1985 deals with police powers and offences in connection with alcohol, articles capable of causing injury, flares, and other articles; whereas at designated football matches, the Football (Offences) Act 1991 deals with offences such as throwing missiles, indecent/racist chanting, or going onto the pitch, and the Football Spectators Act 1989 controls admission through football banning orders.

7.18.1 Possess alcohol/article or drunk at sporting event

Section 7 of the Sporting Events (Control of Alcohol) Act 1985 provides the police with powers of entry, stop, and search in connection with the Act.

Offences

(1) A person who has alcohol or an article to which this section applies in his possession—
   (a) at any time during the period of a designated sporting event when he is in any area of a designated sports ground from which the event may be directly viewed, or
   (b) while entering or trying to enter a designated sports ground at any time during the period of a designated sporting event at that ground, is guilty of an offence.

(2) A person who is drunk in a designated sports ground at any time during the period of a designated sporting event at that ground or is drunk while entering or trying to enter such a ground at any time during the period of a designated sporting event at that ground is guilty of an offence.

Sporting Events (Control of Alcohol) Act 1985, s 2

Points to prove

s 2(1)(a) offence

✓ possessed
✓ alcohol/article to which s 2 applies
✓ during period of designated sporting event
✓ in area of designated sports ground
✓ with a direct view of the event

7.18.1 Possess alcohol/article or drunk at sporting event

---

s 2(1)(b) offence
- ✓ possessed
- ✓ alcohol/article to which s 2 applies
- ✓ while entering/trying to enter
- ✓ a designated sports ground
- ✓ during period of designated sporting event

s 2(2) offence
- ✓ drunk
- ✓ in/while entering/trying to enter
- ✓ a designated sports ground
- ✓ during period of a designated sporting event

Powers

(1) A constable may, at any time during the period of a designated sporting event at any designated sports ground, enter any part of the ground for the purpose of enforcing the provisions of this Act.
(2) A constable may search a person he has reasonable grounds to suspect is committing or has committed an offence under this Act.
(3) A constable may stop a public service vehicle (within the meaning of section 1 of this Act) or a motor vehicle to which section 1A of this Act applies and may search such a vehicle or a railway passenger vehicle if he has reasonable grounds to suspect that an offence under that section is being or has been committed in respect of the vehicle.

Sporting Events (Control of Alcohol) Act 1985, s 7

Meanings

Alcohol (see 9.1.1)

Article to which s 2 applies

Applies to any article capable of causing injury to a person struck by it, being:
- a bottle, can, or other portable container (including such an article when crushed or broken) which is for holding any drink, and when empty, is normally discarded or returned/recovered by, the supplier; or
- part of any of the above articles;
- but does not apply to anything that holds medicinal/veterinary products.

Designated sporting event

Is a sporting event or proposed sporting event for the time being designated, or of a class designated, by order made by the Secretary of State, and the order may apply to events or proposed events outside GB as well as those in England and Wales.

Period of a designated sporting event

This is the period beginning two hours before the start of the event or (if earlier) two hours before the time at which it is advertised to start and ending one hour after the end of the event.

Designated sports ground

Means any place used (wholly or partly) for sporting events where accommodation is provided for spectators, and for the time being designated, or of a class designated, by order made by the Secretary of State. Such an order may include the outer limit of any designated sports ground.

Drunk (see 7.2.1)

Offence under this Act (see 'Practical considerations')

Public service vehicle (PSV)

Means a motor vehicle (other than a tramcar), used for carrying passengers for hire or reward, and either adapted to carry more than eight passengers; or not so adapted, which in the course of business carries passengers at separate fares.

Motor vehicle

Means a mechanically propelled vehicle intended or adapted for use on roads.

Explanatory notes

- Article 2 of the Sports Grounds and Sporting Events (Designation) Order 2005 designates the classes of sports grounds in Sch 1 and sporting events in Sch 2 with regards to offences under the 1985 Act.
  - ✦ Sch 1 refers to any sports ground in England and Wales.
  - ✦ Sch 2 lists sporting events—FA matches at sports grounds, being within or outside England and Wales, in which one or both of the participating teams represents a club which is for the time being a member (whether a full or associate member) of the:—
    - ✦ Football League;
    - ✦ Football Association Premier League;
    - ✦ Football Conference National Division;
    - ✦ Scottish Professional Football League;
    - ✦ Welsh Premier League; or
    - ✦ represents a country or territory.
  - ✦ FA matches in competition for the FA Cup (other than in a preliminary or qualifying round).
- Whilst this Act was aimed primarily at football matches, it can also apply to other sporting events.

Practical considerations

- **Offences under this Act** are s 2 (above), and:
  - ✦ s 1—Where a vehicle, being a PSV or train, is mainly used for carrying passengers for the whole or part of a journey to or from a designated sporting event; then if the operator/hirer or their servant/ agent, knowingly causes/permits alcohol to be carried on the vehicle they will commit an offence. An offence is also committed if a person is drunk or in possession of alcohol on the vehicle.
  - ✦ s 1A—Where a motor vehicle, which is not a PSV but is adapted to carry more than eight passengers, is mainly used for carrying two or more passengers for the whole or part of a journey to or from a designated sporting event; then a person who knowingly causes/ permits alcohol to be carried on the motor vehicle is guilty of an offence if they are the driver, if not the driver but is the keeper or their servant/agent or a person to whom it is made available (by hire, loan or otherwise) by its keeper or their servant/agent. An offence is also committed if a person is drunk or in possession of alcohol on the motor vehicle.
  - ✦ s 2A—This offence replicates the s 2(1) offence, but instead of alcohol or connected receptacle, it applies to flares, fireworks, or an article/ substance that emits smoke or visible gas (eg distress flares, fog signals, or pellets/capsules used for testing pipes or as fumigators).
- Consider CPS charging standards and guidance for these offences.
- A constable may, at any time during the period of a designated sporting event at any designated sports ground, enter any part of the ground for the purpose of enforcing the provisions of this Act.
- A constable may search a person he has reasonable grounds to suspect is committing or has committed an offence under this Act, all of which are summary offences.

 Summary   6 months

 s 2(1) offence

> 3 months' imprisonment and/or level 3 fine
> s 2(2) offence
> Level 2 fine

7.18.2 **Throw object—designated football match/football banning orders**

Offences

It is an offence for a person at a designated football match to throw anything at or towards—

(a) the playing area, or any area adjacent to the playing area to which spectators are not generally admitted, or

(b) any area in which spectators or other persons are or may be present,

without lawful authority or lawful excuse (which shall be for him to prove).

Football (Offences) Act 1991, s 2

Points to prove

✓ while at a designated football match
✓ without lawful authority/excuse
✓ threw missile/object
✓ at/towards

s 2(a) offence

✓ first four 'Points to Prove' (above)
✓ the playing area/area adjacent to playing area
✓ where spectators not generally admitted

s 2(b) offence

✓ first four 'Points to Prove' (above)
✓ an area where spectators/other persons
✓ were/may be present

Meaning of designated football match

Means an association football match designated, or of a description designated, for the purposes of this Act by order of the Secretary of State.

Explanatory notes

- Article 3 of the Football (Offences) (Designation of Football Matches) Order 2004 provides the definition of a designated match, which is an FA match:
  + in which one or both of the participating teams represents a club which is for the time being a member (whether a full or associate member) of the Football League, the Football Association Premier League, the Football Conference, the Scottish Football League, the Welsh Premier League, or whose home ground is for the time being situated outside England and Wales or represents a country or territory.
  + in competition for the FA Cup (other than in a preliminary or qualifying round).
- Offences under this Act can only be committed in England and Wales. The Act covers acts done within a period of two hours before the start of the match (or two hours before the advertised start, if earlier) and ending one hour after the end of the match. Offences could also apply where the match is cancelled, if it has been advertised to start at a particular time on a particular day, in which case it will apply within a period beginning two hours before and ending one hour after the advertised starting times.

Practical considerations

- **Offences under this Act** are s 2 (above), and:
  + s 3—It is an offence to engage or take part in **chanting** of an indecent or **racialist nature** at a designated football match. For this purpose:
    + **chanting** means the repeated uttering of any words or sounds (whether alone or in concert with one or more others); and
    + **racialist nature** means consisting of or including matter which is threatening, abusive, or insulting to a person by reason of his colour, race, nationality (including citizenship), or ethnic or national origins.
  + s 4—It is an offence for a person at a designated football match to go onto the playing area, or any area adjacent to the playing area to which spectators are not generally admitted, without lawful authority or lawful excuse (which shall be for him to prove).
- The act of throwing the missile/object constitutes the s 2 offence. There is no need to prove that it was directed at anyone, or that anyone was likely to be alarmed or distressed by it.
- Be aware of 'ticket touting' offences under s 166 of the Criminal Justice and Public Order Act 1994, where it is an offence for an unauthorised person to sell a ticket for a designated football match, or otherwise to dispose of such a ticket to another person.

Football banning orders

- The Football Spectators Act 1989 controls the admission of spectators to designated football matches by means of a national membership scheme. For the purpose of preventing violence or disorder at or in connection with both designated and regulated football matches, it empowers the courts to make a 'banning order'. A banning order prohibits the person who is subject to the order from entering any premises for the purpose of attending regulated football matches in the UK and, in relation to regulated football matches outside the UK, can require that person to report at a police station as directed by the court.
- Section 14A of the 1989 Act applies where a person (the offender) is convicted of a **relevant offence**. Then if the court is satisfied that there are reasonable grounds to believe that making a banning order would help to prevent violence or disorder at or in connection with any regulated football matches, it must make such an order in respect of the offender.
- Schedule 1 to the 1989 Act provides the list of **relevant offences** in relation to applications for banning orders:
  + breaches/offences regarding banning orders under this Act;
  + s 2 or 2A offence under the 1985 Act (see **7.18.1**);
  + any offence under the 1991 Act (see above);

+ any offence under s 166 of the Criminal Justice and Public Order Act 1994 (sale of tickets by unauthorised persons) which relates to tickets for a football match.
+ the following offences committed during a period relevant to a designated football match while the accused was at any premises or was entering/leaving or trying to enter/leave the premises:
  + under s 4A (see **7.7**) or s 5 (see **7.8**) of the Public Order Act 1986 (harassment, alarm, or distress) or ss 17 to 29 (see **7.9**) of that Act (racial hatred);
  + the use or threat of violence by the accused towards another person (see **2.1**) or property (see **4.4**);
  + the use, carrying, or possession of an offensive weapon (see **8.9**) or a firearm (see **8.1**);
+ the following offences committed while the accused was on a journey to or from a designated football match, being an offence which the court declares related to football matches:
  + under s 12 of the Licensing Act 1872 (drunk in highway or public place) (see **7.2.2**);
  + under s 91(1) of the Criminal Justice Act 1967 (drunk and disorderly in a public place) (see **7.2.1**);
  + under s 1 of the 1985 Act (see **7.18.1**);
  + under s 4A (see **7.7**) or s 5 (see **7.8**) of the Public Order Act 1986 (harassment, alarm, or distress) or ss 17–29 (see **7.9**) of that Act (racial hatred);
  + under s 4 (see **10.10.1**), s 5 (see **10.11.1**), or s 5A (see **10.11.2**) of the Road Traffic Act 1988 (drive while unfit through drink or drugs, while over the alcohol prescribed limit, or above the drugs specified limit);
  + the use or threat of violence by the accused towards another person (see **2.1**) or property (see **4.4**);
  + the use, carrying, or possession of an offensive weapon (see **8.9**) or a firearm (see **8.1**);
+ the following offences, which do not apply to any of the above circumstances, but were committed during a period relevant to a designated football match, and the court declares that the offence related to that match or to that match and any other football match which took place during that period:
  + under s 4A (see **7.7**) or s 5 (see **7.8**) of the Public Order Act 1986 (harassment, alarm, or distress) or ss 17–29 (see **7.9**) of that Act (racial hatred);
  + the use or threat of violence by the accused towards another person (see **2.1**) or property (see **4.4**);
  + the use, carrying, or possession of an offensive weapon (see **8.9**) or a firearm (see **8.1**).

 Summary   6 months

 Level 3 fine

Links to alternative subjects and offences

Chapter 8

Firearms, Fireworks, and Weapons

8.1 'Section 1 Firearms' Offences

The Firearms Act 1968 provides various offences connected with firearms, air weapons, shotguns, and associated ammunition.

8.1.1 Possessing s 1 firearm/ammunition without certificate

This offence involves being in possession of a firearm/ammunition without a valid firearm certificate. Any weapon or ammunition applicable to s 1 is commonly known as a 'section 1 firearm/ammunition'.

Offences

Subject to any exemption under this Act, it is an offence for a person—

(a) to have in his possession, or to purchase or acquire, a firearm to which this section applies without holding a firearm certificate in force at the time, or otherwise than as authorised by such a certificate;

(b) to have in his possession, or to purchase or acquire, any ammunition to which this section applies without holding a firearm certificate in force at the time, or otherwise than as authorised by such a certificate, or in quantities in excess of those so authorised.

Firearms Act 1968, s 1(1)

Points to prove

✓ possessed/purchased/acquired
✓ s 1 firearm/ammunition
✓ without/not authorised by/in quantities exceeding those authorised by
✓ a firearms certificate

Meanings

Exemptions

This includes: antique firearms; rifles loaned on private land; carriers, auctioneers, and warehousemen; Crown servants; police; BTP; Civil Nuclear Constabulary; armed forces; athletics and other approved activities; museums; police permits; registered firearms dealers; rifle and pistol clubs; ship and aircraft equipment; licensed slaughterers; theatres and cinemas; Northern Ireland firearms certificate holder; visiting forces; visitors' permits.

Possession

This has a wide meaning. The term has two distinct elements:
- *The mental element*: whereby the defendant must know of the existence of the firearm but cannot claim ignorance that it was technically 'a firearm'.
- *The practical element*: this term is broader than actual physical possession; a person can 'possess' a firearm in a house or premises under their control, even though they are not at the premises. Similarly, the same firearm could be 'possessed' by two people at the same time, such as the firearm's lawful owner and also its custodian who keeps the firearm at his home (see **5.2.1** notes on '**constructive possession**' of drugs).

Purchase

This is not defined and should be given its natural meaning.

Acquire

Means hire, accept as a gift, or borrow.

Firearm to which s 1 applies

This section applies to every **firearm** except:
- normal shotguns (see **8.2.1** for description);
- normal air weapons (see **8.7.2** for description).

Firearm

Means
(a) a lethal barrelled weapon (see below);
(b) a prohibited weapon;

(c) a relevant component part in relation to a lethal barrelled weapon or prohibited weapon;

(d) an accessory to a lethal barrelled weapon or a prohibited weapon where the accessory is designed or adapted to diminish the noise or flash by firing the weapon.

Lethal barrelled weapon

Means a barrelled weapon of any description from which a shot, bullet, or other missile, with kinetic energy of more than one joule at the muzzle of the weapon, can be discharged.

Shot, bullet, or other missile

These terms are not defined and should be given their natural meaning:
- 'shot' usually means round pellets;
- 'bullet' is normally discharged from a weapon with a rifled barrel;
- 'missile' is a more general term—darts and pellets have been held to be missiles.

Prohibited weapons

- Prohibited weapons require an authority from the Secretary of State and are listed under s 5, being weapons such as: machine gun; self-loading or pump-action rifled gun (other than a 0.22 rifle); rocket launcher; CS spray; electric stun gun (applying contacts/probes directly to the body to achieve incapacitation) or conducted energy device (CED); air weapon with self-contained gas cartridge system; grenade; any weapon of whatever description designed or adapted for the discharge of any noxious liquid, gas, or other thing.
- This written authority will have conditions imposed so as not to endanger the public safety or the peace.
- A person commits an offence under s 5 if, without an authority from the Secretary of State, they possess, purchase, acquire, manufacture, sell, or transfer any prohibited weapon. This offence does not apply unless, (a) the person carries on a business as a firearms dealer, and (b) the firearm is in his or her possession for the purposes of the business.
- Failure to comply with any condition imposed by this authority is an offence under s 5(5).
- The Secretary of State may revoke an authority by notice in writing. Failure to return the authority within twenty-one days is an offence under s 5(6).
- The Anti-social Behaviour, Crime and Policing Act 2014, s 108, inserted s 5(2A) so that an offence will be committed if, without authority a person manufactures; sells or transfers; possesses, purchases, or acquires for sale or transfer, any prohibited weapon or prohibited ammunition. This offence carries a sentence of life imprisonment if a person manufactures, distributes, or possesses for distribution any prohibited weapons or ammunition. HOC 9/2014 provides further details.

8.1.1 Possessing s 1 firearm/ammunition without certificate

Component part

Each of the following items is a relevant component part in relation to a lethal barrelled weapon or a prohibited weapon:

(a) a barrel, chamber or cylinder;
(b) a frame, body or receiver;
(c) a breech block, bolt or other mechanism for containing the pressure of discharge at the rear of the chamber;

but only where the item is capable of being used as part of a lethal barrelled weapon or a prohibited weapon.

Accessory

This is given its natural meaning and includes such accessories as a silencer or flash eliminator.

Firearm certificate

Means a certificate granted by a chief officer of police in respect of any firearm or ammunition to which s 1 applies.

Ammunition to which s 1 applies

This section applies to any **ammunition** for a firearm, except the following articles, namely:

• cartridges containing five or more shot, none of which exceeds 0.36 inch in diameter;
• ammunition for an air gun, air rifle, or air pistol; and
• blank cartridges not more than one inch in diameter.

Ammunition

Means ammunition—being any shot, bullet, or other missile—for any firearm and includes grenades, bombs, and other like missiles, whether capable of use with a firearm or not, and also includes prohibited ammunition.

Explanatory notes

• This is an offence of strict liability (*R v Gregory* [2011] EWCA Crim 3276, CA).
• A telescopic laser/night sight is **not** a component part or accessory that requires a firearm certificate.
• Whether a silencer or flash eliminator can be an accessory will be a question of fact to be determined in all the circumstances (ie whether it could be used with that firearm and did the defendant have it with them for that purpose). It is the accessory that must be 'so designed or adapted', not the weapon.
• Blank cartridges are cases with primer (small explosive charge at the end of the cartridge) and gunpowder; or primed cartridges (as blank but without the gunpowder) both able to be used in a firearm and producing an explosive effect when fired.

- It is a summary offence under s 35 of the Violent Crime Reduction Act 2006 for a person to sell or purchase a cap-type primer designed for use in metallic ammunition for a firearm being either:
  + a primer to which this section applies;
  + an empty cartridge case incorporating such a primer unless that person: is a registered firearms dealer; it is their trade or business; produces a certificate authorising possession; is in Her Majesty's Services and entitled to do so; or shows that they are entitled by virtue of any enactment.
- Blank cartridges greater than 1 inch in diameter are s 1 ammunition.
- The diameter of a cartridge is obtained by measuring immediately in front of the cannelure or rim of its base.
- An airsoft gun, being a barrelled weapon of any description which is designed to discharge only a small plastic missile (see s 57A Firearms Act 1968) is not regarded as a firearm for the purposes of this Act.

Defences

There is no statutory defence as it is an offence of strict liability (*R v Gregory* [2011] EWCA Crim 3276, CA).

Related cases

R v Heddell [2016] EWCA Crim 443 It was held in this case that an imitation firearm could still be a prohibited firearm within the meaning of the Act where it was readily convertible without the use of specialist knowledge or skills. With only minor repairs or alterations required to make the conversion, such as in this case, adding a steel bolt to the front chamber which took only 20 to 30 seconds to complete, this would mean it was a weapon within the meaning of s 57(1) (see meaning of firearm above).

R v Deyemi and Edwards [2007] All ER 369, CA The defendants were in possession of an electrical stun gun which discharged electricity through electrodes (a prohibited weapon under s 5(1)(b)). In their defence, the defendants said that they believed it was a torch. It was held that possession of a prohibited weapon is an absolute offence, and this was clear in the wording of ss 1 and 5 of the Act.

Price v DPP [1996] 7 CL 49 In this case the defendant had someone else's rucksack containing s 1 ammunition. Although unaware of the contents of the rucksack, the offence was still committed.

Moore v Gooderham [1960] 3 All ER 575, QBD This case considered what constituted a lethal barrelled weapon. It was held that the test to be applied was:

'Is this a weapon which, however misused, may cause injury from which death may result?' If the answer is 'Yes' the weapon should be classed as a 'lethal barrelled weapon'.

Practical considerations

- The prosecution need only prove knowledge of the existence of the item, as opposed to its nature. Similarly, there is no onus to prove that the defendant knew that the article was a firearm.
- In practice, forensic testing will determine whether weapons are lethal or not. The main characteristic that is measured is the muzzle velocity (the speed at which the projectile leaves the barrel).
- Certain imitation or replica firearms may be s 1 firearms (see **8.1.4**).
- A s 1 firearm can only be possessed by a firearms certificate holder or some other lawful authority such as a registered firearms dealer, member of the armed forces, or police officer.
- If someone had a silencer in their possession with no evidence linking it to a suitable weapon, possession alone is unlikely to be an offence.
- All repeating shotguns holding more than two cartridges (eg pump-action and revolver shotguns) are 's 1 firearms'.

 Either way   None

 Summary: 6 months' imprisonment and/or a fine

Indictment: 5 years' imprisonment and/or a fine

8.1.2 Aggravated s 1 offences/registered firearms dealers

The offences of possessing, purchasing, or acquiring a s 1 firearm carry a greater punishment if they are aggravated by the shotgun barrel being less than 24 inches long (creating a 'sawn-off' shotgun) or illegally converting anything having the appearance of a firearm into a s 1 firearm.

Offences

(1) Subject to this section [see 'Defences'], it is an offence to shorten the barrel of a shotgun to a length less than 24 inches.

(3) It is an offence for a person other than a registered firearms dealer to convert into a firearm anything, which though having the appearance of being a firearm, is so constructed as to be incapable of discharging any missile through its barrel.

(4) A person who commits an offence under section 1 of this Act by having in his possession, or purchasing or acquiring, a shotgun which has been shortened contrary to subsection (1) above or a firearm which has been converted as mentioned in subsection (3) above (whether by a registered firearms dealer

or not), without holding a firearm certificate authorising him to have it in his possession, or to purchase or acquire it, shall be treated for the purposes of provisions of this Act relating to the punishment of offences as committing that offence in an aggravated form.

Firearms Act 1968, s 4

Points to prove

✓ possessed/purchased/acquired
✓ a shortened shotgun barrel (to length less than 24 inches) or a thing converted into a firearm
✓ without holding/not authorised by
✓ a firearm certificate

Meanings

Registered

Means registered, as a **firearms dealer**, under s 33 of this Act; and references to 'the register', 'registration', and a 'certificate of registration' shall be construed accordingly, except in s 40.

Firearms dealer

Means a person who, by way of trade or business:
• manufactures, sells, transfers, repairs, tests, or proves firearms, or ammunition to which s 1 of this Act applies, or shotguns; or
• sells or transfers air weapons.

Explanatory notes

• This offence could apply to weapons such as starting pistols or imitation firearms which have been converted to s 1 firearms. For example, the Olympic 0.38 is manufactured as a non-lethal blank-firing pistol for use in sports or drama but has been classified as readily convertible into a lethal barrelled firearm.
• A shotgun which has a barrel shortened to less than 24 inches becomes a s 1 firearm. The length of the barrel is determined by measuring from the muzzle to the point at which the charge is exploded on firing the cartridge.

Defences

It is not an offence under subsection (1) above for a registered firearms dealer to shorten the barrel of a shotgun for the sole purpose of replacing a defective part of the barrel so as to produce a barrel not less than 24 inches in length.

Firearms Act 1968, s 4(2)

Practical considerations

- Section 3(1) makes it an offence, if by way of trade or business, a person—
  - ✦ manufactures, sells, transfers, repairs, tests, or proves any firearm or ammunition to which s 1 of this Act applies, or a shotgun;
  - ✦ exposes for sale or transfer, or has in his possession for sale, transfer, repair, test, or proof any such firearm or ammunition, or a shotgun; or
  - ✦ sells or transfers an air weapon, exposes such a weapon for sale or transfer, or has such a weapon in his possession for sale or transfer;

  without being registered under this Act as a firearms dealer.
- Consider confiscation of cash and property for the s 3(1) offence (above), as this is given as a 'criminal lifestyle' offence under Sch 2 to the Proceeds of Crime Act 2002 (see **5.5** for details).
- Section 32 of the Violent Crime Reduction Act 2006 makes it a summary offence to sell air weapons by way of trade or business other than face-to-face to an individual who is not a registered firearms dealer. This allows an air weapon to be sent from one registered firearms dealer to another to make the final transfer in person to the buyer. Guidance is given on ss 31 and 32 in HOC 31/2007.

 Either way   None

 Summary: 6 months' imprisonment and/or a fine

Indictment: 7 years' imprisonment and/or a fine

8.1.3 Restrictions on s 1 firearms/ ammunition to under 14 years

Sections 22(2) and 24(2) of the Firearms Act 1968 place tight restrictions on persons under the age of 14 years from possessing, or receiving as gifts or on loan, any s 1 firearm/ammunition.

Offences

Possession by under 14

It is an offence for a person under the age of 14 to have in his possession any firearm or ammunition to which section 1 of this Act or section 15 of the Firearms (Amendment) Act 1988 applies, except where under section 11(1) or (4) of this Act he is entitled to have possession of it without holding a firearm certificate.

Firearms Act 1968, s 22(2)

Make gift, lend, or part with possession to under 14

It is an offence—
(a) to make a gift of or lend any firearm or ammunition to which section 1 of this Act applies to a person under the age of 14; or
(b) to part with the possession of any such firearm or ammunition to a person under that age, except in circumstances where that person is entitled under section 11(1) or (4) of this Act or section 15 of the Firearms (Amendment) Act 1988 to have possession thereof without holding a firearm certificate.

Firearms Act 1968, s 24(2)

Points to prove

Possess

✓ being a person under the age of 14 years
✓ possessed
✓ any s 1 firearm or ammunition

Make gift/lend/part with possession

✓ make a gift/lend/part with possession
✓ a s 1 firearm or ammunition
✓ to a person under the age of 14 years

Meanings

Possession

This has a wide meaning (see **8.1.1**).

Section 1 firearm or ammunition (see 8.1.1)

Section 15 of the Firearms (Amendment) Act 1988

This provides the mechanism for the creation of approved rifle and **muzzle-loading pistol** clubs where members can, if they wish, use such weapons without being the holder of a firearm certificate.

Muzzle-loading pistol

Means a pistol designed to be loaded at the muzzle end of the barrel or chambered with a loose charge (such as gun powder) and a separate ball (or other missile).

Explanatory notes

- These restrictions are in addition to those imposed on persons under 18 and 15 years of age.
- Both offences can be committed anywhere and not just in a public place.
- The 1968 Act **s 11 exceptions**, applicable to both offences are:
  ✦ carrying a firearm or ammunition belonging to a certificate holder (18 or over) under instructions from, and for the use of, that person for sporting purposes only;

8.1.4 Imitation/replica firearm—convertible to s 1 firearm

- ✦ a person conducting or carrying on a miniature rifle range (whether for a rifle club or otherwise) or shooting gallery at which no firearms are used other than air weapons or miniature rifles not exceeding .23 inch calibre, may possess, purchase, or acquire, such miniature rifles and ammunition suitable for that purpose; and any person using such rifles/ammunition at such a range or gallery.
- Section 11A of the Firearms Act 1968 was introduced by the Policing and Crime Act 2017 and provides additional provisions for the authorised lending and possession of firearms for hunting.
- Any firearm or ammunition found on a person for these offences may be confiscated by the court.

Defences

Both offences

The s 11 exceptions (see **'Explanatory notes'** above) may apply.

Section 24(2) offence

Under s 24(5) having reasonable grounds to believe that the person was 14 years of age or over (see **8.7.1**).

SSS

 Summary   48 months (consent of DPP required after 6 months)

 6 months' imprisonment and/or a fine

8.1.4 **Imitation/replica firearm—convertible to s 1 firearm**

Section 1 of the Firearms Act 1982 controls imitation firearms that can be readily converted to become a working s 1 firearm.

Offences

This Act applies to an imitation firearm if it—
(a) has the appearance of being a firearm to which section 1 of the 1968 Act (firearms requiring a certificate) applies; and
(b) is so constructed or adapted as to be readily convertible into a firearm to which that section applies.

Firearms Act 1982, s 1(1)

Points to prove

✓ possessed/purchased/acquired
✓ an imitation firearm
✓ having the appearance of a s 1 firearm **and**
✓ is constructed/adapted so as to be readily converted into a s 1 firearm
✓ without holding a firearms certificate

Meanings

Imitation firearm (see 8.3.3)

Section 1 firearm (see 8.1.1)

Certificate (see 8.1.1)

Readily convertible into a firearm

Section 1(6) states that an imitation firearm shall be regarded as readily convertible into a firearm to which s 1 of the 1968 Act applies if:

(a) it can be so converted without any special skill on the part of the person converting it in the construction or adaptation of firearms of any description; and

(b) the work involved in converting it does not require equipment or tools other than such as are in common use by persons carrying out works of construction and maintenance in their own homes.

Explanatory notes

- A readily convertible imitation firearm that can be turned into a s 1 firearm will require a firearms certificate.
- The Firearms Act 1982, s 1 was enacted because some 'replica' weapons could be converted into s 1 working firearms with no specialist skill/tools.
- Excepting s 4(3) and (4), ss 16–20 and s 47 of the 1968 Act shall apply in relation to an imitation firearm to which this Act applies as it applies to a 's 1 firearm'.
- Apart from excepted air weapons, component parts, and accessories, any expression given a meaning for the purposes of the 1968 Act has the same meaning in this Act.

Defences

It shall be a defence for the accused to show that he did not know and had no reason to suspect that the imitation firearm was so constructed or adapted as to be readily convertible into a firearm to which s 1 of that Act applies.

Firearms Act 1982, s 1(5)

Related cases

R v Howells [1977] 3 All ER 417, CA In this case the defendant bought a revolver in 1974 in good faith, which he believed to be an antique and did not require a firearm certificate. At his trial, expert evidence was given that the gun was a modern reproduction and consequently, he was convicted of the s 1 offence. On appeal, the conviction was upheld and the court held that s 1 was an offence of strict liability and to allow a defence of reasonable belief would defeat the object of the section.

 Either way

🕐 None

Summary: 6 months' imprisonment and/or a fine

Indictment: 5 years' imprisonment and/or a fine

Aggravated offence (see **8.1.2**): 7 years' imprisonment and/or a fine

8.1.5 **Failing to comply with firearm certificate conditions**

Offences

It is an offence for a person to fail to comply with a condition subject to which a firearm certificate is held by him.

Firearms Act 1968, s 1(2)

Points to prove

✓ failed to comply with condition
✓ subject to which firearm certificate is held

Meaning of firearm certificate (see **8.1.1**)

Explanatory notes

- Section 27(2) of the 1968 Act stipulates that a firearm certificate shall be in the prescribed form and shall specify the **conditions** subject to which it is held. Those conditions are set out in the Firearms Rules 1998 (SI 1941/1998) and HOC 41/1998, with prescribed forms under HOC 16/2013.
- A statutory **condition** under the Firearms (Amendment) Act 1988, s 14 also imposes a duty on auctioneers, carriers, or warehousemen to take reasonable care of the custody of firearms and/or ammunition

which they have in their possession without holding a certificate; being an offence if they fail to keep them in safe custody or fail to notify any loss or theft forthwith to the police.

Related cases

DPP v Houghton-Brown [2010] EWHC 3527, QBD In this case the defendant left a loaded 0.22 rifle under a pile of clothing on the back seat of a parked secure car. It was held by magistrates that this was considered to be keeping the firearm in safe custody. The DPP appealed but the case was dismissed. It was held that it was a fact-sensitive decision. To assess the risk and consequences of the defendant's actions involved looking at factors such as where he had parked, the extent to which the gun was concealed, and the likelihood of somebody wanting to steal clothing from his car. The magistrates had local knowledge of the place where he had parked, and whether the type of car that he had was likely to be broken into in that location.

R v Chelmsford Crown Court, ex parte Farrer [2000] 1 WLR 1468, CA In this case, the defendant's mother had knowledge of where the key to her son's gun cabinet was kept and so could gain access to the weapons. It was held that the Chief Constable was right to refuse firearm certificate renewals on the grounds of a breach of the condition to prevent, as far as is reasonably practicable, access to the guns by an unauthorised person.

Hall v Cotton [1976] 3 WLR 681, QBD In this case, the defendant (A) owned two shotguns and held a shotgun certificate. He took the guns to (B) his friend's house for safe keeping and they went on holiday together. The police checked the guns some six weeks later. It was held that A remained in possession of the firearms even though he did not have physical control of them while they were at his friend's house, and B had custodial possession of the guns without a certificate even while he was on holiday, and that they had, therefore, been 'transferred' to him.

 Summary   48 months

 6 months' imprisonment and/or a fine

Links to alternative subjects and offences

8.1.5 Failing to comply with firearm certificate conditions

8.2 **Shotgun Offences**

The Firearms Act 1968 provides various offences connected with firearms, associated ammunition, air weapons, and shotguns.

8.2.1 **Shotgun without a certificate**

Section 2 of the Firearms Act 1968 creates the offence of possessing, purchasing, or acquiring a shotgun when not being the holder of a relevant certificate.

Offences

Subject to any exemption under this Act, it is an offence for a person to have in his possession or to purchase or acquire a shotgun without holding a certificate under this Act authorising him to possess shotguns.

Firearms Act 1968, s 2(1)

Points to prove

✓ possessed/purchased/acquired
✓ a shotgun
✓ without a certificate

Meanings

Exemptions (see 8.1.1)

Possession (see 8.1.1)

Purchase (see 8.1.1)

Acquire (see 8.1.1)

Shotgun

Means a smooth-bore gun (not being an air gun), which:
• has a barrel not less than 24 inches in length and does not have any barrel with a bore exceeding 2 inches in diameter;
• either has no magazine or has a non-detachable magazine incapable of holding more than two cartridges; **and**
• is not a **revolver** gun.

Revolver

In relation to a smooth-bore gun, means a gun containing a series of chambers which revolve when the gun is fired.

8.2.1 Shotgun without a certificate

Shotgun certificate

Means a certificate granted by a chief officer of police under this Act authorising a person to possess shotguns.

Explanatory notes

- The length of the barrel of a firearm is measured from the muzzle to the point at which the charge is exploded on firing and, in the case of a shotgun that length must not be less than 24 inches, otherwise it becomes a s 1 firearm (see **8.1.2**).
- Some antique shotguns may be classed as an 'antique firearm' and thus be exempt from shotgun offences. However, if 'modern' cartridges can be bought and fired using an antique shotgun it cannot be exempt. This exemption does not cover a modern replica of an antique weapon.
- For a full definition of antique firearms see s 58 Firearms Act 1968.
- An auctioneer cannot sell shotguns without either being a registered firearms dealer or obtaining a police permit.
- A person may, without holding a shotgun certificate, borrow a shotgun from the occupier of private premises and use it on that land in the occupier's presence; but where the person borrowing the shotgun is under the age of 18, this subsection applies only if the occupier is aged 18 or over (s 11(5)).
- A person may, without holding a shotgun certificate, use a shotgun at a time and place approved for shooting at artificial targets by the chief officer of police for the area in which the place is situated (s 11(6)).

Practical considerations

- All repeating shotguns holding more than two cartridges (eg pump-action and revolver shotguns) are s 1 firearms.
- Offences may be committed in relation to persons under 15 years where they have an assembled shotgun with them or for a person to give them a shotgun/ammunition as a gift (see **8.2.2**).
- Any offence involving a shotgun that has an illegally shortened barrel (less than 24 inches), thus creating a 'sawn-off' shotgun, will be an 'aggravated offence' (see **8.1.2**) carrying a greater penalty. It will also make the shotgun a s 1 firearm.
- A shotgun is deemed to be loaded if there is a cartridge in the barrel or approved magazine that can feed the cartridge into the barrel by manual or automatic means.
- A shotgun adapted to have a magazine must bear a mark on the magazine showing approval by the Secretary of State.
- 'Shotgun' includes any component part and any accessory for a shotgun designed or adapted to diminish the noise or flash caused by firing the gun.

Either way   None

 Summary: 6 months' imprisonment and/or a fine

Indictment: 5 years' imprisonment and/or a fine

8.2.2 Shotgun restrictions to under 15 years

Sections 22 and 24 of the Firearms Act 1968 impose shotgun restrictions relating to persons under 15.

Offences

Under 15 have with them

It is an offence for a person under the age of 15 to have with him an assembled shotgun, except while under the supervision of a person of or over the age of 21, or while the shotgun is so covered with a securely fastened gun cover that it cannot be fired.

Firearms Act 1968, s 22(3)

Make gift to under 15

It is an offence to make a gift of a shotgun or ammunition for a shotgun to a person under the age of 15.

Firearms Act 1968, s 24(3)

Points to prove

Have with them

✓ person under 15
✓ had with them
✓ assembled shotgun

Make gift

✓ made a gift of
✓ shotgun/ammunition for a shotgun
✓ to a person under 15

Meanings

With him (see 8.3.6)

Shotgun (see 8.2.1)

Defence for person making gift (see s 24(5), 8.7.1)

Practical considerations

- Unless exempted, or s 11(5) and (6) applies (see **8.2.1**), the person concerned must also be the holder of a shotgun certificate before they can possess, purchase, or acquire a shotgun.
- Offences in relation to air weapons/firearms are imposed on persons under 18 years (see **8.7.1** and **8.7.2**).
- Both ss 22(3) and 24(3) offences can be committed anywhere and not just in a public place.
- A court can order the destruction of any shotgun and ammunition to which this offence relates.
- Restrictions also apply to persons under 14 years in relation to s 1 firearms (see **8.1.3**).

SSS

 Summary   6 months

 Level 3 fine

8.2.3 **Fail to comply with shotgun certificate conditions**

Section 2 of the Firearms Act 1968 creates an offence of failing to comply with a condition imposed by a shotgun certificate.

Offences

It is an offence for a person to fail to comply with a condition subject to which a shotgun certificate is held by him.

Firearms Act 1968, s 2(2)

Points to prove
✓ failed to comply with condition
✓ subject to which shotgun certificate is held

Meaning of shotgun certificate (see 8.2.1)

Practical considerations

- Regarding public safety, the two main **conditions** applying to shotgun certificate holders are the failure to keep the shotgun(s) and/or cartridges in safe custody or in failing to notify any loss forthwith to the police.

- Under s 28(1) a chief officer of police has to be satisfied that the applicant can be permitted to possess a shotgun without danger to the public safety or to the peace.
- Section 28(1A) states that no certificate shall be granted or renewed if the chief officer of police has reason to believe that the applicant is prohibited from possessing a shotgun; **or** does not have a good reason for possessing, purchasing, or acquiring one. However, a certificate can be extended for a period of 8 weeks beginning with the day after the day at the end of which the certificate was due to expire, allowing time for the chief officer to make a decision.
- It is an offence, under s 28A(7), to knowingly or recklessly make a false statement for the purpose of procuring the grant or renewal of a certificate.
- There is a presumption in favour of granting unless the police can prove any of the exemptions.
- The certificate must contain a description of the weapon including any identity numbers.

 Summary   48 months

 6 months' imprisonment and/or a fine

Links to alternative subjects and offences

8.3 **Criminal Use of Firearms**

There is a raft of legislation which has been put in place to try and curb possession of firearms by criminals: some of these measures are discussed below.

8.3.1 **Ban on possession by convicted person**

Section 21 of the Firearms Act 1968 creates an offence for the possession of any firearm or ammunition by convicted criminals. The section first provides three types of ban: total; five years from date of release; and while under a licence, order, or binding-over condition.

Lengths of ban

Total ban

Anyone sentenced to custody for life or preventive detention, imprisonment, or corrective training for a term of three years or more; or to youth custody or detention in a young offender institution for such a term, shall not **at any time** have a firearm or ammunition in his possession—s 21(1).

Five years

- A person who has been sentenced to imprisonment for a term of three months or more but less than three years, or to youth custody or detention in a young offender institution for such a term, or who has been subject to a secure training order or a detention and training order, shall not at any time before the expiration of the period of five years from **the date of release** have a **firearm** or **ammunition** in their **possession**—s 21(2).
- A person who has been sentenced to imprisonment for a term of three months or more, and the sentence is suspended under s 189 of the CJA 2003, shall not have a firearm or ammunition in his possession at any time during the period of five years beginning with the second day after the date on which the sentence is passed—s 21(2C).

Other bans

- A person while:
    - (a) discharged on licence, being holder of licence, issued for detention of children and young persons convicted of serious crime;
    - (b) subject of recognisance to keep peace or be of good behaviour, or community order with a condition not to possess, use, or carry a firearm;

    shall not have a firearm or ammunition in their possession—s 21(3).

Offences

Possess whilst banned

It is an offence for a person to contravene any of the foregoing provisions of this section [*contravene above bans*].

Firearms Act 1968, s 21(4)

Sell/transfer/repair/test/prove for banned person

It is an offence for a person to sell or transfer a firearm or ammunition to, or to repair, test or prove a firearm or ammunition for, a person whom he knows or has reasonable ground for believing to be prohibited by this section from having a firearm or ammunition in his possession.

Firearms Act 1968, s 21(5)

Points to prove

Possess whilst banned

✓ being person sentenced to
✓ imprisonment/youth custody/detention in YOI/detention and training order/secure training order/suspended sentence or other sentence subject to s 21(3)
✓ for a term of [period]
✓ possessed a firearm and/or ammunition namely [description]
✓ while banned/before the expiration of ban

Sell/transfer/repair/test/prove for banned person

✓ sell/transfer **or** repair/test/prove
✓ firearm or ammunition for
✓ a person
✓ prohibited by s 21 from possessing

Meanings

Date of release

Details vary and are as follows:
• normal sentence—actual date a prisoner leaves prison;
• part imprisonment and part suspended sentence—date of release from prison;
• a 'secure training order' or 'detention and training order' whichever is the latest of the following:
  ◆ actual date of release;
  ◆ date the person was released from the order because of a breach;
  ◆ date halfway through the total period of the order.

Possession (see **8.1.1**)

Firearm or ammunition (see **8.1.1**)

Practical considerations

- A person given a suspended sentence of three months or more imprisonment will be subject to a five-year ban under s 21(2C).
- Where there are several short sentences, it is the total sentence that counts.
- Anyone who is banned by these provisions can apply to the Crown Court under s 21(6) for removal of the ban.
- Do not confuse the terms 'firearm' or 'ammunition' with 's 1 firearms or ammunition'. This section includes **all** firearms including air weapons and shotguns.
- If it is an air weapon, it must be proved that it can discharge a shot or missile and that it is a lethal barrelled weapon, capable of causing injury from which death could result.

 Either way

 None

 Summary: 6 months' imprisonment and/or a fine

Indictment: 5 years' imprisonment and/or a fine

8.3.2 **Possession with intent to endanger life**

Section 16 of the Firearms Act 1968 creates the offence of possession of a firearm or ammunition with intent to endanger life.

Offences

It is an offence for a person to have in his possession any firearm or ammunition with intent by means thereof to endanger life or to enable another person by means thereof to endanger life, whether any injury has been caused or not.

Firearms Act 1968, s 16

Points to prove

✓ possessed firearm/ammunition
✓ with intent
✓ to endanger life/enable another to endanger life thereby

Meanings

Possession (see **8.1.1**)

Firearm or ammunition

Includes all firearms and ammunition (see **8.1.1**).

Intent (see **4.1.2**)

Endanger life

Life need not actually be endangered, although if there is danger to life this may assist in proving intent. There is no need to prove any harm or injury to the victim.

Explanatory notes

The intention to endanger life need not be immediate, but it must result from the firearm/ammunition (eg if the defendant possesses the firearm or ammunition but intends to endanger life some other way, say by arson, this offence is **not** committed).

Related cases

R v Salih [2007] EWCA Crim 2750, CA It was held in this case that the law would be seriously impaired if a person who reasonably thought that, at some point, they may be unlawfully attacked, was allowed to carry a weapon. However, if a person carrying a firearm or offensive weapon, is at that time in fear of an imminent attack and is carrying the weapon for self-protection against an explicit and specific threat then that might be a different matter.

R v El-hakkaoui [1975] 2 All ER 146, CA It was held in this case that it is an offence under s 16 for a person [in the UK] to have in his possession a firearm/ammunition with intent to endanger the life of people outside the UK.

Practical considerations

- Intention to endanger life in another country is also an offence under this section.
- The offence of possession for another to endanger life requires the firearm to be specifically held intending that the other should endanger life with it. If the firearm/ammunition is simply held for someone known to be involved in crime, that will be insufficient for this offence.
- Consider the alternative offences of possession:
  + with intent to cause fear of violence (which covers a wider set of circumstances) (see **8.3.3**);
  + at the time of committing/being arrested for a relevant offence (see **8.3.5**).

  Indictable   🕐 None

▥ Life imprisonment and/or a fine

8.3.3 **Possession with intent to cause fear of violence**

Section 16A of the Firearms Act 1968 creates an offence of possessing a firearm (or imitation firearm) with intent to cause others to fear unlawful violence being used against them.

Offences

It is an offence for a person to have in his possession any firearm or imitation firearm with intent—
(a) by means thereof to cause; or
(b) to enable another person by means thereof to cause

any person to believe that unlawful violence will be used against him or another person.

Firearms Act 1968, s 16A

Points to prove

✓ had in your possession
✓ a firearm/imitation firearm
✓ with intent
✓ to cause/enable another to cause
✓ any person
✓ to believe unlawful violence will be used
✓ against them or another person

Meanings

Possession (see **8.1.1**)

Firearm

Means all firearms, not just s 1 firearms (see **8.1.1**).

Imitation firearm
Means any thing that has the appearance of being a firearm (other than appearance of prohibited weapon under s 5(1)(b) for discharge of any noxious liquid, gas, or other thing) whether or not it is capable of discharging any shot, bullet, or other missile.

Intent (see **4.1.2**)

Unlawful violence

Means the unlawful exercise of physical force so as to cause injury or damage to property.

Practical considerations

• The offence can be committed anywhere and does not require intent to commit any specific criminal offence.

- It does not matter if the weapon is an imitation, inoperative, or unloaded.

 Indictable None

 10 years' imprisonment and/or a fine

8.3.4 **Using a firearm to resist or prevent a lawful arrest**

Section 17(1) of the Firearms Act 1968 creates the offence of using a firearm or imitation firearm to resist or prevent a lawful arrest.

Offences

It is an offence for a person to make or attempt to make any use whatsoever of a firearm or imitation firearm with intent to resist or prevent the lawful arrest or detention of himself or another person.

Firearms Act 1968, s 17(1)

Points to prove

✓ made/attempted to make use
✓ of a firearm/an imitation firearm
✓ with intent
✓ to resist/prevent lawful arrest/detention
✓ of self/another

Meanings

Firearm

Means all firearms, not just s 1 firearms (see **8.1.1**). Although it does not include component parts and accessories designed or adapted to diminish the noise or flash caused by firing the weapon.

Imitation firearm (see **8.3.3**)

Intent (see **4.1.2**)

Explanatory notes

It has to be proved that the firearm was being used intentionally to resist/prevent the lawful arrest of the offender or another person.

🦽 Indictable　　　　　🕐 None

▦ Life imprisonment and/or a fine

8.3.5 **Possession at time of committing/ being arrested**

Section 17(2) of the Firearms Act 1968 makes it an offence to be in possession of a firearm or imitation firearm at the time of arrest for certain specified offences.

> ### Offences
>
> If a person at the time of his committing or being arrested for an offence specified in schedule 1 to this Act, has in his possession a firearm or imitation firearm he shall be guilty of an offence under this subsection unless he shows that he had it in his possession for a lawful object.
>
> Firearms Act 1968, s 17(2)

Points to prove

✓ at the time of being arrested for/committing
✓ a Sch 1 offence
✓ possessed firearm/imitation firearm

Meanings

Schedule 1 offences

- Criminal Damage Act 1971, s 1—Damage; damage with intent to endanger life; arson.
- Offences Against the Person Act 1861—
    ✦ s 20—Wounding/GBH;
    ✦ s 21—Criminal intent choke/strangle;
    ✦ s 22—Criminal use of stupefying drugs;
    ✦ s 30—Laying explosive to building, etc;
    ✦ s 32—Endangering persons by tampering with railway;
    ✦ s 38—Assault with intent to resist lawful arrest;
    ✦ s 47—Assault occasioning actual bodily harm.
- Child Abduction Act 1984, Pt 1—Abduction of children.
- Theft Act 1968—burglary; blackmail; theft: robbery; taking of motor vehicles.
- Police Act 1996—assaulting/impeding a police officer.
- Criminal Justice Act 1991—assault prisoner custody officer.

- Criminal Justice and Public Order Act 1994—assault secure training centre custody officer.
- Criminal Justice and Courts Act 2015—assault secure college custody officer.
- Sexual Offences Act 2003:
  - ✦ rape;
  - ✦ assault by penetration;
  - ✦ cause person to engage in sexual activity involving penetration;
  - ✦ rape of a child under 13;
  - ✦ assault of a child under 13 by penetration;
  - ✦ cause/incite child under 13 to engage in sexual activity involving penetration;
  - ✦ sexual activity with a mentally disordered person involving penetration;
  - ✦ cause/incite mentally disordered person to engage in penetrative sexual activity.
- Aiding and abetting any of the Sch 1 offences.
- Attempting to commit any of the Sch 1 offences.

Possession (see **8.1.1**)

Firearm (see **8.3.4**)

Imitation firearm (see **8.3.3**)

> ### Defences
> Proving possession of the firearm or imitation firearm for a lawful reason or purpose.

Explanatory notes

- In this section, 'firearm' means a complete weapon and does not include component parts, and such items as silencers and flash eliminators.
- There is no need to prove any use or intended use of the firearm. Possession of it may be completely unconnected with the other offence committed by the person or for which they are arrested.

Related cases

R v Nelson [2000] 2 Cr App R 160, CA In this case it was held that when the defendant is arrested for a 'relevant' Sch 1 offence there is no need to prove the Sch 1 offence itself.

 SSS   E&S

 Indictable   🕐 None

 Life imprisonment and/or a fine

8.3.6 **Carrying firearm—criminal intent/ resist arrest**

Section 18 of the Firearms Act 1968 makes it an offence to carry a firearm or imitation firearm with criminal intent or to resist/prevent arrest.

Offences

It is an offence for a person to have with him a firearm or imitation firearm with intent to commit an indictable offence, or to resist arrest or prevent the arrest of another, in either case while he has the firearm or imitation firearm with him.

Firearms Act 1968, s 18 (1)

Points to prove
✓ had with them
✓ a firearm/imitation firearm
✓ with intent
✓ to commit an indictable offence/resist arrest/prevent the arrest of another

Meanings

Has with him

This is a narrower definition than 'possession' (see **8.1.1**). Here there is a need to prove:
- a knowledge of the existence of the article;
- that the article was 'to hand and ready for use' (eg it might be hidden a few feet away: it does not have to be physically on the defendant's person).

Firearm (see **8.3.3**)

Imitation firearm (see **8.3.3**)

Intent (see **4.1.2**)

Indictable offence

This includes either way offences.

Related cases

R v Duhaney, R v Stoddart (1998) 2 Cr App R 25, CA In this case the defendant with another, attempted to rob a Securicor van. He had upon him an imitation firearm but did not use it during commission of the robbery. In interview, he admitted having the firearm but contended that he had not intended to use it. On appeal the convictions were upheld, and the court held that mere possession of a firearm is not sufficient for an offence under s 18 to be made out. There must also be the intent to commit an indictable offence. Notwithstanding this requirement the section was enacted so as to encompass the actions of those who set out to commit an indictable offence while intentionally carrying a firearm regardless of whether there was also present the intent to use that firearm.

R v Pawlicki and Swindell [1992] 3 All ER 903, CA It was held in this case that the exact distance between a criminal and his gun should not be the main factor—the accessibility of the gun should be judged in common sense terms in the context of criminals embarking on a joint enterprise to commit an indictable offence. This is a matter of fact for the jury to decide.

Practical considerations

- Proof that the defendant had a firearm or imitation firearm with them and intended to commit the offence, or to resist or prevent arrest, is evidence that they intended to have it with them while doing so.
- Consider 'possess firearm with intent to cause the fear of unlawful violence' (see **8.3.3**), which has a much wider scope.

 Indictable   None

 Life imprisonment and/or a fine

8.3.7 **Using person to mind a firearm/weapon**

Section 28 of the Violent Crime Reduction Act 2006 makes it an offence to use another person to look after, hide, or transport a dangerous weapon, subject to an agreement that it would be available when required for an unlawful purpose.

Offences

(1) A person is guilty of an offence if—

    (a) he uses another to look after, hide or transport a dangerous weapon for him; and

    (b) he does so under arrangements or in circumstances that facilitate, or are intended to facilitate, the weapon's being available to him for an unlawful purpose.

Violent Crime Reduction Act 2006, s 28

8.3.7 Using person to mind a firearm/weapon

Points to prove

✓ uses another person to
✓ look after/hide/transport
✓ dangerous weapon and
✓ under arrangements made or facilitation agreed/intended
✓ the weapon is made available
✓ for an unlawful purpose

Meanings

Dangerous weapon (s 28(3))

In this section 'dangerous weapon' means:
(a) a firearm (see **8.1.1**) **other than** an air weapon or a component part of, or accessory to, an air weapon (see **8.1.2**); or
(b) a weapon to which s 141 (see **8.9.2**) or s 141A (see **8.10.2**) of the Criminal Justice Act 1988 applies (specified offensive weapons, knives, and bladed weapons).

Available for an unlawful purpose (s 28(2))

For the purposes of this section the cases in which a dangerous weapon is to be regarded as available to a person for an unlawful purpose include any case where:
(a) the weapon is available for him to take possession of it at a time and place; **and**
(b) his possession of the weapon at that time and place would constitute, or be likely to involve or to lead to, the commission by him of an offence.

E&S

 Indictable   None

4 to 10 years' imprisonment and/or a fine (details given in s 29)

Links to alternative subjects and offences

8.4 Trespassing with Firearms

The Firearms Act 1968 provides various offences connected with firearms, air weapons, shotguns, and associated ammunition. Some such offences involve trespassing.

8.4.1 Trespass with any firearm in a building

Section 20 of the Firearms Act 1968 creates two offences of trespassing with firearms, one of which is concerned with trespass in buildings.

Offences

A person commits an offence if, while he has a firearm or imitation firearm with him, he enters or is in any building or part of a building as a trespasser and without reasonable excuse (the proof whereof lies on him).

Firearms Act 1968, s 20(1)

Points to prove

✓ had with them
✓ firearm/imitation firearm
✓ entered or was in
✓ building/part of building
✓ as a trespasser
✓ without reasonable excuse

Meanings

Firearm (see **8.3.3**)

Imitation firearm (see **8.3.3**)

Has with him (see **8.3.6**)

Explanatory notes

- A firearm in these circumstances means any firearm—shotgun, air weapon, prohibited weapon, and s 1 firearm.
- The terms 'enters', 'building', 'part of a building', and 'trespasser' should be interpreted as terms used in legislation/case law relating to burglary (see **3.3.1**).

Defence

Reasonable excuse (the burden of proof lies with the defendant). This defence could include saving life/property or self-defence (eg the police carrying out a planned firearms operation).

Practical considerations

- It is important to note that although this is an either way offence, if the weapon is an air weapon or imitation firearm it is triable summarily only.
- The burden of proof lies with the defendant if they claim to have a reasonable excuse. Whether an excuse is reasonable would be for the court to decide having considered all the circumstances.
- Unless it is an imitation, there needs to be some evidence that the weapon is a firearm.
- Consider the offences of aggravated burglary (see **3.3.2**) or attempt aggravated burglary (see **4.1.1**) (especially if an imitation or air weapon is used—greater penalty).

 Either way   None

 Summary: 6 months' imprisonment and/or a fine

 Indictment: 7 years' imprisonment and/or a fine

Air weapons/imitation firearms

 Summary   48 months

 6 months' imprisonment and/or a fine

8.4.2 **Trespass with firearm on land**

Section 20(2) of the Firearms Act 1968 creates an offence of trespass with a firearm on land.

Offences

A person commits an offence if, while he has a firearm or imitation firearm with him, he enters or is on any land as a trespasser and without reasonable excuse (the proof whereof lies on him).

Firearms Act 1968, s 20(2)

8.4.2 Trespass with firearm on land

> **Points to prove**
> ✓ had with them
> ✓ firearm/imitation firearm
> ✓ entered/was on land
> ✓ as a trespasser
> ✓ without reasonable excuse

Meanings

Firearm (see **8.3.3**)

Imitation firearm (see **8.3.3**)

Has with him (see **8.3.6**)

Land

This includes land covered with water.

Trespass (see **3.3.1**)

Explanatory notes

A firearm in these circumstances means any firearm—shotgun, air weapon, prohibited weapon, and s 1 firearm.

> **Defence**
> Reasonable excuse (see **8.4.1**).

Practical considerations

- In order to prove a trespass, it must be shown that the defendant knew that they were a trespasser or was reckless as to whether the facts existed which made them a trespasser.
- If a defence of reasonable excuse is claimed, the burden of proof lies with the defendant.
- Unless it is an imitation firearm, there needs to be some evidence that the weapon is 'a firearm'.

SSS

 Summary

 48 months

 3 months' imprisonment and/or a level 4 fine

Links to alternative subjects and offences

8.5 **Possess Firearm or Imitation Firearm in a Public Place**

Section 19 of the Firearms Act 1968 provides various offences relating to the possession of shotguns, air weapons, firearms, and imitation firearms in a public place.

Offences

A person commits an offence if, without lawful authority or reasonable excuse (the proof whereof lies on him) he has with him in a public place—
(a) a loaded shotgun,
(b) an air weapon (whether loaded or not),
(c) any other firearm (whether loaded or not) together with ammunition suitable for use in that firearm, or
(d) an imitation firearm.

Firearms Act 1968, s 19

Points to prove

✓ without lawful authority/reasonable excuse
✓ had with you in a public place
✓ firearm (together with suitable ammunition) **or**
✓ loaded shotgun **or**
✓ loaded/unloaded air weapon **or**
✓ an imitation firearm

Meanings

Has with him (see 8.3.6)

Public place

This includes any highway and any other premises or place to which at the material time the public have or are permitted to have access, whether on payment or otherwise.

Loaded

Means if there is a cartridge in the barrel or approved magazine that can feed the cartridge into the barrel by manual or automatic means.

Shotgun (see 8.2.1)

Air weapon (see 8.7.2)

Other firearm (see 8.1.1)

Imitation firearm (see 8.3.3)

Explanatory notes

In this offence the requirement for the weapons to be loaded or not varies:

- the requirement for a loaded weapon only applies to shotguns;
- for air weapons, there is no need to have ammunition for them;
- for other firearms, the defendant must have ammunition suitable for use with that firearm.

Defences

Having lawful authority or reasonable excuse (the burden of proof lies with the defendant). This defence could include saving life/property or self-defence (eg the police carrying out a planned firearms operation). Whether an excuse is reasonable would be for the court to decide having considered all the circumstances.

Related cases

R v Harrison [1996] Crim LR 200 During a robbery, one of the robbers had a loaded sawn-off shotgun which the other knew nothing about. On police arrival, the other offender took possession of the gun and it was held that only the knowledge of the fact of possession was needed to prove an offence under s 19 rather than the nature or quality of what was possessed. Once the prosecution has shown that a person had the shotgun the fact that it was loaded, as a result of the offence being absolute, made it a breach of the section.

R v Jones [1995] 2 WLR 64, CA It was held in this case that a firearms certificate does not give the holder a defence of 'lawful authority' against a charge under s 19.

R v Morris and King (1984) 149 JP 60, 79 Cr App Rep 104, CA It was held in this case that the key word in these definitions is 'appearance'. The test is whether the thing looked like a firearm at the time when the defendant had it with him. It is ultimately for the jury to decide, what a witness believed about the object, and/or any admissions made by the defendant as to his reason for carrying it.

Practical considerations

- Section 161 of the Highways Act 1980 deals with the offence of discharging any firearm within 50 feet from the centre of a highway (see **8.8.6**).
- Section 28 of the Town Police Clauses Act 1847 deals with the offence of reckless discharge of a firearm in the street to the annoyance or danger of residents or passengers (see **8.8.6**).
- The 'guilty knowledge' that the prosecution must prove is knowledge of existence of the firearm, not the nature and quality of the weapon.

8.5 Possess Firearm or Imitation Firearm in a Public Place

- The prosecution must prove that the firearm is 'to hand and able to be used'.
- With an imitation firearm, the key issue is whether it looked like a firearm at the time of the offence. It is for the jury to decide on the circumstances of each case.
- Imitation or replica weapons that can be converted into working firearms will be classed as s 1 firearms (see **8.1.4**).
- Unless it is an imitation firearm, there needs to be some evidence that the weapon is a firearm (see **8.1.1**).

 Either way   None

 Summary: 6 months' imprisonment and/or a fine

Indictment: 7 years' imprisonment and/or a fine

Imitation firearm: 12 months' imprisonment and/or a fine

Air weapons

 Summary   48 months

 6 months' imprisonment and/or a fine

Links to alternative subjects and offences

8.6 Police Powers—Firearms

The Firearms Act 1968 provides various offences and powers connected with firearms, air weapons, shotguns, and associated ammunition.

8.6.1 Requirement to hand over firearm/ammunition

Section 47 of the Firearms Act 1968 deals with police powers to stop and search for firearms and provides an offence for failure to do so.

> **Police stop and search powers**
>
> A constable may require any person whom he has reasonable cause to suspect—
> (a) of having a firearm, with or without ammunition, with him in a public place; or
> (b) to be committing or about to commit, elsewhere than in a public place, an offence relevant for the purposes of this section,
>
> to hand over the firearm or any ammunition for examination by the constable.
>
> Firearms Act 1968, s 47(1)

Meanings

Reasonable cause to suspect

There must be objective grounds for the suspicion based on facts, information, or intelligence that are relevant to the likelihood of finding the article(s) (see **1.3.2**).

Firearm/ammunition (see **8.1.1**)

Has with him (see **8.3.6**)

Public place (see **8.5**)

Relevant offence

This refers to s 18 and s 20 offences, being either having a firearm or imitation firearm:
- with intent to commit an indictable offence, or to resist arrest, or prevent the arrest of another (see **8.3.6**);
- with them and entering either a building, or part of a building, or land as a trespasser (see **8.4**).

8.6.1 Requirement to hand over firearm/ammunition

Offences

It is an offence for a person having a firearm or ammunition with him to fail to hand it over when required to do so by a constable under subsection (1) above.

Firearms Act 1968, s 47(2)

Points to prove

✓ failed to hand over
✓ a firearm/ammunition for a firearm
✓ in possession
✓ when required to do so
✓ by a constable

Section 47 of the Firearms Act 1968 also provides qualified powers to search both people and vehicles for firearms and detain them for that purpose.

Police search and detain powers

Person

If a constable has reasonable cause to suspect a person of having a firearm with him in a public place, or to be committing or about to commit elsewhere than in a public place an offence relevant for the purposes of this section, the constable may search that person and may detain him for the purpose of doing so.

Firearms Act 1968, s 47(3)

Vehicle

If a constable has reasonable cause to suspect that there is a firearm in a vehicle in a public place, or that a vehicle is being or is about to be used in connection with the commission of an offence relevant for the purposes of this section elsewhere than in a public place, he may search the vehicle and for that purpose require the person driving or in control of it to stop it.

Firearms Act 1968, s 47(4)

Explanatory notes

- In exercising these powers, s 47(5) also gives a constable power to enter any place.
- The police also have the power to demand the production of shotgun or firearm certificates (see **8.6.2**).
- The power to stop the vehicle is not restricted to a constable in uniform.
- Officers should ensure that the stop and search procedures comply with PACE and the relevant Code (see **1.3.1**).

- With regard to premises a search warrant will have to be obtained under s 46 (see **8.6.3**).

 Summary   48 months

 3 months' imprisonment and/or a level 4 fine

8.6.2 **Police powers—firearms/shotgun certificates**

Section 48 of the Firearms Act 1968 gives a constable power to demand from a person they believe to be in possession of a s 1 firearm/ammunition or shotgun the production of a valid certificate or European pass or to show that they are exempt.

> ### Production of certificate
>
> A constable may demand, from any person whom he believes to be in possession of a firearm or ammunition to which section 1 of this Act applies, or of a shotgun, the production of his firearm certificate or, as the case may be, his shotgun certificate.
>
> Firearms Act 1968, s 48(1)

Meanings

Demand production

Where a person upon whom a demand has been made by a constable under subsection (1) and whom the constable believes to be in possession of a firearm fails—

(a) to produce a firearm certificate or, as the case may be, a shotgun certificate;
(b) to show that he is a person who, by reason of his place of residence or any other circumstances, is not entitled to be issued with a document identifying that firearm under any of the provisions which in the other member states correspond to the provisions of this Act for the issue of European firearms passes; or
(c) to show that he is in possession of the firearm exclusively in connection with the carrying on of activities in respect of which, he or the person on whose behalf he has possession of the firearm, is recognised, for the purposes of the law of another member state relating to firearms, as a collector of firearms or a body concerned in the cultural or historical aspects of weapons,

the constable may demand from that person the production of a document which has been issued to that person in another member state under any such corresponding provisions, identifies that firearm as a firearm to which it relates and is for the time being valid.

Firearms Act 1968, s 48(1A)

Believes

This is a more stringent requirement than 'suspects' and requires stronger grounds.

Section 1 firearm/ammunition (see **8.1.1**)

Firearm certificate (see **8.1.1**)

Shotgun (see **8.2.1**)

Shotgun certificate (see **8.2.1**)

Offences

It is an offence for a person who is in possession of a firearm to fail to comply with a demand under subsection (1A) above.

Firearms Act 1968, s 48(4)

Points to prove

✓ being in possession
✓ of a firearm/shotgun
✓ failed
✓ to comply with a demand
✓ by constable
✓ to produce a valid certificate/document or show exemption

Seize/detain weapon and require details

If a person upon whom a demand is made fails to produce the certificate or document, or to permit the constable to read it, or to show that he is entitled by virtue of this Act to have the firearm, ammunition or shotgun in his possession without holding a certificate, the constable may seize and detain the firearm, ammunition or shotgun and may require the person to declare to him immediately his name and address.

Firearms Act 1968, s 48(2)

Offences

If under this section a person is required to declare to a constable his name and address, it is an offence for him to refuse to declare it or to fail to give his true name and address.

Firearms Act 1968, s 48(3)

Points to prove

✓ having possession
✓ of a firearm/shotgun
✓ failed/refused
✓ to divulge
✓ when required by a constable
✓ their name and address

Explanatory notes

- A firearm certificate also includes a Northern Ireland Certificate.
- As the requirement is to declare 'immediately' their name and address, it is taken that the demand to produce a valid certificate/document or show exemption and (if applicable) the subsequent seizure of the firearm, ammunition, or shotgun will also follow the same immediacy.

SSS

 Summary   6 months

 Level 3 fine

8.6.3 **Premises search warrant**

Section 46 of the Firearms Act 1968 deals with the issue of premises search warrants for firearms and authorities attached thereto.

Granting of warrant

If a justice of the peace is satisfied by information on oath that there is reasonable ground for suspecting—
(a) that an offence relevant for the purposes of this section has been, is being, or is about to be committed; or
(b) that, in connection with a firearm or ammunition, there is a danger to the public safety or to the peace,

he may grant a warrant for any of the purposes mentioned in subsection (2) below.

Firearms Act 1968, s 46(1)

8.6.3 Premises search warrant

Meanings

Relevant offences

All offences under this Act except an offence under s 22(3) (unsupervised 15-year-old possessing shotgun—see **8.2.3**) or an offence relating specifically to air weapons.

Purposes of warrant

A warrant under this section may authorise a constable or civilian officer—

(a) to enter at any time any premises or place named in the warrant, if necessary by force, and to search the premises or place and every person found there;

(b) to seize and detain anything which he may find on the premises or place, or on any such person, in respect of which or in connection with which he has reasonable ground for suspecting—

   (i) that an offence **relevant** for the purposes of this section has been, is being or is about to be committed; or

   (ii) that in connection with a firearm, imitation firearm, or ammunition, there is a danger to the public safety or to the peace.

Firearms Act 1968, s 46(2)

Offences

It is an offence for any person intentionally to obstruct a constable or civilian officer in the exercise of his powers under this section.

Firearms Act 1968, s 46(5)

Points to prove

✓ intentionally obstruct
✓ constable/civilian officer
✓ whilst exercising their powers under s 46

Meaning of civilian officer

Means a person employed by a police authority or the Corporation of the City of London who is under the direction and control of a chief officer of police.

Explanatory notes

• Ensure that the application and execution of the warrant complies with PACE and the COP (see **1.6**).
• In some forces inspections of gun clubs and other routine firearms enquiries are performed by civilian staff rather than police officers.

Summary 48 months

 6 months' imprisonment and/or a fine

Links to alternative subjects and offences

8.7 **Firearms, Air Weapons, Imitation Firearms—Age Restrictions**

The Firearms Act 1968 provides various offences connected with firearms, imitation firearms, air weapons, shotguns, and associated ammunition. Invariably restrictions are in place as to the age of the person involved.

8.7.1 **Purchase/hire or supply by/to under 18**

Sections 22(1) and 24(1) of the Firearms Act 1968 prohibit purchase/hire or supply (sell or let on hire) of any firearm or ammunition by or to a person under 18 years of age.

> **Offences**
>
> *Purchase/hire by under 18*
>
> It is an offence for a person under the age of 18 to purchase or hire any firearm or ammunition.
>
> Firearms Act 1968, s 22(1)
>
> *Supplier (sell/hire) to under 18*
>
> It is an offence to sell or let on hire any firearm or ammunition to a person under the age of 18.
>
> Firearms Act 1968, s 24(1)

Points to prove

Purchase/hire

✓ being a person under the age of 18
✓ purchased/hired
✓ any firearm/ammunition

Supplier (sell/hire)

✓ sold/let on hire, either
✓ any firearm/ammunition
✓ to a person under the age of 18

Meanings of firearm/ammunition

Air weapons and air pellets/darts (see 8.7.2)

Shotguns and cartridges (see 8.2.1)

Section 1/other firearms or ammunition (see 8.1.1)

Defence for supplier under s 24

In proceedings for an offence under any provision of this section it is a defence to prove that the person charged with the offence believed the other person to be of or over the age mentioned in that provision and had reasonable ground for the belief.

Firearms Act 1968, s 24(5)

Practical considerations

- The Firearms (Amendment) Regulations 2010 (SI 1759/2010) increased the age to 18 for lawfully purchasing or hiring all firearms and ammunition under ss 22(1), 24(1) (above), and for s 11 exemptions (see 8.1.3, 8.2.1). Details are given in HOC 12/2010.
- Further prohibition on minors possessing, acquiring, or being supplied with firearms and/or ammunition is given in other s 22 and s 24 offences:
  + **section 1 firearms/ammunition (under 14)**—possessing, making a gift of, lending, or parting with possession (see 8.1.3).
  + **shotgun/cartridges (under 15)**—having an assembled shotgun without being supervised (by a person aged 21 years or over), or securely fastened in a gun cover or making a gift of a shotgun or cartridges to such person (see 8.2.2).
  + **air weapons/ammunition (under 18)**—having, making a gift of, or parting with possession (see 8.7.2).
- It is an offence under s 24A for a person under 18 to purchase or to be sold an imitation firearm (see 8.7.5).

 Summary 48 months (6 months if air weapon/ammunition)

 If firearm/ammunition by/to a person aged 17
3 months' imprisonment and/or a fine.

If air weapon/ammunition or any other case
6 months' imprisonment and/or a fine

8.7.2 **Air weapons—further offences (others)/under 18 restrictions**

The Firearms Act 1968 provides exceptions for young people to possess air weapons, but generally it is an offence for a person under 18 to have with them, or be given, an air weapon or ammunition for an air weapon.

Possess, make gift, or part with possession

Offences

Under 18 have with them

Subject to section 23, it is an offence for a person under the age of 18 to have with him an air weapon or ammunition for an air weapon.

Firearms Act 1968, s 22(4)

Make gift/part with possession to under 18

It is an offence—
(a) to make a gift of an air weapon or ammunition for an air weapon to a person under the age of 18; or
(b) to part with the possession of an air weapon or ammunition for an air weapon to a person under the age of 18 except where by virtue of section 23 of this Act the person is not prohibited from having it with him.

Firearms Act 1968, s 24(4)

Points to prove

Have with them

✓ being under 18 years of age
✓ had with them
✓ an air weapon or ammunition for an air weapon

Make a gift

✓ made a gift
✓ of an air weapon/ammunition for an air weapon
✓ to a person under the age of 18

Part with possession (not s 23 excepted)

✓ parted with possession
✓ of an air weapon/ammunition for an air weapon
✓ to a person under the age of 18
✓ being prohibited from having possession

Meanings

Section 23 (see 'Fire missile beyond premises' below)

Has with him (see 8.3.6)

Air weapon

Most air weapons are firearms, but not s 1 firearms (see **8.1.1**). Part of the definition of a s 1 firearm (s 1(3)(b) of the Firearms Act 1968) relates to every firearm, except air weapons: 'an air weapon that is to say, an air rifle, air gun or air pistol which does not fall within s 5(1) [*being a prohibited weapon—having compressed gas cartridge system*] and which is not of a type declared by rules [*sets the power levels at which an air weapon becomes a s 1 firearm*] made by the Secretary of State under s 53 of this Act to be specially dangerous'.

Defences

Sections 22(4) and 24(4)(b)

Consider s 23 (see **'Fire missile beyond premises'** section).

Section 24

Consider s 24(5) (see **8.7.1**).

Fire missile beyond premises

Offences

Fire missile beyond premises (any age)

A person commits an offence if——
(a)   he has with him an air weapon on any premises; and
(b)   he uses it for firing a missile beyond those premises.

Firearms Act 1968, s 21A(1)

Section 23 exceptions and supervisor offence

(1)   It is not an offence under section 22(4) of this Act for a person to have with him an air weapon or ammunition while he is under the supervision of a person of or over the age of 21; but where a person has with him an air weapon on any premises in circumstances where he would be prohibited from having it with him but for this subsection, it is an offence for the person whose supervision he is to allow him to use it for firing any missile beyond those premises.

(2)   It is not an offence under section 22(4) of this Act for a person to have with him an air weapon or ammunition at the time when—
    (a)   being a member of a rifle club or miniature rifle club for the time being approved by the Secretary of State for the purposes of this section or section 15 of the Firearms (Amendment) Act 1988, he is engaged as such a member in or in connection with target shooting; or

(b) he is using the weapon or ammunition at a shooting gallery where the only firearms used are either air weapons or miniature rifles not exceeding 0.23 inch calibre.

(3) It is not an offence under section 22(4) of this Act for a person of or over the age of 14 to have with him an air weapon or ammunition on private premises with the consent of the occupier.

Firearms Act 1968, s 23

Points to prove

s 21A(1) offence (anyone)

✓ had with them on premises
✓ an air weapon
✓ which they used for firing missile(s)
✓ beyond those premises

s 23(1) offence (supervisor)

✓ being person 21 or over
✓ supervising person under 18 who had an air weapon
✓ on premises (specify)
✓ allowed them to fire a missile beyond those premises

Defences

Offences under s 23(1) or s 21A(1)

It shall be a defence for him to show that the only premises into or across which the missile was fired were premises the occupier of which had consented to the firing of the missile (whether specifically or by way of a general consent).

Firearms Act 1968, ss 23(1A) and 21A(2)

Fail to prevent under 18 from having air weapon

Offences

It is an offence for a person in possession of an air weapon to fail to take reasonable precautions to prevent any person under the age of 18 from having the weapon with him.

Firearms Act 1968, s 24ZA(1)

Points to prove

✓ having possession of air weapon
✓ failed to take reasonable precautions
✓ to prevent person under 18
✓ from having air weapon

Defences

(2) Subsection (1) does not apply where by virtue of section 23 [*above*] of this Act the person under the age of 18 is not prohibited from having the weapon with him.

(3) In proceedings for an offence under subsection (1) it is a defence to show that the person charged with the offence—
  (a) believed the other person to be aged eighteen or over; and
  (b) had reasonable ground for that belief.

(4) For the purposes of this section a person shall be taken to have shown the matters specified in subsection (3) if—
  (a) sufficient evidence of those matters is adduced to raise an issue with respect to them; and
  (b) the contrary is not proved beyond a reasonable doubt.

Firearms Act 1968, s 24ZA

Explanatory notes

- Section 46 of the Crime and Security Act 2010 inserted s 24ZA, this makes it an offence for the person in possession of the air weapon to fail to take reasonable precautions to prevent a person under the age of 18 from gaining unauthorised access to it. HOC 4/2011 provides guidance and further details on this offence.
- HOC 31/2007 provides guidance in relation to air weapons as to: raising the age limits to 18; firing air weapons beyond premises; sales or transfer to be only through a registered firearms dealer by 'face-to-face' transactions (see **8.1.2**).
- As 'air gun', 'air rifle', and 'air pistol' are not defined in the Firearms Act 1968, each case will have to be considered on its own facts and the article in question. Whether a weapon falls into these categories, the court will have to be aware of the following:
  + an 'air gun' is generally a weapon that has an unrifled barrel;
  + an 'air rifle' is a weapon that does have a rifled barrel; and
  + an 'air pistol' is a weapon designed to be fired by using one hand and having the appearance of a pistol;
  + air weapons using or designed/adapted for use with a self-contained compressed gas cartridge system will be prohibited weapons (see **8.7.3**).
- An air weapon is deemed to be loaded if there is ammunition in the chamber or barrel.

Practical considerations

- The prosecution has to prove that the air weapon was a lethal barrelled weapon capable of discharging a shot or missile.
- In practice, forensic testing will determine whether weapons are lethal or not. The main characteristic which is measured is the muzzle velocity (the speed at which the projectile leaves the barrel).
- An air weapon normally fires a projectile by compressed air/gases and is a firearm, namely 'a lethal barrelled weapon of any description from

which any shot, bullet, or other missile can be discharged' (do not confuse a 'firearm' with the narrower definition of a s 1 firearm).

- Certain air weapons can be subject to the prohibition under rules denoting them as especially dangerous.
- Air weapons using, or designed/adapted for use with, a self-contained compressed gas cartridge system will be prohibited weapons (**8.7.3**).
- Application may be made to the court for a confiscation order in relation to a seized air weapon or ammunition.
- For police powers relating to firearms/ammunition (see **8.6**).
- Normally it is an offence for a person under 18 years to have an air weapon and/or ammunition anywhere. However, a young person may possess one if accompanied by someone of or over 21 years of age.
- On premises the person under 18 years old is allowed to fire the weapon, but the missiles must not go beyond those premises—otherwise an offence is committed by the supervisor (subject to defence). Furthermore, the user (who must be at least 14 years old) may have with them an air weapon or ammunition on private premises with permission of the occupier.
- Section 21A(1) (above) makes it an offence for **any person** to use an air weapon on premises which fires a missile beyond those premises, although it is a defence if the occupier of the premises into or across which the missile was fired had consented.
- Under s 19 it is an offence for a person to have with them in a public place an air weapon (loaded or not) or imitation firearm without lawful authority or reasonable excuse (see **8.5**).

 Summary   6 months

 Level 3 fine

8.7.3 **Air weapons deemed prohibited weapons**

Any person who has with him any air rifle, air gun, or air pistol that uses, or is designed or adapted for use with, a self-contained compressed gas cartridge system (SCGC) will be in possession of a prohibited weapon under s 5(1)(af) of the Firearms Act 1968 (see **8.1.1**).

Explanatory notes

- Weapons that use a CO_2 bulb system are not affected because CO_2 bulbs do not contain a projectile and are not therefore self-contained.
- A CO_2 bulb system that gives a pressure less than 12 ft/lbs on air rifles or 6 ft/lbs on air pistols is not restricted, but over that pressure they become s 1 firearms.
- If the air weapon contains a brass cartridge system and uses a self-contained gas cartridge system that can be converted to fire

conventional ammunition, say, then this would make it a prohibited weapon under s 5(1)(af).

- If the weapon comes under s 5(1)(af), then it cannot be possessed, purchased, acquired, manufactured, sold, or transferred without a written authority from the Secretary of State. However, under special arrangements, a person might have been granted permission to possess such a weapon under the terms of a firearms certificate.
- Further details on this matter are given in HOC 1/2004.

8.7.4 'BB guns'

BB guns derived their name from guns that fired ball bearings by different methods such as compressed air or an electrical system, some even firing 4.5 mm lead shot. Such weapons would almost certainly be firearms for the purposes of s 1(3) (see **8.1.1**).

If the method of propulsion is a self-contained compressed gas cartridge, the BB gun may be a prohibited weapon (see **8.7.3**). However, most gas BB guns do not have cartridges: the built-in gas container is recharged by an external aerosol, which is not the same thing.

A more common and readily available BB gun is designed to fire plastic or aluminium pellets which may be too powerful to be officially classed as a toy. These are unlikely to be lethal barrelled weapons (see **8.1.1**) because they are usually too low-powered to be 'lethal'. This type of BB gun will normally have a power rating of about 0.06 ft/lbs. Compare this to a BSA Airsporter 0.22 air rifle that has a power rating of 10.07 ft/lbs (150 times more powerful).

If required, forensic testing of the BB gun can ascertain its power rating, categorise the gun, and say whether or not it is lethal.

As some BB guns closely resemble other firearms, if one is being used in a public place, consider the offence of possession of an imitation firearm in a public place (see **8.5.1**).

8.7.5 Under 18—sell/buy an imitation firearm

Section 24A of the Firearms Act 1968 makes it an offence to sell an imitation firearm to a person under the age of 18, or for a young person under the age of 18 to purchase one.

Offences

(1) It is an offence for a person under the age of 18 to purchase an imitation firearm.

(2) It is an offence to sell an imitation firearm to a person under the age of 18.

Firearms Act 1968, s 24A

> **Points to prove**
>
> *s 24A(1) under 18 purchase*
> ✓ being a person under 18 years of age
> ✓ purchased an imitation firearm
>
> *s 24A(2) sell to under 18*
> ✓ sold an imitation firearm
> ✓ to a person under 18 years of age

Meaning of imitation firearm

Means any thing which has the appearance of being a firearm whether or not it is capable of discharging any shot, bullet, or other missile.

Explanatory notes

Imitation firearms have been increasingly misused to threaten and intimidate others. Although offences and controls exist relating to imitation firearms, s 24A seeks to tackle the problem at source by restricting the sale of imitation firearms.

> **Defence for seller**
>
> In proceedings for an offence under subsection (2) it is a defence to show that the person charged with the offence—
> (a) believed the other person to be aged eighteen or over; and
> (b) had reasonable ground for that belief.
>
> Firearms Act 1968, s 24A(3)

Practical considerations

- The onus is on the prosecution to show that the seller did not take sufficient steps (eg producing ID) to establish that the purchaser was 18 or over.
- Under the Violent Crime Reduction Act 2006:
    - ✦ s 36 makes it an offence to manufacture, import, or sell a realistic imitation firearm;
    - ✦ s 37 provides a defence to s 36 if it is shown that the only purpose of making the imitation firearm was for:
        - ✦ a museum or gallery;
        - ✦ theatrical performances and rehearsals;
        - ✦ production of films or television programmes;
        - ✦ an organisation for holding historical re-enactments;
        - ✦ Crown servants;
    - ✦ s 38 defines realistic imitation firearm (for ss 36 and 37) as an imitation firearm which appears so realistic that it can only be distinguished from a real firearm by:
        - ✦ an expert or on close examination; or

+ attempting to load or fire it; and
+ it is not a deactivated firearm or an antique.
• The Violent Crime Reduction Act 2006 (Realistic Imitation Firearms)
  Regulations 2007 (SI 2606/2007) provide defences, burden of proof,
  details on historical re-enactments, size, and colours of imitation
  firearms. HOC 31/2007 gives guidance on ss 36–41 (realistic
  imitation firearms and supplying to those aged under 18).

 Summary   48 months

 6 months' imprisonment and/or a fine

Links to alternative subjects and offences

8.8 Fireworks

The Fireworks Regulations 2004 and the Pyrotechnic Articles (Safety) Regulations 2015 give firework prohibitions that are enforced by the Fireworks Act 2003 and Consumer Protection Act 1987 respectively. The Highways Act 1980 and Town Police Clauses Act 1847 also deal with offences involving fireworks in a street or highway.

8.8.1 Categories of fireworks

There are different categories of fireworks in relation to supply or possession offences. Category 1, 2, and 3 fireworks are considered suitable for use by the public: whereas a Category 4 firework is only for use by people with specialist knowledge.

Category 1 fireworks present very low hazard, negligible noise level, and are intended for use in confined areas: including fireworks which are intended for use inside domestic buildings (Indoor Fireworks). These are innocuous fireworks (eg cap, cracker snap, novelty match, party popper, serpent, sparkler, or throw-down).

Category 2 fireworks present a low hazard and low noise level and are intended for outdoor use in confined areas (Garden Fireworks). They normally require a minimum spectator distance of 5 metres.

Category 3 fireworks present a medium hazard, are intended for outdoor use in large open areas, and the noise level is not considered harmful to human health (Display Fireworks). They normally require a minimum spectator distance of 25 metres.

Category 4 fireworks present a high hazard, are intended for use only by people with specialist knowledge and have a noise level that is not considered harmful to human health (Fireworks for professional use). The general public is prohibited from possessing these fireworks.

Firework means a **pyrotechnic article** intended for entertainment purposes.

Pyrotechnic article means any article containing explosive substances or an explosive mixture of substances designed to produce heat, light, sound, gas, or smoke or a combination of such effects through self-sustained, exothermic chemical reactions.

8.8.2 Under 18 years—possessing 'adult' fireworks

Offences

Any person who contravenes a prohibition imposed by fireworks regulations is guilty of an offence.

Fireworks Act 2003, s 11(1)

Points to prove

✓ breached a reg 4 prohibition, namely
✓ being a person under the age of 18
✓ in a public place
✓ possessing an adult firework

Prohibition

Subject to regulation 6 below, no person under the age of eighteen years shall possess an adult firework in a public place.

Fireworks Regulations 2004, reg 4(1)

Meanings

Regulation 6

- Regulations 4 and 5 shall not prohibit the possession of any firework by any person who is employed by/in trade or business as:
  - ◆ professional organiser or operator of firework displays;
  - ◆ manufacture of fireworks or assemblies;
  - ◆ supply of fireworks or assemblies;
  - ◆ local authority/government department/forces of the Crown for use at a firework display or national public celebration/commemorative event;
  - ◆ special effects in the theatre, on film, or on television;
  - ◆ acting on behalf of and for purposes of exercising enforcement powers of local authority or enforcement body;
  - ◆ government department use for research or investigations;
  - ◆ supplier of goods designed and intended for use in conjunction with fireworks or assemblies for testing and safety purposes.

Adult firework

Means any firework, except Category 1 Indoor Fireworks (see **8.8.1**).

Public place

Includes any place to which at the material time the public have or are permitted access, whether on payment or otherwise.

Explanatory notes

- This offence prohibits any person under the age of 18 years, from possessing any firework in a public place (except Category 1 Indoor Fireworks) (see **8.8.1**).
- Those people listed in reg 6 (above) are exempted from liability for this offence and are not prohibited from possession.

Practical considerations

- Any breach of the prohibitions in the Fireworks Regulations 2004 is a criminal offence under the Fireworks Act 2003, s 11(1).
- Consider stop, search, and seizure powers under s 1(8B) of PACE (see **1.3.2**).

 Summary   12 months

6 months' imprisonment and/or a fine

8.8.3 **Ban on possession of Category 4 fireworks**

Offences

Any person who contravenes a prohibition imposed by fireworks regulations is guilty of an offence.

Fireworks Act 2003, s 11(1)

Points to prove

✓ breached a reg 5 prohibition, namely
✓ possessed a Category 4 firework
✓ when not exempt from such possession

Prohibition

Subject to regulation 6, no person shall possess a Category 4 firework.

Fireworks Regulations 2004, reg 5

Explanatory notes

- Those people listed in reg 6 (see **8.8.2**) are exempted from liability for this offence and are not prohibited from possession.
- Unless exempted by reg 6, this prohibits a person of any age from possessing **anywhere** a Category 4 firework and an offence will be committed by that person if they breach that regulation.

Practical considerations

- Any breach of the prohibitions in the Fireworks Regulations 2004 is a criminal offence under s 11(1) of the Fireworks Act 2003.
- Consider issuing a PND for this offence (see **7.1.1**).
- Consider stop, search, and seizure powers under s 1(8B) of PACE (see **1.3.2**).
- Category 4 fireworks are for specialist use only (see **8.8.1**).

 6 months' imprisonment and/or a fine

Summary   12 months

8.8.4 **Use firework after 11 p.m.**

Offences

Any person who contravenes a prohibition imposed by fireworks regulations is guilty of an offence.

Fireworks Act 2003, s 11(1)

Points to prove

✓ breached a reg 7(1) prohibition, namely
✓ used an adult firework
✓ during night hours

Prohibition

Subject to paragraph (2) [*exception*] below, no person shall use an adult firework during night hours.

Fireworks Regulations 2004, reg 7(1)

Meanings

Exception (reg 7(2))

Regulation 7(1) above shall not prohibit the use of a firework:

(a) during a permitted fireworks night; or
(b) by any person who is employed by a local authority and who uses the firework in question:

(i) for the purposes of putting on a firework display by that local authority; or

(ii) at a national public celebration or a national commemorative event.

Adult firework (see **8.8.2**)

Night hours

Means the period beginning at 11 p.m. and ending at 7 a.m. the following day.

Permitted fireworks night

Means a period beginning at 11 p.m.:
- on the first day of the Chinese New Year and ending at 1 a.m. the following day;
- and ending at midnight on 5 November;
- on the day of Diwali and ending at 1 a.m. the following day;
- on 31 December and ending at 1 a.m. the following day.

Explanatory notes

- This prohibits the use of a firework (except Category 1 Indoor Fireworks) (see **8.8.1**) after 11 p.m. at night and an offence being committed by that person if they breach that regulation.
- Exceptions are New Year's Eve, Diwali, Chinese New Year (extended 11 p.m.–1 a.m.); Bonfire Night (extended 11 p.m.–midnight); or the local authority putting on a firework display.
- This offence is not restricted to a public place and will be committed if a person breaches this prohibition in their own private garden/land.

Practical considerations

- A breach of this prohibition is a criminal offence under s 11(1) of the Fireworks Act 2003, for which a PND can be issued (see **7.1.1**).
- Consider stop, search, and seizure powers under s 1(8B) of PACE (see **1.3.2**).

 Summary   12 months

 6 months' imprisonment and/or a fine

8.8.5 **Supply of fireworks and pyrotechnic article offences**

The Pyrotechnic Articles (Safety) Regulations 2015 creates prohibitions on the supply of various categories of Christmas crackers, fireworks and pyrotechnic articles to people under the age of 12, 16, or 18 years.

Regulation 31 states that an **economic operator** must not make a **pyrotechnic article** available on the market in the United Kingdom to a person younger than the following minimum age limits—

(a) for a Christmas cracker, 12 years;
(b) for a category F1 firework other than a Christmas cracker, 16 years;
(c) for a category F2 firework or a category F3 firework, 18 years;
(d) for a category T1 theatrical pyrotechnic article, 18 years;
(e) for a category P1 other pyrotechnic article, 18 years.

Regulation 62 provides the offences that can be committed by an economic operator or conformity assessment body, including failing to comply with a notice, intentionally obstruct an enforcing authority/ HMRC, provide false misleading statement/information/document/ record, and purporting to exercise powers under these regulations when not authorised to do so.

Meanings

Economic operator

A manufacturer, importer, or distributor.

Christmas cracker

A paper or foil tube, crimped at each end, enclosing novelties and with one or more snaps running along the length of the tube.

Pyrotechnic article (see **8.8.1**) Category F1, F2, and F3 fireworks (see **8.8.1**)

Category T1 theatrical pyrotechnic articles

Theatrical pyrotechnic articles which present a low hazard.

Category P1 other pyrotechnic articles

Pyrotechnic articles, other than fireworks and theatrical pyrotechnic articles, which present a low hazard.

Defence

Regulation 64 provides a defence of due diligence for a person to show that they took all reasonable steps and exercised all due diligence to avoid committing the offence. It also sets out the circumstances when they may not rely on this defence.

Practical considerations

- Breaching the prohibitions under these regulations is an offence under regulation 62. None of the supply offences is subject to the PND procedure.

 Category 1, 2 or 3 fireworks: Summary
Other Pyrotechnic articles: Either way

 Category 1, 2 or 3 fireworks: 12 months
Other Pyrotechnic articles: None

 Category 1, 2 or 3 fireworks offences:
3 months' imprisonment and/or a fine

Other pyrotechnic articles:
Summary: 3 months' imprisonment and/or a fine
Indictment: 2 years imprisonment and/or a fine

8.8.6 **Other fireworks/firearms offences (in a highway/street)**

Explosives Act

Section 80 of the Explosives Act 1875 creates various offences relating to throwing, casting, or firing any fireworks in the highway or public place.

> #### Offences
> If any person throw, cast, or fire any fireworks in or into any highway, street, thoroughfare, or public place, he shall be guilty of an offence.
>
> Explosives Act 1875, s 80

Points to prove
- ✓ throw/cast/fire
- ✓ a firework
- ✓ in/into a highway/street/thoroughfare/public place

Practical considerations

Consider issuing a PND for this offence—'Throwing fireworks in a thoroughfare' (see **7.1.1**).

Summary   6 months

 Fine

Highways Act

Section 161 of the Highways Act 1980 creates various offences relating to causing danger on the highway.

> ### Offences
>
> If a person without lawful authority or excuse—
> (a) lights any fire on or over a highway which consists of or comprises a carriageway; or
> (b) discharges any firearm or firework within 50 feet of the centre of such a highway,
>
> and in consequence a user of the highway is injured, interrupted or endangered, that person is guilty of an offence.
>
> Highways Act 1980, s 161(2)

Points to prove

- ✓ without lawful authority/excuse
- ✓ discharged a firework or firearm
- ✓ within 50 ft of centre of highway
- ✓ comprising a carriageway
- ✓ as a result, user injured/interrupted/endangered

Meanings

Highway (see 10.22.1)

Carriageway

Means a way constituting or comprised in a highway, being a way (other than a cycle track) over which the public have a right of way for the passage of vehicles.

 Summary   6 months

 Level 3 fine

Town Police Clauses Act

Section 28 of the Town Police Clauses Act 1847 creates numerous offences.

8.8.7 Possession of pyrotechnic articles at musical events

> **Offences**
>
> Every person who wantonly (without lawful motive and thoughtless as to possible consequences) throws or sets fire to a firework in the street to the obstruction, annoyance, or danger of residents or passengers will commit an offence.
>
> *Town Police Clauses Act 1847, s 28*

> **Points to prove**
> - ✓ in street
> - ✓ wantonly
> - ✓ threw/set fire to a firework
> - ✓ to the obstruction/annoyance/danger of residents/passengers

Meaning of street

Street includes any road, square, court, alley, thoroughfare, public passage, carriageway, and footways at the sides.

Explanatory notes

- Section 28 of the Town Police Clauses Act 1847 also states that every person who wantonly (recklessly, without regard for consequences) discharges a **firearm** in the street to the obstruction, annoyance, or danger of residents or passengers will commit an offence.
- None of the Town Police Clauses Act offences are complete unless it can be proved that they would obstruct, annoy, or cause danger to any residents or passengers.

Related cases

Mantle v Jordan [1897] 1 QB 248 The Town Police Clauses Act offences can only be committed in the street, but the annoyance may be to 'residents', meaning the occupiers of houses in the street, although the residents might not be in the street at the time.

 Summary   6 months

 14 days' imprisonment or a level 3 fine

8.8.7 **Possession of pyrotechnic articles at musical events**

The Policing and Crime Act 2017 (Possession of Pyrotechnic Articles at Musical Events) Regulations 2017 create offences relating specifically to musical events.

Offence

It is an offence for a person to have a pyrotechnic article in his or her possession at any time when the person is—

(a) at a place where a qualifying musical event is being held, or

(b) at any other place that is being used by a person responsible for the organisation of a qualifying musical event for the purpose of—

(a) regulating entry to, or departure from, the event, or

(ii) providing sleeping or other facilities for those attending the event.

Policing and Crime Act 2017 s 134(1)

Points to prove

✓ Has possession of a pyrotechnic article

✓ at a place where a qualifying musical event is being held, or

✓ at any other place being used by a person responsible for the organisation of a qualifying musical event for regulating entry to, or departure from, the event, or providing sleeping or other facilities for those attending the event.

Meanings

Pyrotechnic article

Pyrotechnic article (see **8.8.1**), other than a match or article/description as specified in regulations made by the Secretary of State.

Qualifying musical event

An event at which one or more live musical performances take place and which is specified, or of a description specified, in regulations made by statutory instrument by the Secretary of State.

Premises licence

Has the meaning given in s 11 of the Licensing Act 2003.

The provision of regulated entertainment

Has the meaning given in Sch 1(2) to the Licensing Act 2003.

Explanatory notes

- This offence does not apply to a person responsible for organising the event (organiser) or a person who has the article in their possession with the consent of the organiser.
- A qualifying musical event applies to an event that is provided for members of the public or a section of the public, on premises which has a premises licence that authorises regulated entertainment in the form of a performance of live music.

8.8.7 Possession of pyrotechnic articles at musical events

 Summary

 6 months

 3 months' imprisonment and/or level 3 fine

Links to alternative subjects and offences

8.9 **Offensive Weapons and Crossbows**

Possession of or threatening with offensive weapons in a public place, the manufacture and sale of offensive weapons, trespassing with a weapon of offence, and offences involving crossbows form a key part of operational policing.

8.9.1 **Offensive weapons in public place—possess/threaten**

The Prevention of Crime Act 1953 deals with offences regarding possession of or threatening with offensive weapons in a public place.

Offences

Possess

1(1) Any person who without lawful authority or reasonable excuse, the proof whereof shall lie on him, has with him in any public place any offensive weapon shall be guilty of an offence.

Threaten

1A(1) A person is guilty of an offence if that person—
(a) has an offensive weapon with him or her in a public place,
(b) unlawfully and intentionally threatens another person with the weapon, and
(c) does so in such a way that there is an immediate risk of serious physical harm to that other person.

Prevention of Crime Act 1953, ss 1(1) and 1A(1)

Points to prove

Possess (s 1(1))
- ✓ without lawful authority/reasonable excuse
- ✓ had with them
- ✓ in a public place
- ✓ an offensive weapon

Threaten (s 1A(1))
- ✓ had with them an offensive weapon in a public place
- ✓ unlawfully and intentionally threaten another person with the weapon
- ✓ in a way that there was immediate risk of serious physical harm
- ✓ to that other person

8.9.1 Offensive weapons in public place-possess/threaten

Meanings

Has with him (see 8.3.6)

Public place

Includes any highway and any other premises or place to which at the material time the public have or are permitted to have access, whether on payment or otherwise.

Offensive weapon

Means any article **made** or **adapted** for use for causing injury to the person or **intended** by the person having it with them for such use by them, or by some other person.

Intentionally (see 4.1.2)

Serious physical harm (see 8.10.3)

Serious harm amounting to grievous bodily harm (see 2.3.1)

Explanatory notes

- Within the meaning of 'offensive weapon' particular terms used, and case law have provided meanings to those terms as follows:
  + **'made'** includes articles that have been specifically created for the purpose of causing injury, and includes knuckledusters, flick knives, butterfly knives, sword sticks, truncheons, daggers, bayonets, and rice flails. All of these items are generally classed as offensive weapons per se ('by themselves');
  + **'adapted'** consists of articles that have generally been altered in some way with the intention of causing injury, such as smashing a bottle to make the broken end into a weapon for causing injury;
  + **'intended'** these can be otherwise inoffensive articles that the defendant proposes to use to cause injury to a person, such as a bunch of keys held in the fist with the keys projecting through the fingers (making it an impromptu knuckleduster).
- The primary aim of the s 1 possession offence is the **carrying** of such weapons rather than their **use** in the heat of the moment.
- The s 1A offence involves a person having the weapon and unlawfully and intentionally threatening another person with it in such a way that there is an immediate risk of grievous bodily harm to that other person.

Defences

Possess (s 1)

Lawful authority

This extends to people such as an on-duty police officer with a baton.

Reasonable excuse

Whether an excuse is reasonable is for the court to decide having heard all the circumstances. These could include:

- people carrying the tools of their trade (eg hammer/saw by a carpenter or filleting knife by a fishmonger);
- self-defence—if there is an imminent threat, this defence may be available.

Threaten (s 1A)

The use of the weapon must be unlawful; this allows the person to raise relevant defences such as self-defence, defence of others or of property, and prevention of crime.

Related cases

R v Tucker [2016] EWCA Crim 13 The defendant was aware of an affray taking place outside his flat and in anger he went out with a cricket bat with intent to injure another person. While the offence of possessing an offensive weapon does not occur where it is used in the heat of the moment (see the case of *Ohlson v Hylton* below as an example), it was held in this case that where a person introduces an article into a public place to use it offensively there, this would be an offence under s 1 of the Act. The defendant was not at the time carrying the bat for innocent purposes.

DPP v Christof [2015] EWHC 4096 (Admin) The defendant had a belt buckle in the form of a knuckleduster that could be detached from the belt. He was charged with the s 1 offence but acquitted on the basis it was being used as a belt buckle and the fact that the belt had to be disassembled in order to use it as a weapon negated the idea that it was a weapon at all. On appeal by the DPP the Court held that the item in question appeared to have unusual features for a knuckleduster and it was possible that it had been made or designed for the purpose of causing injury, even though it was being put to another use. If it was a fashion item that was widely worn, then those who wore them needed to know that they were potentially at risk of prosecution.

Ohlson v Hylton [1975] 2 All ER 490, QBD and **R v Veasey [1999] Crim LR 158, CA** The defendant was a carpenter who was on his way home from work carrying his tools in a bag. As he was trying to get onto a tube train he got involved in an argument with another passenger. A scuffle ensued and the two of them fell over. The defendant took a hammer from his bag and hit the other man with it. He was convicted of assault but acquitted of possession of an offensive weapon. It was held that the acquittal was correct. If the defendant seized a weapon for 'instant use' on the victim or grabbed something innocuous (like a hammer or snooker cue) in the heat of the moment, then the 'weapon' was not carried unlawfully with prior intent.

R v Allamby and R v Medford [1974] 3 All ER 126, CA The defendants were frightened of a girl's new boyfriend and took four kitchen

8.9.1 Offensive weapons in public place-possess/threaten

knives with them to visit her. During the return journey, the car was stopped by the police and the knives were found. They were charged with possessing offensive weapons at the time and place that the car was stopped. They were acquitted. It was held that it was necessary to prove that *at the time and place* specified in the charge they intended to use the knives as offensive weapons. The kitchen knives were not offensive weapons '*per se*' and, therefore, intent had to be proved.

Practical considerations

- For further information regarding this offence see MOJ Circular 8/2012.
- If a person is found not guilty of the s 1A (threaten) offence (whether on indictment or not), but it is proved that the person committed the s 1 (possess) offence, then they may be convicted of the s 1 offence.
- Consider stop, search, and seizure powers under s 1 of PACE (see **1.3.2**).
- For the s 1 possession offence, where an article is 'made' or 'adapted' to cause injury (offensive per se), the prosecution does not need to prove intent to cause injury as merely having it with them is sufficient.
- The 'intended' use requires an element of intent to use the article to cause injury, which must be proved. An instant use of an innocent article will need proof of a prior intent otherwise no offence is committed, either by possessing or threatening with the weapon.
- Upon conviction the court may make an order for the forfeiture or disposal of any weapon in respect of which the offence was committed.
- If appropriate, consider the offence of possession of a blade/pointed article in a public place (see **8.10**).
- There is a need to prove a knowledge of the existence of the article and that the article is 'to hand and ready for use' (eg it may be hidden a few feet away; it does not have to be physically on the defendant's person).
- The burden of proof for lawful authority or reasonable excuse lies with the accused and it is for the prosecution to disprove it (*R v Archbold* [2007] EWCA Crim 2137, CA).

 Either way None

 Summary: 6 months' imprisonment and/or a fine

  Indictment: 4 years' imprisonment and/or a fine

8.9.2 **Offensive weapons— provide/trade/manufacture**

Transferring ownership, trading in, importing, or manufacturing certain offensive weapons is an offence.

Offences

Any person who manufactures, sells or hires or offers for sale or hire, exposes or has in his possession for the purpose of sale or hire, or lends or gives to any other person, a weapon to which this section applies shall be guilty of an offence.

Criminal Justice Act 1988, s 141(1)

Points to prove

✓ manufactured/sold/hired/lent/gave

or

✓ possessed/exposed/offered
✓ for sale/hire
✓ an offensive weapon

Meaning of weapon to which s 141 applies

The Criminal Justice Act 1988 (Offensive Weapons) Order 1988 specifies weapons to which s 141 applies (see **8.9.3**).

Explanatory notes

- The importation of weapons to which s 141 applies is prohibited.
- Some will also fall into the category of being a bladed/pointed article (see **8.10**).
- See also a warrant to search for and a power to stop/search/seize these weapons (see **8.11**).
- It is an offence to lend, give, or trade in flick or gravity knives (see **8.10.2**).
- This section does not apply to any weapons subject to the Firearms Act 1968 (see **8.1**) or crossbows (see **8.9.5**).
- Consider the offence of using another person to look after, hide, or transport a firearm, offensive/bladed weapon or knife, so that it would be available when required for an unlawful purpose (see **8.3.7**).

Defences

This applies to an offence under s 141(1) or s 50(2) or (3) of the Customs and Excise Management Act 1979 (improper importation) if it can be shown that their conduct was only for the purposes of:
- functions carried out on behalf of the Crown or of a visiting force;
- making the weapon available to a museum or gallery;
- making the weapon available for the purposes specified in s 141(11B).

Defence notes

- A person acting on behalf of a **museum or gallery** can use the above defence if they had reasonable grounds to believe that the person to whom they lent or hired it would use it only for cultural, artistic, or educational purposes. The defence will only apply if the **museum or gallery** does not distribute profits.
- **Museum or gallery** includes any institution which has as its purpose, or one of its purposes, the preservation, display, and interpretation of material of historical, artistic, or scientific interest; and gives the public access to it.
- The purposes under s 141(11B) are for theatrical performances and rehearsals for such performances or for the production of films or television programmes.
- An antique weapon is exempt (more than 100 years old).

 Summary   6 months

 6 months' imprisonment and/or a fine

8.9.3 The Criminal Justice Act 1988 (Offensive Weapons) Order 1988

This order provides a list of weapons where their sale, hire, offering for sale/hire, exposing, or importation is prohibited. The order excludes antique weapons and provides that a weapon is an antique if it was manufactured more than 100 years before the date of any offence alleged to have been committed in respect of that weapon.

This list only applies to s 141 offences (see **8.9.2**) and is not a list of all offensive weapons per se: knuckleduster; sword stick; butterfly knife; death star; belt buckle knife; hollow kubotan (cylinder holding sharp spikes); push dagger; kusari (rope, cord, wire, or chain with hooked knife, sickle, hard weight or hand grip fastened at one end); foot or hand claw; blowpipe; telescopic truncheon; disguised knife; baton;

stealth knife (non-metallic); disguised knife (blade or sharp point concealed within an everyday object such as a comb, brush, writing instrument, cigarette lighter, key, lipstick, or telephone); various types of zombie knives, and a sword with a curved blade.

Explanatory notes

- There are exceptions even if the weapon is on this list.
- The list given above is not an exhaustive or descriptive list; it just gives an idea of the type of weapons included in this Order.
- Stealth knives are non-metallic hunting or stiletto knives, made of a range of materials, such as nylon zytel or high-impact plastic. Although they look like conventional knives, they are difficult to detect by security apparatus. Their design and construction mean that their possession in public may be an offence under:
  - ✦ s 1(1) of the Prevention of Crime Act 1953 (**8.9.1**); or
  - ✦ s 139(1) of the Criminal Justice Act 1988 (**8.10**).
- The 2008 Weapons Amendment Order (SI 973/2008) added a sword with a curved blade of 50 cm or over in length to the list, the length of the blade being measured in a straight line from the top of the handle to the tip of the blade. It is a defence if a person can show that:
  - ✦ the sword was made in Japan before 1954 or at any other time using traditional Japanese methods of forging swords; and
  - ✦ an organisation requires the use of the weapon for a permitted activity (historical re-enactment or a sporting activity), and that public liability insurance was in force which indemnified those taking part in the activity.

8.9.4 **Trespassing with weapon of offence**

Section 8 of the Criminal Law Act 1977 creates the offence of 'trespassing with a weapon of offence'.

Offences

A person who is on any premises as a trespasser, after having entered as such, is guilty of an offence if, without lawful authority or reasonable excuse, he has with him on the premises any weapon of offence.

Criminal Law Act 1977, s 8(1)

Points to prove

✓ on premises as trespasser
✓ having entered as such
✓ had weapon of offence
✓ without lawful authority or reasonable excuse

Meanings

Premises

This consists of any:

- building/part of a building (under separate occupation);
- land adjacent to and used/intended for use in connection with a building;
- site comprising any building(s) together with ancillary land;
- fixed structure; and
- moveable structure, vehicle, or vessel designed, or adapted for residential purposes.

Trespasser (see 3.3.1)

Has with him (see 8.3.6)

Weapon of offence (see 3.3.2)

Practical considerations

- This offence is worth bearing in mind if the carrying of offensive weapons in a public place/school premises or aggravated burglary does not apply.
- Consider stop, search, and seizure powers under s 1 of PACE (see **1.3.2**).
- Entry must have been as a trespasser—it does not extend to a person who has entered lawfully and later becomes a trespasser (eg being asked to leave by the occupier).

 Summary   6 months

 3 months' imprisonment and/or a fine

8.9.5 **Crossbows**

Crossbows are extremely accurate weapons and potentially as lethal as a firearm. This legislation creates offences in relation to persons under 18 years possessing, hiring, or purchasing crossbows.

Sell, purchase, or hire crossbow

Offences

Sell/hire to under 18

A person who sells or lets on hire a **crossbow** or part of a crossbow to a person under the age of 18 is guilty of an offence unless he believes him to be 18 years of age or older and has reasonable grounds for that belief.

Crossbows Act 1987, s 1

Purchase/hire by under 18

A person under the age of 18 who buys or hires a crossbow, or a part of a crossbow is guilty of an offence.

Crossbows Act 1987, s 2

Points to prove

Sell/hire (s 1)

✓ sold/let on hire or sold/let on hire part(s) of
✓ a crossbow
✓ to person under 18 years of age

Purchase/hire (s 2)

✓ person under 18 years of age
✓ hired/purchased or purchased/hired part(s) of
✓ a crossbow

Meaning of crossbow

Does not apply to crossbows with a draw weight of less than 1.4 kg.

Defences (sell/hire)

Reasonable grounds to believe that the person is 18 years or older.

Practical considerations

- Proof required of age (eg ID card or birth certificate).
- Only applies to crossbows of a certain strength, having a draw weight of 1.4kg or over.
- The draw weight limit is very low and can be determined by the forensic testing; only toys will be excluded by this definition.

 Summary　　　 6 months

 Sell/hire (s 1):
6 months' imprisonment and/or a fine

Purchase/hire (s 2):
Level 3 fine

Under 18—possess a crossbow

Offences

A person under the age of 18 who has with him—
(a) a crossbow which is capable of discharging a missile, or
(b) parts of a crossbow which together (and without any other parts) can be assembled to form a crossbow capable of discharging a missile,

is guilty of an offence, unless he is under the supervision of a person who is 21 years of age or older.

Crossbows Act 1987, s 3

8.9.5 Crossbows

> **Points to prove**
> ✓ being under the age of 18
> ✓ had with them
> ✓ a crossbow/crossbow parts (able to form a crossbow)
> ✓ capable of discharging a missile

Meanings

Has with him (see **8.3.6**)

Crossbow (see s 1 above)

Explanatory notes

- This offence can be committed anywhere and not just in public.
- No offence will be committed if under supervision of person age 21 or over.

Practical considerations (see also ss 1 and 2 above)

Although the Act may allow a person of 18 or over to possess a crossbow in public, it may be an offence under s 139 of the Criminal Justice Act 1988 (pointed article/blades, see **8.10.1**) due to the crossbow bolts.

SSS

 Summary   6 months

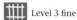 Level 3 fine

Crossbows—search and seizure powers

Section 4 of the Crossbows Act 1987 gives police officers quite wide powers of search, detention, seizure, and entry onto land if a person under 18 years is unsupervised and is in possession of a crossbow/parts.

> **Powers**
> (1) If a constable suspects with reasonable cause that a person is committing or has committed an offence under section 3, the constable may—
>   (a) search that person for a crossbow or part of a crossbow;
>   (b) search any vehicle, or anything in or on a vehicle, in or on which the constable suspects with reasonable cause there is a crossbow, or part of a crossbow, connected with the offence.
> (2) A constable may detain a person or vehicle for the purpose of a search under subsection (1).

(3) A constable may seize and retain for the purpose of proceedings for an offence under this Act anything discovered by him in the course of a search under subsection (1) which appears to him to be a crossbow or part of a crossbow.

(4) For the purpose of exercising the powers conferred by this section a constable may enter any land other than a dwelling-house.

Crossbows Act 1987, s 4

Explanatory notes

• A constable may detain a person or vehicle for the search.
• A constable may seize and retain anything found during the search which appears to be a crossbow or part of a crossbow.
• In exercising this power, a constable may enter on any land **other than** a dwelling house.

Practical considerations (see also ss 1, 2, and 3 above)

Consider powers under s 1 of PACE and ensure compliance with the PACE Codes procedures relating to stop and searches (see **1.3**).

Links to alternative subjects and offences

8.10 Bladed Articles/ Knives Offences

The Criminal Justice Act 1988 deals with offences of having knives/ bladed articles in a public place or on school premises, and sale to persons under 18 years.

8.10.1 Possession of bladed/pointed article in public place

Section 139 of the Criminal Justice Act 1988 creates an offence of having a bladed or pointed article in a public place.

Offences

Subject to subsections (4) and (5) [Defences] below, any person who has an article to which this section applies with him in a public place shall be guilty of an offence.

Criminal Justice Act 1988, s 139(1)

Points to prove

✓ had with them
✓ without good reason/lawful authority
✓ an article being bladed/sharply pointed
✓ in a public place

Meanings

Article

Applies to any article which has a **blade** or is sharply pointed, including a folding pocket knife if the cutting edge of the blade exceeds 3 inches (7.62 cm).

Blade

Examples of this will be the blade of a knife, sword.

Has with him (see 8.3.6)

Public place

Includes any place to which at the material time the public have or are permitted access, whether on payment or otherwise.

Explanatory notes

- A folding pocket knife does not include a lock knife, regardless of the blade length (*Harris v DPP* [1993] 1 WLR 82, QBD).
- Possession of a multi-tool incorporating a prohibited blade/pointed article is capable of being an offence under this section, even if there are other tools on the instrument that may be of practical use (such as a bottle-opener). It is for the defendant to show that s/he had good reason for possession (*R v Giles* [2003] EWCA Crim 1287, CA).

Defences

(4) It shall be a defence for a person charged with an offence under this section to prove that he had good reason or lawful authority for having the article with him in a public place.

(5) Without prejudice to the generality of subsection (4) above, it shall be a defence for a person charged with an offence under this section to prove that he had the article with him—
   (a) for use at work;
   (b) for religious reasons; or
   (c) as part of any national costume.

Criminal Justice Act 1988, s 139

Defence notes

The burden of proof is with the defendant to show good reason or lawful authority for having the blade/pointed article with them. Examples of s 139(5) could be:
- **for use at work**—fishmonger, carpet fitter, chef;
- **for religious reasons**—members of the Sikh religion having a kirpan;
- **as part of a national costume**—the skean dhu in Highland dress.

Related cases

R v Henderson [2016] EWCA Crim 443 The defendant was in a private flat, but he had a knife in his car parked in a public place. In determining whether the weapon was '*with him*' for the purpose of s 139 the court should bear in mind that: possession of an article is a wider concept than that of a person '*having an article with him*' but is broader than 'carrying' an article; the proximity between the person and the weapon; whether the weapon was immediately available; accessibility of the weapon; the context of the criminal enterprise embarked upon; and the purpose of the legislation. It was held in this case that there was no evidence that the knife was 'immediately available' to the defendant. He had not shortly left or was to shortly to return to the car and the knife was not linked in any way to his presence in the flat.

R v Clancy [2012] EWCA Crim 8, CA Fear of attack can constitute good reason under s 139. The defendant's state of mind was relevant and 'good reason' should be allowed a natural meaning.

R v McAuley [2009] EWCA Crim 2130, CA It was held in this case that it could amount to a good reason if someone was carrying a knife for personal protection and was able to show, on the balance of probabilities, that he was in fear of an imminent attack. It was for the jury to decide how imminent, likely, and serious any possible attack might be.

R v Davis [1998] Crim LR 564, CA It was held in this case that a screwdriver is not a 'bladed article'. A blade needs to fall within the same category as a sharply pointed item or the blade on a folding pocket knife having a cutting edge.

Practical considerations

- Consider stop, search, and seizure powers under s 1(8A) of PACE (see **1.3.2**).
- Consider s 139AA if offences relate to threats made when in possession of articles/offensive weapons in public or on school premises (see **8.10.3**).
- Sections 52–55A of the Courts Act 2003 give a court security officer powers to search, exclude, remove, or restrain person(s) in a court building with regard to an article/knife in their possession, including seizing any article or knife found by that officer.

 Either way   None

 Summary: 6 months' imprisonment and/or a fine

Indictment: 4 years' imprisonment and/or a fine

8.10.2 **Sale of knives/blades to persons under 18**

Section 141A of the Criminal Justice Act 1988 creates the offence of selling knives or certain articles with a blade or point to people under the age of 18.

Offences

Any person who sells to a person under the age of 18 years an article to which this section applies shall be guilty of an offence.

Criminal Justice Act 1988, s 141A(1)

Points to prove

✓ sold to person under 18 years
✓ knife/axe/knife blade/razor blade or
✓ bladed, sharply pointed article being made/adapted for use for causing injury

Meanings

Article to which this section applies

Subject to **subsection (3)** below, this section applies to:

(a) any knife, knife blade, or razor blade;
(b) any axe; and
(c) any other article which has a blade, or which is sharply pointed, and which is made or adapted for use for causing injury to the person.

Subsection (3)

This section does not apply to any article described in:

(a) s 1 of the Restriction of Offensive Weapons Act 1959;
(b) an order made under s 141(2) of this Act; or
(c) an order made by the Secretary of State under this section.

Explanatory notes

- Section 1 of the Restriction of Offensive Weapons Act 1959 makes lending, giving, or trading of flick or gravity knives a summary offence.
- An order made under s 141(2) of this Act (see **8.9.2**) relates to weapons given in the Criminal Justice Act 1988 (Offensive Weapons) Order 1988 such as knuckledusters, sword sticks, belt daggers (see **8.9.3**).
- The Criminal Justice Act 1988 (Offensive Weapons) (Exemption) Order 1996, states that this section does not apply to:
  ✦ folding pocket knives if the cutting edge of the blade does not exceed 7.62 cm (3 inches);
  ✦ razor blades permanently enclosed in a cartridge or housing where less than 2 mm of any blade is protruding.

Defences

To prove that they took all reasonable precautions and exercised all due diligence to avoid the commission of the offence.

Criminal Justice Act 1988, s 141A(4)

Practical considerations

- The above defence goes beyond appearance or enquiring about the age of the purchaser, such as proving age by ID card.
- Consider the offence of using another person to look after, hide, or transport a firearm, offensive/bladed weapon, or knife, so that it would be available when required for an unlawful purpose (see **8.3.7**).

 SSS

 Summary   ⏱ None

🏛 6 months' imprisonment and/or a fine

8.10.3 **Threaten with article in public place/school premises**

Section 139AA of the Criminal Justice Act 1988 creates the offence of threatening another person with an article in a public place or on school premises, if there is immediate risk of serious physical harm to that other person.

Offences

A person is guilty of an offence if that person—
(a) has an article to which this section applies with him or her in a public place or on school premises,
(b) unlawfully and intentionally threatens another person with the article, and
(c) does so in such a way that there is an immediate risk of serious physical harm to that other person.

Criminal Justice Act 1988, s 139AA(1)

Points to prove

✓ had with them
✓ a bladed/sharp-pointed article
✓ in a public place/on school premises
✓ unlawfully and intentionally threatened another person with it
✓ in a way that there was an immediate risk of
✓ serious physical harm to that person

Meanings

Article to which this section applies

- In a public place: means an article to which s 139 applies (see **8.10.1**)
- On school premises means:
  ✦ an article to which s 139 applies (see **8.10.1**);
  ✦ an offensive weapon (see **8.9.1**).

Public place (see **8.10.1**)

School premises (see **8.10.4**)

Intentionally (see **4.1.2**)

Serious physical harm

Means harm amounting to grievous bodily harm (see **2.3.1**).

Explanatory notes

- The meaning of an article will depend on if it occurs in a public place or on school premises (see above).

- If a person is found not guilty of an offence under this section (whether on indictment or not), but it is proved that the person committed an offence under s 139 (see **8.10.1**) or s 139A (see **8.10.4**), then the person may be convicted of that offence.

Defences

The use of the weapon must be unlawful, so this allows the person to raise relevant defences such as self-defence, defence of others or of property, and prevention of crime.

Practical considerations

- For further information regarding this offence see MOJ Circular 8/2012.
- Consider the offence of possessing article/weapon on school premises (see **8.10.4**) and causing/permitting a nuisance/disturbance on school premises (see **8.10.5**).
- There is a specific police power under s 139B to enter and search school premises regarding s 139A and s 139AA offences (see **8.11.2**).
- Consider stop, search, and seizure powers under s 1(8A) of PACE (see **1.3.2**).

 Either way   None

 Summary: 6 months' imprisonment and/or a fine

Indictment: 4 years' imprisonment and/or a fine

8.10.4 **Possess weapon/blade/sharp point on school premises**

Section 139A of the Criminal Justice Act 1988 creates the offence of possessing an article with a blade or sharp point, or an offensive weapon on school premises.

Offences

(1) Any person who has an article to which section 139 of this Act applies with him on school premises shall be guilty of an offence.

(2) Any person who has an offensive weapon within the meaning of section 1 of the Prevention of Crime Act 1953 with him on school premises shall be guilty of an offence.

Criminal Justice Act 1988, s 139A

8.10.4 Nuisance/disturbance/powers at school premises

> **Points to prove**
> ✓ without good reason/lawful authority
> ✓ had with them
> ✓ on school premises
> ✓ an offensive weapon/article being a blade/sharply pointed

Meanings

Has with him (see 8.3.6)

School premises

Means land used for the purposes of a **school**, excluding any land occupied solely as a dwelling by a person employed at the school.

School (Education Act 1996, s 4)

Means an educational institution which is outside the further or higher education sector and is an institution for providing:

(a) primary education;
(b) secondary education; or
(c) both primary and secondary education;

whether or not the institution also provides further education.

Article (see 8.10.1)

Offensive weapon (see 8.9.1)

Explanatory notes

- School premises can include open land, such as playing fields or schoolyards. However, dwellings occupied within the premises by employees, such as caretakers' or wardens' houses, are outside the scope of this section.
- The offence applies to both publicly maintained and independent schools.
- This offence can be committed at any time of the day or night, during term time or holidays; it does not have to be during school hours.
- Many schools do not allow access to the general public outside or even during, school hours: so these offences cover the situation where such weapons are carried on school premises that are not public places.

Defences

(3) It shall be a defence for a person charged with an offence under subsection (1) or (2) above to prove that he had good reason or lawful authority for having the article or weapon with him on the premises in question.

(4) Without prejudice to the generality of subsection (3) above, it shall be a defence for a person charged with an offence under subsection (1) or (2) above to prove that he had the article or weapon in question with him—
(a) for use at work,
(b) for educational purposes,
(c) for religious reasons, or
(d) as part of any national costume.

Criminal Justice Act 1988, s 139A

Practical considerations

- If threats are used, when in possession of the article or offensive weapon, then consider the s 139AA offence (see **8.10.3**).
- Consider the offence of causing/permitting a nuisance/disturbance on school premises and power to remove offenders (see **8.10.5**).
- Section 139B gives the police power to enter and search school premises in connection with the s 139A and s 139AA offences (see **8.11.2**).
- Consider powers given to teachers at schools, and members of staff at higher education establishments (see **8.10.5**).

 Either way None

 Summary: 6 months' imprisonment and/or a fine

Indictment: 4 years' imprisonment and/or a fine

8.10.5 Nuisance/disturbance/powers at school premises

Section 547 of the Education Act 1996 creates the offence of causing a nuisance or disturbance on school premises and provides the police with a power to remove offenders.

Offences

Any person who without lawful authority is present on premises to which this section applies and causes or permits nuisance or disturbance to the annoyance of persons who lawfully use those premises (whether or not any such persons are present at the time) is guilty of an offence.

Education Act 1996, s 547(1)

8.10.5 Nuisance/disturbance/powers at school premises

Points to prove
- ✓ without lawful authority
- ✓ was present on
- ✓ premises of local authority maintained/grant-maintained school
- ✓ and permitted/caused
- ✓ a nuisance/disturbance
- ✓ to the annoyance of persons lawfully using those premises

Power to remove offenders

If a police constable, or an authorised person (of appropriate authority) has reasonable cause to suspect that any person is committing or has committed an offence under this section, he may remove him from the premises in question.

Education Act 1996, s 547(3)

Explanatory notes

- Section 139B gives the police a power (see **8.11.2**) to enter school premises and search people on those premises in relation to offences under s 139A (see **8.10.4**) or s 139AA (see **8.10.3**).
- **Premises** includes playgrounds, playing fields, and other premises for outdoor recreation of any—
  - ✦ school maintained by a local authority;
  - ✦ special school not so maintained;
  - ✦ independent school; and
  - ✦ an Academy (not independent school).
- **Premises** also applies to those provided by the local education authority and used wholly or mainly in connection with instruction or leadership in sporting, recreational, or outdoor activities.

School staff members' powers

- Education Acts give school teachers and members of staff at higher education premises various powers.
- Section 93 of the Education and Inspections Act 2006 gives members of staff powers to restrain pupils to prevent the pupil from: committing an offence; causing personal injury/damage to another pupil or personal property; or engaging in any behaviour prejudicial to the maintenance of good order and discipline at the school.
- In England ss 550ZA and 550ZB of the Education Act 1996 allow the head teacher or authorised member of staff to use reasonable force to search a pupil if they have reasonable grounds to suspect that the pupil has a prohibited item in their possession. A prohibited item is a bladed article/knife (see **8.10.1**); offensive weapon (see **8.9.1**); alcohol (see **9.1.1**); controlled drugs (see **5.2.1**); stolen goods

(see **3.5**); an article likely to be used to commit an offence or cause personal injury or damage to property; an article as specified in regulations (see below); any item which the school rules identify as an item for which a search may be made.

- The Schools (Specification and Disposal of Articles) Regulations 2012 (SI 951/2012) list further items that are prohibited under ss 550ZA. They are tobacco and cigarette papers, fireworks, and a pornographic image.
- The above regulations and s 550ZC give power to seize and retain, and give directions as to disposal of, any prohibited items found.
- In Wales s 550AA of the 1996 Act applies and only allows a search of pupils for a bladed article/knife or an offensive weapon. It also provides conditions for such a search, together with powers to seize, retain, and directions as to dispose of any such items found.
- Similar powers exist under the Further and Higher Education Act 1992:
  - ✦ under s 85A a person who is causing a nuisance or disturbance on higher educational premises will commit an offence. The Act also gives a constable or authorised person power to remove such a person from those premises;
  - ✦ in England ss 85AA–85AB gives the principal or authorised member of staff in a further education institution the same powers to search further education students and their possessions for the same prohibited items as given in ss 550ZA–550ZB (above). Section 85AC gives power to seize, retain, and dispose of any prohibited items found;
  - ✦ in Wales s 85B of the 1992 Act applies and only allows staff to search for weapons as given in s 550AA above. Section 85B also gives power to seize, retain, and dispose of such items found.

 Summary   6 months

 Level 2 fine

Links to alternative subjects and offences

8.10.5 Nuisance/disturbance/powers at school premises

8.11 Stop and Search Powers—Knives and Weapons

The Criminal Justice Act 1988 deals with premises search warrants and stop and search powers for school premises.

8.11.1 Search warrant for premises

Section 142 of the Criminal Justice Act 1988 creates a search power in respect of premises.

Grounds for issue of warrant

If on an application made by a constable a justice of the peace is satisfied that there are reasonable grounds for believing—
(a) that there are on premises specified in the application—
   (i) knives such as are mentioned in section 1(1) of the Restriction of Offensive Weapons Act 1959; or
   (ii) weapons to which section 141 applies; and
(b) that an offence under section 1 of the Restriction of Offensive Weapons Act 1959 or section 141 above has been or is being committed in relation to them; and
(c) that any of the conditions specified in subsection (3) below applies, he may issue a warrant authorising a constable to enter and search the premises.

Criminal Justice Act 1988, s 142(1)

Meaning of conditions

The conditions relate to any of the following, in that:
- it is not practicable to communicate with any person entitled to grant entry to the premises or grant access to the knives or weapons to which the application relates;
- entry to the premises will not be granted unless a warrant is produced;
- the purpose of a search may be frustrated or seriously prejudiced unless a constable arriving at the premises can secure immediate entry to them.

Explanatory notes

- Restriction of Offensive Weapons Act 1959 refers to any flick knife, flick gun, or gravity knife (see **8.10.2**).
- Weapons under s 141 are listed in the Offensive Weapons Order 1988 (see **8.9.2** and **8.9.3**).

- A constable may seize and retain anything for which a search has been authorised under s 142(1) above.

8.11.2 **Powers for article/weapon on school premises**

Section 139B of the Criminal Justice Act 1988 provides a power of entry to school premises to search for offensive weapons or articles with a blade or sharp point, and to seize/retain any weapon/article found.

Enter and search

A constable may enter school premises and search those premises and any person on those premises for—
(a)   any article to which section 139 of this Act applies, or
(b)   any offensive weapon within the meaning of section 1 of the Prevention of Crime Act 1953,
if he has reasonable grounds for suspecting that an offence under section 139A or 139AA of this Act is being, or has been, committed.

Criminal Justice Act 1988, s 139B(1)

Seize and retain

If, in the course of a search under this section, a constable discovers an article or weapon which he has reasonable grounds for suspecting to be an article or weapon of a kind described in subsection (1) above, he may seize and retain it.

Criminal Justice Act 1988, s 139B(2)

Explanatory notes

- A constable may use reasonable force, if necessary, in the exercise of the power of entry conferred by this section.
- For the offence under s 139A and s 139AA see **8.10.3**.
- An article under s 139 is a bladed/sharply pointed article (see **8.10.1**).
- For offensive weapon under the Prevention of Crime Act 1953, s 1 see **8.9.1**.

Practical considerations

- Powers under s 139B are additional to entry and search powers under s 17 of PACE (see **1.5.2**).
- If a large number of people are involved, causing fear of a serious public order situation, then consider stop and search powers under the Criminal Justice and Public Order Act 1994, s 60 (see **8.11.3**).
- Consider the offence and power to remove a person who causes or permits a nuisance or disturbance on school premises (see **8.10.5**).

8.11.3 **Stop and search—serious violence/offensive weapon**

Section 60 of the Criminal Justice and Public Order Act 1994 allows senior police officers to authorise constables to stop and search people or vehicles in a specific area, either where a serious public order problem is likely to arise, has taken place, or where people are carrying offensive weapons or sharp-pointed blades. An offence will be committed if that person fails to comply with a constable's requirements.

Authorisation

If a police officer of or above the rank of inspector reasonably believes—

(a) that incidents involving serious violence may take place in any locality in his police area, and that it is expedient to give an authorisation under this section to prevent their occurrence,

(aa) that
  (i) an incident involving serious violence has taken place in England and Wales in his police area;
  (ii) a dangerous instrument or offensive weapon used in the incident is being carried in any locality in his police area by a person; and
  (iii) it is expedient to give an authorisation under this section to find the instrument or weapon; or

(b) that persons are carrying dangerous instruments or offensive weapons in any locality in his police area without good reason,

he may give an authorisation that the powers conferred by this section are to be exercisable at any place within that locality for a specified period not exceeding 24 hours.

Criminal Justice and Public Order Act 1994, s 60(1)

Explanatory notes

- Where a serious violent incident has occurred, and the weapon used in the incident is believed to still be in the locality, this power assists in locating the weapon used and in apprehending the offender before they leave the area or disperse.
- If an authorisation has been given orally under s 60(1)(aa) it needs to be in writing as soon as practicable. Authorisations made under s 60(1)(a) or (b) will still need to be made in writing.
- The inspector giving an authorisation must, as soon as practicable, inform an officer of or above the rank of superintendent.
- If it appears to an officer of or above the rank of superintendent that it is expedient to do so, they may direct that the authorisation shall continue being in force for a further twenty-four hours. This shall be recorded in writing as soon as practicable.

- Any authorisation shall be in writing signed by the officer giving it, and shall specify the grounds, locality, and the period during which the powers are exercisable.

Power to stop and search pedestrian/vehicle

(4)   This section confers on any constable in uniform power—
   (a)   to stop any pedestrian and search him or anything carried by him for offensive weapons or dangerous instruments;
   (b)   to stop any vehicle and search the vehicle, its driver and any passenger for offensive weapons or dangerous instruments.

(5)   A constable may, in the exercise of the powers conferred by subsection (4) above, stop any person or vehicle and make any search he thinks fit whether or not he has any grounds for suspecting that the person or vehicle is carrying weapons or articles of that kind.

Criminal Justice and Public Order Act 1994, s 60

Power to seize

If in the course of such a search under this section a constable discovers a dangerous instrument or an article which he has reasonable grounds for suspecting to be an offensive weapon, he may seize it.

Criminal Justice and Public Order Act 1994, s 60(6)

Offences

A person who fails to stop, or to stop a vehicle, when required to do so by a constable in the exercise of his powers under this section commits an offence.

Criminal Justice and Public Order Act 1994, s 60(8)

Points to prove

✓ failed to stop (person) or vehicle
✓ when required to do so
✓ by a constable in uniform
✓ in exercising powers of stop/search

Meanings

Offensive weapon (see **8.9.1**)

For incidents involving serious violence under s 60(1)(aa)(i)—means any article used in the incident to cause or threaten injury to any person or otherwise to intimidate.

Dangerous instrument

Means instruments which have a blade or are sharply pointed.

Vehicle

This has its natural meaning (see **1.3.2**) and includes a caravan.

Explanatory notes

- Once a written authority has been given for searches, under s 60(5) a constable can stop any person/vehicle or make any search that they think fit, whether or not there are grounds for suspecting that the person or vehicle is carrying weapons or articles.
- Ensure compliance with paras 2.12–2.14B of Code A in relation to searches of persons and vehicles under s 60. Persons involved are entitled to a written statement as to being stopped and/or searched under s 60, if they apply within twelve months.
- A person carries a dangerous instrument or an offensive weapon if they have it in their physical possession.

Related cases

R (on the application of Roberts) v Commissioner of Police for the Metropolis [2015] UKSC 79 In this case the defendant failed to co-operate with a search being carried out under the authority granted by a superintendent in accordance with s 60. She was convicted and appealed on the basis that the stop and search powers were incompatible with ECHR Arts 5 (right to liberty and security) and 8 (right to respect for private and family life) (**see 1.1**). The appeal was dismissed. It was held that the use of force when exercising a power under s 60 was not incompatible with Convention rights.

R (on the application of Laporte) v CC of Gloucestershire [2006] UKHL 55, HL (see 'Related cases' under **7.3** for further details).

Practical considerations

- Apart from BT police, only inspectors and superintendents from Home Office forces may authorise these powers to be exercised, although officers from other police forces (RMP, Civil Nuclear Constabulary) may be involved in such searches.
- With the necessary modifications, s 60 also applies to ships, aircraft, and hovercraft as it applies to vehicles.
- Powers conferred by s 60 are in addition to and do not derogate from any other statutory powers.
- Where a s 60 authority is in force, then s 60AA can be utilised, whereby any items, masks, or disguises which are used in order to conceal identity can be removed and seized. An offence will be committed if a person fails to remove an item worn by them when required to do so by a constable under s 60AA(7).

8.11.3 Stop and search—serious violence/offensive weapon

 Summary   6 months

1 month imprisonment and/or a level 3 fine

Links to alternative subjects and offences

Chapter 9

Alcohol and Licensing

9.1 Alcohol Restrictions on Persons under 16/18

The sale and supply of alcohol is regulated by the Licensing Act 2003 which creates several offences relating to children, young people, alcohol, drunkenness, and disorderly conduct.

The following offences protect children both on and off licensed premises; some of them apply anywhere and are not restricted to licensed premises.

9.1.1 Unaccompanied children prohibited from certain premises

It is an offence to admit children under 16 to certain categories of relevant premises if they are not accompanied by an adult or allow them to be on these premises between midnight and 5 a.m., and those premises are open for the supply of alcohol for consumption therein.

Offences

A person to whom subsection (3) applies commits an offence if—
(a) knowing that relevant premises are within subsection (4), he allows an unaccompanied child to be on the premises at a time when they are open for the purposes of being used for the supply of alcohol for consumption there, or
(b) he allows an unaccompanied child to be on relevant premises at a time between the hours of midnight and 5 a.m. when the premises are open for the purposes of being used for the supply of alcohol for consumption there.

Licensing Act 2003, s 145(1)

9.1.1 Unaccompanied children prohibited from certain premises

> **Points to prove**
> ✓ being a person to whom subsection (3) applies
> ✓ knowing they were relevant premises
> ✓ allowed an unaccompanied child to be on premises
> ✓ when open **or** open between midnight and 5 a.m.
> ✓ when used for supplying alcohol for consumption therein

Meanings

Person to whom subsection (3) applies

Any person who:
- works at the premises in a capacity, whether paid or unpaid, which authorises them to request the unaccompanied child to leave the premises;
- in the case of licensed premises, is the holder of a premises licence in respect of the premises, and the designated premises supervisor (if any) under such a licence;
- in the case of premises in respect of which a club premises certificate has effect, is any member or officer of the club which holds the certificate who is present on the premises in a capacity which enables him to make such a request;
- in the case of premises which may be used for a permitted temporary activity by virtue of Pt 5, is the premises user in relation to the temporary event notice in question.

Relevant premises

Means premises that:
- are licensed; or
- have a club premises certificate in force; or
- may be used for a permitted temporary activity (under Pt 5).

Relevant premises within subsection 4

Relevant premises are within this subsection if they are:
- exclusively or primarily used for the supply of alcohol for consumption on the premises; or
- open for the purposes of the supply of alcohol for consumption on the premises by virtue of Pt 5 (permitted temporary activities) and, at the time the temporary event notice has effect, they are exclusively or primarily used for such supplies.

Child

Means an individual aged under 16.

Alcohol (s 191)

Means spirits, wine, beer, cider, or any other fermented, distilled, or spirituous liquor (in any state), but does **not** include:
- alcohol which is of a strength not exceeding 0.5 per cent at the time of the sale or supply in question;
- perfume;

- flavouring essences recognised by HMRC as not being intended for consumption as or with dutiable alcoholic liquor;
- aromatic flavouring essence commonly known as Angostura bitters;
- alcohol which is, or is included in, a medicinal product, or a veterinary medicinal product;
- denatured alcohol;
- methyl alcohol;
- naphtha; or
- alcohol contained in liqueur confectionery.

Unaccompanied

Means not in the company of an individual aged 18 or over.

Supply of alcohol

Means the sale by retail of alcohol, or the supply of alcohol by or on behalf of a club to, or to the order of, a member of the club.

Explanatory notes

No offence is committed if the unaccompanied child is on the premises solely for the purpose of passing to or from some other place to or from which there is no other convenient means of access or exit.

Defences—s 145(6)–(8)

- That the conduct was by act or default of some other person and the defendant exercised all due diligence to avoid committing it.
- Where the defendant by reason of their own conduct—
  + believed that the unaccompanied child was aged 16 or over or that an individual accompanying the child was aged 18 or over; and
  + either:
    + had taken all reasonable steps to establish the individual's age; or
    + nobody could reasonably have suspected from the individual's appearance that they were aged under 16 or, as the case may be, under 18.

Defence notes

- A person is treated as having 'taken all reasonable steps' to establish an individual's age if:
  + they asked the individual for evidence of their age; and
  + the evidence would have convinced a reasonable person.
- This defence will fail if the prosecution prove that the evidence of age was such that no reasonable person would have been convinced by it—for example, if the proof of age was either an obvious forgery or clearly belonged to another person (see **11.3.1**).
- The defence also applies in situations where the child looks exceptionally old for his or her age.

Practical considerations

Age to be confirmed by ID card, driving licence, or similar document.

Summary

 12 months

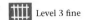 Level 3 fine

9.1.2 **Sale of alcohol to person under 18**

The sale of alcohol to a person under 18 anywhere is an offence.

Offences

A person commits an offence if he sells alcohol to an individual aged under 18.

Licensing Act 2003, s 146(1)

Points to prove

✓ sold alcohol
✓ to person under the age of 18

Meaning of alcohol (see 9.1.1)

Explanatory notes

- Similar offences apply where a club supplies alcohol to persons under 18 by itself or on its behalf (s 146(2)) or where a person supplies to persons under 18 on behalf of the club (s 146(3)).
- The sale of alcohol to children is an offence, not only if it occurs on relevant licensed premises, but **anywhere**.

Defences—s 146(4)–(6)

- Where a defendant by reason of their own conduct:
  - ✦ believed that the individual was aged 18 or over, and either:
    - ✦ they had taken all reasonable steps to establish the individual's age; or
    - ✦ nobody could reasonably have suspected from the individual's appearance that they were aged under 18.
- That the offence was committed by act or default of some other person and that the defendant exercised all due diligence to avoid committing it.

Defence notes

- For 'having taken all reasonable steps' (see **9.1.1 'Defence notes'**).
- The second part of the defence could be where the actual sale was made by a barman and the manager had exercised all due diligence to avoid this offence being committed.

Practical considerations

- Age to be confirmed by ID card, driving licence, or similar document.
- This offence can be dealt with by PND (see **7.1.1**).

 Issue for s 146(1), (3) offences only (**not** s 146(2) club offences)

 Summary   12 months

 Fine

9.1.3 **Allowing the sale of alcohol to children**

Offences

A person to whom subsection (2) applies commits an offence if he knowingly allows the sale of alcohol on relevant premises to an individual aged under 18.

Licensing Act 2003, s 147(1)

Points to prove

- ✓ being person to whom subsection (2) applies
- ✓ on relevant premises
- ✓ knowingly allowed the sale of alcohol
- ✓ to a person under the age of 18

Meanings

Person to whom subsection (2) applies

Any person who works at the premises in a capacity, whether paid or unpaid, which authorises them to prevent the sale.

Knowingly

Means having knowledge (see '**Related cases**' below), an awareness, informed, consciously, intentionally, or an understanding.

Alcohol (see **9.1.1**)

Relevant premises (see **9.1.1**)

Explanatory notes

- There are no statutory defences to this offence. The mental element 'knowingly' applies only to allowing the sale; it does not require

9.1.3 Allowing the sale of alcohol to children

knowledge that the individual was under 18. The prosecution need only prove that the individual was under 18.

- Similar offences apply under s 147(3) where an employee or member/ officer of a club fails to prevent supply on relevant premises by or on behalf of the club to a member/individual who is aged under 18.

Related cases

Ross v Moss and others [1965] 3 All ER 145, QBD The defendant held a licence for a private members' club and it was common for alcohol to be sold there in contravention of the licence. While away on holiday, the defendant delegated the management of the club to his father who continued to sell alcohol in contravention of the licence. It was held that, it makes no difference if one is on the premises and turns one's head or if one is elsewhere in the country if the intention is that the practice continues to occur in one's absence. Where a licence holder delegates management s/he cannot get out of his duty by absenting themselves from the premises and placing another person in charge.

Practical considerations

- Age to be confirmed by ID card, driving licence, or similar document.
- **Persistently selling alcohol to children (under 18):** a summary offence will be committed under s 147A if on two or more different occasions, within a period of three consecutive months, alcohol is unlawfully sold on the same premises to an individual aged under 18.
- The following procedural requirements under s 147A also apply:
  + The premises must be either licensed premises or authorised premises for a permitted temporary activity by virtue of Pt 5, and the offender must hold the premises licence or be the named premises user for a temporary event notice.
  + The same sale may not be counted as different offences for this purpose.
  + The following shall be admissible as evidence that there has been an unlawful sale of alcohol to an individual aged under 18 on any premises on any occasion:
    + a conviction for a s 146 offence in respect of a sale to that individual on those premises on that occasion;
    + a caution in respect of such an offence; or
    + PND issue/payment in respect of such a sale.
- Section 147B provides that if the holder of a premises licence is convicted of a s 147A offence for sales on those premises, the court may order that the premises licence is suspended for a period not exceeding three months.
- A closure notice for persistently selling alcohol to children under 18 can be issued (see **9.3.4**).

 Summary   12 months

 Fine

9.1.4 **Purchase of alcohol by or on behalf of person under 18**

Offences are committed by a person under 18, or a person on behalf of the under-18, who purchases or attempts to purchase alcohol anywhere. Similarly, it is an offence for a person to buy or attempt to buy alcohol for consumption by a person who is under 18 on licensed premises.

Offences

(1)(a) An individual aged under 18 commits an offence if he buys or attempts to buy alcohol.

(3)(a) A person commits an offence if he buys or attempts to buy alcohol on behalf of an individual aged under 18.

(4)(a) A person commits an offence if he buys or attempts to buy alcohol for consumption on relevant premises by an individual aged under 18.

Licensing Act 2003, s 149

Points to prove

s 149(1)(a) offence

✓ being a person under the age of 18
✓ bought **or** attempted to buy alcohol

s 149(3)(a) offence

✓ bought **or** attempted to buy alcohol
✓ on behalf of individual under the age of 18

s 149(4)(a) offence

✓ bought **or** attempted to buy alcohol
✓ for consumption on relevant premises
✓ by an individual under the age of 18

Meanings

Alcohol (see 9.1.1)

Relevant premises (see 9.1.1)

Explanatory notes

- Offences in s 149(1)(a) and s 149(3)(a) may be committed **anywhere**.
- 'On behalf of' does not mean that the purchase must be instigated by the child; the alcohol need only be bought for a child.
- Section 149(2) states that the s 149(1) offence does not apply to an individual aged under 18 who buys or attempts to buy the alcohol at the request of a constable or a weights and measures inspector who are acting in the course of their duty. This exception allows test-purchasing operations to take place (see **9.3.1**).

9.1.4 Purchase of alcohol by or on behalf of person under 18

- Similarly, s 149(5) states that a s 149(4) offence does not apply if:
    + the relevant person is aged 18 or over;
    + the individual is aged 16 or 17;
    + the alcohol is beer, wine, or cider;
    + its purchase or supply is for consumption at a **table meal** on **relevant premises**; and
    + the individual is accompanied at the meal by an individual aged 18 or over.
- **Table meal** means a meal eaten by a person seated at a table, or at a counter or other structure which serves the purpose of a table and is not used for the service of refreshments for consumption by persons not seated at a table or structure serving the purpose of a table.
- Bar snacks do not amount to a table meal.
- Similar offences apply to clubs, under s 149(1)(b), (3)(b), and (4)(b) respectively, where a member of a club is supplied with alcohol by or on behalf of that club for:
    + that member (being under 18), as a result of his act, default, or attempts to do so;
    + an individual aged under 18 as a result of his making, or attempting to make such arrangements; and
    + consumption on relevant premises by an individual aged under 18, by his act, default or attempts to do so.

Defences—s 149(6)

Section 149(3) and (4) offences only

The defendant had no reason to suspect that the individual was aged under 18.

Related cases (on test purchases see 9.3.1)

Practical considerations

Consider issuing a PND for the s 149(3)(a) and (4) offences (see **7.1.1**), but not the s 149(1) offence, as PNDs can no longer be issued to a person under 18.

 s 149(3)(a) and (4) only

 Summary   12 months

s 149(1) offence: Level 3 fine

s 149(3) and s 149(4) offences: Fine

9.1.5 **Consumption of alcohol by person under 18**

Persons aged under 18 are not allowed to consume alcohol on relevant premises.

Offences

(1) An individual under 18 commits an offence if he knowingly consumes alcohol on relevant premises.
(2) A person to whom subsection (3) applies commits an offence if he knowingly allows the consumption of alcohol on relevant premises by an individual aged under 18.

Licensing Act 2003, s 150

Points to prove

s 150(1) offence

✓ being a person under the age of 18
✓ knowingly consumed alcohol on relevant premises

s 150(2) offence

✓ being a person to whom subsection (3) applies
✓ knowingly allowed
✓ an individual under the age of 18
✓ to consume alcohol on relevant premises

Meanings

Knowingly (see 9.1.3)

Alcohol (see 9.1.1)

Relevant premises (see 9.1.1)

Person to whom subsection (3) applies

This subsection applies:
(a) to a person who works at the premises in a capacity, whether paid or unpaid, which authorises him to prevent the consumption; and
(b) where the alcohol was supplied by a club to or to the order of a member of the club, to any member or officer of the club who is present at the premises at the time of the consumption in a capacity which enables him to prevent it.

Explanatory notes

• The s 150(1) knowingly consumed offence will not be committed if the individual inadvertently consumes alcohol, for example if the drink is spiked.

- Section 150(4) states the s 150(1) and (2) offences do not apply if:
  - ✦ the individual is aged 16 or 17;
  - ✦ the alcohol is beer, wine, or cider;
  - ✦ its consumption is at a **table meal** on relevant premises; and
  - ✦ the individual is accompanied at the meal by an individual aged 18 or over.
- Both offences under s 150(1) and (2) also apply to clubs.

Practical considerations

- Knowledge must be proved for both offences, either to 'knowingly' consume or to 'knowingly' allow consumption of the alcohol.
- Age to be proved by ID card, driving licence, or similar documentation.
- Consider issuing a PND for the s 150(2) offence (see **7.1.1**), but not the s 150(1) offence as PNDs can no longer be issued to a person under 18.

 s 150(2) only

 Summary   12 months

 s 150(1) offence: Level 3 fine

s 150(2) offence: Fine

9.1.6 **Delivering alcohol to person under 18**

It is an offence for certain people to deliver or allow delivery of alcohol to a person under 18.

> ### Offences
>
> (1) A person who works on relevant premises in any capacity, whether paid or unpaid, commits an offence if he knowingly delivers to an individual aged under 18—
>   (a) alcohol sold on the premises, or
>   (b) alcohol supplied on the premises by or on behalf of a club to or to the order of a member of the club.
> (2) A person to whom subsection (3) applies commits an offence if he knowingly allows anybody else to deliver to a person under 18 alcohol sold on relevant premises.
>
> Licensing Act 2003, s 151

Points to prove

s 151(1) offence

✓ being a person who worked in a capacity, whether unpaid or paid
✓ on relevant premises
✓ knowingly delivered to an individual under the age of 18
✓ alcohol sold on those premises **or**
✓ supplied on those premises (by or on behalf of a club/order of member)

s 151(2) offence

✓ being a person to whom subsection (3) applies
✓ on relevant premises
✓ knowingly allowed another person to deliver
✓ to an individual under the age of 18
✓ alcohol sold on those premises

Meanings

Relevant premises (see 9.1.1)

Knowingly (see 9.1.3)

Alcohol (see 9.1.1)

Person to whom subsection (3) applies

Any person who works on the premises in a capacity, whether paid or unpaid, which authorises him to prevent the delivery of the alcohol.

Explanatory notes

- Offences in this section cover various situations; for example, under s 151(1)(a) a child takes delivery of a consignment of alcohol bought by a parent from an off-licence (unless the defence applies); or a person authorises a delivery of that sort, under s 151(2).
- An offence similar to s 151(2) is to knowingly allow somebody else to deliver alcohol supplied by a club under s 151(4).

Defences—s 151(6)

Subsections (1), (2), and (4) do not apply where—
(a) the alcohol is delivered at a place where the buyer or, as the case may be, person supplied lives or works, or
(b) the individual aged under 18 works on the relevant premises in a capacity, whether paid or unpaid, which involves the delivery of alcohol, or
(c) the alcohol is sold or supplied for consumption on the relevant premises.

Licensing Act 2003, s 151(6)

Defence notes

This covers cases where, for example, a child answers the door and signs for the delivery of an order for the house, or where a 16-year-old office worker is sent to collect an order for their employer.

Practical considerations

- Knowledge must be proved for all the offences, either to 'knowingly' (see **9.1.3**) deliver or to 'knowingly' allow anybody else to deliver the alcohol.
- Age to be proved by ID card, driving licence, or similar document.
- Consider issuing a PND for these offences (see **7.1.1**).

 Summary   12 months

 Fine

9.1.7 **Sending person under 18 to obtain alcohol**

A person under 18 must not be sent to obtain alcohol.

> **Offences**
>
> A person commits an offence if he knowingly sends an individual aged under 18 to obtain—
> (a) alcohol sold or to be sold on relevant premises for consumption off the premises, or
> (b) alcohol supplied or to be supplied by or on behalf of a club to or to the order of a member of the club for such consumption.
>
> Licensing Act 2003, s 152(1)

> **Points to prove**
> ✓ knowingly sent an individual under the age of 18
> ✓ to obtain alcohol
> ✓ sold/to be sold on relevant premises or
> ✓ supplied/to be supplied (by/on behalf of club/order of member)
> ✓ for consumption off those premises

Meanings

Knowingly (see **9.1.3**)

Alcohol (see 9.1.1)

Relevant premises (see 9.1.1)

Explanatory notes

- Section 152(3) allows an individual under 18 who works on the relevant premises in a capacity (whether paid or unpaid) that involves delivery of alcohol.
- Similarly, s 152(4) states that no offence will be committed if an individual aged under 18 is sent by a constable or a weights and measures inspector who are acting in the course of their duty. This exception allows test-purchasing operations to take place (see **9.3.1**).

Related cases (on test purchases see 9.3.1)

Practical considerations

- This offence covers, for example, circumstances where a parent sends their child (being under 18) to an off-licence to buy and collect alcohol for them.
- Knowledge must be proved as to 'knowingly' send an individual aged under 18 to obtain alcohol sold or supplied from the relevant premises.
- It is an offence under s 153 to knowingly allow a person under 18 to sell or, in the case of a club, to supply alcohol unless each sale or supply is approved by a responsible person.
- It is no longer an offence under s 148 to sell liqueur confectionery (chocolate liqueurs) to children under 16 as it has been repealed by the Deregulation Act 2015, s 70.

 Summary   12 months

Fine

Links to alternative subjects and offences

9.2 **Drunkenness on Licensed Premises**

The Licensing Act 2003 creates several offences relating to alcohol and offences concerning drunkenness and disorderly conduct.

9.2.1 **Sale of alcohol to person who is drunk**

It is an offence to sell or attempt to sell alcohol to a person who is drunk, or to allow alcohol to be sold to such a person, on relevant premises.

Offences

A person to whom subsection (2) applies commits an offence if, on relevant premises, he knowingly—
(a) sells or attempts to sell alcohol to a person who is drunk, or
(b) allows alcohol to be sold to such a person.

Licensing Act 2003, s 141(1)

Points to prove

✓ person to whom subsection (2) applies
✓ knowingly sold/attempted to sell/allowed sale of alcohol
✓ on relevant premises to a person who was drunk

Meanings

Person to whom subsection (2) applies:

- Any person who works at the premises in a capacity, whether paid or unpaid, which gives him authority to sell the alcohol concerned.
- In licensed premises, clubs, or permitted temporary activity premises, the same persons as given in s 145(3) (see **9.1.1**).

Relevant premises (see **9.1.1**)

Knowingly (see **9.1.3**)

Alcohol (see **9.1.1**)

Drunk (see **7.2.1**)

Explanatory notes

- In each case, drunkenness will be a question of fact for the court to decide.

- It is also an offence, under s 141(3), to supply alcohol by or on behalf of a club or to the order of a member of the club to a person who is drunk.

Practical considerations

- If the person is under 18 consider offences under s 145 (see **9.1.1**).
- Knowledge must be proved as to 'knowingly' sell, attempt to sell, or allow to be sold alcohol to a person who is drunk.
- This offence can be dealt with by PND (see **7.1.1**).
- Details of the licence holder and/or the designated premises supervisor should be clearly displayed in the premises.
- Under s 142 it is also an offence to knowingly obtain or attempt to obtain alcohol on relevant premises for consumption on those premises by a person who is drunk.

 Summary 12 months

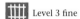 Level 3 fine

9.2.2 **Failure to leave licensed premises**

People who are drunk or disorderly may be requested to leave certain premises and commit an offence if they fail to do so.

Offences

A person who is drunk or disorderly commits an offence if, without reasonable excuse—
(a) he fails to leave relevant premises when requested to do so by a constable or by a person to whom subsection (2) applies, or
(b) he enters or attempts to enter relevant premises after a constable or a person to whom subsection (2) applies has requested him not to enter.

Licensing Act 2003, s 143(1)

Points to prove

✓ without reasonable excuse while drunk or disorderly ✓ failed to comply with request
✓ by a constable or a person to whom subsection (2) applies
✓ to leave **or** not to enter/attempt to enter relevant premises

---

9.2.3 Allowing disorderly conduct on licensed premises

Meanings

Drunk (see 7.2.1)

Disorderly (see 7.2.1)

Relevant premises (see 9.1.1)

Person to whom subsection (2) applies

- Any person who works at the premises in a capacity, whether paid or unpaid, which authorises them to make such a request.
- In licensed premises, clubs, or permitted temporary activity, the same persons as given in s 145(3) (see **9.1.1**).

Explanatory notes

- An offence may not be committed if the person has a reasonable excuse, for example if they are physically prevented by serious disability or injury from leaving the premises.
- Apart from licensed premises, this offence also applies to clubs and premises being used for a permitted temporary activity.
- Whether a person is drunk and/or disorderly will be a question of fact for the court to decide.

Practical considerations

- On being requested to do so by the appropriate person, a constable must help to expel from relevant premises a person who is drunk/disorderly or help to prevent such a person from entering relevant premises.
- Consider either drunk and disorderly in a public place (see 7.2.1) or drunk on licensed premises/public place (see 7.2.2)—both can be dealt with by PND (see 7.1.1).

 Summary   12 months

 Level 1 fine

9.2.3 **Allowing disorderly conduct on licensed premises**

It is also an offence to knowingly allow disorderly conduct on relevant premises.

> ### Offences
>
> A person to whom subsection (2) applies commits an offence if he knowingly allows disorderly conduct on relevant premises.
>
> Licensing Act 2003, s 140(1)

Points to prove

✓ being a person to whom subsection (2) applies
✓ knowingly allowed disorderly conduct on relevant premises

Meanings

Person to whom subsection (2) applies:

* Any person who works at the premises in a capacity, whether paid or unpaid, which authorises them to prevent the conduct.
* In licensed premises, clubs, or permitted temporary activity, the same persons as given in s 145(3) (see **9.1.1**).

Knowingly (see **9.1.3**)

Disorderly (see **7.2.1**)

Relevant premises (see **9.1.1**)

Explanatory notes

* Apart from licensed premises, this offence also applies to clubs and premises which may be used for a permitted temporary activity.

 Summary   12 months

 Level 3 fine

Links to alternative subjects and offences

9.3 **Powers to Enter/Close Licensed Premises and Test Purchases**

The Licensing Act 2003 provides a variety of offences relating to alcohol and powers to enter/close licensed premises/clubs and allows test purchases.

9.3.1 **Test purchases**

Sections 149 and 152 allow the police and trading standards officers to use individuals under 18 to make test purchases to ascertain if such individuals can buy or be supplied with alcohol from on/off-licensed premises, certified club premises, or premises used for a permitted temporary activity without any offences being committed.

Authorities

149(2) But subsection (1) [see 9.1.4] does not apply where the individual buys or attempts to buy the alcohol at the request of—
  (a) a constable, or
  (b) a weights and measures inspector,
who is acting in the course of his duty.

152(4) Subsection (1) [see 9.1.7] also does not apply where the individual aged under 18 is sent by—
  (a) a constable, or
  (b) a weights and measures inspector,
who is acting in the course of his duty.

Licensing Act 2003, ss 149(2) and 152(4)

Explanatory notes

This statutory authority allows test-purchasing operations to establish whether licensees and staff working in relevant licensed premises are complying with the prohibition on the sale/supply of alcohol to individuals aged under 18.

Related cases

R v Loosely/A-G's Reference (No 3 of 2000) [2001] UKHL 53, HL This was a case of entrapment; police officers must not instigate or incite the commission of an offence. To do this would also amount to a breach of Art 6 of the ECHR (see **1.1**). But if the police do no more than what an ordinary customer would do this will not generally be subject to successful challenge.

DPP v Marshall [1988] 3 All ER 683, QBD In this case, police in plain clothes bought four cans of lager and a bottle of wine from the defendant's shop where he was licensed to sell liquor by the case, but not in individual containers. It was argued that evidence should be excluded under s 78 of PACE, as the officers had not revealed the fact that they were policemen at the time of the purchase and this was unfair. It was held that evidence of police officers had been wrongly excluded; it had not been shown that the evidence would have had an adverse effect on the proceedings.

Practical considerations
- Consider the protection of children engaged in such operations.
- Assess the reliability of their evidence.

9.3.2 **Powers to enter licensed premises and clubs**

The Licensing Act 2003 contains provisions dealing with powers of entry to investigate licensable activities or immigration offences:
- Section 179(1) gives power to a constable or an authorised person to enter premises, if they have reason to believe that they are being, or are about to be, used for a licensable activity, in order to see whether the activity is being carried on in accordance with the authorisation. However, this does not apply to clubs, unless there is other authorisation apart from a club premises licence.
- Similarly, under s 180(1) a constable may enter and search any premises in respect of which they have **reason to believe** that an offence under the Licensing Act has been, is being, or is about to be committed. A constable exercising a power conferred by this section may, if necessary, use reasonable force.
- Section 97(1) allows a constable to enter and search club premises if they have reasonable cause to believe that that an offence under s 4(3)(a), (b), or (c) of the Misuse of Drugs Act 1971 (supplying or offering to supply, or being concerned in supplying or making an offer to supply, a controlled drug) has been, is being, or is about to be, committed there (see **5.1.1**), or that an offence under s 5(1) or (2) of the Psychoactive Substances Act 2016 (supplying, or offering to supply, a psychoactive substance) (see **5.3.4**) has been, is being, or is about to be, committed there, or that there is likely to be a breach of the peace (see **7.3**).

Explanatory notes
- It is not necessary to obtain a warrant.
- Police have lawful authority to require production of a premises licence, club premises certificate, or temporary event notice.
- The police may lawfully enter premises to inspect them before a licence or certificate is granted.

Meanings

Authorisation

(a) a premises licence,

(b) a club premises certificate, or

(c) a temporary event notice in respect of which the conditions of
s 98(2) to (4) are satisfied.

Authorised person

(a) An officer of the licensing authority in whose area the premises are
situated, or

(b) if the premises are situated in the area of more than one licensing
authority, an officer of any of those authorities, authorised for the
purposes of this Act.

9.3.3 **Police powers—closure notice**

Where an offence of persistently selling alcohol to children (under
18) has been committed under s 147A (see **9.1.3**) then a closure notice
can be issued by a superintendent (or above) to close the premises.

> ### Closure notice
>
> A relevant officer may give a notice under s 169A(1) (a 'closure notice')
> applying to any premises if—
>
> (a) there is evidence that a person ('the offender') has committed an
> offence under section 147A in relation to those premises;
>
> (b) the relevant officer considers that the evidence is such that, if the
> offender were prosecuted for the offence, there would be a realistic
> prospect of his being convicted; and
>
> (c) the offender is still, at the time when the notice is given, the holder
> of a premises licence in respect of those premises, or one of the
> holders of such a licence.
>
> Licensing Act 2003, s 169A(1)

Meaning of relevant officer

Means a police officer of the rank of superintendent or above; or an appointed inspector of weights and measures.

Explanatory notes

- The **closure notice** will:
  + prohibit sale of alcohol on the premises, for at least 48 hours but
  no more than 336 hours; and
  + if accepted will discharge all criminal liability in respect of the s
  147A offence (see **9.1.3**).

- A closure notice must:
  + be in the form as prescribed by regulations;
  + specify the premises and circumstances surrounding the offence;
  + specify the length of the period during which it is proposed that sales of alcohol should be prohibited on those premises and when that period would begin if the prohibition is accepted;
  + explain the consequences/penalties of the prohibition and any sale of alcohol on the premises during the period for which it is in force;
  + explain the rights of that person; and how those rights may be exercised.

Practical considerations

- The period specified for which it is proposed that sales of alcohol should be prohibited on those premises must be at least must be at least 48 hours but not more than 336 hours; and the time specified as the time from which that period would begin must be not less than 14 days after the date of the service of the closure notice.
- Service of the closure notice may be served on the premises by a constable or trading standards officer to a person having control/responsibility for the premises, and only when licensable activities are being carried on there. A copy must be served on the licence holder of the premises.
- A closure notice must not be given more than three months after the s 147A offence.
- No more than one closure notice may be given in respect of offences relating to the same sales; nor may such a notice be given in respect of an offence in respect of which a prosecution has already been brought.
- Section 169B prescribes other matters when a closure notice has been issued:
  + no proceedings may be brought for the s 147A offence or any **related offence** at any time before the time when the prohibition proposed by the notice would take effect;
  + if the premises' licence holder accepts the proposed prohibition in the manner specified in the notice then that prohibition takes effect (as specified) and no proceedings may be brought against that person for the alleged offence or any related offence;
  + '**related offence**' means an offence under s 146 (see **9.1.2**) or s 147 (see **9.1.3**) in respect of any of the sales to which the alleged offence relates.

Links to alternative subjects and offences

9.3.3 Police powers—closure notice

9.4 Public Spaces Protection Order—Alcohol Restrictions

9.4.1 Power to require person to cease drinking alcohol

Powers

(1) This section applies where a constable or an authorised person reasonably believes that a person (P)—

    (a) is or has been consuming alcohol in breach of a prohibition in a public spaces protection order, or

    (b) intends to consume alcohol in circumstances in which doing so would be a breach of such a prohibition.

(2) The constable or authorised person may require P—

    (a) not to consume, in breach of the order, alcohol or anything which the constable or authorised person reasonably believes to be alcohol;

    (b) to surrender anything in P's possession which is, or which the constable or authorised person reasonably believes to be, alcohol or a container for alcohol.

Anti-social Behaviour, Crime and Policing Act 2014, s 63(1)

Meanings

Authorised person

Means a person authorised for the purposes of this section by the local authority that made the public spaces protection order.

Alcohol (see 9.1.1)

Public spaces protection order (PSPO) (see 7.15.2)

Explanatory notes

- A requirement imposed by a constable or an authorised enforcement officer is not valid if they are asked by P to show evidence of their authorisation, and they fail to do so.
- Local authorities are responsible for making a PSPO and will have to be satisfied, on reasonable grounds, that activities in a public space: have had or will be likely to have a detrimental effect on the quality of life of those in the locality; it is, or is likely to be, persistent or continuing in nature, such as to make the activities unreasonable; and the order justifies the restrictions imposed (see **7.15.2**).
- The person must be informed that failure to comply with the officer's request, without reasonable excuse, is an offence (see **9.4.2**).

- A prohibition in a PSPO on consuming alcohol does not apply to:
  - ✦ premises (other than council-operated) which have a premises licence or club premises certificate for the supply of alcohol; or
  - ✦ a place within the curtilage of those premises;
  - ✦ a place where the sale of alcohol is for the time being authorised by a temporary event notice or was so authorised within the last thirty minutes;
  - ✦ a place where facilities/activities relating to the sale/consumption of alcohol are permitted by a permission granted under s 115E of the Highways Act 1980.
- A constable or an authorised person may dispose of anything surrendered to them under s 63(2)(b) in such manner as they consider appropriate.
- Consider using the power to confiscate alcohol from people under 18 years of age (see **9.5**).

9.4.2 **Failure to comply with alcohol requirements**

Example of constable's requirement

'This is a restricted area in a public place and I have reason to believe that you are/have been consuming or intend to consume alcohol in breach of a prohibition in a public spaces protection order. I require you to stop drinking and give me the container from which you are/have been drinking and any other containers (sealed or unsealed). I must inform you that failure to comply with my request, without reasonable excuse, is an offence.'

> **Offences**
>
> A person who fails without reasonable excuse to comply with a requirement imposed on him or her under subsection 63(2) [see **9.4.1**] commits an offence.
>
> Anti-social Behaviour, Crime and Policing Act 2014, s 63(6)

Points to prove

Surrender alcohol

✓ without reasonable excuse
✓ failed to surrender
✓ something that was or reasonably believed to be
✓ alcohol or container for such
✓ in their possession
✓ in a restricted area subject to a PSPO
✓ when required by a constable or an authorised person

Consume alcohol

✓ without reasonable excuse

✓ failed to comply with requirement

✓ imposed by constable or an authorised person

✓ not to consume in a restricted area of a PSPO

✓ something that was or reasonably believed to be alcohol

Practical considerations

- A constable or an authorised person who imposes the requirement shall inform the person concerned that failing without reasonable excuse to comply with the requirement is an offence.
- A CSO or CSV has a conferred power to search a person for alcohol or a container for alcohol if after a requirement to surrender alcohol or a container is made under s 63(2) the person fails to comply with the requirement. The CSO or CSV must reasonably believe that the person has alcohol or a container for alcohol in his or her possession (see **11.1.4**).
- The seizure and disposal of alcohol in both sealed and unsealed containers is allowed, although officers should follow their own force orders or LA procedure in relation to disposal.
- Consider issuing an FPN under s 68 for this offence (see **7.15.2**).

Links to alternative subjects and offences

 PND

 Summary 6 months

 Level 2 fine

9.5 Alcohol in Public Place (under 18)—Offences/ Confiscation

The Confiscation of Alcohol (Young Persons) Act 1997 allows the police to confiscate alcohol from people under 18 years in certain public places, with a failure to comply offence, while s 30 of the Policing and Crime Act 2009 makes it an offence for a person under 18 to persistently possess alcohol in a public place.

9.5.1 Offences/confiscation of alcohol (under 18)

Power

(1) Where a constable reasonably suspects that a person in a relevant place is in possession of alcohol and that either—
   (a) he is under the age of 18; or
   (b) he intends that any of the alcohol should be consumed by a person under the age of 18 in that or any other relevant place; or
   (c) a person under the age of 18 who is, or has recently been, with him has recently consumed alcohol in that or any other relevant place, the constable may require him to surrender anything in his possession which is, or which the constable reasonably believes to be, alcohol or a container for alcohol.

(1AA) A constable who imposes a requirement on a person under subsection (1) shall also require him to state his name and address.

Confiscation of Alcohol (Young Persons) Act 1997, s 1(1) and (1AA)

Offences

(3) A person who fails without reasonable excuse to comply with a requirement imposed on him under subsection (1) or (1AA) commits an offence.

Confiscation of Alcohol (Young Persons) Act 1997, s 1(3)

Points to prove

✓ without reasonable excuse
✓ failed to comply with requirement
✓ imposed by constable
✓ to surrender
✓ alcohol/suspected alcohol **or** a container for such
✓ in their possession
✓ and/or state their name and address

Meanings

Relevant place

Means any **public place**, other than **licensed premises**; or any place, other than a public place, to which the person has unlawfully gained access.

Licensed premises

Means premises which may by virtue of Pt 3 or Pt 5 of the Licensing Act 2003 (premises licence; permitted temporary activity) be used for the **supply of alcohol.**

Supply of alcohol (see 9.1.1)

Public place

For this purpose, a place is a public place if at the material time the public or any section of the public has access to it, on payment or otherwise, as of right, or by virtue of express, or implied permission.

Possession

At common law possession is defined as: **actual** or **potential** physical control and an intention to possess. In practice, visible or external signs of possession, which can be demonstrated to a court, must support the two conditions above (*Jowett's Dictionary of English Law*).

Alcohol (see 9.1.1)

Recently

Defined by the *Oxford English Dictionary* as 'lately' or 'comparatively near to the present time'.

Explanatory notes

- Officers can seize sealed and open containers, as well as the alcohol they hold, and dispose of both in an appropriate manner. Where a young person has, for example, a sealed six-pack under his arm, officers should still consider who sold it, and whether there are any child welfare issues, and act as appropriate.
- A constable may dispose of anything surrendered in such manner as s/he considers appropriate.
- When imposing a requirement to surrender a constable must inform the person of the suspicion and that failing without reasonable excuse to comply with the requirement as to surrender of alcohol and/or to state their name and address is an offence.

Example of officer's requirement

'I have reason to suspect that you are in possession of alcohol and that either you are under 18 years of age or you intend that any of the alcohol will be consumed or it has recently been consumed by a person under 18 in this or any other relevant place. (If applicable) You must stop drinking immediately. I require you to give me that can/bottle/

plastic cup, etc and to give me your name and address. I must warn you
that failure to comply with my requirements is an offence.'

Practical considerations

- A constable imposing a requirement under s 1(1) may, if the
  constable reasonably suspects that person to be under the age of 16,
  remove that person to their place of residence or a place of safety.
- Officers should follow their own force orders in relation to disposal.
- A CSO or CSV has the same powers as a police constable under this
  section (other than the arrest power) (see **11.1.4**).

 Summary   6 months

 Level 2 fine

9.5.2 **Persistently possess alcohol in public (under 18)**

Offences

A person under the age of 18 is guilty of an offence if, without
reasonable excuse, the person is in possession of alcohol in any relevant
place on 3 or more occasions within a period of 12 consecutive months.

Policing and Crime Act 2009, s 30(1)

Points to prove

- ✓ person under 18
- ✓ without reasonable excuse
- ✓ in **possession** of **alcohol**
- ✓ in any **relevant place**
- ✓ on three or more occasions
- ✓ within a twelve-month (consecutive) period

Meanings

Possession (see **9.5.1**)

Alcohol (see **9.1.1**)

Relevant place

Means any public place, other than **excluded premises**; or any place, other
than a **public place**, to which the person has unlawfully gained access.

Excluded premises

Means premises which may by virtue of the Licensing Act 2003:
• Pt 3 or 5 (premises licence or permitted temporary activity) should be used for the supply of alcohol;
• Pt 4 (club premises certificate) should be used for the supply of alcohol to members or guests.

Public place (see 9.5.1)

Explanatory notes

This offence only applies to people under the age of 18 if they possess alcohol in a relevant public place; and this has occurred on three or more occasions within a twelve-month period.

 Summary   6 months

 Level 2 fine

Links to alternative subjects and offences

Chapter 10

Road Traffic

10.1 Meanings: Roads, Public Places, Vehicles, and Drives

10.1.1 Roads

The term 'road' has many meanings within various pieces of legislation.

Meaning of road

'Road' is defined in several Acts. The two most commonly used meanings of a road are:
- any highway and any other road to which the public has access, and includes bridges over which a road passes (Road Traffic Act 1988, s 192(1));
- any length of highway and any other road to which the public has access and includes bridges over which a road passes (Road Traffic Regulation Act 1984, s 142(1)).

Explanatory notes
- 'Road' includes public highways, footpaths, and bridleways maintained by government agencies or local authorities.
- The term 'public road' in the Vehicle Excise and Registration Act 1994 means a road repairable at public expense.
- The physical nature of a road provides a defined or definable route, or way to which the general public has legal access, being a route allowing travel between two places.
- A field used for parking at an agricultural show was held not to be a road, as it had no definable way.
- A privately owned hotel forecourt used as a shortcut between two streets is a road.
- Walking or driving must take place on the road and such walking or driving must be lawful.

- Case decisions regarding roads need to be considered very carefully. As questions of 'fact', usually taken by lower courts, these decisions are heavily dependent on the individual circumstances of the case.

Related cases

Hallett v DPP [2011] EWHC 488 (Admin), QBD A 'service road' ran alongside another road, with twenty houses leading off this 'service road'. It was open at both ends and had 'give way' road markings at the entrance/exit. Residents were responsible, by covenant, to maintain this 'service road', but it had no barriers or 'private road' signs in place. Actual use of the road by the public must be evidenced for it to be a public road.

Sadiku v DPP [2000] RTR 155, QBD A paved area used as a thoroughfare by pedestrians can be a road.

Cutter v Eagle Star Insurance Company Ltd [1998] 4 All ER 417, HL and **Clarke v Kato and others [1998] 4 All ER 417, HL** A part of a car park may be a road but the whole of the car park will not necessarily be (ie properly designated parking bays will not be a road, but a definable route (direction arrows, lane markings, etc) may make the rest of the car park a road).

McGurk and another v Coster [1995] CLY 2912, CC Access to a temporary car park on a beach by driving over part of the beach between the sea and sand dunes was held not to be a road.

Practical considerations

- What are the physical characteristics, function, and public access of the place involved?
- Public access alone is not sufficient to make a place a road; similarly, some form of private use will not necessarily prevent it from being a road.
- Most important road traffic legislation relates to 'public places' as well—this is a wider and different definition that should be considered in each case (see **10.1.2**).
- The footway, lay-by, or verge is normally part of the road.
- The mode of transport is not relevant and such travellers may be on foot, riding on animals, or in a vehicle.
- In instances of real doubt, the courts have to decide on a case-by-case basis.

10.1.2 **Public place**

Meaning of public place

The term 'public place' has, for the purposes of the Road Traffic Act 1988, been interpreted as: 'any place to which the public have open access is a public place, even if payment must be made to gain entry'.

Explanatory notes

- Whether a place to which the public have limited, or restricted, access is a public place is a question of fact and degree in each case.
- The time at which the place was being used is important in dealing with 'public place' considerations. The car park of a public house may be a public place during licensing hours but may not be so outside those hours.
- An off-road parking bay adjacent to a highway with no physical impediment between the bay and the road is a public place.
- Lanes at a ferry port could be a public place or road as the public have access to them.

Related cases

Cowan v DPP [2013] EWHC 192 (Admin) QBD No evidence was provided for the court to conclude that a university campus was a public place, so it was unable to convict for an offence of driving a motor vehicle while OPL.

R v Spence [1999] Crim LR 975, CA A company car park in an industrial estate, used by employees, customers, and visitors on business, but not the general public, was held not to be a public place.

Practical considerations

- The test for whether or not it is a public place is to consider: 'do the people gaining access there have a special characteristic or personal reason which is not possessed by the general public?'
- Public use of the area must be shown evidentially.

10.1.3 Vehicles/motor vehicles/ mechanically propelled vehicles

Meaning of vehicles

General

The *Oxford English Dictionary* defines a 'vehicle' as a conveyance, usually with wheels, for transporting people, goods, etc; a car, cart, truck, carriage, sledge, etc; any means of carriage or transport; a receptacle in which something is placed in order to be moved.

For vehicle excise duty purposes

In the following provisions of this Act 'vehicle' means:
- a mechanically propelled vehicle, or
- any thing (whether or not it is a vehicle) that has been, but has ceased to be, a mechanically propelled vehicle.

Vehicle Excise and Registration Act 1994, s 1(1B)

Explanatory notes

The above definitions of 'vehicle' should not be confused with the meaning of 'motor vehicle' or 'mechanically propelled vehicle'.

- **Motor vehicle** means as follows:
  - ✦ subject to s 20 of the Chronically Sick and Disabled Persons Act 1970 (which makes special provision about invalid carriages, within the meaning of that Act), a **mechanically propelled vehicle** intended or adapted for use on roads (Road Traffic Act 1988, s 185);
  - ✦ any mechanically propelled vehicle, whether or not it is intended or **adapted for use on a road** (Police Reform Act 2002, s 59).
- **Mechanically propelled vehicle**—this is not legally defined, but it has a wider meaning than 'motor vehicle', as a mechanically propelled vehicle does not have to be 'intended or adapted for use on a road'. It means a vehicle which can be propelled by mechanical means and would include electric or steam-powered vehicles. Whether it is a mechanically propelled vehicle will have to be determined by the court.
- **Adapted for use on a road** means fit and apt for use on a road.
- A sidecar is part of a motor vehicle when attached to a motorbike and is not a trailer (Road Traffic Act 1988, s 186(1)).
- Conversely, the semi-trailer of an articulated vehicle is a trailer and not part of the towing vehicle (Road Traffic Act 1988, s 187(1)).
- An articulated bus ('bendy bus') should be treated as one vehicle (Road Traffic Act 1988, s 187(2)).
- A hovercraft is a motor vehicle (Road Traffic Act 1988, s 188).
- Certain specialised vehicles may be used as invalid carriages on pavements without being classified as motor vehicles.

Related cases

DPP v King [2008] EWHC 447 (Admin), QBD A 'City Mantis' electric scooter that looked like a bicycle, except that it did not have any pedals or other means of manual propulsion and was capable of speeds up to 10 mph, was held to be a motor vehicle.

CC of North Yorkshire Police v Saddington [2001] Crim LR 41, QBD A 'Go-Ped' (which resembles a child's scooter with an engine) has been held to be a motor vehicle. Despite a warning on it that it was not intended for use on a road, the correct test would be whether a reasonable person would say that one of its uses would be some general use on a road.

Reader v Bunyard [1987] RTR 406, QBD A motor vehicle remains a mechanically propelled vehicle unless there was evidence that there was no likelihood of it being so used again. The onus is on the prosecution to prove that the vehicle is capable of being repaired or used.

Thomas v Hooper [1986] RTR 1, QBD A vehicle may no longer be a motor vehicle if it has none of the normal vehicular controls operative.

Burns v Currell [1963] 2 All ER 297, QBD When deciding whether one of the uses of a vehicle would be on a road a 'reasonable person' test should be applied to the vehicle and not the intentions of the specific user at the time it was stopped.

Practical considerations

* What was the vehicle intended for and to what use is it currently being put?
* The onus of proving that a motor vehicle remained a mechanically propelled vehicle lies with the prosecution.
* Pedestrian-controlled mowing machines, other pedestrian-controlled vehicles and electrically assisted pedal cycles approved by the Secretary of State are **not** motor vehicles (Road Traffic Act 1988, s 189).
* It is a matter of fact and degree for the court to decide whether or not a vehicle is a motor vehicle or mechanically propelled vehicle at the time of a specific incident.
* In such cases, include evidence of the characteristics of the vehicle, which may be a photograph if appropriate.

10.1.4 **Drives/driving**

Meaning of drives/driving

* The statutory definition of a 'driver'—where a separate person acts as a steersman of a motor vehicle—includes (except for the purposes of s 1 of this Act) that person as well as any other person engaged in the driving of the vehicle, and 'drive' is to be interpreted accordingly (Road Traffic Act 1988, s 192(1)).
* This means that a driver is any person who is engaged in the driving of the vehicle including, where a separate person acts as a steersman of a motor vehicle, that person.
* Case law provides matters to consider but the principal test is:
  + 'the essence of driving is the use of the driver's controls for the purpose of directing the movement of the car however the movement is produced' (R v McDonagh [1974] 2 All ER 257, CA).
* Whether or not a person was driving is ultimately a matter of fact and degree. It is for the court or jury to decide on the facts in each case (*Edkins v Knowles* [1973] 2 All ER 503, QBD).

Explanatory notes

* The vehicle does not have to be moving. A driver is still driving until he has completed the normal operations, such as applying the handbrake, that occur at the end of a journey.
* A vehicle may halt temporarily such as at traffic lights, so consider:
  + What was the purpose of the stop?
  + How long was the vehicle stopped?

✦ Did the driver get out of the vehicle?
- It is also possible for two people to be driving the same vehicle.

Related cases

Avery v CPS [2011] EWHC 2388 (Admin), DC In this case, a car driven on a private driveway collided with a parked car on the adjacent road, with the collision being caused by the protruding boot of the car. It was held that although the tyres of the car remained on private land and only part of the car (the boot) encroached onto the road, the driver was still found to have driven the vehicle 'on' a road.

Cawthorn v DPP [2000] RTR 45, QBD A driver left his vehicle for a few minutes, set the handbrake and switched on the hazard warning lights, but the passenger released the handbrake. The vehicle rolled down a hill and hit a brick wall. It was held that this intervening act did not make that person the driver, as the passenger did not have sufficient control to fulfil the definition of driving. The defendant still remained the driver until the journey was complete or someone else had taken over the driving. Whether someone was a driver at any particular time was a question of fact for the court or jury to decide.

DPP v Hastings (1993) 158 JP 118, QBD It was held in this case that a passenger snatching the wheel momentarily is not a 'driver' because this action does not constitute the act of driving.

Burgoyne v Phillips [1983] RTR 49, QBD The defendant had set the car in motion, was sitting in the driving seat, and was trying to control the car. It was held that the fact that the steering was momentarily locked did not prevent the defendant from 'driving' the car.

McQuaid v Anderton [1980] 3 All ER 540, QBD It was held in this case that steering a car being towed can be 'driving'. The essence of 'driving' was the use of the driver's controls in order to direct the movement of the car, the method of propulsion being irrelevant.

Tyler v Whatmore [1976] RTR 83, QBD Two people can be driving a vehicle at the same time. The defendant (the front seat passenger) was leaning across steering the car, whilst the other driver manipulated the controls. In this case neither person had full control of both the brakes and the steering and although the passenger could not control the propulsion, there was some control over the handbrake and ignition system. The passenger was, therefore, driving the vehicle.

Practical considerations

- If there is some doubt as to whether a person is driving or not, the circumstances must be looked at individually.
- As a general rule there are three elements to driving:
    ✦ control of the steering; *and*
    ✦ control of the propulsion; *and*
    ✦ the actions of the person must fall within the everyday meaning of driving.

Links to alternative subjects and offences

10.2 Powers to Stop/Direct Vehicles and Pedestrians

The Road Traffic Act 1988 provides various powers to stop vehicles; and offences of drivers neglecting or refusing to comply with traffic directions given by a police constable.

10.2.1 Drivers to comply with traffic directions

Section 35 of the Road Traffic Act 1988 provides for drivers who refuse or neglect to comply with traffic directions given by a police constable.

Offences

(1) Where a constable or traffic officer is for the time being engaged in the regulation of traffic in a road, a person driving or propelling a vehicle who neglects or refuses—
   (a) to stop the vehicle; or
   (b) to make it proceed in, or keep to, a particular line of traffic, when directed to do so by the constable in the exercise of his duty or the traffic officer (as the case may be) is guilty of an offence.

(2) Where—
   (a) a traffic survey of any description is being carried out on or in the vicinity of a road, and
   (b) a constable or traffic officer gives a person driving or propelling a vehicle a direction—
      (i) to stop the vehicle,
      (ii) to make it proceed in, or keep to, a particular line of traffic, or
      (iii) to proceed to a particular point on or near the road on which the vehicle is being driven or propelled,
   being a direction given for the purposes of the survey (but not a direction requiring any person to provide any information for the purposes of a traffic survey),
the person is guilty of an offence if he refuses or neglects to comply with the direction.

Road Traffic Act 1988, s 35

Points to prove

s 35(1) offence

✓ constable or traffic officer
✓ engaged in the regulation of traffic in a road

10.2.1 Drivers to comply with traffic directions

✓ driver/rider of vehicle neglected/refused
✓ to stop vehicle/proceed/keep to particular line of traffic
✓ as directed

s 35(2) offence

✓ traffic survey on/in vicinity of a road
✓ driver/rider of vehicle
✓ refused/failed/neglected to comply
✓ with directions given by constable or traffic officer
✓ for purposes of the survey

Meanings

Traffic officer

Person designated under the Traffic Management Act 2004, s 2.

Road (see 10.1.1)

Driving (see 10.1.4)

Vehicle (see 10.1.3)

Explanatory notes

- The constable/traffic officer must be engaged in the regulation of traffic and acting in the execution of their duty.
- A constable may direct a person to disobey a traffic sign if it is reasonably necessary for the protection of life.
- The prosecution needs to show that the given signal was obvious and should have been evident to the motorist, not that the motorist saw it.
- Although a constable/traffic officer can direct a driver/rider to a specific point for a traffic survey, they cannot direct any person to supply information for the survey.
- Any direction in connection with a traffic survey must not cause undue delay to a person who indicates that they are unwilling to give information for the survey.

Practical considerations

- Offences under s 35 are not confined to mechanically propelled vehicles.
- Stop does not automatically mean the driver must remain stationary until signaled to proceed, unless the direction was to remain stationary.
- Notice of intended prosecution (NIP) to be issued (see **10.5**).
- Consider issuing a TFPN (see **10.4.1**).

Summary   6 months

 Level 3 fine

> *If committed in a motor vehicle:*
> Discretionary disqualification and obligatory endorsement of 3
> penalty points

10.2.2 **Directions to pedestrians**

Section 37 of the Road Traffic Act 1988 empowers a constable in uniform
or traffic officer engaged in the direction of vehicular traffic on a road to
also direct a pedestrian walking along or across the carriageway to stop.

Offences

Where a constable in uniform or traffic officer is for the time being
engaged in the regulation of vehicular traffic in a road, a person on
foot who proceeds across or along the carriageway in contravention
of a direction to stop given by the constable in the execution of
his duty or the traffic officer (as the case may be), either to persons
on foot or to persons on foot and other traffic, is guilty of an
offence.

Road Traffic Act 1988, s 37

Points to prove

✓ being a pedestrian proceeded along/across carriageway
✓ contravened direction of constable or traffic officer
✓ engaged in direction of vehicular traffic on a road

Meanings

Traffic officer (see 10.2.1)

Road (see 10.1)

Explanatory notes

- Reference to a constable includes reference to a traffic
  warden.
- A suitably designated PCSO has the same powers as a constable
  under s 37.

Practical considerations

- A pedestrian breaching s 37 may be required to give their name and address.
- The constable must be in uniform—include details in evidence.

 Summary   6 months

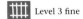 Level 3 fine

10.2.3 **Testing the condition of vehicles on a road**

Section 67 of the Road Traffic Act 1988 empowers authorised vehicle examiners to test motor vehicles on the road, but any vehicle stopped for a test must be stopped by a constable in uniform or 'stopping officer'.

> **Offences**
>
> If a person obstructs an authorised examiner acting under this section or fails to comply with a requirement of this section or Schedule 2 (deferred tests of conditions of vehicles) to this Act, he is guilty of an offence.
>
> Road Traffic Act 1988, s 67(9)

Meanings

Authorised vehicle examiner

Includes a constable authorised by or on behalf of the chief officer of police.

Test

Includes inspect or inspection.

Vehicle (see 10.1.3)

Includes a trailer drawn by it.

Explanatory notes

- Vehicle examiners may test all motor vehicles that are on the road.
- A vehicle shall not be required to stop for a test except by a constable in uniform or a 'stopping officer'. The Road Vehicles (Powers to Stop) Regulations 2011 (SI 996/2011) provides for appointment of **'stopping officers'** under s 66B, with powers to stop

certain commercial vehicles for specific checks by vehicle examiners and other authorised persons.

Related cases

Sadiku v DPP [2000] RTR 155, QBD It was held in this case that a constable requiring the test to be carried out, may ask for the keys while awaiting the arrival of the authorised examiner.

Practical considerations

- An authorised examiner may test a motor vehicle on a road to ascertain whether it meets construction and use requirements, and its condition does not involve a danger of injury to any person.
- For the purpose of testing a vehicle the examiner may require the driver to comply with reasonable instructions, and drive the vehicle.
- The driver may elect for the test to be deferred to a time and place in accordance with Sch 2. However, if the vehicle has been involved in an accident on a road or is so defective that it ought not to be allowed to proceed, the constable may require that the vehicle shall not be taken away until the test has been carried out.
- A constable who is not an authorised examiner cannot use s 67 to carry out this test. However, a constable can still enforce regulations concerning construction and use where the driver is cooperative.
- This section applies to vehicles registered outside Great Britain.

 Summary   6 months

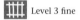 Level 3 fine

10.2.4 **Police powers to stop a vehicle on a road**

Section 163 of the Road Traffic Act 1988 empowers a police constable in uniform or a traffic officer to stop a mechanically propelled vehicle on a road.

Offences

(1) A person driving a mechanically propelled vehicle on a road must stop the vehicle on being required to do so by a constable in uniform or a traffic officer.

(2) A person riding a cycle on a road must stop the cycle on being required to do so by a constable in uniform or a traffic officer.

(3) If a person fails to comply with this section he is guilty of an offence.

Road Traffic Act 1988, s 163

10.2.4 Police powers to stop a vehicle on a road

Points to prove

✓ drove mechanically propelled vehicle/rode cycle
✓ on a road
✓ required by constable or traffic officer
✓ to stop the vehicle/cycle
✓ failed to do so

Meanings

Driving (see 10.1.4)

Mechanically propelled vehicle (see 10.1.3)

Road (see 10.1.1)

Traffic officer (see 10.2.1)

Explanatory notes

- 'Mechanically propelled vehicle' is not defined in the Act and is a matter of fact and degree to be decided by the court (see 10.1.3).
- Plain-clothed police officers can use the common law to stop vehicles they reasonably believe to be involved in crime (eg a stolen car) (*R (on the application of Rutherford) v IPCC* [2010] EWHC 2881).

Practical considerations

Consider issuing a traffic fixed penalty notice (TFPN) (see 10.4.1).

 E&S **TFPN**

 Summary 6 months

 Fine level 5 (level 3 fine if a cycle)

Links to alternative subjects and offences

10.3 **Fail to Comply with Traffic Signs**

Section 36 of the Road Traffic Act 1988 creates an offence of failing to comply with certain traffic signs.

> **Offences**
>
> Where a traffic sign, being a sign—
> (a) of the prescribed size, colour and type, or
> (b) of another character authorised by the Secretary of State under the provisions in that behalf of the Road Traffic Regulation Act 1984,
>
> has been lawfully placed on or near a road, a person driving or propelling a vehicle who fails to comply with the indication given by the sign is guilty of an offence.
>
> Road Traffic Act 1988, s 36(1)

Points to prove

✓ authorised traffic sign lawfully placed
✓ on or near a road
✓ driver/rider of vehicle on that road
✓ failed to comply with the direction of that sign

Meanings

Traffic sign

As given in the Traffic Signs Regulations and General Directions 2016.

Lawfully placed

A sign will not be lawfully placed unless it indicates a statutory prohibition, restriction, or requirement, or a provision of the Traffic Acts specifically states that it is a sign to which this section applies.

Road (see **10.1.1**)

Driving (see **10.1.4**)

Vehicle (see **10.1.3**)

Explanatory notes

- Some of the traffic signs to which this section applies are: double white line markings; box junction markings; traffic lights (including temporary traffic lights at roadworks); 'stop' sign (including manually operated at roadworks); flashing red 'stop' lights on motorways or automatic tram/railway crossing; no entry sign; give way sign; directional arrow; keep left/right sign; bus/cycle/tramcar route sign; weight/height restriction sign.

- This section applies to traffic survey signs and emergency traffic signs put out by police (eg football matches, processions).
- A single dotted white line in the centre of the road separating two carriageways does not fall into this section.
- For contravention of a 'stop' sign or red traffic light signal it is necessary to prove that the vehicle did not stop at the stop line or, if the stop line is not visible, before entering the major road or that it stopped beyond the mounting of the primary signal respectively.
- Emergency vehicles may be exempted from the requirement to conform to a red traffic light but must proceed so as not to cause danger to the driver of another vehicle or to cause such driver to change their speed or direction to avoid an accident, or cause danger to non-vehicular traffic.
- Failure by the driver to see the traffic sign is not a defence, except in very limited situations (see *Coombes v DPP* [2006] EWHC 3263, QBD below) and will generally be evidence to support an offence of driving without due care and attention (see **10.6**).

Defences

This section creates absolute offences except for the possible defences of mechanical defect, automatism, or not seen due to badly located signage.

Defence notes

- 'Automatism' has been defined as 'the involuntary movement of a person's body or limbs' and its source or cause must be something of which the driver was unaware or something that they could not reasonably be expected to foresee.
- Falling asleep whilst driving a vehicle does not amount to automatism.
- In very limited situations where a driver fails to see the sign (see *Coombes v DPP* [2006], EWHC 3263, QBD).

Related cases

R v McKay (2015) unreported CA It was held in this case that the defence of automatism was not available to an offender who had induced a state of automatism through taking drink or drugs.

Peake v DPP [2010] EWHC 286 (Admin), QBD If the prosecution establishes the route taken by the driver, it would only have to show that compliant signs provided adequate guidance, at the point of enforcement, for someone taking that route. Otherwise, they would have to show that there were compliant signs on all routes which the driver might have taken.

10.3 Fail to Comply with Traffic Signs

McKenzie v DPP [1997] Crim LR 232, QBD A vehicle can stop on a road where double white lines are present to drop/pick up passengers, load/unload goods, to carry out road/building work, or to remove obstructions.

A-G's Reference (No 2 of 1992) [1993] 4 All ER 683, CA Driving without awareness (such as falling asleep) is not a case where automatism could be used as a defence.

Practical considerations

- Traffic signs placed on or near a road are deemed to be of the correct specification and to have been lawfully placed unless the contrary is proved.
- A stop sign at a junction indicates that a vehicle must at least momentarily stop at the stop line and not merely slow down.
- Section 87 of the Road Traffic Regulation Act 1984 exempts fire, ambulance, responding to an emergency for NHS ambulance service, and police vehicles from speed limits if observance would hinder the use of the vehicle for the purpose it was being used for on that occasion. The Deregulation Act 2015 amended s 87 to include providing a response to an emergency at the request of an NHS ambulance service.
- Consider issuing a TFPN (see **10.4.1**).
- Is the traffic sign one that is specified for this section?
- Is the contravention evidence of a more serious offence (eg dangerous driving, driving without due care and attention)?
- An NIP must be served for offences of failing to comply with some types of traffic signs (see **10.5**).

 Summary 6 months

 Level 3 fine

Discretionary disqualification, obligatory endorsement—3 penalty points

Links to alternative subjects and offences

10.4 **Traffic Fixed Penalty Notices**

Traffic Fixed Penalty Notices (TFPNs) and procedures with regard to road traffic offences are covered by ss 51–90 of the Road Traffic Offenders Act 1988.

10.4.1 **Traffic Fixed Penalty Notices**

Section 54 of the Act allows a constable in uniform who has reason to believe that a person is committing or has committed a fixed penalty offence to then issue a TFPN in respect of that offence.

Offences

A person is guilty of an offence if he removes or interferes with any notice fixed to a vehicle under this section, unless he does so by or under the authority of the driver or person in charge of the vehicle or the person liable for the fixed penalty offence in question.

Road Traffic Offenders Act 1988, s 62(2)

A person who, in a response to a notice to owner, provides a statement which is false in a material particular and does so recklessly or knowing it to be false in that particular is guilty of that offence.

Road Traffic Offenders Act 1988, s 67

Points to prove

s 62(2) offence

✓ without authority of driver/person in charge or liable for TFPN
✓ removed/interfered with TFPN fixed to vehicle

s 67 offence

✓ in response to notice to owner
✓ provided false statement
✓ recklessly/knowing it to be false

Meaning of 'Traffic Fixed Penalty Notice'

Means a notice offering the opportunity of the discharge of any liability to conviction of the offence to which the notice relates by payment of a fixed penalty in accordance with Pt 3 of this Act.

Explanatory notes

- TFPNs apply where a constable in uniform believes that a person is committing or has committed a **relevant offence** (see below) and may be issued either at the time of the offence or at a police station.
- If the offence involves obligatory endorsement the constable may only issue a TFPN if the offender produces and surrenders their driving licence to the constable and is not liable to disqualification under s 35—the 'totting up' procedure.
- Where the offender has no licence with them, the constable may issue a notice requiring its production within seven days at a specified police station and, if certain requirements are met, can then be issued with a TFPN.
- A TFPN must give details of the offence, **suspended enforcement period**, penalty payable, and how it should be paid.
- '**Suspended enforcement period**' means the period following the date of the offence during which no proceedings will be brought against the offender.
- Where the penalty has not been paid or a hearing elected during the suspended enforcement period, the penalty plus 50 per cent may be registered against them.
- If the offence involves obligatory endorsement, the person receiving the surrendered licence must issue a receipt and forward the surrendered licence on to the fixed-penalty clerk.
- If the licence holder is liable to disqualification under the 'totting up' (see **10.13**) system, the fixed-penalty clerk must forward the licence on to the chief officer of police who may commence proceedings. Where such proceedings are commenced any action already taken (eg registration as a fine) is void.
- At the end of the suspended enforcement period, if the penalty has not been paid or a hearing requested by the driver at the relevant time, a notice to owner may be served on the owner.
- A notice to owner must include particulars as to the offence, TFPN issued, response time allowed (minimum twenty-one days), penalty if it is not paid, requesting a hearing.
- If the person on whom the notice to owner was served was not the owner of the vehicle at the time of the offence and provides a statutory statement of ownership to that effect, they are not liable for the fine registered against them.
- If a notice to owner has been served, proceedings may not be brought against anybody else in relation to that offence unless they are identified as the driver at the relevant time in a statutory statement of facts.

Relevant offences

Schedule 3 to this Act lists the TFPN offences:

10.4.1 Traffic Fixed Penalty Notices

Highways Act 1835

s 72—Driving/cycling on footway.

Transport Act 1968

s 96(11)—Contravened drivers' hours.
s 96(11A)—Contravened periods of driving.
s 97(1)—Contravened recording equipment regs.
s 98(4)—Contravened drivers' hours written records regs.
s 99(4)—Fail to produce records/obstruction.
s 99ZD(1)—Fail to comply with requirements/obstruction.
s 99C—Fail to comply with prohibition/direction.

Road Traffic (Foreign Vehicles) Act 1972

s 3(1)—Drive foreign GV or PSV in contravention of prohibition.

Greater London Council (General Powers) Act 1974

s 15—Parking vehicles on footways, verges, other related offences.

Highways Act 1980

s 137—Obstruction of highway committed in respect of a vehicle.

Public Passenger Vehicles Act 1981

s 12(5)—Use PSV on road without PSV operator's licence.

Road Traffic Regulation Act 1984

s 5(1)—Traffic regulation order outside Greater London.
s 8(1)—Traffic regulation order in Greater London.
s 11—Experimental traffic order.
s 13—Breach of experimental traffic scheme.
s 16(1)—Temporary prohibition or restriction.
s 17(4)—Wrongful use of special road.
s 18(3)—One-way traffic order on trunk road.
s 20(5)—Prohibition/restriction of driving on certain classes of road.
s 25(5)—Breach of pedestrian crossing regulations, except offence
   in respect of moving motor vehicle, other than contravention of
   regs 23, 24, 25, and 26 of the Zebra, Pelican and Puffin Pedestrian
   Crossings Regulations and General Directions 1997.
s 29(3)—Street playground order.
s 35A(1)—Local authority parking place on a road.
s 47(1)—Parking place designation order.
s 53(5)—Parking place designation order under s 53(1)(a).
s 53(6)—Designation order authorised parking on road without charge.
s 88(7)—Minimum speed limit.
s 89(1)—Speeding.

Road Transport (International Passenger Services)

Regulations 1984

reg 19(1)—Use vehicle for carriage of passengers without authorisation/certificate.

reg 19(2)—Use vehicle for carriage of passengers without passenger waybill.

Road Traffic Act 1988

s 3—Driving mechanically propelled vehicle on a road/public place without due care and attention, or reasonable consideration.

s 14—Seat belt regulations.

s 15(2)—Restriction re children in front of vehicles.

s 15(4)—Restriction re children in rear of vehicles.

s 16—Crash helmet regulations re motorcycle rider/passenger.

s 18(3)—Breach use of eye protector regulations on motorcycles.

s 19—Parking heavy commercial vehicle on verge/footway.

s 22—Leave vehicle in dangerous position.

s 23—Unlawfully carry passenger on motorcycle.

s 24—Carry more than one person on pedal cycle.

s 34—Drive mechanically propelled vehicle elsewhere than on road.

s 35—Fail to comply with traffic directions.

s 36—Fail to comply with prescribed traffic signs (see **10.3**).

s 40A—Use vehicle where condition; purpose used; passengers carried; load involves danger of injury.

s 41A—Breach of requirements re brakes, steering-gear, or tyres.

s 41B—Breach of weight requirement re goods and passenger vehicles.

s 41D—Breach of requirements re control, view of road, or use hand held device.

s 42—Breach of other construction and use regulations.

s 47—Using vehicle without a test certificate.

s 71(1)—Contravened prohibition order or fail comply order.

s 87(1)—Drive vehicle otherwise than in accordance with licence.

s 143—Using a motor vehicle without insurance.

s 144A—Keeping a vehicle that does not meet insurance requirements

s 163—Fail to stop vehicle when required by officer in uniform.

s 172—Failed to give information re driver of motor vehicle.

Road Traffic Offenders Act 1988

s 90D(6)—Drive in contravention of prohibition or fail to comply direction.

Goods Vehicles (Community Authorisations) Regulations 1992

reg 3—Use goods vehicle without community authorisation.

reg 7—Use vehicle contravening regulations under community authorisation.

10.4.1 Traffic Fixed Penalty Notices

Vehicle Excise and Registration Act 1994

s 34—Use trade licence for unauthorised purposes/circumstances.
s 42—Driving/keeping vehicle without required registration mark.
s 43—Drive/keep vehicle with registration mark obscured.
s 43C—Offence of using an incorrectly registered vehicle.
s 59—Fail to affix prescribed registration mark to vehicle.

Goods Vehicles (Licensing of Operators) Act 1995

s 2(5)—Use GV on road for carriage of goods—no operator's licence.

Public Service Vehicles (Community Licences) Regulations 1999

reg 3—Use PSV on road without community licence.
reg 7—Use PSV under community licence—contravened licence
conditions.

Road Transport (Passenger Vehicles Cabotage) Regulations 1999

reg 3—Using vehicle on road for UK cabotage operations—no EC
licence.
reg 4—Using vehicle on road for UK cabotage operations—no control
document.
reg 7(1)—Fail to produce EC licence when requested.
reg 7(3)—Failed to produce control document when requested.

Vehicle Drivers (Certificates of Professional Competence)

Regulations 2007

reg 11(7)—Driver of relevant vehicle failed to produce evidence/
document.

Practical considerations

- Consider the seriousness of the offence. There is no obligation to
  issue a TFPN—it is at the discretion of the constable.
- Is the fixed penalty scheme appropriate?
- Is the offence endorsable—if so, is the offender with the vehicle?
- Only a non-endorsable TFPN may be attached to a vehicle.
- Is the offender liable to disqualification under the totting up
  system?

 Summary

s 62 offence:
6 months

s 67 offence:
If statutory declaration is made, 6 months from date of declaration, up to a maximum of 12 months from the original offence. In all other cases—6 months.

 s 62 offence:
Level 2 fine

s 67 offence:
Fine not exceeding level 5

10.4.2 Control of vehicle and use of hand-held device

Offences

A person who contravenes or fails to comply with a construction and use requirement—

(a) as to not driving a motor vehicle in a position which does not give proper control or a full view of the road and traffic ahead, or not causing or permitting the driving of a motor vehicle by another person in such a position, or

(b) as to not driving or supervising the driving of a motor vehicle while using a hand-held mobile telephone or other hand-held interactive communication device, or not causing or permitting the driving of a motor vehicle by another person using such a telephone or other device is guilty of an offence.

Road Traffic Act 1988, s 41D

Points to prove

s 41D(a) offence

✓ contravened/failed to comply with requirement
✓ by driving a motor vehicle on a road
✓ without proper control of vehicle or full view **or**
✓ caused/permitted the above offences

s 41D(b) offence

✓ contravened/failed to comply with requirement
✓ being the driver/driving supervisor
✓ of a motor vehicle on a road
✓ **used hand-held** mobile/similar device **or**
✓ caused/permitted above offence

10.4.2 Control of vehicle and use of hand-held device

Meaning of 'construction and use requirement'

Means requirement imposed by regulations made under s 41 of the Road Traffic Act 1988, being mainly the Road Vehicles (Construction and Use) Regulations 1986.

Explanatory notes

- Not being in a position to have proper control of the vehicle or a full view of the road and traffic ahead comes under reg 104 of the Road Vehicles (Construction and Use) Regulations 1986.
- Using a hand-held mobile telephone or similar device comes under reg 110 of the Road Vehicles (Construction and Use) Regulations 1986.

Practical considerations

- These offences provide for obligatory endorsement and disqualification (at the court's discretion).
- A two-way radio, which performs an interactive communication function by transmitting and receiving data, is not a device under reg 110.
- Regulation 110(5) states that a person does not contravene reg 110 if:
  - ✦ they are using the telephone or device to call the police, fire, ambulance, or other emergency service on 112 or 999;
  - ✦ they are acting in response to a genuine emergency; and
  - ✦ it is unsafe or impracticable for them to cease driving in order to make the call.
- A mobile telephone or other device is to be treated as hand-held if it is, or must be, held at some point during the course of making or receiving a call or performing any other interactive communication function.
- A person who supervises the holder of a provisional licence must be at least 21 years of age and hold a full EC/EEA licence for that type of vehicle (including manual or automatic). The supervisor must not speak (hand-held) on their mobile, or text, while supervising a learner.

 TFPN

 Summary   6 months

Level 4 fine for goods vehicle or vehicle carrying more than eight passengers

Level 3 fine in any other case

Discretionary disqualification

Obligatory endorsement—3 penalty points for an offence under s 41D(a) and 6 penalty points for an offence under s 41D(b)

10.4.3 Graduated fixed penalties, penalty deposits, and immobilisation

The Road Safety Act 2006 introduced the graduated fixed penalty scheme, roadside deposits, and vehicle immobilisation.

Schedule 2 to the Fixed Penalty Order 2000 lists the graduated fixed penalties and graduates the level of specified fixed penalties based on the seriousness of the offending. It increases the level of fine for some offences to above the default amount (£100 endorsable and £50 non-endorsable). Initially these graduated fixed penalties only apply to specific offences relating to commercial and PSV vehicles.

Any officer appointed by their force or a DVSA officer will have responsibility for dealing with graduated fixed penalties.

Roadside deposits

The Road Traffic Offenders Act 1988, ss 90A–90D provide enforcement powers under what is termed the 'roadside deposit scheme'.

> **Offences**
>
> A person who—
> (a) drives a vehicle in contravention of a prohibition under this section,
> (b) causes or permits a vehicle to be driven in contravention of such a prohibition, or
> (c) fails to comply within a reasonable time with a direction under subsection (5) above, is guilty of an offence.
>
> Road Traffic Offenders Act 1988, s 90D(6)

> **Points to prove**
>
> ✓ drives a vehicle or causes/permits vehicle to be driven
> ✓ in contravention of a prohibition or
> ✓ fails to comply within a reasonable time with a direction under s 90D(5)

Meanings

Prohibition

This section applies where a person on whom a financial penalty deposit requirement is imposed does not make an immediate payment of the appropriate amount in accordance with section 90B(1) of this Act (and any order made under it).

The constable or vehicle examiner by whom the requirement was imposed may prohibit the driving on a road of any vehicle of which the person was in charge at the time of the offence by giving to the person notice in writing of the prohibition.

The prohibition—

(a) shall come into force as soon as the notice is given, and
(b) shall continue in force until the happening of whichever of the events in subsection (4) below occurs first.

Those events are—

(a) the person making a payment of the appropriate amount in accordance with section 90B(1) of this Act (and any order made under it) at any time during the relevant period,
(b) (where a fixed penalty notice was given, or a conditional offer handed, to the person in respect of the offence) payment of the fixed penalty,
(c) the person being convicted or acquitted of the offence,
(d) the person being informed that he is not to be prosecuted for the offence, and
(e) the coming to an end of the prosecution period.

Direction

A constable or vehicle examiner may by direction in writing require the person to remove the vehicle to which the prohibition relates (and, if it is a motor vehicle drawing a trailer, also to remove the trailer) to such place and subject to such conditions as are specified in the direction; and the prohibition does not apply to the removal of the vehicle (or trailer) in accordance with the direction.

Road Traffic Offenders Act 1988, s 90D

Explanatory notes

- Section 90A gives a constable in uniform or a vehicle examiner power to require the payment of a deposit from a person, whom they believe is committing or has committed an offence in relation to a motor vehicle, and who is unable to provide a satisfactory address in the UK at which they can be found. Furthermore, the police officer or vehicle examiner must also believe that the person, the offence, and the circumstances in which the offence is committed are of a description specified by order made by the Secretary of State.
- Under s 90B a financial penalty deposit, of an amount specified by order, can be paid to the constable or examiner. That person must then be given either a fixed penalty notice or written notice as to proposed court proceedings for the offence.
- The specified amounts are:
  - ✦ when it is a TFPN, the amount of that fixed penalty;
  - ✦ in other cases, it is a maximum of £500 per offence, to a maximum of £1,500 per vehicle stoppage.
- Once payment is made, s 90C stipulates that the person must be issued with a written receipt and notice outlining the process that applies through the various provisions of s 90C.

- If the driver does not contest the roadside deposit within twenty-eight days, then the deposit is paid into court and that is the end of the matter. Alternatively, should the driver contest and the court decide in their favour or if the case did not go to court within a year (or less than this if a shorter prosecution period applies), then the deposit would be refunded with the relevant interest. Similarly, if the court decided against them, the deposit would be retained to be offset against all, or part, of the fine imposed.
- Under s 90D, if a person does not make an immediate roadside deposit payment of the appropriate amount, the constable or vehicle examiner may then give the person a prohibition notice which prohibits the moving of the vehicle, though the vehicle/trailer may be moved to a specified place by way of a written direction.
- This prohibition will remain in force until one of the following occurs:
  + payment of the appropriate amount, during the relevant period;
  + payment of the fixed penalty notice;
  + conviction or acquittal of the offence;
  + driver informed that they will not be prosecuted; or
  + the prosecution period has expired.

Practical considerations

- This legislation provides enforcement powers against both UK and non-UK drivers who do not have a satisfactory UK address and were previously able to avoid payment of fixed penalties and prosecution as a result. It applies to both fixed penalty offences and other traffic offences.
- Enforcement of this scheme is through prohibition notices and vehicle immobilisation, removal, and disposal powers.
- Under the Road Safety (Immobilisation, Removal and Disposal of Vehicles) Regulations 2009 a vehicle may be immobilised when the vehicle is being driven:
  + whilst unfit for service or overloaded;
  + in contravention of the drivers' hours rules;
  + in contravention of international transport requirements;
  + by a person who has failed to pay the financial penalty deposit.
- Immobilisation will physically prevent a prohibition being disregarded, but the vehicle cannot be immobilised simply because it appears that the driver is likely to abscond.
- Therefore, where a driver does not make a payment under the roadside deposit scheme, the prohibition and immobilisation powers can be applied by the enforcement officer until the prohibition requirements are satisfied or, in cases of offenders who do not have a reliable UK address, until a deposit is paid, or the case is settled in court.
- Prior to this scheme, prohibitions were usually imposed for breaches of drivers' hours or when the vehicle was not roadworthy.
- Payment will normally be made by cash or debit cards, as payment by credit cards can be cancelled prior to the transfer taking place.

10.4.3 Graduated fixed penalties etc

 (including graduated TFPN)

 Summary

 6 months

 Fine

Discretionary disqualification

Links to alternative subjects and offences

10.5 **Notice of Intended Prosecution**

Section 1 of the Road Traffic Offenders Act 1988 requires a notice of intended prosecution to be given to a defendant for certain offences.

Requirement

Subject to section 2 of this Act, a person shall not be convicted of an offence to which this section applies unless—

(a) he was warned at the time the offence was committed that the question of prosecuting him for one or other of the offences to which this section applies would be taken into consideration, or

(b) within 14 days of the commission of the offence a summons for the offence was served on him, or

(c) within 14 days of the commission of the offence a notice of the intended prosecution specifying the nature of the alleged offence and the time and place where it is alleged to have been committed, was—

    (i) in the case of an offence under section 28 or 29 of the Road Traffic Act 1988 (cycling offences) [see 10.12], served on him,

    (ii) in the case of any other offence, served on him or on the person, if any, registered as the keeper of the vehicle at the time of the commission of the offence.

Road Traffic Offenders Act 1988, s 1(1)

Meanings

Subject to section 2

This section will not apply if:

- at the time of the offence or immediately after it, the vehicle concerned was involved in an accident;
- a fixed penalty notice or a notice under the fixed penalty scheme requiring production of the defendant's licence and counterpart at a police station is issued (see **10.4**).

Within 14 days

Means the notice must be posted to reach the defendant within 14 days of the offence.

Explanatory notes

- Notices of intended prosecution (NIPs) may be served personally, or by registered post, recorded delivery, or first-class post to their last known address.

- A NIP sent by registered post or recorded delivery is deemed served if addressed to them at their last known address even if it is returned undelivered or not received by them for some other reason.
- Requirements of s 1 are met unless the contrary is proved or if the defendant is charged and given a copy of the charge within fourteen days of the commission of the offence.
- A NIP posted the day after the offence, which failed to arrive within the fourteen days, was good service; whereas one sent by recorded delivery on the fourteenth day was deemed not 'served'.
- Failure to comply with s 1 is not a bar to conviction if the name and address of the defendant or the registered keeper could not be ascertained with due diligence in time to comply, or that the accused's conduct contributed to the failure.
- If an alternative verdict is returned by the court and the alternative offence requires NIP this is not a bar to conviction, providing the original offence did not require NIP.

Related cases

R v Myers [2007] EWCA Crim 599, CA There must be a causal link between a traffic offence and the accident, otherwise the driver requires serving with NIP.

Relevant offences

Schedule 1 to the Road Traffic Offenders Act 1988 lists the offences for which NIP is required under s 1, being:

Road Traffic Regulation Act 1984

s 16—Contravene speed restriction at road works.
s 17(4)—Contravene motorway speed limit.
s 88(7)—Contravene minimum speed limit.
s 89(1)—Exceeding speed limit.

Road Traffic Act 1988

s 2—Dangerous driving.
s 3—Careless, and inconsiderate, driving.
s 22—Leaving vehicles in dangerous position.
s 28—Dangerous cycling.
s 29—Careless, and inconsiderate, cycling.
s 35—Failing to comply with traffic directions.
s 36—Failing to comply with traffic signs prescribed under s 36 (see **10.3**).

Practical considerations

- If the offence arises out of an accident of which the driver may not be aware NIP required (*Bentley v Dickinson* [1983] RTR 356).

- No NIP required if a TFPN (see **10.4**) is issued or notice that one will be issued on production and surrender of driving licence, and counterpart at a police station is issued.
- There is no need to quote exact Act and section of the offence—keep it simple.

Links to alternative subjects and offences

10.6 Driving without Due Care and Attention

Section 3 of the Road Traffic Act 1988 relates to the offence of driving without due care and attention or without reasonable consideration for other users of the road or public place. Section 168 requires a person alleged to have committed this offence to give their details to any person having reasonable grounds for obtaining them.

10.6.1 Driving without due care and attention

Offences

If a person drives a mechanically propelled vehicle on a road or other public place without due care and attention, or without reasonable consideration for other persons using the road or public place, he is guilty of an offence.

Road Traffic Act 1988, s 3

Points to prove

✓ drove mechanically propelled vehicle
✓ on road/other public place
✓ without due care and attention/reasonable consideration for other road users

Meanings

Drives (see 10.1.4)

Mechanically propelled vehicle (see 10.1.3)

Road (s 192) (see 10.1.1)

Public place (see 10.1.2)

Driving without due care and attention or reasonable consideration

(1) This section has effect for the purposes of sections 2B, 3, and 3A.
(2) A person is to be regarded as driving without due care and attention if (and only if) the way he drives falls below what would be expected of a competent and careful driver.
(3) In determining for the purposes of subsection (2) above what would be expected of a careful and competent driver in a particular case, regard shall be had not only to the circumstances of which he

could be expected to be aware but also to any circumstances shown
to have been within the knowledge of the accused.

(4) A person is to be regarded as driving without reasonable consideration for other persons only if those persons are inconvenienced
by his driving.

Road Traffic Act 1988, s 3ZA

Explanatory notes

- Breaching certain road traffic regulations (eg crossing central white
  lines without explanation) can be enough to prove this offence.
- Section 168 of the Road Traffic Act 1988 empowers the obtaining of
  the defendant's name and address (see **10.6.2**).
- Riding a pedal cycle without due care and attention is an offence
  under s 29 (see **10.12.2**).

Defences

The defences of automatism, unconsciousness and sudden illness, duress,
sudden mechanical defect, assisting in the arrest of offenders, and taking
part in an authorised motoring event may be used.

Defence notes

- 'Automatism' means an affliction which overcomes the driver and
  causes them to lose control of the vehicle. It must be sudden and
  something that they were unaware of and could not reasonably be
  expected to foresee.
- 'Unconsciousness and sudden illness' applies if a driver is rendered
  unconscious and unable to control the vehicle. For example, a blow
  to the head or sudden and unforeseen epileptic fit may cause this.
- The defence of 'duress' may be split into two parts—duress by threat
  or duress of necessity (of circumstances).
    ◆ For duress by threat to apply a person cannot deliberately put
      themselves in a position where they are likely to be subject to
      threats and, if they can escape the duress by escaping the threats,
      they must do so.
- 'Sudden mechanical defect' applies if a sudden and unexpected
  defect in the motor vehicle causes the driver to totally lose control.
  It does not apply to a defect already known to the driver or one that
  could be easily discovered with reasonable prudence.
- The defence of 'assisting in the arrest of offenders' may be available to
  a driver if their driving, though careless or inconsiderate, amounted to
  reasonable force assisting in the arrest of an offender (see **1.2.1**).
- Section 13A(1) states that a person shall not be guilty of an offence
  under s 1, s 1A, s 2, s 2B, or s 3 of this Act by virtue of driving a
  vehicle in a public place other than a road if they show that they were
  driving in accordance with an authorisation for a motoring event
  given under regulations made by the Secretary of State (currently the
  Motor Vehicles (Off Road Events) Regulations 1995 (SI 1371/1995)).

10.6.1 Driving without due care and attention

Related cases

R v McKay (2015) unreported CA (see **10.3**).

DPP v Harris [1994] 158 JP 896, QBD A detective constable driving an unmarked police car was covertly following a vehicle carrying suspects planning to commit an armed robbery when the defendant went through a red traffic light and collided with another vehicle. It was held that care due in these circumstances would involve edging slowly forwards, being prepared to stop if required. For the defence of 'necessity' it would be necessary to show that actions were reasonable and proportionate in the light of a threat of death or serious injury.

Kay v Butterworth (1945) 110 JP 75, CA If a driver falls asleep whilst driving, they are guilty of at least driving without due care and attention.

McCrone v Riding [1938] 1 All ER 157, KBD It was held in this case that the standard of driving required from a driver is an objective one, fixed in relation to the safety of other users of the highway. It does not relate to the degree of proficiency or experience attained by the individual driver.

Practical considerations

- This offence requires NIP to be served (see **10.5**).
- This offence can be dealt with by TFPN (see **10.4.1**).
- Although there is no special standard for emergency vehicles, the courts have made it clear that public safety must be paramount (see 'Related cases' above).
- This section creates two offences and it is bad for duplicity to charge both of them as alternatives.
- Other persons using the road includes other drivers, passengers, pedestrians, or cyclists.
- Section 38(7) of the Road Traffic Act 1988 states that failure to observe a provision of the Highway Code shall not render that person liable to criminal proceedings, but any such failure may be relied upon by any party to any proceedings (civil or criminal) as tending to establish or negate any liability which is in question in those proceedings.
- Consider CPS guidance on prosecuting cases of bad driving.
- In s 3ZA, the statutory meaning of driving without due or reasonable consideration for others also applies to s 3A (death by careless driving when under influence) (see **10.8.2**) and s 2B (death by careless driving) (see **10.8.3**).

	£100 and licence endorsed with 3 penalty points

Summary	6 months

 Fine

Discretionary disqualification, obligatory endorsement—3 to 9 penalty points

10.6.2 **Request details after reckless, careless, or inconsiderate driving or cycling**

Offences

Any of the following persons—
(a) the driver of a mechanically propelled vehicle who is alleged to have committed an offence under section 2 or 3 of this Act, or
(b) the rider of a cycle who is alleged to have committed an offence under section 28 or 29 of this Act,
who refuses, on being so required by any person having reasonable ground for so requiring, to give his name and address, or gives a false name and address, is guilty of an offence.

Road Traffic Act 1988, s 168

Points to prove

✓ driver of mechanically propelled vehicle/rider of cycle
✓ commits offence under ss 2/3 or 28/29 of RTA 1988
✓ when required by person having reasonable grounds
✓ refused to give name and address/gave false details

Meanings

Mechanically propelled vehicle (see **10.1.3**)

Driver (see **10.1.4**)

Explanatory notes

Above offences applicable to this section are:
• Dangerous driving, s 2 (see **10.7.1**).
• Driving without due care and attention/without reasonable consideration, s 3 (see **10.6.1**).
• Sections 28 and 29 involve similar offences to above but riding pedal cycles (see **10.12**).

 Summary   6 months

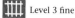 Level 3 fine

Links to alternative subjects and offences

10.7 Dangerous Driving/Cause Serious Injury

10.7.1 Dangerous driving

Section 2 of the Road Traffic Act 1988 relates to dangerous driving.

> **Offences**
>
> A person who drives a mechanically propelled vehicle dangerously on a road or other public place is guilty of an offence.
>
> Road Traffic Act 1988, s 2

Points to prove

✓ being driver of a mechanically propelled vehicle
✓ drove dangerously
✓ on a road/other public place

Meanings

Drives (see **10.1.4**)

Mechanically propelled vehicle (see **10.1.3**)

Driving dangerously (s 2A)

For the purposes of ss 1, 1A, and 2 a person is regarded as driving dangerously if the driving falls far below what would be expected of a competent and careful driver, and it would be obvious to a competent and careful driver that driving in that way and/or driving the vehicle in its current state would be dangerous.

Road (s 192) (see **10.1.1**)

Public place (see **10.1.2**)

Explanatory notes

- In considering the state of the vehicle, anything attached to or carried in or on it, and the manner of it being so attached or carried are also relevant.
- 'Dangerous' refers to danger either of injury to any person or serious damage to property.
- Consideration will be taken not only of the circumstances which a competent and careful driver could be expected to be aware of, but also any circumstances shown to be within the defendant's knowledge.
- There is an offence of dangerous cycling under s 28 (see **10.12.1**).
- Section 168 empowers obtaining of driver's name and address (see **10.6.2**).

Defences (see **10.6.1**)

Defence notes (see **10.6.1**)

Related cases

DPP v Milton [2006] EWHC 242 (Admin), QBD Excessive speed alone is insufficient for dangerous driving; the driving must be considered with all the circumstances.

R v Pleydell [2005] EWCA Crim 1447, CA Evidence that a driver had taken cocaine was, by itself, admissible as the defendant had driven dangerously because of being adversely affected by drugs.

R v Strong [1995] Crim LR 428, CA The danger is 'obvious' only if it can be seen or realised at first glance, or is evident to the competent or careful driver, or the defendant knew of it.

R v Woodward [1995] 3 All ER 79, CA Evidence of consumption of alcohol is admissible only where it is to the effect that the defendant had drunk so much of it as would adversely affect a driver.

R v Spurge [1961] 2 All ER 688, CA A driver aware of a mechanical defect, which caused the vehicle to be dangerous, could not use this defence.

Practical considerations

- This offence requires NIP to be served (see **10.5**).
- Consider CPS guidance on prosecuting cases of bad driving.
- A court may convict of an alternative offence under s 3 (see **10.6.1**).
- Consider any CCTV evidence that may be available.
- Forfeiture of the vehicle used may also be ordered.

 Either way None

 Summary: 6 months' imprisonment and/or a fine

Indictment: 2 years' imprisonment and/or a fine. Obligatory disqualification until test passed

Obligatory endorsement—3 to 11 penalty points (unless special reasons apply)

10.7.2 Cause serious injury by dangerous driving

Section 1A of the Road Traffic Act 1988 relates to causing serious injury by dangerous driving.

Offences

A person who causes serious injury to another person by driving a
mechanically propelled vehicle dangerously on a road or other public
place is guilty of an offence.

Road Traffic Act 1988, s 1A

Points to prove

✓ being driver of a mechanically propelled vehicle
✓ caused serious injury to another person
✓ by driving dangerously
✓ on a road/other public place

Meanings

Serious injury

Physical harm which amounts to grievous bodily harm (see **2.3.1**).

Drives (see **10.1.4**)

Mechanically propelled vehicle (see **10.1.3**)

Driving dangerously (see **10.7.1**)

Road (s 192) (see **10.1.1**)

Public place (see **10.1.2**)

Explanatory notes (see 10.7.1)

This offence was created by the Legal Aid, Sentencing and Punishment
of Offenders Act 2012. It came into force on 3 December 2012, and only
applies to s 1A driving after that date.

Defences (see **10.6.1**)

Defence notes (see **10.6.1**)

Related cases (see **10.7.1**)

Practical considerations (see 10.7.1)

• A court may convict of an alternative offence under s 2 (see **10.7.1**)
  or s 3 (see **10.6.1**).
• For further information see MOJ Circular 8/2012.

 Either way   None

Summary: 12 months' imprisonment and/or a fine

Indictment: 5 years' imprisonment and/or a fine. Obligatory disqualification until test passed

Obligatory endorsement—3 to 11 penalty points (unless special reasons apply)

10.7.3 **Wanton or furious driving**

Section 35 of the Offences Against the Person Act 1861 provides for the offence of wanton or furious driving.

Offences

Whosoever, having the charge of any carriage or vehicle, shall by wanton or furious driving or racing, or other wilful misconduct, or by wilful neglect, do or cause to be done any bodily harm to any person whatsoever, shall be guilty of an offence.

Offences Against the Person Act 1861, s 35

Points to prove

✓ in charge of a carriage/vehicle
✓ by wanton/furious driving/racing or other wilful misconduct/neglect
✓ did/caused bodily harm to be done to another

Meanings

Vehicle (see **10.1.3**)

Wanton

Means without any lawful motive and being thoughtless as to the possible consequences.

Driving (see **10.1.4**)

Bodily harm (see **2.1.2**)

Explanatory notes

A person riding a pedal cycle in a wanton or furious manner resulting in injuries to another person may be convicted under this section.

Practical considerations

• This offence can be committed anywhere.
• Consider CPS guidance on prosecuting cases of bad driving.

Indictment None

 2 years' imprisonment

If a mechanically propelled vehicle—discretionary disqualification and obligatory endorsement of 3 to 9 penalty points

Links to alternative subjects and offences

10.8 **Fatal Road Traffic Collision Incidents**

A driver involved in a fatal road traffic incident has the same obligations as a driver involved in any other reportable road traffic collisions (RTC) (see **10.9**). Offences connected with deaths caused by road traffic incidents are found in s 1 (dangerous driving); s 2B (due care); s 3A (careless driving when under influence of drink or drugs); s 3ZB (no licence/insurance); and s 3ZC (disqualified).

10.8.1 **Causing death by dangerous driving**

Causing death by dangerous driving is an offence created by s 1 of the Road Traffic Act 1988.

> **Offences**
>
> A person who causes the death of another person by driving a mechanically propelled vehicle dangerously on a road or other public place is guilty of an offence.
>
> Road Traffic Act 1988, s 1

Points to prove

✓ caused the death of another person
✓ by driving a mechanically propelled vehicle dangerously
✓ on a road/public place

Meanings

Another person

Means anybody, other than the defendant. It has been held to include a foetus in utero (still in the uterus) and subsequently born alive, but who later dies of their injuries.

Driving (see **10.1.4**)

Mechanically propelled vehicle (see **10.1.3**)

Driven dangerously (see **10.7.1**)

Road (s 192) (see **10.1.1**)

Public place (see **10.1.2**)

Explanatory notes

- The death of the person concerned must be shown to have been caused in some way by the incident to which the charge relates.
- The cause of death does not need to be a substantial cause, but neither should it be a slight or trifling link. It will suffice if the driving was a cause of the death even though it was not the sole or even a substantial cause.
- A person charged with this offence may be convicted of the alternative offences of dangerous driving (see **10.7**); death by driving without due care (see **10.8.3**); or careless, and inconsiderate, driving (see **10.6**).

Defences (see **10.6.1**)

Defence notes (see **10.6.1**)

Related cases (see also 'Dangerous driving' cases **10.7.1**)

R v Buono [2005] EWCA Crim 1313, CA In this case, a fatal collision had been caused by the defendant taking a bend in the middle of the road at excessive speed. Similar fact evidence was admitted showing the way the car had been driven earlier—swerving across the road and driving at excessive speed. Such evidence had considerable probative force, which undoubtedly outweighed any prejudice to the defendant.

R v Hennigan [1971] 3 All ER 133, CA In this case, a vehicle on the main road was travelling at an excessive speed and collided with a vehicle emerging from the side road, killing the driver. The other driver was convicted of s 1, even though the deceased was mainly to blame; excessive speed and dangerous driving by the defendant was partly to blame.

Practical considerations

- This section applies to tramcars and trolley vehicles operating under a statutory power.
- If appropriate, consider manslaughter (see **2.7**) for this offence.
- Theoretically, two different drivers could cause the same death.
- *R v Beckford* (1994) 159 JP 305, CA (see **10.8.2**) also applies to this offence.
- Consider CPS guidance on prosecuting cases of bad driving.
- When dealing with the incident follow **force policy**, preserve the scene, involve supervision, scenes of crime, CID, and other agencies.
- Check for CCTV evidence that may be available.
- Consider seizing the vehicle as it may be forfeited. This will also ensure that the vehicle can be examined for any mechanical defect defences before eventual disposal.

Indictment None

 14 years' imprisonment

Obligatory disqualification until extended test passed

Obligatory endorsement—3 to 11 penalty points

10.8.2 **Causing death by careless driving when under influence**

Section 3A of the Road Traffic Act 1988 provides an offence of causing the death of another by careless driving when under the influence of drink or drugs or failing to provide or give permission for a specimen.

Offences

If a person causes the death of another person by driving a mechanically propelled vehicle on a road or other public place without due care and attention, or without reasonable consideration for other persons using the road or place, and—

(a) he is, at the time when he is driving, unfit to drive through drink or drugs, or

(b) he has consumed so much alcohol that the proportion of it in his breath, blood or urine at that time exceeds the prescribed limit, or

(ba) he has in his body a specified controlled drug and the proportion of it in his blood or urine at that time exceeds the specified limit for that drug, or

(c) he is, within 18 hours after that time, required to provide a specimen in pursuance of section 7 of this Act [see 10.11.2], but without reasonable excuse fails to provide it, or

(d) he is required by a constable to give his permission for a laboratory test of a specimen of blood taken from him under section 7A of this Act [see 10.11.2], but without reasonable excuse fails to do so,

he is guilty of an offence.

Road Traffic Act 1988, s 3A(1)

Points to prove

✓ caused the death of another person

✓ by driving a motor vehicle

✓ on a road/public place

✓ without due care or reasonable consideration for other road users and

> ✓ at the time of driving was unfit through drink/drugs **or**
> ✓ was over the prescribed (alcohol) or specified (drugs) limit
> ✓ within eighteen hours of incident failed to provide specimen **or**
> ✓ on being required failed to give permission to take specimen
>   of blood

Meanings

Another person (see **10.8.1**)

Driving (see **10.1.4**)

Mechanically propelled vehicle (see **10.1.3**)

Road (s 192) (see **10.1.1**)

Public place (see **10.1.2**)

Without due care and attention or reasonable

consideration (see **10.6.1**)

Unfit to drive

When the ability to drive properly is impaired.

Through drink or drugs (see **10.10**)

Exceeds the prescribed limit (alcohol) (see **10.11.1**)

Exceeds the specified limit (drugs) (see **10.11.2**)

Explanatory notes

- The careless or inconsiderate driving (see **10.6**) must be a cause of the death of another person, as must being under the influence of drink/drugs or failing to provide or give permission for a specimen.
- Section 3A(3) states that s 3A(1)(b), (ba), (c), and (d) do not apply to a mechanically propelled vehicle. They only apply to a motor vehicle (see **10.1.3**).
- It is not necessary for the intoxication to be a direct cause of the careless/inconsiderate driving.
- A person charged with this offence may be convicted of the alternative driving offences of careless and inconsiderate (see **10.6**); unfit through drink/drugs (see **10.10**); excess alcohol in breath/blood/urine (see **10.11.1**); while over the specified (drugs) limit in blood/urine (see **10.11.2**); or failing to provide a specimen (see **10.11.3**).

Defences (see **10.6.1**)

Defence notes (see **10.6.1**)

Related cases

R v Ash [1999] RTR 347, QBD Where only one blood sample is taken, the analysis result can still be used under s 3A. The requirement to take two samples under s 15 of the Road Traffic Offenders Act 1988 does not apply to s 3A.

R v Beckford (1994) 159 JP 305, CA In this case, a vehicle was scrapped shortly after being involved in a fatal collision. The defendant relied upon a defence of 'mechanical defect' where the steering had locked. The court stated that police 'procedures' should ensure that cars are not scrapped unless the police give permission; this will not be given where serious criminal charges are to be brought which may involve a mechanical defect in the car.

Practical considerations

- Consider CPS driving offences charging standards.
- As with all fatal RTCs, protect and prevent contamination of the scene.
- Seize the vehicle as it may be forfeited.
- Consider CCTV evidence, if available.

 Indictment None

 14 years' imprisonment and/or fine

Obligatory disqualification until extended test passed

Obligatory endorsement—3 to 11 penalty points

10.8.3 **Causing death by driving: disqualified driver**

Section 3ZC of the Road Traffic Act 1988 provides for the offence of causing the death of another person by driving a motor vehicle on a road while at the time disqualified from driving.

> **Offences**
>
> A person is guilty of an offence under this section if he or she—
> (a) causes the death of another person by driving a motor vehicle on a road, and
> (b) at that time, is committing an offence under section 103(1)(b) of this Act (driving while disqualified).
>
> Road Traffic Act 1988, s 3ZC

Points to prove

✓ caused the death of another person
✓ by driving a motor vehicle
✓ on a road
✓ whilst disqualified

Meanings

Another person (see 10.8.1)

Driving (see 10.1.4)

Motor vehicle (see 10.1.3)

Road (s 192) (see 10.1.1)

Explanatory notes

This offence is subject to a fatal RTC and committing an offence under s 103(1)(b) driving whilst disqualified (see **10.13.1**). It has effect only in relation to driving which occurs on or after 13 April 2015.

Practical considerations

- Consider CPS driving offences charging standards.
- Protect and prevent contamination of the scene. Consider CCTV, if available.
- This offence requires some element of fault by the driver that they caused the death of another person (*R v Hughes* [2013] UKSC 56, see **10.8.5**), not just driving a motor vehicle whilst disqualified.
- Annex A of MOJ Circular 1/2015 provides guidance on this matter.

E&S

 Indictment   None

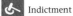 10 years' imprisonment and/or fine

Obligatory disqualification until extended test passed

Obligatory endorsement—3 to 11 penalty points

10.8.4 Causing death by driving without due care

Section 2B of the Road Traffic Act 1988 provides for the offence of causing death by driving without due care and attention or reasonable consideration for others.

> ### Offences
>
> A person who causes the death of another person by driving a mechanically propelled vehicle on a road or other public place without due care and attention, or without reasonable consideration for other persons using the road or place is guilty of an offence.
>
> Road Traffic Act 1988, s 2B

10.8.4 Causing death by driving without due care

> **Points to prove**
> ✓ caused the death of another person
> ✓ by driving a mechanically propelled vehicle
> ✓ on a road/public place
> ✓ without due care and attention/reasonable consideration
>   for others

Meanings

Another person (see 10.8.1)

Driving (see 10.1.4)

Mechanically propelled vehicle (see 10.1.3)

Road (s 192) (see 10.1.1)

Public place (see 10.1.2)

Without due care and attention or reasonable consideration
(see 10.6.1)

Explanatory notes (see 10.6.1)

Defences (see **10.6.1**)

Practical considerations (see also **10.6.1** and **10.8.2**)

- This section may be an alternative verdict to an offence under:
  + s 1 (causing death by dangerous driving—see **10.8.1**);
  + s 3A (causing death by driving without due care when under the
    influence—see **10.8.2**).
- Ensure compliance with the law in relation to reporting RTCs
  (see **10.9**).

 Either way   None

 Summary: 12 months' imprisonment and/or a fine

Obligatory disqualification and obligatory endorsement with 3
to 11 penalty points

Indictment: 5 years' imprisonment and/or a fine.
Obligatory disqualification and obligatory endorsement with 3
to 11 penalty points

10.8.5 **Causing death by driving: no insurance or licence**

Section 3ZB of the Road Traffic Act 1988 provides for the offence of causing the death of another person by driving a motor vehicle on a road otherwise than in accordance with a licence, or without insurance.

Offences

A person is guilty of an offence under this section if he causes the death of another person by driving a motor vehicle on a road and, at the time when he is driving, the circumstances are such that he is committing an offence under—

(a) section 87(1) of this Act (driving otherwise than in accordance with a licence), …, or

(b) section 143 of this Act (using motor vehicle while uninsured or unsecured against third party risks).

Road Traffic Act 1988, s 3ZB

Points to prove

✓ caused the death of another person
✓ by driving a motor vehicle
✓ on a road
✓ without driving licence/insurance

Meanings

Another person (see 10.8.1)

Driving (see 10.1.4)

Motor vehicle (see 10.1.3)

Road (s 192) (see 10.1.1)

Explanatory notes

This offence is subject to a fatal RTC by **causing** the death by their driving and committing an offence under:

• s 87(1)—Driving otherwise than in accordance with a licence (see **10.14.1**); or

• s 143—Using motor vehicle without insurance (see **10.16.1**).

Related cases

R v Hughes [2013] UKSC 56, SC It was held in this case that the s 3ZB offence requires at least some act or omission in respect of the control of

10.8.5 Causing death by driving without due care

the car. The act/omission must involve some element of fault, whether amounting to s 3 driving or not, and must contribute in more than a minimal way to the death but does not necessarily have to be the principal cause of death.

Practical considerations

- Consider CPS driving offences charging standards.
- Protect and prevent contamination of the scene.
- Consider powers of seizure and removal under s 165A (see **10.16.6**).
- This offence requires some element of fault by the driver (*R v Hughes* [2013] UKSC 56) of causing the death.
- Consider CCTV evidence, if available.

 Either way   None

Summary: 12 months' imprisonment and/or a fine

Obligatory disqualification and obligatory endorsement with 3 to 11 penalty points

Indictment: 2 years' imprisonment and/or a fine

Obligatory disqualification and obligatory endorsement with 3 to 11 penalty points

Links to alternative subjects and offences

10.9 Road Traffic Collisions

Section 170 of the Road Traffic Act 1988 imposes duties on the driver of a mechanically propelled vehicle involved in certain RTCs on a road or other public place.

10.9.1 Incidents to which applicable

Collisions which apply

If owing to the presence of a mechanically propelled vehicle on a road or other public place, an accident occurs by which—

(a) personal injury is caused to a person other than the driver of that mechanically propelled vehicle, or

(b) damage is caused—

    (i) to a vehicle other than that mechanically propelled vehicle or a trailer drawn by that mechanically propelled vehicle, or

    (ii) to an animal other than an animal in or on that mechanically propelled vehicle or a trailer drawn by that mechanically propelled vehicle, or

    (iii) to any other property constructed on, fixed to, growing in or otherwise forming part of the land on which the road or place in question is situated or land adjacent to such land.

Road Traffic Act 1988, s 170(1)

Meanings

Mechanically propelled vehicle (see 10.1.3)

Road (s 192) (see 10.1.1)

Public place (see 10.1.2)

Accident

This is an unintended occurrence having an adverse physical result.

Injury

Includes any actual bodily harm and may well include nervous shock.

Driver (see 10.1.4)

Animal

Means horse, cattle, ass, mule, sheep, pig, goat, or dog.

Practical considerations

- There must be some link between the presence of the vehicle and the occurrence of the accident.
- 'Vehicle', in respect of the other vehicle damaged, may include a pedal cycle.
- If attending a potential fatal RTC (see **10.8**).

10.9.2 **Duties of driver after accident**

Offences

(2) The driver of the mechanically propelled vehicle must stop and, if required to do so by any person having reasonable grounds for so requiring, give his name and address and also the name and address of the owner and the identification marks of the vehicle.

(3) If for any reason the driver of the mechanically propelled vehicle does not give his name and address under subsection (2) above, he must report the accident.

(4) A person who fails to comply with subsection (2) or (3) above is guilty of an offence.

Road Traffic Act 1988, s 170

Points to prove

✓ being the driver of a mechanically propelled vehicle
✓ involved in a road traffic accident
✓ failed to stop **and**
✓ on being requested by a person having grounds to do so
✓ failed to provide details, as required

Meanings

Driver (see **10.1.4**)

Mechanically propelled vehicle (see **10.1.3**)

Accident (see **10.9.1**)

Explanatory notes

- If the driver does not stop immediately they must do so as soon as it is safe and convenient to do so.
- If personal injury is involved and the vehicle is a motor vehicle, and the driver does not, at the time of the collision, produce evidence of insurance to a constable or some person having reasonable grounds for requiring them to do so, they must report the collision and produce such evidence (see **10.9.3**).

- After stopping, the driver must remain there long enough to enable them, if required, to furnish the relevant information.

Related cases

DPP v Hay [2005] EWHC 1395 (Admin), QBD The defendant was driving a vehicle involved in an accident and was taken to hospital without exchanging details or reporting the collision to the police, and subsequently, failed to report the accident after being discharged from hospital. It was held that the defendant failed to comply with s 170, even though the police observed the RTC and had made no request for information.

DPP v McCarthy [1999] RTR 323, DC The requirement to give a name and address has a wider meaning than just the driver's home address. An address needs to be somewhere where a person can be contacted.

Practical considerations

- The driver does not commit this offence if they are unaware that the RTC has occurred.
- These two subsections create two separate offences (failing to stop and give information **and** failing to report). Therefore, the driver may be charged with either one or both. A further offence may be committed in a s 170(1)(a) injury accident where the driver fails to comply with s 170(5) (see **10.9.3**).
- The scene of the RTC is the place in the road or public place where the collision occurs. Remember the vehicles themselves may also be 'scenes'.

 Summary 6 months

 6 months' imprisonment and/or a fine not exceeding level 5

Discretionary disqualification and obligatory endorsement with 5 to 10 penalty points

10.9.3 **Duty of driver to report the incident**

Section 170 provides for the obligation and a subsequent offence where a reportable RTC occurs.

Offences

(5) If, in a case where this section applies by virtue of subsection (1)(a) above [*injury*, see **10.9.1**], the driver of a motor vehicle does not at the time of the accident produce such a certificate of insurance or security, or other evidence, as is mentioned in section 165(2)(a) of this Act—

  (a) to a constable, or

10.9.3 Duty of driver to report the incident

Points to prove

✓ being driver of a motor vehicle
✓ involved in a relevant road traffic accident
✓ did not at the time of the accident
✓ produce to a constable/person with grounds for requiring
✓ relevant evidence of insurance **or**
✓ failed to report the accident and produce relevant insurance

Meanings

Driver (see 10.1.4)

Motor vehicle (see 10.1.3)

Accident (see 10.9.1)

Insurance/security (see 10.16.1)

Section 165(2)(a) (see 10.16.5)

Explanatory notes

- To comply with the requirement to produce the relevant proof of insurance, s 170(6) states that the driver must do so at a police station or to a constable, which must be done as soon as is reasonably practicable and, in any case, within twenty-four hours of it occurring.
- A person will not be convicted of this offence only because they failed to produce the relevant insurance document if, within seven days following the accident it is produced at a police station specified by them at the time they reported the accident.
- The obligation to report the accident includes where there is nobody else about to whom the driver can give the details (eg damage to street furnishings).

Practical considerations

- Note that whereas s 170(2) and (3) create offences in relation to a mechanically propelled vehicle, this offence is in relation to the use of a motor vehicle.
- This requirement does not apply to an invalid carriage.
- 'At a police station' means the motorist should report it in person at a police station or to a constable; a report by telephone will not suffice.

Summary 6 months

 6 months' imprisonment and/or a fine not exceeding level 5.

Discretionary disqualification and obligatory endorsement with
5 to 10 penalty points

Links to alternative subjects and offences

10.10 Drive/Attempt to Drive/ in Charge of Vehicle While Unfit through Drink/Drugs

10.10.1 Drive while unfit drink/drugs

Section 4 of the Road Traffic Act 1988 provides for the offences of driving, attempting to drive, and being in charge of a mechanically propelled vehicle on a road or public place while unfit through drink or drugs.

Offences

(1) A person who, when driving or attempting to drive a mechanically propelled vehicle on a road or other public place, is unfit to drive through drink or drugs is guilty of an offence.

(2) Without prejudice to subsection (1) above, a person who, when in charge of a mechanically propelled vehicle which is on a road or other public place, is unfit to drive through drink or drugs is guilty of an offence.

Road Traffic Act 1988, s 4

Points to prove

s 4(1) offence

✓ drove/attempted to drive
✓ a mechanically propelled vehicle
✓ on a road/other public place
✓ when unfit to drive through drink/drugs

s 4(2) offence

✓ in charge of a mechanically propelled vehicle
✓ on a road/public place
✓ being unfit to drive through drink/drugs

Meanings

Driving (see 10.1.4)

Mechanically propelled vehicle (see 10.1.3)

Road (s 192) (see 10.1.1)

Public place (see 10.1.2)

In charge

There is no legislation or test for what constitutes 'in charge' for the purposes of being in charge of a vehicle under s 4, s 5, or s 5A (see **10.11**), but a close connection between the defendant and control of the vehicle is required.

Explanatory notes

- A person is **unfit to drive** properly if their ability is for the time being impaired. The prosecution must give evidence of unfitness.
- It needs to be ascertained whether the person is in charge of the vehicle by virtue of being the owner, lawful possessor, or recent driver. Are they still in charge or have they relinquished charge at the relevant time; have they assumed charge?
- Factors that need to be considered in establishing whether the person was in charge include:
  - ◆ Who is the registered keeper of the vehicle; who is insured to drive it; where were the other insured drivers (if any)?
  - ◆ What were their immediate and future intended movements?
  - ◆ If away from their home/accommodation, how did they propose to return without driving?
  - ◆ How had the vehicle got to where it was; when did they last drive it; are they in possession of a key which fits the ignition?
  - ◆ What was their position in relation to the car; were they in the vehicle; if not how far away were they?
  - ◆ Was anyone else in or around the vehicle; what were they doing at the relevant time?
  - ◆ Is there evidence of an intention to take control of the vehicle?
  - ◆ When and where had they been drinking; time of last drink; what had they been doing since then?
- The evidence of a doctor who examines the defendant at the request of the police is admissible even if they had to persuade the defendant to allow the examination.

Defences

For the purposes of subsection (2) above, a person shall be deemed not to have been in charge of a mechanically propelled vehicle if he proves that at the material time the circumstances were such that there was no likelihood of his driving it so long as he remained unfit to drive through drink or drugs.

Road Traffic Act 1988, s 4(3)

Defence notes

- In the case of *Sheldrake v DPP (A-G's Reference No 4 of 2002)* [2005] 1 Cr App R 28 it was held that the burden of proof should remain on the defendant, to be decided on the balance of probabilities. This imposition did not contravene the presumption of innocence and was compatible with the ECHR.

10.10.1 Drive while unfit drink/drugs

- The court, in determining whether there was a likelihood of a person driving whilst still unfit through drink or drugs, should disregard any injury to them and any damage to the vehicle (ie it is not the practical possibility of the person being able to drive the vehicle that is relevant here, but rather the possibility of that person driving at all while still impaired).

Related cases

R v Ealing, ex parte Woodman (1994) 158 JP 997, QBD It was held in this case that, if there was sufficient proof that a driver had taken more than their normal dose of insulin and failed to counterbalance it with food intake, insulin would be treated by the court as a drug under this section.

Smith v Mellors and another [1987] RTR 210, QBD If the driver cannot be identified and each occupant of the car is over the prescribed limit, each one can be charged with the relevant drink driving offence and alternatively with aiding and abetting the other(s) to commit the drink driving offence. However, evidence of the aiding must be put to the court.

Practical considerations

- A charge under this section, which uses both the alternatives of 'drink or drugs', is not bad for duplicity.
- The CPS are unlikely to take the case forward unless there is evidence that the suspect was likely to drive whilst under the influence of drink/drugs. Similarly, if in charge, ensure that the s 4(3) defence can be countered if raised.
- This section applies to trolley vehicles operated under statutory powers, but not to tramcars.
- An indictment containing a charge under s 1 of the Road Traffic Act 1988 (see **10.8**) should not include a charge under this section, as this section is triable summarily only.
- A non-expert witness may give evidence of the defendant's condition, but not of their fitness to drive.

 Summary   6 months

 s 4(1) offence: 6 months' imprisonment and/or a fine
Obligatory disqualification

Obligatory endorsement—3 to 11 penalty points

s 4(2) offence: 3 months imprisonment and/or a level 4 fine

Discretionary disqualification, obligatory endorsement—10 penalty points

10.10.2 **Preliminary test powers**

Section 6 of the Road Traffic Act 1988 provides for the requiring of preliminary tests for alcohol, impairment, or drugs to drivers of motor vehicles. Sections 6A–6C relate to the specific tests, whilst s 6D provides a power of arrest and s 6E a power of entry.

Offences

A person commits an offence if without reasonable excuse he fails to co-operate with a preliminary test in pursuance of a requirement imposed under this section.

Road Traffic Act 1988, s 6(6)

Points to prove

✓ without reasonable excuse
✓ failed to cooperate with a preliminary test
✓ when required under this section

Meanings

Fails

Fail includes refuse.

Preliminary test

This refers to any of the tests described in ss 6A–6C and means a preliminary test of breath/impairment or for drugs.

Requirements

Under s 6(1)–(5) a constable may require a person to cooperate with any one or more preliminary tests administered to them by that constable or another constable, if the constable reasonably suspects that:

• they are driving, attempting to drive, or are in charge of a motor vehicle on a road or other public place, and have alcohol or a drug in their body or are under the influence of a drug; **or**
• they had been driving, attempting to drive, or in charge of a motor vehicle on a road or other public place while having alcohol or a drug in their body, or while unfit to drive because of a drug, and still have alcohol or a drug in their body, or are still under the influence of a drug; **or**
• they are or have been driving, attempting to drive, or in charge of a motor vehicle on a road or other public place, and have committed a **traffic offence** while the vehicle was in motion; or
• an accident has occurred owing to the presence of a motor vehicle on a road or other public place, and a constable reasonably believes that they were driving, attempting to drive, or in charge of the vehicle at the time of the accident.

10.10.2 Preliminary test powers

Traffic offence

Means an offence under the Public Passenger Vehicles Act 1981, Pt 2 (ss 6–29); Road Traffic Regulation Act 1984; Road Traffic Offenders Act 1988 (except Pt 3—fixed penalties); or Road Traffic Act 1988 (except Pt 5—driving instruction).

Explanatory notes

- Only a constable in uniform may administer a preliminary test, except if it relates to an accident under s 6(5).
- A preliminary breath test (s 6A) is a procedure by which the person taking the test provides a specimen of breath, using a device approved by the Secretary of State, to ascertain whether the proportion of alcohol in their breath or blood is likely to exceed the prescribed limit.
- For a preliminary impairment test (s 6B) the constable requesting it observes the person taking it performing tasks specified by the constable and makes any observations of the person's physical state as they think is expedient. The constable shall have regard to the code of practice issued by the Secretary of State which governs preliminary impairment tests.
- For a preliminary drug test (s 6C) a specimen of sweat or saliva is obtained (using a device approved by the Secretary of State) to ascertain whether the person tested has a drug in their body; if so, whether it is a specified controlled drug; if it is, whether the proportion of it in their blood or urine is likely to exceed the specified limit for that drug. Up to three preliminary drug tests may be administered at or near the place where the test requirement is imposed or if expedient at a specified police station.
- A person will not be required at random to provide a specimen of breath for a breath test.
- An asthma sufferer who is incapable of providing a sample has a duty to inform the officer requiring it.
- A person who refuses (without good cause) to take a test is deemed to have failed to take it.
- While in hospital, no person will be requested to supply a breath sample or laboratory specimen without the knowledge and permission of the doctor in charge of their case.

Power of arrest

(1) A constable may arrest a person without warrant if as a result of a preliminary breath test or preliminary drug test the constable reasonably suspects that—

   (a) the proportion of alcohol in that person's breath or blood exceeds the prescribed limit, or

   (b) the person has a specified controlled drug in his body and the proportion of it in the person's blood or urine exceeds the specified limit for that drug.

(2) A constable may arrest a person without warrant if—
   (a) the person fails to co-operate with a preliminary test in pursuance of a requirement imposed under s 6, and
   (b) the constable reasonably suspects that the person has alcohol or a drug in his body or is under the influence of a drug.

Road Traffic Act 1988, s 6D

Power of entry (after injury accident)

A constable may enter any place (using reasonable force if necessary) for the purpose of—

(a) imposing a requirement by virtue of section 6(5) following an accident in a case where the constable reasonably suspects that the accident involved injury of any person, or

(b) arresting a person under section 6D following an accident in a case where the constable reasonably suspects that the accident involved injury of any person.

Road Traffic Act 1988, s 6E(1)

Related cases

DPP v Wilson [2009] EWHC 1988 (Admin), QBD The defendant was breathalysed at hospital following an RTC; it showed a positive result and he was arrested. The doctor consented to blood being taken and the result confirmed that he was OPL. It was argued that the arrest was unlawful per s 6D(3), and consequently, the blood result could not be used as evidence. It was held that the fact that an arrest is prohibited does not prevent the blood and breath test procedures; provided they are taken in accordance with statutory requirements, they remain valid.

Gearing v DPP [2008] EWHC 1695 (Admin), QBD There is clear conflict between s 58 of PACE as to consulting a solicitor and requirements under the 1988 Act. What is important is the public interest of evidential testing as soon as possible. Safeguards accompany the procedure itself.

R v Beckford [1995] RTR 251, CA In this case, a constable questioned a driver who had been involved in a fatal accident as to how much alcohol he/she had consumed. No caution was given before the questioning. The defendant replied 'three pints' which then gave rise to a requirement that a caution be given before any further questions were put.

Practical considerations

- A constable can arrest a person under s 6D(1A) if specimens of breath have been provided under s 7 (see **10.11.3**) and the constable imposing the requirement has reasonable cause to believe that the approved device used for analysis did not produce a reliable result.

10.10.2 Preliminary test powers

- A preliminary breath test requested because a constable suspects that a person has alcohol or a drug in their body or is under the influence of a drug may only be given at or near the place where it is requested.
- Following an RTC a preliminary breath test, preliminary impairment test, or preliminary drugs test may be given at or near the place where it is requested or, if the constable requesting it thinks it expedient, at a police station specified by them.
- Only a constable approved by their chief officer may give a preliminary impairment test, which must satisfy the COP.
- A person arrested under the above powers may, instead of being taken to a police station, be detained at or near the place where the preliminary test was, or would have been, administered, to impose a requirement there under s 7 on them (see **10.11.3**).
- A person may not be arrested under s 6D(3) while at a hospital as a patient.
- A constable may enter any place (by reasonable force if necessary) to impose a requirement by virtue of an RTC having occurred, or to arrest a person under s 6D following an RTC, where they reasonably suspect that such RTC involved injury to a person.
- If a motorist supplies enough breath for the device to give a reading they cannot be said to have failed to cooperate.
- Evidential specimens can be obtained at the roadside.

 E&S

 Summary   6 months

 Level 3 fine

Discretionary disqualification, obligatory endorsement—4 penalty points

Links to alternative subjects and offences

10.11 Drive/Attempt to Drive/ in Charge While over the Prescribed/Specified Limit

10.11.1 Drive motor vehicle while over the prescribed (alcohol) limit

Section 5 of the Road Traffic Act 1988 provides the offences of driving, attempting to drive, and being in charge of a motor vehicle on a road or public place while over the prescribed limit of alcohol in blood, breath, or urine.

Offences

If a person—
(a) drives or attempts to drive a motor vehicle on a road or other public place, or
(b) is in charge of a motor vehicle on a road or other public place,

after consuming so much alcohol that the proportion of it in his breath, blood or urine exceeds the prescribed limit he is guilty of an offence.

Road Traffic Act 1988, s 5(1)

Points to prove

✓ drove/attempted to drive/in charge of motor vehicle
✓ on a road/public place
✓ proportion of alcohol in blood/breath/urine exceeded prescribed limit

Meanings

Drive (see 10.1.4)

Motor vehicle (see 10.1.3)

Road (s 192) (see 10.1.1)

Public place (see 10.1.2)

In charge (see 10.10.1)

Consuming

With regard to alcohol primarily means by mouth but can include other means of ingesting it into the blood, breath, or urine.

Prescribed limit

For driving offences, the limits are:
- 35 microgrammes of alcohol in 100 millilitres of breath;
- 80 milligrammes of alcohol in 100 millilitres of blood;
- 107 milligrammes of alcohol in 100 millilitres of urine.

Power of arrest (see **10.10.2**)

Explanatory notes

- Be aware of the powers to administer a preliminary breath test (see **10.10.2**).
- Being so hopelessly drunk that they are incapable of driving a motor vehicle is not a defence to this offence.
- If the offence is under s 5(1)(b) then it needs to be ascertained whether the person is in charge of the vehicle (see '**Explanatory notes**', **10.10.1**).
- Evidence of the proportion of alcohol at the time of driving other than that provided by the specimen is admissible.
- Where it is established that the defendant was driving and has given a positive sample, it is assumed that the amount of alcohol at the time of the alleged offence is not less than the specimen provided.

Defence—being in charge

It is a defence for a person charged with an offence under subsection (1)(b) above to prove that at the time he is alleged to have committed the offence the circumstances were such that there was no likelihood of his driving the vehicle whilst the proportion of alcohol in his breath, blood or urine remained likely to exceed the prescribed limit.

Road Traffic Act 1988, s 5(2)

Defence notes (see also **10.10.1**)

- The burden of proof is on the defendant.
- In determining whether there was any likelihood of them driving, the court may ignore any injury to them or damage to the vehicle.

Related cases (see also **10.1.4** and **10.10** cases)

Croitoru v CPS [2016] EWHC 1645 (Admin) In this case the rider of a mechanically propelled invalid carriage was charged and convicted with the s 5 offence. It was held that if the use of the carriage was in accordance with the proscribed conditions contained within s 20 of the Chronically Sick and Disabled Persons Act 1970, it was exempt from being classified as a motor vehicle under that section. However, drunk driving was not included in these exemptions, so the conviction was upheld.

CPS v Thompson [2007] EWHC 1841 (Admin), QBD The defendant was found asleep in his car by police. He was intoxicated but stated that he had had no intention of driving while he knew he was over the legal limit. He was arrested, and a subsequent breath sample showed he was over the prescribed limit. He was acquitted but the prosecution appealed. It was held that by merely focusing on the evidence given by the defendant (that he had no intention of driving until he had felt alright) the court had failed to focus sufficiently on the wording of s 5(2) when considering whether he had satisfied the defence. The court's conclusion that he had no intention of driving at the time he got into the vehicle, or when the police had awoken him, did not meet the statutory test and s 5(2) is not primarily concerned with the person's intentions.

DPP v Mullally [2006] EWHC 3448 (Admin), QBD In this case, the defendant, acting in fear for her sister who had been assaulted, drove a car to her sister's house while over the prescribed limit and then called the police. When the police arrived, she drove away. Once a defence of duress is raised the burden of proof rests upon the prosecution to dispel the evidence. The court must consider:

- Was s/he forced to act as they did because of a genuine belief that death or serious injury would result if they had not acted in that manner?
- Would a sober person of reasonable firmness have been forced into acting in the same way?

The court held in this case that the defendant had a genuine fear but her response to that genuine fear had not been reasonable. She had not been entitled to drive away after the police had arrived at her sister's house.

DPP v H [1997] 1 WLR 1406, QBD Insanity cannot be used as a defence against a s 5 offence as there is no requirement for any intent; the offence is one of strict liability.

Lafferty v DPP [1995] Crim LR 430, QBD In a claim that the intoximeter reading was inaccurate, the court may consider evidence of the roadside breath test.

DPP v Johnson (1994) 158 JP 891, QBD The 'consumption' of alcohol may be by injection.

Sharpe v DPP (1994) JP 595, QBD If an officer is a trespasser at the time of the screening test it may invalidate the procedure.

DPP v Wilson [1991] Crim LR 441, QBD An officer is entitled to form an opinion that a driver has been drinking from information from an anonymous caller.

Practical considerations

- The CPS are unlikely to take the case forward unless there is evidence of a likelihood of driving whilst under the influence of drink or drugs. Similarly, if in charge, ensure that the s 5(2) defence can be countered if raised.
- A person acting as a supervisor of a provisional licence holder is 'in charge' of the vehicle and can commit that offence under this section.
- 'Lacing' a person's drink without their knowledge may constitute an offence of aiding and abetting the commission of an offence under this section, if there is proof that the intent was to bring about the offence.

- Be aware of the 'Hip Flask Defence' (where the suspect claims to have had an alcoholic drink since driving but before providing a specimen). Ascertain amount drunk and inform the laboratory so the appropriate calculations can be made.
- A power of entry is available for the provision of a preliminary test in cases which involve an injury accident. Reasonable force may be used to effect entry under s 6E or carry out a preliminary test and arrest a person under s 6D (see **10.10.2**).

 Summary   6 months

 s 5(1)(a) offence: 6 months' imprisonment and/or a fine not exceeding level 5 on the standard scale

Obligatory disqualification, obligatory endorsement—3 to 11 penalty points

s 5(1)(b) offence: 3 months imprisonment and/or a level 4 fine

Discretionary disqualification, obligatory endorsement—10 penalty points

10.11.2 **Drive motor vehicle while over the specified (drugs) limit**

Section 5A of the Road Traffic Act 1988 provides the offences of driving, attempting to drive, and being in charge of a motor vehicle on a road or public place while over the specified limit of a specified controlled drug in blood or urine.

Offences

(1) This section applies where a person ('D')—
  (a) drives or attempts to drive a motor vehicle on a road or other public place, or
  (b) is in charge of a motor vehicle on a road or other public place, and there is in D's body a specified controlled drug.
(2) D is guilty of an offence if the proportion of the drug in D's blood or urine exceeds the specified limit for that drug.

Road Traffic Act 1988, s 5A

Points to prove

✓ drove/attempted to drive/in charge of motor vehicle
✓ on a road/public place
✓ proportion of specified controlled drug in blood/urine
✓ exceeded specified limit for that drug

10.11.2 Over the specified (drugs) limit

Meanings

Drive (see 10.1.4)

Motor vehicle (see 10.1.3)

Road (s 192) (see 10.1.1)

Public place (see 10.1.2)

In charge (see 10.10.1)

Specified

Means specified in regulations made by the Secretary of State.

Controlled drug (see 5.1.1)

Specified controlled drug/limit

The Drug Driving (Specified Limits) Regulations 2014, reg 2 (SI 2868/2014) specifies the controlled drugs and specified limits (microgrammes per litre of blood) that apply to the s 5A offence: amphetamine (250); benzoylecgonine (50); Clonazepam (50); cocaine (10); delta-9-tetrahydrocannabinol (2); Diazepam (550); Flunitrazepam (300); ketamine (20); Lorazepam (100); lysergic acid diethylamide (1); methadone (500); methylamphetamine (10); methylenedioxymethamphetamine (10); 6-monoacetylmorphine (5); morphine (80); Oxazepam (300); and Temazepam (1000).

Explanatory notes

- Officers can screen for specified drugs at the roadside by using an approved device under s 6C (see **10.10.2**).
- If the offence is under s 5A(1)(b) then it needs to be ascertained whether the person is in charge of the vehicle (see '**Explanatory notes**', **10.10.1**).
- The s 5A offence makes it easier for police to detect and prosecute drug-drivers, being an offence to drive/attempt to drive or being in charge while over the limit for drugs (as specified), as it is for drink driving over the prescribed limit (see **10.11.1**).
- There is no requirement to provide proof of impairment for this offence.

Power of arrest (see 10.10.2)

> ### Defences
>
> (3) It is a defence for a person ('D') charged with an offence under this section to show that—
> (a) the specified controlled drug had been prescribed or supplied to D for medical or dental purposes,
> (b) D took the drug in accordance with any directions given by the person by whom the drug was prescribed or supplied, and with

      any accompanying instructions (so far as consistent with any such directions) given by the manufacturer or distributor of the drug, and

    (c) D's possession of the drug immediately before taking it was not unlawful under section 5(1) of the Misuse of Drugs Act 1971 (restriction of possession of controlled drugs) because of an exemption in regulations made under section 7 of that Act (authorisation of activities otherwise unlawful under foregoing provisions).

(4) The defence in subsection (3) is not available if D's actions were—

    (a) contrary to any advice, given by the person by whom the drug was prescribed or supplied, about the amount of time that should elapse between taking the drug and driving a motor vehicle, or

    (b) contrary to any accompanying instructions about that matter (so far as consistent with any such advice) given by the manufacturer or distributor of the drug.

(5) If evidence is adduced that is sufficient to raise an issue with respect to the defence in subsection (3), the court must assume that the defence is satisfied unless the prosecution proves beyond reasonable doubt that it is not.

(6) It is a defence for a person ('D') charged with an offence by virtue of subsection (1)(b) to prove that at the time D is alleged to have committed the offence the circumstances were such that there was no likelihood of D driving the vehicle whilst the proportion of the specified controlled drug in D's blood or urine remained likely to exceed the specified limit for that drug.

(7) The court may, in determining whether there was such a likelihood, disregard any injury to D and any damage to the vehicle.

Road Traffic Act 1988, s 5A

Defence notes (see also **10.10.1**)

- The burden of proof is on the defendant to show that the drug had been prescribed or supplied to them for medical or dental purposes, was taken as directed, and they complied with the accompanying instructions; but this defence is not available if their actions were contrary to the advice or instructions given.

- If there is sufficient evidence to show a valid defence under s 5A(3), then the prosecution would have to prove beyond reasonable doubt that this is not the case.

- It is a defence for a person charged with the s 5A(1)(b) offence that the circumstances were such that there was no likelihood of them driving the vehicle whilst over the specified limit for that drug. In determining whether there was any likelihood of them driving, the court may ignore any injury to them or damage to the vehicle.

10.11.2 Over the specified (drugs) limit

Related cases (see **10.1.4**, **10.10**, and **10.11** cases)

Practical considerations

- The CPS are unlikely to take the case forward unless there is evidence of a likelihood of driving whilst under the influence of drink or drugs. Similarly, ensure that the s 5A(3)–(7) defences are considered and can be countered if raised.
- A person acting as a supervisor of a provisional licence holder is 'in charge' of the vehicle and can commit that offence under this section.
- The s 5A offence will work alongside the existing s 4 offence (see **10.10.1**) of being unfit through drink or drugs, which will continue to be used for drugs which are not specified controlled or prescribed drugs, including 'legal highs'.
- Limits are set at very low levels for the illegal drugs including cocaine, cannabis, ecstasy, and ketamine; while some legally prescribed drugs, including Diazepam and methadone, are included, as certain strong medication can affect people's ability to drive safely.
- As s 5A sets limits for specified legal drugs, it's vital that anyone taking prescribed medication reads the instructions carefully and keeps to the prescribed dosage. If anyone is unsure as to whether their medication affects their ability to drive they should obtain advice from a doctor or pharmacist.
- The medication specified in s 5A is usually prescribed for the following treatments: Clonazepam (epilepsy); Diazepam, Lorazepam (anxiety/insomnia); Oxazepam (anxiety); Flunitrazepam, Temazepam (insomnia); morphine (severe pain); methadone (severe pain/heroin substitute).
- A power of entry is available for the provision of a preliminary test in cases involving an injury accident. Reasonable force may be used to effect entry under s 6E or carry out a preliminary test and arrest a person under s 6D (see **10.10.2**).

 Summary 6 months

 s 5(1)(a) offence:
51 weeks imprisonment and/or a level 5 fine
Obligatory disqualification, obligatory endorsement—3 to 11 penalty points

s 5(1)(b) offence:
51 weeks imprisonment and/or a level 4 fine
Discretionary disqualification, obligatory endorsement—10 penalty points

10.11.3 Provision of specimens for analysis

Section 7 of the Road Traffic Act 1988 deals with the provision of evidential specimens and s 7A details the provisions in relation to the taking of specimens of blood from persons incapable of consenting.

Offences

A person who, without reasonable excuse, fails to provide a specimen when required to do so in pursuance of this section is guilty of an offence.

Road Traffic Act 1988, s 7(6)

Points to prove

✓ without reasonable excuse
✓ failed/refused to provide specimen
✓ when lawfully required to do so

Meanings

Fails (see 10.10.2)

Specimen

Specimens taken under s 7 may consist of two specimens of breath for analysis by an approved device (alcohol) or a specimen of blood or urine for laboratory analysis (alcohol or drugs).

Explanatory notes

Specimens may be required from a person suspected of having committed an offence under:
- s 3A—Causing death by careless driving when under influence of drink or drugs (see **10.8.2**);
- s 4—Driving, attempting to drive or being in charge, when under influence of drink or drugs (see **10.10.1**);
- s 5—Driving, attempting to drive or being in charge of a motor vehicle with alcohol concentration above prescribed limit (see **10.11.1**);
- s 5A—Driving, attempting to drive or being in charge of a motor vehicle with specified controlled drug being over specified limit (see **10.11.2**).

Related cases

DPP v Camp [2017] EWHC 3119 Self-induced intoxication does not amount to a reasonable excuse for failing to provide a specimen of breath for analysis under section 7(6) of the Road Traffic Act 1988.

10.11.3 Provision of specimens for analysis

Chalupa v CPS [2009] EWHC 3082 (Admin), QBD Only in exceptional circumstances (where a solicitor is readily available) could a breath test be delayed allowing an individual to take legal advice as there is a public interest requirement that a test be undertaken promptly.

DPP v Baldwin [2000] RTR 314, QBD The purpose of the requirement to provide a specimen of urine one hour after the first specimen is to give the motorist a finite time. If this period is extended, that extension does not make any findings inadmissible.

DPP v Furby [2000] RTR 181, QBD A medical condition of which they are unaware cannot later be used as an excuse for failing to provide the required sample.

Francis v DPP [1997] RTR 113, QBD A request can be legitimately made of a mentally unstable person if they understand what is happening.

Hague v DPP [1997] RTR 146, QBD Breath samples were taken on an intoximeter machine. The officer believed the machine to be faulty and requested blood or urine, which was refused. The machine was examined and found to be working correctly so the readings were still admissible.

DPP v Coyle [1996] RTR 287, CA It is not necessary to wait for the intoximeter machine to 'time out' before a suspect's refusal or failure to give a sample of breath will be complete.

DPP v Wythe [1996] RTR 137, QBD If a medical reason is put forward by the suspect, the final decision as to whether blood can be taken is the doctor's.

Wade v DPP [1996] RTR 177, QBD A defendant on medication may have a medical reason for not providing a specimen of blood.

DPP v Garrett [1995] RTR 302, QBD Where the blood sample procedure was flawed, but the sample was not taken and used, it did not affect the request for a urine sample.

DPP v Nesbitt and Duffy [1995] 1 Cr App R 38, QBD Where a request for blood or urine is made at a hospital the required warnings must explain the procedures in full, with reasons, and state the consequences of failing to comply.

DPP v Smith, The Times, 1 June 1994, QBD A defendant cannot insist that blood should be taken by their own GP.

Practical considerations

- On requiring a person to provide a specimen under this section, a constable **must** warn them that failure to provide it may render them liable to prosecution.
- A requirement for a specimen of breath can only be made at a police station, a hospital, or at or near a place where a relevant breath test has been given to the person concerned or would have been so given but for their failure to cooperate.

- The constable requiring the breath sample must be in uniform or have imposed a requirement on the defendant to cooperate with a breath test as a result of an accident.
- Where a requirement has been imposed for a person to cooperate with a relevant breath test at any place, the constable may remain at or near there to impose a requirement under this section.
- If a requirement is made for two samples of breath for analysis by an approved device at a place other than a police station, it may revert to being made at a police station if a device or reliable device is not available there, or it is not practicable to use one there, or the constable making the previous requirement believes that the device has not produced a reliable result.
- Under this section, a requirement for a specimen of blood or urine can only be made at a police station or a hospital.
- A requirement for a sample of blood or urine can be made at a police station unless: the constable requiring it believes that for medical reasons it cannot or should not be made; specimens of breath have not been provided elsewhere and an approved device is not available there; an approved device has been used but the constable believes the result to be unreliable; the constable believes, following a preliminary drugs test, that the defendant has a drug in their body; or, if the offence is under s 3A, s 4, or s 5A of the Act and the constable has been informed by a medical practitioner that the person's condition might be due to some drug.
- The above requirement may be made even if the defendant has been required to supply two specimens of breath.
- If a specimen other than breath is required, the question as to whether it is blood or urine (and, if it is blood, who will take it) will be decided by the constable making the requirement.
- If a medical or health care practitioner thinks that, for medical reasons, blood cannot or should not be taken the requirement will not be made. A urine sample may then be required instead.
- A specimen of urine must be provided within an hour of its being required and after the provision of a previous such specimen.
- In cases involving a failure to provide breath, consider retaining the mouthpiece as a possible exhibit.
- If a person is involved in a traffic accident and their medical condition prevents them from giving consent, then s 7A(1) allows taking a blood specimen from that person—providing blood could have been requested under s 7.
- If blood has been taken by a 'police medical or health care practitioner' under s 7A(1), then under s 7A(5) a constable must require the person to give permission for a laboratory test of the blood specimen taken, and warn that failure to give this permission may render them liable to prosecution under s 7A(6).
- **Section 7A(6) offence**—A person who, without reasonable excuse, fails to give his permission for a laboratory test of a specimen of blood taken from him under this section is guilty of a summary offence.

10.11.3 Provision of specimens for analysis

 Summary 6 months

 Driving or attempting to drive:
6 months' imprisonment and/or a fine not exceeding level 5

Obligatory disqualification, obligatory endorsement—3 to 11 penalty points

In all other cases:
3 months' imprisonment and/or a level 4 fine

Discretionary disqualification, obligatory endorsement—10 penalty points

Links to alternative subjects and offences

10.12 Pedal Cycle Offences

Sections 28, 29, and 30 of the Road Traffic Act 1988 provide similar offences for cyclists to those contained in ss 1, 2, and 3 for motorists. Additionally, there is the offence of driving or cycling on a footpath under s 72 of the Highways Act 1835.

10.12.1 Dangerous cycling

Section 28 creates an offence of dangerous cycling on a road.

Offences

A person who rides a cycle on a road dangerously is guilty of an offence.

Road Traffic Act 1988, s 28(1)

Points to prove

✓ rode a cycle
✓ on a road
✓ dangerously

Meanings

Cycle

Means a bicycle, a tricycle, or a cycle having four or more wheels, not being in any case a motor vehicle.

Road (s 192) (see 10.1.1)

Dangerously

A person is to be regarded as riding dangerously if and only if:
- the way that they ride falls far below what would be expected of a competent and careful cyclist; **and**
- it would be obvious to a competent and careful cyclist that riding in that way would be dangerous.

Explanatory notes

- The term 'danger' refers to danger either of injury to any person or of serious damage to property.
- To determine what would be obvious to a competent and careful cyclist in a particular case regard shall be had not only to the circumstances of which they could be expected to be aware, but also to any shown to have been within their knowledge.
- A person may be convicted of the alternative offence of careless, and inconsiderate, cycling (see 10.12.2).

Practical considerations

- NIP to be issued (see **10.5**).
- This offence must be on a road—it does not extend to a public place.
- Section 168 empowers obtaining of cyclist's name and address (see **10.6.2**).
- Section 163 of the Road Traffic Act 1988 empowers a police constable in uniform to stop a cycle on a road. A person who fails to stop the cycle will be guilty of an offence (see **10.2.4**).

 Summary   6 months

 Level 4 fine

10.12.2 **Careless, and inconsiderate, cycling**

Section 29 creates an offence of cycling on a road without due care and attention or without reasonable consideration for other road users.

> **Offences**
>
> If a person rides a cycle on a road without due care and attention, or without reasonable consideration for other persons using the road, he is guilty of an offence.
>
> Road Traffic Act 1988, s 29

Points to prove

- ✓ rode a cycle
- ✓ on a road
- ✓ without due care and attention/reasonable consideration for other road users

Meanings

Cycle (see **10.12.1**)

Road (s 192) (see **10.1.1**)

Without due care and attention

Means that their cycling falls below the level of care, skill, and attention that would have been exercised by a competent and careful cyclist.

Without reasonable consideration

Requires other persons to be inconvenienced by the defendant's cycling.

Explanatory notes

- Cycling on a road without due care and attention is a question of fact for the court to decide on the evidence as to whether or not the cycling is careless. The standard of care and attention is an objective one.
- Cycling on a road without reasonable consideration for other road users is a subjective test that has to be decided by the court on the evidence before it. The other persons using the road can include drivers or passengers in vehicles, pedestrians, or other cyclists. It can include giving a misleading signal, cutting across a car, or causing a pedestrian to stop.

Practical considerations (see 10.12.1)

 Summary   6 months

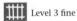 Level 3 fine

10.12.3 **Cycling when under the influence of drink or drugs**

Section 30 creates an offence of cycling on a road or public place while unfit through drink or drugs.

Offences

A person who, when riding a cycle on a road or other public place, is unfit to ride through drink or drugs (that is to say, is under the influence of drink or a drug to such an extent as to be incapable of having proper control of the cycle) is guilty of an offence.

Road Traffic Act 1988, s 30(1)

Points to prove

✓ rode a cycle
✓ on a road/other public place
✓ while unfit to ride through drink/drugs

Meanings

Road (s 192) (see 10.1.1)

Public place (see 10.1.2)

Practical considerations

- As there is no power to require a specimen of breath, blood, or urine, other methods of calculating the extent to which the defendant is under the influence of drink or drugs need to be used.
- Section 163 of the Road Traffic Act 1988 empowers a police constable in uniform to stop a cycle on a road. A person who fails to stop the cycle will be guilty of an offence (see **10.12.1**).
- This offence does not extend to being in charge of a cycle as it would with other forms of transport.
- A bicycle or tricycle is a carriage under the Licensing Act 1872. Therefore, consider the offence of being drunk in charge of a carriage on any highway or other public place under s 12 of that Act (see **7.2.2**).

 Summary   6 months

 Level 3 fine

10.12.4 **Riding or driving on the footpath**

Section 72 of the Highways Act 1835 creates an offence of wilfully riding or driving on the footpath.

Offences

If any person shall wilfully ride upon any footpath or causeway by the side of any road, made or set apart for the use or accommodation of foot passengers; or shall wilfully lead or drive any horse, ass, sheep, mule, swine, cattle or carriage of any description, or any truck or sledge, upon any such footpath or causeway or tether any horse, ass, mule, swine or cattle on any highway so as to suffer or permit the tethered animal to be thereon, he shall be guilty of an offence.

Highways Act 1835, s 72

Points to prove

✓ wilfully rode/drove/led/tethered
✓ carriage of any description, truck, sledge, or animal (as described)
✓ upon a footpath/causeway
✓ by the side of a road
✓ made/set apart
✓ for the use/accommodation of foot passengers

Meanings

Wilfully

'Wilful' under this section means 'purposely'.

Footpath

A footpath is part of a highway, if it is beside a road.

Carriage of any description

This includes bicycles, tricycles, motor vehicles, and trailers.

Explanatory notes
- Section 72 applies not only to the riding of bicycles or tricycles on the footpath/causeway, but also to the riding/driving of motor vehicles/trailers/truck/sledge and leading/tethering any animals as described.
- A Segway is a 'carriage' for the purposes of s 72 (*Coates v CPS* [2011] EWHC 2032 (Admin)).
- This offence requires proof of wilfully riding, driving a carriage, or leading/tethering animals as specified.
- Proceedings may be instituted by anyone.
- Consider issuing a TFPN for driving or cycling on the footway (see **10.4.1**). A PCSO can stop a cyclist and issue a TFPN for cycling on a footway.

 Summary 6 months

Level 2 fine

Links to alternative subjects and offences

10.13 **Driving While Disqualified/Cause Serious Injury**

10.13.1 **Obtain licence/drive on a road— while disqualified**

Section 103 of the Road Traffic Act 1988 creates the offences of obtaining a driving licence while disqualified from driving and driving a motor vehicle on a road while so disqualified.

Offences

A person is guilty of an offence if, while disqualified for holding or obtaining a licence, he—
(a) obtains a licence, or
(b) drives a motor vehicle on a road.

Road Traffic Act 1988, s 103(1)

Points to prove

✓ while disqualified for holding/obtaining a licence
✓ obtained a licence/drove a motor vehicle on a road

Meanings

Disqualified

Means disqualified for holding or obtaining a licence and, where the disqualification relates only to vehicles of a particular class, a licence to drive vehicles of that particular class.

Licence (see **10.14.1**)

Drives (see **10.1.4**)

Motor vehicle

This is defined by s 185 (see **10.1.3**).

Road (s 192) (see **10.1.1**)

Explanatory notes

- An under-age driver (unless disqualified by the court) should be charged with the offence of 'driving otherwise than in accordance with a licence' (see **10.14.1**).

- Subsection (1)(b) does not apply to a person disqualified for obtaining a licence authorising them to drive a motor vehicle of a specific class while they hold another licence to drive that class of vehicle.
- Such a person is disqualified for obtaining such a licence even if the licence held is suspended (s 102).
- Disqualification given in England and Wales applies to all of Great Britain, even if they hold a foreign or international driving licence or permit or service driving licence.
- A driver disqualified in a foreign country would not be guilty of this offence but may be guilty of driving without a licence.
- Disqualification by a court is usually for a specified period as punishment for a road traffic offence.
- If penalty points imposed by the court, together with any to be taken into account on that occasion, total twelve or more (the 'totting up' system) the court must, other than in exceptional circumstances, disqualify the defendant for at least a **minimum period** (Road Traffic Offenders Act 1988, s 35).
- **Minimum period** is six months if no previous disqualification, one year if one such period is to be taken into account, and two years if two or more such periods are taken into account.
- The court may order a driver to be disqualified until they pass a driving test. Such driver may not drive during the disqualification period; after this period, they can only drive on a provisional licence. Thereafter, if they fail to comply with the provisional licence conditions they may be guilty of driving whilst disqualified. Disqualification will only come to an end after they have passed the driving test.

Related cases (see also **10.1.4** cases)

Pattison v DPP [2005] EWHC 2938 (Admin), QBD Prosecution must prove that the defendant was a disqualified driver. Identification of the defendant as the person convicted in court may be established by admission, fingerprints, or by a person in court at time of conviction.

DPP v Barker [2004] EWHC 2502 (Admin), QBD If a person was disqualified until they had passed a driving test, the burden of proof was on the driver to show that they had a provisional licence and were driving in accordance with the licence conditions.

Practical considerations

- This offence is committed only if the defendant drives a motor vehicle of a class that is subject to the disqualification, although a disqualification by order of the court will not normally be limited to a particular class of vehicle.
- A licence obtained by a disqualified person is not valid.
- Proving beyond reasonable doubt that the person named on the certified court extract is the accused is an essential element of the prosecution case, although there is no prescribed way in which identity must be proved.

10.13.2 **Causing serious injury by driving: disqualified driver**

- Proof that the defendant knew of the disqualification is not necessary.
- A person is disqualified for holding or obtaining a licence to drive a certain class of motor vehicle if they are under the age stipulated for that class (s 101), but the offence would be contrary to s 87(1) (see **10.14.1**).
- Minimum ages for driving specified classes of motor vehicles are shown in **10.14.2**.

 Summary

 Normally 6 months but no more than 3 years after the offence

 s 103(1)(a) offence:
Level 3 fine

s 103(1)(b) offence:
6 months' imprisonment and/or a fine not exceeding level 5
Discretionary disqualification, obligatory endorsement—6 penalty points

10.13.2 **Causing serious injury by driving: disqualified driver**

Section 3ZD of the Road Traffic Act 1988 provides for the offence of causing the serious injury of another person by driving a motor vehicle on a road and at the time being disqualified from driving.

Offences

(1) A person is guilty of an offence under this section if he or she—
   (a) causes serious injury to another person by driving a motor vehicle on a road and,
   (b) at that time, is committing an offence under section 103(1)(b) of this Act (driving while disqualified).

Road Traffic Act 1988, s 3ZD

Points to prove

✓ caused the serious injury of another person
✓ by driving a motor vehicle
✓ on a road
✓ whilst disqualified

Meanings

Serious injury

Physical harm which amounts to grievous bodily harm (see **2.3.1**).

Another person (see **10.8.1**)

Driving (see 10.1.4)

Motor vehicle (see 10.1.3)

Road (s 192) (see 10.1.1)

Explanatory notes

- This offence is subject to driving a motor vehicle on a road and **causing** serious injury to another person whilst disqualified from driving under s 103(1)(b) (see **10.13.1**). It has effect only in relation to driving which occurs on or after 13 April 2015.

Practical considerations

- Consider CPS driving offences charging standards.
- Consider drive disqualification offence matters (see **10.13.1**).
- This offence requires some element of fault by the driver for causing the death of another person (*R v Hughes* [2013] UKSC 56; see **10.8.5**), not just driving a motor vehicle whilst disqualified.
- Annex A of MOJ Circular 1/2015 provides further guidance on this offence.

 Summary None

 Summary: 12 months' imprisonment and/or a fine
Obligatory disqualification
Obligatory endorsement—3 to 11 penalty points

Indictment: 4 years' imprisonment and/or a fine.
Obligatory disqualification
Obligatory endorsement—3 to 11 penalty points

Links to alternative subjects and offences

10.14 Driving Not in Accordance with a Driving Licence

Section 87 of the Road Traffic Act 1988 requires all people driving a motor vehicle on a road to hold a driving licence for that class of vehicle and to comply with any conditions attached to it.

10.14.1 Drive motor vehicle of a class not authorised

Offences

(1) It is an offence for a person to drive on a road a motor vehicle of any class otherwise than in accordance with a licence authorising him to drive a motor vehicle of that class.

(2) It is an offence for a person to cause or permit another person to drive on a road a motor vehicle of any class otherwise than in accordance with a licence authorising that other person to drive a motor vehicle of that class.

Road Traffic Act 1988, s 87

Points to prove

s 87(1) offence

✓ drove motor vehicle
✓ on a road
✓ otherwise than in accordance with licence
✓ authorising driving of that class of vehicle

s 87(2) offence

✓ caused/permitted
✓ another person to commit s 87(1) offence

Meanings

Drive (see 10.1.4)

Road (s 192) (see 10.1.1)

Motor vehicle (see 10.1.3)

Class (see 10.14.2)

Cause

Means involving some degree of control or dominance by or some express mandate from the causer. It also requires some positive action and knowledge by the defendant (*Price v Cromack* [1975] 1 WLR 988).

Permit

Is less direct or explicit than 'causing' and involves leave or licence to do something. Permission can be express or inferred. A person cannot permit a vehicle to be used unless they are in a position to forbid and no one can permit what he cannot control.

Licence

Means a licence to drive a motor vehicle under Pt 3 of the Road Traffic Act 1988 or a **community licence**.

Community licence

Means a document issued by an EEA state (other than the UK) by authority of the EEA state authorising the holder to drive a motor vehicle.

Full licence

Means a licence other than a **provisional licence**.

Provisional licence

Means a licence issued to enable an applicant to drive motor vehicles with a view to passing a test of competence to drive.

Explanatory notes

- The holder of a convention driving permit, a domestic driving licence/permit issued by a country outside the UK, or a British Forces driving permit who is resident outside the UK may drive any class of vehicle specified in the permit or licence for twelve months.
- A person who is an EU citizen and holds a driving licence or permit issued in another EU country may drive on that licence or permit in this country in accordance with that licence or permit. They would not need to exchange the licence or permit for a UK licence no matter how long they stayed here.
- Under s 88 a person who has held a driver's licence, a community licence, a Northern Ireland licence, a British external licence, a British Forces licence, or an exchangeable licence may, in certain circumstances, still drive a relevant vehicle even if the licence and its counterpart have been surrendered or revoked. This includes where a qualifying application has been received at DVLA or their licence to drive that class of vehicle and its counterpart has been revoked or surrendered for renewal; was granted in or contains an error; or for amendment of a requirement or the holder's name and address.

Practical considerations

- Where a person is charged with driving without a licence, the burden of proving that they have a licence is with that person (*John v Humphreys* [1955] 1 All ER 793, QBD).
- The police have powers to seize and remove a motor vehicle if the driver has no driving licence or there is no insurance in force for the vehicle (see **10.16.6**).
- It is an offence for a person not to produce their driving licence (see **10.16.4**).
- A TFPN can be issued for the s 87(1) offence (see **10.4**).
- This offence includes circumstances where the driver is driving under age.
- The classes of vehicles which a licence holder is authorised by it to drive are stated on the licence itself.
- A licence is valid only when it is used in accordance with its conditions of use.

 Summary   6 months

 s 87(1) offence:
Level 3 fine.
Discretionary disqualification, obligatory endorsement—3 to 6 penalty points

s 87(2) offence:
Level 3 fine

10.14.2 Minimum ages for holding/obtaining driving licences

Section 101 of the Road Traffic Act 1988 provides that a person is disqualified from holding or obtaining a licence to drive a motor vehicle of a class specified if he is under the age specified. The class of motor vehicle and minimum ages are as follows:
- Invalid carriage—16 years.
- Moped—16 years.
- Motor bicycle—17 years.
  - ✦ Where the motor bicycle is a large motor bicycle that age becomes 21 years (see **Appendix 2**), unless it is used for military purposes.
- Agricultural or forestry tractor—17 years.
  - ✦ However, that age will be 16 years, if it is a wheeled tractor (not tracked) and is not more than 2.45 metres wide or has a trailer

which is either two-wheeled or close-coupled, four-wheeled (maximum 840 mm gap), and both have a maximum width of 2.45 metres, **and** the person has passed, or is going to, taking, or returning from a test for a category F vehicle.

- Small vehicles (cars)—17 years.
  - ✦ This age may become 16 years if driven by a person in receipt of the higher-rate component of the disability living allowance without a trailer.
- Medium-sized goods vehicles—18 years, except:
  - ✦ where vehicle is towing a trailer and the maximum authorised mass of the combination exceeds 7.5 tonnes that age will be 21 years; or
  - ✦ if the vehicle is being used for military purposes the minimum age will be 17 years.
- Other motor vehicles—21 years.

This age will be 18 years for:

- a vehicle which carries more than eight passengers if the driver holds a full licence for that category **and** is carrying passengers on a regular 50-kilometre route or driving a vehicle in category D1;
- a passenger-carrying vehicle if the driver has a provisional licence for that category and there are no passengers;
- a vehicle which is a category D1 vehicle AND is an ambulance;
- a vehicle in category *C1 + E* with a maximum mass not exceeding 7.5 tonnes;
- a person who is part of a training scheme for large goods vehicle drivers either with their employer or an authorised school.

This age will be 17 years if:

- the vehicle is being used for military purposes or the vehicle is a road roller propelled otherwise than by steam, has no wheel fitted with pneumatic, soft, or elastic tyres, does not exceed 11.69 tonnes unladen, and only carries tools and equipment for its own use.

Explanatory notes

- If a person under the minimum age for driving a particular class of motor vehicle drives that vehicle without such a licence he commits the offence of driving without a licence for that class under s 87(1) (see **10.14.1**).
- The Motor Vehicles (Driving Licences) (Amendment) Regulations 2012 (SI 977/2012) amended the principal 1999 Regulations, in particular regarding driving mopeds and motorcycles; these regulations came into effect from 19 January 2013 (see Appendix 2).

Links to alternative subjects and offences

10.15 **Drive with Defective Eyesight**

Section 96 of the Road Traffic Act 1988 creates an offence of driving with defective eyesight.

Offences

Drive with uncorrected defective eyesight

(1) If a person drives a motor vehicle on a road while his eyesight is such (whether through a defect which cannot be or one which is not for the time being sufficiently corrected) that he cannot comply with any requirement as to eyesight prescribed under this Part of this Act for the purposes of tests of competence to drive, he is guilty of an offence.

Refuse to submit to eyesight test

(2) A constable having reason to suspect that a person driving a motor vehicle may be guilty of an offence under subsection (1) above may require him to submit to a test for the purpose of ascertaining whether, using no other means of correction than he used at the time of driving, he can comply with the requirement concerned.

(3) If that person refuses to submit to the test he is guilty of an offence.

Road Traffic Act 1988, s 96

Points to prove

s 96(1) offence

✓ drove a motor vehicle
✓ on a road
✓ while unable to meet eyesight requirements

s 96(3) offence

✓ being the driver of a motor vehicle
✓ on a road
✓ and being required to take eyesight test
✓ by a constable under s 96(2)
✓ refused to take such test

Meanings

Drives (see 10.1.4)

Motor vehicle (see 10.1.3)

Road (s 192) (see 10.1.1)

10.15 Drive with Defective Eyesight

Explanatory notes

- This section creates two offences
  - ♦ driving with defective eyesight;
  - ♦ refusing to submit to an eyesight test.
- The **requirement** as to **eyesight prescribed** can be found in reg 72 of the Motor Vehicles (Driving Licences) Regulations 1999. This requires a person to be able to read, in good light (with visual aids if used), a number plate on a vehicle containing characters of the **prescribed size**.
- **Prescribed size** means characters which are 79 mm high and 50 mm wide.
- The distance from which the number plate should be read is 20 metres, but for a category K vehicle (eg mowing machine and pedestrian-controlled vehicle) it is 12 metres.
- Spectacles or contact lenses may be used for the test if they were wearing them while driving.
- For the purposes of this offence it does not matter whether the defect is one that can be corrected or not. The important matter is the state of their eyesight at the time they were driving.
- Knowledge of the defect by the defendant is not necessary, although this may be used in mitigation if the defendant has suffered a gradual and unnoticed deterioration in their eyesight.
- However, under s 92(1) any person holding or applying for a licence has a duty to inform the DVLA of any prescribed disability likely to cause the driving of a vehicle by them in accordance with the licence to be a source of danger to the public. This includes a 'prospective' disability such as a condition that does not at the time amount to a relevant disability, but which is likely to deteriorate to that level in the course of time.

Practical considerations

- The degree by which the defendant's eyesight fails to meet the requirement is particularly relevant as this will reflect the degree of risk taken or danger created by them.
- The more severe the defect the more difficult it will be for the defendant to mitigate the offence.
- An inability to read the characters in the test will amount to a prescribed disability and the person will have to inform the DVLA under s 92(1).

 Summary   6 months

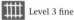 Level 3 fine

Discretionary disqualification, obligatory endorsement— 3 penalty points

Links to alternative subjects and offences

10.16 Vehicle Document Offences and Seizure of Vehicles

10.16.1 No insurance (use, cause, or permit)

Section 143 of the Road Traffic Act 1988 requires the user of a motor vehicle to be insured or secured against third party risks.

> **Offences**
>
> (1) Subject to the provisions of this Part of this Act—
>   (a) a person must not use a motor vehicle on a road or other public place unless there is in force in relation to the use of the vehicle by that person such a policy of insurance or such a security in respect of third party risks as complies with the requirements of this Part of this Act, and
>   (b) a person must not cause or permit any other person to use a motor vehicle on a road or other public place unless there is in force in relation to the use of the vehicle by that other person such a policy of insurance or such a security in respect of third party risks as complies with the requirements of this Part of this Act.
> (2) If a person acts in contravention of subsection (1) above he is guilty of an offence.
>
> Road Traffic Act 1988, s 143

Points to prove

✓ used/caused/permitted another to use
✓ motor vehicle
✓ on a road/public place
✓ without insurance/security for third party risks

Meanings

Use

Means the driver of a vehicle, the driver's employer while it is being used for their business, the vehicle owner if they are in it while somebody else is driving it, or the steersman of a broken-down vehicle which is being towed.

Motor vehicle (see 10.1.3)

Road (s 192) (see 10.1.1)

Public place (see 10.1.2)

Policy of insurance

This includes a cover note.

Security

This section does not apply to a vehicle owned by a person who has deposited and keeps deposited with the Accountant General of the Senior Courts the sum of £500,000, at a time when the vehicle is being driven under the owner's control.

Cause (see 10.14.1)

Permit (see 10.14.1)

Explanatory notes

- This section does not apply to invalid carriages.
- Section 144 states that s 143 does not apply to:
  - ✦ a vehicle owned by a county or county district council, Broads Authority, City of London Common/Borough Council, National Park Authority, Inner London Education Authority, London Fire and Emergency Planning Authority, joint (local government) waste authorities, or a joint authority, or a joint board or committee which includes member representatives of such council—at a time when the vehicle is being driven under the owner's control;
  - ✦ a vehicle owned by a local policing body when it is being driven under the owner's control, or a vehicle being driven for police purposes by or under the direction of a constable, by civilian staff of a police force or a member of staff of the police and crime commissioner's/Mayor's office (within the meaning of Pt 1 of the Police Reform and Social Responsibility Act 2011);
  - ✦ a vehicle being driven to or from a place for the purposes of salvage under the Merchant Shipping Act 1995;
  - ✦ a vehicle owned by a health service body or Local Health Board—at a time when the vehicle is being driven under the owner's control;
  - ✦ an ambulance owned by an NHS Trust or Foundation Trust at a time when the vehicle is being driven under the owner's control;
  - ✦ a vehicle made available to a person, body, or local authority under s 12 or s 80 of the National Health Service Act 2006 (s 10 or s38 of the National Health Service (Wales) Act 2006) while being used in accordance with the terms under which it was made available;

✦ a vehicle owned by the Care Quality Commission, at a time when the vehicle is being driven under the owner's control.
- Section 144(2)(b), on its plain and ordinary meaning, exempts a police officer on duty using his own vehicle for police purposes, from the requirement for third party insurance (*Jones v Chief Constable of Bedfordshire* [1987] RTR 332).

Defences

A person charged with using a motor vehicle in contravention of this section shall not be convicted if he proves—

(a) that the vehicle did not belong to him and was not in his possession under a contract of hiring or of loan,

(b) that he was using the vehicle in the course of his employment, and

(c) that he neither knew nor had reason to believe that there was not in force in relation to the vehicle such a policy of insurance or security as is mentioned in subsection (1) above.

Road Traffic Act 1988, s 143(3)

Related cases

DPP v Hay [2005] EWHC 1395 (Admin), QBD It is for the defendant to show that there was in force a policy of insurance, once it has been proved that they used the motor vehicle on a road or public place.

Dodson v Peter H Dodson Insurance Services [2001] 1 WLR 1012, CA In the absence of a condition in the policy of insurance making it clear that the policyholder would only be covered while they were the owner of the relevant vehicle, the policy is valid until expiry.

Plumbien v Vines [1996] Crim LR 124, QBD A vehicle left on a road for several months such that it could not be moved is still at the disposal of the owner and so requires insurance (and test certificate).

Practical considerations

- Read the conditions on the insurance very carefully as they may, for example, cover a person who is not a current driving licence holder. Similarly, a valid insurance certificate may not cover that person for the vehicle being used or for that particular purpose.
- A TFPN for the s 143(1)(a) 'using' offence can be issued (see **10.4**).
- The policy must be issued by an authorised insurer (eg a member of the Motor Insurers' Bureau).
- It is an offence to fail to produce insurance (see **10.16.5**).
- The motor vehicle can be seized if no insurance is in force for the vehicle (see **10.16.6**).

s 143(1)(a) offence only

 Summary

 36 months

 Fine not exceeding level 5
Discretionary disqualification, obligatory endorsement—3 to 8 penalty points

10.16.2 **No insurance (registered keeper)**

Section 144A makes it an offence to keep a registered vehicle which is not insured or secured against third party risks.

> ### Offences
>
> If a motor vehicle registered under the Vehicle Excise and Registration Act 1994 does not meet the insurance requirements, the person in whose name the vehicle is registered is guilty of an offence.
>
> Road Traffic Act 1988, s 144A(1)

Points to prove

✓ person in whose name a motor vehicle is registered
✓ failed to ensure
✓ insurance requirements met for vehicle

Meanings

Motor vehicle (see 10.1.3)

Registered

Means a vehicle registered with the Secretary of State under s 21 of the Vehicle Excise and Registration Act 1994.

Insurance requirements

A vehicle meets the insurance requirements if:
• covered by a **policy of insurance** or **security** in respect of third party risks as complies with the requirements of Pt 6 of this Act **and**
• **either** of the following conditions is satisfied:
  ✦ **first condition** is that the policy or certificate of insurance or security identifies the vehicle by its registration mark as a vehicle covered by the policy or security;

10.16.2 No insurance (registered keeper)

+ **second condition** is that the vehicle is covered by the policy or security, which covers any vehicle, or vehicle of a particular description; the owner being named in that policy or certificate of insurance or security, and the vehicle is owned by that person.

Policy of insurance (see **10.16.1**)

Security (see **10.16.1**)

Explanatory notes

- For the purposes of this section a vehicle is covered by a policy of insurance or security if the policy of insurance or security is in force in relation to the use of the vehicle.
- Section 144B provides exceptions for either the registered keeper or owner of the vehicle regarding the s 144A offence under the following conditions:
    + owns vehicle and a security is in force or most of the exceptions to s 144 apply (see **10.16.1 'Explanatory notes'**);
    + owns vehicle with the intention that it should be used for the purposes of salvage under the Merchant Shipping Act 1995 or for NHS or social care purposes;
    + not keeping vehicle, required details provided;
    + keeping vehicle, but not used on a road/public place, required details provided;
    + vehicle stolen before relevant time, not recovered, and theft reported as required;
    + keeping vehicle, no VEL in force on or since 31 January 1998 and not used or kept on a road after that date.

Practical considerations

- The Motor Vehicles (Insurance Requirements) (Immobilisation, Removal and Disposal) Regulations 2011 (SI 1120/2011) provide for the immobilisation and/or removal of uninsured vehicles found stationary on roads and other public places.
- Sections 144A–144D of this Act give DVLA and the MIB, who administer the Motor Insurance Database, powers to deal with registered keepers of vehicles that are taxed but not insured, through the introduction of Continuous Insurance Enforcement (CIE).
- Where a vehicle is taxed, but uninsured, the MIB will issue an 'Insurance Advisory Letter' to the registered keeper advising them as follows:
    + if not insured, insure immediately.
    + if insured, contact insurance provider immediately to check that the Motor Insurance Database has been correctly updated.
    + send a SORN to DVLA so the vehicle is not included in CIE.
    + if they no longer have the vehicle, notify DVLA in writing.
- If the keeper fails to act and the vehicle remains taxed but not insured, DVLA will issue a £100 fixed penalty notice to the keeper (reduced to £50 if paid within twenty-one days).

• These sections only apply to GB (vehicles registered in Northern Ireland, Channel Islands, and Isle of Man are excluded as they have their own registration authorities).

 Summary   6 months

 Level 3 fine

Fixed penalty ticket: £100.

Note: A fixed penalty notice for this offence shall be treated as having been paid if the amount of £50 is paid before the end of the period of 21 days following the date the notice is given.

10.16.3 **No test certificate**

Section 47 creates an offence relating to motor vehicles over three years old being on a road without a valid test certificate in force, and s 53 creates a similar offence for goods vehicles over twelve months old.

Offences

Motor vehicle

A person who uses on a road at any time, or causes or permits to be so used, a motor vehicle to which this section applies, and as respects which no test certificate has been issued within the appropriate period before that time, is guilty of an offence.

Road Traffic Act 1988, s 47(1)

Goods vehicle

If any person at any time on or after the relevant date—
(a) uses on a road a goods vehicle of a class required by regulations under s 49 to have been submitted for a goods vehicle test, or
(b) causes or permits to be used on a road a goods vehicle of such a class,
and at that time there is no goods vehicle test certificate in force for the vehicle, he is guilty of an offence.

Road Traffic Act 1988, s 53(2)

Points to prove

s 47(1) offence

✓ used/caused to use/permitted to use
✓ a motor vehicle to which s 47 applies
✓ on a road
✓ without a valid test certificate

10.16.3 **No test certificate**

---

s 53(2) offence

✓ used/caused to use/permitted to use
✓ a goods vehicle as specified by regulations under s 49
✓ on a road
✓ without a valid goods vehicle test certificate

Meanings

Uses (see **10.16.1**)

Road (see **10.1.1**)

Causes (see **10.14.1**)

Permits (see **10.14.1**)

Motor vehicles to which section 47 applies

Motor vehicles (see **10.1.3**) (not being goods vehicles) which have been registered under the Vehicles Excise and Registration Act 1994 for not less than three years or were manufactured at least three years ago and have been used on roads (whether in GB or elsewhere) before being so registered.

Appropriate period

Means a period of twelve months or shorter as may be prescribed.

Related cases

Plumbien v Vines [1996] Crim LR 124, QBD (see **10.16.1**)

Explanatory notes

Motor vehicles

- Types of motor vehicles to which s 47 applies are:
  - ✦ passenger vehicles with not more than eight seats (excluding the driver's seat);
  - ✦ rigid goods motor cars—unladen weight does not exceed 1,525 kg;
  - ✦ dual-purpose vehicles, motor cycles (including three-wheelers, mopeds), and motor caravans.
- These vehicles (unless exempt) must obtain a test certificate annually, after the first test certificate.
- Similarly, a motor vehicle used to carry passengers and having more than eight seats excluding the driver's seat, a taxi licensed to ply for hire or an **ambulance**, is required to be submitted for an annual test from the first anniversary of its registration or manufacture.
- 'Ambulance' means a motor vehicle that is constructed or adapted, and primarily used, for the carriage of persons to a place where they will receive, or from a place where they have received, medical or dental treatment, and which, by reason of design, marking, or equipment is readily identifiable as a vehicle so constructed or adapted.

Goods vehicles

- Heavy motor cars, motor cars constructed or adapted to form part of an articulated vehicle, other heavy motor cars that exceed 3,500 kg design weight, semi-trailers, converter dollies manufactured on or after 1 January 1979, and trailers exceeding 1,020 kg unladen weight **all require a goods vehicle test certificate**.
- All vehicles requiring a goods vehicle test certificate must be submitted for their first test, in the case of a motor vehicle, before the last day of the calendar month in which falls the first anniversary of its date of registration, and in relation to trailers, before the last day of the calendar month in which falls the first anniversary of the date on which it was first sold or supplied by retail.

Practical considerations

- Vehicles exempted from a s 47 test certificate are vehicles:
  - ✦ being driven to a pre-arranged test;
  - ✦ being tested by an authorised examiner;
  - ✦ where a test certificate is refused, vehicles:
    - ✦ being driven from the test;
    - ✦ being delivered by pre-arranged delivery to or from a place where work is to be or has been done to remedy the defects;
    - ✦ delivering or towing to a place to be scrapped;
  - ✦ being removed under a statutory power;
  - ✦ being tested by a motor trader under a trade licence;
  - ✦ that are imported and that are being driven from entry port to the owner's residence;
  - ✦ detained/seized by police and HMRC;
  - ✦ exempt from testing by order under s 44 (see below).
- Vehicles exempted from testing are described in reg 6(1) of the Motor Vehicles (Tests) Regulations 1981, being: vehicles that are temporarily in GB (not exceeding twelve months); manufactured before 1 January 1960; proceeding to a port for export; used on a public road only to travel between land in occupation of the vehicle keeper n/e aggregate of 6 miles per calendar week; provided for police purposes by a police authority and maintained in approved workshops; provided for NCA; heavy locomotive; light locomotive; motor tractor; track laying vehicle; goods vehicle exceeding 3,500 kg design gross weight (subject to goods vehicle testing); articulated vehicle not being an articulated bus; works truck; pedestrian-controlled vehicle; invalid carriage n/e 306 kg u/w (510 kg u/w if supplied by NHS); visiting forces' or imported Armed Forces' vehicles; current Northern Ireland test certificate; electrically propelled goods vehicle n/e 3,500 kg design gross weight; licensed hackney carriage or private hire car which undergoes testing by the local authority; agricultural motor vehicle; street cleansing, refuse, and gully cleaning vehicle constructed and not merely adapted, being either a three-wheeled vehicle or maximum design speed of 20 mph, or inside track width less than 810 mm; tramcar and trolley vehicles.
- Vehicles exempt from goods vehicle testing are given in Sch 2 to the Goods Vehicle (Plating and Testing) Regulations 1988. Nearly

forty categories of vehicles are listed and, in some instances, they are similar to those given above.

- It is an offence to fail to produce (if required) the test certificate, plating certificate, or goods vehicle test certificate (see **10.16.5**).
- The date of manufacture is taken to be the last day of the year in which its final assembly is completed.
- Consider issuing a TFPN for a motor vehicle s 47 offence (see **10.4**).
- A TFPN **cannot** be issued for a goods vehicle s 53 offence.
- Authorised examiners may carry out roadside tests on vehicles under s 67 (see **10.2.3**).
- Under s 68(4) a vehicle examiner or police officer in uniform may direct a goods vehicle or PSV to proceed to a suitable place for inspection, provided it is within 5 miles from where the requirement has been made. It is a summary offence to obstruct the examiner under s 68(3) or refuse/fail to comply with request under s 68(5).

 s 47(1) offence

 Summary 6 months

 s 47(1) offence:
Level 3 fine. Level 4 if vehicle adapted to carry more than eight passengers

s 53(2) offence:
Level 4 fine

10.16.4 **Fail to produce driving licence**

Section 164 empowers a constable or vehicle examiner to require production of a driving licence and a certificate of completion of a motorcycle course.

Offences

If a person required under the preceding provisions of this section to produce a licence or state his date of birth or to produce his certificate of completion of a training course for motorcyclists fails to do so he is, subject to subsections (7) to (8A) *[defences]*, guilty of an offence.

Road Traffic Act 1988, s 164(6)

Points to prove

✓ when required by a constable/vehicle examiner
✓ failed to state date of birth or produce driving licence, motorcycle training certificate

Meanings

Required to produce

Any of the following persons—
(a) driving a motor vehicle on a road,
(b) whom a police constable or vehicle examiner has reasonable cause
    to believe to have been the driver of a motor vehicle at a time
    when an accident occurred owing to its presence on a road,
(c) whom a constable or vehicle examiner has reasonable cause to
    believe to have committed an offence in relation to the use of a
    motor vehicle on a road, or
(d) a person—
    (i) who supervises the holder of a **provisional licence** while the
        holder is driving a motor vehicle on a road, or
    (ii) whom a constable or vehicle examiner has reasonable cause
        to believe was supervising the holder of a provisional licence
        while driving, at a time when an accident occurred owing to the
        presence of the vehicle on a road or at a time when an offence
        is suspected of having been committed by the holder of the
        provisional licence in relation to the use of the vehicle on a road,

must, on being so required by a constable or vehicle examiner, produce
his licence for examination, so as to enable the constable or vehicle
examiner to ascertain the name and address of the holder of the licence,
the date of issue, and the authority by which they were issued.

Road Traffic Act 1988, s 164(1)

State date of birth (s 164(2))

A person required by a constable under s 164(1) to produce their licence
must in **prescribed circumstances**, on being required by the constable,
state their date of birth.

Prescribed circumstances

The circumstances in which a constable may require a person's date of
birth are given in reg 83(1) of the Motor Vehicles (Driving Licences)
Regulations 1999. Where the person:
• fails to produce their licence for immediate examination;
• produces a licence which the constable suspects was not granted to
  that person, was granted to them in error, or contains an alteration
  in particulars entered on the licence made with intent to deceive or
  where the driver number has been altered, removed, or defaced; or
• is a supervisor under s 164(1)(d) and the constable suspects they are
  under 21 years of age.

Provisional licence (see 10.14)

Explanatory notes

Other preceding provisions for failing to produce offences under s 164(6) are:
• s 164(3): where a licence has been revoked by the Secretary of State,
  a constable may require its production, and, if it is produced, may
  seize it and deliver it to the Secretary of State;

10.16.4 Fail to produce driving licence

- s 164(4): if a constable reasonably believes that a licence holder, or any other person, has knowingly made a false statement to obtain a licence (s)he may require the holder to produce it to them;
- s 164(4A): where a provisional licence is produced by a motorcyclist and a constable reasonably believes that the holder was not riding the motorcycle as part of an approved training course, the constable may require production of his certificate of completion of a training course for motorcyclists;
- s 164(5): if a person has been required to produce their licence to a court and fails to do so, a constable may require them to produce it and, when it is produced, may seize it and deliver to the court.

Defences

(7) Subsection (6) [*offences*] above does not apply where a person required on any occasion under the proceeding provisions of this section to produce a licence—

   (a) produces on that occasion a current receipt for the licence issued under section 56 of the Road Traffic Offenders Act 1988 and, if required to do so, produces the licence in person immediately on its return at a police station that was specified on that occasion, or

   (b) within 7 days after that occasion produces such a receipt in person at a police station that was specified by him on that occasion and, if required to do so, produces the licence in person immediately on its return at a police station.

(8) In proceedings against any person for the offence of failing to produce a licence it shall be a defence for him to show that—

   (a) within 7 days after the production of his licence was required he produced it in person at a police station that was specified by him at the time its production was required, or

   (b) he produced it in person there as soon as was reasonably practicable, or

   (c) it was not reasonably practicable for him to produce it there before the day on which the proceedings were commenced.

(8A) Subsection (8) above shall apply in relation to a certificate of completion of a training course for motorcyclists as it applies in relation to a licence.

Road Traffic Act 1988, s 164

Practical considerations

- Since 8 June 2015 the driving licence paper counterpart has no longer been issued with driving licences. Endorsements will no longer be entered onto counterparts, as they will be entered onto a person's electronic driving record, maintained by the DVLA. GB licence holders will no longer be required to retain or produce the paper counterpart.
- In certain circumstances reference to a constable includes reference to a TW.

Summary   6 months

Level 3 fine

10.16.5 Fail to provide details or produce vehicle documents

Section 165 empowers a constable or vehicle examiner to require production of insurance and vehicle test documents.

Requirements

Any of the following persons—
(a) driving a motor vehicle (other than an invalid carriage) on a road, or
(b) whom a constable or vehicle examiner has reasonable cause to believe to have been the driver of a motor vehicle (other than an invalid carriage) at a time when an accident occurred owing to its presence on a road or other public place, or
(c) whom a constable or vehicle examiner has reasonable cause to believe to have committed an offence in relation to the use on a road of a motor vehicle (other than an invalid carriage),

must, on being so required by a constable or vehicle examiner, give his name and address and the name and address of the owner of the vehicle and produce the following documents for examination.

Road Traffic Act 1988, s 165(1)

Offences

Subject to subsection (4) [*defences*], a person who fails to comply with a requirement under subsection (1) is guilty of an offence.

Road Traffic Act 1988, s 165(3)

Points to prove
✓ being a person falling under s 165(1)
✓ failed when required by a constable/vehicle examiner
✓ to give name and address or name and address of vehicle owner **and/or**
✓ produce for inspection a test certificate or goods vehicle test certificate or certificate of insurance, or certificate of security

Meanings

Owner

In relation to a vehicle which is the subject of a hiring agreement this includes each party to the agreement.

10.16.6 Seize and remove motor vehicle

Documents (s 165(2))

The documents specified in subsection (1) are:
- a relevant certificate of insurance or certificate of security;
- a test certificate required by s 47; and
- a plating certificate or goods vehicle test certificate required by s 53.

Explanatory notes

- Under s 165(5) a supervisor of a provisional licence holder must, on being required by a constable/vehicle examiner, give their name and address, and the name and address of the owner of the vehicle.
- If the supervisor fails to comply with the name and address requirements, then under s 165(6) they will commit an offence.

Defences

A person shall not be convicted of an offence under subsection (3) by reason only of failure to produce any certificate or other evidence in proceedings against him for the offence if he shows that—

(a) within 7 days after the date on which the production of the certificate or other evidence was required it was produced at a police station that was specified by him at the time when its production was required, or

(b) it was produced there as soon as was reasonably practicable, or

(c) it was not reasonably practicable for it to be produced there before the day on which the proceedings were commenced,

and for the purposes of this subsection the laying of the information shall be treated as the commencement of the proceedings.

Road Traffic Act 1988, s 165(4)

Practical considerations

- In the above defence, the question of whether a defendant produced documents 'as soon as was reasonably practicable' will be a question of fact for the court to decide in each case.
- Reference to a constable includes, in certain circumstances, a TW.

 Summary   6 months

 Level 3 fine

10.16.6 Seize and remove motor vehicle (no insurance/driving licence)

Section 165A empowers a constable to seize and remove a motor vehicle, which they believe is being used without a driving licence or insurance.

Powers

Seizure conditions

Under s 165A a constable may seize a motor vehicle under this section if any of the following sections apply—

- s 164, on being required by a constable in uniform to produce their licence for examination (see **10.16.3**), a person fails to do so, and the constable reasonably believes that they are or were driving without a licence (see **10.14**);
- s 165, on being required by a constable in uniform to produce evidence of insurance, a person fails to do so (see **10.16.4**), and the constable reasonably believes that the vehicle was being driven without such insurance (see **10.16.1**);
- s 163, on being required by a constable in uniform to stop a vehicle, the driver fails to do so (see **10.2.4**) or fails to do so long enough for the constable to make appropriate enquiries, and the constable reasonably believes that they are or were driving without a licence or insurance.

Removal

The Road Traffic Act 1988 (Retention and Disposal of Seized Motor Vehicles) Regulations 2005, made under s 165B, specifically provide for the retention, safe keeping, and disposal by the police or persons authorised by them, of vehicles seized under s 165A.

Explanatory notes

- Before seizing the motor vehicle, the driver or person appearing to be the driver must be warned of the consequences of failure to immediately produce their driving licence, or provide evidence of insurance, unless circumstances make it impracticable to give the warning.
- If the vehicle fails to stop or drives off, and cannot be seized immediately, it may be seized at any time within twenty-four hours of the original incident.
- To seize the vehicle a constable may enter any premises (except a private **dwelling house**) on which they reasonably believe the vehicle to be. If necessary, reasonable force may be used in the exercise of this power.
- A **dwelling house** does not include a garage or other structure occupied with the dwelling house or land belonging to it.

Related cases

Pryor v CC of Greater Manchester Police [2011] EWCA Civ 749, CA
In this case, the defendant lent his recently acquired motor vehicle to another person with written authority and they were stopped by the police. Although the other person's insurance policy allowed him to drive a car not owned by him (with consent of the owner), the police still seized the car under s 165A for no insurance, as PNC showed no

current keeper and no insurance in force. The defendant was awarded damages for wrongful interference with his car, as the police had failed to establish grounds for seizure.

Practical considerations

- In this section motor vehicle does not include an invalid carriage.
- A constable must be in uniform and may use reasonable force, if necessary, to exercise these powers.
- The police are under a duty to ensure the retention and safe keeping of a seized vehicle until it is released to the owner or otherwise disposed of under the 2005 Regulations (see '**Removal**' above).
- Regulation 4 of the 2005 Regulations states that when the vehicle is seized, a seizure notice shall be given to the driver of the seized vehicle, unless the circumstances make it impracticable to do so. It also gives the procedure to follow in respect of seized vehicles.
- Where practicable a seizure notice must be given to the registered keeper and the owner.

Links to alternative subjects and offences

10.17 **Seat Belts**

Section 14 of the Road Traffic Act 1988 relates to the wearing of seat belts in motor vehicles by adults and s 15 by children.

10.17.1 **Seat belts—adults**

Section 14 empowers the Secretary of State to make regulations concerning the wearing of seat belts in motor vehicles by adults and creates an offence of failing to comply with such regulations.

> **Offences**
>
> A person who drives or rides in a motor vehicle in contravention of regulations under this section is guilty of an offence; but notwithstanding any enactment or rule of law, no person other than the person actually committing the contravention is guilty of an offence by reason of the contravention.
>
> Road Traffic Act 1988, s 14(3)

Points to prove

✓ drove/rode in a motor vehicle
✓ contravened regulations made under s 14

Meanings

Drives (see **10.1.4**)

Motor vehicle

Defined by s 185 (see **10.1.3**), **but** for s 14 or s 15(1) **does not include** a motorcycle (with or without a sidecar).

Regulations

(1) Subject to the following provisions of these regulations, every person—
   (a) driving a motor vehicle; or
   (b) riding in a front or rear seat of a motor vehicle;
   shall wear an adult belt.
(2) Paragraph (1) **does not apply** to a person under the age of 14 years.

Motor Vehicles (Wearing of Seat Belts) Regulations 1993, reg 5

Exemptions

Regulation 6 of the above regulations gives exemptions from reg 5 requirements to:

- person holding a medical certificate;
- driver/passenger in a motor vehicle constructed or adapted for carrying goods, being on a journey which does not exceed 50 metres used for delivery or collection;
- driver of a vehicle performing a manoeuvre including reversing;
- qualified driver supervising provisional licence holder who is performing a manoeuvre including reversing;
- driving test examiner conducting a test of competence to drive and wearing a seat belt would endanger the examiner or any other person;
- person driving or riding in a vehicle being used for fire and rescue authority, police, or NCA purposes, or for carrying a person in lawful custody;
- person riding in a motor ambulance while they are providing medical attention or treatment to a patient which cannot be delayed;
- driver of a licensed taxi used for seeking hire, or answering a call for hire, or carrying a passenger for hire, or driver of a private hire vehicle used to carry a passenger for hire;
- person riding in a vehicle, used on trade plates to investigate or remedy a fault in the vehicle;
- disabled person wearing a disabled person's belt;
- person riding in a vehicle taking part in a procession organised by or on behalf of the Crown;
- person driving a vehicle if the driver's seat is not provided with an adult belt;
- person riding in the front/rear of a vehicle if no adult belt is available for them;
- person riding in a small or large bus which is:
  - ✦ being used to provide a local service in a built-up area; or
  - ✦ constructed or adapted for the carriage of standing passengers and on which the operator permits standing.

Explanatory notes

- Regulation 47(1) of the Road Vehicles (Construction and Use) Regulations 1986 stipulates that seatbelts are required to be fitted to a motor vehicle to which reg 46 applies.
- Regulation 46 applies to a motor vehicle, which is not an **excepted vehicle** and is:
  - ✦ a bus first used on or after 1 April 1982;
  - ✦ a wheeled motor car first used on or after 1 January 1965;
  - ✦ a three-wheeled motorcycle having an u/w exceeding 255 kg, first used on or after 1 September 1970; or
  - ✦ a heavy motor car first used on or after 1 October 1988.
- **Excepted vehicles** are listed in reg 46(2), being a goods vehicle (except a dual-purpose vehicle) being first used before 1 April 1967 or 1 April 1980–1 October 1988 (exceeding 3,500 kg max gross wt) or u/

w exceeding 1,525 kg before 1 April 1980 (but if manufactured before 1 October 1979 then first used before 1 April 1982); motor tractor; works truck; goods vehicle (electrically propelled—first used before 1 October 1988); pedestrian-controlled vehicle; vehicle used on roads outside GB (being driven from port of entry place of residence of owner or driver, or to prearranged place for fitting of anchorage points and seat belts as required by regs 46 and 47); vehicle having max speed n/e 16 mph; locomotive or agricultural motor vehicle.

- The holder of a medical certificate cannot rely on the reg 5 exception unless they produce the certificate to the constable at the time of being reported for summons, or produce it within seven days or as soon as practicable after being reported at a police station specified by them, or where it is not so produced it is not reasonably practicable to produce it there before the commencement of proceedings.

Practical considerations

- Consider issuing a TFPN for this offence (see **10.4**).
- Each passenger is responsible for wearing a seatbelt and liable for the s 14(3) offence, except passengers under the age of 14 years (see **10.17.2**) where the responsibility is then with the driver.
- Regulation 5 above does not apply where there is no adult seat belt available in that part of the vehicle.

 Summary   6 months

 Level 2 fine

10.17.2 **Seat belts—children**

Section 15 creates offences concerning the wearing of seat belts by children in motor vehicles.

Offences

Seated in front

(1) Except as provided by regulations, where a child under the age of 14 years is in the front of a motor vehicle, a person must not without reasonable excuse drive the vehicle on a road unless the child is wearing a seat belt in conformity with regulations.

(1A) Where—
    (a) a child is in the front of a motor vehicle other than a bus,
    (b) the child is in a rear-facing child restraining device, and

---

(c) the passenger seat where the child is placed is protected by a front air bag,

a person must not without reasonable excuse drive the vehicle on a road unless the air bag is deactivated.

(2) It is an offence for a person to drive a motor vehicle in contravention of subsection (1) or (1A) above.

Seated in rear

(3) Except as provided by regulations, where—
   (a) a child under the age of three years is in the rear of a motor vehicle, or
   (b) a child of or over that age but under the age of fourteen years is in the rear of a motor vehicle and any seat belt is fitted in the rear of that vehicle,

   a person must not without reasonable excuse drive the vehicle on a road unless the child is wearing a seat belt in conformity with regulations.

(3A) Except as provided by regulations, where—
   (a) a child who is under the age of 12 years and less than 150 cm in height is in the rear of a passenger car,
   (b) no seat belt is fitted in the rear of the passenger car, and
   (c) a seat in the front of the passenger car is provided with a seat belt but is not occupied by any person,

   a person must not without reasonable excuse drive the passenger car on a road.

(4) It is an offence for a person to drive a motor vehicle in contravention of subsection (3) or (3A) above.

Road Traffic Act 1988, s 15

Points to prove

s 15(2) offence (seated in front)

✓ without reasonable excuse
✓ drove a motor vehicle
✓ on a road
✓ child under 14 years
✓ in the front of the vehicle
✓ not wearing a seat belt or
✓ in a rear-facing restraining device and front airbag not deactivated

s 15(4) offence (seated in rear)

✓ per first four points of s 15(2)
✓ in the rear of the vehicle
✓ a child under the age of 3 years **or** aged 3 years to 13 years
✓ not wearing a fitted seat belt

or

✓ motor vehicle was a passenger car
✓ child under 12 years and less than 150 cm tall
✓ with no rear seat belt fitted and
✓ a front seat (with belt) was available

Meanings

Motor vehicle (see **10.17.1**)

Road (see **10.1.1**)

Seat belt

This includes any description of restraining device for a child.

Bus

Means a motor vehicle that:
- has at least four wheels;
- is constructed or adapted for the carriage of passengers;
- has more than eight seats in addition to the driver's seat; and
- has a maximum design speed exceeding 25 kilometres per hour.

Passenger car

Means a motor vehicle which:
- is constructed or adapted for use for the carriage of passengers and is not a goods vehicle;
- has no more than eight seats in addition to the driver's seat;
- has four or more wheels;
- has a maximum design speed exceeding 25 kilometres per hour; and
- has a **maximum laden weight** not exceeding 3.5 tonnes.

Maximum laden weight

In relation to a vehicle or combination of vehicles means:
- in respect of which a gross weight not to be exceeded in GB is specified in construction and use requirements, **that weight**;
- in respect of which **no such weight is specified** in construction and use requirements, the weight which the vehicle, or combination of vehicles, is designed or adapted not to exceed when in normal use and travelling on a road laden.

Regulations (seated in front)

Motor Vehicles (Wearing of Seat Belts by Children in Front Seats) Regulations 1993. Regulation 5 describes the belt or restraint to be worn.

Regulations (seated in rear)

Motor Vehicles (Wearing of Seat Belts) Regulations 1993.

Small child

A child under the age of 12 years and under 135 cm in height.

Large child

Is a child who is not a small child.

10.17.2 Seat belts—children

Explanatory notes

- The concept of a small child and a large child has been added by the above regulations. This has resulted in the lowering of the height from 150 cm down to 135 cm for a small child. This only affects the type of restraint that a small child should wear.
- Sections 15(3) and 15(3A) rear seat prohibitions do not apply to:
  + a child for whom there is a medical certificate;
  + a small child aged **under 3 years** who is riding in a licensed taxi or licensed hire car, if no appropriate seat belt is available for them in the front or rear of the vehicle;
  + a small child aged **3 years or more** who is riding in a licensed taxi, a licensed hire car, or a small bus and wearing an adult belt if an appropriate seat belt is not available for them in the front or rear of the vehicle;
  + a small child aged **3 years or more** who is wearing an adult belt and riding in a passenger car or light goods vehicle where the use of child restraints by the child occupants of two seats in the rear of the vehicle prevents the use of an appropriate seat belt for that child and no appropriate seat belt is available for them in the front of the vehicle;
  + a small child riding in a vehicle being used for the purposes of the police, security, or emergency services to enable the proper performance of their duty;
  + a small child aged **3 years or more** who is wearing an adult belt and who, because of an unexpected necessity, is travelling a short distance in a passenger car or light goods vehicle in which no appropriate seat belt is available for them; or
  + a disabled child who is wearing a disabled person's belt or whose disability makes it impracticable to wear a seat belt where a disabled person's belt is unavailable to them.
- Prohibitions in s 15(1) do not apply to:
  + a small child aged **3 years or more** who is riding in a bus and is wearing an adult belt if an appropriate seat belt is not available for them in the front or rear of the vehicle;
  + a child for whom there is a medical certificate;
  + a disabled child who is wearing a disabled person's belt;
  + a child riding in a bus which is being used to provide a local service in a built-up area, or which is constructed/adapted for the carriage of standing passengers and on which the operator permits standing; or
  + a large child if no appropriate seat belt is available for them in the front of the vehicle.
- The driver of a motor vehicle has the same opportunity to produce a medical certificate for a child not wearing a seat belt as an adult (see **10.17.1**).

Practical considerations

- Consider issuing a TFPN for this offence (see **10.4**).
- The seat belt must be appropriate for a child of a particular weight and height travelling in a particular vehicle.

- A seat is regarded as provided with child restraint if the child restraint is:
  - ✦ fixed in such a position that it can be worn by an occupier of that seat; or
  - ✦ elsewhere in or on the vehicle but could readily be fixed in such a position without the aid of tools, and is not being worn by a child for whom it is appropriate and who is occupying another seat.
- A seat belt is considered appropriate in relation to:
  - ✦ **a small child**, if it is a child restraint of a description prescribed for their height and weight by reg 5;
  - ✦ **a large child**, if it is a child restraint of a description prescribed for their height and weight by reg 5 or an adult belt; or
  - ✦ **a person aged 14 years or more**, if it is an adult belt.
- In relation to ages and height, subject to exceptions/requirements:
  - ✦ **aged under 3** must travel in front or rear in an appropriate baby/child seat:
    - ◆ EU-approved and selected according to weight;
    - ◆ where a rear-facing baby seat is in the front seat, the airbag has to be deactivated;
  - ✦ **aged 3 to 11 and under 135 cm**, in rear using appropriate child seat, booster seat, or booster cushion;
  - ✦ **aged 12 to 13 or under 12 but over 135 cm**, in front or rear using adult seat belt, if no suitable child restraint is available;
  - ✦ **aged 14 and over**, adult regulations apply (see **10.17.1**).

TFPN

 Summary   6 months

 s 15(2) offence:
Level 2 fine

s 15(4) offence:
Level 2 fine

Links to alternative subjects and offences

10.18 Motorcycle—No Crash Helmet/Eye Protectors

Section 16 of the Road Traffic Act 1988 empowers the Secretary of State to make regulations concerning the wearing of crash helmets by motorcyclists and an offence of breaching such regulations.

Offences

A person who drives or rides on a motor cycle in contravention of regulations under this section is guilty of an offence; but not withstanding any enactment or rule of law no person other than the person actually committing the contravention is guilty of an offence by reason of the contravention unless the person actually committing the contravention is a child under the age of 16 years.

Road Traffic Act 1988, s 16(4)

Points to prove
✓ drove/rode on motorcycle
✓ contravened regulations under s 16

Meanings

Drives (see 10.1.4)

Motorcycle

Means a **mechanically propelled vehicle**, not being an invalid carriage, having less than four wheels and the unladen weight does not exceed 410 kg.

Mechanically propelled vehicle (see 10.1.3)

Regulations

Every person driving or riding (otherwise than in a sidecar) on a **motor bicycle** when on a **road** shall wear protective headgear (Motor Cycles (Protective Helmets) Regulations 1998, reg 4).

Road (see 10.1.1)

Explanatory notes

- 'Motor bicycle' means a two-wheeled **motorcycle**, whether or not having a sidecar attached, although where the distance measured between the centre of the area of contact with the road surface of any two wheels of a motorcycle is less than 460 mm, those wheels are counted as one wheel.
- This section does not include people riding in a sidecar, or people of the Sikh religion while wearing a turban.

- A British/EU standards mark must be on the helmet.
- Regulation 4 does not apply to a mowing machine or if propelled by a person on foot.
- If the vehicle is being propelled by 'scooter' style (eg the rider sat astride the machine and propelling it by pushing on the ground with their foot/feet) then a helmet should be worn.
- **Eye protectors offence**—Motor Cycles (Eye Protectors) Regulations 1999, reg 4 creates an offence under s 18(3) of not wearing approved eye protectors. Each person driving or riding on a motor bicycle (otherwise than in a sidecar) is required to wear eye protectors of a prescribed type.

Related cases

DPP v Parker [2005] RTR 1616, QBD A motorcycle fitted with enhanced safety features (eg a roof) does not negate the requirement to wear protective headgear.

Practical considerations

- In general, the rider of a quad bike would not be required to wear a crash helmet.
- Consider issuing a TFPN for these offences (see **10.4**).
- Any helmet worn must be securely fastened using straps or other means of fastening provided.
- If the helmet has a chin cup it must have an additional strap to fit under the jaw.
- Eye protectors/visors marked 'Daytime Use' or bearing a symbol of the same meaning should only be used in daytime.
- Visors that transmit less than 50 per cent of visible light cannot be legally used on the road.

 TFPN

 Summary   6 months

 Level 2 fine

Links to alternative subjects and offences

10.19 Improper Use of Trade Plates

The Vehicle Excise and Registration Act 1994 provides for the registration and excise duty payable in respect of motor vehicles. Section 34 relates to offences committed in relation to trade licences.

Offences

A person holding a trade licence or trade licences is guilty of an offence if he—

(a) uses at any one time on a public road a greater number of vehicles (not being vehicles for which vehicle licences are for the time being in force) than he is authorised to use by virtue of the trade licence or licences,

(b) uses a vehicle (not being a vehicle for which a vehicle licence is for the time being in force) on a public road for any purpose other than a purpose which has been prescribed under section 12(2) (b), or

(c) uses the trade licence, or any of the trade licences, for the purposes of keeping on a public road in any circumstances other than circumstances which have been prescribed under section 12(1)(c) a vehicle which is not being used on that road.

Vehicle Excise and Registration Act 1994, s 34(1)

Points to prove

s 34(1)(a) offence

✓ being the holder of trade licence(s)
✓ used on a public road
✓ by virtue of that licence
✓ more vehicles than authorised by the licence

s 34(1)(b) offence

✓ being the holder of trade licence(s)
✓ used a vehicle on a public road
✓ by virtue of that licence
✓ for purposes other than as prescribed in the licence

s 34(1)(c) offence

✓ being the holder of trade licence(s)
✓ kept a vehicle on a public road
✓ by virtue of that licence
✓ when the vehicle was not being used on that road

Meanings

Trade licence

Is a licence issued under s 11.

Uses (see 10.16.1)

Public road (s 62)

Means a road repairable at public expense.

Road (s 192) (see 10.1.1)

Vehicle (s 1(1B))

Means a mechanically propelled vehicle, or anything (whether or not it is a vehicle) that has been, but has ceased to be, a mechanically pro-pelled vehicle.

Section 12(2)(b)

Regulations giving purposes for which the holder of a trade licence may use a vehicle under that licence.

Section 12(1)(c)

Holder of a trade licence is not entitled to keep any vehicle on a road if it is not being used on the road for the purposes prescribed by regulations.

Regulations

Currently these are the Road Vehicles (Registration and Licensing) Regulations 2002 (SI 2742/2002).

Explanatory notes

- A trade licence will only be issued to a motor trader (including a vehicle manufacturer), vehicle tester, or person intending to start a business as a motor trader or vehicle tester.
- Where the conviction is for a continuing offence the offence will be taken as committed on the latest date to which the conviction relates.
- The trade licence holder who changes their name or the name and/ or address of their business must notify the Secretary of State and submit the licence for amendment.
- It is an offence under s 44 for a person to forge, fraudulently alter or use, or fraudulently lend or allow to be used by another person any trade plate.
- Nothing that can be mistaken for a trade plate should be displayed on a vehicle.

Practical considerations

- Consider issuing a TFPN (see 10.4.1) for offences under s 34.

10.19 Improper Use of Trade Plates

- A trade licence is valid only for vehicles temporarily in the possession of a motor trader (including a vehicle manufacturer) or vehicle tester in the course of their business.
- A trade licence only authorises the use of one vehicle at any one time under s 12(1)(a), but a person may hold more than one licence.
- A vehicle and semi-trailer superimposed thereon counts as only one vehicle.
- If a question arises as to the number of vehicles used, their character, weight or cubic capacity (cc) rating, the seating capacity, or the purpose for which they were being used, s 53 places the burden of proof on the defendant.
- Section 29 creates the offence of using/keeping an unlicensed vehicle (including trade licence) on a public road (see **10.20.1**).

 Summary   36 months

 Level 3 fine or 5 times VEL duty amount

Links to alternative subjects and offences

10.20 Vehicle Excise/Trade Licences and Registration Marks/Documents

The Vehicle Excise and Registration Act 1994 offences include failing to fix a registration mark to a vehicle, or to produce a registration document, and using or keeping an unlicensed vehicle on a road or a vehicle bearing an obscured/misrepresented registration mark.

10.20.1 Using/keeping unlicensed vehicle

Section 29 creates the offence of using or keeping an unlicensed vehicle on a public road.

> **Offences**
>
> If a person uses, or keeps, a vehicle which is unlicensed he is guilty of an offence.
>
> Vehicle Excise and Registration Act 1994, s 29(1)

Points to prove

✓ used/kept a vehicle
✓ without VEL or trade licence being in force

Meanings

Uses (see 10.16.1)

Vehicle (see 10.19)

Unlicensed

If there is no vehicle licence or trade licence in force for vehicle.

Exempt vehicles (exempt from vehicle excise duty)

Applies to the following vehicles listed under Sch 2:
- certain historic vehicles constructed 40 years or more ago;
- electrically assisted pedal cycles;
- vehicles not used or adapted for carrying a driver or passenger;
- emergency vehicles;
- disabled persons' vehicles;
- a vehicle on test;
- a vehicle travelling between parts of private land;

10.20.1 Using/keeping unlicensed vehicle

- a vehicle for export or imported by members of foreign armed forces;
- an off-road vehicle after notifying DVLA (SORN);
- tractor, light agricultural vehicle, agricultural engine;
- mowing machine;
- steam-powered vehicles;
- electrically propelled vehicle, trams, and snow ploughs.

Explanatory notes

- Various people can 'use' a vehicle, being the driver, employer if the vehicle is being used for the employer's business, owner being driven by another person while owner is in the vehicle, or steersman where a broken-down vehicle is being towed.
- Where a vehicle licence has expired, and the vehicle is not to be used/kept on a road, the vehicle keeper must send a SORN to the Secretary of State.

Practical considerations

- All exempt vehicles require a nil licence except trams; electrically assisted pedal cycles; vehicles that do not carry a driver or passenger; vehicles going to, from, or taking a test of road worthiness or pollution; or vehicles which are zero-rated whilst awaiting export. It is an offence under s 43A to use/keep a vehicle that requires a nil licence without such licence.
- The Finance Act 2014, Sch 19 omitted ss 10 and 33 from 1 October 2014. This means that when a vehicle changes ownership the VEL cannot be transferred to the new owner anymore, so the buyer will have to get a new VEL, and the seller can obtain a VEL refund once they notify DVLA. It also means it is no longer an offence to fail to display a VEL or trade licence—as a result these paper licences have stopped being issued.
- The burden of proof that the defendant was the keeper of the vehicle on the relevant day is on the prosecutor, but it is on the defendant to prove that a VEL was in force for the vehicle.
- Under s 53 the burden of proof is on the defendant if a question arises as to the character, weight, cubic capacity (cc) rating, or seating capacity of the vehicle or the purpose for which it was being used.
- If offences involve misuse of trade plates under s 34 see **10.19**.

TFPN

 Summary   6 months

 Level 5 fine

10.20.2 **No registration mark on vehicle/ fail to produce registration document**

Section 42 relates to the fixing of the registration mark to a vehicle and creates an offence of failure to do so.

Offences

If a registration mark is not fixed on a vehicle as required by virtue of section 23, the relevant person is guilty of an offence.

Vehicle Excise and Registration Act 1994, s 42(1)

Points to prove

✓ drove/kept
✓ vehicle on a road
✓ registration mark not fixed to front/rear of vehicle as required

Meanings

Registration mark required by section 23(1)

A vehicle registered under s 21(1) shall be assigned a registration mark indicating the registered number of that vehicle.

Vehicle (see 10.19)

Relevant person

Driver of vehicle or, if not being driven, the keeper.

Explanatory notes

- The Road Vehicles (Display of Registration Marks) Regulations 2001 govern how such marks must be displayed on vehicles first registered on or after 1 October 1938, such as the size, shape, and character of the lettering and the manner by which the registration marks are to be displayed and rendered easily distinguishable (whether by day or by night) (see 10.20.3).
- A registration plate must be fixed to the rear of the vehicle or, if towing a trailer or trailers, the rear of the rearmost trailer, in a vertical position or, if that is not practicable, as close to vertical as possible, and in such position that, in normal daylight, the characters are easily distinguishable.
- Similarly, except a motorcycle, a registration plate must be fixed to the front of the vehicle in a vertical position or, if that is not practicable, as close to vertical as possible, and in such position that,

in normal daylight, the characters are easily distinguishable from every part of the relevant area.

Defences

(4) It is a defence for a person charged with an offence under subsection (1) to prove that—
  (a) he had no reasonable opportunity to register the vehicle under this Act, and
  (b) the vehicle was being driven for the purpose of being so registered.

(5) It is a defence for a person charged with an offence under subsection (1) in relation to a vehicle to which s 47 of the Road Traffic Act 1988 applies by virtue of subsection (2)(b) of that section (vehicles manufactured before the prescribed period and used before registration) to prove that he had no reasonable opportunity to register the vehicle under this Act and that the vehicle was being driven in accordance with subsection (6).

Vehicle Excise and Registration Act 1994, s 42

Defence notes

A vehicle is driven under s 42(6) if it is being driven for, or in connection with, examination under s 45 of the Road Traffic Act 1988 (MOT tests) in circumstances in which its use is exempted from s 47(1) of that Act by regulations.

Practical considerations

- Consider issuing a TFPN (see **10.4**).
- The Regulations concerning the displaying of registration marks do not apply to invalid vehicles or pedestrian-controlled vehicles.
- A motorcycle first registered on or after 1 September 2001 **must not** have a registration plate fixed to the front, and one first registered before that date does not need to have a front registration plate fixed to it.
- If an agricultural machine is towing a trailer the registration plate on the rear of the trailer may show the registration mark of any similar machine owned by the keeper.

Produce registration document

- Section 28A of the Act makes it a summary offence if, when using (eg driver or keeper) a vehicle, they fail to produce the registration document for inspection on being so required by a constable or authorised person (authorised by the Secretary of State).
- Like other document production offences, s 28A does not apply if the registration document is produced at a police station specified by the person required to produce, within seven days of the request or as soon as reasonably practicable.

Summary   6 months

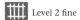 Level 2 fine

10.20.3 Obscured/misrepresented registration marks

Section 43 requires a registration plate fixed to a vehicle to be unobscured, easily distinguishable, and not be misrepresented.

Offences

If a registration mark fixed on a vehicle as required by virtue of section 23 is in any way—
(a) obscured, or
(b) rendered, or allowed to become, not easily distinguishable,
the relevant person is guilty of an offence.

Vehicle Excise and Registration Act 1994, s 43(1)

Points to prove

✓ drove/kept
✓ vehicle on a road
✓ registration mark obscured/rendered/allowed to become indistinguishable

Meanings

Registration mark required by section 23 (see **10.20.2**)

The Road Vehicles (Display of Registration Marks) Regulations 2001 have been made under s 23.

Vehicle (see **10.19**)

Relevant person (see **10.20.2**)

Defences

It is a defence for a person charged with an offence under this section to prove that he took all steps which it was reasonably practicable to take to prevent the mark being obscured or rendered not easily distinguishable.

Vehicle Excise and Registration Act 1994, s 43(4)

10.20.3 Obscured/misrepresented registration marks

Practical considerations

- Examples of this offence could be where the registration plate is obscured by the tow bar/ball, or covered by a pedal cycle rack, or is covered by dirt/mud and is allowed to remain there.
- Officers should use their discretion when dealing with this type of offence.
- The Vehicles (Crime) Act 2001 concerns the control of registration plate suppliers. It is an offence under s 28 of that Act to sell a plate where the registration mark is misrepresented. Prosecution to show that the supplier knew of the defective plate or was reckless as to the nature of the plate.
- DVLA has issued guidelines for tackling misrepresented number plates. Action should be considered where the number plate may be unreadable by ANPR, uses bolts/screws to change appearance of characters, has illegal font, looks foreign (on GB vehicle), is patterned or textured, has incorrectly spaced/sized characters, does not show plate supplier, displays illegal graphics, or appears offensive.
- Where s 43 offences are dealt with by TFPN (see **10.4**) or report for summons, photographic evidence should be obtained (where possible) and the driver issued with a DVLA form V796. Send an offence notification report form to DVLA, accompanied by photograph and details of plate supplier. DVLA will then take follow-up action, including revocation of registration mark for repeat offences or repeat use of misrepresented plates; but DVLA will take no action if it is dealt with by VDRS.
- The BS for number plates states that characters must be a 'Shade of Black'. 3D characters meet this description and are acceptable, but patterns, such as stripes, are not allowed. Plates with 3D characters must comply with other BS requirements.
- If a vehicle is liable for vehicle excise duty or is an exempt vehicle that requires a nil licence to be in force (see **10.20.1**), s 43C makes it a summary offence to use such a vehicle on a public road/place if the keeper details are incorrect or not recorded in the DVLA vehicle register. A TFPN can be issued for this offence (see **10.4.1**).

 Summary   6 months

 Level 3 fine

Links to alternative subjects and offences

10.21 Obstruction of the Road/Footpath

Obstruction of a road is catered for by the Highways Act 1980 and the Road Vehicles (Construction and Use) Regulations 1986.

10.21.1 Wilful obstruction of the highway

Section 137 of the Highways Act 1980 provides an offence of wilful obstruction of the highway.

Offences

If a person, without lawful authority or excuse, in any way wilfully obstructs the free passage along a highway he is guilty of an offence.

Highways Act 1980, s 137(1)

Points to prove

✓ without lawful authority/excuse
✓ wilfully obstructed
✓ free passage of the highway

Meanings

Person

Includes a body corporate.

Wilfully

Means purposefully, deliberately.

Highway

Means the whole or part of a highway other than a ferry or waterway. Where a highway passes over a bridge or through a tunnel, that bridge or tunnel is taken to be part of the highway.

Explanatory notes

- Stopping someone from using the highway by fear alone is insufficient to commit obstruction: there should be some physical obstruction.

10.21.1 Wilful obstruction of the highway

- The highway does not need to be completely blocked, only made less convenient or roomy.
- If a person is convicted under s 137 and the obstruction is continuing, the court may, instead of or in addition to imposing any punishment, order them to remove it within a fixed period under s 137ZA. Failure to comply with this order, without reasonable excuse, will be an offence.

Related cases

Birch v DPP [2000] Crim LR 301, QBD People at a demonstration sat in the road blocking traffic. The defendant was one of the demonstrators and admitted obstructing the traffic but claimed to have a lawful excuse to do so. It was held that a person could not unreasonably obstruct a highway and had no right to demonstrate in such a way. The term 'lawful excuse' embraces activities otherwise lawful in themselves which may or may not be reasonable in all the circumstances.

Torbay Borough Council v Cross (1995) 159 JP 882, QBD In this case, the defendant owned a shop and he displayed goods out on the street projecting approximately 5 per cent of the street width in front of the premises. It was held that the *de minimis* rule (ie that the law is not concerned with trifling matters) was not appropriate because it would apply to minor fractional obstructions and in this case the obstruction was held to have been substantial. Although the display was narrow, it was 8 metres long, and anything which substantially prevented the public from having free access to the whole of the highway and which was not purely temporary in its nature (such as a person looking in a shop, a stationary push chair or a street cleaner's cart) was capable of amounting to an unlawful obstruction.

Nagy v Weston [1965] 1 All ER 78, QBD It was held in this case that the test for determining whether a particular use of the highway amounts to an obstruction is if, in the particular circumstances, such use is unreasonable. Circumstances would include duration, position of the obstruction, its purpose, and whether it caused an actual or potential obstruction.

Practical considerations

- Consider whether the obstruction is wilful or deliberate (as opposed to accidental) or without lawful excuse.
- If a motor vehicle is involved, consider issuing a TFPN (see **10.4**).
- If it can be proved the obstruction was with the consent or connivance of an officer of a body corporate, then they may have committed the offence as well as the body corporate.
- Duration and extent of the obstruction are important considerations.
- The Town Police Clauses Act 1847, s 28 obstruction offences have been repealed by the Deregulation Act 2015, Sch 23.

Summary

 6 months

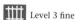 Level 3 fine

10.21.2 **Builders' skips on the highway**

Section 139 of the Highways Act 1980 controls the use of builders' skips deposited on the highway.

Offences

(3) If a builder's skip is deposited on a highway without a permission granted under this section, the owner of the skip is, subject to subsection (6) below, guilty of an offence.

(4) Where a builder's skip has been deposited on a highway in accordance with a permission granted under this section, the owner of the skip shall secure—

    (a) that the skip is properly lighted during the hours of darkness and, where regulations made by the Secretary of State under this section require it to be marked in accordance with the regulations (whether with reflecting or fluorescent material or otherwise), that it is so marked;

    (b) that the skip is clearly and indelibly marked with the owner's name and with his telephone number or address;

    (c) that the skip is removed as soon as practicable after it has been filled;

    (d) that each of the conditions subject to which that permission was granted is complied with;

and, if he fails to do so, he is, subject to subsection (6) below, guilty of an offence.

Highways Act 1980, s 139

Points to prove

s 139(3) offence

✓ deposited builder's skip on a highway
✓ without permission under s 139

s 139(4) offence

✓ owner of a builder's skip
✓ deposited skip on a highway
✓ with a permission granted under s 139
✓ failed to secure that the skip was
✓ properly lighted during the hours of darkness; **or**
✓ clearly and indelibly marked with owner's details; **or**
✓ removed as soon as practicable after being filled; **or**
✓ not complying with each of the conditions

10.21.2 Builders' skips on the highway

Meanings

Builder's skip

Means a container designed to be carried on a road vehicle and to be placed on a highway or other land for the storage of builders' materials, or for the removal and disposal of builders' rubble, household waste, and other rubbish or earth.

Highway (see 10.21.1)

Owner

In relation to a builder's skip, subject of a hiring agreement, being an agreement for a hiring of not less than one month, or a hire purchase agreement, means the person in possession of the skip under that agreement.

Hours of darkness

Half an hour after sunset and half an hour before sunrise.

> #### Power to move skip
>
> Under s 140, the highways authority or a constable in uniform may require the owner of a skip to remove or reposition it; or cause it to be so removed or repositioned themselves. This applies even though it has been deposited with a permission granted under s 139.

Explanatory notes

- A permission under s 139 authorises a person to whom it is granted to deposit, or cause to be deposited, a skip on a highway specified therein.
- Such permission may be granted unconditionally or with specified conditions such as: siting of skip; its dimensions; manner in which it must be marked to be visible to oncoming traffic; care and disposal of contents; way in which it must be lighted or guarded; and its removal at the expiry of the permission.
- Permission must be in writing and blanket permission is not allowed (*York City Council v Poller* [1976] RTR 37).
- Nothing in this section authorises the creation of a nuisance or a danger to users of the highway or imposes on a highway authority granting permission any liability for any injury caused, damage, or loss resulting from the presence on a highway of a skip to which the permission relates.

> #### Defences
>
> (6) In any proceedings for an offence under this section it is a defence, subject to subsection (7) below, for the person charged to prove that the commission of the offence was due to the act or default of another person and that he took all reasonable precautions and exercised all due diligence to avoid the commission of such an offence by himself or any person under his control.

(7) A person charged with an offence under this section is not, without leave of the court, entitled to rely on the defence provided by subsection (6) above unless, within a period ending 7 clear days before the hearing, he has served on the prosecutor a notice in writing giving such information identifying or assisting in the identification of that other person as was then in his possession.

(8) Where any person is charged with an offence under any other enactment for failing to secure that a builder's skip which has been deposited on a highway in accordance with a permission granted under this section was properly lighted during the hours of darkness, it is a defence for the person charged to prove that the commission of the offence was due to the act or default of another person and that he took all reasonable precautions and exercised all due diligence to avoid the commission of such an offence by himself or any person under his control.

(9) Where a person is charged with obstructing, or interrupting any user of, a highway by depositing a builder's skip on it, it is a defence for the person charged to prove that the skip was deposited on it in accordance with a permission granted under this section and either—

(a) that each of the requirements of subsection (4) above had been complied with; or

(b) that the commission of any offence under that subsection was due to the act or default of another person and that he took all reasonable precautions and exercised all due diligence to avoid the commission of such an offence by himself or any person under his control.

Highways Act 1980, s 139

Practical considerations

- If a person commits an offence under s 139 because of an act or default of another person, that other person is guilty of the offence, and may be charged with and convicted of the offence whether or not proceedings are taken against the first-mentioned person.
- Requirement for a skip to be moved must be made face to face (*R v Worthing Justices, ex parte Waste Management Ltd* (1988) 152 JP 362, DC).

 Summary   6 months

Level 3 fine

10.21.3 **Cause injury/danger/annoyance on the highway**

Section 161 of the Highways Act 1980 creates various offences that relate to causing danger on a highway, including annoyance by playing games on the highway.

10.21.3 Cause injury/danger/annoyance on the highway

Offences

(1) If a person, without lawful authority or excuse, deposits any thing whatsoever on a highway in consequence of which a user of the highway is injured or endangered, that person is guilty of an offence.

(2) [See **8.8.6**]

(3) If a person plays at football or any other game on a highway to the annoyance of a user of the highway he is guilty of an offence.

(4) If a person, without lawful authority or excuse, allows any filth, dirt, lime or other offensive matter or thing to run or flow on to a highway from any adjoining premises, he is guilty of an offence.

Highways Act 1980, s 161

Points to prove

s 161(1) offence

✓ without lawful authority/excuse
✓ deposits any thing whatsoever on a highway
✓ thus injuring/endangering user of the highway

s 161(3) offence

✓ played football/a game on a highway
✓ thus annoying a user of the highway

s 161(4) offence

✓ without lawful authority/excuse
✓ allowed any filth, dirt, lime, or other offensive matter or thing
✓ to run or flow on to a highway
✓ from any adjoining premises

Meaning of highway (see **10.21.1**)

Explanatory notes

- The s 161(2) offences relate to lighting any fire on/over a highway or discharging any firearm or firework within 50 feet of the centre of a highway and are dealt with in **8.5** and **8.8.6**.
- Section 161A creates another offence of lighting a fire on any land (not part of a highway/carriageway) and as a result the user of any highway being injured, interrupted, or endangered by smoke from that fire.
- Any rope, wire, or other apparatus placed across a highway so as to cause danger to users of the highway is an offence under s 162, unless adequate warning has been given of this danger.
- The s 161(3) offence is very wide and covers all types of 'game'. For example, a mock hunt with a man dressed as a stag being chased by people in fancy dress and with trumpets has been held to be a game (*Pappin v Maynard* (1863) 27 JP 745).

Summary

 6 months

s 161(1) offence:
Level 3 fine

s 161(3) and (4) offences:
Level 1 fine

10.21.4 **Unnecessary obstruction**

Regulation 103 of the Road Vehicles (Construction and Use) Regulations 1986 creates an offence of causing an unnecessary obstruction.

Offences

No person in charge of a motor vehicle or trailer shall cause or permit the vehicle to stand on a road so as to cause any unnecessary obstruction of the road.

Road Vehicles (Construction and Use) Regulations 1986, reg 103

Points to prove

✓ in charge of a motor vehicle/trailer
✓ caused/permitted vehicle
✓ to stand on a road
✓ so causing an unnecessary obstruction on road

Meanings

Motor vehicle (see **10.1.3**)

Mechanically propelled vehicle intended or adapted for use on roads.

Trailer

Vehicle drawn by a motor vehicle but does not apply to any part of an articulated bus.

Road

Includes the footpath.

Explanatory notes

• A motor vehicle left on a road for an unreasonable time may be an unreasonable obstruction.
• Consider the use to which the highway was being put by the vehicle causing the obstruction. The highway is intended as a means of transit, not a store (*Nelmes v Rhys Howells Transport Ltd* [1977] RTR 266).

10.21.4 Unnecessary obstruction

- Where a motorist parks their vehicle on one side of the road and the subsequent parking of vehicles on the opposite side of the road causes an obstruction, no offence under this regulation was committed by the parking of the original vehicle (*Langham v Crisp* [1975] Crim LR 652).

Related cases

Carey v CC of Avon and Somerset [1995] RTR 405, CA The purpose of the Removal and Disposal of Vehicles Regulations 1986 is to clear the road of an 'obstruction' as a matter of urgency even if no one is really at fault. They do not apply to s 137 of the Highways Act 1980 and reg 103 of the Road Vehicles (Construction and Use) Regulations 1986, which relate to obstruction of the highway without a lawful excuse and constitute an unreasonable use of the highway.

Practical considerations

Consider the offence of wilfully obstructing the free passage of the highway, without lawful authority or excuse, under s 137(1) of the Highways Act 1980 (see **10.21.1**). A TFPN can be issued for this offence (see **10.4.1**).

 Summary 6 months

 Level 4 fine if goods vehicle or a vehicle adapted to carry more than eight passengers. Level 3 fine in any other case

Links to alternative subjects and offences

10.22 **Off-Road Driving/ Immobilise Vehicles on Land**

Section 34 of the Road Traffic Act 1988 prohibits the driving of motor vehicles elsewhere than on a road.

Offences

Subject to the provisions of this section, if without lawful authority a person drives a mechanically propelled vehicle—

(a) on to or upon any common land, moorland or land of any other description, not being land forming part of a road, or

(b) on any road being a footpath, bridleway or restricted byway, he is guilty of an offence.

Road Traffic Act 1988, s 34(1)

Points to prove

✓ without lawful authority
✓ drove a mechanically propelled vehicle
✓ on to/upon common land/moorland/land
✓ not being land forming part of a road or
✓ on a road being a footpath/bridleway/restricted byway

Meanings

Drives (see **10.1.4**)

Mechanically propelled vehicle (see **10.1.3**)

Excluding a pedestrian-controlled vehicle, a pedestrian-controlled mowing machine, or an electrically assisted pedal cycle.

Common land

Land that is:

- subject to '**rights of common**' whether those rights are exercisable at all times or only during limited periods; and
- waste land of a manor not subject to 'rights of common'.

Rights of common

These include:

- rights of sole or several vesture, or herbage (rights to take vegetation or flowers from the land);
- rights of sole or several pasture (allowing animals to be put out to pasture on the land);

- cattlegates and beastgates (a particular right, mainly existing in northern England, to graze an animal on common land).

They do not include rights held for a term of years or from year to year.

Road (see **10.1.1**)

Footpath

Means a highway over which the public have a right of way on foot only, not being a footway.

Bridleway

A way over which the public have the following, but no other, rights of way: a right of way on foot and a right of way on horseback, or leading a horse, with or without a right to drive animals of any description along the way.

Restricted byway

A way over which the public have restricted byway rights within the meaning of Pt 2 of the Countryside and Rights of Way Act 2000, with or without a right to drive animals of any description along the way, but no other rights of way.

Explanatory notes

- A way shown in a definitive map and statement as a footpath, bridleway, or restricted byway is taken to be so, unless the contrary is shown.
- Nothing in s 34 prejudices the rights of the public over commons and waste lands, or any by-laws applying to any land, or affects the law of trespass to land, or any right or remedy to which a person may by law be entitled in respect of any such trespass, or in particular confers a right to park a vehicle on any land.
- It is not an offence under s 34 to drive on any land within 15 yards of a road, for purpose only of parking the vehicle on that land (s 34(3)).
- Police powers concerning the stopping, seizure, and removal of a motor vehicle that is used in contravention of s 34, which is causing, or likely to cause, alarm, distress, or annoyance to members of the public can be used under s 59 of the Police Reform Act 2002 (see **7.14**).

Defences

(2A) It is not an offence under this section for a person with an interest in land, or a visitor to any land, to drive a mechanically propelled vehicle on a road if, immediately before the commencement of section 47(2) of the Countryside and Rights of Way Act 2000, the road was—

  (a) shown in a definitive map and statement as a road used as a public path, and

(b) in use for obtaining access to the land by the driving of mechanically propelled vehicles by a person with an interest in the land or by visitors to the land.

(3) It is not an offence under this section to drive a mechanically propelled vehicle on land within 15 yards of a road, being a road on which a motor vehicle may legally be driven, for the purpose only of parking the vehicle on that land.

(4) A person shall not be convicted of an offence under this section with respect to a vehicle if he proves to the satisfaction of the court that it was driven in contravention of this section for the purpose of saving life or extinguishing fire or meeting any other like emergency.

Road Traffic Act 1988, s 34

Practical considerations

- **Interest in land**—includes any estate in land and any right over land (whether exercisable by virtue of the ownership of an estate or interest in the land or by virtue of a licence or agreement) and, in particular, includes rights of common and sporting rights.
- Consider issuing a TFPN (see **10.4**).
- A power of entry to premises to exercise the powers of seizure and removal of the motor vehicle is granted by s 59 of the Police Reform Act 2002. Reasonable force may be used, if necessary, to stop, seize, or remove the motor vehicle or for the power of entry (see **7.14**).
- **Immobilise vehicles left on land**: Section 54 of the Protection of Freedoms Act 2012 provides that a person commits an offence, if without lawful authority they immobilise a motor vehicle by attaching an immobilising device (eg wheel clamp), or move or restrict the movement of such a vehicle by any means, intending to prevent or inhibit the removal of the vehicle by a person otherwise entitled to remove it.
- The restriction of movement of the vehicle offence does not apply to a lawfully erected fixed barrier in place at the time of parking. In this section 'motor vehicle' means a mechanically propelled vehicle or a vehicle designed or adapted for towing by a mechanically propelled vehicle.

 Summary   6 months

 Level 3 fine

Links to alternative subjects and offences

Chapter 11

General: Patrol

11.1 Police Powers for Civilian Staff and Volunteers

The Policing and Crime Act 2017 amends s 38 of the Police Reform Act 2002 (the exercise of police powers etc by civilians). The amendments came into force in December 2017. Under the new provisions under s 38, there is no longer a list of standard powers for Community Support Officers (CSOs).

Section 38(1) allows for the designation of a person as a community support officer (CSO) or a community support volunteer (CSV).

Powers

The powers and duties that may be conferred or imposed on a person designated under s 38 are—

(a) **any power or duty of a constable**, other than a power or duty specified in Part 1 of Schedule 3B (excluded powers and duties) (see **11.1.1**);

(b) where the person is designated as a community support officer or a community support volunteer, **any power or duty that is described in Sch 3C** as a power or duty of a community support officer or community support volunteer.

Police Reform Act 2001 s 38(6B)

Schedule 3C—Powers that may be conferred or imposed

Schedule 3C—sets out the powers and duties that may be conferred or imposed on a designated CSO or CSV and include:
- Issue fixed penalty notices (see **11.1.2**)
- Require names and addresses (see **11.1.3**)
- Search for and seize alcohol and tobacco (see **11.1.4**)
- Seize and detain in relation to controlled drugs (see **11.1.5**)
- Seize and detain in relation to psychoactive substances (see **11.1.6**)
- Detain pending arrival of a constable etc (see **11.1.7**)

- Search individuals detained (see **11.1.8**)
- Powers re persons detained in relation to park trading offences (see **11.1.9**)
- Powers in relation to road traffic (see **11.1.10**)
- Power to use reasonable force (see **11.1.11**).

Meanings

CSO

A person designated by a chief officer of police as a community support officer under section 38.

CSV

A person designated by a chief officer of police as a community support volunteer under section 38.

The relevant police area

In relation to a CSO or CSV, means the police area for which the police force in question is maintained.

Explanatory notes

- The chief officer of police of any police force may designate a **relevant employee** as either or both of the following—a community support officer; or a policing support officer; or designate a **police volunteer** as either a community support volunteer; or a policing support volunteer.
- Section 38(4) states that a chief officer of police shall not designate a person under this section unless he is satisfied that that person is a suitable person to carry out the functions for the purposes of which he is designated; is capable of effectively carrying out those functions; and has received adequate training in the carrying out of those functions and in the exercise and performance of the powers and duties to be conferred on him by virtue of the designation.
- **Transitional provision**: Any designations made under this section prior 15 December 2017 remain effective until they are amended or revoked under this section as it applies after that date. However, the excluded powers and duties of constables listed in part 1 of Sch 3B (see **11.1.1**) must not be used; the transitional provision does not apply to powers which are prohibited by virtue of section 38(6B)(a) and listed in part 1 of Schedule 3B with the effect that those powers cease to be conferred or imposed under this section.
- Section 38(6E) states that any power or duty of a constable that is conferred or imposed on a person designated under this section by a chief officer of police of a police force may (subject to provision included in the designation under subsection (6F)) (*see below*) be exercised or performed by the person—in the area of that police

force, and in any cases or circumstances in which it could be exercised or performed by a constable who is a member of that force.
- Under s 38(6F), a designation under this section may provide that any power or duty of a constable that is conferred or imposed by the designation may be exercised or performed by the person designated—in such areas outside the area of the police force in question as are specified in the designation (as well as within the area of the police force); only in such parts of the area of that police force as are specified in the designation; and only in cases or circumstances so specified.
- Failing to comply with any powers exercised by a CSO etc that are conferred or imposed under Sch 3C is a summary offence (see **11.1.11**).

11.1.1 Schedule 3B—restricted designations under section 38

Schedule 3B to the Police Reform Act 2002 lists the 'core' powers and duties of constables ('excluded powers and duties') that **cannot** be given to persons designated under s 38, ie to community support officers, policing support officers, community support volunteers, and policing support volunteers.

The powers which **cannot** be given to the person designated under s 38 are specified in part 1 of Schedule 3B and are:

1. Any power or duty of a constable to make an arrest.
2. Any power or duty of a constable to stop and search an individual or a vehicle or other thing.
3. The power of a constable, under s 36(4) of the Police and Criminal Evidence Act 1984, to perform the functions of a custody officer at a designated police station if a custody officer is not readily available to perform them.
4. Any power that is exercisable only by a constable of a particular rank.
5. Any power of a constable under—
   (a) the Terrorism Act 2000; (except for cordons – see **11.1.11** in explanatory notes);
   (b) the Terrorism Act 2006;
   (c) the Counter-Terrorism Act 2008;
   (d) the Terrorism Prevention and Investigation Measures Act 2011;
   (e) the Counter-Terrorism and Security Act 2015.
6. Any power of a constable under the Official Secrets Acts 1911 to 1989, (Official Secrets Act 1911, Official Secrets Act 1920, Official Secrets Act 1939 and the Official Secrets Act 1989).
7. The power of a constable to make an application on behalf of the Commissioner of Police of the Metropolis under s 19 or 21 of the Investigatory Powers Act 2016 (applications for warrants under Chapter 1 of Part 2 of that Act).

Apart from the powers and duties listed above, any power or duty of a constable may be conferred or imposed on a person designated under section 38 and the statutory provisions are to be interpreted in a way to ensure the power works as intended—see part 2 of Schedule 3 B:

Part 2 Application of legislation

Section 8(1) of Sch 3B, Pt 2 of the Police Reform Act 2002 Where a power or duty of a constable is conferred or imposed on a person designated under s 38—

(a) a reference to a constable (however expressed) in legislation relating to the power or duty includes a reference to the person designated under section 38;

(b) a reference in legislation to anything done in the exercise or purported exercise of the power, or in the performance or purported performance of the duty, includes a reference to anything done in the exercise or purported exercise of the power, or the performance or purported performance of the duty, by the person designated under s 38.

11.1.2 **Powers to issue fixed penalty notices etc**

- **Paragraph 2 of Sch 3C** provides for powers to issue fixed penalty notices.
- **Paragraph 2(1)** A CSO or CSV has the power of an authorised officer of a litter authority to give a notice under s 88 of the Environmental Protection Act 1990 (fixed penalty notices in respect of **litter**) in relation to an individual whom the CSO or CSV has reason to believe has committed an offence under s 87 of that Act at a place within the relevant police area (see **7.16.2**).
- **Paragraph 2(2)** A CSO or CSV has the power of an authorised officer of a local authority to give a notice under s 43(1) of the Anti-social Behaviour Act 2003 (penalty notices in respect of **graffiti or fly-posting**) in relation to an individual whom the CSO or CSV has reason to believe has committed an offence that is a relevant offence for the purposes of s 43(1) at a place within the relevant police area.
- **Paragraph 2(3)** A CSO or CSV designated under s 38 by the Commissioner of Police of the Metropolis has the power of an authorised officer of a borough council to give a notice under s 15 of the London Local Authorities Act 2004 in relation to an individual whom the CSO or CSV has reason to believe has committed an offence under **s 38(1) of the London Local Authorities Act 1990**.
- **Paragraph 2(4)** A CSO or CSV designated under s 38 by the Commissioner of Police for the City of London has the power of an authorised officer of a borough council to give a notice under s 15 of the London Local Authorities Act 2004 in relation to an individual whom the CSO or CSV has reason to believe has committed

an offence under s 27(1) of the City of Westminster Act 1999 (**unlicensed street trading**).

- **Paragraph 2(5)** A CSO or CSV has the power of an authorised officer of an authority to give a notice under s 237A of the Local Government Act 1972 or under s 12 of the Local Government Byelaws (Wales) Act 2012 (fixed penalty notices in relation to offences against certain byelaws) in relation to an individual whom the CSO or CSV has reason to believe has committed an **offence against a listed byelaw** at a place within the relevant police area.

Explanatory notes

- **Paragraph 2(6)** A byelaw is a 'listed byelaw' for the purposes of sub-paragraph (5) if, at the time the CSO or CSV gives the notice—
  a. It is a byelaw to which s 237A of the Local Government Act 1972 or to which s 12 of the Local Government Byelaws (Wales) Act 2012 (fixed penalty notices in relation to offences against certain byelaws) applies, and
  b. the chief officer of police for the relevant police area and the authority that made the byelaw have agreed to include it in a list of byelaws kept for the purposes of sub-paragraph (5).
- **Paragraph 2(7)** The chief officer of police for the relevant police area must publish the list of byelaws kept for the purposes of sub-paragraph (5) in such a way as to bring it to the attention of members of the public in localities where the byelaws in the list apply.

11.1.3 **Powers to require the names and addresses**

Paragraph 3 of Sch 3C provides for powers to require the names and addresses of persons believed to have committed a relevant offence.

Power

A CSO or CSV may require a person to give his or her name and address if the CSO or CSV has reason to believe that—

(a) the person has committed a relevant offence in the relevant police area, or

(b) the person has committed a relevant licensing offence (whether or not in the relevant police area).

Police Reform Act 2002 Sch 3C para 3(1)

Meanings

Relevant offence

Means any of the following offences—

(a) an offence in respect of which the CSO or CSV is authorised to give a penalty notice (whether in consequence of paragraph 2 of

---

this Schedule or in consequence of provision included in his or her designation in reliance on s 38(6B)(a));

(b) an offence under s 3 or 4 of the Vagrancy Act 1824;

(c) an offence committed in a specified park which by virtue of s 2 of the Parks Regulation (Amendment) Act 1926 is an offence against the Parks Regulation Act 1872;

(d) an offence under s 39 of the Anti-social Behaviour, Crime and Policing Act 2014 (see **7.15.1**);

(e) an offence under a listed byelaw;

(f) an offence the commission of which appears to the CSO or CSV to have caused—
   (i) injury, alarm or distress to any other person, or
   (ii) the loss of, or any damage to, any other person's property.

Relevant licensing offence

Means an offence under any of the following provisions of the Licensing Act 2003—

(a) s 141 [Sale of alcohol to a person who is drunk] (otherwise than by virtue of subsection (2)(c) or (3) of that section) (see **9.2.1**);

(b) s 142 [knowingly obtain or attempt to obtain alcohol on relevant premises for consumption on those premises by a person who is drunk] (see **9.2.1**);

(c) s 146(1) [Sale of alcohol to a person under 18] (see **9.1.2**);

(d) s 149(1)(a), (3)(a), or (4)(a) [Purchase of alcohol by or on behalf of person under 18] (see **9.1.4**);

(e) s 150(1) [Consumption of alcohol by person under 18 on relevant premises] (see **9.1.5**);

(f) s 150(2) [Allows consumption of alcohol on relevant premises by individual aged under 18] (otherwise than by virtue of subsection (3)(b) of that section) (see **9.1.5**);

(g) s 152(1) [Sending person under 18 to obtain alcohol] (excluding paragraph (b)) (see **9.1.7**).

Listed byelaw

A byelaw is a 'listed byelaw' for the purposes of sub-paragraph (3)(e) if, at the time the CSO or CSV requires a person to give his or her name and address—

(a) it is a byelaw which has been made by a relevant body with authority to make byelaws for any place within the relevant police area, and

(b) it is included in the list of byelaws published for the purposes of this paragraph by the chief officer of police for the relevant police area.

Explanatory notes

- In the case of a relevant offence that is an offence under a listed byelaw (see sub-paragraphs (3)(e) and (5)), the power to impose a requirement under sub-paragraph (1) is exercisable only in a place to which the byelaw relates.

- In its application in relation to an offence in respect of which the CSO or CSV is authorised to give a penalty notice under s 444A of the Education Act 1996 (penalty notice in respect of failure to secure regular attendance at school of registered pupil), sub-paragraph (1)(a) of this paragraph has effect as if the words 'in the relevant police area' were omitted.

11.1.4 Powers to search for and seize alcohol and tobacco

Paragraph 4 of Sch 3C allows for search and seizure of alcohol or containers for alcohol and tobacco or cigarette papers. Failure to consent to being searched is an offence.

- **Paragraph 4(1)** A CSO or CSV may search a person for alcohol or a container for alcohol if—
  - (a) the CSO or CSV has (in consequence of provision included in his or her designation in reliance on s 38(6B)(a)) imposed a requirement on a person to surrender alcohol or a container for alcohol under s 63(2) of the Anti-social Behaviour, Crime and Policing Act 2014 (see **9.4.1**) or under s 1 of the Confiscation of Alcohol (Young Persons) Act 1997 (see **9.5.1**),
  - (b) the person has failed to comply with the requirement, and
  - (c) the CSO or CSV reasonably believes that the person has alcohol or a container for alcohol in his or her possession.
- **Paragraph 4(2)** A CSO or CSV may search a person for tobacco or cigarette papers where—
  - (a) the CSO or CSV has (in consequence of provision included in his or her designation in reliance on s 38(6B)(a)) sought to seize the tobacco or cigarette papers under s 7(3) of the Children and Young Persons Act 1933 (seizure of tobacco from young persons) (**see explanatory notes below**),
  - (b) the person from whom the CSO or CSV sought to seize the item has failed to surrender it, and
  - (c) the CSO or CSV reasonably believes that the person has it in his or her possession.
- **Paragraph 4(3)** The power to search under sub-paragraph (1) or (2)—
  - (a) is to do so only to the extent that is reasonably required for the purpose of discovering whatever the CSO or CSV is searching for, and
  - (b) does not authorise the CSO or CSV to require a person to remove any of his or her clothing in public other than an outer coat, jacket or gloves.
- **Paragraph 4(5)** A CSO or CSV who proposes to exercise a power to search a person under sub-paragraph (1) or (2) must inform him or her that failing without reasonable excuse to consent to being searched is an offence.

- **Paragraph 4(6)** If the person in question fails to consent to being searched, the CSO or CSV may require him or her to give the CSO or CSV his or her name and address.
- **Paragraph 4(7)** If on searching the person the CSO or CSV discovers what he or she is searching for, the CSO or CSV may seize it and dispose of it.

Explanatory notes

Section 7(3) of the Children and Young Persons Act 1933 provides that it shall be the duty of a constable and of a park-keeper being in uniform to seize any tobacco or cigarette papers in the possession of any person apparently under the age of sixteen (16) years whom he finds smoking in any street or public place, and any tobacco or cigarette papers so seized shall be disposed of, if seized by a constable, in such manner as the local policing body may direct, and if seized by a park-keeper, in such manner as the authority or person by whom he was appointed may direct.

11.1.5 **Powers to seize and detain—controlled drugs**

Paragraph 5 of Sch 3C provides for powers to seize and detain controlled drugs and makes it an offence to fail to give name and address when required under this paragraph.

- **Paragraph 5(1)** A CSO or CSV may exercise the powers conferred by sub-paragraph (2) or (3) in the relevant police area.
- **Paragraph 5(2)** If the CSO or CSV—
  - (a) finds a controlled drug in a person's possession (whether or not the CSO or CSV finds it in the course of searching the person in the exercise of a power or duty conferred or imposed by his or her designation under s 38), and
  - (b) reasonably believes that it is unlawful for the person to be in possession of it,
  the CSO or CSV may seize it and retain it.
- **Paragraph 5(3)** If the CSO or CSV—
  - (a) either—
    - (i) finds a controlled drug in a person's possession (as mentioned in sub-paragraph (2)(a)), or
    - (ii) reasonably believes that a person is in possession of a controlled drug, and
  - (b) reasonably believes that it is unlawful for the person to be in possession of it,
  the CSO or CSV may require the person to give the CSO or CSV his or her name and address.
- **Paragraph 5(4)** If, in exercise of the power conferred by sub-paragraph (2), the CSO or CSV seizes and retains a controlled drug, the CSO or CSV must—

(a) if the person from whom it was seized maintains that he or she was lawfully in possession of it, tell the person where inquiries about its recovery may be made, and

(b) comply with a constable's instructions about what to do with it.

Meanings

Controlled drug

The same meaning as in the Misuse of Drugs Act 1971 (see **5.1.1**).

11.1.6 Powers to seize and detain— psychoactive substances

Paragraph 6 of Sch 3C allows for seizure and detention of psychoactive substances (see **5.3.6**) and makes it an offence not to give name and address when required under this paragraph.

- **Paragraph 6(1)** A CSO or CSV may exercise the powers conferred by sub-paragraph (2) or (3) in the relevant police area.
- **Paragraph 6(2)** If the CSO or CSV—
    (a) finds a psychoactive substance in a person's possession (whether or not the CSO or CSV finds it in the course of searching the person in the exercise of a power or duty conferred or imposed by his or her designation under s 38), and
    (b) reasonably believes that it is unlawful for the person to be in possession of it,
  the CSO or CSV may seize it and retain it.
- **Paragraph 6(3)** If the CSO or CSV—
    (a) either—
        (i) finds a psychoactive substance in a person's possession (as mentioned in sub-paragraph (2)(a)), or
        (ii) reasonably believes that a person is in possession of a psychoactive substance, and
    (b) reasonably believes that it is unlawful for the person to be in possession of it,
  the CSO or CSV may require the person to give the CSO or CSV his or her name and address.
- **Paragraph 6(4)** If, in exercise of the power conferred by sub-paragraph (2), the CSO or CSV seizes and retains a psychoactive substance, the CSO or CSV must—
    (a) if the person from whom it was seized maintains that he or she was lawfully in possession of it—
        (i) tell the person where inquiries about its recovery may be made, and
        (ii) explain the effect of ss 49 to 51 and 53 of the Psychoactive Substances Act 2016 (retention and disposal of items), and

(b) comply with a constable's instructions about what to do with it.

- **Paragraph 6(5)** Any substance seized in exercise of the power conferred by sub-paragraph (2) is to be treated for the purposes of ss 49 to 53 of the Psychoactive Substances Act 2016 as if it had been seized by a police or customs officer under s 36 of that Act.
- Section 50 of the Psychoactive Substances Act 2016 [Power of police, etc. to dispose of seized psychoactive substances] applies in relation to any such substance as if the reference in subsection (1)(b) to the police or customs officer who seized it were a reference to the CSO or CSV who seized it.
- **Paragraph 6(7)** In this paragraph, police or customs officer and psychoactive substance have the same meaning as in the Psychoactive Substances Act 2016.

11.1.7 **Powers to detain pending arrival of a constable etc**

Paragraph 7 of Sch 3C makes provision for the detention of persons while waiting for the arrival of a constable and creates offences of making off.

Power

A CSO or CSV may require a person to wait with the CSO or CSV, for a period not exceeding 30 minutes, for the arrival of a constable where—
(a) the CSO or CSV has required the person to give his or her name and address (whether in consequence of paragraph 3, 4(6), 5(3) or 6(3) or in consequence of provision included in his or her designation in reliance on section 38(6B)(a))), and
(b) either—
  (i) the person has failed to comply with the requirement, or
  (ii) the CSO or CSV has reasonable grounds for suspecting that the person has given a name or address that is false or inaccurate.

Police Reform Act 2002 Sch C para 7(1)

Explanatory notes

- **Paragraph 7(2)** Sub-paragraph (1) does not apply if the requirement to give a name and address was imposed in connection with a relevant licensing offence mentioned in paragraph 3(4)(a), (c), or (f) which the CSO or CSV believes to have been committed on licensed premises (within the meaning of the Licensing Act 2003).
- **Paragraph 7(3)** A CSO or CSV may require a person to wait with the CSO or CSV, for a period not exceeding 30 minutes, for the arrival of a constable where—
  (a) the CSO or CSV has reason to believe that the person is committing an offence under s 3 [begging in a public place] or s 4 [lodging outdoors] of the Vagrancy Act 1824,

    (b) the CSO or CSV requires the person to stop doing whatever
        gives rise to that belief, and
    (c) the person fails to stop as required.
- Paragraph 7(4) A person who has been required under sub-paragraph (1) or (3) to wait with a CSO or CSV may, if requested to do so, elect that (instead of waiting) he or she will accompany the CSO or CSV to a police station in the relevant police area.
- Paragraph 7(5) Where the person does not elect to accompany the CSO or CSV to the police station, and the constable arrives within the period of 30 minutes, the CSO or CSV is under a duty to remain with the person and the constable until the CSO or CSV has transferred control of the person to the constable.
- Paragraph 7(6) Where the person does elect to accompany the CSO or CSV to the police station—
    (a) the CSO or CSV is under a duty to remain at the police station until the CSO or CSV has transferred control of the person to the custody officer there,
    (b) until control is transferred, the CSO or CSV is treated for all purposes as having the person in his or her lawful custody, and
    (c) for so long as the CSO or CSV remains at the police station or in its immediate vicinity (whether before control of the person is transferred or afterwards), the CSO or CSV is under a duty to prevent the person's escape and to assist in keeping the person under control.

11.1.8 Powers to search etc—individuals detained

Powers and duties that may be conferred or imposed on a community support officer or community support volunteer as provided for in s 38(6B)(b).
- **Paragraph 8(1)** A CSO or CSV may exercise the powers set out in sub-paragraphs (2) and (3) in relation to a person whom the CSO or CSV has required to wait for the arrival of a constable under paragraph 7(1) or (3) (whether or not that person makes an election under paragraph 7(4)).
- **Paragraph 8(2)** If the CSO or CSV has reasonable grounds for believing that the person may present a danger to himself or herself or to others, the CSO or CSV may search the person.
- **Paragraph 8(3)** If the CSO or CSV has reasonable grounds for believing that the person may have concealed on him or her anything which might be used to assist in escaping from lawful custody, the CSO or CSV may search the person for that thing.
- **Paragraph 8(4)** The power conferred by sub-paragraph (2) or (3)—
    (a) does not authorise a CSO or CSV to require a person to remove any of his or her clothing in public other than an outer coat, jacket or gloves;
    (b) does authorise a search of a person's mouth.

- **Paragraph 8(5)** A CSO or CSV searching a person under sub-paragraph (2) may seize and retain anything that is found, if the CSO or CSV has reasonable grounds for believing that the person searched might use it to cause physical injury to himself or herself for to any other person.
- **Paragraph 8(6)** A CSO or CSV searching a person under sub-paragraph (3) may seize and retain anything that is found, other than an item subject to legal privilege, if the CSO or CSV has reasonable grounds for believing that the person might use it to assist in escaping from lawful custody.
- **Paragraph 8(7)** If a CSO or CSV seizes or retains anything under sub-paragraph (5) or (6), the CSO or CSV must—
  - (a) tell the person from whom it was seized where inquiries about its recovery may be made, and
  - (b) comply with a constable's instructions about what to do with it.

11.1.9 **Persons detained for park trading offences**

Powers and duties that may be conferred or imposed on a community support officer or community support volunteer as provided for in s 38(6B)(b).

- **Paragraph 9(1)** If a CSO or CSV reasonably suspects that a person required to wait for the arrival of a constable under paragraph 7(1) has committed a park trading offence, the CSO or CSV may take possession of anything of a non-perishable nature which—
  - (a) the person has in his or her possession or under his control, and
  - (b) the CSO or CSV reasonably believes to have been used in the commission of the offence.
- **Paragraph 9(2)** The CSO or CSV may retain possession of the thing in question for a period not exceeding 30 minutes unless the person makes an election under para 7(4), in which case the CSO or CSV may retain possession of the thing in question until he or she is able to transfer control of it to a constable.
- **Paragraph 9(3)** In this paragraph park trading offence means an offence committed in a specified park which is a park trading offence for the purposes of the Royal Parks (Trading) Act 2000.

Meanings

Specified park

The same meaning as in s 162 of the Serious Organised Crime and Police Act 2005 and includes a park, garden, recreation ground, open space or other land in the metropolitan police district.

11.1.10 **Road traffic powers**

Powers and duties that may be conferred or imposed on a community support officer or community support volunteer as provided for in s 38(6B)(b). Paragraph 10 provides for powers in relation to the removal of abandoned vehicles.

- Paragraph 10 of Sch 3C states that a CSO or CSV has in the relevant police area the powers conferred on persons designated by regulations under s 99 of the Road Traffic Regulation Act 1984 (**removal of abandoned vehicles**) (see also **11.1.11**).

11.1.11 **Power to use reasonable force**

Paragraph 11 of Sch 3C provides for the use of reasonable force when exercising powers under paragraph 7 or 8 (see above).

Paragraph 11 A CSO or CSV has power to use reasonable force—

- (a) to prevent a person whom the CSO or CSV has required under paragraph 7(1) or (3) (see **11.1.7**) to wait for a constable from making off, or to keep the person under control, at any time while the person is subject to the requirement;
- (b) where such a person elects under paragraph 7(4) to accompany a CSO or CSV to a police station, to prevent the person from making off, or to keep the person under control, while the person is accompanying the CSO or CSV to the police station;
- (c) where a CSO or CSV is fulfilling a duty imposed under paragraph 7(5) or (6), to prevent the person from making off (or escaping) and to keep him or her under control;
- (d) where a CSO or CSV is exercising a power conferred by paragraph 8 (see **11.1.8**).

Explanatory notes

- PACE Codes of Practice have to be observed by designated officers when exercising powers, see s 67(9A) of PACE.
- Special constables—designated officers should be distinguished from special constables, who have much wider policing powers and different terms of employment; see the Special Constables Regulations 1965.
  - ✦ Section 54(3)(ba) and (g) of the Firearms Act 1968 make it clear that police civilian volunteers do not need a certificate or authorisation in order to carry a defensive spray.
  - ✦ Guidance on relevant experience and qualifications appropriate for a person to have before being designated as a community support volunteer or policing support volunteer, and the training that should be undertaken, may be issued by the College of Policing, see s 53F of the Police Act 1996.

11.1.11 Power to use reasonable force

- ✦ Volunteers designated as community support volunteers or policing support volunteers are within the definition of individuals serving with the police and are subject to the police complaints system set out in part 2 of the Police Reform Act 2002, see s 12(7)(d) of the Police Reform Act 2002.
- Paragraph 14 of Sch 4 of the Act provides that where a designation applies, that person shall, in relation to any cordoned area in the relevant police area, have all the powers of a constable in uniform under section 36 of the Terrorism Act 2000 (enforcement of cordoned area) to give orders, make arrangements or impose prohibitions or restrictions (see **1.3**).
- Section 38(7A) A relevant employee authorised or required to do anything by virtue of a designation under this section—
  - (a) shall not be authorised or required by virtue of that designation to engage in any conduct otherwise than in the course of that employment, and
  - (b) shall be so authorised or required subject to such restrictions and conditions (if any) as may be specified in his designation.
- Where any power exercisable by any person in reliance on his designation under this section is a power which, in the case of its exercise by a constable, includes or is supplemented by a **power to use reasonable force**, any person exercising that power in reliance on that designation shall have the same entitlement as a constable to use reasonable force. Police Reform Act 2002 s 38(8).
- Where any power exercisable by any person in reliance on his designation under s 38 includes power to use force to enter any premises, that power **shall not** be exercisable by that person except—
  - (a) in the company, and under the supervision, of a constable; or
  - (b) for the purpose of saving life or limb or preventing serious damage to property. Police Reform Act 2002 s 38(9).
- Section 38(9A) The chief officer of police of a police force must ensure that no person designated by the chief officer under this section is authorised to use a firearm, within the meaning given by s 57(1) of the Firearms Act 1968, in carrying out functions for the purposes of the designation and (9B) for limitations.
- Section 38(9B) However, subsection (9A) does not apply to—
  - (a) the use of a weapon, designed or adapted for the discharge of either of the following substances, for the purpose of discharging either of those substances
    - (i) the substance, commonly known as CS spray, that is produced by the use of 2-chlorobenzalmalononitrile;
    - (ii) the substance, commonly known as PAVA spray, that is produced by the use of pelargonic acid vanillylamide;
  - (b) the use of a weapon for a purpose specified in regulations made by the Secretary of State;
  - (c) the use of a weapon of a description specified in regulations made by the Secretary of State, whether generally or for a purpose so specified.

Practical considerations

- Section 46 of the Police Reform Act 2002 makes it an offence to assault/resist/obstruct a designated or accredited person in execution of duty (see **2.2.5**).
- It is an offence for a person to fail to comply with any powers exercised under Sch 3C paras 3 to 9 inclusive.

 Summary   6 months

 Level 3 fine

Links to alternative subjects and offences

11.2 Mental Health Act— Removal etc of Mentally Disordered Persons without a Warrant

The Mental Health Act 1983 provides for police powers to act in respect of people experiencing a mental health crisis for the purposes of ensuring their care and safety.

A person experiencing a mental health crisis should receive the best possible care at the earliest possible point. The legal changes to the Mental Health Act 1983 introduced by the Policing and Crime 2017 Act are intended to improve immediate service responses to people who need urgent help with their mental health in cases where police officers are the first to respond.

Powers

(1) If a person appears to a constable to be suffering from mental disorder and to be in immediate need of care or control, the constable may, if he thinks it necessary to do so in the interests of that person or for the protection of other persons—
   a) remove the person to a place of safety within the meaning of section 135, or
   b) if the person is already at a place of safety within the meaning of that section, keep the person at that place or remove the person to another place of safety.

(1A) The power of a constable under subsection (1) may be exercised where the mentally disordered person is at any place, other than—
   a) any house, flat or room where that person, or any other person, is living, or
   b) any yard, garden, garage or outhouse that is used in connection with the house, flat or room, other than one that is also used in connection with one or more other houses, flats or rooms.

(1B) For the purpose of exercising the power under subsection (1), a constable may enter any place where the power may be exercised, if need be by force.

(1C) Before deciding to remove a person to, or to keep a person at, a place of safety under subsection (1), the constable must, if it is practicable to do so, consult—
   a) a registered medical practitioner,
   b) a registered nurse,
   c) an approved mental health professional, or
   d) a person of a description specified in regulations made by the Secretary of State.

Mental Health Act 1983, s 136

Permitted period of detention

Under s 136(2) a person removed to, or kept at, a place of safety under this section may be detained there for a period not exceeding the **permitted period of detention** for the purpose of enabling him to be examined by a registered medical practitioner and to be interviewed by an approved mental health professional and of making any necessary arrangements for his treatment or care.

Section 136(2A) states that the permitted period of detention means—

a) the period of **24 hours** beginning with—
   i) in a case where the person is removed to a place of safety, the time when the person arrives at that place;
   ii) in a case where the person is kept at a place of safety, the time when the constable decides to keep the person at that place; or
b) where an authorisation is given in relation to the person under s 136B, that period of 24 hours and such further period as is specified in the authorisation.

Under s 136(3) A constable, an approved mental health professional or a person authorised by either of them for the purposes of this subsection may, before the end of the permitted period of detention mentioned in subsection (2) above, take a person detained in a place of safety under that subsection to one or more other places of safety.

Under s 136(4) A person taken to a place of safety under subsection (3) above may be detained there for a purpose mentioned in subsection (2) above for a period ending no later than the end of the permitted period of detention mentioned in that subsection.

Protective Search Powers

Section 136C(3) Where a person is detained under section 136(2) or (4), a constable may search the person, at any time while the person is so detained, if the constable has reasonable grounds for believing that the person—

    (a) may present a danger to himself or herself or to others, and
    (b) is concealing on his or her person an item that could be used to cause physical injury to himself or herself or to others.

(4) The power to search conferred by subsection ... (3) is only a power to search to the extent that is reasonably required for the purpose of discovering the item that the constable believes the person to be concealing.

(5) The power to search conferred by subsection ... (3)—
    (a) does not authorise a constable to require a person to remove any of his or her clothing other than an outer coat, jacket or gloves, but
    (b) does authorise a search of a person's mouth.

(6) A constable searching a person in the exercise of the power to search conferred by subsection ... (3) may seize and retain anything found, if he or she has reasonable grounds for believing that the

> person searched might use it to cause physical injury to himself or
> herself or to others.
> (7) The power to search a person conferred by subsection . . . (3) does
> not affect any other power to search the person.
>
> Mental Health Act s 136C

Use of police stations as places of safety

- Section 136A(1) [states that] **a child** may not, in the exercise of a
  power to which this section applies, be removed to, kept at or taken
  to a place of safety that is a police station.
- Section 136A(2) The Secretary of State may by regulations—
  a) provide that **an adult** may be removed to, kept at or taken to a
     place of safety that is a police station, in the exercise of a power
     to which this section applies, only in circumstances specified in
     the regulations;
  b) make provision about how adults removed to, kept at or taken
     to a police station, in the exercise of a power to which this
     section applies, are to be treated while at the police station,
     including provision for review of their detention.
- The power to which this section applies includes the power under s
  136(3) where a constable, an approved mental health professional or a
  person authorised by either of them for the purposes of this subsection
  may, before the end of the permitted period of detention mentioned in
  subsection (2) [**see above**], take a person detained in a place of safety
  under that subsection to one or more other places of safety.

Meanings

Child

A person aged under 18.

Adult

A person aged 18 or over.

Mental disorder

Means any disorder or disability of the mind, and 'mentally disordered'
shall be construed accordingly.

Place of safety

Means residential accommodation provided by a local social services
authority, a hospital as defined by this Act, a police station, an **independent hospital** or **care home** for mentally disordered persons, or any
other suitable place. A house, flat or room where a person is living **may
not** be regarded as a suitable place unless—

a) if the person believed to be suffering from a mental disorder is
   the sole occupier of the place, that person agrees to the use of the
   place as a place of safety;

b) if the person believed to be suffering from a mental disorder is an occupier of the place but not the sole occupier, both that person and one of the other occupiers agree to the use of the place as a place of safety;

c) if the person believed to be suffering from a mental disorder is not an occupier of the place, both that person and the occupier (or, if more than one, one of the occupiers) agree to the use of the place as a place of safety.

A place other than a), b), and c) above may not be regarded as a suitable place unless a person who appears to the constable exercising powers under this section to be responsible for the management of the place agrees to its use as a place of safety.

Approved mental health professional

Means a person approved under s 114(1) by any local social services authority.

Care home/independent hospital

These have the same meaning as in the Care Standards Act 2000.

Explanatory notes

- The protective search powers under s 136C(1) also apply where a warrant is issued under s 135.
- While s 136A(1) prevents the use of police stations as place of safety in any circumstances where the person is under 18, s 136A(2) allows the Secretary of State to make regulations to restrict circumstances in which police cells may be used as a place of safety for persons aged 18 and over. The prohibition in s 136A(1) means that children must not be removed to any part of a police station as a place of safety under this Act.
- The powers under s 136(1) apply to any public or private place other than dwellings. Public or private place would therefore include private work premises, schools, rooftops of commercial or business buildings, on railway lines, in hospital emergency departments, schools, non-residential parts of residential buildings with restricted entry and police custody. A place of safety could not be a private room in a care or a residential home where a person lives.
- Although s 136(1) requires that a constable consults with a health care professional before taking a person into detention, it may not always be practicable. The reasons include:
  - ✦ whether there are established local arrangements for undertaking such consultation (eg street triage schemes),
  - ✦ the time it is likely to carry out the consultation,
  - ✦ whether the person appearing to suffer from a mental disorder is likely to remain cooperative and present during the time taken to undertake the consultation; and

✦ whether it is safe to undertake a consultation or whether the behaviour of the person requires immediate action in the interests of safety.

The Home Office guidance [Oct 2017] for the 'changes to police powers and places of safety provisions in the mental health act 1983' provides more detail on places of safety and advice on welfare for persons detained at police stations.

Practical considerations

- The Mental Health Act 1983: Codes of Practice (England) (Last Updated 31 October 2017). Chapter 16 of the Code is the most relevant for the police and relates to police powers and places of safety. The Code of Practice issued under s 118 of the Mental Health Act 1983 provides guidance to professionals on how to carry out their responsibilities under the Act. It guides patients, their families and carers on their rights and has been revised reflecting the changes in legislation, case law, policy and professional practice since its last revision in 2008. Although the Code remains in force, the revised legislation under the Policing and Crime Act 2017 will mean that parts of the Code will require updating in due course.
- When a person is detained under this section an ambulance should be requested to transport the person, accompanied by a police officer, to the place of safety.
- Although the maximum period of detention is 24 hours, this can be extended if a doctor certifies that an extension of up to 12 hours is necessary.
- Section 135 deals with an application for a warrant on suspicion that a person is suffering from a mental disorder and has been, or is being, ill-treated, neglected, or kept otherwise than under proper control, in any place or being unable to care for him/herself, is living alone in any such place. The warrant may authorise any constable to enter the place, if need be by force in order to take that person to a place of safety.
- A person cannot be deemed to be suffering from mental disorder by reason only of their promiscuity, immoral conduct, sexual deviancy, or dependence on alcohol or drugs.
- If an offence has also been committed, the PACE powers of arrest (or other relevant power to arrest) could be considered.
- Legality of detention issues:
  ✦ People removed from public places under s 136 should be assessed as soon as possible. If that assessment is to take place in a police station, an approved mental health professional and registered medical practitioner **must** be called to carry out the interview and examination (PACE Code C 3.16). Once interviewed, examined, and suitable arrangements made for their treatment or care they can no longer be lawfully detained under s 136.
  ✦ The person should not be released until they have been assessed by an approved mental health professional and the registered medical practitioner.

✦ If the decision has been made that the person is not 'mentally disordered', admittance for treatment can only be affected with that person's consent.

Links to alternative subjects and offences

11.3 **Illegal Entry into the UK/Identity Documents**

Legislation relating to immigration is vast. However, three major aspects potentially affect everyday policing and include: illegal entry into the UK, illegal entry by deception, and assisting and harbouring an illegal immigrant.

11.3.1 **Illegal entry into the UK/identity documents/powers relating to passports**

Section 24 of the Immigration Act 1971 creates offences in relation to illegal entry.

Offences

A person who is not a British citizen shall be guilty of an offence in any of the following cases—

(a) if contrary to this Act he knowingly enters the UK in breach of a deportation order or without leave;

(b) if, having only a limited leave to enter or remain in the UK, he knowingly either—
   (i) remains beyond the time limited by the leave; or
   (ii) fails to observe a condition of the leave;

(c) if, having lawfully entered the UK without leave by virtue of section 8(1), he remains without leave beyond the time allowed by section 8(1);

(d) if, without reasonable excuse, he fails to comply with any requirement imposed on him under Sch 2 to this Act to report to a medical officer of health, or to attend, or submit to a test or examination, as required by such an officer;

(e) if, without reasonable excuse, he fails to observe any restriction imposed on him under Sch 2 or 3 to this Act as to residence, as to his employment or occupation or as to reporting to the police to an immigration officer or to the Secretary of State;

(f) if he disembarks in the UK from a ship or aircraft after being placed on board under Sch 2 or 3 to this Act with a view to his removal from the UK;

(g) if he embarks in contravention of a restriction imposed by or under an Order in Council under section 3(7) of this Act.

Immigration Act 1971, s 24(1)

Points to prove

✓ not being a British citizen
✓ committed one or more of the acts in s 24(1)

Explanatory notes

- European Union nationals and those exercising EU rights do not need leave to enter or remain in the UK.
- A person commits an offence under s 24(1)(b)(i) on the day when they first know that the time limited by the leave has expired and continues to commit it throughout any period during which they remain in the UK; but that person shall not be prosecuted more than once in respect of the same limited leave.
- Section 24B creates a summary offence for a person subject to immigration control of work if s/he has not been granted leave to enter or remain, the leave to enter or remain is invalid, has ceased to have effect, or is subject to a condition preventing him/her from doing that kind of work, and s/he knows or has reasonable cause to suspect that s/he is disqualified from working by reason of immigration status. Where a person has been arrested for an offence under this section, there is a power to search business premises without a warrant. Wages paid to illegal workers could be recoverable under the Proceeds of Crime Act 2002 (see **5.5**).

Related cases

R v Uxbridge Magistrates' Court, ex parte Sorani; Adimi and Kaziu [1999] 4 All ER 529, QBD Provides guidance on the prosecution of asylum seekers as illegal immigrants (see below).

Practical considerations

- Illegal entrants should not be prosecuted for offences of illegal entry or travelling on false documents if they are claiming political asylum, arriving directly from a place where they were in danger, present themselves immediately, and show good reason for their entry. This is in line with the UN Convention relating to refugee status and was followed in the case of *R v Uxbridge Magistrates' Court, ex parte Sorani, Adimi and Kaziu* [1999] 4 All ER 529, QBD. This only applies to offences relating to asylum seekers who face charges relating to illegal entry and the use of false travel documents; they are still subject to prosecution for other offences in the usual way.
- Section 25D provides that where a person has been arrested for assisting in illegal entry (see **11.3.3**) or any of the following offences:
  ◆ s 25—Assist in unlawful immigration to Member State/does act in breach of immigration law;

11.3.1 Illegal entry into the UK/identity documents/powers

+ s 25A—For gain, help an asylum seeker to enter the UK;
+ s 25B—Assist arrival/entry/remain in UK in breach of deportation/
  exclusion order; then any vehicle, ship, or aircraft used when
  committing these offences may be seized and detained by a police
  constable or senior immigration officer, pending a court order for
  their forfeiture.
- Consider confiscation of cash and property for the s 25, s 25A,
  or s 25B Immigration Act 1971 (assisting unlawful immigration)
  offences. These and other people trafficking offences are given as
  'criminal lifestyle' offences under Sch 2 to the Proceeds of Crime Act
  2002 (see **5.5** for details).

Identity documents

- Section 4 of the Identity Documents Act 2010 makes it an indictable
  offence for a person with an improper intention to have in their
  possession or control an **identity document** that is false, improperly
  obtained, or relates to someone else.
- Section 6 of the Identity Documents Act 2010 makes it an 'either
  way' offence for a person, without reasonable excuse, to have in their
  possession or control an **identity document** that is false, improperly
  obtained, relates to someone else, or any apparatus/article which is
  specially designed or adapted for the making of false identity documents.
- An **identity document** means any document that is or purports to
  be an immigration document, UK passport, passport for a country
  or territory outside the UK, a document that can be used instead of
  a passport, UK driving licence, or driving licence for a country or
  territory outside the UK.
- HOC 4/2010 provides guidance on the entry, search, and seizure powers,
  relating to nationality or identity documents, which are available to a
  constable or the UKBA under ss 44–47 of the UK Borders Act 2007.

Powers relating to passports

- Schedule 8 of the Anti-social Behaviour, Crime and Policing Act
  2014 provides search powers in relation to passports and if required
  to seize and retain the passport/travel document.
- HOC 4/2014 provides guidance for the police and immigration
  and customs officials in applying these powers at ports; and for
  the police to seize/retain passports that have been cancelled by the
  Secretary of State where a person is suspected of involvement in
  activities contrary to the public interest.

Powers of search and seizure at ports (para 2)

- An **examining officer** may exercise any of the following powers in
  the case of a person at a **port** whom the officer believes to be there
  in connection with entering or leaving GB or Northern Ireland, or
  travelling by air within GB or Northern Ireland. The powers are to:
  + require the person to hand over all travel documents in their
    possession for inspection by the officer;

+ search for travel documents, and take possession to inspect any found by the officer;
+ (subject to para 4) retain any **travel document** taken from the person, while its validity is checked or which the examining officer believes to be **invalid**.
- To search for travel documents, the officer has a power to search:
  + the person;
  + anything that the person has with them;
  + any vehicle in which the examining officer believes the person to have been travelling or to be about to travel.
- An examining officer may:
  + stop a person or vehicle and if necessary use reasonable force for the purposes of exercising the above powers;
  + authorise a person to carry out a search on behalf of the officer.
- An examining officer, other than a constable, in exercising the above powers has the same powers of arrest (without warrant) as a constable in relation to offences under s 4 or s 6 of the Identity Documents Act 2010 (above).

Meanings

Examining officer

Means a constable, immigration officer, or a general customs official.

Port

Means:
- an airport, sea port, hoverport, heliport;
- a railway station where passenger trains go to/from places outside the UK; or
- any other place at which a person is able, or attempting, to get on or off any craft, vessel, or vehicle in connection with entering or leaving GB or Northern Ireland.

Travel document

Means anything that is, or appears to be, a passport or other document which has been issued by or for HM Government, or the government of another state, and enables or facilitates travel from one state to another.

Invalid travel document

A travel document is invalid if: it has been cancelled or expired; it was not issued by the government or authority by which it purports to have been issued; or it has undergone an unauthorised alteration.

Constable's search and seizure powers (para 3)

- A constable may exercise any of the below powers, at a place that is not a port, if the constable reasonably believes that a person is in possession of a passport which:
  + was issued by or for HM Government;

11.3.1 Illegal entry into the UK/identity documents/powers

+ has been cancelled by the Secretary of State on the basis that the person to whom it was issued has or may have been, or will or may become, involved in activities so undesirable that it is contrary to the public interest for the person to have access to passport facilities; and
+ is specified in an authorisation issued by the Secretary of State for the use of the powers under this paragraph.
+ The powers are to:
+ require the person to hand over all travel documents in their possession for inspection by the constable;
+ search for travel documents and to take possession of any that the constable finds;
+ inspect any travel document taken from the person and to retain it while its validity is checked;
+ (subject to para 4) retain any travel document taken that the constable believes to be invalid.
• The power to search for travel documents is a power to search:
  + the person;
  + anything that the person has with them;
  + any vehicle in which the constable believes the person has travelled in or is about to travel;
  + any premises on which the constable is lawfully present.
• A constable may:
  + if necessary use reasonable force for the purpose of exercising the above powers;
  + authorise a person to carry out the above search powers on the constable's behalf.

Retention or return of documents seized (para 4)

• If a travel document is retained under para 2 or 3 while its validity is checked, the checking must be carried out as soon as possible.
• If such a travel document is valid, or is invalid only because it has expired, it must be returned to the person straight away.
• A travel document taken under para 2 or 3 must be returned to the person before the end of the period of seven days beginning with the day on which it was taken, unless during that period it is established that the document is invalid for some reason other than expiry.
• A requirement to return an expired travel document does not apply where the officer concerned reasonably believes that the person from whom they took the document, or some other person, intends to use it for purposes for which it is no longer valid.
• A requirement to return a travel document has effect subject to any provision not in this Sch under which the document may be lawfully retained.

Schedule 8 offences (para 5)

• A person who is required under para 2 or 3 to hand over all travel documents in their possession commits an offence if they fail without reasonable excuse to do so.

• A person who intentionally obstructs, or seeks to frustrate, a search under para 2 or 3 commits an offence.

Illegal entry/Passports

SSS

 Summary   6 months

 6 months' imprisonment and/or a fine

Identity documents

E&S

 s 4 Indictable; s 6 Either way   None

 s 4 offence
Indictment: 10 years' imprisonment and/or a fine

 s 6 offence
Summary: 6 months' imprisonment and/or a fine
Indictment: 2 years' imprisonment and/or a fine

11.3.2 **Illegal entry by deception**

> **Offences**
>
> A person who is not a British citizen is guilty of an offence if, by means which include deception by him—
> (a) he obtains or seeks to obtain leave to enter or remain in the UK; or
> (b) he secures or seeks to secure the avoidance, postponement or revocation of enforcement action against him.
>
> Immigration Act 1971, s 24A(1)

> **Points to prove**
> ✓ not being a British citizen
> ✓ by any means including deception
> ✓ obtained/sought to obtain leave to enter/remain in UK
> **or**
> ✓ secured/sought to secure the avoidance/postponement/ revocation of enforcement action

11.3.3 Assisting illegal entry

Meaning of enforcement action

Enforcement action in relation to a person means:
- giving of directions for removal from the UK;
- making of a deportation order under s 5; or
- removal from UK from directions or deportation order.

 Either way   None

 Summary: 6 months' imprisonment and/or a fine

Indictment: 2 years' imprisonment and/or a fine

11.3.3 **Assisting illegal entry**

Section 25 of the Immigration Act 1971 deals with assisting unlawful immigration to a Member State of the EC.

Offences

A person commits an offence if he—
(a) does an act which facilitates the commission of a breach of immigration law by an individual who is not a citizen of the European Union,
(b) knows or has reasonable cause for believing that the act facilitates the commission of a breach of immigration law by the individual, and
(c) knows or has reasonable cause for believing that the individual is not a citizen of the European Union.

Immigration Act 1971, s 25(1)

Points to prove
✓ did an act
✓ which facilitated breach of immigration law
✓ by a person
✓ who was not a citizen of the EU
✓ knowing/having reasonable cause for believing
✓ that the act facilitated breach of immigration law
✓ by that person
✓ knowing/having reasonable cause for believing
✓ that person was not a citizen of the EU

Meanings

Immigration law (s 25(2))

Means a law which has effect in a **Member State** and which controls, in respect of some or all persons who are not nationals of the state, entitlement to enter, transit across, or be in the state.

Member State

Apart from an EC Member State, it also includes a state named on a list known as the 'Section 25 List of Schengen Acquis States'.

Citizen of the European Union

Includes a reference to a person who is a national of a state on the s 25 list (see **'Practical considerations'**).

Practical considerations

- Section 25(4) states that s 25(1) applies to things done whether inside or outside the UK.
- The 'Section 25 List of Schengen Acquis States' are regarded as Member States for the purposes of s 25, and they are **Norway** and **Iceland**. This means that, although both states are only members of the European Free Trade Association and are outside the EU, the Schengen rules apply to them.
- Section 25A of the Immigration Act 1971 creates an offence of knowingly and for gain facilitating the arrival/entry into the UK of an individual and knowing/having reasonable cause to believe that the individual is an asylum seeker.
- Section 25D gives a power to seize the means of transport used for this offence and s 25C provides the court with a power to order forfeiture of this transport (see **11.3.1**).
- Consider confiscation of cash and property for the s 25 offences of assisting unlawful immigration/entry. This and other people trafficking offences are given as 'criminal lifestyle' offences under Sch 2 to the Proceeds of Crime Act 2002 (see **5.5** for details).

 Either way   None

 Summary: 6 months' imprisonment and/or a fine

Indictment: 14 years' imprisonment and/or a fine

Links to alternative subjects and offences

11.4 **Wasting Police Time**

This section considers two aspects of taking up police resources on false pretenses: those of wasting police time and of carrying out a bomb hoax.

11.4.1 **Wasting police time**

Section 5(2) of the Criminal Law Act 1967 creates the offence of the wasteful employment of the police by making false reports.

Offences

Where a person causes any wasteful employment of the police by knowingly making to any person a false report tending to show that an offence has been committed or to give rise to apprehension for the safety of any persons or property or tending to show that he has information material to any police inquiry, he commits an offence.

Criminal Law Act 1967, s 5(2)

Points to prove

✓ knowingly caused
✓ wasteful employment of police
✓ by false report
✓ that offence committed **or**
✓ giving apprehension for safety of persons/property **or**
✓ that had information material to police enquiry

Explanatory notes

'Giving rise to apprehension for safety of any persons or property' could apply where a person falsely reports a house fire in order to commit a burglary or a mother falsely reports that her child is missing in an attempt to get her estranged husband back.

Practical considerations

- Consent of DPP is required before commencing a prosecution.
- If suitable, consider issuing a PND (see **7.1.1**).
- Decisions to prosecute are often inconsistent and may bear no relation to the number of hours wasted on the investigation.
- Consider other similar offences such as hoax bomb calls (see **11.4.2**) or false messages (see **7.12**).

Summary 6 months

 6 months' imprisonment and/or a level 4 fine

11.4.2 **Bomb and terrorist-type hoaxes**

Bomb hoaxes

Section 51 of the Criminal Law Act 1977 concerns bomb hoaxes.

> **Offences**
>
> A person who—
> (a) places any **article** in any place whatever; or
> (b) dispatches any article by post, rail or any other means whatever of sending things from one place to another,
> with the **intention** (in either case) of inducing in some other person a belief that it is likely to explode or ignite and thereby cause personal injury or damage to property is guilty of an offence.
>
> A person who communicates any information which he knows or believes to be false to another person with the intention of inducing in him or any other person a false belief that a bomb or other thing liable to explode or ignite is present in any place or location whatever is guilty of an offence.
>
> Criminal Law Act 1977, s 51

Points to prove

s 51(1) offence

✓ placed in any place or dispatched by post/rail/other means of sending things
✓ an article
✓ with intent
✓ to induce in another the belief
✓ that the article
✓ was likely to explode/ignite
✓ and cause personal injury/damage to property

s 51(2) offence

✓ communicated
✓ information to another person
✓ knew/believed to be false
✓ with intent
✓ of inducing a false belief in that person/any other person
✓ that bomb/thing was in place or location and
✓ was liable to explode/ignite at that place/location

11.4.2 Bomb and terrorist-type hoaxes

Meanings

Article

This includes substance.

Intention (see **4.1.2**)

Person

It is not necessary to have any particular person in mind as the person in whom they intend to induce the belief in question.

Explanatory notes

- Section 51(1) concerns the placing or dispatching of articles with the intention that people believe that they are bombs or explosive devices; whereas s 51(2) concerns people who communicate false information intending others to believe there is a bomb or explosive device likely to explode.
- This section does not require a specific place or location to be given.

Related cases

R v Webb [1995] 27 LS Gaz R 31, CA The hoax message does not have to give a specific place or location.

Terrorist-type hoaxes

Section 114 of the Anti-terrorism, Crime and Security Act 2001 has created a similar offence for biological, chemical, and nuclear hoaxes. These include actions such as sending powders or liquids through the post and claiming that they are harmful.

Offences

(1) A person is guilty of an offence if he—
   (a) places any substance or other thing in any place; or
   (b) sends any substance or other thing from one place to another (by post, rail or any other means whatever);
   with the intention of inducing in a person anywhere in the world a belief that it is likely to be (or contain) a noxious substance or other noxious thing and thereby endanger human life or create a serious risk to human health.

(2) A person is guilty of an offence if he communicates any information which he knows or believes to be false with the intention of inducing in a person anywhere in the world a belief that a noxious substance or other noxious thing is likely to be present (whether at the time the information is communicated or later) in any place and thereby endanger human life or create a serious risk to human health.

Anti-terrorism, Crime and Security Act 2001, s 114

Points to prove

s 114(1) offence

✓ placed **or** sent
✓ a substance/thing
✓ intending
✓ to induce in a person
✓ a belief that it is likely to be/contain a noxious substance/thing
✓ and thereby endanger human life/create a serious risk to human health

s 114(2) offence

✓ communicated information
✓ knew/believed to be false
✓ intending
✓ to induce in a person
✓ anywhere in the world
✓ a belief that a noxious substance/thing
✓ was likely to be present in any place
✓ thereby endanger human life/create a serious risk to human health

Meanings

Substance

Includes any biological agent and any other natural or artificial substance (whatever its form, origin, or method of production).

Intention (see 4.1.2)

Person (see 'Bomb hoaxes' above)

Practical considerations

- A related offence is food contamination contrary to s 38 of the Public Order Act 1986. It is an offence under s 38(1) to intend to cause alarm, injury, or loss by contamination of or interference with **goods,** or by making it appear that goods have been contaminated or interfered with, in a place where goods of that description are consumed, used, sold, or otherwise supplied. It is also an offence under s 38(2) to make threats or claims relating to s 38(1) or to possess materials under s 38(3) with a view to committing a s 38(1) offence.
- Section 38 concerns 'consumer terrorism' which could involve animal rights activists or an individual trying to blackmail a manufacturer or supermarket chain. **Goods** includes substances whether natural or manufactured and whether or not incorporated in or mixed with other goods.
- The court should be made aware of the disruptions and anxiety caused by the hoax.
- How much time and expense were wasted by the hoax?

11.4.2 Bomb and terrorist-type hoaxes

 Either way   None

 Summary: 6 months' imprisonment and/or a fine

Indictment: 7 years' imprisonment and/or a fine

Links to alternative subjects and offences

11.5 Supplying Tobacco

11.5.1 Supplying butane lighter refills and tobacco

The Cigarette Lighter Refill (Safety) Regulations 1999 (SI 1844/1999) make it an offence to supply butane lighter refills to people under 18. The Children and Young Persons Act 1933 makes it an offence to sell tobacco or cigarette papers to a person under 18, with a power to search and seize from people under 16 found smoking in a street or public place.

Offences

No person shall supply any cigarette lighter refill canister containing butane or a substance with butane as a constituent part to any person under the age of 18 years.

Cigarette Lighter Refill (Safety) Regulations 1999, reg 2

Points to prove

✓ supplied
✓ cigarette lighter refill canister containing butane
✓ to person aged under 18 years

Explanatory notes

- These Regulations prohibit the supply of cigarette lighter refill canisters containing butane to persons under the age of 18.
- Contravention of these Regulations is an offence under s 12 of the Consumer Protection Act 1987.

Defences

It shall be a defence for that person to show that he took all reasonable steps and exercised all due diligence to avoid committing the offence.

Consumer Protection Act 1987, s 39(1)

Possession of tobacco or cigarette papers

- Section 7 of the Children and Young Persons Act 1933 makes it an offence to sell to a person under the age of 18 any tobacco or cigarette papers, whether for their own use or not. It is a defence

11.5.1 Supplying butane lighter refills and tobacco

for the seller to prove that they took all reasonable precautions and exercised all due diligence to avoid committing the offence.

- A power of seizure exists, but there is an anomaly in that it only applies to a person who appears to be under 16. A constable in uniform can seize any tobacco or cigarette papers from a person who appears to be under 16, whom they find smoking in any street or public place and can dispose of any seized tobacco or cigarette papers as directed by the police authority.
- CSOs and CSVs have conferred powers to seize tobacco or cigarette papers from any person who appears to be under 16, whom they find smoking in any street or public place. CSOs and CSVs have an additional power to search, if they reasonably believe the person has tobacco/cigarette papers in their possession (see **11.1.4** and **9.5.1**).
- Section 91 of the Children and Families Act 2014 makes it an offence to purchase tobacco, nicotine products, etc on behalf of persons under 18 (so-called 'proxy purchasing').
- The EU Tobacco Products Directive (2014/40/EU) states that electronic cigarettes which contain nicotine will be regulated by the Tobacco Products Directive and, consequently, need to meet new standards set by the Tobacco and Related Products Regulations 2016 for packaging etc. Electronic cigarettes that are purely herbal are not included. The Directive acknowledges the risks to children due to the sudden popularity of vaping, and there have been concerns that they could become popular with school children as smoking begins to appear 'cool' again.

 Summary 6 months

 Butane refills: 6 months' imprisonment and/or a fine

    Tobacco: Level 4 fine

Links to alternative subjects and offences

11.6 **Animal Welfare and Control of Dogs**

The Animal Welfare Act 2006 is discussed in the first subject area, and the remaining topics deal with dangerous dogs, orders for their control, and guard dogs.

11.6.1 **Animal welfare offences**

The Animal Welfare Act 2006 has introduced several offences that are intended to prevent harm and distress to animals. The offence of unnecessary suffering under s 4 is dealt with, but other offences within the Act are given in a bullet point/précis form so that the reader is at least aware of them.

Unnecessary suffering

> #### Offences
>
> (1) A person commits an offence if—
>   - (a) an act of his, or a failure of his to act, causes an **animal** to suffer,
>   - (b) he knew, or ought reasonably to have known, that the act, or failure to act, would have that effect or be likely to do so,
>   - (c) the animal is a **protected animal**, and
>   - (d) the **suffering** is unnecessary.
> (2) A person commits an offence if—
>   - (a) he is **responsible** for an animal,
>   - (b) an act, or failure to act, of another person causes the animal to suffer,
>   - (c) he permitted that to happen or failed to take such steps (whether by way of supervising the other person or otherwise) as were reasonable in all the circumstances to prevent that happening, and
>   - (d) the suffering is unnecessary.
>
> Animal Welfare Act 2006, s 4

> #### Points to prove
>
> *s 4(1) offence*
> - ✓ did an act/failed to act
> - ✓ that caused a protected animal to suffer
> - ✓ knowing/ought to have known by this act/failure to act
> - ✓ caused/was likely to cause this suffering and
> - ✓ the suffering is unnecessary

11.6.1 Animal welfare offences

> **s 4(2) offence**
> ✓ being responsible for an animal where
> ✓ another person did an act/failed to act
> ✓ that caused the animal to suffer
> ✓ permitted/failed to prevent this suffering happening
> ✓ it caused/was likely to cause this suffering and
> ✓ the suffering is unnecessary

Meanings

Animal

Means a vertebrate other than man. It does not apply to an animal while in a foetal or embryonic form.

Protected animal

An animal if it is:
- of a kind which is commonly domesticated in the British Islands;
- under the control of man whether permanent or temporary; or
- not living in a wild state.

Suffering

Means physical or mental suffering.

Responsible

A person is responsible for an animal:
- whether on a permanent or temporary basis;
- when they are in charge of it;
- when they own it;
- when they have actual care and control of a person under the age of 16 who is responsible for it.

Explanatory notes

- An offence under subsection 4(1) would only be committed through a failure to act if that failure to act causes unnecessary suffering. An example would be a dog owner who fails to feed his pet who then starves as a result. However, a person who encounters a starving dog in public and chooses not to act is unlikely to be guilty of the offence as their failure to act is not the cause of the animals suffering.
- Matters to consider whether suffering is unnecessary include:
  + Could it have been avoided or reduced?
  + Was there compliance with legislation/licence/code of practice?
  + Was it for a legitimate purpose, such as benefiting the animal, or protecting a person, property, or another animal?
  + Was it proportionate to the purpose of the conduct concerned?
  + Was the conduct that of a reasonably competent and humane person?

- This section does not apply to the destruction of an animal in an appropriate and humane manner.

Related cases

Riley v CPS [2016] EWHC 2513 (Admin) In this case it was held that partners in a business could not be liable for events in their absence where there was no allegation of a systematic failure or a proper joint charge.

RSPCA v Colchester magistrates' court and orders [2015] EWHC 1418 (Admin) A search under a warrant may only be a search to the extent required for the purpose for which the warrant was issued unless 'expressly' relying upon s 19 PACE powers of general seizure (see **1.5.4**).

Other animal welfare offences

Section 5—Mutilation

- It is an offence if a person carries out/causes to be carried out a prohibited procedure on a protected animal.
- Similarly, the person responsible for the animal will commit an offence if they carry out the procedure or permit/fail to prevent this happening.
- The procedure involves interference with the sensitive tissues or bone structure of the animal, otherwise than for its medical treatment.

Section 6—Docking of dogs' tails

- With certain exceptions, it is an offence if a person removes/causes to be removed all/part of a dog's tail.
- Similarly, the person responsible for the dog is liable if the dog's tail is docked or permits/fails to prevent this happening.

Section 7—Administration of poisons or injurious drug/substance

- It is an offence if a person, without lawful authority or reasonable excuse administers or causes to be taken any poisonous or injurious drug or substance to/by a protected animal, knowing it to be poisonous or injurious.
- Similarly, a person responsible for an animal commits an offence if:
  + without lawful authority or reasonable excuse, another person administers a poisonous or injurious drug or substance to the animal or causes the animal to take such a drug or substance; **and**
  + they permitted that to happen or, knowing the drug or substance to be poisonous or injurious, they failed to take such steps (whether by way of supervising the other person or otherwise) as were reasonable in all the circumstances to prevent that happening.
- A poisonous or injurious drug or substance includes a drug or substance which, by virtue of the quantity or manner in which it

is administered or taken, has the effect of a poisonous or injurious drug or substance.

Section 8—Offences involving animals fighting

- A person commits an offence if they:
    + cause an **animal fight** to take place, or attempt to do so;
    + knowingly receive money for admission to an animal fight;
    + knowingly publicise a proposed animal fight;
    + provide information about an animal fight to another with the intention of enabling or encouraging attendance at the fight;
    + make or accept a bet on the outcome of an animal fight, or on the likelihood of anything occurring or not occurring in the course of an animal fight;
    + take part in an animal fight;
    + have in their possession anything designed or adapted for use in connection with an animal fight with the intention of its being so used;
    + keep or train an animal for use for or in connection with an animal fight;
    + keep any premises for use for an animal fight.
- A person commits an offence if, without lawful authority or reasonable excuse, they are present at an animal fight.
- '**Animal fight**' means an occasion on which a protected animal is placed with an animal, or with a human, for the purpose of fighting, wrestling, or baiting.
- Section 22(1) gives a constable power to seize any animal that appears to have been involved in fighting, where an offence under s 8 has been committed.
- An animal must be under some degree of control and not wild and while this section is aimed at animal fights that are organised or controlled the payment of money does not have to be involved but if it was, it would be an aggravating factor. If a fight or intended fight was to fall within the meaning of s 8 of the Act, it could not be the by-product of a chance meeting but had to be a contrived or artificial creation specifically for the purpose of a fight during which the other animal had no natural means of escape (see *RSPCA v McCormick and others* [2016] EWHC 928 (Admin)).
- A person could commit an offence under s 8 if they kept or trained an animal for use in connection with an animal fight, through an agent (see *Wright v Reading Crown Court* [2017] EWHC 2643 (Admin).

Section 11—Transfer animals by sale/transaction/prize to under 16

- A person commits an offence if they sell an animal to a person they have reasonable cause to believe to be under the age of 16 years:
    + selling includes transferring ownership in consideration of entering into another transaction.
- It is an offence to enter into an arrangement with a person there is reasonable cause to believe to be under the age of 16 years,

where the 16-year-old has the chance to win an animal as a prize, unless it is:

+ in the presence of and they are accompanied by a person over 16 years; or
+ in the belief that the person who has care and control has consented; or
+ arranged in a family environment.

Practical considerations

- Section 18 gives a constable powers to take such steps as appear to be immediately necessary to alleviate a protected animal's suffering. It is an offence to intentionally obstruct a person exercising the s 18 powers.
- Section 19 allows a constable to enter premises (except a part which is used as a private dwelling) to search for a protected animal in order to exercise their s 18 power, having reasonable belief that the animal is on the premises and is suffering or likely to suffer. A constable may use reasonable force to gain entry, but only if it appears that entry is required before a warrant can be obtained (under s 23) and executed.
- Section 54 states that a constable in uniform may stop and detain a vehicle for the purpose of entering and searching it in the exercise of a search power conferred under:
    + s 19 for a protected animal believed to be suffering; or
    + s 22 for an animal, believed involved in fighting under s 8.
- A vehicle may be detained for as long as is reasonably required to permit a search or inspection to be carried out (including the exercise of any related power under this Act) either at the place where the vehicle was first detained or nearby.
- Section 17(1)(c)(v) of PACE (see **1.5.2**) gives further power to a constable in order to enter and search premises for the purpose of arresting a person for offences under ss 4, 5, 6(1) and (2), 7, and 8(1) and (2) of this Act.

Applies to s 4, s 5, s 6, s 7, and s 8 offences

 E&S

 Summary

 Maximum of three years from date of offence, **but** six months from date on which evidence which the prosecutor thinks is sufficient to justify the proceedings comes to his knowledge.

 maximum 51 weeks imprisonment and/or fine not exceeding £20,000

11.6.2 Dangerous dogs not under control

The Dangerous Dogs Act 1991 imposes restrictions on keeping dogs which are a danger to the public and creates offences relating to a dog being dangerously out of control.

Offences

If a dog is dangerously out of control in any place in England or Wales (whether or not a public place)—

(a) the owner; and

(b) if different, the person for the time being in charge of the dog,

is guilty of an offence, or, if the dog while so out of control injures any person or assistance dog, an aggravated offence, under this subsection.

Dangerous Dogs Act 1991, s 3(1)

Points to prove

Standard offence

✓ owner/person in charge of dog

✓ dangerously out of control

✓ in any place

Aggravated offence

✓ while out of control caused injury to any person or assistance dog

Meanings

Dangerously out of control

Means when there are grounds for reasonable apprehension that the dog will injure any person or **assistance dog**, whether or not it actually does so.

Public place

Means any street, road, or other place (whether or not it is enclosed) to which the public have or are permitted to have access, whether for payment or otherwise, including the common parts of a building containing two or more separate dwellings.

Owner

Where a dog is owned by a person who is under 16, any reference to its owner shall include a reference to the head of the household, if any, of which that person is a member.

Assistance dog

Means a dog which has been trained:

- to guide a blind person;
- to assist a deaf person;

- by a prescribed charity to assist a disabled person with a disability that consists of epilepsy or otherwise affects their mobility, manual dexterity, physical coordination, or ability to lift, carry, or otherwise move everyday objects;
- to assist a disabled person who has a disability of a prescribed kind (not given above), and the dog is of a prescribed category.

Explanatory notes

- The Anti-social Behaviour, Crime and Policing Act 2014, s 106 extended the s 3 offence to not just a public place, or a private place where the dog is not permitted to be, but to all places including private property.
- The exemptions given in ss 3(1A) and (1B) (see **'Defences'**) cover cases where a dog becomes dangerously out of control when a trespasser is inside, or is in the process of entering, a building that is a place where a person lives. It does not matter whether the person was a trespasser; if the owner is in the building when the dog becomes out of control and believes that the person is a trespasser that is sufficient.
- People who live in buildings which serve a dual purpose as a place of residence and a place of work (eg a shopkeeper and his or her family who live above the shop) can rely on the defence of self-defence given in s 76(8B) of the Criminal Justice and Immigration Act 2008 (see **1.2.1**) regardless of which part of the building they were in when they were confronted by an intruder, providing that there is internal means of access between the two parts of the building.

Defences

(1A) A person ('D') is not guilty of an offence under subsection (1) in a case which is a householder case.

(1B) For the purposes of subsection (1A) 'a householder case' is a case where—

    (a) the dog is dangerously out of control while in or partly in a building, or part of a building, that is a dwelling or is forces accommodation (or is both), and

    (b) at that time—

        (i) the person in relation to whom the dog is dangerously out of control ('V') is in, or is entering, the building or part as a trespasser, or

        (ii) D (if present at that time) believed V to be in, or entering, the building or part as a trespasser.

Section 76(8B) to (8F) of the Criminal Justice and Immigration Act 2008 (use of force at place of residence) [see 1.2.1] apply for the purposes of this subsection as they apply for the purposes of subsection (8A) of that section (and for those purposes the reference in section 76(8D) to subsection (8A)(d) is to be read as if it were a reference to paragraph (b)(ii) of this subsection).

> (2) In proceedings for an offence under subsection (1) above against a person who is the owner of a dog, but was not at the material time in charge of it, it shall be a defence for the accused to prove that the dog was, at the material time, in the charge of a person whom he reasonably believed to be a fit and proper person to be in charge of it.
>
> Dangerous Dogs Act 1991, s 3

Destruction and disqualification orders

> (1) Where a person is convicted of an offence under section 1 or 3(1) above the court—
>   (a) may order the destruction of any dog in respect of which the offence was committed and, subject to subsection (1A) below, shall do so in the case of an offence under section 1 or an aggravated offence under section 3(1) above; and
>   (b) may order the offender to be disqualified, for such period as the court thinks fit, for having custody of a dog.
> (1A) Nothing in subsection (1)(a) above shall require the court to order the destruction of a dog if the court is satisfied that the dog would not constitute a danger to public safety.
> (1B) For the purposes of subsection (1A)(a), when deciding whether a dog would constitute a danger to public safety, the court—
>   (a) must consider—
>   (i) the temperament of the dog and its past behaviour, and
>   (ii) whether the owner of the dog, or the person for the time being in charge of it, is a fit and proper person to be in charge of the dog, and
>   (b) may consider any other relevant circumstances.
>
> Dangerous Dogs Act 1991, s 4

Related cases (see **11.6.4** for further cases)

L v CPS [2010] EWHC 341, DC In this case, the defendant took his dog into a public place and asked the co-defendant to take the dog's lead. The co-defendant released the dog and shouted, 'Get him', and the dog attacked and injured the victim. Although the co-defendant took physical control of the dog, the defendant remained 'in charge'. He had been in charge of the dog during the whole incident, both before and after the co-defendant had taken physical control. The defendant would have remained in control of the dog if, for example, it was let off its lead in a park, and there was no reason why he did not remain in charge even where, for a short period, he put the dog under another's physical control. The defendant could have taken control of the dog at any time because the dog reacted to his commands, and if he had given such commands, he would have been able to control it.

R v Gedminintaite [2008] EWCA Crim 814, CA In this case, the defendant owned two Rottweiler dogs and with the assistance of another person, was taking them for a walk. During the walk, the dog that was under the control of the other person bit a child. It was held that the behaviour of the dog, and the fact that the defendant had no proper control over it, was sufficient evidence that the dog was dangerously out of control in a public place.

R v Bezzina; R v Codling; R v Elvin [1994] 3 All ER 964, CA In this case it was held that the s 3(1) offence imposes strict liability, as no 'mens rea' is required on the part of the owner or handler of dogs.

Practical considerations

- In considering whether a dog is dangerously out of control, references to a dog injuring a person or assistance dog or there being grounds for reasonable apprehension that it will do so, do not include references to any case in which the dog is being used for a lawful purpose by a constable or a person in the service of the Crown.
- An order under s 2 of the Dogs Act 1871 (order on complaint that a dog is dangerous and not kept under proper control) (see **11.6.3**) may be made whether or not the dog is shown to have injured any person; and may specify measures for keeping the dog under proper control, whether by muzzling, keeping on a lead, excluding it from specified places, requiring it to be neutered, or otherwise.
- If animals are injured, apart from an assistance dog, consider using powers under s 2 of the 1871 Act (see **11.6.3**).
- Section 1 of the Dogs (Protection of Livestock) Act 1953 provides an offence for the owner (person in charge) of a dog that has worried livestock on agricultural land. This could be attacking or chasing livestock or being at large in a field or enclosure in which there are sheep. Any dog found under such circumstances (without an owner/ person in charge on any land) may be seized and detained by a police officer under s 2 of that Act.

Standard offence

 Summary 6 months

 6 months' imprisonment and/or a fine

Aggravated offence

 E&S

 Either way None

 Summary: 6 months' imprisonment and/or a fine

Indictment: If a person dies as a result of being injured: 14 years' imprisonment and/or a fine

Where a person is injured: 5 years' imprisonment and/or a fine

Where an assistance dog is injured/dies: 3 years' imprisonment and/or a fine

11.6.3 **Dog control orders**

Section 2 of the Dogs Act 1871 allows magistrates' courts to make orders in respect of dangerous dogs.

> ### Complaint
>
> Any magistrates' court may hear a complaint that a dog is dangerous and not kept under proper control, and if satisfied that it is dangerous, may order that it be kept under proper control by the owner, or destroyed.
>
> Dogs Act 1871, s 2

Meanings

Dangerous

Is not limited to meaning dangerous to people. It could include other animals.

Proper control

Proper control is also a question of fact for the court. If a dog is kept under proper control, an order cannot be made in respect of it.

Explanatory notes

The expression '**dangerous**' will be a question of fact for the courts to determine. It includes:

- being dangerous to livestock, birds, and other dogs (*Briscoe v Shattock* [1999] 1 WLR 432, QBD);
- however, a dog that killed two pet rabbits on only one occasion was held not to be dangerous, as it was in the nature of dogs to chase and kill other small animals;
- a dog could be dangerous on private property to which people have a right of access.

Practical considerations

- Where a court orders a dog to be destroyed, it may appoint a person to undertake the seizure and destruction and require any person with custody to deliver it up, and in addition may disqualify the owner from having custody of a dog, under s 1 of the Dangerous Dogs Act 1989, or under s 4(1)(b) of the 1991 Act (see **11.6.2**).
- In a statement of complaint, the victim must identify the dog. It is usually necessary for the victim to then identify the dog in the presence of the owner and the investigating officer. Any injuries should be examined by the officer and described in both their statement and that of the victim. This is a complaint rather than an offence, but it is advisable to interview the owner under the provisions of PACE.
- If there has been a genuine transfer of ownership of the dog, an order could only be made against the new owner.

11.6.4 **Restrictions on dangerous dog breeds**

The Dangerous Dogs Act 1991 imposed restrictions on keeping dogs that are a danger to the public. Section 1 created offences relating to dogs bred for fighting.

Offences

(2) No person shall—
- (a) breed, or breed from, a dog to which this section applies;
- (b) sell or exchange such a dog or offer, advertise or expose such a dog for sale or exchange;
- (c) make or offer to make a gift of such a dog or advertise or expose such a dog as a gift;
- (d) allow such a dog of which he is the owner or for the time being in charge, to be in a public place without being muzzled and kept on a lead; or
- (e) abandon such a dog of which he is the owner or, being the owner or for the time being in charge of such a dog, allow it to stray.

(3) No person shall have any dog to which this section applies in his possession or custody except—
- (a) in pursuance of the power of seizure; or
- (b) in accordance with an order for its destruction under the subsequent provisions of this Act.

(7) Any person who contravenes this section is guilty of an offence.

Dangerous Dogs Act 1991, s 1

Points to prove

s 1(2) offence

- ✓ breed from/sell/exchange/offer/advertise/make a gift of **or**
- ✓ allow in public place without muzzle and kept on lead **or**
- ✓ abandon/allow to stray
- ✓ a fighting dog (as defined in s 1(1))

s 1(3) offence

- ✓ had in possession/custody
- ✓ a fighting dog (as defined in s 1(1))

Meanings

Dog to which this section applies

- Any dog of—
  - (a) the type known as the **Pit Bull Terrier**;
  - (b) the type known as the **Japanese Tosa**; and

11.6.4 Restrictions on dangerous dog breeds

    (c)   any dog of any type designated for the purposes of this section by an order of the Secretary of State, being a type appearing to him to be bred for fighting or to have the characteristics of a type bred for that purpose.

Dangerous Dogs Act 1991, s 1(1)

- SI 1743/1991 added two more dogs to s 1(1) above:
  - ✦ the type known as the **Dogo Argentino**; and
  - ✦ the type known as the **Fila Braziliero**.

Advertise

This includes any means of bringing a matter to the attention of the public.

Public place (see **11.6.2**)

> **Defences**
>
> The above does not apply to dogs being used for lawful purposes by a constable or any other person in the service of the Crown, such as dogs being used by the police, prison service, military police, and Customs & Excise.

Related cases (see 11.6.2 for further cases)

R v Haringey Magistrates' Court, ex parte Cragg (1996) 161 JP 61, QBD and R v Trafford Magistrates' Court, ex parte Riley (1996) 160 JP 418, QBD These two cases were concerned with dog destruction orders. It was held that where the owner of a dog is known, the owner must be informed of any court proceedings which may result in an order for destruction of the dog. The court suggested that had the owner been present during the proceedings against her friend, she may have been able to convince the court to come to a different decision. Even though the legislation makes no provision for informing the owner of such proceedings, not giving them this opportunity is against the rules of natural justice.

DPP v Kellet (1994) 158 JP 1138, QBD A dangerous dog wandered into a public place because the defendant was drunk and had left their front door open. It was held that voluntary intoxication is not a defence.

Bates v DPP (1993) 157 JP 1004, QBD An unmuzzled pit bull terrier was found loose in the back of a car and the defendant was convicted under s 1(2)(d). It was held that a dog in a vehicle may be deemed to be in a public place if the vehicle itself is in a public place.

Practical considerations

- The Dangerous Dogs Exemption Schemes (England and Wales) Order 2015 (SI 138/2015) states that the prohibition in s 1(3) of the Act shall not apply if the Agency (DEFRA) has issued a certificate of exemption in respect of a dog.
- A certificate of exemption can be issued by DEFRA (see **Appendix 1**) if it is satisfied that: a court has determined that the dog is not a danger to public safety and the person is a fit and proper person

to be in charge of the dog; a court has made the dog subject to a contingent destruction order under s 4A; and that the dog has been neutered, microchipped, and third party insurance is in force regarding death or bodily injury to any person caused by the dog.

- For further guidance on this Act see HOC 29/1997.
- The word **'type'** has a wider meaning than **'breed'** in that behavioural characteristics can also be considered: *Brock v DPP* [1993] 4 All ER 491, QBD.
- If it is alleged that a dog is of a type to which this section applies, it is presumed to be so until the owner proves to the contrary. If there is any doubt, the dog may be seized and taken to kennels where the owner may have it examined at his own expense.
- DEFRA (see **Appendix 1**) have guidance on their website to help police and local authorities enforce dangerous dog laws more effectively and crack down on irresponsible dog owners. It provides:
  + an outline and explanation of current law;
  + best practice for the main enforcement authorities;
  + guidance on identifying pit bull terrier-type dogs; and local initiatives.

 Summary   6 months

 6 months' imprisonment and/or a fine

11.6.5 **Guard dogs**

The Guard Dogs Act 1975 was introduced to regulate the use of guard dogs.

Offences

1(1) A person shall not use or permit the use of a guard dog at any premises unless a person ('the handler') who is capable of controlling the dog is present on the premises, and the dog is under the control of the handler at all times while being so used, except while it is secured so that it is not at liberty to go freely about the premises.

1(2) The handler of a guard dog shall keep the dog under his control at all times while it is being used as a guard dog at any premises, except—
   (a) while another handler has control over the dog; or
   (b) while the dog is secured so that it is not at liberty to go freely about the premises.

1(3) A person shall not use or permit the use of a guard dog at any premises unless a notice containing a warning that a guard dog is present is clearly exhibited at each entrance to the premises.

5(1) A person who contravenes section 1 or 2 of this Act shall be guilty of an offence.

Guard Dogs Act 1975, ss 1 and 5

11.6.5 Guard dogs

Points to prove

s 1(1) offence

✓ use/permit the use of
✓ a guard dog(s)
✓ on premises without a capable controller present and not under control
✓ of handler at all times

s 1(2) offence

✓ handler of guard dogs(s) fail
✓ to keep dogs
✓ under control at all times
✓ on premises

s 1(3) offence

✓ use/permit the use of
✓ a guard dog(s)
✓ on premises
✓ when warning notice(s) that a guard dog was present
✓ was/were not clearly exhibited at each entrance

Meanings

Guard dog

Means a dog which is being used to protect premises, or property kept on the premises, or a person guarding the premises or such property.

Premises

Means land other than **agricultural land** and land within the curtilage of a dwelling house; and buildings, including parts of buildings, other than dwelling houses.

Agricultural land (see **11.6.2**)

Section 2

This states that a person shall not keep a dog at guard dog kennels unless a licence under s 3 is held in respect of the kennels.

Related cases

Hobson v Gledhill [1978] 1 All ER 945, QBD It was held in this case that the handler is not required to be on the premises whilst the dog is properly secured. Whether a dog is secured so that it is not at liberty to go freely about the premises will depend on the facts of each case.

Summary   6 months

 Fine

Links to alternative subjects and offences

11.7 **Drones**

Popularly known as drones, but also referred to as remotely piloted aircraft systems or unmanned aerial vehicles, these vehicles come in a variety of shapes and sizes, ranging from small hand-held types, to large aircraft, potentially a similar size to airliners.

Just like any other aircraft, an unmanned aircraft must always be flown in a safe manner, both with respect to other aircraft in the air and to people and properties on the ground. The CAA's primary aim is to enable the full and safe integration of all UAS operations into the UK's total aviation system (Civil Aviation Authority).

The problems associated with the use of drones have become more common when they are flown near to airliners or when used to deliver tobacco, drugs, mobile phones etc to prisons. The governance of, and offences in relation to their use, is contained in the recent Air Navigation Order 2016.

Under the terms of the Police (Collaboration: Specified Functions) Order 2012 (SI 2012/1690) the National Police Air Service is ultimately responsible for drones used by the police.

11.7.1 **Small unmanned aircraft**

Offences

(1) A person must not cause or permit any article or animal (whether or not attached to a parachute) to be dropped from a small unmanned aircraft so as to endanger persons or property.

(2) The person in charge of a small unmanned aircraft may only fly the aircraft if reasonably satisfied that the flight can safely be made.

(3) The person in charge of a small unmanned aircraft must maintain direct, unaided visual contact with the aircraft sufficient to monitor its flight path in relation to other aircraft, persons, vehicles, vessels and structures for the purpose of avoiding collisions.

Article 94 of the Air Navigation Order 2016

Points to prove

Art 94(1)

✓ date and location
✓ cause/permit
✓ article/animal (whether or not attached to parachute) to be dropped
✓ from a small unmanned aircraft
✓ so as to endanger persons/property

Art 94(2)

✓ date and location
✓ in charge of a small unmanned aircraft
✓ flew the aircraft in circumstances
✓ when not reasonably satisfied that the flight could be made safely

Art 94(3)

✓ date and location
✓ in charge of small unmanned aircraft
✓ fail to maintain direct, unaided visual contact
✓ sufficient to monitor its flight path
✓ in relation to other aircraft/persons/vehicles/vessels/structures
✓ for the purpose of avoiding collisions

Meanings

Small unmanned aircraft

Means any unmanned aircraft, other than a balloon or a kite, having a mass of not more than 20 kg without its fuel but including any articles or equipment installed in or attached to the aircraft at the commencement of its flight.

Flight and to fly

Have the meanings respectively assigned to them by Art 3.

Explanatory notes

- Article 94(4) provides restrictions relating to small unmanned aircraft which has a mass of more than 7 kg.
- Article 94(5) states that a person in charge of a small unmanned aircraft must not fly the aircraft for the purposes of commercial operations except in accordance with a permission granted by the CAA.

11.7.2 **Small unmanned surveillance aircraft**

Offence

- The person in charge of a small unmanned surveillance aircraft must not fly the aircraft in any of the circumstances described in paragraph 95(2) except in accordance with a permission issued by the CAA.

Article 95 of the Air Navigation Order 2016

11.7.2 Small unmanned surveillance aircraft

> **Points to prove**
> ✓ date and location
> ✓ in charge of a small unmanned surveillance aircraft
> ✓ fly aircraft in circumstances as described in Art 95(2)
> ✓ other than in accordance with permission issued by CAA

Meanings

Small unmanned aircraft (see 11.7.1)

A small unmanned surveillance aircraft

A small unmanned aircraft which is equipped to undertake any form of surveillance or data acquisition.

Congested area

In relation to a city, town, or settlement, means any area which is substantially used for residential, industrial, commercial, or recreational purposes.

Explanatory notes

- Article 95(2) states that the circumstances referred to in para 95(1) are:
    - (a) over or within 150 metres of any congested area;
    - (b) over or within 150 metres of an organised open-air assembly of more than 1,000 persons;
    - (c) within 50 metres of any vessel, vehicle, or structure which is not under the control of the person in charge of the aircraft; or
    - (d) subject to paras (3) and (4), within 50 metres of any person.
- Article 95(3) states that subject to para (4), during take-off or landing, a small unmanned surveillance aircraft must not be flown within 30 metres of any person.
- This offence does not apply to the person in charge of the small unmanned surveillance aircraft or a person under the control of the person in charge of the aircraft (both of whom may be standing within 30 metres of the aircraft).
- A small unmanned surveillance aircraft means a small unmanned aircraft which is equipped to undertake any form of surveillance or data acquisition.
- Article 95(4) states that paras 95(2)(d) and 95(3) do not apply to the person in charge of the small unmanned surveillance aircraft or a person under the control of the person in charge of the aircraft.

Practical considerations

- Section 79 of the Serious Crime Act 2015 provides for an offence under s 40CB(1) of the Prison Act 1952 to throw or project any article or substance into a prison and this includes drones used for that purpose. Articles that may be brought into this new offence include psychoactive substances (see **5.3.2**).

- Under Art 257 of the 2016 Order, if it appears to a constable that any aircraft is intended or likely to be flown in contravention of the above rules and, consequently, is a cause of danger to any person or property, or the aircraft is in a condition unfit for the flight, the constable may direct the operator not to permit the aircraft to make the flight or any other flight of such description as may be specified in the direction, until the direction has been revoked. Following such a direction, a constable is also empowered to take such steps as are necessary to detain the aircraft.

- An offence under Art 241 could also be considered, though more difficult to prove, if a person recklessly or negligently caused or permitted an aircraft to endanger any person or property. This is an either way offence which can result in two years' imprisonment.

- The advice issued by the NPCC is to identify the pilot of any drone causing concern and instruct them to land it. Failure to comply with such an instruction may result in an offence of obstruction being committed. The guidance states that an officer should only attempt to take control of a drone in exceptional circumstances, owing to the risk of their inadvertently causing an accident while in control.

- When drones are used by individuals for their private purposes there is a risk that images of citizens are collected without their consent but more importantly where drones are used in a commercial setting whether it be for the management of landed estates, the delivery of commercial products or the review of commercial buildings, the Information Commissioner's Office (ICO) have identified that without appropriate practices the use of drones will infringe the data protection rights of individuals and render the commercial operator of drones non-compliant with the Data Protection Act 1998.

- The use of drones is included in the latest CCTV Code of Practice published by the ICO. The Code states that the use of drones has a high potential for collateral intrusion by recording images of individuals unnecessarily and therefore can be highly privacy intrusive and the ICO advise that it is very important that users can provide a strong justification for the use of drones.

- Apart from data protection issues, the fact that drones may inadvertently or otherwise capture information relating to the property and activities of individuals may be an infringement of their rights under Art 8 of the ECHR.

- It should also be borne in mind that recordings from drones need to be stored in a secure manner to comply with the seventh principle of the Data Protection Act 1998, and businesses that store drone camera footage need to apply the same rigorous information security controls as they would in respect of general CCTV footage.

 Summary (United Kingdom only)   6 months

 fine not exceeding level 4 on the standard scale

Links to alternative subjects and offences

Useful Contacts

ACPO (See **NPCC**)

Alcohol Concern
<http://www.alcoholconcern.org.uk> accessed 11 April 2018
Telephone: 020 7566 9800
Helpline (Drinkline): 0300 123 1110

Ask the police FAQ (see **PNLD**)

British Association of Women Police
<http://www.bawp.org> accessed 11 April 2018
Telephone: 07790 505204

CEOP (Child Exploitation and Online Protection Centre)
<http://www.ceop.police.uk> accessed 11 April 2018
Telephone: 0870 000 3344

Childline
<http://www.childline.org.uk> accessed 11 April 2018
Telephone: 0800 1111

Citizens Advice Bureau (provides local links)
<http://www.citizensadvice.org.uk> accessed 11 April 2018

CPS (Crown Prosecution Service)
<http://www.cps.gov.uk> accessed 11 April 2018
Telephone: 020 3357 0000

Crime Stoppers
<http://www.crimestoppers-uk.org> accessed 11 April 2018
Telephone: 0800 555 111

DEFRA (Department for Environment, Food and Rural Affairs)
<https://www.gov.uk/government/organisations/department-for-environment-food-rural-affairs> accessed 11 April 2018
Telephone: 03459 33 55 77

Department for Transport (see **Transport**)

Disclosure and Barring Service (DBS)
<https://www.gov.uk/government/organisations/disclosure-and-barring-service/> accessed 11 April 2018
Telephone: 03000 200 190

Appendix 1: Useful Contacts

Domestic Violence (see **National Domestic Violence Helpline**)

DVLA (Driver and Vehicle Licensing Agency)
<https://www.gov.uk/government/organisations/driver-and-vehicle-licensing-agency> accessed 11 April 2018
Provides links to service required

DVSA (Driver and Vehicle Standards Agency)
<https://www.gov.uk/government/organisations/driver-and-vehicle-standards-agency> accessed 11 April 2018
Provides links to service required

Equality and Human Rights Commission (EHRC)
<http://www.equalityhumanrights.com> accessed 11 April 2018
Telephone (Equality Advisory Support Service): 0808 800 0082

European Commission
<http://ec.europa.eu/index_en.htm> accessed 11 April 2018
Telephone: 00800 67891011

Forced Marriage Unit (see **Honour Network** for victim support)
<https://www.gov.uk/forced-marriage> accessed 11 April 2018
Telephone: 020 7008 0151 Outside office hours: 020 7008 1500

Foreign & Commonwealth Office
<http://www.gov.uk/government/organisations/foreign-commonwealth-office> accessed 11 April 2018
Telephone: 020 7008 1500

GMB (Union)
<http://www.gmb.org.uk> accessed 11 April 2018
Telephone: 020 7391 6700

GOV.UK (Government official information)
<https://www.gov.uk> accessed 11 April 2018

GOV.UK (Driving licence categories/ages/rules)
Categories <https://www.gov.uk/driving-licence-categories>
Ages <https://www.nidirect.gov.uk/articles/minimum-ages-you-can-ride-or-drive-vehicles accessed> 11 April 2018

Hate crime (Stop Hate UK)
<http://www.stophateuk.org> accessed 11 April 2018
Telephone: 0113 293 5100

Highways Agency
<http://www.highways.gov.uk> accessed 11 April 2018
Telephone: 0300 123 5000

HMCTS (Her Majesty's Courts & Tribunals Service)
<https://www.gov.uk/government/organisations/hm-courts-and-tribunals-service> accessed 11 April 2018
Provides links to courts/tribunals and other justice agencies

HMIC (HM Inspectorate of Constabulary)
<http://www.justiceinspectorates.gov.uk/hmic> accessed 11 April 2018
Telephone: 020 3513 0500

HM Prison Service
<https://www.gov.uk/government/organisations/hm-prison-service>
accessed 11 April 2018
Telephone: 0300 047 6325

HMRC (HM Revenue & Customs)
<https://www.gov.uk/government/organisations/hm-revenue-customs>
accessed 11 April 2018
Telephone: 0800 59 5000 (fraud)

Home Office
<http://www.gov.uk/government/organisations/home-office>   accessed
11 April 2018
Telephone: 020 7035 4848

Homophobic abuse (London)
<http://www.galop.org.uk> accessed 11 April 2018
Telephone: 020 7704 2040

Honour Network (honour violence and forced marriages)
<http://www.karmanirvana.org.uk> accessed 11 April 2018
Telephone: 0800 5999 247

Hope for Justice (human trafficking and slavery)
<http://www.hopeforjustice.org.uk> accessed 11 April 2018
Telephone: 0845 519 7402

HSE (Health and Safety Executive)
<http://www.hse.gov.uk> accessed 11 April 2018
Incident Contact Centre: 0345 300 9923

Human Trafficking Centre (UK)
<http://www.nationalcrimeagency.gov.uk/about-us/what-we-do/
specialist-capabilities/uk-human-trafficking-centre/national-
referral-mechanism> accessed 11 April 2018
Telephone: 0370 496 7622

Identity and Passport Service (Agency of the Home Office)
<https://www.gov.uk/government/organisations/hm-passport-office>
accessed 11 April 2018
Telephone: 0300 222 0000

Information Commissioner (data protection/freedom of information)
<http://www.ico.org.uk> accessed 11 April 2018
Telephone: 0303 123 1113

Appendix 1: Useful Contacts

Intellectual Property Office
<http://www.gov.uk/government/organisations/intellectual-property-office> accessed 11 April 2018
Telephone: 0300 300 2000

International Police Association
<http://www.ipa-uk.org> accessed 11 April 2018
Telephone: 0115 981 3638

IOPC (Independent Office for Police Conduct)
< https://www.policeconduct.gov.uk > accessed 11 April 2018
Telephone: 030 0020 0096

Law Society
<http://www.lawsociety.org.uk> accessed 11 April 2018
Telephone: 020 7242 1222

Legislation
<http://www.legislation.gov.uk/> accessed 11 April 2018

Mental illness advice (SANE)
<http://www.sane.org.uk> accessed 11 April 2018
Telephone: 020 7375 1002 Helpline: 0300 304 7000

MIB (Motor Insurers' Bureau)
<http://www.mib.org.uk> accessed 11 April 2018

Ministry of Justice
<https://www.gov.uk/government/organisations/ministry-of-justice>
accessed 11 April 2018
Provides links to MOJ and other justice agencies
Telephone: 020 3334 3555

Missing persons (National Missing Persons Helpline)
<https://www.missingpeople.org.uk> accessed 11 April 2018
Telephone: 020 8392 4590 or Freefone: 116 000

National Black Police Association
<http://www.nbpa.co.uk> accessed 11 April 2018
Telephone: 07921 095262

National Domestic Violence Helpline (women and children)
<http://www.womensaid.org.uk> accessed 11 April 2018
Telephone: 0808 2000 247

National Domestic Violence Helpline (men)
<http://www.mankind.org.uk> accessed 11 April 2018
Telephone: 01823 334244

National Stalking Helpline
<http://www.stalkinghelpline.org> accessed 11 April 2018
Telephone (Support): 0808 802 0300

NCA (National Crime Agency)
<http://www.nationalcrimeagency.gov.uk> accessed 11 April 2018
Telephone: 0370 496 7622

NPCC (National Police Chiefs' Council—formerly **ACPO**)
<http://www.npcc.police.uk> accessed 11 April 2018
Telephone: 020 7084 8950

NSPCC (National Society for Prevention of Cruelty to Children)
<https://www.nspcc.org.uk> accessed 11 April 2018
Telephone: 0808 800 5000
ChildLine: 0800 1111

Parliament
<http://www.parliament.uk> accessed 11 April 2018

PNLD (Police National Legal Database)
<http://www.pnld.co.uk> accessed 11 April 2018
email: <pnld@westyorkshire.pnn.police.uk>
Telephone: 01924 294086

PNLD (Ask the police FAQ database)
<https://www.askthe.police.uk> accessed 11 April 2018

Police Federation
<http://www.polfed.org> accessed 11 April 2018
Telephone: 01372 352000

Rape (rape counselling and advice service)
<http://www.rapecrisis.org.uk> accessed 11 April 2018
Telephone: 0808 802 9999

Revenue & Customs (see **HMRC**)

RNID (Royal National Institute for Deaf People)
<http://www.actionhearingloss.org.uk> accessed 11 April 2018
Telephone: 0808 808 0123 Textphone: 0808 808 9000

RSPB (Royal Society for the Protection of Birds)
<https://www.rspb.org.uk> accessed 11 April 2018
Telephone: 01767 693 690

RSPCA (Royal Society for the Prevention of Cruelty to Animals)
<http://www.rspca.org.uk> accessed 11 April 2018
Telephone: 0300 1234 999

Samaritans (organisation)
<http://www.samaritans.org> accessed 11 April 2018
Telephone: 08457 90 90 90

Sentencing Council (Sentencing Guidelines)
<http://www.sentencingcouncil.org.uk> accessed 11 April 2018
Telephone: 020 7071 5793

Appendix 1: Useful Contacts

Stonewall (lesbian, gay, and bisexual charity)
<https://www.stonewall.org.uk> accessed 11 April 2018
Telephone: 0800 050 2020

Superintendents' Association
<http://www.policesupers.com> accessed 11 April 2018
Telephone: 0118 984 4005

Trading Standards
<http://www.tradingstandards.uk> accessed 11 April 2018
Provides advice/contact details

Transport (Department for Transport)
<https://www.gov.uk/government/organisations/department-for-transport> accessed 11 April 2018
Provides aviation, rail, roads, and shipping links
Telephone: 0300 330 3000

UK Intellectual Property Office
<https://www.gov.uk/government/organisations/intellectual-property-office> accessed 11 April 2018
Telephone: 0300 300 2000

UKMPB (UK Missing Persons Bureau)
<http://missingpersons.police.uk> accessed 11 April 2018
Telephone: 0845 000 5481

Victim Support
<https://www.victimsupport.org.uk> accessed 11 April 2018
Telephone: 0808 1689 111

VIPER® Video Identification Parade Electronic Recording
<http://www.viper.police.uk> accessed 20 Feb 2018
Telephone: 01274 373880

VOSA (see **DVSA**)

Youth Justice Board
<https://www.gov.uk/government/organisations/youth-justice-board-for-england-and-wales> accessed 11 April 2018
Telephone: 020 3334 5300

Traffic Data—Vehicle Categories and Minimum Ages

Motorcycles and three- or four-wheeled light vehicles

Minimum age		
Category	Description	Minimum age
AM	**Mopeds**—Two- or three-wheel vehicles with a maximum design speed over 25 km/h but not more than 45 km/hLight Quadricycles (**Quad Bikes**)—A four-wheeled vehicle with an unladen weight of not more than 350 kg (not including the mass of the batteries in the case of electric vehicles), whose maximum design speed is over 25 km/h and less than 45 km/h	16*
A1	**Light motorcycles** with an engine size of up to 125 cc and a power output of up to 11 kW (14.6bhp) with a power weight ratio not exceeding 0.1 kW (including tricycles up to 15 kW)	17*
A2	**A motorcycle** of a power not exceeding 35 kW and with a power/weight ratio not exceeding 0.2 kW/kg and not derived from a vehicle of more than double its power	19*
A	**A motorcycle** of a power exceeding 35 kW. A motor tricycle over 15 kW	24 (21 via Progressive Access)

* Must have completed Compulsory Basic Training (CBT) and the certificate must be valid for the relevant motorcycle category.

Appendix 2: Traffic Data—Vehicle Categories and Minimum Ages

Other categories

Category	Description	Minimum age
F	Agricultural tractors	17*
K	Mowing machine or vehicle controlled by a pedestrian	16
P	Moped	16
Q	Motor vehicles with less than four wheels which if propelled by an internal combustion engine, has a cylinder capacity less than 50cc and maximum speed not exceeding 25 km/h	16

* Age 16 for tractors less than 2.45-m-wide pulling trailers less than 2.45–m-wide with two wheels, or four close-coupled.

Cars or light vans, with and without trailers

Category	Description	Minimum age
B	Motor vehicle with a maximum authorised mass (the total weight of the vehicle plus the maximum load it can carry safely) of up to 3,500 kg, no more than eight passenger seats, with or without a trailer—weighing no more than 750 kg Or, as above, but with a trailer weighing more than 750 kg. The total weight of the vehicle and the trailer together can't weigh more than 3,500 kg. The weight of the trailer, when fully loaded, can't weigh more than the unladen weight of the vehicle	17*
B auto	As category B with automatic transmission	17*
B96	Combinations of a motor vehicle and trailer where: • the tractor vehicle is in category B • the maximum authorised mass of the trailer exceeds 750 kg • the maximum authorised mass of the combination exceeds 3.5 tonnes but does not exceed 4.25 tonnes	17

Appendix 2: Traffic Data—Vehicle Categories and Minimum Ages

Category	Description	Minimum age
B+E	Combination of a motor vehicle (being a tractor vehicle in category B) and a trailer or semi-trailer where: • the combination does not fall within Category B • the maximum authorised mass of the trailer or semi-trailer does not exceed 3,500 kg	17

* Age 16 if currently receiving a Disability Living Allowance at the higher rate (mobility component).

These tables contain public sector information licensed under the Open Government Licence v3.0 and are a summary of the data provided for guidance only—more information regarding other categories and relevant ages is available online at www.gov.uk/driving-licence-categories and; https://www.nidirect.gov.uk/articles/minimum-ages-you-can-ride-or-drive-vehicles [accessed on 11 April 2008].

Firearms Offences Relating to Age

Under 18 Offence

- Using a firearm for a purpose not authorised by the European weapons directive (despite lawful entitlement to possess—being the holder of a firearms/shotgun certificate).

Any firearm/ammunition

- Purchase or hire any firearm or ammunition (see **8.7.1**).
- Sell or let on hire any firearm or ammunition (see **8.7.1**).

'Section 1 firearm/ammunition'

- Purchase or hire s 1 firearm/ammunition (see **8.7.1**).
- Sell or let on hire or hire s 1 firearm/ammunition (see **8.7.1**).

Shotgun/cartridges

- Purchase or hire shotgun/cartridges (see **8.7.1**).
- Sell or let on hire or hire shotgun/cartridges (see **8.7.1**).

Air weapon/ammunition

- Purchase or hire an air weapon or ammunition for an air weapon (see **8.7.1**).
- Sell or let on hire or hire an air weapon or ammunition for an air weapon (see **8.7.1**).
- Make a gift of an air weapon or ammunition for an air weapon (see **8.7.2**).
- Part with possession of an air weapon or ammunition for an air weapon *subject to exceptions below* (see **8.7.2**).
- Have an air weapon or ammunition for an air weapon (see **8.7.2**), *except if*:
  - ✦ that person is under the supervision of a person of or over the age of 21;
  - ✦ member of approved rifle clubs;
  - ✦ using at authorised shooting galleries (not exceeding 0.23 inch calibre);
  - ✦ that person has attained the age of 14 and is on private premises with the consent of the occupier, and is under the supervision of a person of or over the age of 21, but it is an offence for the

supervisor to allow him to fire any missiles beyond those premises (subject to defence—see **8.7.2**).

Imitation firearm

- Purchase an imitation firearm (see **8.7.5**).
- Sell an imitation firearm (see **8.7.5**).

Under 15 Offences (shotgun/cartridges)

- Have an assembled shotgun except while under the supervision of a person of or over the age of 21, or while the shotgun is so covered with a securely fastened gun cover that it cannot be fired (see **8.2.2**).
- Make a gift of a shotgun or ammunition for a shotgun to a person under the age of 15 (see **8.2.2**).

Under 14 Offences ('s 1 firearm/ammunition')

- Possess s 1 firearm or ammunition (see **8.1.3**), except for:
  - ✦ use of a certificate holder, being under their instructions, and for sporting purposes only;
  - ✦ a member of an approved cadet corps when engaged as a member of the corps in or in connection with drill or target shooting;
  - ✦ a person conducting or carrying on a miniature rifle or shooting gallery for air weapons or miniature rifles not exceeding 0.23 inch calibre;
  - ✦ using such rifles/ammunition at such a range or gallery.
- Part with possession of a s 1 firearm or ammunition to a person under 14, subject to above exceptions (see **8.1.3**).
- Make a gift of or lend s 1 firearm or ammunition to a person under 14 (see **8.1.3**).

Appendix 4
Religious Dates/Events

Advisory notes: These dates are provided for guidance purposes only. Some dates may vary as the festivals are guided by the lunar calendar and some local customs may also vary the date. The religions are listed alphabetically.

	2018	**2019**
Baha'I		
World Religion Day	21 January 2018	20 January 2019
Naw-Rúz (New Year)	20 March 2018	21 March 2019
First Day of Ridvan	20 April 2018	21 April 2019
Last Day of Ridvan	2 May 2018	2 May 2019
Declaration of the Báb	23 May 2018	24 May 2019
Ascension of Baha'u'llah	28 May 2018	29 May 2019
Martyrdom of the Báb	8 July 2018	10 July 2019
Birth of the Báb	19 October 2018	29 October 2019
Birth of Baha'u'llah	9 November 2018	30 October 2019
Day of the Covenant	25 November 2018	26 November 2019
Ascension of 'Abdu'l-Baha	26 November 2018	28 November 2019
Buddhist		
Mahayana Buddhist New Year	12–15 January 2018	21–23 January 2019
Parinirvana Day	8 February 2018	8 February 2019
Nirvana Day (alternative date)	15 February 2018	15 February 2019
Magha Puja Day	31 March 2018	9 Febrauary 2019
Therevadin Buddhist New Year	30 April 2018	19 April 2019
Wesak (Buddha Day)	29 May 2018	19 May 2019
Asalha (Puja Day)	8 July 2018	16 July 2019
Obon (Ulambana)	13–15 July 2018	15 August 2019
Bodhi Day (Rohatsu)	8 December 2018	8 December 2019
Catholic		
Mary Mother of God	1 January 2018	1 January 2019
Blessing of the Animals (Hispanic)	17 January 2018	17 January 2019
Corpus Christi	31 May 2018	31 May 2019
Sacred Heart of Jesus	8 June 2018	8 June 2019
St Benedict Day	11 July 2018	11 July 2019

	2018	2019
Assumption of Blessed Virgin Mary	15 August 2018	15 August 2019
St Francis' Day	4 October 2018	4 October 2019
All Souls' Day	2 November 2018	2 November 2019
Immaculate Conception of Mary	8 December 2018	8 December 2019
Feast Day—Our Lady of Guadalupe	12 December 2018	12 December 2019
Feast of the Holy Family	30 December 2018	30 December 2019

Chinese

Lunar New Year	16 February 2018	5 February 2019

Christian

Twelfth Night	5 January 2018	5 January 2019
Epiphany	6 January 2018	6 January 2019
Shrove Tuesday	13February 2018	5 February 2019
Ash Wednesday (Lent begins)	14 February 2018	6 February 2019
St David's Day	1 March 2018	1 March 2019
St Patrick's Day	17 March 2018	17 March 2019
Palm Sunday	25 March 2018	14 April 2019
Maundy Thursday	29 March 2018	18 April 2019
Good Friday	30 March 2018	19 April 2019
Easter Day	1 April 2018	21 April 2019
St George's Day	23 April 2018	23 April 2019
Ascension Day	10 May 2018	30 May 2019
Whit Sunday (Pentecost)	20 May 2018	9 June 2019
Trinity Sunday	27 May 2018	16 June 2019
Lammas	1 August 2018	1 August 2019
All Hallows Eve	31 October 2018	31 October 2019
Advent Sunday	2 December 2018	1 December 2019
St Andrew's Day	30 November 2018	30 November 2019
Christmas Day	25 December 2018	25 December 2019

Hindu

Vasant Panchami (Saraswati's Day)	22 February 2018	10 February 2019
Maha Shivaratri	13 February 2018	4 March 2019
Holi	1 March 2018	20 March 2019
New Year	18 March 2018	7 March 2019
Ramayana Begins	18 March 2018	4 April 2019
Ramanavami	26 March 2018	12 April 2019

Appendix 4: Religious Dates/Events

	2018	2019
Hanuman Jayanti	31 March 2018	19 April 2019
Guru Purnima	27 July 2018	16 July 2019
Raksha Bandhan	26 August 2018	15 August 2019
Krishna Janmashtami	3 September 2018	24 August 2019
Ganesa Chaturthi	13 September 2018	1 September 2019
Navaratri first Day	9 October 2018	29 September 2019
Navaratri Ends	18 October 2018	8 October 2019
Dasera	19 October 2018	7 October 2019
Diwali (Deepavali)	7 November 2018	27 October 2019

Islam

Mawlid-al-Nabi (Birth of Prophet)	20 November 2018	10 November 2019
Lailat Al-Isra wa Al-Miraj (Ascension to Heaven)	13 April 2018	3 April 2019
Lailat al Bara'ah (Night of Emancipation)	1 May 2018	1 May 2019
Commencement of Ramadhan (Fasting)	16 May 2018	6 May 2019
Laylat el qadr	10 June 2018	31 May 2019
Eid Al-Fitr (Completion of Fasting)	14 June 2018	4 June 2019
Waqf al Arafa (Hajj—Pilgrimage Day)	20 August 2018	10 August 2019
Eid-al-Addha (Day of Sacrifice)	21 August 2018	11 August 2019
Muharram (Islamic New Year)	11 September 2018	31 August 2019
Day of Ashura	20 September 2018	9 September 2019

Jehovah's Witness

Lord's Evening Meal	11 April 2018	11 April 2019

Jewish

Notes: All Jewish holidays commence/start on the evening before the actual day specified, as the Jewish day actually begins at sunset on the previous night.

Rosh Chodesh Sh'vat	16 January 2018	6 January 2019
Tu B'Shvat	30 January 2018	21 January 2019
Shabbat Shekalim	9 February 2018	2 March 2019
Rosh Chodesh Adar	15 February 2018	5 February 2019
Ta'anit Esther	28 February 2018	20 March 2019
Shabbat Zachor	23 February 2018	16 March 2019
Purim	28 February 2018	21 March 2019
Shushan Purim	28 March 2018	22 March 2019

Appendix 4: Religious Dates/Events

	2018	**2019**
Shabbat Parah	9 March 2018	30 March 2019
Shabbat HaChodesh	16 March 2018	6 April 2019
Rosh Chodesh Nisan	16 March 2018	6 April 2019
Shabbat HaGadol	23 March 2018	13 April 2019
Ta'anit Bechorot	30 March 2018	19 April 2019
Pesach	30 March 2018	19 April 2019
Yom HaShoah	11 April 2018	2 May 2019
Rosh Chodesh Iyyar	14 April 2018	6 May 2019
Yom HaAtzma'ut	18 April 2018	9 May 2019
Yom HaZikaron	17 April 2018	8 May 2019
Lag B'Omer	2 May 2018	23 May 2019
Yom Yerushalayim	12 May 2018	2 June 2019
Rosh Chodesh Sivan	14 May 2018	4 June 2019
Shavuot	19 May–21 May 2018	8 June–10 June 2019
Rosh Chodesh Tamuz	12 June 2018	3 July 2019
Tzom Tammuz	1 July 2018	21 July 2019
Rosh Chodesh Av	12 July 2018	2 August 2019
Shabbat Hazon	20 July 2018	10 August 2019
Tish'a B'Av	21 July 2018	11 August 2019
Shabbat Nachamu	27 July 2018	17 August 2019
Rosh Chodesh Elul	10 August 2018	31 August 2019
Rosh Hashana	9–11 September 2018	29 September–1 October 2019
Tzom Gedaliah	12 September 2018	2 October 2019
Shabbat Shuva	14 September 2018	5 October 2019
Yom Kippur	18 September 2018	9 October 2019
Sukkot	23 September 2018	14 October 2019
Shmini Atzeret	30 September 2018	21 October 2019
Simchat Torah	1 October 2018	22 October 2019
Rosh Chodesh Cheshvan	8 October 2018	29 October 2019
Rosh Chodesh Kislev	7 November 2018	28 November 2019
Chanukah	2–10 December 2018	22–30 December 2019

Sikh

Birthday of Guru Gobind Singh Ji	5 January 2018	5 January 2019
Maghi	14 January 2018	13 January 2019
Hola Mohalla	2 March 2018	22 March 2019
Baisakhi (Vaisakhi)	14 April 2018	14 April 2019
Martyrdom of Guru Arjan Dev Ji	16 June 2018	16 June 2019

Appendix 4: Religious Dates/Events

	2018	2019
Installation of Scriptures as Guru Granth	20 October 2018	20 October 2019
Diwali (Deepavali)	19 October 2018	27 October 2019
Birthday of Guru Nanak Dev Ji	23 November 2018	12 November 2019
Martyrdom of Guru Tegh Bahadur Ji	4 December 2018	24 November 2019

Index

Index

Index

Index

Index

Index

Index

Index

Index

Index

Index

Index

Index

Index

Index

Index

Index

Index

Index

Index

Index

Index

Index

Index

Index

Index

Index

Index